S0-ACO-065

MOVIES

**FROM THE SILENT CLASSICS OF THE SILVER SCREEN
TO THE DIGITAL AND 3-D ERA**

GENERAL EDITOR
PHILIP KEMP

FOREWORD BY
SIR CHRISTOPHER FRAYLING

MOVIES

FROM THE SILENT CLASSICS OF THE SILVER SCREEN TO THE DIGITAL AND 3-D ERA

UNIVERSE

First published in the United States of America in 2011 by
UNIVERSE PUBLISHING
A Division of Rizzoli International Publications, Inc.
300 Park Avenue South
New York, NY 10010
www.rizzoliusa.com

Copyright © 2011 Quintessence

All rights reserved. No part of this publication may be reproduced, stored
in a retrieval system or transmitted in any form or by any means, electronic,
mechanical, photocopying, recording, or otherwise, without the permission
of the copyright holder.

2011 2012 2013 2014 / 10 9 8 7 6 5 4 3 2 1

ISBN: 978-0-7893-2262-3

Library of Congress Control Number: 2011923856

QSS.TICI

This book was designed and produced by
Quintessence Editions Ltd.
226 City Road
London EC1V 2TT

Project Editor	Simon Ward
Assistant Editors	Robert Dimery, Becky Gee, Simon Hartley, Carol King, Louise Larchbourne, Fiona Plowman
Editorial Assistants	Helena Baser and Olivia Young
Designer	Nicole Kuderer
Design Assistants	Tom Howey and Alison Hau
Production Manager	Anna Pauletti
Editorial Director	Jane Laing
Publisher	Tristan de Lancey

Color reproduction by Chroma Graphics (Overseas) Pte. Ltd
Printed in China by Toppan Leefung Printers Ltd

CONTENTS

FOREWORD

When I was growing up in early 1950s South London, there was a children's encyclopedia on our shelves that included a section on "the seven arts." Not the nine Muses, but the seven arts. These arts were Literature, Music, Opera, Dance, Drama, Visual Art—and Film, which was described as THE art form of the twentieth century, an art form that had its origins as an end-of-pier sort of entertainment but that through a mixture of technological change, fashion, industrial organization, and human creativity had long since matured into the seventh art. The nameless encyclopedist predicted that before long film history—like art history—would surely enter the hallowed portals of mainstream culture through museums, exhibitions, scholarly publications based on primary, secondary, and tertiary sources, and the kinds of critical seriousness that were routinely applied to the other six arts. In my early teens, I was an avid reader of the magazine *Films and Filming*, which introduced me to serious film criticism and which in the process made much the same point: it was one part of a stable of publications devoted to "the seven arts."

Half a century later, only some of these predictions have come true. Where the arts establishment is concerned, there are still "the arts" (the six), there are a few films made by artists, and then there is something called cinema or film or the movies; not quite sure which. When theater companies perform live adaptations of well-known films, popular culture somehow morphs into art. When Tate Modern put on a survey exhibition about the painter Edward Hopper, the images illustrating his undoubted influence on film were placed outside the exhibition proper; next to the cafeteria, actually. For a subsequent exhibition on "Dalí and Film," which included material on Walt Disney (1901–66) and Alfred Hitchcock (1899–1980), the promotional material reduced the size of the words "and Film" for fear they might put off the art crowd.

The reasons for this sense of a cultural hierarchy are complex, involving as they do—among many other things—the fact that film isn't collectible in the traditional sense; it isn't normally about communication from person to person nor about individual artistic creativity, except at a metaphorical level; it can be as much about business as culture and often is; what you are seeing is not exactly an artifact; it is part of what used to be called mass culture, which ever since the Frankfurt School of social researchers and philosophers in the interwar years has tended to be contrasted with the authentic individual experience; it doesn't have a centuries-old back catalogue; it isn't live. And it is democratic. The fact that most of this could be said of much contemporary art is quietly forgotten. Such hierarchies go deep, especially in British culture, which is odd, considering how the traditional boundaries are becoming fuzzy just about everywhere else. But, when they are allied with the current hue and cry over media studies—which has taken over from sociology as the whipping boy of choice for those who want to lament the decline of standards in higher education—they begin to become serious.

All of which might explain the somewhat defensive tone of many published studies of film: the yearning to show off academic credentials and be taken seriously by better established surrounding disciplines—usually literature and history rather than art history or visual studies. This defensiveness coincided with new waves of theory coming from Europe, which seemed to provide an instant, intellectual résumé for film studies—one that was highly suspicious for various methodological reasons of archives, dictionaries, encyclopedias, and narrative histories. The result was that film studies inherited a suspicion of its basic building blocks before they even existed.

The rise of home entertainment, together with the maturing of film studies—at last!—has created a strong demand for clearly written, jargon-free, reliable reference works about film history, to counter the blandness of most DVD extras about "the making of . . . ," to place the anecdote of the viewing experience in some kind of broader cinematic or cultural context, and to provide a well-researched alternative to gushingly promotional film reviews, star ratings, and gossip about budgets or on-set arguments. And perhaps, above all, to take stock at a time when the distribution, screening, technologies, and viewing of film are all at a turning point. Freeze-frame has certainly led to close scrutiny, closer than the filmmakers intended in most cases, but it has usually been close scrutiny of anachronisms and continuity errors that can make the viewer feel superior: the assistant in a coat and tie as the Persians attack Babylon in *Intolerance* (1916); Ilsa wearing a suit not a dress in the Paris flashback of *Casablanca* (1942); a blind man wearing a wristwatch in *The Ten Commandments* (1956), and numerous soldiers wearing them in *Spartacus* (1960); modern tire tracks in countless Westerns, including *Stagecoach* (1939). And can you spot the glass reflection of David Lean (1908–91) and crew in *Doctor Zhivago* (1965)? This book does something much more interesting with freeze-frame by judiciously selecting "key scenes" from individual films and explaining their significance.

Movies provides a chronological account of the story of film, from the first public screening of the Lumiere Brothers' films in 1895 right through to post-9/11 American films, CGI, and 3D, and postmillennial European cinema. Not a "names and dates" story about Hollywood—the usual approach—but a symphonic narrative of world cinema, emphasizing film cultures in the plural rather than film culture in the singular. This rich material is organized thematically by period, region, or genre. There are introductions by specialists, which place the films in their historical context, essays on individual films, timelines of key events, profiles of individual filmmakers, and sidebars on matters arising ("page to screen," relationship with art movements of the day, music, cinematography, and so on). One feature of *Movies* is the emphasis on how each generation of filmmakers is in conversation with earlier ones—with flashforwards to and flashbacks from today. Another is the high quality of the illustrations, taken for granted in histories of art but not until recently in histories of film.

The celebrated opening words of Ernst Gombrich's *The Story of Art* are: "There really is no such thing as Art. There are only artists. . . . Art with a capital A has come to be something of a bogey and a fetish." By the same token, this book isn't about "Cinema" or "Film" in the abstract. It is about filmmakers and films, and their still underrated importance in all our lives. This has involved very careful selection of case studies, which is always a brave thing to do.
PROFESSOR SIR CHRISTOPHER FRAYLING

HISTORIAN, CRITIC, AND BROADCASTER, LONDON, UNITED KINGDOM

INTRODUCTION

Has any art form caught on so rapidly or so universally as cinema? Although the exact moment of its genesis is disputed, most accounts agree on 1895: the year in which brothers Louis (1864–1948) and Auguste (1862–1954) Lumière (opposite) projected *La sortie des usines Lumière* to members of the Société d'Encouragement pour l'Industrie Nationale, on March 22, and then, on June 10, gave private demonstrations of their films to the Photographic Congress at Lyons. Six months later, on December 28 at the Hotel Scribe in Paris, they mounted the first-ever public showing of films to a paying audience.

Within a mere twenty years of these pioneering ventures—a blink of an eye in the history of literature or art—films were being watched by mass audiences across the globe. Production was under way in all the major European countries, in the United States, Canada, India, China, Japan, Turkey, Mexico, Brazil, Argentina, and Australia, and was already supported by a substantial industry in many of those countries. So immediate was the appeal of moving pictures that Charlie Chaplin (1889–1977, below) stepped before a movie camera for the first time in January 1914 as a young English vaudeville artist, and by the end of that year had become the most widely recognized person in the world.

Paradoxically, one major factor in cinema's rapid rise to universality was its chief limitation: silence. Silent films were easily and cheaply adaptable: slot in a few translated intertitles and a film could play to any audience anywhere. Even low levels of literacy were rarely a barrier; filmgoers soon became used to the murmur of helpful audience members reading out the intertitles for their less literate neighbors. (The Japanese, idiosyncratic as ever, employed official readers known as *benshi*, whose job was to stand beside the screen and recount the plot to the audience.) One can speculate that had cinema been born in full "talkie" mode it might have taken far longer to achieve worldwide acceptance. As it was, by the time the "talkies" came in, the habit of going to the movies was too firmly ingrained to be discouraged by language barriers.

The chief cinematic genres emerged early, too. Within months of the Lumière brothers' screenings, the ex-stage magician Georges Méliès (1861–1938) was creating fantasy, horror, and science fiction movies. Documentary,

▶ Charlie Chaplin, a pivotal figure in early cinema, on set at Keystone Studios in 1914. His iconic screen character The Tramp was instantly recognizable by his ill-fitting suit, bowler hat, and bamboo cane.

◄ Auguste and Louis Lumière in Lyons, France, in 1892. The brothers developed a camera to make motion pictures and were among cinema's earliest filmmakers. Their first film (1895) showed workers leaving the Lumière factory.

of course, existed from the start, as many early filmmakers simply pointed their cameras at the world around them. Comedy swiftly followed, along with costume drama, romance, thrillers, psychological drama, war movies, farce, Ancient World epics, and even pornography. Prestige literary adaptations not surprisingly abounded, drawn from the stage and the page alike. Westerns were a natural choice for US filmmakers, especially once the industry shifted its center to California. Animation soon arrived, its first appearance generally credited to J. Stuart Blackton (1875–1941) with *Humorous Phases of Funny Faces* (1906). By 1910, virtually every genre that we now recognize had been established, although some were in primitive form.

The same can be said of the main cinematic techniques. It took remarkably little time for filmmakers to discover the manifold tricks that the camera could play. Close-ups, panning shots, slow motion, speeded-up motion, split-screen, multiple exposure, superimposition, stop-action, freeze-frames, dissolves, fades, and iris-outs all made their debut appearances in those initial decades. It could well be argued that every key technical development—with the exception of sound, color, and 3D—had been devised by 1914. Likewise with narrative techniques: flashbacks and flashforwards, parallel editing (simultaneous events shown sequentially), subjective shots, dream sequences, and the like were all present in embryo form. All that has happened since has been in terms of vastly greater sophistication and technical agility. Youngest and most dynamic of the major arts, cinema has gone from primitivism to postmodernism in barely a century, still bearing the imprint of its origins.

The revolution that overtook the cinema in its third decade of existence had little to do with technique, but was played out in terms of national market dominance. Before World War I, Europe's film industries dominated the international market, with France, Italy, and Denmark the chief producers. The United States was a net importer of films: in 1907, of the 1,200 films released in the United States only some 400 were US-made. This all changed with the war. With the activities of European filmmakers curtailed by the effects of the conflict, the nascent US film industry—lavishly funded and newly established on the West Coast—seized its chance. By the 1920s, Hollywood, with its unrivaled financial and technical resources, had gained pole position in world cinema and had become an irresistible magnet for overseas talent—a situation that remains largely the case today.

▶ Howard Hawks on the set of *The Big Sleep* (1946) with Lauren Bacall and Humphrey Bogart. The director often produced his own films and improvised scenes on the spot without the approval of the censorship authorities.

Almost from the beginning, it was recognized that cinema was unique in its immediacy and accessibility. For some, this was a matter for celebration. "This is the marvel of the motion pictures," rhapsodized the *American Magazine* in 1913, "it is art democratic, art for the race. Here the masses of mankind enter through the rhythm of vivid motion the light that flies before and the beauty that calls the spirit of the race." However, a medium so widely disseminated and influential soon fell under suspicion—of vulgarizing, dumbing down, sensationalism, lubricity, political propaganda, encouraging mindless aspirational consumerism, and corrupting the minds and morals of the young. (Much the same, a couple of centuries previously, was being said about the novel and live theater, now linchpins of high culture.)

Such condemnations were sweeping in the extreme. Motion pictures "[are] without a redeeming feature to warrant their existence," growled the *Chicago Tribune* in 1907. "Sinful and abominable rubbish" was British prime minister Ramsay MacDonald's dismissal of Hollywood's output, and as late as 1958 the influential *Journal of Education* dismissed the art of cinema in toto as "ephemeral" and "parasitic." From politicians, preachers, and teachers came demands for control, for systems of censorship, often resulting in the setting-up of self-regulatory bodies. The most famous of these was the Motion Producers and Distributors of America, which drew up a list of caveats known as the Hays Code. Even so, far from being trammeled by these petty "dos" and "don'ts," many filmmakers—such as Ernst Lubitsch (1892–1947, opposite above) and Howard Hawks (1896–1977, above)—took delight in subtly circumventing them.

A more lasting, and in many ways more restrictive, curb on the creativity of filmmakers lay within the structure of the industry itself. In some ways the medium's very popularity told against it; once it became evident what potential profits stood to be made from films, the business side of the industry set out to secure a stranglehold over its more experimental or artistic elements.

While the three main branches of production, distribution, and exhibition remained separate from each other, there was room for maneuver; however, as the power of the studios increased and vertical integration became common, the scope for independence rapidly narrowed. Almost from its earliest years, the history of cinema offers all too frequent examples of original talent either hindered, frozen out, or co-opted into the bland populist mainstream. In almost every decade and every country, filmmaking is a pitched battle between the financiers, who want to maximize their returns, and the creative artists, who want to make something of which they can be proud. The money men would be happy to dispense with the artists, if they could, but few accountants know how to write a script or direct a film. (Not that this incapacity, all too often, has stopped them from trying.)

It therefore says a lot for the sheer irrepressible vitality of the medium that, both within and outside the studio system, so many exceptional films have been made and, it is worth emphasizing, are still being made today. In cinema, as in so many other activities, the myth of the "golden age" continues to hold sway: that legendary era when classic after classic was produced and overall creative standards were vertiginously high. On examination, the myth is generally the product of selective memory, and so it is here. Take, for example, the supposed golden age of Hollywood, the studio era of the 1930s: yes, it produced *Scarface* (1932) and *The Bride of Frankenstein* (1935), *Queen Christina* (1933) and *Bringing up Baby* (1938), and *Gone with the Wind* (below) and *The Wizard of Oz* (both 1939); but these are the films that have rightly survived. Alongside them was a great mass of humdrum competence, mediocrity, and ill-made dross that no one would think deserved reviving today. At any time, probably no more than 5 percent of the world's annual output of films is worthy of even passing attention, and that may well be an overestimate.

Nonetheless, there have been a number of cinematic golden ages, and *Movies* sets out to highlight some of them: those periods—they seldom seem to last longer than a decade—when a national film industry is, through a mix of social, technical, historical, and economic factors, buoyed up on a wave of creative originality. Besides Hollywood in the 1930s, we could single out Germany and Soviet Russia in the 1920s, France in the 1930s, Britain and the Italy of Neo-Realism in the late 1940s, Japan in the 1950s, France again with the Nouvelle Vague of the 1960s, the films of the Prague Spring in mid-1960s Czechoslovakia,

▲ Ernst Lubitsch with Jeanette MacDonald in 1932. The German-born director was renowned for his elegant comedies of manners. The risqué subject matter and oblique, suggestive dialogue of his films perplexed the censors.

◄ Clark Gable reading Margaret Mitchell's best-selling book *Gone With the Wind* in 1939. The film, in which he played Rhett Butler, won ten Academy Awards and remains one of the most popular Hollywood films of all time.

▶ Jean-Luc Godard (center) with Eddie Constantine and Anna Karina in 1965. Like other Nouvelle Vague directors, Godard challenged traditional cinema, inspiring filmmakers from Wim Wenders (b. 1945) to Quentin Tarantino (b. 1963).

Germany again with the New German Cinema of the 1970s, the Hollywood of the "movie brats" such as Martin Scorsese (b. 1942, opposite below) and Robert Altman (1925–2006) in the same decade, and the Chinese cinema of the Fifth Generation in the 1980s. More recent decades have seen flowerings of filmmaking talent from Iran, South Korea, Thailand, Latin America, and Romania.

At other times—and not always coinciding with a specific golden age— certain genres and styles enjoy an ascendance, often in response to a national mood. Looking at Hollywood, a social historian could trace the way in which Film Noir—that haunted emanation of the American psyche—emerged in the shadows of imminent world conflict just as the perky sassiness of 1930s screwball comedy reached the end of its cycle, and then continued into the paranoid years of the Cold War, overlapping with—and even infecting—the more optimistic all-American genres of the musical and the Western. Likewise, one could link the cycle of "J-horror" films that began with *Ringu* (*The Ring*, 1998) by Hideo Nakata (b. 1961) to the increase in national uncertainty and disillusionment that followed the crisis in the Japanese economy.

The second century of cinema seems likely to see revolutionary changes within the art form and possibly even its metamorphosis into something radically different. Within the last three decades, with the rise and growing sophistication of computer-generated imagery (CGI), cinema has become increasingly technology driven. This, it could be argued, is unprecedented. The earlier major developments in cinematic technology—sound, color, and widescreen—though far-reaching in their impact, remained subordinate to the filmmaking process. Even when their words could be heard and their actions seen in Technicolor on huge screens, actors still performed in front of a camera, on a set or on location, just as before. However, computers have revolutionized live-action movies perhaps more than they have changed animation. After all, the makers of *Toy Story* (1995) and its successors are still painting moving pictures, as were Disney's artists in *Bambi* (1942); all that has changed are the tools.

In live-action films, not only can huge monsters and vast armies (as in the attack on Helm's Deep in *Lord of the Rings: The Two Towers*, 2002) be created on-screen, but also actors can appear on complex landscapes despite never having seen them. Even the actors themselves can be fabricated through motion capture—witness Andy Serkis's performance as Gollum in the same film—and might even become superfluous as the techniques of CGI and motion capture become more sophisticated. Before long, the first wholly convincing computer-generated "human" actor in a live-action film may be seen, and deceased stars could be resurrected to give new performances. Marilyn Monroe may yet star in a movie with Humphrey Bogart. Meanwhile, the movie-house may be going the way of the music-hall: in fifty years' time films as we now know and experience them may become outmoded.

At this juncture, though, it can credibly be claimed that the twenty-first century is something of a golden age for cinephiles. The development of video, DVDs, and downloads means that more of the riches of world cinema, past and present, are readily available to us than at any previous time. Not so long ago, catching up with vintage or foreign-language movies generally meant living within reach of an arthouse cinema in a major city, or relying on chance screenings on television. Today, it is likely that readers of this book will be able to watch or rewatch virtually all the films featured in these pages, decide for themselves on our inclusions and omissions, and reach their own conclusions on our verdicts.

The aim of this volume has been to give an overview of cinema, from its beginnings to the present day, and to give some idea of its ever-expanding scope. It is, of course, an ambitious task: cinema is too protean and multifarious to be encompassed in a single volume, and far too elusive to be defined. Cinema, Jean-Luc Godard (b. 1930, opposite) remarked, is "the truth twenty-four times a second"— which sounds impressive until you consider how it might apply to, say, the anti-Semitic *Jud Süss* (1940) by Veit Harlan (1899–1964). Sam Fuller (1912–97, right) perhaps came closer when he described cinema as "a battleground: love, hate, action, death. In a word: emotion." Though even this would scarcely cover the abstract animations of Hans Richter (1919–2008) or Oskar Fischinger (1900–67).

In *Movies* we have opted for a series of establishing shots, each presenting a significant phase or element within the history of the medium—a crucial decade, trend, genre, or highpoint in a particular country or region's output— before moving in to close-ups on key films within that frame. In choosing the latter, the criterion has been to go for the most illuminatingly representative specimens rather than what might be considered "the best." Readers, and critics, will have no trouble spotting omissions: in a book of this kind, deciding what to leave out is a more painful process than deciding what to put in. Film arouses as many passionate arguments and disagreements as any of the other arts, more perhaps. If this book sparks discussions, suggestions, or furious objections; if it leads to reassessments, for or against; or if it inspires readers to seek out films, filmmakers, genres, or entire national cinemas that they might otherwise have ignored—it will have served its purpose. **PK**

▲ Sam Fuller on the set of his World War II movie *The Big Red One* (1980). Fuller's low-budget, hard-hitting movies reflect his original career in tabloid journalism.

◄ Martin Scorsese (center) on the set of *Mean Streets* (1973) with Robert De Niro and Harvey Keitel. Scorsese wrote the script based on real events that he had witnessed as an adolescent in the Little Italy neighborhood.

1 | 1900 TO 1929

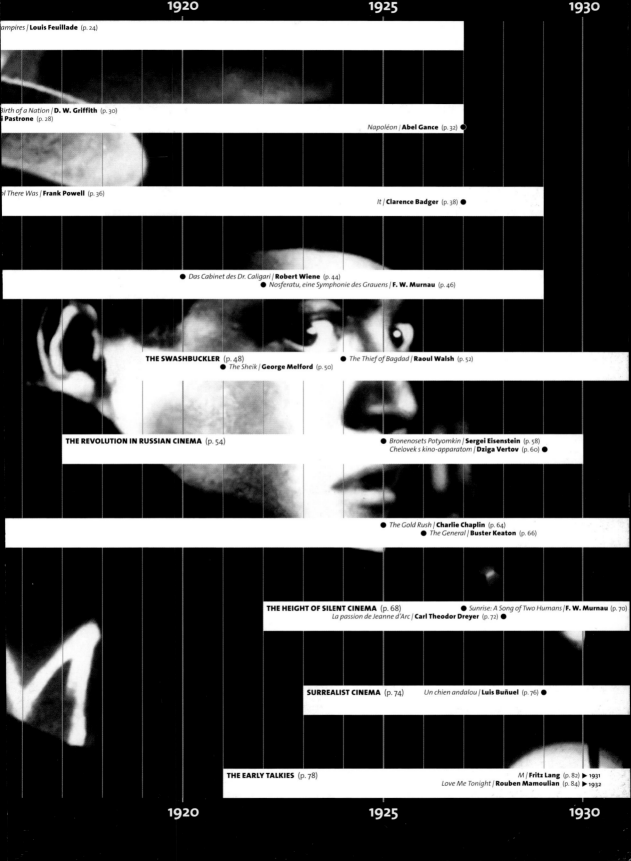

PIONEERING MOTION PICTURES

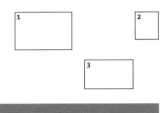

1

2

3

1 An early split-screen shot depicts a flight above the roofs of Belleville, Paris, in Ferdinand Zecca's *A la conquête de l'air*.

2 Note the cockerel in the background of this poster from 1908 for Pathé Frères— it remains the company's motif today.

3 In *L'homme à la tête en caoutchouc* the bellows stand ready in the laboratory as the scientist (Georges Méliès) prepares to experiment with his detached head.

Motion pictures both created and fed an appetite for spectacle, offering the possibility of re-creating the past, reimagining the present, and visualizing the future. The technology for making movies was invented in 1895, but the first films were often just a few seconds long and depicted simple everyday events or trick effects. Films with a recognizable narrative arrived with the twentieth century. The earliest pioneers were not based in Hollywood, which was not then a center of filmmaking, but in Europe. Notable among them were French filmmakers Georges Méliès (1861–1938), Charles Pathé (1863–1957), and Ferdinand Zecca (1864–1947). The latter directed the one-minute short *A la conquête de l'air* (*Conquering the Skies*, 1901, above) in which he flew over the Belleville neighborhood of Paris in a bizarre flying machine. The film was produced for Pathé Frères (opposite above), the film production company founded in 1896 by Charles Pathé and his brother Emile. The brothers were former restaurateurs who, in reference to their culinary origins, used a distinctive cockerel, Le Coq, as their trademark.

A technical difficulty that held back film's potential as an art form was the inability to create continuity of action across successive shots. *Attack on a China Mission—Bluejackets to the Rescue* (1900) was a cinematic milestone. Inspired by China's Boxer Rebellion (1898–1901), it focuses on a group of Christian missionaries under siege by Boxer fighters. It was directed by British

KEY EVENTS

1895	1900	c. 1902	1902	1903	1904
Auguste (1862–1954) and Louis (1864–1948) Lumière screen ten short films in Paris, including *La sortie des usines Lumière*, to a fee-paying public.	The premiere of *Attack on a China Mission—Bluejackets to the Rescue* is held at Hove Town Hall, Sussex. The audience demands a repeat screening.	The average length of a film increases from 50 feet to 600 feet, allowing more time for a narrative to unfold.	Georges Méliès directs *Le couronnement du roi Edouard VII*, a reenactment, using actors, of the recent coronation of British King Edward VII.	Edwin S. Porter's *Life of an American Fireman* is released. It is innovative for its continuous narrative and visual storytelling technique.	*Voyage a travers l'impossible* (*The Impossible Voyage*), directed by Georges Méliès, plays with ideas of space and submarine travel.

film pioneer James Williamson (1855–1933), who created one of the most developed narratives of its time. The film boasted a set in a derelict house, a cast of a couple of dozen people, and action shots aided by simulated explosions and gunshots.

After attending the first public screening of the Lumière brothers' films in 1895, the theater impresario and stage magician Georges Méliès quickly grasped the possibilities for cinema as a vehicle for illusion and fantasy. Méliès's signature was the magician's love of trickery, splicing the fantastic with the macabre. The silent fantasy L'homme à la tête en caoutchouc (The India Rubber Head, 1901, below) features Méliès as a scientist who attaches a rubber tube to his own detached head and inflates it with a pair of bellows. The experiment is repeated by an assistant, who inflates the head until it explodes. In Le voyage dans la lune (The Trip to the Moon, 1902, see p. 20) the image of the rocket ship landing in the moon's eye is a typical Méliès juxtaposition of the whimsical and the visceral. Yet for all the dazzling cinematic innovations that Méliès developed and exploited, his films never truly broke free from his theatrical roots.

The Société Film d'Art was an altogether more high-minded enterprise, formed with the intention of bringing artistic standards to cinema, particularly in the depiction of history. The first and best-known example was L'assassinat du duc de Guise (1908), directed by Charles Le Bargy (1858–1936) and André Calmettes (1861–1942), which was based on an incident in the sixteenth century when Henri III arranged for the assassination of his aristocratic rival. Despite the sensational nature of the subject, the film, with a specially commissioned score by Camille Saint-Saëns and a cast drawn from the Comédie-Française, provided a sober and serious historical pageant.

1910	1912	1912	1914	1918	1927
D. W. Griffith (1875–1948) directs his seventeen-minute short In Old California, the first motion picture filmed in Hollywood.	New York nickleodeon owner William Fox forms the Fox Film Corporation. It will become Twentieth Century Fox in 1935.	Adolph Zukor founds the Famous Players Film Company, the first US company to concentrate on making feature-length films.	Cecil B. DeMille (1881–1959) makes his first motion picture, The Squaw Man.	Jack, Albert, Harry, and Samuel Warner open their first West Coast film studio.	The silent era of films effectively ends with the release of The Jazz Singer, the first widely screened feature-length talkie.

In India the pioneering director D. G. Phalke (1870–1944), inspired by seeing an early film version of the life of Christ, learned the rudiments of filmmaking to make *Raja Harishchandra* (1913). This elaborate costume drama, based on Hindu mythology, marked the start of the Indian film industry. Drawing on a text from the Sanskrit epic the *Mahabharata*, the film tells the story of King Harishchandra, who gives up his kingdom in order to keep his promise to a holy man. Using an all-male nonprofessional cast and filming in the countryside surrounding Mumbai, Phalke created an elaborate Hindu epic of forty-minutes long. The film was an enormous success when it was first shown at the Coronation Cinema in Mumbai. Unfortunately, only the first two reels survive and modern audiences must guess at the ambitions of the finished film.

In Italy early filmmakers were drawn to the mythical and the spectacular. The works of Dante provided a fruitful source of material, the most successful example being *L'inferno* (1911), which is considered to be the first Italian feature-length film. At the same time the historical genre was developing through a series of spectacular short films, notably *La caduta di Troia* (*The Fall of Troy*, 1911) directed by Giovanni Pastrone (1883–1959) and *Gli ultimi giorni di Pompeii* (*The Last Days of Pompeii*, 1913) directed by Mario Caserini (1874–1920).

In the United States *The Great Train Robbery* (1903, see p. 22), directed by Edwin S. Porter (1870–1941), is recognized as the first US narrative film. Porter's innovative camera techniques and editing, location shots, and Western format combined to make an exciting film for audiences of the day. As technology advanced, filmmakers were able to make longer films, sometimes turning to literature for inspiration. In 1907 Canadian director Sidney Olcott (1873–1949) made the first film version of *Ben-Hur* for the New York–based Kalem Company. Adapted from Lew Wallace's novel of 1880, the fifteen-minute film is hard to follow unless the viewer knows the story, and its famous chariot race—filmed from a fixed point—lacks excitement. However, it was popular enough for Kalem to be sued—successfully—for copyright infringement, and the outcome provoked the setting of a precedent for future literary adaptations.

Cramming a lengthy narrative from a novel into a short film was problematic and therefore some of the most satisfying films to emerge were those written specifically for the big screen. *Le moulin maudit* (*The Mill*, 1909), shot for Pathé Frères by French director Alfred Machin (1877–1929), tells a story of revenge. Filmed on location in Belgium, stencil tinted to provide color and running at almost six minutes, the playlet has a self-contained narrative that is easy to follow.

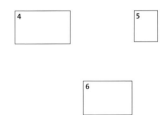

4 A scene from Louis Feuillade's thrilling five-episode crime serial *Fantômas*. The serial was renowned for its suspenseful endings.

5 The poster for adventure serial *Judex*. A master of disguise and man of mystery, this avenger of crime prefigures later celluloid superheroes.

6 The famous chariot race in *Ben-Hur: A Tale of the Christ* has been much imitated on the big screen. The remake in 1959 (see p. 226) re-created the scene almost shot for shot.

As technology advanced, filmmakers produced movies that grew in length, and mini-serials developed. Among the more successful in this format is *Fantômas* (1913–14, opposite), a five-part serial based on one of the most popular characters in French crime fiction, played here by René Navarre. Directed by Louis Feuillade (1873–1925), each episode lasted about an hour and ended grippingly on a cliffhanger. Fantômas is an amoral, murderous villain who has continued to capture the imagination of filmmakers up to the present day. Another Feuillade serial, *Judex* (1916, right), follows the fantastic adventures of a more virtuous and heroic protagonist in what perhaps marks the first appearance of a caped crusader. The prolific French filmmaker also produced the ten-part serial *Les vampires* (1915, see p. 24), which tells the story of a Parisian crime organization known as "Les Vampires." The thriller techniques developed by Feuillade were to influence later masters such as Fritz Lang (1890–1976) and Alfred Hitchcock (1899–1980).

The opportunity to make longer products, the emergence of the Hollywood studios, and larger budgets encouraged filmmakers to produce literary adaptations such as *20,000 Leagues Under the Sea* (1916), directed by Scotsman Stuart Paton (1883–1944) and based on Jules Verne's novel of 1869 and the same author's *The Mysterious Island* (1874). Paton joined forces with two fellow British immigrants to the United States, brothers John and George Williamson, to create the first film showing underwater sequences. The pioneering special effects, location shots, and elaborate sets—including a mock-up of the *Nautilus* submarine—created a film that was truly remarkable for its time.

The appetite for spectacle continued to find expression in epic films such as *The Ten Commandments* (1923) and *Ben-Hur: A Tale of the Christ* (1925, below), forming what would later become known as the sword-and-sandal genre. Directed by Fred Niblo (1874–1978) and an uncredited Charles Brabin (1882–1957), *Ben-Hur: A Tale of the Christ* proved a troubled and costly production for the newly merged Metro-Goldwyn-Mayer. To make the chariot race more exciting, a $100 prize was put up by the studio for the winner; the terrible crash that resulted remains in the final cut of the movie. The spirit of pioneering director Georges Méliès can be glimpsed in such epic films of the 1920s and later in the special effects work of Ray Harryhausen in the 1950s and 1960s. Film techniques have grown more complex and narrative structures ever more sophisticated, but the basic creative rationale of cinema—to reinvent and reinterpret reality—has remained a constant since its earliest days. **CK/DP**

Le voyage dans la lune 1902
The Trip to the Moon GEORGES MÉLIÈS 1861 – 1938

▲ Méliès created a world of fantastical landscapes in the film. Here, a Selenite tries to prevent the capsule returning to Earth.

▼ The most iconic image from the film: a rocket in the eye of the Man in the Moon

LE VOYAGE
DANS LA LUNE

The best-known, most widely seen, most successful (and most pirated) of pioneer *ciné-fantasiste* Georges Méliès's 500-plus films, this fourteen-minute cosmic epic is the forerunner of *Flash Gordon* (1936), *Destination Moon* (1950), *2001: A Space Odyssey* (1968, see p. 292) and *Star Wars* (1977, see p. 366). In a succession of hectic tableaux, an expedition to the Moon is proposed, debated (by sorcerous-looking fellows with pointy hats), and carried out.

The method of space travel is drawn from Jules Verne's book *De la terre à la lune* (*From the Earth to the Moon*, 1865, filmed in 1958), as elderly professors climb into a shell-shaped metal capsule and are fired from a cannon. The world they find is closer to H. G. Wells's *The First Men in the Moon* (1901, filmed in 1919 and 1964), with capering insect-parrot-skeleton Selenites living in a sublunar forest of giant mushrooms and the explorers forced to stand trial at the court of the Grand Lunar. Like all Méliès's films, *Le voyage dans la lune* is childishly violent—the explorers cheerfully murder natives and assassinate the Grand Lunar—and mildly satirical: stress is placed on the pompous ceremonial of the launch and the congratulatory medal-giving and parade to commemorate the safe return.

The Moon is at once a pastry-swathed human face, weeping as the rocket sticks in its eye, and a rugged, magical world. Once there, the explorers bed down and the cosmos passes above them like a speciality act—with pretty girls' faces for the seven stars of Ursa Major. The effects mix ambitious opticals (such as the precedent-setting matting of a cut-out capsule with real sea for the landing) with cut-out animations and cleverly manipulated giant theatrical scenery. **KN**

👁 KEY SCENES

1 LIFT-OFF
A line of sailor-suited chorus girls (hired from the Folies Bergère) loads the bullet-shaped space capsule into a giant cannon for perhaps the most glamorous rocket launch of all time. The surrounding scenery, including the rooftops, had all been painted.

2 MOON LANDING
Once the capsule has crash-landed on the Moon, the astronauts disembark and begin to take in the mysterious rocky lunar landscape. Méliès adds to the drama of the moment in the next shot, which inverts a familiar sight.

3 EARTH RISE
Instead of the Moon rising above the Earth, the latter appears in the darkened sky above the lunar horizon. To emphasize the point, the astronauts' outstretched hands and doffed hats lead the audience's eye to the planet.

4 ALIENS ATTACKED
The Selenites explode in puffs of smoke when struck with an umbrella. Their name is a reference to Selene, the Greek goddess of the Moon, and was previously used in H. G. Wells's novel *The First Men in the Moon*.

5 THE TROPHY
The capsule returns to Earth (with a Selenite attached), lands in the sea, and is towed to shore. At a subsequent celebration, the Selenite is forced to dance for the crowd—rather as Africans brought to Europe were often put on show for Western entertainment.

🕐 DIRECTOR PROFILE

1861–94
Georges Méliès was born in 1861. He became prominent in Paris as a stage magician, founding the Théâtre Robert-Houdin.

1895–1901
Méliès began by shooting footage in the style of the Lumière brothers but then hit on the potential of the camera to create magical illusion—essentially inventing special effects. His first films were simple one-reelers built around magical coups, such as transformations and disappearances.

1902–12
He made more complex films, with special effects set pieces linked by more elaborate plots. His last epics were overlooked.

1913–38
Bankrupt and out of business, Méliès was hailed by Surrealists as a master and granted recognition by the state: in 1931 he was awarded the Légion d'Honneur.

The Great Train Robbery 1903

EDWIN S. PORTER 1870 – 1941

▲ The robbers take control of the train. Despite being a Western, the film was actually shot in New Jersey.

▼ The poster echoes the film's famous closing shot and is reminiscent of classic romantic depictions of the Old West.

Edwin S. Porter's Western marked the arrival of modern filmmaking, with its location shooting, camera movement, and parallel editing, forging a style that would be perfected by Charlie Chaplin (1889–1977), Mack Sennett (1880–1960), and D. W. Griffith over the next two decades.

Adapted from Scott Marble's Broadway success of 1896 and drawing on the real-life seizure of a Union Pacific train by the "Hole in the Wall" gang on August 29, 1900, *The Great Train Robbery* presents all the tropes that would come to define the Western genre over the course of eleven minutes and fourteen single-shot sequences. The film's account of a railroad heist excels in its pacing and suspense, which ensured its success with audiences unused to such gripping entertainment on the screen.

Beyond its technical merits, the film fascinates in the way the robbers are presented. Porter clearly admires their ruthless efficiency and introduces ambiguity to the conventional presentation of good and bad characters. The revelers shooting the floor around the man dancing—the first time this cliché was employed in a film—undermines their role as heroic characters. Such ambivalence on the part of the filmmaker became a mainstay of genre filmmaking, particularly the Hollywood Western (see p. 242), Film Noir (see p. 168), and thrillers. The final shot comes after the robbers have been killed and the narrative is complete: one of the villains appears in close-up, raises his gun, and shoots at the audience. It is one of the most overt examples of cinema's ability to thrill, offering audiences the vicarious adrenaline rush of violence. **IHS**

👁 KEY SCENES

1 A CAREFULLY PLANNED JOB
In the opening scene, the robbers take control of the station office. With ruthless and meticulous planning they hold the telegraph operator and ticket collector hostage. This sets the story in motion and highlights the robbers' efficiency.

2 A POSSE IS FORMED
As the robbers make their getaway, the telegraph operator interrupts a local dance, informing the revelers of what has happened. The scene is an entertaining diversion from the action, introducing the heroes of the day—a posse that pursues the robbers.

3 SHOOTING THE AUDIENCE
The final sequence remains an oddly compelling scene. Breaking the fourth wall (when an actor directly addresses the audience), it offers an early display of cinema's explicit relationship with violence. The shot caused some audience members a little distress at the time.

🕐 DIRECTOR PROFILE

1870–1903
Edwin Stanton Porter was born in 1870. In 1899 he joined the Edison Manufacturing Company, where he took control of the New York Studios. He was involved in every aspect of filmmaking, although his two earliest successes, *Life of an American Fireman* (1903) and *The Great Train Robbery* failed to credit him as director.

1904–8
He experimented with parallel editing in *The Kleptomaniac* (1905) and played with camera angles, close-ups, and lighting set-ups in *The Seven Ages* (1905). *Dream of a Rarebit Fiend* (1906) saw him draw on the work of Georges Méliès for his adaptation of a Winsor McCay comic strip.

1909–16
Porter left Edison to set up a short-lived motion picture company, Rex. In 1912 he joined Adolph Zukor's Famous Players, where he directed the first five-reel US film, *The Prisoner of Zenda* (1913), followed in the same year by *The Count of Monte Cristo*. In his last two years as director, he worked with Mary Pickford and made a star of acclaimed stage actress Pauline Frederick, who appeared in the title role of his final film, *Lydia Gilmore* (1915).

1917–41
Porter became president of the Precision Machine Company, which manufactured the Simplex projector. He continued to develop and invent new technology for cinema until his death, at seventy-one, on April 30, 1941, at the Taft Hotel in New York.

CINEMA'S FIRST WESTERN STAR

Born in Little Rock, Arkansas, on March 21, 1880, Max Aronson (below) was cinema's first Western hero. His break arrived with *The Great Train Robbery*. Edwin S. Porter cast Aronson in three roles in the film. He first appears as the passenger who is shot in the back as he attempts to flee from the robbers; he also plays the dancer whose feet are being shot at, and one of the brakemen on the train. The success of the film led him to direct his own films, but it was his inability to find a lead actor for *Broncho Billy's Redemption* (1910) and the decision to play the role himself that led to stardom.

Dozens of sequels followed, and he became a household name as Broncho Billy, until the character's penultimate outing in *Broncho Billy and the Parson* (1915). Fifty years later Aronson made a final return to the screen in *The Bounty Killer* (1965), when he was eighty-five.

Les vampires 1915

LOUIS FEUILLADE 1873 – 1925

▲ Marta the ballerina—soon to perish, on stage, courtesy of the Grand Vampire.

▼ Musidora's black-clad vamp anticipated the gothic attire of Catwoman and Batman.

LES FILMS MYSTÉRIEUX

LES VAMPIRES · LES YEUX QUI FASCINENT

With rival Pathé set to release a new serial featuring *Perils of Pauline* star Pearl White in France, Leon Gaumont asked Louis Feuillade to invent a new series of sensational criminal exploits. The result: *Les vampires*, a ten-part serial about a gang—not a horror film, despite the title. Dismissed by those seeking a more artistically elevated cinema—and by authorities suspicious of the lack of moralizing—*Les vampires* is now seen as Feuillade's masterpiece: a thoroughly modern example of early cinema.

Crucial to the film's power is the way in which it places fantastic events in real locations. Stories of cannonball attacks, poisoned champagne, and more than one criminal gang terrorizing the homes of respectable citizens were filmed using the streets, houses, and rooftops of Paris. The departure of local citzens to fight in World War I gave the Paris streets an empty, eerie quality. Feuillade used the hero's assistant Mazamette (Marcel Lévesque) to lighten the tone, but the real star is Musidora (a.k.a. Jeanne Roques) as Irma Vep. Here, and later in the serial *Judex* (1916), she gave striking portrayals of feminine evil.

While US films were moving toward a more complex cutting style and camerawork, *Les vampires* makes minimal use of editing and stages action in front of a generally static camera. Just as earlier French film pioneers the Lumière brothers and Georges Méliès had pointed to cinema's alternative possibilities as a means of presenting everyday life or imagining impossible worlds, in *Les vampires* Feuillade demonstrates how filmmakers could document the fantastic. **GB**

KEY SCENES

1 "LA TÊTE COUPÉE"

The severed head of Inspector Durtal is found in the Château de la Chesnaye. Millionairess Mrs. Simpson and Dr. Nox (Jean Aymé) are kept under close guard, but soon Mrs. Simpson is murdered. Dr. Nox flees over the roofs, leaving a card reading, "I am the Grand Vampire."

2 "LE CRYPTOGRAMME ROUGE"

In disguise, young reporter Philippe Guérande (Edouard Mathé) visits the Howling Cat, the seedy nightclub where the Vampire gang meets. Inside, the singing of Irma Vep (an anagram of "vampire") elicits rowdy applause. Guérande returns home.

3 "LES YEUX QUI FASCINENT"

The guests at the hotel du Grand Veneur include the Count Kerlor and his son (actually the Grand Vampire and Irma Vep), and rival criminal Moreno (Fernand Herrmann). The cat-suited Irma Vep searches Werner's room. On leaving, she is captured by Moreno.

4 "LES NOCES SANGLANTES"

Philippe Guérande's wife is captured by the Vampires, who celebrate the wedding of Irma Vep and Vénénos (Frederik Moriss), who is the new Grand Vampire. Guérande, his assistant Mazamette, and the police burst in. This time, the Vampires do not escape.

⏱ DIRECTOR PROFILE

1873–1907

Louis Feuillade was born into a family of vintners in the village of Lunet, in the south of France. After a largely unsuccessful literary career, he entered the film industry by writing screenplays for Alice Guy, then artistic director at the leading French production company, Gaumont Pictures. He took over from Guy in 1907 and remained artistic director until 1918, during which time he produced *Les vampires*, the film series for which he is best remembered today.

1908–12

The prolific Feuillade directed hundreds of short films—his total output has been estimated at more than seven hundred pieces—ranging from "Film esthétique" (historical reenactments, mythological fantasies, and tragedies) to comedies. Feuillade had notable success with the Bébé films (1910–13) starring the child actor René Dary, while his serial *La vie telle qu'elle est* (1911–12) was a groundbreaking combination of domestic melodrama and location shooting. He followed up the Bébé series with sixty-two *Bout-de-Zan* films (1912–16).

1913–16

Feuillade made his name with crime serials such as *Fantômas* (1913–14)—generally regarded as having established the format for his other well-known work—based on the best-selling novels by Pierre Souvestre and Marcel Allain, *Les vampires* (made after a brief service in the trenches), and *Judex*. At the time, they attracted the critics' ire for being tasteless and outmoded compared, for example, to the perceived "high art" of D. W. Griffith's work. Feuillade continued to explore and work in other genres.

1917–25

His final triumphs were two further crime serials: *Tih-Minh* (1918) and *Barrabas* (1919). Feuillade had slipped into obscurity by the time of his death in 1925, but his films continued to delight the Surrealists—in part precisely because of their unrespectable, low-brow reputation—and were rediscovered by a new generation after World War II.

THE EARLY EPIC

1 Epic films require large, elaborate set designs, such as the one featured in the spectacular chariot race in *Quo vadis?*.

2 The film poster for *Civilization*. The war theme worked well on the big screen.

3 Jesus (H. B. Warner) gives his Sermon on the Mount in Cecil B. DeMille's biblical epic *The King of Kings*.

Epic movies are known for their big budgets, towering sets, large casts, breadth of vision, and sometimes their special effects. In the early days of cinema the nascent technology limited what directors could produce, but as it improved directors gave full rein to their imagination. The roots of the epic spring from Europe and in particular Italy, where directors looked back at their country's classical past to make films that were visually extravagant and operatic in scale. Enrico Guazzoni (1876–1949) used five thousand extras in his nine-reel drama *Quo vadis?* (1912, above) set in early Christian Rome. Giovanni Pastrone (1883–1959) filmed *Cabiria: visione storica del terzo secolo AC* (*Cabiria: Historic Vision of the Third Century BC*, 1914, see p. 28) in multiple locations. It is three hours long, sports a cast of hundreds, and features spectacular sets. Pastrone and his Spanish cinematographer Segundo de Chomón were the first to use a dolly-track system, which allows a camera to move. This enabled them to create smooth tracking shots. De Chomón was a great master of optical effects, contributing to *Napoléon* (1927, see p. 32) directed by Abel Gance (1889–1981), an epic film that explored camera techniques extensively. Italian sword-and-sandal epics were a major influence on Hollywood output and inspired Cecil B. DeMille (1881–1959) to make his first version of *The Ten Commandments* (1923), a 136-minute spectacle that dramatizes the biblical story of Moses.

KEY EVENTS

1912	1912	1913	1914	1915	1916
Enrico Guazzoni's 120-minute drama *Quo vadis?* is the first movie to run for two hours.	In Los Angeles, Thomas H. Ince builds Inceville, a city of motion picture sets where he shoots many of his films.	Italians Mario Caserini (1874–1920) and Eleuterio Rodolfi (1876–1933) make the extravagant *Gli ultimi giorni di Pompeii* (*The Last Days of Pompeii*).	*Cabiria* (see p. 28) costs more than one million lira to make and becomes the most expensive film of its day.	*The Birth of a Nation* (see p. 30) runs to 190 minutes and breaks the record for the longest film.	D. W. Griffith responds to accusations of bigotry with his epic *Intolerance: Love's Struggle Throughout the Ages*.

DeMille deployed his sense of showmanship again in 1927 when he directed the spectacular biblical epic—*The King of Kings* (below right)—about the life and death of Jesus Christ.

When World War I broke out in 1914 it disrupted the development of the European film industry but US directors continued to break cinematic barriers. D. W. Griffith (1875–1948) directed a saga about the American Civil War, *The Birth of a Nation* (1915, see p. 30), which was innovative in its technical and narrative style. Yet the United States was not immune to events in Europe and *The Birth of a Nation* was intended to show war as abhorrent. Directors explored the subject of war further with pacifist films such as the allegorical *Civilization* (1916, right) by Thomas H. Ince (1882–1924). Ince was a titan of the early film industry: a film director who also defined the roles of film producer and production executive, helped to develop the Hollywood studio system, and in 1915, cofounded one of Hollywood's first major independent production companies, Triangle Motion Picture Company.

Ince realized the need for a place to make feature films requiring large sets, props, dressing rooms, and stages. He built the first recognizable studio, Inceville, at a ranch in Los Angeles, and filmed *Civilization* there. Set in the imaginary kingdom of Wredpryd, the movie follows the fate of a submarine commander who refuses to fire at a civilian ocean liner suspected of carrying ammunition for his country's enemies, sinks his submarine and finds himself in Purgatory. A showman, Ince promoted his $1 million movie with newspaper advertisements touting the extravagance of its production: "$18,000 Used for Ammunition in One Battle/40,000 People Employed/10,000 Horses in Thrilling Cavalry Charges/40 Aeroplanes in Great Air Battle." The film was a success and its bloody depiction of war so effective that when the United States entered World War I in 1917, it was pulled from distribution.

After the war, directors such as Fritz Lang (1890–1976) made an impact in Europe. *Die Nibelungen: Siegfried* and *Die Nibelungen: Kriemhilds Rache* (*Die Nibelungen: Kriemhild's Revenge*, both 1924) were based on a thirteenth-century poem about the Teutonic warrior Siegfried. Lavish productions, with fantastical set designs, choreographed battle scenes, and mythological creatures, these films laid the foundations for the fantasy epic. However, it was a movie with a World War I theme that became the silent era's biggest blockbuster: *The Big Parade* (1925), directed by King Vidor (1894–1982), achieved an unprecedented ninety-six-week run at New York's Astor Theater. Vidor created an antiwar epic showing the brutality of trench warfare, which strikes an emotional chord because of its effective portrayal of intimacy. The film stars John Gilbert as Jim, a lazy rich kid who is shamed into enlisting. Jim comes of age as he makes friends with fellow soldiers, falls in love with a French girl and faces the reality of losing those he loves. Vidor's focus on the joking camaraderie between the young soldiers adds to the poignancy of their fate when they fall. **CK**

1921	1923	1925	1925	1925	1927
Influenced by *Intolerance*, Carl Theodor Dreyer (1889–1968) makes the multistoried *Blade af Satans Bog* (*Leaves Out of the Book of Satan*).	Cecil B. DeMille's *The Ten Commandments* is an early color movie that amazes and delights audiences with its use of Technicolor inserts.	A version of Fritz Lang's *Siegfried* is released in the United States with a Wagnerian score, which angers the Austrian director.	*The Big Parade* premieres. It takes in $22 million at the box office worldwide to become the highest-grossing silent film ever.	Erich von Stroheim (1885–1957) spends $500,000 to make the ten-hour drama *Greed*. It is released after MGM cuts it to 150 minutes.	Cecil B. DeMille's $1,265,000 epic *The King of Kings*, about the life of Christ and featuring a cast of thousands, is released.

Cabiria 1914

GIOVANNI PASTRONE 1883 – 1959

▲ *Cabiria*'s towering and artful sets established the tone for subsequent epics.

▼ D'Annunzio's name helped sell the film.

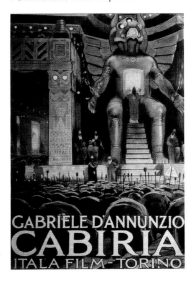

The story of the kidnapping of young Roman noble Cabiria (Carolina Catena) and her nurse Croessa (Gina Marangoni) by Phoenician pirates during the Second Punic War in the third century BCE, and their subsequent rescue by a Roman spy and his slave, the muscular Maciste (Bartolomeo Pagano), *Cabiria: visione storica del terzo secolo AC* (*Cabiria: Historic Vision of the Third Century BC*) is as grandiose, spectacular, and impressive today as it was upon its release in 1914. *Cabiria* was the most visually impressive and daring of a number of flamboyant Italian epics made before World War I that addressed Italy's imperial past, focusing on tales of classical antiquity and imperial opulence. Contemporary advertisements announced a cast of 5,000, 1,000 horses, 200 elephants, and 200 camels in more than 1,200 scenes. These were no idle boasts. Shot over six months and with a sizeable budget, the film has impressive set pieces including a reenactment—with real elephants—of Hannibal crossing the Alps, the eruption of Mount Etna, the defeat of the Roman fleet at Syracuse, and the preparation for Cabiria's sacrifice at the immense Temple of Moloch. The film was so massive in scale that it ran to more than fourteen reels (three hours) at a time when most US films were still shorts.

Director Giovanni Pastrone's camera was, unusually for the time, highly mobile, employing a number of tracking shots. Technically innovative and hugely successful upon release, *Cabiria* was influential upon later filmmakers such as D. W. Griffith, whose *Intolerance* (1916) owes much to *Cabiria*'s grandiose and adventurous spirit. **RH**

1 CABIRIA IS KIDNAPPED

In the chaos that reigns after Mount Etna erupts, a young noblewoman, Cabiria, is separated from her parents and then presumed dead. Later, Cabiria and her nurse Croessa are kidnapped by pirates and sold to Rome's sworn enemies, the Carthaginians.

2 NEAR SACRIFICE

A crowd gathers as the captive Cabiria is selected to be sacrificed at the Carthaginian Temple of Moloch. Before she can be killed a Roman noble and spy, Fulvio Axilla (Umberto Mozzato), and his faithful (muscular) slave Maciste rescue her in a spectacular fight.

3 THE RETURN TO ROME

The Romans defeat the Carthaginians after a ten-year struggle, so the now-adult Cabiria (Lidia Quaranta) and her rescuer Fulvio can return to Rome. As the boat reaches home, the loving couple embrace and watch as angels joyously circle their vessel.

1883–1906

Giovanni Pastrone was born in Montechiaro d'Asti in Piedmont, Italy, where he studied violin and accountancy. In 1905 he began his career working as an administrative assistant at Carlo Rossi & Company in Turin.

1907–8

In two years Pastrone rose to become administrative director and when Carlo Rossi & Company became Itala Film in 1908, Pastrone became joint owner. He was central to the success of the developing company, attracting top French comedian André Deed from Pathé Frères to Itala Film, and bringing in innovative Spanish cinematographer and effects specialist Segundo de Chomón, who later proved crucial to the technical visual wizardry and realism of *Cabiria*.

1909–14

After reorganizing production methods at Itala Film, Pastrone directed a number of popular historical shorts including *Enrico III* (*Henry III*, 1909) and *Giulio Cesare* (*Julius Caesar*, 1909). His ambitious thirty-minute *La caduta di Troia* (*The Fall of Troy*, 1911) was successful in the United States although there was an embargo on foreign films at the time. In 1914 he directed his first feature, *Cabiria*, which was a massive hit.

1915–59

After *Cabiria*, Pastrone directed eight more films, some featuring the superstrong character Maciste, before Itala Film was absorbed into another company. He retired from the film industry in 1923 to become a medical researcher.

GABRIELE D'ANNUNZIO

Although the screenplay for *Cabiria* was written largely by the film's director, Giovanni Pastrone, Italian poet Gabriele d'Annunzio (below) provided the very lyrical and much praised intertitles for the film. His exact contribution has been contested over the years, but it is the film with which his name is associated most closely. D'Annunzio was a true polymath. A celebrated poet, he was also a journalist, novelist, playwright, political thinker, and sometime daredevil. Although only an occasional screenwriter, many of his novels, a poem, and several of his plays were adapted for

the screen and some, such as *La Gioconda* (*Gioconda*, 1899), were transposed several times. D'Annunzio's close association with Fascist ideology in Italy during the rise of Benito Mussolini has clouded the writer's reputation, although his innovative work remains fascinating.

The Birth of a Nation 1915

D. W. GRIFFITH 1875 – 1948

▲ The Ku Klux Klan ride triumphantly through a town defended by black soldiers.

▼ The poster reflects the film's notorious portrayal of the Klan's knights as noble.

The merits of D. W. Griffith's film are somewhat eclipsed by its content. An epic 190-minute account of the American Civil War and subsequent rise of the Ku Klux Klan, the film was adapted from Reverend Thomas Dixon Jr.'s stage play *The Clansman* (1905). It details the problems that arise when blacks and whites are given equal status and celebrates the bravery of a secret society that "saved the South from the anarchy of black rule."

Technically and narratively, the film is a marvel of early cinema. Other directors might have toyed with the potential of film and helped forge a basic language, but it was Griffith who transformed it into grammar, drawing all these techniques together, allowing him to expand his canvas in telling the story of two families torn apart by civil war. However, such innovation is impossible to praise unreservedly in a film the opening scene of which tells the viewer that "The bringing of the African to America planted the first seed of disunion."

The movie is divided into two sections, and part one mostly adheres to the historical retelling of how the North and South came to blows. However, after the president's assassination, Griffith embarks on an alternative history of postwar society, where the "simple" black man is corrupted. Griffith argued that there were no black actors in California at the time, so white actors in makeup play the main black and mixed-race characters. Despite complaints from the National Association for the Advancement of Colored People, the film would eventually gross a record $18 million. It also renewed interest in the Klan, which had all but disappeared by the time of the film's release. **IHS**

👁 KEY SCENES

1 BATTLE CHARGE
Battle sequences, particularly the elaborate charge scene, are infused with a pace and technical virtuosity previously unseen. Griffith understood audiences' ability to grasp even the smallest details quickly.

4 ATTACK ON THE CABIN
Although the Klan's overthrow of Silas Lynch, the mulatto lieutenant governor of South Carolina, and the climactic siege at the log cabin showcase brilliant intercutting, this sequence contains Griffith's most obscene representation of black characters.

🕐 DIRECTOR PROFILE

1875–1914
David Llewelyn Wark Griffith was born in Kentucky in 1875, the son of a Confederate civil war hero. After his initial attempts to pursue a career in the theater as a director or writer foundered, Griffith reluctantly turned to the new medium of film. Although his first script was turned down by Edwin S. Porter (1870–1941), he was given a small part in the director's *Rescued from an Eagle's Nest* (1908). Over the next six years, Griffith directed more than four hundred films and discovered one of the first major stars of US cinema, Mary Pickford, whom he cast in the title role in *The Little Teacher* (1909).

2 LINCOLN ON THE BALCONY
The film prides itself on the accuracy of its historical scenes, replicating every detail of Ford's Theater, where Abraham Lincoln was shot. Although not problematic in itself, such verisimilitude feeds into the presentation of the film's final section as some kind of truth.

1915–18
Griffith followed *The Birth of a Nation* with *Intolerance: Love's Struggle Throughout the Ages* (1916), an ambitious and costly plea for peace around the world. The film failed to ignite public interest and left the director severely bankrupt.

1919–24
Griffith joined forces with Charlie Chaplin, Mary Pickford, and Douglas Fairbanks to form United Artists, enabling them to distribute their films without studio interference. Three of his titles, *Broken Blossoms* (1919), *Way Down East* (1920), and *Orphans of the Storm* (1921), were successes, but never on the scale of *The Birth of a Nation*. After the failure of *Isn't Life Wonderful?* (1924), Griffith departed United Artists to become a director for hire.

3 CONGRESS OPENS
Following coercive tactics that prevent the white electorate from voting and allow South Carolina's State House to be dominated by blacks, the newly elected representatives are presented as lazy, gluttonous, power-obsessed idiots.

1925–48
Griffith made only three more films. *Lady of the Pavements* (1929) experimented with sound, whereas *Abraham Lincoln* (1930) and *The Struggle* (1931) attempted to merge the cumbersome new movie-making technology with Griffith's fluid style of filming, with limited success. In 1936, Griffith was employed to shoot the earthquake sequence in *San Francisco*, directed by Woody van Dyke (1889–1943), for which he was not credited. He died from a cerebral hemorrhage at the Knickerbocker Hotel in Hollywood on July 23, 1948.

Napoléon 1927
ABEL GANCE 1889 − 1981

▲ In one of the film's stunning location shots, Napoleon sets sail from Corsica.

▼ Gance's sense of visual imagery is echoed in the film's poster, as the French leader is painted as both a literal and symbolic hero.

Directed, produced, and written with breathtaking vision by Frenchman Abel Gance, *Napoléon* is a revolutionary work. Innovative use of lighting and special effects, masterful editing, and an exceptional ability to tell a story reveal Gance to be one of cinema's earliest auteurs. Conceived as the first in a series of films depicting the life of Napoleon Bonaparte, *Napoléon* charts the future emperor's schooldays and his role in the Siege of Toulon, the Reign of Terror, and the first Italian campaign. Sadly, the huge cost of *Napoléon* meant that the series was never completed, and the rise of the talkies and the difficulties of projecting in widescreen meant that the film was poorly received. Gance continued to edit and modify it for the rest of his life, resulting in numerous nondefinitive cuts of the film, some as long as five and a half hours.

Napoléon stands out for Gance's pioneering editing and camerawork using handheld cameras, split screens, widescreen triptychs, hand-tinting, jump cuts, dolly shots, close-ups, and superimposed montages. Lingering close-ups of Bonaparte (Albert Dieudonné), soldiers, and people in a crowd create an atmosphere of joy and pain. The camera moves with astonishing speed and grace, taking the viewer to the heart of battle scenes, conjuring the atmosphere of euphoria at a victory ball, and hinting at Bonaparte's lust for his future wife by lingering over the bare legs and behinds of ecstatic dancers. *Napoléon* is epic cinema, with subtle direction, thoughtful acting, spectacular action scenes, and vast sets all combined with a storyline that includes humor, romance, sorrow, compassion, pain, and courage. **CK**

1 PILLOW FIGHT
The young Bonaparte, angry that cadets at his school have released his pet eagle—a recurring symbol of his soaring destiny—engages in a pillow fight. Gance pioneered the use of Polyvision to create a split-screen format. One shot alone required sixty exposures.

2 DEATH OF MARAT
The depiction of the assassination of journalist Jean-Paul Marat mimics that of Jacques-Louis David's painting *The Death of Marat* (1793), bringing its still beauty alive as a moving image. The light on Marat's head creates a halo effect, suggesting his martyrlike role.

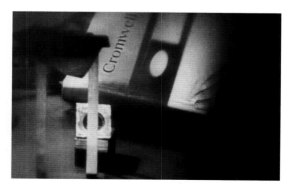

3 SHADOW OF THE GUILLOTINE
After Danton (Alexandre Koubitzky) is executed, Saint-Just (Gance) and Robespierre (Edmond van Daële) observe the shadow of a guillotine cast onto a book about Cromwell. Bonaparte refuses to join forces with them during the Reign of Terror.

4 COLOR TRIPTYCH
The film culminates in a triptych sequence, changing from black and white to hand-tinted blue, white, and red in imitation of the French flag, celebrating Bonaparte's triumphant Italian campaign. Gance used multiple exposures to create the changing images.

🕐 DIRECTOR PROFILE

1889–1909
Born in Paris, Abel Gance worked as a solicitor's clerk before pursuing a career as an actor on the stage and in films. Gance made his debut, as both an actor and a writer, in the short *Molière* (1909), directed by Léonce Perret (1880–1935).

1910–15
Gance secured a one-season contract as an actor at the Théâtre Royal du Parc in Brussels but continued to write film scenarios; he also directed a historical drama, *La digue* (*The Dam*, 1911). During this period, Gance wrote and directed an experimental short, *La folie du docteur Tube* (*Dr Tube's Folly*, 1915), about the hallucinations of a scientist, using a variety of distorted lenses and mirrors to create hallucinatory effects. He also continued to make films and experiment with lighting, editing, and camera techniques.

1916–26
After the drama *La dixième symphonie* (*The Tenth Symphony*, 1918), Gance made the antiwar movie *J'accuse* (*I Accuse*, 1919). Assisted by cinematographer Léonce-Henry Burel, Gance's climactic scenes of the dead reawakening on the battlefield—some sites had seen genuine battles—struck a painful chord with postwar audiences worldwide. During a trip to the United States in 1921, Gance met D. W. Griffith. In 1923 he directed a drama about a father and daughter, *La roue* (*The Wheel*), which was innovative for its quick-fire cuts.

1927–81
Following the release of *Napoléon*, Gance forged a patchy career in talkies, including *Lucrèce Borgia* (1935), and returned to the theme of Bonaparte with *Austerlitz* (1960). After the failure of science fiction movie *La fin du monde* (*The End of the World*, 1931), however, his popularity waned. Interest in Gance's work was revived when French Nouvelle Vague (see p. 248)directors rediscovered his silents. In 1979 a newly edited five-hour version of *Napoléon* was screened, restoring his reputation and introducing his legacy to a new legion of admirers only two years before he died from tuberculosis.

SILENT HEROINES

1 Theda Bara in trademark revealing garb as the Egyptian queen in *Cleopatra*, directed by J. Gordon Edwards (1867–1925).

2 Greta Garbo as beautiful but destructive cheat Elena in the romantic drama *The Temptress*, by Fred Niblo (1874–1948).

3 The German poster for *Die Büchse der Pandora*, a melodrama about a naive yet dangerous young woman.

The virgins portrayed soulfully by Lillian Gish and playfully by Mary Pickford during the silent era were countered by two comparatively modish manifestations of the sexual woman. In the mid-teens came the vamp, the voracious destroyer of upper-class men, iconically portrayed by Theda Bara in *A Fool There Was* (1915, see p. 36). In the 1920s the vamp ceded her place to the flapper, a hedonistic but far from malign figure espoused most famously by Colleen Moore and Clara Bow, the "It girl."

Virgins and vamps were holdovers from Victorian melodrama, fantasy creations rooted in idealized and demonized notions of femininity. Arriving after World War I, the flapper was one face of the emancipated New Woman who worked, voted, smoked, drank, danced to jazz, and had sex. The other face was the sophisticated wife, played most adventurously by the elaborately costumed Gloria Swanson in six Cecil B. DeMille (1881–1959) boudoir comedies beginning with *Don't Change Your Husband* (1919). The sexy, working girl and the liberated wife morphed into the fast-talking modern women of 1930s screwball comedy.

Just as the femme fatale of 1940s Film Noir (see p. 168) was the product of male anxieties during a time of national upheaval, the vamp was a sociological construct. Unlike the femme fatale, however, she would not later be redeemed by feminist scholars. She emerged as a cinematic phantom, via Sir Philip

KEY EVENTS

1912	1913	1915	1917	1919	1920
Clara Pontoppidan plays cinema's first-known vamp in the influential Danish erotic melodrama *Vampyrdanserinden* (*The Vampire Dancer*).	Alice Hollister stars in the silent short *The Vampire*, which establishes the ruination formula of the US vamp film.	Theda Bara becomes the definitive US vamp, scourge of wealthy capitalists, in *A Fool There Was* (see p. 36).	Known for her risqué costumes, Bara sports a metal snake bra revealing most of her breasts in the epic *Cleopatra*.	Gloria Swanson gives marital comedy a knowing edge in *Don't Change Your Husband*, the first of her flamboyant Cecil B. DeMille comedies.	Olive Thomas plays a schoolgirl infatuated with an older man in *The Flapper*. The same year, she dies from accidental poisoning at the age of twenty-five.

Burne-Jones's painting *The Vampire*, the poem of that name by his cousin Rudyard Kipling, and Bram Stoker's novel *Dracula*, all from 1897. Kipling's poem inspired Porter Emerson Browne's Broadway hit of 1909, *A Fool There Was*. Browne's play drew on the Social Darwinist theories of influential sociologist William Graham Sumner, which suggested that the vampiric nature of female sexuality threatened the capitalistic energies of the evolutionary Aryan male. Implicating Browne's play and Frank Powell's film of 1915, cultural historian Bram Dijkstra has traced how the teachings of Sumner and his contemporaries, embracing racism and misogyny, eventually fed the Nazi genocide.

Whether or not Bara considered the social ramifications of her performance, the movie's success enabled William Fox to found his studio and made her a star. She exploited her vampish traits with an array of kohl-eyed domestic temptresses and exotics, most famously *Cleopatra* (1917, opposite). However, she was not US cinema's first vamp. Alice Hollister had preempted her in *The Vampire* (1913), in which vaudeville dancers Alice Eis and Bert French re-created their notorious "Vampire Dance" of 1909. As an otherworldly woman who sucks the life force from a lawyer, Bara was the most erotic of fatal women—despite her ponderousness—until 1926 when Greta Garbo starred in *The Temptress* (right) and *Flesh and the Devil*. Betty Blythe (Bara's skimpily attired replacement at Fox), Helen Gardner, and Myrna Loy were among those who played variations on the vamp without challenging Bara's cultural impact. Imported from Germany in 1922, Pola Negri brought a darkly passionate presence to her Paramount films but she was more imperious than deadly.

In 1920 F. Scott Fitzgerald symbolically launched the roaring twenties with his sensational debut novel *This Side of Paradise* and Olive Thomas, who had originated the "baby vamp" in *Upstairs and Down* (1919), played a schoolgirl imitating a jazz baby in *The Flapper*—the first use of that word in the United States (from the party girl's defiant habit of leaving galoshes unfastened). Fitzgerald credited Colleen Moore as the quintessential flapper for her performance in *Flaming Youth* (1923). Moore became a box-office phenomenon, but she was wholesome rather than seductive. That could not be said of Bow in films like *It* (1927, see p. 38), in which Bow excelled as a department store employee out to snare its owner, and writer Elinor Glyn showed up on screen to explain the meaning of "It," her euphemism for sex appeal. Bow had this in abundance: she was a whirligig of winks, smiles, pouts, and wiggles, but she never crossed the line into vulgarity or made desirability threatening.

On another plane was the dazzling, sybaritic Louise Brooks. Having played flappers in *A Social Celebrity* (1926), *Love 'Em and Leave 'Em* (1926), and *Rolled Stockings* (1927), she was summoned to Berlin to star in *Die Büchse der Pandora* (*Pandora's Box*, 1929, right), by G. W. Pabst (1885–1967). Haplessly promiscuous, Brooks's Lulu destroys men not deliberately but because she cannot help it. Her performance carried the flapper into the realm of the love goddess. **GF**

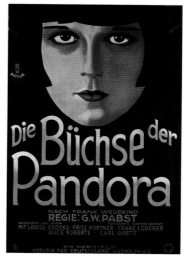

1923	1924	1926	1927	1928	1929
Colleen Moore enjoys huge success as a flapper in *Flaming Youth*, based on Walter Fabian's novel of 1923 about contemporary "petting party" culture.	Pola Negri stars as a vampy Catherine the Great in the drama *Forbidden Paradise*, directed by Ernst Lubitsch (1892–1947).	Greta Garbo is a lethal femme fatale in *The Temptress* and torments John Gilbert with love—on and off camera—in *Flesh and the Devil*.	Clara Bow's shop girl wins her wealthy boss in *It* (see p. 38)—named after the quality defined by Edwardian authoress Elinor Glyn.	The flapper played by Joan Crawford in *Our Dancing Daughters* combines outward sexual aggressiveness and inner virtue.	Louise Brooks's insouciant bobbed-hair Lulu lacerates German manhood—and one woman—in G. W. Pabst's *Die Büchse der Pandora*.

A Fool There Was 1915

FRANK POWELL 1877 – 1964

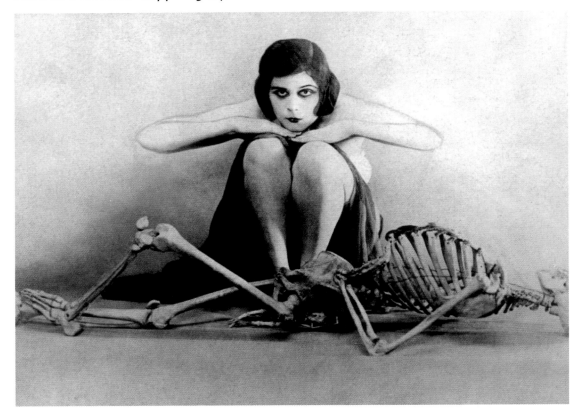

▲ Theda Bara was a phenomenon of early cinema. Studio publicity created and promoted her mysterious, exotic image.

▼ The film's poster illustrates the seductive but dangerous charms of Theda Bara.

In an acid reminiscence about early cinema, scriptwriter to the Marx Brothers S. J. Perelman characterized *A Fool There Was* thus: "What gave the picture significance, assuming that it had any, was neither its story, which was paltry, nor its acting, which was aboriginal, but a pyrogenic half-pint by the name of Theda Bara, who immortalized the vamp just as Little Egypt, at the World's Fair in 1893, had the hoochie-coochie." Although, as Perelman's piece makes clear, the erotic charge of the film may have diminished over the years, there is no denying the influence that Bara's film debut exerted on the nascent industry. She is little known today, largely because most of her films are lost.

Shot at the William Fox studios in Fort Lee, New Jersey, the film was based on a play of the same name, which in turn was inspired by Rudyard Kipling's poem "The Vampire." Bara is the unnamed suburban succubus (described in the film as "a certain woman of the vampire species") who seduces a wealthy businessman, John Schuyler (Edward José), pursuing him from the United States to Europe, where he becomes her slave. Dismissed from his job, Schuyler returns to New York, where he installs his demanding mistress. Despite interventions from his wife and daughter, he sinks into his final degradation.

Although it declared itself as a psychological drama, the film is more concerned with sensation than psychology and for this reason it is Bara's film. Equipped with an exotic biography courtesy of the studio publicity machine, she became one of the screen's earliest sex symbols, and the first in a long line of femmes fatales. **DP**

👁 KEY SCENES

1 THE DOMESTIC IDYLL
In suburban Larchmont, businessman John Schuyler is spending his summer in domestic contentment with his wife and daughter. Meanwhile, the Vampire is in the process of discarding one lover and turning her attention to Schuyler.

2 SUICIDE ON THE BOAT
The Vampire's abandoned lover follows her on the steamer and confronts her. She laughs in his face, and the title reads "Kiss me, my fool." He shoots himself, and Schuyler, boarding the boat, sees the body being carried off.

3 THE DENOUEMENT
Bringing her infant daughter with her, Schuyler's wife makes a last-minute attempt to free her husband from the clutches of the Vampire. He is about to go with them when the Vampire returns and once again he sinks under her spell.

🕐 STAR PROFILE: THEDA BARA

1885–1914
Theda Bara was born Theodosia Burr Goodman in Cincinnati, Ohio, the daughter of a prosperous tailor who had emigrated from Poland. She attended the University of Cincinnati where she developed an interest in theater. She moved to New York and made her Broadway debut in 1908 in *The Devil*.

1915–18
She made her film debut in *A Fool There Was*—an immediate hit thanks to the Fox publicity machine, which created a pedigree for her as the Egyptian-raised daughter of a French actress and an Italian sculptor. The profits from the film helped William Fox set up the Fox Film Foundation, and Bara became one of his biggest stars. Her first films were shot in the Fox studio in Fort Lee, Florida. She relocated to the West Coast for *Cleopatra* (1917), her most famous role. She made some forty films with Fox; the majority (including *Cleopatra*) are lost. Her last film for the company is *The She Devil* (1918).

1919–26
After leaving Fox she made only two more films, *The Unchastened Woman* (1925) and *Madame Mystery* (1926) in which she burlesqued her vamp persona.

1927–55
After appearing on Broadway in *The Blue Flame* in 1927 Bara effectively retired. Having married film director Charles Brabin (1882–1957) in 1921, she spent the rest of her life with him, moving between Hollywood and New York. She never made another film. She died in Los Angeles in 1955.

BY ANY OTHER NAME

Theda Bara was neither the first nor the last star to be renamed by the Hollywood studios. Florence Lawrence, "the Biograph girl," who in 1910 became the first star to be named on screen, was really Florence Annie Bridgwood. Many others were given—or more rarely chose—screen names. At times it was for reasons of euphony: Julius Ulman became Douglas Fairbanks and Frances Gumm metamorphosed into Judy Garland (below). Some names had unfortunate associations: Hedwig Kiesler's surname was thought too close to "kiester" (slang for "backside")—hence Hedy Lamarr.

Only when the grip of the old studio system began to weaken could actors, such as Jack Lemmon, refuse rechristening. More recently, such stars as Arnold Schwarzenegger and Renée Zellweger have forged stellar careers while proudly retaining their surnames.

It 1927
CLARENCE BADGER 1880 – 1964

▲ Betty Lou demonstrates that she has "It."

▼ Clara Bow's name dominates the poster.

Of the six silent movies Clara Bow starred in during 1927, *It* created a Jazz Age icon, earning Bow, then Paramount's top earner, her "It girl" sobriquet at the age of twenty-one. She thus became one of cinema's first sex symbols. Although she is more incorrigibly flirtatious in other pictures, *It* was the vehicle that assured her place in film history.

But for Bow's vitality and "Madame" Elinor Glyn's cameo, the film would have been a routine comedy of misunderstanding and class difference, deftly directed though it was by Clarence Badger. Bow's Betty Lou, a Manhattan department store salesgirl, falls for her dapper boss Cyrus (Antonio Moreno). Despite being involved with a socialite, Cyrus is drawn to Betty Lou. The romance stalls when Cyrus receives false information from his upper-class-twit friend (William Austin) that Betty Lou has a baby, but the déclassée darling will not be denied winning her man.

Glyn, celebrity author of erotica, invented the notion of "It" (in her novel of the same name) and sold it to Paramount for $50,000. She defines "It" as "Self-confidence and indifference as to whether you are pleasing or not—and something in you that gives the impression you are not all cold." Two more, equally vague explanations are provided via titles. Suffice to say, "It" is a mercurial alloy of charisma, magnetism, and unself-consciousness amounting to sex appeal. Bow bursts with these qualities, but she is also loyal, moral, moving, and funny. That she was sublimely sexy was a given—but her appeal was multifaceted. **GF**

1 LOVE AT FIRST SIGHT

Department store salesgirl Betty Lou (second from left) takes one look at her new boss, Cyrus T. Waltham, and proclaims: "Sweet Santa Claus, give me him." She plots an introduction to him at the Ritz that evening through his gawky friend Monty (William Austin).

2 GETTING FRESH

After a fun night out bumping against each other on Coney Island's amusement park rides, Cyrus drives Betty home to her cheap lodging house. When he kisses her in his car she slaps him, but after he has driven away she touches her lips with rapture.

3 THAT'S MY BABY

When welfare workers threaten to seize the baby of Betty Lou's sickening roommate Molly (Priscilla Bonner), Betty Lou shows her loyalty and claims the child is hers. The incident is witnessed by Monty, who tells Cyrus that Betty Lou is an unmarried mother.

4 NOT THAT KIND OF GIRL

After Cyrus snubs Betty Lou, she flirts with him and they admit their love for each other. When Cyrus offers her diamonds, she thinks he wants her as his mistress and walks out. She later resolves to win him back when she learns about the confusion over Molly's baby.

5 "IT" WILL FIND A WAY

Betty Lou wrangles her way onto Cyrus's yacht *Itola*. When the hapless Monty rams a passing ship, Betty Lou and Cyrus's girlfriend Adela are thrown into the ocean. Betty Lou rescues Adela and climbs onto the yacht's anchor. Betty Lou and Cyrus come together for a clinch.

🕒 DIRECTOR PROFILE

1880–1916

Clarence Badger was born in San Francisco. In 1914 he became a gag writer for Mack Sennett. He directed many short comedies for him but left to join Goldwyn, for whom he directed his first feature, *A Modern Enoch Arden* (1916).

1917–27

He directed for Goldwyn, Paramount, and Warner Bros, specializing in light romantic comedies.

1928–32

Badger directed Clara Bow in *It*—his (and her) best-remembered film—and in *Red Hair* (1928) and *Three Weekends* (1928). The latter two films are now lost.

1933–64

His career flagging, he directed his final Hollywood film, *When Strangers Marry* (1933). He emigrated to Australia where he directed two last films before retiring in 1941. He died in 1964.

CINEMA OF THE FANTASTIC

1 *Häxan: Witchcraft Through the Ages* was banned in the United States and censored in other countries for its graphic scenes of torture and nudity.

2 The film poster for the 1920 version of *Der Golem* features an expressionistic illustration of the Prague ghetto.

3 The experimental Japanese film *Kurutta ippeiji* starred the renowned stage and film actor Masao Inoue.

E arly on in the evolution of cinema, certain pioneers realized how perfectly suited the medium was to presenting the uncanny, ghastly, fantastic, and supernatural. French filmmaker Georges Méliès (1861–1938) was the first to explore this territory, latching on to the possibilities of slow motion, speeded-up motion, double exposure, superimposition, stop-action, dissolves, and all the other cunning tricks that the moving camera could play on delighted, bemused, or terrified audiences. As early as 1896, while Louis Lumière (1864–1948)—sober prose to Méliès's mischievous poetry—was showing the exciting spectacle of *Neuville-sur-Saône: Débarquement du congrès des photographes à Lyon* (*The Photographical Congress Arrives in Lyon*, 1895), Méliès was luring his patrons with *Le manoir du diable*. It is significant that while the Lumière brothers started out as industrial chemists, Méliès was a stage conjuror by profession. Imaginative though they were, however, there was always something of the pantomime about Méliès's films, and it is hard to imagine that many people were ever seriously scared or disturbed by them.

During the early twentieth century, most of the classic figures of fantasy made their screen debut: *Frankenstein* in 1910, in a sixteen-minute version directed by J. Searle Dawley (1877–1949) and produced by Thomas Edison; *The Werewolf* in 1913, directed by Henry McRae (1876–1944); and Dr. Jekyll and Mr.

KEY EVENTS

1901	1910	1918	1919	1920	1921
Georges Méliès's *L'homme a la tête en caoutchouc* (*The India Rubber Head*), in which a chemist inflates his own head, is released.	The first Frankenstein movie is directed by J. Searle Dawley for Thomas Edison.	The defeat of Germany and Austro-Hungary brings World War I to an end. The kaiser abdicates and the Austrian Empire falls apart.	Robert Wiene directs *Das Cabinet des Dr. Caligari* (see p. 44) with a twist ending provided by writer Fritz Lang.	F. W. Murnau makes *Der Januskopf*, based on R. L. Stevenson's *The Strange Case of Dr. Jekyll and Mr. Hyde*. Regrettably, this is one of Murnau's lost films.	F. W. Murnau shoots *Nosferatu, eine Symphonie des Grauens* (see p. 46), starring Max Schreck as the vampire Count Orlok.

Hyde in 1914 as *Ein seltsamer Fall*, directed by Max Mack (1884–1973). Vampires, however, had to wait until the next decade and *Nosferatu, eine Symphonie des Grauens* (1922, see p. 46), directed by F. W. Murnau (1888–1931). *Der Golem* (1915), directed by Henrik Galeen (1881–1949), offered a variant on the Frankenstein story, based on the legend of a giant clay figure brought to life in 1580 to save the Jews of Prague from a pogrom. The makers of this version were obliged to update the story to the twentieth century—to the dissatisfaction of Paul Wegener (1874–1948), who coscripted it and played the title role. In 1920 he remade *Der Golem* (right), this time as director, returning the story to its fifteenth-century origins to far more potent effect. The monstrous clay giant (Wegener) has a lumbering pathos that anticipates Boris Karloff's Monster in the Frankenstein films directed by James Whale (1889–1957) in the 1930s, while designer Hans Poelzig and cinematographer Karl Freund (two of the period's finest technicians) created a shadowy, claustrophobic vision of old Prague.

Witchcraft was another subject that fueled the emerging creativity of fantasy cinema. Danish director Benjamin Christensen (1879–1959) decamped to Hollywood, but not before making his masterpiece. *Häxan: Witchcraft Through the Ages* (1922, opposite), with its surreal mix of documentary and richly dramatized sequences, often infused with the spirit of Hieronymus Bosch or Francisco de Goya, mounted an impassioned attack on religious bigotry but found room for mocking humor—especially with the director himself popping up as Satan, performing stark naked. Most of Christensen's Hollywood films are lost, but *Seven Footprints to Satan* (1929) is one of the better haunted-house spoofs.

Madmen, and especially mad scientists, often figured in early fantasy films. Abel Gance (1889–1981) came up with *La folie du docteur Tube* (1915), about a scientist who discovers how to change the appearance of people and objects (cue much use of distorting lenses). The fantasy tales of Edgar Allan Poe were a popular resource for adaptation, one of the earliest being *Le système du docteur Goudron et du professeur Plume* (1913, directed by Maurice Tourneur, 1873–1961), taken from Poe's "The System of Dr. Tarr and Professor Fether," in which a visitor to a lunatic asylum has trouble distinguishing between guards and inmates. The asylum later reappeared as a setting in *Kurutta ippeiji* (*A Page of Madness*, 1926, right), an astonishingly avant-garde drama by Japanese director Kinugasa Teinosuke (1896–1982) about an ex-sailor who works as a janitor in an asylum to be near his insane wife. Spurning intertitles and challenging the viewer with jump-cut images that predate Jean-Luc Godard (b. 1930) by more than thirty years, Kinugasa's film deploys expressionistic distortions to put the viewer inside the madwoman's head. Even today it looks startlingly modern.

Many of the early scripts by Fritz Lang (1890–1976), such as *Die Pest in Florenz* (1919)—another Poe adaptation, of "The Masque of the Red Death"— showed an obsession with death. Lang had seen active wartime service in the Austrian army and sustained serious wounds: "For four years I saw life stripped

1922	1923	1924	1926	1927	1929
Drama documentary *Häxan: Witchcraft Through the Ages* is released, based partly on a fifteenth-century German guide for inquisitors.	In November Hitler mounts an abortive putsch in Munich. In December Germany reaches hyperinflation, causing economic and social instability.	Paul Leni directs *Das Wachsfigurenkabinett*. It was to be Leni's last film made in Germany. In 1927 he emigrated to the United States.	Mizoguchi Kenji (1898–1956) directs *Kyoren no onna shisho*. Two lovers are driven to a grim death by the ghost of a woman spurned by the man.	In Hollywood Lon Chaney stars in Tod Browning's *The Unknown*, about a carnival knife thrower. Paul Leni directs *The Cat and the Canary*.	In September Paul Leni dies, at the age of forty-four, from blood poisoning in Los Angeles.

to its rawest—hunger, desperation, and death." In *Hilde Warren und der Tod* (1917, directed by Joe May, 1880–1954) Lang himself took the role of Death, although his acting was found unimpressive. For *Der Totentanz* (1919) and *Lilith und Ly* (1919), two more death-haunted fantasies, he stuck to scripting. His directorial career was getting under way, and he was slated to direct *Das Cabinet des Dr. Caligari* (*The Cabinet of Dr. Caligari*, 1920, see p. 44). In the event the assignment went to Robert Wiene (1873–1938), but not before Lang had suggested the film's cruel final twist. With *Das Cabinet des Dr. Caligari*, the cinema of the fantastic definitively took off—especially in postwar Germany. The film's skewed, expressionistic sets, rejecting all pretence at realism, the fractured narrative, the hyper-stylized acting, and the sense of paranoid uncertainty all expressed the mood of a defeated, traumatized nation, unsure of its identity, seeing enemies within and without. The painted shadows of this movie and its successors during the silent period seemed to prefigure—as Siegfried Kracauer and other critics have pointed out—the shadows that would deepen over the collective German psyche in the coming years.

Not surprising then if Death, either in the form of the Grim Reaper himself or as various of his demonic avatars, dominated German cinema during its most creative period. Released the same year as *Nosferatu, eine Symphonie des Grauens*, Lang's *Der müde Tod* (*Destiny*, 1921) has Death offer to a young woman, whose bridegroom he has taken, three chances of rescuing him. But the stories he shows her—set in Caliphate Baghdad, Renaissance Venice, and fairy-tale China—prove only the impossibility of rescuing a doomed life, and at last the bride accepts death so as to be reunited with her lover. The "triple story in a framework" format was copied by Paul Leni (1885–1929) for *Das Wachsfigurenkabinett* (*Waxworks*, 1924), where the stories of three of the effigies are told—Harun al-Raschid (Emil Jannings), Ivan the Terrible (Conrad Veidt), and Jack the Ripper (Werner Krauss). Krauss and Veidt, two of the key German actors of the period, had starred in *Das Cabinet des Dr. Caligari*, as the doctor and his homicidal somnambulant respectively.

Jack the Ripper would also feature in *Die Büchse der Pandora* (*Pandora's Box*, 1928) directed by G. W. Pabst (1885–1967), one of the two films he made with the luminous Louise Brooks. Before that, however, Pabst directed *Geheimnisse einer Seele* (*Secrets of a Soul*, 1926, opposite above), one of the earliest attempts to deal with psychoanalysis on screen. A chemistry professor (Krauss), troubled

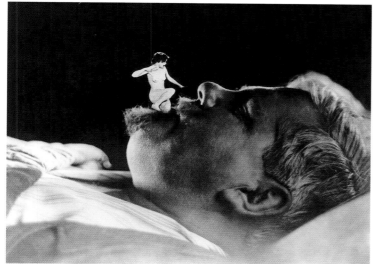

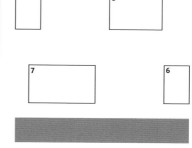

by dreams of murder, consults an analyst: the near-documentary presentation of the case history contrasts with the depiction of the dreams, all fevered sexual symbolism, whirling multiple exposures, and virtuoso expressionistic set designs. The US émigré Arthur Robison (1883–1935) attempted something similar in *Schatten* (*Warning Shadows*, 1923), about a psychotically jealous husband who undergoes hypnosis, but the film was far stronger on atmosphere than on plot.

Henrik Galeen, who directed the first Golem movie, returned to Prague for *Der Student von Prag* (*The Student of Prague*, 1926, opposite below), an adaptation of Edgar Allan Poe's "William Wilson" in which Conrad Veidt plays a student who sells his own mirror image, only to find it doing terrible things in his name. Galeen's team, designer Hermann Warm (who had worked on *Das Cabinet des Dr. Caligari*) and cinematographer Günther Krampf, conjured up a swirling, hallucinatory world where everything seems about to shift and dissolve.

In the whole rich crop of fantasy films of the German silent period there is a sense of dark forces taking over, of things out of control and sliding inexorably toward the edge of a fatal abyss—inevitable, again, to relate this to the nightmare that would soon engulf the country. Not that the German cinema had a monopoly on fantasy at this time. Hollywood produced a run of films starring the protean Lon Chaney, who established himself as one of the most powerful performers of the era. In one of his most memorable performances, Chaney played the facially deformed Phantom in *The Phantom of the Opera* (1925, opposite above) directed by Rupert Julian (1879–1943). Chaney garnered critical acclaim in the part not only for his acting abilities, but also for his artistry in applying his own innovative makeup.

Although these Hollywood fantasies featured morbid and fantastical elements, they were essentially grotesque tales within realistic settings, and lacked the unnerving sense of an entire world slipping out of kilter that was so potent in the German cinema of the period. A rare exception was *The Man Who Laughs* (1928, right), directed by Paul Leni with Conrad Veidt in the title role, a piece of perverse Grand Guignol adapted from Victor Hugo's novel of the same name. Veidt plays Gwynplaine, the son of a disgraced English nobleman who has offended King James II. On the king's orders, Gwynplaine is disfigured and left with a permanent rictus grin. Gwynplaine's freakish grin was later to influence the designers of comic book character the Joker, in Batman comics, and film portrayals, such as Heath Ledger's in *The Dark Knight* (2008). **PK**

4 Lon Chaney's groundbreaking makeup in *The Phantom of the Opera* was designed to resemble a human skull.

5 Director G. W. Pabst juxtaposed startling, surrealistic images in filming the dream sequence of *Geheimnisse einer Seele*.

6 The poster for *The Man Who Laughs* promotes the film as a romantic melodrama rather than a horror feature.

7 The atmospheric use of light and shadow in *Der Student von Prag* demonstrated the technical progress made in German cinema after the earlier version of 1913.

Das Cabinet des Dr. Caligari 1920
The Cabinet of Dr. Caligari   ROBERT WIENE 1873 – 1938

▲ Dr. Caligari spoon-feeds Cesare. Remarkably, most of the dynamic, dreamlike sets were made from paper.

▼ This poster, designed by Ledl Bernhard, clearly draws on Expressionist imagery.

In a secluded garden, Francis (Friedrich Feher), a young man, tells an older, haunted neurotic about events that have traumatized him. Some time earlier, the small town of Holstenwall was visited by Dr. Caligari (Werner Krauss), a fairground mountebank, with his prize specimen, the psychic somnambulist Cesare (Conrad Veidt). During Caligari's sideshow lecture, Cesare delivers prophecies of death that later come true—because the sinister showman sends his zombielike slave out to commit the murders he predicts. The pair set their sights on Jane (Lil Dagover), Francis's girlfriend, and the hero has to rescue her—and then Francis is ultimately revealed to be an inmate of an insane asylum, his whole story a demented fantasy populated by the other inmates and the staff.

Writers Carl Mayer and Hans Janowitz conceived *Das Cabinet des Dr. Caligari* as an indictment of an insane, hypocritical world; the "unrealistic" sets, with painted shadows and distorted perspectives, were a stratagem to disturb audiences. Fritz Lang, attached to direct before Robert Wiene took over, devised the frame story (similar to one he was to use in *The Woman in the Window*, 1944) as an "explanation" for the unique look of the film. It made the movie an early art-house/mainstream crossover—an hour of fractious weirdness capped with an explanation to satisfy the bourgeois tastes the writers had wanted to assail.

A key film in the development of the cinema of the imagination, *Das Cabinet des Dr. Caligari* pioneered many tropes of the horror film. Its influence can be felt in works from *Murders in the Rue Morgue* (1932), by Robert Florey (1900–79), to *The Usual Suspects* (1995), by Bryan Singer (b. 1965). **KN**

1 INSIDE THE CABINET

Dr. Caligari opens his cabinet, to reveal Cesare the somnambulist, a black-clad wraith with unsettling eyes. Krauss and Veidt became iconic horror stars with these roles. Cesare's deathly makeup and emergence from a coffinlike box anticipate later screen zombies.

3 A CHASE OVER THE ROOFTOPS

Cesare abducts the heroine and carries her across the rooftops of the town, pursued by the hero and a torch-wielding mob. Similar chase scenes would be reprised in a host of subsequent horror films, from *Frankenstein* (1931, see p. 92) onward.

2 THE SOMNAMBULIST'S PROPHECY

During Caligari's performance/lecture, Cesare gives a disturbing answer to one particular question. "How long will I live?" asks Francis's best friend, Alan (Hans Heinrich von Twardowski). "Until dawn tomorrow," comes the ominous reply.

4 A MADMAN'S VISION

Francis, the narrator, is revealed to be an inmate in an asylum. The story has been his distorted vision; Caligari is actually the director of the institute. But doubts persist—the madman's distrust of his physician may have some basis in fact. The glint of Caligari remains.

CALIGARISM AND EXPRESSIONISM

Critics came to refer to the weird, fantastical films that were made in Germany in the 1920s as exhibiting elements of "Caligarism." Such films were linked in the public mind with the Expressionist art movement, exemplified by the works of Wassily Kandinsky and Franz Marc (*Fate of the Animals*, 1913, right). The movement extended beyond the theatrical flats of *Das Cabinet des Dr. Caligari* to films shot on location, such as *Nosferatu, eine Symphonie des Grauens* (1922, see p. 46), directed by F. W. Murnau, or with elaborate studio sets, such as the medieval monster movie *Der Golem* (1920) by Paul Wegener. Fritz Lang continued to draw on Expressionism in films such as *Der müde Tod* (*Destiny*, 1921), the Dr. Mabuse movies of 1922 to 1933 and *Metropolis* (1927).

Nosferatu, eine Symphonie des Grauens 1922
Nosferatu   F. W. MURNAU 1888 – 1931

▲ The rays of the new dawn mean death for Count Orlok—Nosferatu (Bird of Death).

▼ An enigmatic poster for Prana's first—and last—feature film.

Through *Nosferatu, eine Symphonie des Grauens*, wrote critic Béla Balázs, "there blows a chill draught from the world beyond." Countless versions of the Dracula story have been made since, many with greater technical sophistication, but F. W. Murnau's film remains the most disturbingly unearthly. At one point, as the hero nears the sinister castle, the film slips into negative, with ghastly white trees waving stricken limbs as if even nature had been sucked dry. Two brief episodes of jerky speeded-up action cause figures to move with a deranged clockwork rapidity. For the most part Murnau relies on subtly off-center framings and disorienting camera angles to convey the menace of his vision.

Max Schreck's vampire is unforgettably grotesque from the first, with no hint of the superficial urbanity of Béla Lugosi or Christopher Lee. Tall, cadaverously thin, bald, bat-eared, rabbit-toothed, he moves with short convulsive steps, taloned hands close to his sides, as if permanently confined by the shape of his diurnal coffin. The effect is near ludicrous, chilling, and even pitiful—the creature's need for blood, for living warmth, seems urgent to the point of agony.

Following *Das Cabinet des Dr. Caligari* (*The Cabinet of Dr. Caligari*, 1920, see p. 44), most German horror films of the period were claustrophobic, studio-bound, filled with heavy shadows and distorted expressionistic sets. By contrast, much of *Nosferatu* was filmed on location, in mountain landscapes and the quiet streets of old north German towns. As film critic David Thomson suggests, "Murnau's greatness lies in the realization that it is possible to photograph the real world yet invest it with a variety of poetic, imaginative, and subjective qualities." **PK**

👁 KEY SCENES

1 COUNT ORLOK IS THIRSTY

Thomas Hutter (Gustav von Wangenheim) has been sent from Wisborg to Carpathia to sell a property to Count Orlok. On his second night in Orlok's castle, Hutter is terrified to see his bedroom door swing open and the vampire advance toward his bed.

2 THE CAPTAIN'S LAST STAND

While Hutter travels overland back to Wisborg, Nosferatu goes by sea, along with a cargo of coffins. One by one the crew of the ship is killed—when only the captain is left, he lashes himself to the wheel and awaits his fate.

3 THE SHADOW OF THE VAMPIRE

Hutter's wife Ellen has learned that only a pure woman can defeat the vampire, by luring him to stay with her until the sun rises. In perhaps the movie's scariest scene, Nosferatu approaches her bedroom, represented by a huge, spiderlike shadow.

🕐 DIRECTOR PROFILE

1888–1918

Born Friedrich Wilhelm Plumpe in Bielefeld, Murnau took his surname from that of a southern German town. After studying art history and literature at Heidelberg, he joined Max Reinhardt's Deutsches Theater company. Drafted into the infantry at the outbreak of World War I, Murnau later became a pilot. In 1917 he accidentally crash-landed in Switzerland, where he was interned and released at the Armistice.

1919–26

Murnau formed his own production company, Murnau-Veidt Filmgesellchatt, with actor Conrad Veidt, and in 1919 directed his first feature, *Der Knabe in Blau* (*The Blue Boy*). Several of his early films are now lost; the oldest survivors are *Der Gang in die Nacht* (*The Dark Road*, 1920) and *Schloß Vogelöd* (*The Haunted Castle*, 1921). Murnau established his reputation with *Nosferatu, eine Symphonie des Grauens. Der letzte Mann* (*The Last Laugh*, 1924) made him internationally famous. He followed it with *Herr Tartüff* (1925, adapted from Molière's play *Tartuffe*) and *Faust* (1926).

1927–31

Invited to Hollywood, Murnau made his masterpiece, *Sunrise* (1927, see p. 70), for Fox. His next two films, *Four Devils* (1928) and *Our Daily Bread/City Girl* (1930), were mutilated by the studio. After quitting Fox, Murnau teamed up with Robert Flaherty to make *Tabu: A Story of the South Seas* (1931) in Tahiti. He died in a car crash a week before its premiere. The film later won an Oscar for its cinematographer, Floyd Crosby.

PAGE TO SCREEN

The script of *Nosferatu, eine Symphonie des Grauens*, by Henrik Galeen, broadly follows the outline of Bram Stoker's classic vampire novel *Dracula* (1897), although it simplifies the plot and eliminates or marginalizes a number of characters. Jonathan Harker, the young hero, becomes Hutter; Professor Van Helsing, Dracula's powerful nemesis, shrinks to the ineffectual Professor Bulwer. The film's theme of female self-sacrifice (Ellen, Hutter's wife, gives herself to the vampire in order to destroy him) does not feature in the novel. The setting is changed: Whitby becomes the fictional Baltic port of "Wisborg." In particular, Dracula himself becomes Count Orlok, presumably to disguise the fact that the filmmakers had lifted Stoker's plot without permission. If so, the disguise was ineffectual: Stoker's estate successfully sued for breach of copyright, and all prints of the film were ordered to be destroyed. The production company Prana (Sanskrit for "life force") was bankrupted, making *Nosferatu, eine Symphonie des Grauens* its first and only release.

THE SWASHBUCKLER

1 The athletic actor Douglas Fairbanks (in mask) worked with a fencing coach to perfect his swordsmanship for *The Mark of Zorro*, the first swashbuckler movie.

2 Ronald Colman stars in the title role of *Beau Geste*, which was based on the novel of the same name by P. C. Wren.

3 John Gilbert plays a rakish marquis in *Bardelys the Magnificent*.

A whole new movie genre was born with *The Mark of Zorro* (1920, above) —the swashbuckler. Adventure films, packed with action and romance, these tales of derring-do featured pirates, bandits, musketeers, and knights. They also prompted a wealth of comedy spoofs. Zorro was the brainchild of Douglas Fairbanks, who produced and starred in the movie, and the film was the first to be released by United Artists, the studio he cofounded with his wife, actress Mary Pickford, actor-director Charlie Chaplin (1889–1977), and director D. W. Griffith (1875–1948). Fairbanks stars as the mild-mannered nobleman Don Diego Vega, who puts on a black mask and cape to become his alter ego, Zorro, and champion the rights of the poor. The film is packed with beautifully choreographed and often amusing fight scenes where Zorro leaps across tables and sips wine while battling his arch-foe, Captain Juan Ramon (Robert McKim), and Ramon's hapless sidekick, Sergeant Pedro Gonzales (Noah Beery Sr.).

Based on *The Curse of Capistrano*, a story serialized in a pulp magazine that Fairbanks read and helped adapt for the big screen, the film was a huge risk for the star, who was then known as a romantic lead in contemporary dramas. Such was his concern about audience reaction to his outing as Zorro that he filmed a romantic comedy, *The Nut*, the same year, but waited to release it until after *The Mark of Zorro* in case the adventure bombed at the box office.

KEY EVENTS

1919	1921	1922	1922	1922	1926
Fairbanks, Pickford, Chaplin, and Griffith found United Artists in an effort to have more control over their creative output.	Valentino gets his big break in *Four Horsemen of the Apocalypse*. He appears in *The Sheik* (see p. 50) the same year; women faint while watching it.	Comedian Max Linder (1883–1925) makes *The Three Must-Get-Theres* —a parody of Fairbanks's *The Three Musketeers*—on the original sets.	*Robin Hood*, starring Douglas Fairbanks, is released and breaks box-office records for a Hollywood movie.	John Gilbert stars as the count, Edmond Dantès, in *Monte Cristo*, an adaptation of Alexandre Dumas's classic novel.	Greta Garbo jilts lover John Gilbert at the altar. Reports suggest that an argument broke out between Gilbert and studio head Louis B. Mayer.

He need not have worried; Zorro provided his best box-office receipts to date. The public's appetite was whetted and Fairbanks starred in a string of hits as a swashbuckling hero, including *The Three Musketeers* (1921), *Robin Hood* (1922), *The Thief of Bagdad* (1924, see p. 52) and *Don Q, Son of Zorro* (1925).

Other studios were quick to capitalize on the public's thirst for romance and action. Famous Players–Lasky Corporation's *The Sheik* (1921, see p. 50), starring Rudolph Valentino, located events in the Arabian desert and showed that the romantic action hero could have as much, if not more, appeal to women as to men by adding sexual tension into the mix. Such was the film's success that Valentino reprised his role in a sequel, *Son of the Sheik* (1926), which proved even more popular.

Although Fairbanks and Valentino are still remembered today as the classic adventurers of the silent era, they were not alone. Ronald Colman and John Gilbert were also big box-office draws during the 1920s. Colman starred in Paramount Pictures's *Beau Geste* (1926, right), which became the studio's hit of the year. It tells the story of the three Geste brothers, Michael "Beau" (Colman), Digby (Neil Hamilton), and John (Ralph Forbes), who join the French Foreign Legion after a scandal engulfs them when a family heirloom is stolen from their home and Beau is fingered as the thief. Feeding the appetite for films with exotic desert locations generated by *The Sheik*, *Beau Geste* eclipses its predecessor in terms of visual style and deft camerawork. The opening sequence is a breathtaking shot of a camel train snaking through sand dunes as director Herbert Brenon (1880–1958) and cinematographer Roy Hunt establish the tone for a movie full of expertly choreographed crowd scenes and impressive sets. Colman's nuanced performance, as the most dashing legionnaire among his ragtag comrades, is outstanding in a film that offers mystery, comedy, and sentimental touches as well as exciting action scenes (although Beery Sr.'s portrayal of the tyrannical Sergeant Lejaune almost steals the show).

Gilbert came to prominence in war epic *The Big Parade* (1925), directed by King Vidor (1894–1982), in which the actor showed more than pretty-boy looks. His and Vidor's fifth collaboration, MGM's *Bardelys the Magnificent* (1926, right), was set in France during the reign of Louis XIII. Gilbert plays the Marquis de Bardelys, who woos frosty noblewoman Roxalanne de Lavedan (Eleanor Boardman) in an effort to make her his wife and win a wager. In a story of secret identities, twists and turns, Bardelys melts the heart of the icy Roxalanne. Gilbert's charisma and aptitude for realistic on-screen passion make the movie and he became almost as popular a sex symbol as Valentino. A former stage actor, Colman went on to have a successful career when sound came to the screen, winning an Oscar nomination for his first talkie, *Bulldog Drummond* (1929). Gilbert was less fortunate and his star waned when the talkies arrived. It was claimed his voice was inadequate, although there have been suggestions he fell out of favor with MGM studio boss Louis B. Mayer. **CK**

1926	1926	1927	1929	1929	1931
The Black Pirate is the first movie filmed entirely in two-tone Technicolor, at that time a highly expensive process.	Valentino dies on August 23. Riots break out when almost 80,000 mourners attend his funeral and some of his grieving fans commit suicide.	Fairbanks is elected the first president of the Academy of Motion Picture Arts and Sciences, and a year later presents the first Academy Awards.	"I'm Unlucky at Gambling," from Cole Porter's Broadway musical *Fifty Million Frenchmen*, includes the line: "I like John Gilbert a lot—don't you?"	Fairbanks stars in his last silent film, *The Iron Mask*. It is, in fact, part talkie and includes two short speeches by Fairbanks, a musical score, and sound effects.	In Stan Laurel and Oliver Hardy's short, *Beau Hunks* (later *Beau Chumps*), they join the French Foreign Legion in a parody of *Beau Geste*.

The Sheik 1921
GEORGE MELFORD 1877 – 1961

▲ Rudolph Valentino and Agnes Ayres at the height of their emotional turmoil.

▼ The poster plays to stereotype, depicting a noble savage who is romantic at heart.

Director George Melford's *The Sheik*, set in the Sahara desert and featuring Rudolph Valentino as Sheik Ahmed Ben Hassan opposite Agnes Ayres as feisty Lady Diana Mayo, was a huge hit worldwide when it was released—despite being panned by the press, which did not warm to Valentino's toothy smile and fey acting style. The movie cost $200,000 to produce and made $1 million at the box office in its first year, bestowing international superstardom on Valentino.

The Sheik achieved its stellar success as an archetypal woman's film. Based on a best-selling romantic novel of the same name by Edith M. Hull (published in 1919), it was scorned by highbrow critics for its focus on the repressed sexual desire of a socialite who finds love in the arms of a macho Arab sheik when she is kidnapped by him while on an expedition to the deserts of Araby. Casting the handsome Valentino as the sheik helped attract crowds of women who swooned at his devilish charm and the depiction of a noble savage turned hero-rescuer by the bewitching power of love.

From a modern perspective Valentino's rolling eyes and exaggerated gestures seem unbelievable, yet it is not difficult to imagine the effect his sexually charged performance had on a contemporary female audience. Melford reveals himself as a capable director, with fine location-shot scenes of swathes of sand dunes punctuated by palm trees and men on horseback. The film never appears labored and the narrative unfolds in a briskly pleasing fashion, confirming *The Sheik* as a pioneering action-adventure movie with a romantic twist. **CK**

◉ KEY SCENES

1 THE SHEIK

Ahmed Ben Hassan uses binoculars to spy on Lady Diana Mayo as she says good-bye to her brother, Sir Aubrey, before continuing her desert expedition alone. Valentino's effeminate features, exaggerated by his long, flowing robes, incurred criticism.

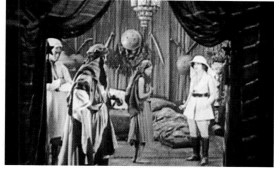

2 KIDNAPPED

When Diana is held captive in the sheik's tent, her "hour of anguished revolt" is flagged up by a title card. In the original novel, the sheik subdues the high-spirited aristocrat by raping her. This scene is not shown in the film for fear of falling foul of the censors.

3 THE SHEIK'S TENT

The multilayered, loose-fitting, gauzy costumes and exotic drapery as depicted in the scene in the sheik's tent led to a craze for orientalism. Valentino's style—slicked-back, brilliantined hair—was copied too, although some men were critical of his feminine appearance.

◷ DIRECTOR PROFILE

1877–1914

Born to German immigrants in Rochester, New York, as George Henry Knauff, Melford worked as a stage actor before making his screen debut in *The Wayward Daughter* (1909) for the Kalem Company, a studio in New York. He wrote and codirected his first short film, a Western, *Arizona Bill*, two years later. He went on to direct another thirty films for Kalem.

1915–24

Having established a reputation as a capable director, in 1915 Melford was hired by Jesse L. Lasky's Feature Play Company, later to evolve into Paramount Pictures. The same year Melford became one of the twenty-six founding directors of the Motion Picture Directors Association. He found success with the romantic drama *To Have and To Hold* (1916), starring one of silent cinema's dashing action heroes, Wallace Reid, who played opposite future star Mae Murray in her film debut. In 1921 Melford directed *The Sheik*, his best-known movie.

1925–45

Melford joined Universal Studios and made his first talkie, *Love in the Desert*, in 1929. He directed four Spanish-language films for the studio including an acclaimed version of *Drácula* (1931).

1946–61

Having directed more than 130 films, Melford gave up directing, but such was his passion for the industry that he worked as a character actor until a year before his death from heart failure, even taking a small role as a nobleman in the epic *The Ten Commandments* (1956), directed by Cecil B. DeMille (1881–1959).

THE FIRST SCREEN IDOL

Born in 1895, Rudolph Valentino became Hollywood's first male sex symbol. He was an Italian immigrant, and his Mediterranean looks and gigolo roles earned him the nickname "The Latin Lover." Before long he came to represent the ultimate in cinematic exotic charm. Despite being criticized for his effeminate style, he was the first actor to acquire celebrity status, thanks to legions of adoring female fans, and was twice married and divorced. Accusations of bigamy, a relationship with high-profile actress Pola Negri, and a one-man strike against the Famous Players–Lasky studio meant he was

as infamous off screen as he was famous on-screen. His untimely death from peritonitis in 1926 at the age of thirty-one guaranteed him iconic status and enduring fame. Some 80,000 people— mainly women— attended his funeral in New York.

The Thief of Bagdad 1924
RAOUL WALSH 1887 – 1980

▲ Julanne Johnston, in all her finery, is enthralled by Douglas Fairbanks's thief.

▼ Groundbreaking special effects help conjure a fantasy world.

A silent action movie directed by the maestro of actioners, Raoul Walsh, *The Thief of Bagdad* stars the agile Douglas Fairbanks as a swashbuckling thief who turns hero when he falls in love with a princess, played by a swooning Julanne Johnston. The thief experiences various trials before he gets the girl, fighting off competition from the Indian prince (Noble Johnson), Persian prince (French-born actress Mathilde Comont, playing in drag), and devious Mongol prince (Sôjin), who is aided in his scheme to conquer Baghdad by a duplicitous handmaiden to the princess, superbly portrayed by Anna May Wong.

Fairbanks also cowrote and produced this epic fantasy, which was one of the most expensive films of the decade to make owing to its extravagant costumes, state-of-the-art special effects, lavish sets, and crowd scenes requiring a large cast. Fairbanks was assisted in the ambitious project by his engineer brother, Robert, who worked as technical director, and groundbreaking cinematographer Arthur Edeson. Together they pushed contemporary technology to its limit with the use of slow-motion photography, double exposure, animation, and incorporation of miniatures. Their scenes, which include a flying carpet, a winged horse, a smoke-breathing dragon, and an invisible cloak, look dated today but they wowed audiences at the time. Walsh was known for his pioneering camerawork, seen in this movie in an impressive tracking shot of the thief's magic army that is seven seconds long. The film's direction, sets, and stylized appearance still have a strong visual appeal. **CK**

1 THE THIEF JUMPS OVER POTS
Fairbanks's athleticism is illustrated when the bare-chested thief, on the run in a Baghdad market, bounces in and out of a series of clay pots. Small trampolines were placed inside each pot so that the star could jump from one to the other with apparent ease.

4 FLYING CARPET
In this scene the princess's three suitors are shown flying from the desert to Baghdad to revive the dying princess. Creating such special effects was expensive and the movie's budget reached $2 million. It was the first film to cost more than $1 million.

2 ENTERING THE CALIPH'S PALACE
The thief makes his way into the palace to steal its treasures. After taking a string of pearls he is drawn by curiosity to the princess's bedroom where he falls in love with her. This leads to the realization that material riches are nothing compared to the treasure of love.

🕐 **DIRECTOR PROFILE**

1887–1913
Born Albert Edward Walsh, Raoul Walsh worked as a stage actor from 1909 before switching to films four years later. He made his directorial debut with *The Pseudo Prodigal* (1913).

1914–26
In 1914 Walsh directed his first feature, *The Life of General Villa*, which included genuine footage of combat between Pancho Villa's men and Mexican federal soldiers. He subsequently became an assistant to director D. W. Griffith (1875–1948). Working as both assistant director and editor on Griffith's epic *The Birth of a Nation* (1915, see p. 30), Walsh also played the role of John Wilkes Booth, Lincoln's assassin. His direction of one of the earliest gangster movies, *Regeneration* (1915), garnered acclaim for its innovative camerawork.

1927–38
Walsh established a name as a top Hollywood director and in 1927 cofounded the Academy of Motion Picture Arts and Sciences. In 1928 he acted in his first film since 1915—opposite Gloria Swanson—in *Sadie Thompson*, which he also directed. An accident on the set of *In Old Arizona* (1928) cost him his lead role and his right eye, ending his acting career. He gave John Wayne his first important role as the lead in the first widescreen film, the Western *The Big Trail* (1930).

1939–53
Walsh moved from Paramount Pictures to Warner Bros., where he directed a string of classics over a variety of genres, including *The Roaring Twenties* (1939), *Dark Command* (1940), *High Sierra* (1941), *They Died with Their Boots On* (1941), and *White Heat* (1949), furthering the acting careers of James Cagney, Humphrey Bogart, and Errol Flynn.

1954–80
After Walsh left Warner Bros., he continued to direct, notably Clark Gable in the Western *The Tall Men* (1955); he also produced the film version of Norman Mailer's *The Naked and the Dead* in 1958. Walsh's career as a director ended in 1964, although he lived until 1980, dying in California.

3 TREACHEROUS HANDMAIDEN
Wong wears sexy flapper-style outfits for her role as a scheming Mongol slave. Her performance brought her critical plaudits and international fame. She became a fashion icon and went on to become Hollywood's leading Asian actress in the 1930s.

THE REVOLUTION IN RUSSIAN CINEMA

1 *Mat* is an adaptation of a novel by Maxim Gorky about a woman's struggle to rescue her son from prison during the Russian Revolution of 1905.

2 The simple geometric forms of the poster for Sergei Eisenstein's *Stachka* reflect the dynamism of contemporary Soviet art.

3 Soviet party leaders, including Stalin (seated center), with the documentary filmmakers Soyuzkinokhronika in 1929.

As, decade by decade, the name of Sergei Eisenstein (1898–1948), the most famous and influential of all Russian directors, falls down the critics' lists of all-time great directors, it is increasingly tempting to revise, downplay, or forget the part he and his fellow Russian filmmakers and theorists have played in the development of cinema. Yet the impact of the films and ideas they produced during the 1920s, the high point of the silent movie era and the most innovative decade in Russia's cinematic history to date, was immense. It has been said that their influence was as often cautionary as it was exemplary. The filmmakers, and the films they made, were a product of the conditions prevailing in immediately post-revolutionary Russia. Those conditions—famine; war, both external and civil; political, social and economic upheaval; and institutional instability balanced by the dutiful optimism required in the building of a new socialist state—provided an overwhelming necessity that bred a commensurate level of invention, which flourished until it was snuffed out by the iron fist of Joseph Stalin (opposite below) when he came to power.

That invention applied to all elements of filmmaking, in theory and in practice: acting technique and cinematography, costume, art and production design, as well as the two most celebrated advances made by Soviet cinema in documentary filmmaking and in the art of montage (the effects brought

KEY EVENTS

1917	1917	1919	1921	1922	1924
The Russian Revolution begins. Tsar Nicholas II of Russia abdicates and is replaced by a provisional government in the first revolution in February.	In October the Bolsheviks take over and establish the Proletkult to marshal the arts in the service of the "dictatorship of the proletariat."	Soviet cinema is nationalized and the world's first film school, the All-Union State Institute of Cinematography, is founded in Moscow.	Domestic film production is still at a 1918-level low. Vladimir Lenin introduces the New Economic Policy to prevent Soviet economic collapse.	Lev Kuleshov publishes his essay "Americanism," advocating an "organic link with contemporary life" by the use of close-ups, rapid editing, and montage.	Lev Kuleshov employs US cinematic idioms in his movie *Neobychainye priklyucheniya mistera Vesta v strane bolshevikov.*

by the juxtaposition of images). The innovation, daring, and accomplishment of Soviet films released from 1924 to 1930—including such masterpieces as *Mat* (*Mother*, 1926, opposite) by Vsevolod Pudovkin (1893–1953), Eisenstein's *Oktyabr* (*October: Ten Days That Shook the World*, 1928), *Chelovek s kino-apparatom* (*Man with a Movie Camera*, 1929, see p. 60) by Dziga Vertov (1896–1954), and *Zemlya* (*Earth*, 1930) by Alexander Dovzhenko (1894–1956)—were the results of a lengthy and arduous apprenticeship.

The film industry the Bolsheviks inherited was in disarray. Many of the pre–October 1917 generation of producers, filmmakers, and actors had fled Russia. The early years of the Soviet era saw the domestic exhibition circuit in disrepair, film distributors and production companies in limbo in expectation of nationalization, and film stock virtually nonexistent until German imports were agreed in 1922. The foreign film imports that had dominated the market before 1917 dried up, and the production of domestic movies stalled.

It was in these conditions that a young avant-garde generation of filmmakers was given opportunity, freedom, and power at unprecedented levels. Many learned their craft making *agitki* propaganda films, from a combination of old film stock, newsreel, and newly shot documentary footage, to be screened on film trains sent to remote locations around the country. Lev Kuleshov (1899–1970), Pudovkin, Eisenstein, and Vertov, as well as directors Leonid Trauberg (1902–90) and Grigory Kozintsev (1905–73), all worked on these agitational films and this experience of making films aimed at largely illiterate audiences with available resources for instructional and ideological purposes had a profound and formative effect on their later radical stylistic, intellectual, and aesthetic approach to cinema.

That approach was revolutionary in a number of ways. One was the extent to which, and speed with which, they were able to absorb, adapt, and incorporate some of the frenzied excitement, radical ideas, trends, practices, and techniques of the established arts. Simultaneous revolutions occurred in art, design, poetry, literature, and theater. The dynamic geometricism of Constructivist art, the work of theater directors Vsevolod Meyerhold and Constantin Stanislavsky, and Futurist writer and poet Vladimir Mayakovsky were powerfully influential. The acrobatics, Grand Guignol episodes, shock effects, narrative fragmentation, choreographed movement, and use of symbol and characteristic faces Eisenstein deploys in *Stachka* (*Strike*, 1925, above right) can be traced to his experience working and directing for Meyerhold, whose theory of "biomechanics" stressed physical expression rather than the psychological motivation favored by Stanislavsky.

In 1919 Kuleshov, the anti-Naturalist, anti-Stanislavsky "father of Russian cinema," co-founded the All-Union State Institute of Cinematography film school in Moscow. The lack of film stock contributed to his early practice of shooting "filmless" movies and encouraging his students to reedit cut-up

1925	1926	1928	1928	1929	1930
Sergei Eisenstein's first feature films appear: *Stachka* is released on April 28 followed by *Bronenosets Potyomkin* (see p. 58) on December 24.	Vsevolod Pudovkin's feature debut *Mat* is released, in which he develops the montage theories that would make him famous.	Eisenstein's *Oktyabr* is released in January to celebrate the tenth anniversary of the 1917 October Revolution.	The tracking shots and fast cuts of Dziga Vertov's experimental movie, *Chelovek s kino-apparatom* (see p. 60), change cinematic language.	Grigory Kozintsev and Leonid Trauberg make their first film with the support of the Soviet government, the propagandist and witty *Novyy Vavilon*.	Joseph Stalin reorganizes the Soviet film industry and quenches innovative filmmaking regarded as criticizing his tyrannical regime.

copies of D. W. Griffith (1875–1948) movies. One of the first films Kuleshov's workshop produced was his witty parody *Neobychainye priklyucheniya mistera Vesta v strane bolshevikov* (*The Extraordinary Adventures of Mr. West in the Land of the Bolsheviks*, 1924, above) relating the madcap adventures of an American in Soviet Moscow. Kuleshov's most outstanding student was Pudovkin, a skilled user of montage in his films. Kuleshov's experiments in the assemblage and serial editing of film stock began a debate on the theory and practice of montage that became central to Russian cinema of the 1920s. Kuleshov's ideas were taken up by others, notably by Eisenstein, who went on to analyze them into their various components—metric, rhythmic, tonal, and intellectual—in a debate that was eventually deemed deviationist and dangerously "formalist" by the state film apparatus.

The other central revolutionary element was the development of the documentary film. Vertov worked on Russia's first newsreel series, *Kino-nedelya* (1919), and became an avid and vocal advocate of the "non-acted" film, the superior educational role and more perfect presentation of reality provided by documentary film. With his wife, Elizaveta Svilova, and his Kinoks (Cinema Eyes) group he created his own newsreel series, *Kino-pravda* (1922–25). Vertov's masterwork *Chelovek s kino-apparatom* is the culmination of his kinetic wizardry and the bravura expression of his innovative montage techniques and camera movement. The use of handheld and mobile cameras necessitated by the documentary work of Vertov and his collaborators influenced the development of tracking shots used by the new generation of filmmakers, most famously in the shot introducing the fall of the baby carriage down the Odessa Steps in Eisenstein's *Bronenosets Potyomkin* (*Battleship Potemkin*, 1925, see p. 58).

Whether the absence of stars from the revolutionary period's films was a necessity—most were in exile; new film stars were hard to establish—or intellectual and aesthetic preference is debatable. Eisenstein adopted a representational approach, elaborating the theory of "typage," eschewing the use of trained actors in favor of *naturshchik* "models" who could convey to an audience character, role, or class. The director chose to cast the inexpressive worker Vasili Nikandrov to impersonate Vladimir Lenin in *Oktyabr* purely for his facial resemblance, and the masses themselves to play the "collective hero."

Nevertheless, other directors came to rely far more on the elements of script and performance. Pudovkin's debut *Mat* highlights Vera Baranovskaya's expressive depiction of the mother, an eponymous heroine spurred into

4 The American Mr. West and his companions meet the Bolsheviks in Lev Kuleshov's *Neobychainye priklyucheniya mistera Vesta v strane bolshevikov*.

5 *Arsenal* relates the story of the Kiev Arsenal uprising of workers during the Russian Civil War in 1918 when they aided the Bolshevik army.

6 Grigory Kozintsev and Leonid Trauberg's allegorical *Novyy Vavilon* focuses on the tragic fate of two lovers, a shopgirl and a soldier, separated by the barricades of the Paris Commune in 1871.

revolutionary action by personal tragedy and loss. Alumni of the experimental theater group at the Leningrad FEKS (Factory of the Eccentric Actor), such as Trauberg and Kozintsev, traced the trajectory of individual experience and destiny within the popular dramatic forms of satirical comedy, romantic adventure, and melodrama in films such as *Chyortovo koleso* (*The Devil's Wheel*), *Shinel* (*The Overcoat*, both 1926) and the eccentric, shop girl's view of the Paris Commune in 1871 shot by Andrei Moskvin, *Novyy Vavilon* (*The New Babylon*, 1929, below), for which composer Dmitri Shostakovich wrote his first film score. The Ukrainian director Dovzhenko's fascination with the relationship between man and his natural environment led him, in films such as *Arsenal* (1929, right) and *Zemlya*, to adopt a more leisurely, painterly and poetic approach to cinema, augmenting his tales of class struggle with elements of ritual, myth, and folklore.

Many of the films cited have proved enduring classics but few were popular with ordinary people. They preferred less didactic entertainments in the form of stirring adventure stories, such as *Tsiteli eshmakunebi* (*The Red Imps*, 1923) by Georgian-Greek director Ivan Perestiani (1870–1959), science fiction melodramas, such as the popular Constructivist-designed extravaganza *Aelita* (*Aelita: Queen of Mars*, 1924) by Yakov Protazanov (1881–1945), and romantic satirical comedies, including *Dom na Trubnoy* (*The House on Trubnaya*, 1928) by Kuleshov experimental workshop member Boris Barnet (1902–65). This film seditiously uses a lively tale of mistaken identity involving a newly arrived Moscow housemaid to lampoon the absurdities of Lenin's New Economic Policy, which allowed limited free enterprise to boost the Soviet economy.

As the decade progressed, such explicitly or covertly critical visions of life in the USSR became harder, or more dangerous, to produce. The productive debates and expressions of artistic difference between filmmakers were replaced by dogmatic ideological quarrels and restrictive production covenants between those filmmakers and their political masters. The apparatchiks of the Soviet People's Commissariat for Enlightenment, run since 1917 by Anatoli Lunacharsky, focused their attention on coercing the film industry into adapting to the demands of "socialist construction," enforcing ideological conformity and eradicating inaccessible formalist experimentation. The strictures grew tighter as Stalin consolidated his power: Lunacharsky was replaced in 1930 by the hard-line Boris Shumyatsky, purges in the industry began, and the reign of comparative freedom and experimentation enjoyed by the revolutionary generation of filmmakers came to a close. **WH**

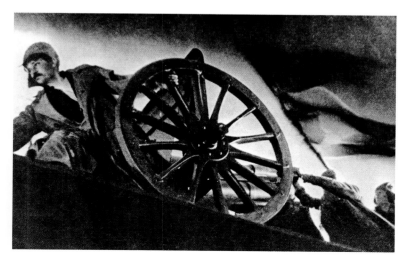

Bronenosets Potyomkin 1925
Battleship Potemkin   SERGEI EISENSTEIN 1898 – 1948

▲ Looming large in cinema: the titanic *Potemkin* casts a formidable shadow in revolutionizing cinematic techniques.

▼ Classic Soviet artwork depicts the titular ship and its rebel crew.

Commissioned to mark the twentieth anniversary of a rebellion by the crew of the *Potemkin*, who rose up against the tsarist-controlled officer class, Sergei Eisenstein's dramatic reenactment is the most famous of all Soviet silent films and also a skilled example of propagandist filmmaking. In accordance with the film's aim of showing the power of the people over the divine authority of a monarch, characterization is less important than the actions of the masses. The exception is the heroic Vakulinchuk (Aleksandr Antonov), a Stakhanovite symbol of proletariat strength, whose refusal to pay heed to his superiors and subsequent death become the catalyst for the general uprising among the citizens of Odessa. Other roles are merely ciphers in Eisenstein's presentation of class oppression and the fight for justice. And although there was no massacre on the Odessa Steps, the sequence became a symbol of the ruthless tactics used against the common man.

Eisenstein edited the film to emphasize rhythm over narrative. The effect may seem odd to contemporary audiences, but the approach served the director's intentions of creating a work that engaged the mind, creating a rallying call to arms.

For many years the film was deemed too dangerous to screen. In Russia, Leon Trotsky's written introduction was excised after he fell foul of Joseph Stalin, while the film's violence was edited heavily in Germany before it was banned under the Nazis. In Britain, the film remained banned until 1954, then was given an "X" (18) certificate, which was not rescinded until 1978. **IHS**

👁 KEY SCENES

1 TROUBLE IN THE RANKS
The first seeds of dissent are sown when the noncommissioned ranks complain that their food is infested with worms. The medical officer rejects their claims and Eisenstein skillfully drives a wedge between the workers—and audiences—and the ruling class.

2 MEMORIAL FOR A FALLEN SAILOR
Following Vakulinchuk's murder, his body becomes a focus for a general revolt. Eisenstein's choreography of the mourning crowd effectively demonstrates the spread of a reaction into a movement and finally a groundswell of action against oppressive rule.

3 THE CLIMACTIC ENCOUNTER
The tsar's troops bear down on an unarmed populace, slaughtering them as they descend the Odessa Steps. Heightening the suspense is the fate of a child in a baby carriage, whose nursemaid is killed, causing the carriage to topple down the stairs.

🕐 DIRECTOR PROFILE

1898–1925
After a stint in the military, Sergei Eisenstein entered the theater in 1920. His feature film debut was *Stachka* (*Strike*, 1925), followed in the same year by *Bronenosets Potyomkin*.

1926–36
International acclaim was crucial in securing Eisenstein permission to make *Oktyabr* (*October: Ten Days That Shook the World*, 1928) to mark the tenth anniversary of the October Revolution. Charlie Chaplin (1889–1977) introduced Eisenstein to US novelist Upton Sinclair and together they embarked upon a Mexican project that remains unfinished.

1937–43
A period of teaching and an aborted film, *Bezhin lug* (*Bezhin Meadow*, 1937), reflected Eisenstein's falling out of favor with Stalin. A reprieve saw Eisenstein return with *Alexander Nevsky* (1938, see p.142), a cautionary tale about the menace of the Nazis.

1944–48
Ivan Groznyy (*Ivan the Terrible, Part 1*, 1944) was seen to capture the strength of the Russian people and their indomitable leader. The director finished filming the second part, *Ivan Groznyy: Skaz vtoroy-Boyarskiy zagovor van* (*Ivan the Terrible, Part 2*), in 1946 but its study of leadership descending into tyranny attracted Stalin's ire and it was not released until 1958. Eisenstein suffered a heart attack while working on the third and final part of the movie and died on February 11, 1948. The film was never completed.

THE ODESSA STEPS IN FILM

Few film sequences have been as parodied or homaged as *Bronenosets Potyomkin*'s most famous scene. One of the earliest references appears in *Foreign Correspondent* (1940, see p. 156) by Alfred Hitchcock (1899–1980) with the assassination of Van Meer. A similar assassination takes place in the climactic sequence of *The Godfather* (1972, see p. 342), with Don Barzini being shot. In *Bananas* (1971) by Woody Allen (b. 1935) a political assassination on the steps outside a building is accompanied by on-the-scene narration from sports commentator Howard Cosell. Brian De Palma (b. 1940) homaged the sequence in a crucial scene in *The Untouchables* (1987, below), complete with suspense, murder, and the falling buggy.

Chelovek s kino-apparatom 1929
Man with a Movie Camera   DZIGA VERTOV 1896 – 1954

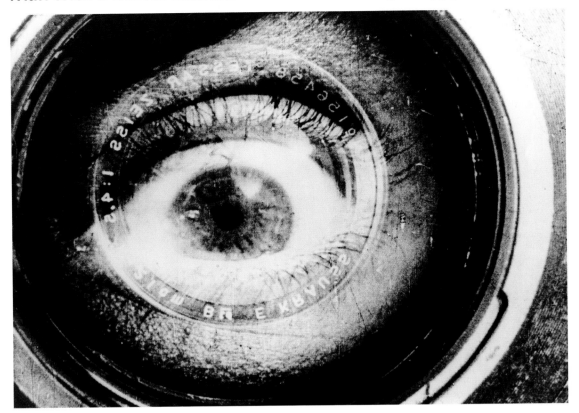

▲ Vertov turns his camera lens, superimposed with a human eye, on the viewer.

▼ The vertiginous images and concentric type emphasize the dynamism of city life.

Soviet filmmaker Dziga Vertov was obsessed with speed and movement. Born Denis Arkadyevich Kaufman, before he embarked on a filmmaking career he changed his name to create a more dynamic identity—"Dziga Vertov" roughly translates to "spinning top." *Chelovek s kino-apparatom* is indeed a symphony of movement and follows an intrepid cameraman who spins his way through Moscow, Kiev, and Odessa filming Soviet life from dawn to dusk. The cameraman puts up his tripod in the face of oncoming traffic, clambers over bridges and shoots trains, trams, and cars. The film shows birth, death, marriage, and divorce, each in the blink of an eye. Vertov believed that the movie camera could plunge into the chaos of modern life and discover meanings hidden from the naked eye. He used every film technique available in order to achieve this, including split-screen, slow motion, reverse action, jump cuts, montage editing, and even animation.

Chelovek s kino-apparatom took four years to make. The result is an avant-garde movie that attempts to distinguish film as an art form from theater: one of the first "city symphony" documentaries focusing on people leading their daily lives within a man-made environment. However, its wild, fast-paced editing, lack of customary linear narrative, and purely visual content infuriated and bemused contemporary audiences and critics alike. Nevertheless, Vertov's work was a precursor to Modernism and has had an immense influence on directors such as Jean-Luc Godard (b. 1930), *cinéma-vérité* documentary makers, composers such as Michael Nyman, and filmmakers of the MTV generation. **GM**

👁 KEY SCENES

1 MAN WITH A MOVIE CAMERA

Vertov did not use actors, sets, intertitles, or a script: the man with the movie camera shown filming trams, bicycles, and horse-drawn carriages crisscrossing the roads of a city from a car with his hand-cranked camera is the only consistent "character" in the film.

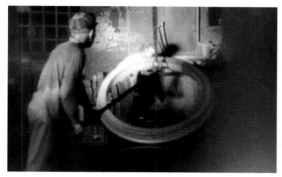

2 WORKER IN A FACTORY

Like the Futurists, Vertov celebrated the speed, mechanization, and industrialization of modern life, and *Chelovek s kino-apparatom* is a paean to labor. Factories are not grimy, sitting on assembly lines is not deadening work, and man marches in step with machine.

3 PEOPLE ON A BEACH

As an ardent Communist and father of the Soviet documentary, when Vertov shows workers at leisure crammed on a beach, he strives to show they are being productive, as they swim or exercise in order to get their bodies trim for the work of building a nation.

🕐 DIRECTOR PROFILE

1896–1916

Dziga Vertov was born in Białystok, Poland (then part of Russia). He trained as a musician and, after his family fled to St. Petersburg to escape the German army, as a neurologist. He began to experiment with sound and was influenced by the work of the Futurists.

1917–21

After the October Revolution he became head of the cinema department of the All-Russian Central Executive Committee, which produced the first Soviet newsreels. There he met his future wife, Elizaveta Svilova. He made his directorial debut in 1919 when he was touring the battlefronts filming documentaries to encourage Communist soldiers.

1922–31

Together with Svilova and his younger brother, Mikhail Kaufman, he formed the Kinoks (Cinema Eyes) unit that combined propaganda with art. They produced twenty-three films in the *Kino-pravda* (1922–25) newsreel series. He made *Odinnadtsatyy* (*The Eleventh Year*, 1928), *Chelovek s kino-apparatom*, and his first sound film, *Entuziazm: Simfoniya Donbassa* (*Enthusiasm: Dombass Symphony*, 1931).

1932–54

Vertov made *Tri pesni o Lenine* (*Three Songs About Lenin*, 1934), considered by many to be his masterpiece. In the era of Socialist Realism, Vertov was accused of formalism and his career began to falter. He continued working on newsreels and compilation films but as an increasingly marginalized figure.

VERTOV AND THE AVANT-GARDE

Vertov's formal radicalism owed much to his early exposure to Futurism and the influence of poet and playwright Vladimir Mayakovsky. A member of the Soviet avant-garde, Mayakovsky had an affair with Lilya Brik, who was immortalized in a poster (below) by artist Alexander Rodchenko. A pioneer of graphic design for propaganda, Rodchenko's use of montage is mirrored in Vertov's innovative montages in contemporary film. The style reflects their adoption of Constructivist principles that emerged after the Russian Revolution, the foremost of which is the rejection of "art for art's sake."

SILENT COMICS

1 Harold Lloyd in one of silent cinema's
most iconic moments—dangling
precipitously from a clock face high
above the city streets in *Safety Last!*

2 Charlie Chaplin and Jackie Coogan
as the scam-artist duo in *The Kid*.

3 The poster for *Sally of the Sawdust*,
which features W. C. Fields as Professor
Eustance McGargle.

S ilent comedy, although so often associated with the stars of its "golden
era" such as Charlie Chaplin (1889–1977) and Buster Keaton (1895–1966),
was in fact one of cinema's earliest and most popular genres. From
cinema's very beginnings, a handful of films, such as *L'arroseur arrosé* (*Tables
Turned on the Gardener*, 1895) directed by Louis Lumière (1864–1948), where
a gardener has a series of mishaps with his garden hose, tended to play upon
single-scene sight gags. These early experiments were a great success, but
many performers who were very popular in the silent era are now largely
forgotten or exist in the shadow of both Chaplin and Keaton. Harold Lloyd's
daring performance in *Safety Last!* (1923, above) and Raymond Griffith's in
Hands Up! (1926) are typical examples of well-crafted comic routines and also
reminders of the way in which iconic performers can fade from public view.

In the early silent period it was in Europe that comedy began to develop
the logic and form that would take it well into the 1920s, with comic actors
such as André Deed and most notably the hugely popular Max Linder making
early headway in the field. However, it was Mack Sennett's Keystone Studios
that developed the tropes that would come to define silent comedy and began
to produce comic films on an industrial scale, with his "Keystone Kops" proving
a favorite with audiences after the founding of the studio in 1912. "Kops" films,

KEY EVENTS

1909	1910	1912	1914	1915	1917
Roscoe "Fatty" Arbuckle makes his screen acting debut in the short comedy film *Ben's Kid*.	Chaplin first tours the United States with the Fred Karno Company. He later returns and is signed by Mack Sennett.	Mack Sennett founds Keystone Studios in Edendale, California. He develops silent comedy on an industrial scale.	Chaplin's "tramp" makes his screen debut in *Kid Auto Races at Venice*.	W. C. Fields stars in and writes *Pool Sharks*. The film is Fields's acting and writing debut and showcases elements of his vaudeville routine.	Mack Sennett leaves the studio in an attempt to form a new entity. It signals the beginning of the end for one phase of silent comedy.

which were often made in a matter of days and which varied immensely in quality, usually consisted of manic chase sequences featuring a series of crazed physical stunts and a cast of people humorously mismatched in size. Sennett was crucial in developing a form of on-screen comedy that relied upon a series of sight gags, reality-defying scenarios, and the use of unconventional-looking character actors. Keystone films were designed to be ephemeral, with new shorts appearing on a weekly basis, often playing upon topical themes or aping famous films of the day. It was Sennett, too, who developed Hollywood's first comedy stars, with performers such as Mack Swain, Ford Sterling, Mabel Normand, Roscoe "Fatty" Arbuckle, Harry Langdon, and Charlie Chaplin all rising to fame making Keystone films.

Chaplin went on to graduate from Keystone's simple knockabout fare and become the preeminent comedy star of the era, eventually commanding a weekly salary in 1915 of $1,250. Crucial to Chaplin's success was the control that his fame allowed him to exert over his own material. As such he increasingly moved away from the broad brushstrokes and overtly slapstick comedies of Keystone (an approach he was never comfortable with) and refined his comic alter ego, a down-at-the-heels but kind-hearted tramp with bowler hat, walking cane, and ill-fitting clothes. Chaplin's *The Gold Rush* (1925, see p. 64) was one of the top-grossing films of the silent era and like many of his films, such as *The Kid* (1921, above right), it explored themes that were close to his heart—not least the effects of poverty, something that resonated with Chaplin's own impoverished background. The film is best known, however, for the "roll dance" where Chaplin's tramp performs an artful "dance" with two forks stuck into two bread rolls. This was typical of Chaplin's comedy, a canny mix of deft, balletic physical comedy and thoughtful, situation-based gags.

Keaton, a former acrobat and vaudeville child performer, differed from Chaplin in that his comedy tended to derive from the contrast between his perpetually deadpan face and the absurdly athletic acts his characters had to perform in order to avoid injury. With Keaton, physical comedy was almost poetic in the thoughtful and skillful performance of increasingly elaborate set pieces that were as dangerous as they were spectacular.

The coming of sound radically changed the careers of many silent comedy performers. Chaplin resisted films with dialogue until as late as 1940 and *The Great Dictator*, preferring instead to use sound effects in films such as *Modern Times* (1936). Keaton found it hard to adjust to dialogue-based comedy and performers such as Harold Lloyd and Harry Langdon lost much of their comic verve and appeal. W. C. Fields, who had featured witty repartee as part of his stage career, was able to move from silent hits such as *Sally of the Sawdust* (1925, right) to a successful career in talkies, such as *The Bank Dick* (1940). Similarly, Laurel and Hardy began working at the end of the silent period, and adapted to the changing medium and initiated the next generation of comic geniuses. **RH**

1919	1921	1923	1925	1926	1936
Chaplin, along with several other Hollywood stars, forms United Artists in an attempt to allow performers more artistic control.	Fatty Arbuckle's career begins to plummet as a result of the Virginia Rappe scandal.	*Safety Last!*, starring Harold Lloyd and produced by Hal Roach, is released.	Chaplin releases *The Gold Rush* (see p. 64), which becomes one of his most iconic and successful films. It is one of the top-grossing films of silent cinema.	Keaton completes *The General* (see p. 66). It receives poor reviews but is later rediscovered and heralded as one of the best films of the silent film era.	Nearly ten years after the first sound film, Chaplin releases *Modern Times*, his first "sound" film. It features only sound effects.

The Gold Rush 1925
CHARLIE CHAPLIN 1889 – 1977

▲ Chaplin savors the laces of an old leather boot for dinner.

▼ Chaplin's special combination of humor and pathos is conveyed in the poster.

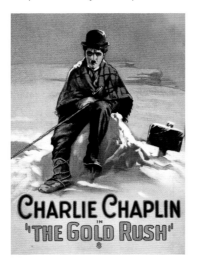

Charlie Chaplin called *The Gold Rush* "the picture I want to be remembered by." Indeed, it has a fair claim to be the quintessential Charlie Chaplin film. It was made after Chaplin's more serious film *A Woman of Paris* (1923), in which he did not star. This movie was spurned by audiences, and Chaplin decided to change tack with *The Gold Rush*, making an epic comedy out of grim subject matter. The film was inspired by the Donner Pass disaster, in which a group of gold prospectors was stranded in the mountains. In his autobiography, Chaplin cheerily notes: "Out of 160 pioneers, only eighteen survived, most of them dying of hunger and cold. Some resorted to cannibalism, eating their dead, others roasted their moccasins to relieve their hunger."

Chaplin plays a bedraggled prospector who ends up stranded in a cabin with the hirsute Big Jim Mackay (Mack Swain) for company. In a celebrated sequence, the tramp serves up his boot as dinner. What makes the scene work so brilliantly is Chaplin's fussiness, as he garnishes the boot and nibbles the laces as if they are strands of spaghetti. Equally inspired is the giddy sequence in which the men's cabin seesaws on a precipice. The plotting is formulaic. There is a rent-a-thug in the shape of Black Larsen, who makes off with Big Jim's gold. The second half of the film is set in a frontier town and follows Chaplin's erratic courtship of a chorus girl (Georgia Hale). The film's strengths are the set pieces and the sheer verve of Chaplin's visual imagination. *The Gold Rush* took an epic fourteen months to make and cost a small fortune, but went on to become one of the biggest money-spinners of the 1920s. **GM**

👁 KEY SCENES

1 THE PROSPECTOR PROSPECTED
In the heights of Alaska, Chaplin beats a weary path up a snow-covered mountain. As he trudges onward to the site of the gold rush, he does not realize that a large bear is following just a few paces behind him.

2 BOOT FOR DINNER
In arguably the movie's most famous scene (and certainly its most parodied), Chaplin cooks his famished partner a sumptuous dinner of roasted boot. The proceedings are carried out with all the formalities of a five-star restaurant.

3 DANCE OF THE BREAD ROLLS
The tramp improvises a high-kicking dance with a pair of bread rolls. With his relaxed, somewhat coy expression, Chaplin makes all the quick-stepping seem effortless. The scene is an imitation of one performed by Fatty Arbuckle in *The Rough House* (1917).

⏱ DIRECTOR PROFILE

1889–1912
Charlie Chaplin was born in Walworth, southeast London. His parents were music-hall artists. In 1910 he began touring the United States with the Fred Karno troupe.

1913–19
He was hired by the Keystone Company in 1913. His tramp character first appeared in *Kid Auto Races at Venice* (1914). Two years later he was paid to make films for the Mutual Film Corporation. In 1919 he cofounded United Artists with Mary Pickford, Douglas Fairbanks, and D. W. Griffith (1875–1948).

1920–36
Chaplin directed five features for United Artists: *A Woman of Paris* (1923), *The Gold Rush*, *The Circus* (1928), *City Lights* (1931), and *Modern Times* (1936), a "silent" film in the "talkie" era.

1937–47
Chaplin made his first real talkie, *The Great Dictator* (1940, see p. 158). In 1947 he played a serial killer in *Monsieur Verdoux*.

1948–67
Limelight (1952) was Chaplin's final US film. He was accused of harboring un-American sympathies and quit the United States for Switzerland. He directed two films in exile—*A King in New York* (1957) and *A Countess from Hong Kong* (1967).

1968–77
He returned to the United States for the first time in twenty years to receive an honorary Oscar. In 1975 he was knighted by Queen Elizabeth II. He died two years later in Switzerland.

CHAPLIN: TAKE TWO

To silent film purists, the decision of Chaplin (below) to re-release *The Gold Rush* in a shortened sound version (complete with changes to the plot) in 1942 was an act of desecration. The director-star provides the voice-over narration himself. Audiences must have been surprised by his rich, actorly tones and the voice-over lends a curious detachment to the storytelling. Chaplin relates the story of his own character in the third person, creating the impression that he is looking down from on high at the characters he first created almost twenty years earlier. The director had remarked in 1929 that

talkies were "spoiling the oldest art in the world—the art of pantomime. They are ruining the great beauty of silence." Yet the sound version of *The Gold Rush* was a huge success with audiences in the 1940s who had not known Chaplin in his silent-era prime.

The General 1926
BUSTER KEATON 1895 – 1966

▲ Keaton invented the mechanical gag, as seen in this cannonball stunt on the train.

▼ Keaton's trademark hangdog expression is depicted in the low-key poster.

One of cinema's strangest love triangles, *The General* tells the story of a man, his girl, and the train engine he drives. Set in the South in the early days of the American Civil War, it finds Buster Keaton's dour hero, Johnnie Gray, wrongly accused of cowardice by his beloved and her family. Only through his attempts to retrieve his engine, stolen by Union spies, is Johnnie able to repair his reputation, his engine, and the relationship he is lost without.

The accurate historical re-creation of the Civil War involved hundreds of extras, dangerous stunt sequences, and the destruction of a train. The story was inspired by *The Great Locomotive Chase,* a novel by William Pittenger, about an engineer who was involved in retrieving his stolen locomotive.

Never seeking fame, fortune, or adventure, the classic Keaton character's one mission is to restore his life to its former state before events spiraled out of control, in the process having to find his way out of various scrapes. Along the way, Keaton stages astonishing stunt sequences, his beguilingly deadpan face never betraying the real danger of the stunts he performed.

The film was a box-office disaster at the time of its release, with audiences more interested in *Flesh and the Devil* (1926), starring Greta Garbo. It also failed to impress critics, who saw little humor in the engine driver's escapades. Keaton was devastated by the response, believing the film to be his best. Now, however, *The General* regularly appears in "best of" lists and, in 1989, it was selected by the Library of Congress to be among the first batch of US films deemed worthy of preservation in the United States National Film Registry. **IHS**

👁 KEY SCENES

1 SETTING UP A ROMANCE
Besotted with the thought of meeting Annabelle, Johnnie is unaware two boys have been following him and that she is present as he tidies his appearance before calling at her door. This illustrates Keaton's typical blend of comedy and drama or, as here, romance.

2 DENIED THE DRAFT
Intent on impressing his love, Johnnie is first in line at the draft office, but is turned down because his job is deemed too important. Annabelle's father and brother assume Johnnie was too cowardly to sign up, thus setting the story in motion.

3 ONE MAN AND HIS MACHINE
In the film's most famous sequence, a spurned Johnnie sits on The General's drive rod. It was a dangerous stunt, as Keaton could have fallen onto the engine's wheel had the train moved too fast. It shows how unfocused Johnnie is without the love of Annabelle.

4 THE FINAL BATTLE
A real train precariously weighs down a bridge before the bridge gives way and the train crashes down into the gorge. This was one of the most expensive sequences of its era. The film's climax has Johnnie accidentally saving the day.

🕑 DIRECTOR PROFILE

1895–1916
Joseph Frank Keaton was born on October 4, 1895. His family were vaudevillians and he first performed on stage in 1899.

1917–22
Keaton appeared in his first film, *The Butcher Boy* (1917), opposite Fatty Arbuckle. His screen persona was already in place, complete with pork-pie hat. His first starring role was in *The Saphead* (1920). Joseph M. Schenck saw promise in the young star and gave him his own production unit, Buster Keaton Comedies.

1923–28
This period was the classic age of Keaton, where his deadpan persona, daring set pieces, and occasional melancholy tone elevated his work above the glut of studio comedies. *Our Hospitality* (1923) was followed by *Sherlock Jr.* and *The Navigator* (both 1924), *College* (1927), *Steamboat Bill, Jr.* and *The Cameraman* (both 1928). Throughout, Keaton's characters are desperate to escape chaos and find solace in a simpler life.

1929–49
A contract with MGM saw executives attempting to curb any excessive spending after the commercial failure of *The General*. Ironically, the pallid teamings with Jimmy Durante, particularly *What! No Beer?* (1933), Keaton's last starring feature, were some of his biggest box-office successes.

1950–65
Apart from a few notable cameos, including an appearance as a cardplayer in *Sunset Boulevard* (1950), Keaton appeared in minor comic roles in a variety of films, among them *Around the World in 80 Days* (1956) and *It's a Mad, Mad, Mad, Mad World* (1963). At the age of sixty-eight he played in the twenty-four-minute *Film* (1965), from Samuel Beckett's script.

1966
His last appearance was alongside Zero Mostel in *A Funny Thing Happened on the Way to the Forum*, directed by Richard Lester (b. 1932). Keaton died on February 1, 1966, in California.

THE HEIGHT OF SILENT CINEMA

1 A still from F. W. Murnau's *Faust*, depicting the angel who places a wager with the Devil for Faust's soul.

2 The fairy-tale ambience of *Die Nibelungen* set the tone for later fantasy epics.

3 The original poster for the cinema release of Fritz Lang's *Metropolis* (1927), featuring the iconic *Machinenmensch* (machine-human).

By the mid-1920s the cinema, denied speech, had developed a form of visual narration as subtle and as expressive as words. While written intertitles supplied dialogue, it was the images that truly carried the narrative and captured emotions. Unconstrained by the requirements of sound recording, the camera, which F. W. Murnau (1888–1931) called "the director's pencil," attained a flexibility that remains unsurpassed. Unable to talk, actors relied on gesture and facial expression, achieving no less subtlety and depth of feeling than they would with the more naturalistic style that came with sound.

Silence, then, was not a limitation. For many aesthetes and film theorists, the uniqueness of cinema was precisely its ability to tell a story through images alone. Murnau's *Der letzte Mann* (*The Last Laugh*, 1924) eschewed intertitles, seeking to create a wholly visual narrative, and this quest for a pure cinema found disciples as far afield as Japan, where the expressionistic *Kurutta ippeji* (*A Page of Madness*, 1926), directed by Kinugasa Teinosuke (1896–1982), used only images to narrate its disorienting story of events inside a lunatic asylum.

Few films went to the lengths of eliminating intertitles altogether, but the glory of late silent cinema was undoubtedly its visual artistry. Murnau's *Faust* (1926, above), despite its literary origins in the legend of the man who sells his soul to the Devil, was most remarkable for its luminous re-creation of medieval

KEY EVENTS

1922	1923	1924	1925	1926	1927
Fritz Lang's two-part *Dr. Mabuse, der Spieler* (*Dr. Mabuse: The Gambler*) creates a claustrophobic fantasy underworld of crime and espionage.	Abel Gance embraces visual grandeur in *La Roue* (*The Wheel*). Mauritz Stiller (1883–1928) makes *Gunnar Hedes Saga* (*The Blizzard*).	German studio UFA produces Fritz Lang's *Die Nibelungen* series and F. W. Murnau's *Der letzte Mann*, which pioneers the "unchained camera."	G. W. Pabst (1885–1967) explores psychological subtlety in *Die freudlose Gasse* (*Joyless Street*). King Vidor (1894–1982) makes *The Big Parade*.	At UFA, Murnau makes a visually splendid *Faust*. The avant-garde film *A Page of Madness* demonstrates the maturity of Japanese silent cinema.	Abel Gance makes *Napoléon* in France. In Hollywood, Murnau makes *Sunrise: A Song of Two Humans* (see p. 70), perhaps the most beautiful silent film.

Europe. This was one of the extravagant productions by leading German studio UFA, which also made the pageantlike *Die Nibelungen: Siegfried* and *Die Nibelungen: Kriemhilds Rache* (*Kriemhild's Revenge*, both 1924, right), by Fritz Lang (1890–1976), and his science fiction epic *Metropolis* (1927, below right). Despite a penny-dreadful plot, the latter remains one of cinema's most visually impressive evocations of the future. French cinema also often aspired to an epic mode, never more so than in the work of Abel Gance (1889–1981), whose *Napoléon* (1927, see p. 32) took the stylistic elaboration of silent cinema to an extreme. The emperor's career is told in a series of set pieces, including the remarkable "storm in the convention"—Napoleon's voyage on a stormy sea is juxtaposed with thunderous debates between French politicians. Danish director Carl Theodor Dreyer (1889–1968) dramatized French history in *La passion de Jeanne d'Arc* (*The Passion of Joan of Arc*, 1928, see p. 72), but largely eschewed spectacle for a single-minded focus on the emotional registers conveyed by the human face.

Indeed, the remarkable thing about late silent film was its ability to combine visual grandeur with emotional intimacy. This was true of Hollywood too, where some of the best masterpieces were directed by European émigrés. Murnau came from Germany to work for Fox, and in the romantic melodramas *Sunrise: A Song of Two Humans* (1927, see p.70) and *City Girl* (1930) he combined stylistic beauty with delicate attention to human feelings. The Swede Victor Sjöström (1879–1960), known for his studies of Scandinavian rural life, opted for a similarly remote setting in one of the last great US silents, *The Wind* (1928), a powerful melodrama shot on location in the Mojave desert.

The excellence of silent film during the late 1920s helps to explain why many saw the coming of sound as a backward step. Most of *Lonesome* (1928), another tale of US urban life by a European émigré (Paul Fejos, 1897–1963), showed the flair of late silent cinema, but the mood was shattered by some terribly banal dialogue sequences. As critic Andrew Sarris wrote, "It is possible to appreciate the depth of an aesthete's despair at a time when the medium seemed a mess."

Sound opened up new possibilities for film and by 1930 the new medium had won out in the United States and Western Europe, but it was years before filmmakers had the technology to combine sound with the visual fluency of the late silents. The point is confirmed by the outstanding work of the few mature film industries that made silent films after 1930. Until the mid-1930s, Soviet cinema produced fine silents, such as *Schastye* (*Happiness*, 1934), by Alexander Medvedkin (1900–89), with its blend of slapstick, satire, and folklore. In Japan, where sound films were rare until 1935, directors such as Mikio Naruse (1905–69) and Hiroshi Shimizu (1903–66) fused local traditions with the flamboyant camera style learned from Western masters of late silent film. In films such as *Otona no miru ehon—Umarete wa mita keredo* (*I Was Born, But...*, 1932), Yasujiro Ozu (1903–63) showed that silent cinema was capable of a realism as authentic as that achieved with sound in the Neo-Realist (see p. 178) films of postwar Italy. **AJ**

1928	1929	1929	1931	1932	1934
In Hollywood, the changeover to sound begins in earnest, but a few late silent masterpieces emerge, including King Vidor's *The Crowd*.	G. W. Pabst's *Die Büchse der Pandora* (*Pandora's Box*) and *Tagebuch einer Verlorenen* (*Diary of a Lost Girl*) bring a new realism to German silent cinema.	In Britain, Anthony Asquith (1902–68) makes one of his finest films, *A Cottage on Dartmoor*, as a silent, condemning it to instant obsolescence.	Among the last US-produced silents are the Charlie Chaplin (1889–1977) comedy *City Lights* and F. W. Murnau's *Tabu*, shot in Polynesia.	Yasujiro Ozu makes his finest silent film, the bittersweet realist comedy *Otona no miru ehon—Umarete wa mita keredo*.	Alexander Medvedkin's *Schastye* becomes the last Soviet silent film.

Sunrise: A Song of Two Humans 1927

F. W. MURNAU 1888 – 1931

▲ *Sunrise* is renowned for its groundbreaking cinematography and poignant storytelling.

▼ Despite its eye-catching poster, the big-budget *Sunrise* was a box-office failure.

Hollywood, acutely aware of the technical and artistic advances made in European film, recognized that the movies needed visionaries—to the extent of funding the occasional, noncommercial picture simply to advance the art form. German director F. W. Murnau, a leading figure in German Expressionism, was much admired for *Der letzte Mann* (*The Last Laugh*, 1924). The film is an exercise in purely visual storytelling that abjured the silent movie convention of intertitles. Studio head William Fox imported Murnau and gave him studio resources—crucially, including innovative cameramen Charles Rosher and Karl Struss—for *Sunrise: A Song of Two Humans*.

In this film Murnau uses subtle imagery to set the tone of the scenes and titles appear infrequently. The story is a naive fable: in a village by a lake, the Man (George O'Brien) is tempted away from his demure Wife (Janet Gaynor) by the seductive Woman from the City (Margaret Livingston), who is on a summer vacation. He thinks about murdering his Wife, so that he can sell his farmhouse and run away with the Woman from the City, but is overcome by conscience. From this, Murnau spins a dreamlike visual symphony of sustained passages and striking moments—most memorably, when the young couple (now reconciled) cross a crowded, traffic-busy city street, only to have it dissolve into fields as they pause to kiss. The film was awarded Oscars for Best Picture (Unique and Artistic Achievement), Cinematography (Charles Rosher and Karl Struss), and Best Actress (Janet Gaynor) at the first Academy Awards in 1929. **KN**

👁 KEY SCENES

1 IN THE MARSH
The Man and the Woman from the City embrace among the reeds on the lake shore. She seduces him into thinking that he should drown his wife and move with her to the city. Murnau creates a fairy-tale world and images of the metropolis flash above them.

3 STREETCAR
A streetcar journey runs straight from the country to the center of the big city—showing off Murnau's enormous, stylized, and costly set. The film was one of the first to feature sound effects recorded by the Fox Movietone sound-on-film system.

2 ON THE LAKE
The Man rows a boat out on to the lake, intent on drowning his Wife. She is happy to be spending some time with her distant husband. He finds himself unable to go through with the drowning and rows to the shore, where the Wife runs from him in fear.

4 STORM
As the reconciled couple row back across the lake, a sudden storm whips up. They cling to each other in their tiny boat until it capsizes. Thinking his Wife drowned, the Man believes malign fate has fulfilled his earlier evil intent.

THE COMING OF SOUND

Silent pictures were seldom silent and accompaniments ranged from solo piano or organ to full orchestra. During the 1920s, there were attempts to wed dialogue and music to moving images, leading to *The Jazz Singer* (1927, right), which featured songs and scraps of speech. In the rush to convert to sound, many masterpieces of "silent" technical sophistication, including *Sunrise*, were overlooked, their artistry and poetic intertitles overshadowed even by the most primitive uses of sound. Mobile cameras were trapped inside noise-dampeners, and great mimes were displaced by Broadway-trained actors. The careers of actors were ended by an unwelcome accent or speech impediment, and a whole new grammar of film had to be invented.

La passion de Jeanne d'Arc 1928
The Passion of Joan of Arc   CARL THEODOR DREYER   1889 – 1968

▲ Joan (Maria Falconetti) is handed a cross at the stake. "Will I be with you tonight in Paradise?" she asks, wiping away her tears.

▼ As with the film itself, the poster focuses directly on Falconetti's expressive features.

Austere Danish master Carl Theodor Dreyer made *La passion de Jeanne d'Arc* more than eighty years ago, but few would deny that it still marks the gold standard of portraiture in cinema. The film presents the martyred warrior-maiden with the weight of a nation on her shoulders, and does so by having total faith in the expressive capacity of her eyes alone. This is largely down to the anguished and ethereal performance gifted by the enigmatic Maria Falconetti, a theater actress discovered by Dreyer in Paris. (This was not her screen debut, but—perhaps overwhelmed by Dreyer's methods—she never made another film.) Falconetti's palpable on-screen suffering was tortuously refined by— allegedly—making her kneel on cobbled stones and watch rushes of the film over and over again so she had an intimate knowledge of the contours of her face.

Setting his film in Rouen in 1431 and basing it on the manuscripts of Joan's trial, Dreyer works from a palette of unalloyed emotion: Falconetti's expressions speak heartbreaking volumes about Joan's present woes, past glories, and future fears. Often framing her face in close-up and a little off-center, he counterpoints her sorrow by having his camera sidle across the gargoylelike mugs of the judges and theologians gathered to force her confession, generating a claustrophobic and hopeless atmosphere. As with later films such as *Vredens dag* (*Day of Wrath*, 1943) and *Ordet* (*The Word*, 1955, see p. 206), Dreyer addresses questions of faith and spirituality by depicting characters who have supposedly achieved a state of grace being judged by a society of violent sceptics and bigots. The film remains a spellbinding anomaly in the history of European cinema. **DJ**

KEY SCENES

1 THE FIRST TEARS

Having been barraged with sarcastic queries about her claim that she is carrying out orders from God, Joan finally sheds her first tears of the film when asked to recite the Lord's Prayer. Her emotional reaction is ambiguous: Is she infuriated? Exultant? Confident? Sad?

2 THE PRESENCE OF GOD

Back in her cell, Joan catches sight of a shadow on the floor—a cross formed by the bars on her window. This confirms to her that a spiritual presence is close at hand. Later, Dreyer makes the shadow fade from view when one of the wicked cardinals walks over it.

3 TORTURED SOUL

The clerics threaten Joan with torture. The scene cuts between shots of a petrified Joan and the rotating spikes on a torture device. As the wheel speeds up so do the edits, representing the horrendous pressure that Joan is under to renounce her spiritual beliefs.

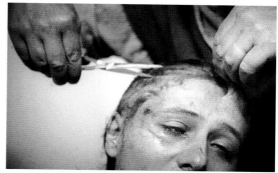

4 AN ACT OF FAITH

In perhaps the most moving scene, Joan is returned to her cell having forcibly signed a decree admitting to heresy. Her hair is cut, but as the shavings are swept away she realizes that she has traded her life for her beliefs and country. She reneges her testimony and is burned alive.

DIRECTOR PROFILE

1889–1909

Born in Copenhagen, the illegitimate son of a Swedish farmer and his housekeeper, Dreyer was orphaned as an infant and fostered at the age of two by Carl Theodor Dreyer Sr., a prominent typographer and strict Lutheran.

1910–20

Having worked as a journalist, scriptwriter, and even a balloon pilot, Dreyer broke into the Danish film industry as a title writer. In 1919 he directed his first feature, *Præsidenten* (*The President*), assembling his cast according to how closely their facial features seemed to match the characters they were to play.

1921–25

Blade af Satans Bog (*Leaves from Satan's Book*, 1921) marked Dreyer's first attempt to delineate the facets of good and evil, while the stunningly assured proto-*Kane*, *Michael* (*Heart's Desire*, 1924), deals with themes of legacy and homoerotic yearning. *Du skal ære din hustru* (*Master of the House*, 1925) was a skittish comic treatment of outmoded patriarchy.

1926–28

Dreyer made *La passion de Jeanne d'Arc* in France; the film was heavily censored upon its release. A complete version remained lost until 1981, when a copy of the original negative was discovered in the closet of a mental institution in Norway.

1929–68

Dreyer was dogged by production troubles until the end of his career, and his output was restricted by his fastidious perfectionism. Nevertheless, he produced a number of singular masterpieces, including *Vampyr* (*Not Against the Flesh* or *Adventures of David Gray*, 1932)—the commercial failure of which drove him back to journalism for a while— *Vredens dag*, *Ordet* and his final film *Gertrud* (1964). The latter achieves the aesthetic purity of *La passion de Jeanne d'Arc*, combined with an investigation into the subtle lyricism of language and cadence. Dreyer died of pneumonia in Copenhagen, at the age of seventy-nine.

SURREALIST CINEMA

The founder of Surrealism, André Breton, viewed cinema as a way of liberating the unconscious. As his collaborator Philippe Soupault wrote, "We thought cinema would propose extraordinary possibilities for expressing, transfiguring and realizing dreams." In 1924 Breton wrote *Le Manifeste du Surréalisme* (*The Surrealist Manifesto*), and the same year filmmaker René Clair (1898–1981) directed *Entr'acte* (above), a blend of slapstick and dream logic. Designed to play during the interval of Francis Picabia's ballet *Relâche* at Paris's Théâtre des Champs-Élysées, the film features cameos from Picabia and fellow artists Man Ray (1890–1976) and Marcel Duchamp. Picabia co-wrote the movie with Clair and intended it to be an attack on Breton, yet *Entr'acte* is regarded as a Surrealist film. It starts with a montage of images and uses skilled editing to create disorienting effects: a ballerina morphs into a bearded man and a runaway hearse travels on the rails of a roller coaster.

Although director Germaine Dulac (1882–1942) was never a member of the Surrealist movement, she shared its interest in the unconscious and used Surrealist Antonin Artaud's screenplay for *La coquille et le clergyman* (*The Seashell and the Clergyman*, 1928, opposite below), a fragmented, lyrical narrative centering on the erotic hallucinations of a cleric. Yet Artaud felt Dulac's fluid camerawork and optical effects were incompatible with Surrealism and staged a noisy protest along with other Surrealists at its premiere.

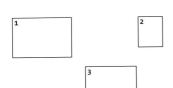

1 Clair used a montage of successive images in *Entr'acte* such as this one of a ballet dancer shot from underneath to create a disorienting effect.

2 The poster for *L'âge d'or* highlights its erotic content.

3 The provocative imagery in *La coquille et le clergyman* blends fantasy and reality to explore the subconscious.

KEY EVENTS

1923	1924	1924	1924	1926	1928
Man Ray films the experimental *Le retour à la raison* using his avant-garde photography technique the "rayograph."	André Breton publishes the first *Manifeste du Surréalisme*, in which he defines Surrealism as "pure psychic automatism."	Artist Fernand Léger and filmmaker Dudley Murphy (1897–1968) make the abstract film *Ballet mécanique*.	René Clair's twenty-two-minute silent, *Entr'acte*, premieres in Paris with a score written by Erik Satie.	Man Ray shoots *Emak-Bakia* in Paris. It consists of a succession of seemingly unrelated images, including dancing legs and fish swimming.	Members of the Surrealist movement protest at the premiere of Germaine Dulac's *La coquille et le clergyman* in Paris in February.

La coquille et le clergyman was overshadowed by the widely applauded
Un chien andalou (1929, see p. 76) directed by Luis Buñuel (1900–83) and cowritten with artist Salvador Dalí. The film helped both men gain acceptance
as Surrealists, and Buñuel's second movie, L'âge d'or (Age of Gold, 1930, right),
was also faithful to Surrealism. Early in the film, two lovers (Gaston Modot
and Lya Lys) roll in the mud and are dragged apart, and the rest of the action
is energized by frustrated desire. At the film's climax an image of Christ is
introduced into a quote from the Marquis de Sade's Les cent vingt journées
de Sodome (The 120 Days of Sodom, 1785). The film caused a scandal and riots
broke out at the premiere, after which it was banned for almost fifty years.
Buñuel broke with the Surrealists in 1932 but continued to produce Surrealist
movies throughout his career. Later an exile from his native Spain, in 1960 he
accepted an invitation from Francisco Franco's government to make a film. Buñuel
showed that he had lost none of his subversive edge and the movie, Viridiana
(1961), with its tableau of rioting tramps posed in imitation of Leonardo da
Vinci's The Last Supper, was banned in Spain during Franco's lifetime.

Surrealism gradually found its way into the mainstream. In 1945 Dalí was
hired to provide a dream sequence for the Freudian thriller Spellbound by Alfred
Hitchcock (1899–1980). A year later Dalí collaborated with Walt Disney on a
short animation, Destino, which was shelved until 2003, when it was finally
completed by Disney animators. Surrealist cinema's influence is significant,
and its dreamlike imagery, non sequiturs, use of Freudian symbolism, and
bizarre juxtaposition are seen in the films of directors such as Federico Fellini
(1920–93), Kenneth Anger (b. 1927), and David Lynch (b. 1946). **DP**

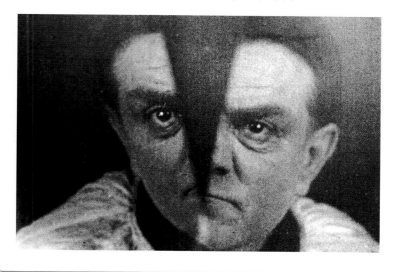

1928	1929	1929	1930	1930	1933
Man Ray's L'étoile de mer (The Starfish) opens in Paris. Based on a poem by Robert Desnos, the film is largely shot deliberately out of focus.	Luis Buñuel's Un chien andalou (see p. 76), scripted by him and Salvador Dalí, premieres in Paris. It proves popular and runs for eight months.	Breton publishes the Second manifeste du Surréalisme (Second Surrealist Manifesto) in an effort to unite Surrealists as the movement fractures.	Buñuel's L'âge d'or opens in Paris and causes an outrage: the Vatican threatens to excommunicate its producer, Charles, Vicomte de Noailles.	Director Jean Cocteau (1889–1963) makes the first part of his Orphic Trilogy, Le Sang d'un poète (The Blood of a Poet), using Surrealist imagery.	Luis Buñuel directs the documentary Las hurdes using a Surrealist approach to emphasize the misery of the Spanish poor.

Un chien andalou 1929
LUIS BUÑUEL 1900 – 83

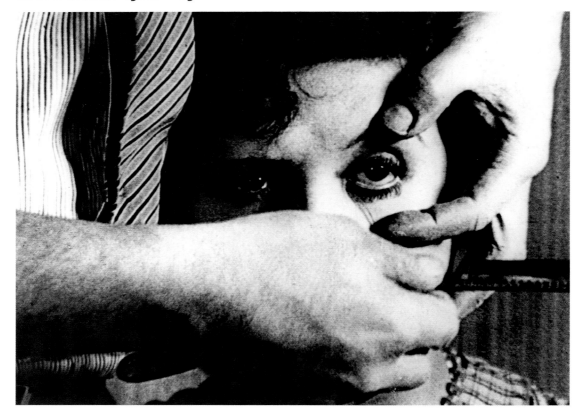

▲ The iconic and gruesome opening scene.

▼ The poster features many of the film's shocking and Surrealist images.

In the summer of 1929, a Parisian audience gathered for the screening of a new film. Behind the screen, the director waited with a bucket full of stones to throw at the audience in case of a hostile reception. On the screen a razor is sharpened on a leather strop. A man with a cigarette dangling from his mouth tests the blade on his thumb, drawing blood. A young woman faces an invisible audience, without expression. A hand prises her eyelids apart. A full moon hangs in the sky and a sharp-edged cloud scuds across it. The razor slices through the eyeball.

In his autobiography Luis Buñuel describes how he and artist Salvador Dalí worked on *Un chien andalou*: "Our only rule was very simple; no idea or image that might lend itself to a rational explanation of any kind would be accepted. We had to open all doors to the irrational and keep only those images that surprised us, without trying to explain why." It offers the illusion of a narrative: opening with that most simple of all invocations to a story, "Once upon a time," and title cards impose an arbitrary and meaningless timeline.

The film is a stream of subversive images: a man in semi-drag, cap and apron over a suit, rides a bicycle through the streets of Paris; an enigmatic young woman pokes at a severed hand lying in the road; ants crawl out of a hole in the palm of a living hand; to reach the object of his desire a man must pull a harness holding two priests and two grand pianos, each topped by a dead donkey. *Un chien andalou* may not have been the first Surrealist film but it is a defining moment in Surrealism. **DP**

👁 KEY SCENES

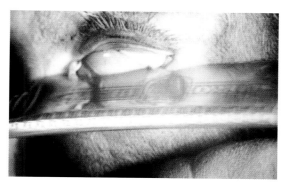

1 "ONCE UPON A TIME"
On a moonlit balcony, a man (Buñuel) sharpens his razor. He then takes hold of a Young Girl (Simone Mareuil) and uses the razor to slice through the woman's eyeball, causing its vitreous humor to spill out. Buñuel said he used the eye of a dead calf for the scene.

4 "SIXTEEN YEARS AGO"
In the apartment the Man shoots his doppelgänger with a book that is transformed into a pistol. When the Man fires, the scene changes from the apartment to a field. As the victim falls he rakes his hand down the back of a naked woman, who then disappears.

🕐 DIRECTOR PROFILE

1900–30
Luis Buñuel Portolés was born in Aragón, Spain. He went to the University of Madrid where he became friends with writer Federico García Lorca and artist Salvador Dalí. Buñuel went to Paris and worked as an assistant to the French filmmaker Jean Epstein (1897–1953). Buñuel collaborated with Dalí on *Un chien andalou*, but after a quarrel during their second film, *L'âge d'or* (*Age of Gold*, 1930), their partnership ended.

1931–45
Buñuel returned to Spain and in 1933 made a short documentary about peasant life, *Las hurdes* (*Land Without Bread*). He wrote the screenplay for a documentary short about the early days of the Spanish Civil War, *España 1936* (1937) directed by Frenchman Jean-Paul Le Chanois (1909–85). Buñuel fled Spain to escape the war and went to Hollywood, where he worked on foreign-language versions of US films.

1946–63
An exile from Spain, Buñuel went to Mexico, where he remained for the rest of his life and made twenty films. In 1952 he won the Best Director award at Cannes Film Festival for his study of street children in Mexico City, *Los olvidados* (*The Young and the Damned*, 1950). In 1960 dictator Francisco Franco invited Buñuel to return to Spain to make a film of his choice. The director made a movie about a young nun about to take her vows, *Viridiana* (1961), which caused a scandal and was banned in Spain, but nevertheless won the Palme d'Or.

2 "EIGHT YEARS EARLIER"
The Young Girl and a Man (Pierre Batcheff) look out an apartment window to the road outside. They watch with increasing excitement as an androgynous young woman stands in the middle of the street holding a box before being mown down by an automobile.

1964–83
He returned to filmmaking in France with *Le journal d'une femme de chambre* (*Diary of a Chambermaid*, 1964). Other films of this period include *Belle de jour* (1967, see p. 282), *Tristana* (1970), *Le charme discret de la bourgeoisie* (*The Discreet Charm of the Bourgeoisie*, 1972) and *Le fantôme de la liberté* (*The Phantom of Liberty*, 1974). After completing *Cet obscur objet du désir* (*That Obscure Object of Desire*) in 1977 he retired from filmmaking to write his autobiography, *Mon dernier soupir* (*My Last Sigh*, 1982). Buñuel died in Mexico City in 1983.

3 "AROUND THREE IN THE MORNING"
The Man lies in bed dressed in nun's clothing and is awoken by the sound of a doorbell. The Young Girl admits his angry doppelgänger (Batcheff) into the apartment; she does not return. The visitor forces the Man to remove his nun's outfit and stand against a wall.

THE EARLY TALKIES

1 *The Jazz Singer* premiered at Warner Bros.' flagship theater in New York City and introduced the sound era.

2 Kitty Lewis (Helene Costello) and Eddie Morgan (Cullen Landis) in the first talkie feature, *Lights of New York*.

3 The poster for *Hallelujah* focuses on the movie's musical element of blues, jazz, honky-tonk, and spirituals.

In his study of the talkies titled *You Ain't Heard Nothin' Yet,* critic Andrew Sarris describes October 23, 1927, when *The Jazz Singer* (above) made its debut in New York, as "a date enshrined in film history, with all the dread decisiveness of Waterloo, Sarajevo, and Pearl Harbor." This hyperbolic verdict reflects the seismic nature of the change that sound would bring and the apocalyptic fears of those who believed that talking pictures would diminish the art of cinema.

Sound had been an aspiration since the infancy of cinema. As far back as 1888 Eadweard Muybridge claimed to have discussed with Thomas Alvah Edison the possibility of using the Edison recorded sound process to accompany his zoopraxiscope movie projector. Throughout the silent era there were many experiments to bring mechanically recorded sound to the cinema, and two sound formats gradually evolved: sound on disc (where sound is provided by a separate phonograph record played in sync with the image) and sound on film (where the sound is physically recorded on the strip of film holding the image). Although sound on disc was initially successful, with the Vitaphone process dominating the industry, it was sound on film that was to prevail.

In 1921, with *Dream Street,* D. W. Griffith (1875–1948) attempted a commercial feature utilizing the sound process. Although released in a silent version, a second version premiered in New York with a spoken introduction by Griffith, as well as a sound sequence featuring a recorded song and various

KEY EVENTS

1921	1923	1925	1926	1927	1928
D. W. Griffith's *Dream Street* is released as a silent film on April 12 and then with sound on May 2.	On April 12, in New York City, US inventor Lee de Forest gives a demonstration of a talking motion picture, using his Phonofilm process.	In April Warner Bros. purchases Western Electric's Vitaphone sound-on-disc system.	Warner Bros. releases a series of Vitaphone film shorts featuring musical numbers by classical musicians and opera stars.	*The Jazz Singer,* directed by Alan Crosland and starring Al Jolson, is released in the United States on October 23.	Bryan Foy's *Lights of New York* opens in the United States. It grosses $47,000 in its first week at the Mark Strand Theater in New York.

sound effects. Like Griffith's *Broken Blossoms* (1919), *Dream Street* was based on the work of Thomas Burke, and shared the earlier film's setting in London's Chinatown, but not its popularity. Utilizing an anachronistic Photokinema sound on disc process, Griffith's experiment proved abortive because most cinemas were unable to accommodate the Photokinema equipment. The first commercial sound film opened in August 1926, when Warner Bros. released *Don Juan* using the Vitaphone system. Directed by Alan Crosland (1894–1936), *Don Juan* was a swashbuckling vehicle for John Barrymore accompanied by a recorded orchestral score and sound effects.

It was, however, Crosland's *The Jazz Singer* that made the move to sound irrevocable. Modern audiences may find it hard to understand the impact of *The Jazz Singer*. Based on Samson Raphaelson's stage play, this heavily sentimental account of a Jewish cantor's son, who alienates his father through his desire to sing "jazz"—the film's definition of jazz comprises sentimental show tunes and old-fashioned blackface minstrelsy—is not really a talkie. There is a musical soundtrack, but, apart from two sequences, the dialogue is conveyed in titles. However, it is the two dialogue sequences that are the key to the film's success. In mid-performance Jakie Rabinowitz (Al Jolson) introduces the next number with stuttering enthusiasm: "Wait a minute, wait a minute, you ain't heard nothin' yet!" Later on, while Rabinowitz serenades his mother to Irving Berlin's hit of 1926, "Blue Skies," he breaks off to tell her that if he is a success, he is going to move her to the Bronx where "there's the Ginsbergs, the Guttenbergs, and the Goldbergs. Oh, a whole lotta Bergs—I don't know 'em all." Both sequences communicate a sense of immediacy and intimacy, while Jolson's ebullient "you ain't heard nothin' yet" provided an irresistible strapline for the age of the talkies.

Lights of New York (1928, above right), a gangster melodrama from Warner Bros., was the first all-talking feature. Originally given permission to make a two-reeler (short), director Bryan Foy (1896–1977) took advantage of the absence of studio heads Harry and Jack Warner to expand it into his first full-length feature film. Successful with the public (it grossed $1.3 million), but not with the critics, *Lights of New York* became an unlikely milestone. As Warner Bros. producer Darryl F. Zanuck put it: "*The Jazz Singer* turned them to sound, *Lights of New York* to talk. It turned the whole goddam tide."

In 1929 Ernst Lubitsch (1892–1947) directed his first sound film, *The Love Parade*, starring Maurice Chevalier and Jeannette MacDonald. Lubitsch brought his trademark wit to a Ruritanian romance, while showing that sound and music need not make the camera static. The first sound film from King Vidor (1894–1982), *Hallelujah* (1929, right), was also a musical. A story based around the lives of black sharecroppers, *Hallelujah* was one of the first Hollywood films to use a completely African American cast and it combined on-location recording with Hollywood post-production.

1929	1930	1930	1931	1931	1932
Blackmail, directed by Alfred Hitchcock, is released in Britain in June. By the end of the year, Hollywood is producing only sound films.	*Der blaue Engel* opens in Germany in April. An English-language version premieres in the United States eight months later.	René Clair's *Sous les toits de Paris* premieres in France and becomes the first French talkie to achieve international success.	G. W. Pabst's *Die 3-Groschen Oper* is released, with different casts in the German- and French-language versions of the film.	Fritz Lang's thriller *M* opens in Germany. To reduce costs only two-thirds of the film is shot with sound and its use of voice-over narration is innovative.	Danish director Carl Theodor Dreyer (1889–1968) makes *Vampyr*. It is filmed three times in three languages: German, French, and English.

One of the most significant directors of the early sound era was Rouben Mamoulian (1897–1987). Starting his career as a stage director, he was courted by the studios because they needed directors who could handle dialogue. His first feature, *Applause* (1929), is a groundbreaking backstage drama set in the world of burlesque, puncturing the illusion of glamour and showing a mastery of sound. The film is full of memorable moments: a chorus line whispering messages under strident music (an effect achieved by recording the singing and whispering on two channels then mixing them so that the audience can hear both); the sequence of two lovers in a dance hall ending their relationship, their dialogue accompanied by the dramatic shadows of dancers moving on the wall behind them.

With the United States making the transition to talkies it was inevitable that the rest of the world would follow. In England the change was more gradual, but what is considered the first British sound film is also one of its masterpieces. *Blackmail* (1929, left) by Alfred Hitchcock (1899–1980) was originally intended to be a silent film and exists today in both silent and sound versions. *Blackmail* is a virtuoso performance from the young Hitchcock, combining naturalistic dialogue capturing the rhythms of lower-middle-class life, with a kind of sonic expressionism. The latter is demonstrated in a sequence where the terrified heroine is subjected to a neighbor's prurient monologue, which merges into a meaningless drone from which the word "knife" emerges with shocking clarity.

In France *The Jazz Singer*'s premiere was not until 1929 and the evolution of sound film was much slower. While studios changed over, sound films were shot elsewhere (notably in England) and silent films were converted. In 1930 two notable avant-garde films appeared: *L'âge d'or* (*Age of Gold*) by Luis Buñuel (1900–83) and *Le sang d'un poète* (*The Blood of a Poet*, opposite above) by Jean Cocteau (1889–1963). Although both films used sound experimentally, neither qualifies as a talkie. The first real French talkie, *Les trois masques* (*The Three Masks*, 1929), directed by André Hugon (1886–1960), was shot in a rented studio in England. René Clair (1898–1981) rapidly established himself as a master of sound with a trio of highly successful films. The first of these, *Sous les*

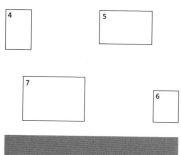

toits de Paris (*Under the Roofs of Paris*, 1930), is a musical set in a working-class neighborhood that opts for poetic rather than realistic dialogue. The second, *Le million* (*The Million*, 1931, below right), is a romantic farce about a missing lottery ticket. The third, the musical satire *A nous la liberté* (*Freedom for Us*, 1931), is an anarchic study of the soul-destroying regimentation of industry that presages *Modern Times* (1936) by Charlie Chaplin (1889–1977).

The coming of talkies was attended by a long list of casualties and a generational shift that constituted, perhaps, the greatest shift in the history of cinema. One early casualty was Abel Gance (1889–1981), whose silent films, including *Napoléon* (1927, see p. 32), had been highly successful. His science fiction film *La fin du monde* (*End of the World*, 1931) had an unintelligible soundtrack that rendered the film's dialogue incomprehensible. Directed by Gene Kelly (1912–96) and Stanley Donen (b. 1924), *Singin' in the Rain* (1952, see p. 202) is famous as an entertaining account of the teething problems that attended the coming of sound. From the cumbersome camera equipment, the problems of recording directly to microphone and the overdubbing of unfeasible accents, the film presents a witty cavalcade of the pitfalls of early talking pictures. The fate of *Singin' in the Rain*'s imperious silent-film diva, Lina Lamont, whose shrill Noo-Yawk accent belies her on-screen beauty, was shared by a generation of stars unable to make the transition to sound.

In Germany, the arrival of sound gave a new impetus to cinema in the last years of the Weimar Republic. *Der blaue Engel* (*The Blue Angel*, 1930, opposite below) by Josef von Sternberg (1894–1969) was an early success that brought international stardom to Marlene Dietrich. Filmed simultaneously in German and English, the story of the downfall of a middle-aged schoolmaster (played by Emil Jannings) through his obsession with Dietrich's cabaret singer Lola Lola was a hit on both sides of the Atlantic. Its success was helped by the inclusion of Friedrich Hollander's plaintive song "Falling in Love Again (Can't Help It)" sung seductively by Dietrich at the start of the film and with remorseless froideur toward the end. The following year saw G. W. Pabst (1885–1967) adapt Bertolt Brecht's *Die 3-Groschen Oper* (*The Threepenny Opera*), which was filmed simultaneously in German and French. The first sound film by Fritz Lang (1890–1976) was *M* (see p. 82), which also appeared in 1931. The film's climax, in which Peter Lorre's killer, gripped by a mixture of anguish and hysteria, tries to explain his compulsion to do evil to a self-appointed court of hardened criminals, is one of the most powerful sequences in early sound cinema and could not have exerted a fraction of the same impact if reduced to intertitles. **DP**

4 *Blackmail*, Hitchcock's twelfth film as director, began production as a silent film but was converted to sound.

5 The provocative imagery of Cocteau's *Le sang d'un poète* caused a religious scandal and delayed its release by a year.

6 The French poster for *Le million* illustrates the romantic rags-to-riches story of a penniless artist.

7 Dietrich's performance as a cabaret artist in Josef von Sternberg's *Der blaue Engel* brought her international fame.

M 1931
FRITZ LANG 1890 – 1976

▲ *M* made Peter Lorre a star but the role typecast him for life as the sinister villain.

▼ Based on real-life murder cases, *M* was written by Lang's wife, Thea von Harbou.

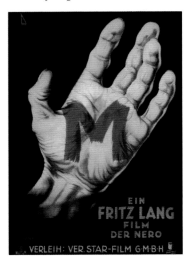

Franz Beckert (Peter Lorre)—a pudgy, pop-eyed, pathetic fellow—wanders the streets of a German city, whistling snatches of Edvard Grieg's "In the Hall of the Mountain King" as he stalks the children he feels compelled to murder. The killings cause outrage among the respectable bourgeoisie, which brings political pressure on the hard-working police. The team is led by tough cop "Fatty" Lohmann (Otto Wernicke), who later returns in director Fritz Lang's *Das Testament des Dr. Mabuse* (*The Testament of Dr. Mabuse*, 1933) to track down a criminal mastermind. As the police generally roust the underworld in search of the murderer, a shadow establishment of crooks sets out to trap the killer because the official crackdown is bad for the ordinary business of crime. Ultimately, the society of criminals puts the murderer on trial for his life and, in a neat paradox, the suspense element of the finale comes from the question of whether the police will swoop on the kangaroo court before sentence is passed. The murderer himself is in peril, and audiences are persuaded to sympathize with the perpetrator of hideous abuses, who is depicted as a small, almost comical individual at the mercy of forces he cannot comprehend.

Ever the innovator, Lang seized on the potential of talkies in a manner that perhaps was inspired by the use of subjective sound in *Blackmail* (1929) by Alfred Hitchcock. Moreover, *M*'s sense of a city in chaos thanks to a serial killer also evokes Hitchcock's *The Lodger* (1927). It is a daring narrative, darting about the city, with vignettes of all levels of society as the crimes resonate horribly, focusing on its central character only when he is forced to explain himself. **KN**

👁 KEY SCENES

1 THE TITLES
Before the first words of this early talkie are even spoken the audience is confronted by the stark, silent, expressionistic titles. Nero-Film Studio's logo appears, followed by the film title and the director's name. As the screen goes black there is a chilling sound.

4 THE NET CLOSES IN
A letter *M* is chalked on Beckert's shoulder by a street crook, identifying him as the murderer to his pursuers. The hunter has become the hunted. At this point Lang starts to raise moral questions and shift the empathy of the audience to the murderer.

2 THE BALLOON
The ensnared balloon symbolizes that a murder has taken place. Lang ratchets up the tension by intercutting from Elsie being led away by Beckert after he has given her the balloon to scenes of her mother's growing anxiety when her little girl does not come home.

5 THE TRIAL
Beckert is put on trial by the criminals and pleads for his life in a powerful monologue. They are criminals by choice, he argues, but he is in the grip of a compulsion: "I can't help myself! I have no control over this, this evil thing inside of me, the fire, the voices, the torment!"

🕐 DIRECTOR PROFILE

1890–1929
Fritz Lang was born in Austria. He trained as a painter and worked for a short time as an actor in Vienna. He wrote scripts and directed his first films while working for producer Erich Pommer. He made thrillers such as *Dr. Mabuse, Der Spieler* (*Dr. Mabuse: The Gambler*, 1922), fantasies such as *Der müde Tod* (*Destiny*, 1921), epics including a two-part *Die Nibelungen* (1924), and science fiction (*Metropolis*, 1927).

1930–56
Unable to continue working under the Nazis, he left for Hollywood, where his blending of German Expressionism and US hard-boiled crime led to Film Noir (see p. 168).

1957–76
He returned to Europe and directed a last Mabuse movie—*Die 1000 Augen des Dr. Mabuse* (*The Thousand Eyes of Dr. Mabuse*, 1960). His career was ended in 1960 by failing eyesight.

3 THE WINDOW DISPLAY
Beckert gazes longingly at a window display of sparkling knives. He then sees a girl's reflection in the shop window and becomes transfixed, a slave to his lustful urges. Lang uses reflections and shadows throughout the film to express atmosphere and emotion.

Love Me Tonight 1932
ROUBEN MAMOULIAN 1897 – 1987

▲ An astonished Maurice takes off his straw boater in wonder as he surveys the splendid decor of the château.

▼ A wry looking Chevalier in the poster of *Love Me Tonight*.

A mere five years separate *Love Me Tonight* from *The Jazz Singer* (1927), but the mastery of sound and image in Rouben Mamoulian's dazzling, musical fairy tale shows how far cinema had advanced in that short period. *Love Me Tonight*'s frothy operetta plot is the springboard for a stream of visual and sonic invention that makes it unique among film musicals.

Maurice Courtelin (Maurice Chevalier) is a sweet-natured Parisian tailor who pursues an aristocratic client, who has not paid a hefty bill, to his château. Among the family is Princess Jeanette (Jeanette MacDonald), a young widow prone to swooning; her father, the duke, is trying to find her a new husband of suitable rank. Forced to adopt the cover of a baron, Maurice educates the princess about life—"You know too much about hunting, etiquette, tradition. You know nothing about style, charm, and love"—and wins her heart in the process.

Love Me Tonight moves through a series of brilliant set pieces. The opening features a symphony of sounds that turns the noises of Paris awakening—a tramp snoring, the swish of a street cleaner's broom, a rug being beaten—into a *musique concrète* overture. The staging of the song "Isn't It Romantic?," which passes from one singer to the next as it accompanies the journey from Maurice's shop to the balcony of Princess Jeanette, is a tour de force. The dialogue slips in and out of verse, and the music and lyrics of Rogers and Hart are incorporated seamlessly into the narrative. The wit and invention of Mamoulian's direction endows *Love Me Tonight* with the key articles of Maurice's manifesto—"style, charm, and love." **DP**

⊙ KEY SCENES

1 THE OVERTURE
A symphony of sounds as Paris awakens leads up to Maurice's first musical number. At his tailor's shop, he learns that the Viscount Gilbert de Varèze (Charles Ruggles), who has ordered an entire wardrobe from Maurice, has no intention of paying the large bill.

2 MEETING THE PRINCESS
Maurice and Jeanette first meet when her carriage overturns. He flirts with her but she haughtily dismisses him. By this, their third film together, Chevalier and MacDonald were such an established star team that their screen characters take their real names.

3 THE HUNT
During the hunt, the princess finds Maurice in a cottage, feeding a stag that he has saved from the hunters. The film speeds up during the hunt sequence and slows down in its aftermath—when Maurice persuades the hunters to leave quietly as the stag needs to rest.

4 THE REAL MAURICE REVEALED
Caught in a compromising position with the princess, Maurice must prove himself by making her an outfit within two hours. He completes the task with such expertise that his true identity is exposed. But can Jeanette accept a man who is only a tailor?

⊙ DIRECTOR PROFILE

1897–1928
Rouben Mamoulian was born in Tiflis, Georgia. He attempted his first stage work while studying at Moscow University. He moved to London in 1922 and then to the United States the following year to help direct the American Opera Company. In 1927 he directed the opening of Edwin DuBose Heyward's *Porgy* for the stage. In this production he first introduced a symphony of natural sounds to present Catfish Row.

1929–35
Mamoulian directed his first film, *Applause* (1929), one of the earliest talkies, at the Astoria Studios, New York. The film introduced the innovative camera movement and sound that characterized his subsequent work, including *Love Me Tonight*. He became a US citizen in 1930. In 1931 he directed what many consider to be the most successful version of *Dr. Jekyll and Mr. Hyde*. He also directed the historical drama *Queen Christina* (1933) and *Becky Sharp* (1935), the first feature to use three-strip Technicolor.

1936–44
Mamoulian directed the operetta *The Gay Desperado* (1936), a musical Western *High, Wide and Handsome* (1937), the swashbuckler *The Mark of Zorro* (1940), and the bullfighting drama *Blood and Sand* (1941). His career suffered a setback when he was dismissed from *Laura* (1944) and replaced as director by the film's producer, Otto Preminger (1905–86).

1945–87
Mamoulian directed only two more films: *Summer Holiday* (1948), a musical version of Eugene O'Neill's play *Ah, Wilderness*, and *Silk Stockings* (1957), a musical version of Ernst Lubitsch's film *Ninotchka* (1939). His maverick's sense of independence increasingly led to clashes with the Hollywood system. Although he continued to find success directing on Broadway, including *Oklahoma!* (1943), his film career ended when he was sacked from *Porgy and Bess* (1959)—again replaced by Preminger—and *Cleopatra* (1963), when he was replaced by Joseph Mankiewicz (1909–93).

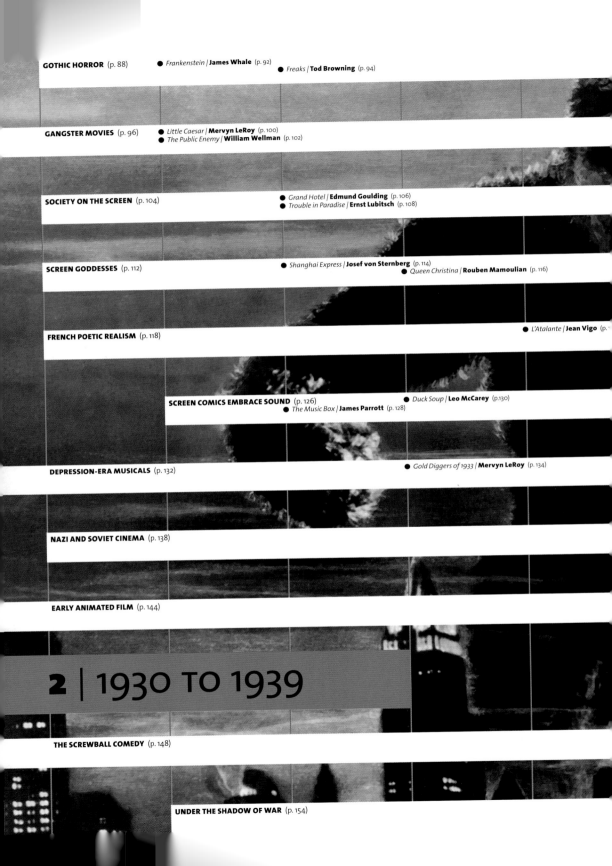

2 | 1930 TO 1939

Citizen Kane | **Orson Welles** (p. 110) ▶ 1941

La règle du jeu | **Jean Renoir** (p. 124) ●

/ **Mark Sandrich** (p. 136)

des Willens | **Leni Riefenstahl** (p. 140)

● *Alexander Nevsky* | **Sergei Eisenstein** (p. 142)

● *Snow White and the Seven Dwarfs* | **David Hand, William Cottrell, Wilfred Jackson, et al.** (p. 146)

● *Bringing Up Baby* | **Howard Hawks** (p. 150)

The Lady Eve | **Preston Sturges** (p. 152) ▶ 1941

Foreign Correspondent | **Alfred Hitchcock** (p. 156) ●

The Great Dictator | **Charlie Chaplin** (p. 158) ●

GOTHIC HORROR

The history of gothic horror cinema is linked to the gothic horror novel. Horace Walpole's *The Castle of Otranto* (1764) and Ann Radcliffe's *The Mysteries of Udolpho* (1794) developed a genre of literature that proved popular because of the way it blended romance and terror. This popularity peaked with Mary Shelley's masterpiece *Frankenstein; or, the Modern Prometheus* (1818). Later manifestations include the writings of Edgar Allan Poe and the music of Hector Berlioz, which combined allusions to exoticism, heresy, and the supernatural with a sense of pessimism and foreboding. Other typical elements were descriptions of madness and a suspicion of new technologies. By 1897, when Bram Stoker's *Dracula* was published, the stylistic and thematic aspects of gothic horror had fanned out across many kinds of storytelling, including Robert Louis Stevenson's *Strange Case of Dr. Jekyll and Mr. Hyde* (1886).

The first decades of cinema's history saw several attempts to adapt gothic novels for the screen, but it was not until the 1920s that a gothic horror film tradition was established with films that owed much to the gothic novels of the eighteenth and nineteenth centuries and the dark, brooding atmosphere of German Expressionist films, such as *Der müde Tod* (*Destiny*, 1921) by Fritz Lang (1890–1976) and *Nosferatu, eine Symphonie des Grauens* (*Nosferatu, a Symphony of Horror*, 1922, see p. 46) by F. W. Murnau (1888–1931). These films demonstrated the cinematic potential of lighting and set design to create shadowy worlds of ruined castles frequented by bats and ghouls. They introduced the character types of the male predator, of which *Nosferatu*'s Max Schreck (whose name means "terror") became the template, and the hysterical female victim.

1 Fredric March's mesmerizing performance as the insane murderer Mr. Hyde in *Dr. Jekyll and Mr. Hyde* is a tour de force.

2 Using only minimal makeup and his naturally thick Hungarian accent, Béla Lugosi portrayed Count Dracula as a suave, yet sinister gentleman.

3 Inspired by the discovery of Tutankhamun's tomb in 1922, *The Mummy* stars Karloff as an ancient Egyptian priest who comes back to life during an archaeological dig.

KEY EVENTS

1930	1930	1931	1931	1932	1932
Lon Chaney, "The Man of a Thousand Faces," dies. The status of horror movie icon is left open for a new generation of actors.	Rupert Julian (1879–1943) and John Willard (1885–1942) direct *The Cat Creeps*, the first sound horror film from Universal.	Jack P. Pierce develops groundbreaking makeup for *Frankenstein* (see p. 92). His artistry proves integral to the success of the "monster movies."	*Dracula* and *Frankenstein* are released. They trigger a rash of gothic horror films made in the hope of imitating their commercial success.	Fredric March wins the Best Actor Oscar for his performance in *Dr. Jekyll and Mr. Hyde*. He is the first horror film actor to win an Academy Award.	*Freaks* is released by MGM. It becomes embroiled in controversy and effectively cuts short the career of its director, Tod Browning.

Hollywood forays into gothic horror followed the example of these films. Immigrant directors such as Paul Leni (1885–1929), with *The Cat and the Canary* (1927), and Benjamin Christensen (1879–1959), with *Seven Footprints to Satan* (1929), introduced the German style in Hollywood. Advances in makeup effects and staging were most notable in the films of actor Lon Chaney, among which was *The Hunchback of Notre Dame* (1923), an early example in cinema of a daring mix of Grand Guignol, gothic romance, sideshows, pantomime, and burlesque vaudeville. Chaney's portrayals of disfiguration and madness (roles for which he famously created his own makeup)—often set within hauntingly Gothic architecture in films such as *The Phantom of the Opera* (1925) and *London After Midnight* (1927)—caused a furor, with audiences allegedly recoiling in terror at the sight of "The Man of a Thousand Faces" in his latest spooky creation.

Before the Hays Office's strict implementation of self-censorship halted experiments in suggestiveness and explicit gore, the early sound era saw gothic horror movies flourish, including Paramount's *Dr. Jekyll and Mr. Hyde* (1931, opposite) starring Fredric March, which is known for its strong sexual content. Most horror movies of the time were made by Universal and the studio released two films in 1931, *Dracula* (right) and *Frankenstein* (see p. 92), that settled the themes, styles and inspirations of gothic horror into a firm template. *Dracula* was directed by Tod Browning (1880–1962), who had worked with Chaney on various films before the latter's untimely death. It was an adaptation of both Stoker's novel and the Broadway stage play that had brought fame for actor Béla Lugosi in 1927. In the film, Lugosi reprised his stage role, and Browning wove around Lugosi's hypnotic, heavily accented performance a mix of theatricality and uncanny moodiness, much of it evoked through careful camera movement, props, and stage design. The most successful and iconic gothic horror film is *Frankenstein* directed by James Whale (1889–1957). The story of a scientist, Henry Frankenstein, who successfully attempts to reanimate the collected body parts of various corpses, focuses on The Monster (Boris Karloff), a kindly but lumbering beast, who kills a young girl by accident and is then hunted down by villagers. While *Dracula* summarized what gothic horror cinema could do, *Frankenstein* added an important new element, that of pity for the monster figure as a victim of society.

The success of *Dracula* and *Frankenstein* initiated a barrage of films that attempted to build upon their narrative and style. Universal's keenness to repeat its hits enshrined the conventions and iconography of the gothic horror film in the public's imagination. Films such as *Murders in the Rue Morgue* (1932), starring Lugosi, and *The Mummy* (1932, right) and *Bride of Frankenstein* (1935), both featuring Karloff, include slight variations on the templates, but remain archetypically gothic in their stories and atmospheres, heightened by exotic locations, macabre props, and odd minor characters.

1933	1933	1935	1936	1938	1941
Claude Rains stars in an adaptation of H. G. Wells's *Invisible Man*.	The use of stop-motion technology takes a giant leap forward when the fantasy horror movie *King Kong* is released.	James Whale's *Bride of Frankenstein* is the first sequel to *Frankenstein* and features a female monster. It is considered to be better than its predecessor.	MGM releases its last horror movie, *The Devil Doll* directed by Tod Browning. It marks the end of Browning's commercial career.	To generate income, Universal re-release *Dracula* and *Frankenstein*, the world's first double bill.	Universal releases *The Wolf Man* starring Lon Chaney Jr., starting the studio's second cycle of horror movies; these films are weaker than the originals.

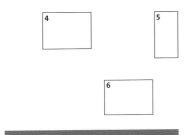

4 The iconic finale of *King Kong*, with the mighty Kong on top of the Empire State Building being attacked by military planes.

5 Such was Boris Karloff's fame when *Bride of Frankenstein* was released that Universal chose to bill him simply by his surname.

6 In *Dracula's Daughter* manservant Sandor (Irving Pichel) stabs his mistress, Countess Marya Zaleska (Gloria Holden), through the heart with an arrow in revenge for her breaking her promise to make him immortal.

Among the more significant innovations was the deepening of female roles. Productions became ever more creative in establishing soiled objects of desire around whom the story would unfold, and this had the effect—at least for many viewers—that the films exuded a sense of sexual repression, impurity, anxiety, and hysteria from both men and women. The visceral, piercing scream of the vulnerable female victim or heroine was first uttered by Fay Wray as the plucky blonde captive, Ann Darrow, opposite a gigantic gorilla, Kong, in RKO's *King Kong* (1933, above) directed by Merian C. Cooper (1893–1973) and Ernest B. Schoedsack (1893–1979). She was encouraged to rehearse her scream, which became the acme of the sexual connotations such films elicited, and Wray became known as the "queen of scream." *King Kong* is also known for its advances in special effects, with its use of stop-motion to animate the dinosaurs and the giant Kong.

Universal's foray into gothic source material made the horror genre a mature form of cinema. The studio instigated a string of legendary franchises that consolidated the studio's status as a stalwart of gothic horror, such as *Dracula's Daughter* (1936, opposite below), starring Gloria Holden as Dracula's daughter, Countess Marya Zaleska, which drew on the vamp tradition in its lesbian overtones. In later years, Universal's horror output appeared in numerous guises, *Son of Frankenstein* (1939), *House of Dracula* (1945), and even the comic *Abbott and Costello Meet Frankenstein* (1948). They tended to disconnect the appeal of the characters from that of the movies in which they were anchored initially, with the result that the personas of Frankenstein or Dracula and, by extension, the concepts of vampire and man-made monster, became separated from their gothic atmospheres. Removing the characters from their settings made them less gothic and less menacing. It also left the original Universal horror films with the respectful status of elders of the tribe—a respect that is illustrated by the enduring dignity of the label "Universal horror" and admiration for original, groundbreaking actors such as Lugosi and Karloff.

Central to the success of Universal's horror were the creative personnel involved with these productions. In Whale, a veteran of World War I, Universal employed an innovative director whose vision and sly, often quirky humor added much to the films he directed. No less crucial to the success of the "monster film" was visionary makeup artist Jack P. Pierce. It was Pierce who designed Karloff's classic square-headed bolt-necked look for *Frankenstein* as well as successfully designing a number of different and innovative makeups for *Bride of Frankenstein* (right) and *The Wolf Man* (1941) among others. For *Bride of Frankenstein* Pierce changed his original design for the Monster to depict the after-effects of a fire by adding scars and making his hair shorter; as the movie progressed, he altered the Monster's makeup to show that his injuries were healing. The makeup sessions were often long and cumbersome. On *Bride of Frankenstein* Pierce worked seven hours a day creating the two monsters over thirty-two days of shooting. The results were spectacular and ensured that Universal's monsters became iconic figures.

Not all gothic horror films, however, were produced under Universal's aegis. Films as diverse as *White Zombie* (1932), *Freaks* (1932, see p. 94), *The Ghoul* (1933), *Cat People* (1942), and *I Walked with a Zombie* (1943) were produced by other, often independent, studios and were accused of trying to "out-Frankenstein *Frankenstein*." *Freaks*, in particular, gained notoriety. The "story within a story" portrayal of a troupe of circus "freaks," played by real people with deformities, enacting revenge upon their bullies so upset the general public that the film was subjected to numerous bans, almost ending director Browning's career.

I Walked with a Zombie also stood out, but for different reasons. As part of a cycle of RKO-distributed horror films produced by Val Lewton, its brief was that of a franchise exploitation movie. However, it does not contain a marketable monster and is almost void of explicit violence, although rife with sexual suggestion. It interiorizes much of the horror that earlier horror films had shown explicitly—with the effect that any anxieties that it arouses become exaggerated. *I Walked with a Zombie* showcases long, dreamlike and silent passages set against a fading colonial backdrop as the heroine Betsy Connell (Frances Dee) and catatonic Jessica Holland (Christine Gordon) wander through the wilderness of an island in the West Indies to the sound of voodoo drums. Only very rarely are there moments of shock: a cadaver, a glance and, finally, one zombie. At the time, *Freaks* and *I Walked with a Zombie* stood apart from their contemporaries and puzzled viewers. Today, both films still stand at the margins of the horror genre, a position that sustains their cult reputations. Tellingly, neither movie has yet been remade. **RH**

Frankenstein 1931

JAMES WHALE 1889 – 1957

▲ Boris Karloff as the Monster. "His face fascinated me," Whale later recalled.

▼ Karloff's name appears on the poster, but he was listed as "?" in the opening credits.

In a still-startling moment, after the crackle of the laboratory scene, the Monster (Boris Karloff) finally appears on screen, walking backward—the viewer sees the back of his flat head first, then views progressive close-ups of the outstanding makeup Jack P. Pierce applied to the Anglo-Indian actor's sad-eyed face. This monster, at once a child and a brute, yearns for the sunlight he reaches out to touch, but learns cruelty and cunning when whipped by the deformed assistant Fritz (Dwight Frye).

Like *Dracula* (1931), directed by Tod Browning, James Whale's film is less an adaptation of the source novel than a fantasy based on its themes, with Mary Shelley filtered through several stage (and silent screen) versions and visual elements from *Der Golem* (1915) and the Faustian *The Magician* (1926). Set in a peculiar European, comic-opera country, with nineteenth-century peasants and lounge suits from 1931, it is a story of overweening ambition, with the febrile Colin Clive playing the mad scientist as a desperate visionary talked by his friends and colleagues into trying to destroy his achievement. Whale, hitherto known for war-themed movies, dresses the monster in the dirty suit and big boots of a disfigured veteran, but constantly homes in on the pain in Karloff's eyes (partly caused by wearing this outfit under arc lights and California sun).

For generations, this was the definitive horror movie, with a cultural legacy encompassing television sitcom *The Munsters* (1964–66), which domesticates the Monster as Herman Munster, and *El espíritu de la colmena* (*The Spirit of the Beehive*, 1973), whose heroine imagines a magical encounter with him. **KN**

👁 KEY SCENES

1 THE CREATION OF THE MONSTER
During an electrical storm, Henry Frankenstein hoists his bandaged creation aloft on a surgical table in his gothic laboratory. When he notices the Monster's hand moving, Frankenstein gasps the keynote line of many horror movies: "It's alive!"

2 THE DOOMED IDYLL BY THE LAKE
The Monster meets a child who is not afraid of him and they play a game floating flowers on a still lake. The abused creature becomes tender and hopeful, but, not understanding that little girls do not float like flowers, tosses the child into the lake. She drowns.

3 THE BURNING MILL
The torch-wielding mob of villagers set fire to the wooden mill where Frankenstein has just confronted the Monster. In panic, fear, and rage, the creature fights against the flames—fire is the element he fears most—but the blaze claims his unnatural life. Until the sequel.

⏱ DIRECTOR — PRODUCER PROFILE

1889–1929
A working-class lad from Dudley, England, James Whale reinvented himself as an "aristocrat" directing amateur theatricals in a World War I prison camp. In the 1920s he had a stage hit with R. C. Sherriff's trenches-set play *Journey's End*.

1930–41
Arriving in Hollywood as a specialist in war subjects, Whale directed the film of *Journey's End* (1930), the talkie scenes of *Hell's Angels* (1930) by Howard Hughes (1905–76), and *Waterloo Bridge* (1931). Given his pick of projects by Universal, Whale took *Frankenstein* (1935), cast the then-unknown Karloff, and founded a genre. He essayed queer (in all senses of the term) gothic humor-horror in *The Old Dark House* (1932), *The Invisible Man* (1933), and *Bride of Frankenstein* (1935). The screwball mystery *Remember Last Night?* (1935) and the musical *Show Boat* (1936) showed his versatility, but his career foundered with the troubled prestige production *The Road Back* (1937), a supposed sequel to *All Quiet on the Western Front* (1930). Bounced from Universal to lesser studios, he directed the camp jungle movie *Green Hell* (1940) and one year later walked off the set of his final feature, *They Dare Not Love*.

1942–57
Whale took a long retirement in his Hollywood villa, occupying himself with painting. His health deteriorating, he was found dead in his swimming pool in 1957, probably a suicide. In 1998 Bill Condon (b. 1955) cast Ian McKellen as Whale in *Gods and Monsters*, a speculative drama about his death.

FRANKENSTEIN ON SCREEN

James Whale's film helped define horror as a cinema genre and he and Karloff returned for *Bride of Frankenstein*. *Son of Frankenstein* (1939, below), with Karloff overshadowed by Basil Rathbone's mad doctor and Béla Lugosi's scene-stealing Ygor, was followed by *Frankenstein Meets the Wolf Man* (1943) and the spoof *Abbott and Costello Meet Frankenstein* (1948). In 1957 Hammer added *The Curse of Frankenstein*. The scientist and his monster have made many outings since— sometimes solemn, as in *Mary Shelley's Frankenstein* (1994), sometimes comic, as in *Young Frankenstein* (1974)—and appear indestructible.

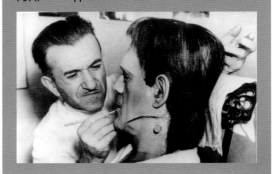

Freaks 1932
TOD BROWNING 1880 – 1962

▲ Cleopatra apprehensively exits her trailer.

▼ The prurient poster (note the tagline) aims to tantalize as much as to shock.

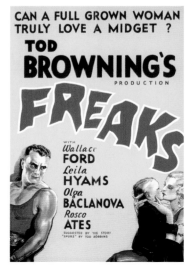

One of the most jarring and unusual films ever backed by a major Hollywood studio, Tod Browning's *Freaks* pulls in two radically different directions at once. This is both an unashamed exploitation pic (billed as "the most startling horror story of the abnormal and the unwanted") and a film that treats its misshapen leads with considerable sensitivity.

MGM's intentions were clear from the outset. "Give me something that will out-horror *Frankenstein*," MGM executive Irving Thalberg reputedly told the filmmakers, mindful of the success that Universal had just enjoyed with its Boris Karloff film. Browning had directed *Dracula* at Universal and had a strange and morbid sensibility, but clearly felt strong sympathy for his characters. This was not a movie that MGM's top talent wanted to be involved with. Myrna Loy, originally cast as Cleopatra the trapeze artist, begged the studio bosses to let her out of the assignment. She was replaced by Olga Baclanova.

The setting is a traveling circus full of clowns, acrobats, and "freaks." Hans (Harry Earles), a dapper dwarf, has inherited a fortune. Cleopatra tries to come between him and his fiancée Frieda (Daisy Earles), while carrying on an affair with Hercules the strongman (Henry Victor). She attempts to poison Hans, but is discovered—and the freaks take a terrible revenge. The strongman is stabbed to death and Cleopatra is turned into a chicken with a human head and arms.

The film proved too extreme for many. After disastrous test screenings, it was heavily cut. Even then, the reception was hostile. Not until the 1960s and the counter-culture era did the film achieve the cult status it enjoys today. **GM**

1 "THE PEACOCK OF THE AIR"

A circus barker sets the scene, inviting onlookers to peer into a mysterious box, from which several of them recoil in horror. "She was once a beautiful woman," he reveals before it cuts to a flashback of the elegant trapeze artist flying through the air.

2 SEEING DOUBLE?

When one of the pretty Siamese twins (Daisy and Violet Hilton) is pinched on the arm, the other feels the pain. Most of the actors who appeared in the film were sideshow or circus performers in real life, and Tod Browning had himself worked in a touring circus.

3 DEATH IN THE RAIN

The freaks take a horrible revenge on Hercules the strongman, who is pursued and stabbed (presumably to death) beneath a wagon's wheels during a thunderstorm. In the original ending he was also castrated—a symbolic reference to his affair with Cleopatra.

4 CHICKEN-WOMAN

At the end, the viewer too is able to look into that enigmatic box and discover the fate that awaits those who break the "code" of the freaks. In a rather happier finale, added at the studio's request, Hans is reunited with Frieda.

🕐 DIRECTOR PROFILE

1880–1913

Tod Browning was born in Kentucky. As a teenager, he left his affluent family to join a carnival and went on to work in vaudeville and burlesque as well as having a brief spell as a jockey. After meeting D. W. Griffith (1875–1948) in New York, Browning began acting in single-reel comedies for the Biograph Company. When Griffith broke from Biograph and headed to California, in 1913, Browning did the same.

1914–18

In 1915 Browning directed his first film, *The Lucky Transfer*, and appeared in Griffith's *Intolerance: Love's Struggle Throughout the Ages* (1916), the follow-up to the notorious *The Birth of a Nation* (1915, see p. 30). The same year, he was involved in a car crash after driving his vehicle into a train at high speed. He sustained serious injuries that put a halt to his filmmaking activities for nearly two years.

1919–25

Browning's *The Wicked Darling* (1919) marked the first of his collaborations with Lon Chaney, "The Man of a Thousand Faces." After a string of less remarkable works, the director enjoyed one of his biggest hits with *The Unholy Three* (1925). Like *Freaks*, this was a circus yarn, with Chaney in the dual role of Echo the ventriloquist and the sweet-natured Mrs. O'Grady. Reviewers relished the fact that, for once, Chaney was not hiding under layers of makeup.

1926–29

London after Midnight (1927) was Browning's first vampire film. *Where East Is East* (1929) marked his last collaboration with Chaney.

1930–62

Browning returned to the vampire genre with *Dracula* (1931), which made a star of another horror movie legend—Béla Lugosi—although the commercial failure of *Freaks* stymied the director's career. His last film of merit was *Devil Doll* (1936) with Lionel Barrymore; *Miracles for Sale* (1939) was his final film.

GANGSTER MOVIES

1 *Scarface* charts the rise and fall of Tony "Scarface" Camonte. It was one of the first movies to feature the Thompson submachine or "tommy" gun.

2 *Underworld* is seen as the first true Hollywood gangster film and the first to feature the gangsters' perspective.

3 Director Michael Curtiz (1886–1962) made the most of atmospheric shadows in *Angels with Dirty Faces* in the scene prior to the capture of Rocky (Cagney).

The early 1930s in Hollywood are sometimes referred to as the "golden age of turbulence"—a period when censorship was in abeyance, Mae West was in her glory days, wildly expressionistic musicals were being made, and gangsters with machine guns were on the prowl. The period's films bring certain images to mind: James Cagney squashing the grapefruit in Mae Clarke's face in *The Public Enemy* (1931, see p. 102), Paul Muni wielding his machine gun in *Scarface* (1932, above) and Edward G. Robinson as the pudgy, felt-hatted mobster boss in *Little Caesar* (1931, see p. 100). These three films form what critics call the "paradigm" of the classic gangster movie.

Although the 1930s was a particularly fertile period for the gangster film, what is widely considered to be the first example of the genre predated the decade by nearly twenty years. *The Musketeers of Pig Alley* (1912) by D. W. Griffith (1875–1948) was a sixteen-minute silent based on the real-life murder of gambler Herman Rosenthal. A pivotal gangster film of the late 1920s was *Underworld* (1927, opposite above) by Josef von Sternberg (1894–1969), scripted by ex-Chicago newspaperman Ben Hecht. "An idea came to me. The thing to do was to skip the heroes and heroines, to write a movie containing only villains and bawds," Hecht explained in a revealing passage in his autobiography. "As a newspaperman, I had learned that nice people—the audience—loved criminals, doted on reading about their love problems as well as their sadism."

KEY EVENTS

1929	1930	1931	1932	1933	1934
Chicago's St. Valentine's Day massacre, a conflict between Al Capone's Italian gang and Bugs Moran's Irish gang, leaves seven people dead.	*Roadhouse Nights*, starring Jimmy Durante, is the first of many gangster films inspired by Dashiell Hammett's novel *Red Harvest* (1929).	*Little Caesar* (see p. 100) sets the template for future gangster films and introduces a new vocabulary—"gats" (guns), "molls" (girls), and "bulls" (cops).	Al Capone begins serving his eleven-year sentence for tax evasion in Atlanta, Georgia. He is released six years later for good behavior.	On December 5 the 21st Amendment to the Constitution repeals Prohibition; it allows the manufacture and sale of liquor in the United States.	After evading police for almost a year, bank robber turned folk hero John Dillinger is gunned down by police. Bonnie and Clyde are also killed this year.

The gangster film of the 1930s had had a boost from an unlikely quarter—the US Congress—a decade before, in the autumn of 1919, when the Volstead Act prohibiting the sale of alcohol was passed. The result of Prohibition was to foster the growth of criminal gangs, who stepped into the breach and provided Americans with illicit access to booze. This was the era of gangster bosses, bootleggers, and speakeasies. It was also a brave new world of opportunity for Hollywood. Certain studios specialized in gangster movies. Pre-eminent among them was Warner Bros, which liked to boast that it made movies "torn from the headlines." *Little Caesar*, directed by Mervyn LeRoy (1900—87) and starring Edward G. Robinson as a pint-sized psychopathic hoodlum, *The Public Enemy*, by William Wellman (1896—1975) with Cagney as a live-wire gangster (both from Warner Bros), and *Scarface*, from United Artists and directed by Howard Hawks (1896—1977), came out quickly one after another and spawned hosts of imitators.

Scarface, scripted by Hecht, was based on the story of gang leader Al Capone (played in swaggering fashion by Muni). "I would like to do the Capone family as if they were the Borgias set down in Chicago," Hawks had told Hecht. Unlike other early gangster films, *Scarface* did fall foul of the censors. "The American public and all conscientious State Boards of Censorship find mobsters and hoodlums repugnant. Gangsterism must not be mentioned in the cinema," Hawks was told by the Hays Office on the eve of production. Hawks shot the film regardless, but then he and producer Howard Hughes faced a Herculean battle to secure its release.

The concessions originally demanded from Hawks and Hughes to allow *Scarface* to be shown set a daunting example for future producers of gangster movies. The censors wanted the film to be retitled "The Shame of a Nation" and for the gangster hero to be revealed as a coward in the final reel and then hanged. Although an alternative ending was shot, Hughes showed the original version to the critics and released it in New Orleans, where it was out of the reach of the Hays Office. In the end, the film was seen in the original cut in many states. The censors could hardly accuse Hollywood of making up its gangster stories in an era when gangsters were regularly front-page news. The lines between the real-life hoodlums and their movie equivalents often seemed to blur. John Dillinger, one of the most notorious gangsters of the era, was shot and killed in 1934 as he came out of a Chicago cinema where he had been watching a Clark Gable gangland film, *Manhattan Melodrama* (1934).

There is a defining tension at the heart of the gangster genre, obvious from the very first gangster films but especially prevalent in the 1930s. On the one hand, gangster heroes are glamorous, charismatic figures with whom audiences are likely to identify. Yet they are invariably revealed as mean and vicious killers who leave physical and emotional destruction in their wake. That is why they need to be punished and why Cagney's gangster in *Angels with Dirty Faces* (1938, right) goes in such cowardly fashion to the electric chair.

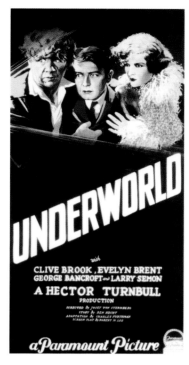

1935	1936	1937	1937	1939	1941
The Warner Bros film "*G*" *Men* celebrates the birth of the newly named FBI—an attempt to counteract the "pernicious" effect of gangster films.	*The Petrified Forest* helps propel actor Humphrey Bogart to stardom as gangster Duke Mantee, whose character is allegedly based on Dillinger.	Gangster "Bugsy" Siegel is sent by the East Coast mob to set up gambling syndicates in California. He is now operating on Hollywood's doorstep.	Urban gangster film *Dead End*, by William Wyler (1902–81), introduces the Dead End Kids—arguably the first teenage rebels of cinema.	*The Roaring Twenties*, directed by Raoul Walsh (1887–1980), is released. It is considered the last of the great gangster movies of the 1930s.	*High Sierra*, scripted by John Huston (1906–87) from the novel by W. R. Burnett, begins cinema's great collaboration between Huston and Bogart.

Or, at least, he seems to. The film ends on an ambiguous note: the viewer never knows whether Cagney's fear is put on for the sake of his boyhood friend Jerry Connolly (Pat O'Brien), now a priest, who has begged him to die whimpering so the kids he is trying to keep on the right side of the law do not idolize him, or whether he feels it for real.

Gangster heroes have a particular fascination for anyone wishing to criticize the status quo. This was evident in critic Robert Warshow's influential essay "The Gangster as Tragic Hero" (1948), just after the golden age of gangster movies of the 1930s and early 1940s. He argued that gangster movies were "an expression of the part of the American psyche which . . . rejects Americanism." The United States as a social and political organization may have been committed to "a cheerful view of life," but Warshow believed that this cheerful view was subverted from within by gangster movies. He wrote about Hollywood gangsters as if they were Shakespearean figures—heroes with fatal flaws: "The gangster is the man of the city, with the city's language and knowledge, with its queer and dishonest skills and its terrible daring, carrying his life in his hands like a placard, a club," Warshow suggested.

If 1930s gangster films created a new kind of Hollywood protagonist—the tough, urban, working-class hero, often from an immigrant background—they also made very evident the US obsession with violence. Guns had been a factor in US movies since *The Great Train Robbery* (1903, see p. 22) by Edwin S. Porter (1870–1941), but the early 1930s boom came just as Hollywood was turning to talkies, and it took sound movies to do justice to the rat-tat-tat of the machine gun fire created by "G-men" and gangsters alike. The gangsters, especially those played by Cagney, used dialogue in an equally reckless and aggressive way. The best gangster movies also had some of the same demotic energy and vivid characterization found in the vernacular writing of Damon Runyon and Ring Lardner stories of the period.

Concerned about the rise of celebrity criminals such as John Dillinger (opposite above), the censors at the Hays Office issued a moratorium on gangster movies in 1935. Hollywood's response was to shift the gangster, or at least the actor who played the gangster, onto the side of the law.

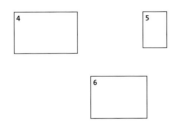

4 In *Bullets or Ballots*, directed by William Keighley (1889–1984), gangster Nick "Bugs" Fenner (Humphrey Bogart, left) and Detective Johnny Blake (Edward G. Robinson) are poised for a shootout when Fenner discovers that Blake is a policeman who has infiltrated his crime organization.

5 A "Wanted" poster issued for the notorious bank robber John Dillinger, who came to epitomize the idea of the hero outlaw for some impoverished Americans during the Depression.

6 The poster for *"G" Men* focuses on star James Cagney as an incorruptible lawyer turned FBI agent, but it does little to indicate a dramatic change in role for the actor from gangster to law man.

"G" Men (1935, below) starred Cagney, one of the archetypal gangster actors, transformed into a government man, a lawyer working for the FBI. Although gangster movies nearly always led to the criminal's downfall, conservatives objected to the freedom and luxury depicted on the big screen as part of the life of crime. Films such as *"G" Men* and *Bullets or Ballots* (1936, opposite) consciously tried to counteract the image of gangsters portrayed in the early 1930s.

The influence of the US gangster movie reached Europe where the shadows of war were looming. Although *Pépé le Moko* (1937), starring Jean Gabin as an infamous Parisian gangster who hides out in the Algiers kasbah, was apparently modeled on its US counterpart, it is more a precursor to Film Noir (see p. 168) than part of the gangster genre. In Hollywood the gangster movie did not begin to give way to the brooding self-consciousness of Film Noir until the 1940s. It is instructive to chart Humphrey Bogart's progress. In *The Petrified Forest* (1936) he was Duke Mantee, "world-famous killer." In *Dead End* (1937), *Angels with Dirty Faces,* and *The Roaring Twenties* (1939), he was still on the side of the demons. However, his screen persona gradually changed. He began to play private eyes rather than hoodlums. As he metamorphosed, so did the gangster genre. The *Scarface*s and *Little Caesar*s gave way to films in which the detectives, not the hoodlums, were the heroes.

In the documentary *A Personal Journey with Martin Scorsese through American Movies* (1995), the director argues that *The Roaring Twenties* was the last "great gangster film before the advent of Film Noir" and that the gangster genre changed as "the gangster turned into a businessman." However, the gangsters in 1920s and 1930s Hollywood movies were businessmen of a sort. Prohibition provided gangsters with a gap in the market that they exploited at the end of a gun. The Depression created a daunting economic environment in which the gangster lifestyle appealed. By the 1950s Prohibition was no more and the United States was more affluent. Gangsters became the dark underbelly of society. The level of sadistic violence began to ratchet higher. In *The Big Heat* (1953), Lee Marvin throws a pot of scalding coffee in Gloria Grahame's face. By 1973, in *The Long Goodbye,* Mark Rydell smashes a bottle into his girlfriend's face—not for anything she has done, just to warn off Elliott Gould's Philip Marlowe. **GM**

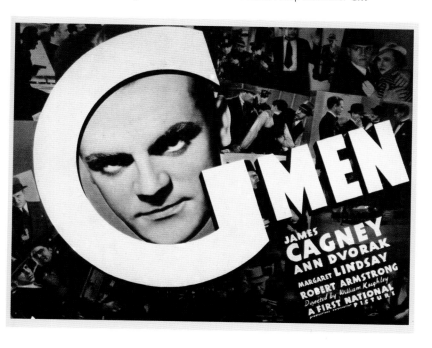

Little Caesar 1931

MERVYN LEROY 1900 – 87

▲ Rico (Edward G. Robinson) was made to look like real-life mobster Al Capone.

▼ The original film poster implies that the good guy, not the gangster, gets the girl.

The gangster movie needed sound to catch on. Audiences who had grown up with silent cinema were bowled over not only by hearing films talk but also by sound effects. *Little Caesar* has the rhythm of snarled, urban street chatter, the rat-tat-tat of tommy guns in drive-by hits, and the screech of getaway tires. Based on the novel (1929) by W. R. Burnett, *Little Caesar* was tougher than previous gangster movies. Producer Darryl F. Zanuck commented, "Every other underworld picture has had a thug with a little bit of good in him. He reforms before the fade-out. This guy is no good at all. It'll go over big." Like most big gangster films, *Little Caesar* is roughly modeled on the plot of *Macbeth*. Thug Caesar Enrico "Rico" Bandello (the frog-faced Edward G. Robinson in a star-making role) is ambitious, gets violent, rises to the top, takes a huge fall, and dies in the gutter. Warner Bros loved stories that were ripped from the headlines, and movies that really moved. Director Mervyn LeRoy has scenes blow up and blow over as fast as a child's tantrum.

Like woman-beating Tom Powers (James Cagney) in *The Public Enemy* (1931, see p. 102) and incestuous Neanderthal Antonio "Tony" Camonte (Paul Muni) in *Scarface* (1932), Rico is not just a crook. For contemporary times he was a sexual deviant, with a simmering gay crush on an ex-partner, Joe Massara (Douglas Fairbanks Jr.), who quits the rackets for Hollywood stardom. This was intended to make the villain creepier, but the closeted streak humanizes him and adds Zanuck's "little bit of good." However, it is charisma and high living, not any moral grounding, that makes Robinson's gangster a great movie archetype. **KN**

👁 KEY SCENES

1 NEW YEAR'S EVE
Keen to win the loyalty of fellow gang members and demonstrate his toughness, the ambitious and brazen Rico undertakes the riskiest jobs. He heists a society party on New Year's Eve—and takes the time to rub out the city's crusading anticrime commissioner.

2 RISE OF CAESAR
When fellow hoods hold a banquet at the Palermo Club in Rico's honor to confirm his new position as a kingpin in the underworld, Rico shares the dais as an equal with other crime lords and reluctantly gives an acceptance speech full of hollow sentiment.

3 ISSUING A THREAT
Rico informs his rival Little Arnie Lorch (Maurice Black) that he is through and that Rico is taking over his territory: "If you ain't out of town by tomorrow morning, you're going to leave in a pine box!" The frightened Lorch leaves town and goes to Detroit the next day.

4 "MOTHER OF MERCY, IS THIS THE END OF RICO?"
Fittingly, a gangster pays for his crimes, as Rico dies in a gutter— shot full of holes by Sergeant Tom Flaherty (Thomas E. Jackson). All subsequent great gangster movies are required to deliver similar operatic death scenes for their monstrous heroes.

🕐 DIRECTOR PROFILE

1900–26
Mervyn LeRoy was born in California to a wealthy Jewish family who were ruined by the San Francisco earthquake in 1906. LeRoy went into vaudeville as a comedian. He entered the film industry with the aid of his cousin, producer Jesse L. Lasky, who hired him at Famous Players–Lasky as a wardrobe assistant and film tinter before he progressed to gag writer, screenwriter, and bit-part actor.

1927–37
At First National (later Warner Bros.) he became a director, initially specializing in comedies including *No Place to Go* (1927) and *Harold Teen* (1928). With *Little Caesar* he invented the 1930s gangster genre and became associated with contemporary, tough dramas, continuing with *Five Star Final* (1931) and *I Am a Fugitive from a Chain Gang* (1932). He carried his fast, down-to-earth, socially relevant tone over into musicals, such as *Gold Diggers of 1933* (1933, see p. 134).

1938–39
He joined MGM as head of production and was responsible for the decision to make *The Wizard of Oz* (1939).

1940–50
LeRoy continued to direct and was nominated for a Best Director Oscar for the drama *Random Harvest* (1942). He won an Honorary Oscar for a short about anti-Semitism, *The House I Live In* (1945).

1951–61
After handling the big-budget spectacle *Quo vadis* (1951), he made musicals such as *Million Dollar Mermaid* (1952) and *Rose Marie* (1954). He took over *Mister Roberts* (1955) from original director John Ford (1894–1973) and returned to darker subjects with *The Bad Seed* (1956) and *The FBI Story* (1959).

1962–87
His last major film was a musical, *Gypsy* (1962), and he was uncredited as director of John Wayne's *The Green Berets* (1968). He died in Beverly Hills in 1987.

The Public Enemy 1931

WILLIAM WELLMAN 1896 – 1975

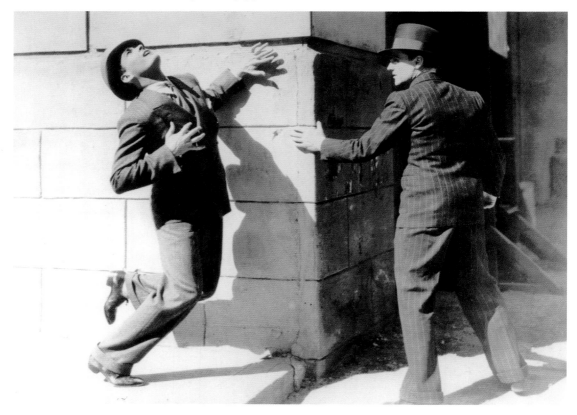

▲ Tom's own death is foreshadowed when his long-time partner is gunned down.

▼ The lurid colors of the poster set the tone for this tale of guns, gangsters, and molls.

William Wellman's Prohibition era–set *The Public Enemy* was not immediately recognized as a classic by contemporary critics. "It is just another gangster film, weaker than most in its story," complained a reviewer in *The New York Times*, seemingly oblivious to its importance in establishing the gangster genre. Its star, James Cagney, who gave a career-defining performance as motor-mouthed hoodlum Tom Powers, also had his reservations. In one of the film's most famous scenes, Cagney is shown shoving half a grapefruit into Mae Clarke's face.

The film was based on the novel *Beer and Blood* by Chicago writers Kubec Glasmon and John Bright, but much of it was taken from actual events. The grapefruit scene was loosely inspired by a real-life incident involving Chicago gangster Hymie Weiss, who had once taken an omelette his girlfriend had just cooked and smeared it across her face.

Like most gangster films of the period, *The Public Enemy* took an ambivalent attitude toward its gangster protagonists. On the one hand, these men were beneath disdain. When the film was re-released in a double bill with *Little Caesar* (1931, see p. 100) in 1954, there was even a foreword explicitly demonizing Cagney's character as a sociological "problem." On the other hand, Cagney's Tom was by far the most dynamic and charismatic character in the film. Audiences loved his punchy delivery, his wit, and his defiance. Watching the film, the audience could not help but root for him. As Wellman acknowledged, "The thing that made it successful was one word—Cagney!" **GM**

KEY SCENES

1 MISSPENT YOUTH
Tom (Cagney) and Matt (Edward Woods) are first shown as kids on the run from the cops. Although Tom grows up to be a ruthless gangster, the audience is introduced to him when he is a mischievous boy and can hence empathize with him to a degree.

2 WHAT'S FOR BREAKFAST?
Tom sneers through the notorious scene in which he cruelly squashes half a grapefruit into Mae Clarke's face. Cagney ruefully reflected in later years that he could not enter a restaurant without some joker sending a grapefruit over to his table.

3 CAGNEY MOVES
When the rival mob lets rip with a machine gun that leaves Matt dying, Tom jumps behind a wall with all the grace and speed of the vaudevillian actor he once had been. Cagney was cast initially as Matt but the roles were soon reversed after the first takes.

4 "I AIN'T SO TOUGH"
Out for revenge, Tom marches through a storm carrying his guns. The audience sees him enter a building, gunshots are heard, and then he stumbles out wounded, back into the rain. As he reels in the gutter, he utters his own epitaph.

5 A DEATHLY DELIVERY
To the accompaniment of the song "I'm Forever Blowing Bubbles," Tom's trussed-up corpse is delivered to his home. To appease the censors, there is no happy ending for the gangster. Tom's way of life is continually contrasted in the film with his law-abiding brother's.

DIRECTOR PROFILE

1896–1919
"Wild Bill" William Wellman was born in Brookline, Massachusetts. A hell-raiser from an early age, he was thrown out of high school. He became a professional ice hockey player for a minor league team in 1914. He later became an ambulance driver and a fighter pilot in World War I.

1920–42
Wellman made his directorial debut (uncredited) with *The Twins of Suffering Creek* in 1920. He won his first Academy Award for Best Picture for *Wings* (1927). In 1937 he showed his versatility directing Hollywood tragedy *A Star Is Born*, which he also scripted, and screwball comedy *Nothing Sacred*.

1943–75
He directed the brilliant Western *The Ox-Bow Incident* (1943), followed by *The Story of GI Joe* (1945), one of Wellman's most underrated films. He died in Los Angeles of leukemia in 1975.

SOCIETY ON THE SCREEN

1 The shackles are checked in hard-hitting prison drama *I Am a Fugitive from a Chain Gang*. The film led to the appeal and release of many chain gang prisoners in the United States.

2 The poster for *Mr. Deeds Goes to Town*. Frank Capra's comedy contrasts traditional, small-town values with the self-interested sophistication of the metropolis.

3 Spencer Tracy turns the tables on the mob that nearly lynches him in *Fury*. It was German exile Fritz Lang's first film in Hollywood.

During the economic hardships of the Great Depression, the movies provided an affordable window on the world, a place where US audiences could get a glimpse of other lives. For the price of a ticket, the average moviegoer could see sophistication and glamour in films such as *Grand Hotel* (1932, see p. 106) and *Trouble in Paradise* (1932, see p. 108) or learn about the lives of great men such as Louis Pasteur and Emile Zola through filmed biographies. With *Citizen Kane* (1941, see p. 110), the public was afforded insight into the world of a contemporary celebrity, the newspaper magnate William Randolph Hearst.

Occasionally, the studio system was prepared to use its influence to educate audiences about some of the darker areas of US society. In 1931 Warner Bros. bought an autobiographical piece by Robert Elliott Burns that appeared in *True Detective* magazine, later published as the book *I Am a Fugitive from a Georgia Chain Gang*. Despite doubts about the subject matter—one director dismissed it as an unsuitable subject for a time "when the whole public is depressed to the extent that many of them are leaping out of windows"—the studio persevered and Burns, while still technically a fugitive, was employed secretly to work on an early draft of the script. The success of *I Am a Fugitive from a Chain Gang* (1932, above), directed by Mervyn LeRoy (1900–87) and with Paul Muni as the fugitive James Allen, shone a powerful light on the brutal penal system in the American South.

KEY EVENTS

1930	1931	1931	1932	1933	1934
The double lynching of two black men in Indiana is the last recorded lynching of black Americans in a northern state.	Despite the Depression, RKO Pictures makes the big-budget *Cimarron*, about the nineteenth-century Oklahoma Land Rush.	*City Lights*, directed by and starring Charlie Chaplin (1889–1977), is one of his most searching explorations of his Tramp persona.	Mervyn LeRoy directs a searing indictment of contemporary penal practices with *I Am a Fugitive from a Chain Gang*.	Thomas Thurmond and John M. Holmes are lynched in San Jose, California, for allegedly murdering Brooke Hart. The lynching is broadcast live on radio.	Biopics *The Barretts of Wimpole Street* and *The House of Rothschild* are released.

Fritz Lang (1890–1976) directed a powerful indictment of another US dirty secret. *Fury* (1936, below) was inspired by the true story of a double lynching in San Jose three years earlier. Spencer Tracy plays Joe Wilson, a man who is wrongly accused of child abduction. When a lynch mob burns down the prison, he escapes but pretends to be dead so that the perpetrators will face a murder charge. In truth the majority of those who suffered at the hands of lynch mobs were black, a fact that no studio was willing to publicize at the time. The unique power of *Fury* manifests itself in the way the audience is forced into an uncomfortable empathy with the mob who also become victims of injustice.

Frank Capra (1897–1991) offered an altogether sunnier vision of the travails of the common man. The historian Robert Sklar ascribes the key to Capra's success as "his ability to convince audiences they were watching their own strengths and foibles, their own dreams and values, their own selves dramatized on the screen." Classic Capra heroes, such as Longfellow Deeds trying to dispose of an inherited $20 million in *Mr. Deeds Goes to Town* (1936, right), are innocents whose good nature is exploited by the rich, the powerful, and the cynical.

Capra's heroes may be victims of corrupt politics and capitalism, but they are not outsiders. Putting the lives of the dispossessed on the screen was more problematic. When Darryl Zanuck acquired the rights to John Steinbeck's novel *The Grapes of Wrath* (1939), the fate of the Dust Bowl refugees was something that many were unwilling to acknowledge. The sensitive film version by John Ford (1894–1973) touched the collective conscience of the nation's cinemagoers in 1940. Woody Guthrie, who rewrote the story in ballad form, summed up its importance: "Go see *Grapes of Wrath*, pardner . . . You was the star in that picture. Go and see your own self and hear your own words and your own song." **DP**

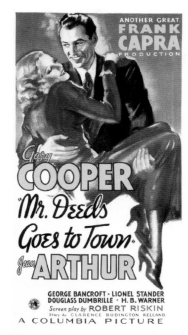

1935	1936	1937	1939	1940	1941
David Copperfield, based on Charles Dickens's novel and directed by George Cukor (1899–1983), is released.	Chaplin charts poverty, strikes, unemployment, political intolerance, and the monotony of machines in his final Little Tramp film *Modern Times*.	William Dieterle (1893–1972) follows up the success of *The Story of Louis Pasteur* (1936) with *The Life of Emile Zola*.	Jefferson Smith tries to use politics to make the world a better place in Frank Capra's *Mr. Smith Goes to Washington*.	*The Grapes of Wrath*, based on John Steinbeck's novel, spotlights the plight of the United States's dispossessed farming communities.	*Citizen Kane* (see p. 110) is released. Having failed to prevent the movie being made, William Randolph Hearst attempts to discredit it.

Grand Hotel 1932
EDMUND GOULDING 1891 – 1959

▲ Greta Garbo at her best as the fading, suicidal ballerina Grusinskaya.

▼ The poster draws attention to the film's selling point—the all-star cast.

Billed as "the show of the century," *Grand Hotel* made cinematic history as the first movie to have an ensemble cast of stars, with a lineup that includes Greta Garbo, John Barrymore, Joan Crawford, Wallace Beery, Lionel Barrymore, Lewis Stone, and Jean Hersholt. MGM producer Irving Thalberg bought the rights to Vikki Baum's popular novel from 1929, *Menschen im Hotel*, based on the lives of guests and staff at a Berlin hotel, for $35,000, hired gifted filmmaker Edmund Goulding to direct, built what was at that time the largest set ever created, and cajoled many of Hollywood's leading actors into working together alongside more than one hundred extras.

The result is a film that follows a disparate group of people over a few days and narrates how their paths cross. The characters include Grusinskaya, a weary Russian ballerina (Garbo) in crisis because her career is waning; the dashing Baron Felix von Geigern (John Barrymore), an aristocrat reluctantly turned jewel thief to pay his gambling debts; the meek-mannered Otto Kringelein (Lionel Barrymore); the nasty industrialist General Director Preysing (Beery), who is desperate to close a business deal; Preysing's blowsy but good-hearted stenographer Flaemmchen (Crawford); and permanent hotel resident, war veteran, and wry observer Doctor Otternschlag (Stone).

The Hollywood premiere included a mock-up of the film's hotel lobby reception desk, where stars attending, including Marlene Dietrich and Clark Gable, had to sign in as they entered. Audiences flocked to see the movie and *Grand Hotel* won the Oscar for Best Picture. **CK**

👁 KEY SCENES

1 OPENING SEQUENCES
The film opens with telephone switchboard operators taking and directing calls, then shifts to show characters making telephone calls. The characters' paths are to cross and their destinies interweave just as the telephone cables crisscross on a switchboard surface.

2 THE LOBBY
Goulding uses overhead shots to establish the scale of the hotel, which itself is like a character in the movie. The grandeur of the concentric structure around a central lobby reflects the unraveling lives of its guests, all keen to project an image of wealth.

3 THE STENOGRAPHER
Flaemmchen begins work for General Director Preysing. This was one of Joan Crawford's early roles and initial reactions indicated that the young actress's gritty, realistic performance threatened to upstage the silent movie acting style of Greta Garbo.

4 GRUSINSKAYA WANTS TO BE ALONE
Garbo as the ballerina tells her manager and assistant, "I want to be alone," and so delivered one of the best-known movie quotes of all time. The phrase came to haunt the actress as a defining statement about her own reclusive behavior.

5 DOCTOR OTTERNSCHLAG SUMS UP
As guests featured in the story depart from the hotel and new ones arrive, Doctor Otternschlag—a permanent resident—sums it all up, saying, "Grand Hotel . . . always the same. People come, people go. Nothing ever happens."

🕐 DIRECTOR PROFILE

1891–1928
Born in England, after World War I Edmund Goulding emigrated to the United States, where he worked as a scriptwriter. Hired by MGM, Goulding made his directorial debut with *Sun-Up* (1925). He became recognized as one of Hollywood's top directors after *Love* (*Anna Karenina*, 1927).

1929–42
In 1937 Goulding joined Warner Bros., where he found success with a remake of the war movie *The Dawn Patrol* (1938) and three classic Bette Davis melodramas: *Dark Victory* (1939), *The Old Maid* (1939), and *The Great Lie* (1941).

1943–59
At Twentieth Century Fox, Goulding mixed genres with the drama *The Razor's Edge* (1946) and the noirish *Nightmare Alley* (1947). Following his last film, the musical *Mardi Gras* (1958), Goulding died in 1959 while undergoing heart surgery.

Trouble in Paradise 1932
ERNST LUBITSCH 1892 – 1947

▲ Sexual intrigue contributes to Gaston Monescu's troubles in paradise in Lubitsch's sophisticated romantic comedy.

▼ An elegant poster for the film, which remained the director's personal favorite.

The romantic comedy as audiences know it today might not have existed if Ernst Lubitsch had not made *Trouble in Paradise*. This luxuriantly amoral creation, however, does not much resemble many films of the genre. For, by twisting the milieu and verbiage of love, Lubitsch extinguishes sentimentality in favor of sly desire.

In a Venice hotel, Gaston Monescu (Herbert Marshall), disguised as a doctor, robs Mr. Filiba (Edward Everett Horton) of his wallet and returns to his room to receive "Countess" Lily (Miriam Hopkins) for supper. The lovers each discover the other as a thief and, besotted, begin their life of crime together. In Paris a year later, Gaston steals a bejeweled bag belonging to perfume heiress Mariette Colet (Kay Francis). When Mariette offers a 20,000 franc reward for the "lost" bag, Gaston goes to collect it, turning on the charm and getting hired as her secretary. But his seduction of Mariette rebounds on him when she proves as much an adept as he. When he discovers that Mr. Filiba is her suitor, Gaston realizes he must vanish before he is recognized as the Venice burglar. His plans to flee with Lily self-destruct when Mariette makes her desire plain and Lily senses the truth.

If the diamond-sharp dialogue is what keeps *Trouble in Paradise* so fresh, Lubitsch's brilliant use of doors and staircases dazzles almost as much. Mariette's poor butler (Robert Greig) never knows which door conceals his mistress and her new secretary, and is forever knocking at the wrong one. There is also plenty of profile acting, of Gaston gazing at Mariette and running through his lexicon of superlatives: "wonderful," "marvelous," etc. **NJ**

👁 KEY SCENES

1 PICKPOCKET PETTING

"Countess" Lily says in "Baron" Gaston's hotel room: "Baron, you are a crook. You robbed the gentleman in 253, 5, 7, and 9." He accuses her in turn: "Countess, you are a thief." An exchange takes place of items that each has stolen from the other, climaxing with Lily's garter.

2 A BAG OF PHOOEY

Mariette advertises a reward for her "lost" bag. A scruffy man asks her if her bag had diamonds on it. When she says yes and asks if he has found it, he yells, "No . . . but let me tell you, any woman who spends a fortune in times like this for a handbag: phooey, phooey, and phooey."

3 SILENT LIES

Gaston is dimming the lights in Mariette's bedroom when Lily arrives. She has guessed that he has a rendezvous with Mariette, and wants the 100,000 francs in the safe. When she gets to the money, she exclaims, "This is what I want. This is real. Cash!"

🕓 DIRECTOR PROFILE

1892–1914

Ernst Lubitsch was born in Berlin, the son of a tailor. He started out in Berlin theater and by 1911 was playing comic Jewish characters for Max Reinhardt (1873–1943) in his Deutsches Theatre. He went on to star in the movie *Der Stolz der Firma* (1914).

1915–22

Lubitsch began directing silent German comedy films, such as *Die Austernprinzessin* (*The Oyster Princess*, 1919). He developed an elegant film style—dubbed "The Lubitsch Touch" (see panel below)—that mocked sexual convention. His breakthrough came with the opulent period film *Madame DuBarry* (1919).

1923–28

Mary Pickford brought Lubitsch to Hollywood to direct *Rosita* (1923). He stayed there and worked for most of the major studios. The visual economy of his social comedies, such as *The Marriage Circle* (1924), transformed the way Hollywood made films. His films often mirrored US society but usually in an imaginary or foreign setting. *The Student Prince* (1927) exemplifies this.

1929–47

Lubitsch's first sound film was the magnificent musical *The Love Parade* (1929). After moving to MGM, he directed *Ninotchka* (1939), one of his best-loved films. His classic romantic comedies include *The Shop Around the Corner* (1940) and *To Be or Not To Be* (1942). Heart trouble made him withdraw to a supervisory role in 1946, and in 1947 it killed him.

THE LUBITSCH TOUCH

Billy Wilder (1906–2002) famously had a sign on his desk saying: "How would Lubitsch do it?" European émigré Ernst Lubitsch (below) brought an urbane sophistication to the Hollywood films he directed. His style has been summed up by writer Leland A. Poague: "Ernst Lubitsch is generally remembered for his cinematic wit, for his gracefully charming and fluid style, for his ingenious ability to suggest more than he showed and to show more than others dared suggest; for all of those qualities and characteristics known collectively as 'The Lubitsch Touch.'" The scene from

triangular love story *Design for Living* (1933), in which George returns home and becomes aware of Gilda's infidelity (e.g. a table set for two) is a fine example of this. The audience knows what has happened, but Lubitsch visualizes George's perception with his sure "touch."

Citizen Kane 1941

ORSON WELLES 1915 – 85

▲ The American dream turns out to be empty for the monstrous newspaper proprietor Charles Foster Kane.

▼ Welles's name dominates the poster of the film for which he tried to take full credit.

Orson Welles's directorial debut *Citizen Kane* has so long been considered "The Greatest Movie Ever Made" that it has become hard to view it clearly. Myths have coalesced around it—that Welles pioneered all kinds of innovative cinematic techniques and that it was dismissed on its initial release as a pretentious failure. Welles was not the first to use deep focus photography, ceilinged sets, sound montage, jump cuts, overlapping dialogue, chiaroscuro lighting, or multiple narrator viewpoints—although no previous director had dared combine them with such gusto and visual inventiveness as Welles. When *Citizen Kane* first came out, most critics raved about it, but its release was sabotaged. Press baron William Randolph Hearst had no trouble recognizing himself in Charles Foster Kane, and in no time the whole crushing weight of the Hearst public-relations machine was grinding into action against Welles's movie, ensuring it never got a decent release.

For such a seminal work the film's underlying message is staggeringly conventional: that the rich should not be envied their wealth and power because they have forfeited the simple pleasures of true love and happiness. Even so, the film deserves its status: first, because Welles's signature is so compelling, so unmistakably inscribed in every frame; and second, because with hindsight audiences can recognize so much of Welles in Kane himself. *Citizen Kane* is still a towering film, but through all the visual grandeur, the baroque showmanship, and look-at-me techniques, dazzling though they are, sounds the howl of Welles's future frustration and blocked genius like an awful premonition. **PK**

KEY SCENES

1 "ROSEBUD"
Dying, Kane (Welles) utters one word, "Rosebud," that sends news reporter Thompson (William Alland) on a quest to find out the "truth" about who Kane really was. The snowglobe links the end of Kane's life to his childhood; it is symbolic of a calmer, simpler life.

2 MARRIAGE MONTAGE
In a deft montage of breakfast scenes over a number of years, Welles shows the steady deterioration of Kane's marriage to his first wife Emily (Ruth Warrick). The film is noted for its nonlinear storytelling and use of flashbacks from multiple points of view.

3 KANE ENTERS POLITICS
Kane runs for the governorship of New York against his political rival, the corrupt "Boss" Jim W. Gettys. This scene is an example of the deep-focus shot Welles used repeatedly in the film. Everything in the foreground and background is in sharp focus.

4 LIFE AT XANADU
Kane builds a baroque palace named "Xanadu" in Florida, where he lives with second wife, Susan, in sterile luxury, but she grows weary of both it and him. Kane's wealth and megalomania isolate him from others, who leave him to die in loneliness at Xanadu.

DIRECTOR PROFILE

1915–39
Orson Welles was born in Kenosha, Wisconsin. A child prodigy, he mounted productions of Shakespeare from the age of ten. He went to study at the Chicago Art Institute in 1930, then acted professionally at the Gate Theatre Dublin. In 1933 he joined Katherine Cornell's rep company and he mounted his *Voodoo Macbeth* in Harlem in 1936. Welles founded the Mercury Theatre Company with John Houseman—their "Fascist Julius Caesar" on Broadway was a sensation. He took up regular radio work; the Mercury radio production of *The War of the Worlds* was so realistic that it caused widespread panic. In 1939 he was invited to direct films in Hollywood for RKO. The studio gave him a two-picture deal with complete artistic control, unheard of for an untried director.

1940–48
He directed, co-wrote, and starred in *Citizen Kane*. His second film, *The Magnificent Ambersons* (1942), was butchered by the studio during his absence in Latin America. Studio interference also compromised his next three films: *The Stranger* (1946), *The Lady from Shanghai* (1948), and *Macbeth* (1948). He quit Hollywood in disgust in 1948.

1949–85
Welles took up a peripatetic career, mainly in Europe, acting in other people's films, notably *The Third Man* (1949), directed by Carol Reed (1906–76). He directed his own films, often in chaotic conditions: *Othello* (1952); *Mr. Arkadin* (1955); *Touch of Evil* (1958, in Hollywood); *Le procès* (*The Trial*, 1962, adapted from Kafka); *Campanadas a medianoche* (*Chimes at Midnight*, 1965, the last of his three Shakespeare films); *The Immortal Story* (1968); and *Vérités et mensonges* (*F for Fake*, 1973). Various projects were left unfinished, including *Don Quixote*, *The Deep*, and *The Other Side of the Wind*. Although a Hollywood outsider, Welles remained in demand as an actor and voice-over narrator. He also worked on several high-profile television commercials. He died on October 10, 1985, of a heart attack, two hours after appearing on *The Merv Griffin Show*.

SCREEN GODDESSES

1 Bette Davis stars opposite Henry Fonda in *Jezebel*. The role gained Davis an Academy Award for best actress.

2 The statuesque Joan Crawford in a publicity still from 1932.

3 Vivien Leigh in historical drama *Fire Over England*, which teamed the actress with her future husband, Laurence Olivier.

When Belgian director Harry Kümel (b. 1940) was preparing his cult vampire movie *Le rouge aux lèvres* (*Daughters of Darkness*, 1971), he told his leading actress Delphine Seyrig that he wanted her to look like a Hollywood star of the 1930s—"because they are immortal." It was an astute observation. Stars such as Greta Garbo, Marlene Dietrich, Joan Crawford (opposite above), Bette Davis (above, in *Jezebel*, 1938), Vivien Leigh, and Katharine Hepburn have a timeless quality that few actors of later generations could match.

Their goddesslike status was not easily won. The Greta Garbo first lured to MGM in the mid 1920s by Louis B. Mayer was a fuzzy-haired, thickset twenty-one-year-old Swede who hardly spoke a word of English. However, what Garbo also had was a beautiful, enigmatic face that looked radiant in close-ups, especially when filmed by William H. Daniels, who became known as "Garbo's cameraman." Starting with *Flesh and the Devil* (1926), he shot twenty films with her, providing the lambent lighting that showed her off to best advantage in films such as *Romance* (1930) and *Queen Christina* (1933, see p. 116).

As Billy Wilder (1906–2002) told Cameron Crowe (b. 1957), he used to joke with Dietrich when he worked with her that she should light her scenes herself. After her films with Josef von Sternberg (1894–1969), such as *Shanghai Express* (1932, see p. 114), she knew as much about camera lighting as any director or cinematographer and gave lighting advice to subsequent directors, who ensured that her beauty did not fade as she aged. She was not the only screen

see p. 116
see p. 114

KEY EVENTS

1930	1931	1932	1933	1934	1935
Der blaue Engel (*The Blue Angel*) kicks off the collaboration between director Josef von Sternberg and his muse Marlene Dietrich.	Jean Harlow appears in her most iconic role in *Platinum Blonde*. Scores of female fans dye their hair in slavish admiration of the star.	Greta Garbo and Joan Crawford appear together with a gaggle of other big MGM names in the quintessential star vehicle—*Grand Hotel*.	Mae West delivers her infamous line "Why don't you come up sometime and see me?" in *She Done Him Wrong*.	Bette Davis, the sourest of screen goddesses, plays the scheming waitress on the make opposite Leslie Howard in *Of Human Bondage*.	Junior screen goddess Shirley Temple receives a special Academy Award—at the age of seven.

goddess to benefit from technology. Merle Oberon, leading actress in *Wuthering Heights* (1939), had a serious car accident in 1937, resulting in problems with her skin. However, her husband, ace cameraman Lucien Ballard, designed a special light (known as the "Obie") that made her on-screen beauty as heavenly as ever.

It has often been pointed out that stars in the silent era had an ethereal quality that enraptured audiences. Gloria Swanson expressed it best when she played the fading movie actress in Billy Wilder's *Sunset Boulevard* (1950): "We did not need dialogue . . . we had faces." There was indeed something transcendent about a close-up of a silent star such as Garbo or Lillian Gish. Some feared the screen goddesses would lose their Olympian luster in the talkie era, when they were forced to speak. This was to become the fate of some stars. Pola Negri's career was derailed by her heavy Polish accent and Norma Talmadge's nasal New Jersey tones did her no favors. Yet sound saw no diminution in the appeal of certain stars. Sceptics were convinced that Garbo would sink in the new era. She proved them wrong playing—of all things—a hard-drinking barfly in *Anna Christie* (1930). "Give me a viskey, ginger ale on the side. Don't be stingy," were her first lines. Audiences found her thick European accent almost as alluring as the famous face. Vivien Leigh's consummate Englishness made her perfect for home-grown period pieces such as *Fire Over England* (1937, below right), and her British accent did not prevent her from snatching one of the most coveted female lead roles of the decade— as Southern belle Scarlett O'Hara in *Gone with the Wind* (1939).

Behind the scenes, publicity departments played a crucial part in the creation of magnetic screen goddesses. MGM, under legendary boss of the 1930s Irving Thalberg, liked to boast that the studio had "more stars than there are in heaven." These stars were pampered and highly paid but had little control over their careers. "We told stars what to say, and they did what we said because they knew we knew best," Howard Strickling, the studio's hard-driving publicity head, later claimed. The screen goddesses were locked into draconian contracts. Strickling and his team policed every aspect of their lives, burying scandals, forging the stars' signatures on publicity pictures, and even brokering their marriages.

Of course, figures such as Garbo, Hepburn, and Dietrich were far too imperious to be bossed around by studio underlings. Hepburn was nicknamed "Katharine of Arrogance" and the other big actresses of her era were equally haughty. This points up the paradox at the heart of the studio system: screen goddesses were very important because they helped bring in the enormous box-office returns studios enjoyed during the 1930s. At the same time, they were relatively powerless hired hands. If a star was difficult to deal with or her beauty fading, her services could be dispensed with quickly. What then? As *Sunset Boulevard* and *What Ever Happened to Baby Jane?* (1962) proved, the fate of the forgotten screen goddess was both poignant and grotesque. **GM**

1937	1937	1938	1939	1940	1941
Vivien Leigh and Laurence Olivier commence their off-screen relationship while playing on-screen lovers in *Fire Over England*.	Jean Harlow dies at the untimely age of twenty-six as a result of uremic poisoning.	After hankering so much after the part of Scarlett O'Hara, Bette Davis wins an Oscar playing another archetypal Southern belle—in *Jezebel*.	Joan Crawford confirms her status as screen diva in an all-female cast in *The Women*, starring as husband stealer Crystal Allen.	Katharine Hepburn's beauty and independent nature are used to great effect in *The Philadelphia Story* by George Cukor (1899–1983).	Greta Garbo bows out of Hollywood with her final film, *Two-Faced Woman*, and becomes a virtual recluse.

Shanghai Express 1932
JOSEF VON STERNBERG 1894 – 1969

▲ The iconic Marlene Dietrich smolders provocatively in this highly charged drama.

▼ The poster portrays allure: both of the star and of Eastern promise.

Josef von Sternberg's fourth outing with muse and star Marlene Dietrich is a lavish soap opera presented as a sophisticated life-or-death drama, in which civil war and sexual jealousy threaten a rekindled love affair. Interestingly, it is less the pre-Hays Code raciness—Shanghai Lily has clearly been around the block, even admitting to her fair share of lovers—than the mere presence of Dietrich and Anna May Wong on the screen that raises the film's temperature. The stars clearly realized that their acting skills were less important than their ability to simmer on demand.

What story there is involves the train being commandeered by a ruthless Chinese rebel, played by future Charlie Chan star Warner Oland. Holding Clive Brook's military surgeon hostage in order to gain leverage over the authorities, he meets his end courtesy of some deft knifework by Wong's Hui Fei.

Emotion is everything in Sternberg's films. Logic and reason are relegated to minor roles, with the director creating "an emotionalized background that would transfer itself into my foreground." Nowhere is this more apparent than in the way Sternberg, with Oscar-winning cinematographer Lee Garmes, shot the film's star. Dietrich's performance is little more than a series of poses and looks. From her entrance in black, with a veil partially covering her face, the viewer is encouraged to bathe in the luminosity of a cinematic icon.

The film marked the commercial high point of the collaboration between director and star. It was subsequently remade as *Night Plane from Chungking* (1943) and as *Peking Express* (1951). **IHS**

⊙ KEY SCENES

1 ALL ABOARD
The ticket office scene introduces the nine passengers as they board the train. They are from a variety of backgrounds, with distinct personalities, and the stock characters include a missionary, an officer, a businessman, and a gambler.

2 BRIEF ENCOUNTER
The first encounter between Shanghai Lily (Dietrich) and Captain Harvey (Brook) is charged with sexual tension as the former lovers indulge the audience with their exploits during their years apart. Note the prolonged handshake and longing stares.

3 THE FINAL CLINCH
After giving up hope that they would ever be together again, the lovers are reunited at last. They conjure up one of cinema's most erotically charged embraces, which breaks the tension that has built up throughout the film.

⊙ DIRECTOR PROFILE

1894–1927
Josef Sternberg was born in Vienna in 1894. He added the "von" to his name after the production of his first script, *By Divine Right* (1924). His directorial debut, *The Salvation Hunters*, was made in the same year and released in 1925. He then worked on a number of uncompleted projects until his first masterpiece, *Underworld* (1927). Ben Hecht won an Oscar for the script and the film launched the gangster genre.

1928–30
Sternberg made a series of powerful dramas, including *The Docks of New York*, *Street of Sin*, and *The Last Command* (all 1928). The latter two featured Emil Jannings, who also starred in *Der blaue Engel* (*The Blue Angel*, 1930) opposite Marlene Dietrich.

1931–35
Sternberg made six more features with Dietrich, ending with *The Devil Is a Woman* (1935). During this period, he also directed a documentary, *The Fashion Side of Hollywood* (1935), and an ambitious, but ultimately unsuccessful, adaptation of Theodore Dreiser's *An American Tragedy* (1931).

1936–69
An attempt to film *I, Claudius* for Alexander Korda was canceled before completion in 1936. It was followed by a series of disappointing features, with the exception of the entertaining *The Shanghai Gesture* (1941). Sternberg's last film was the steamy Japanese war drama *The Saga of Anatahan* (1953). In 1965 he published an acclaimed autobiography, *Fun in a Chinese Laundry*. He died in Hollywood in 1969.

A DIRECTOR AND HIS MUSE

Few collaborations between director and star have been as successful as that of Josef von Sternberg and Marlene Dietrich (below). Sternberg accentuated the mystery of the German-born actress, allowing her to develop a very specific persona: accessible, but enigmatic. Although Sternberg is credited with discovering Dietrich, she had already appeared on stage and in more than a dozen German films. Sternberg sculpted his dramas out of how the star looked as opposed to what she said. So when he told Dietrich, "Count to six and look at that lamp as if you could no longer live without it," he knew it was in her power to leave an audience enraptured.

Queen Christina 1933
ROUBEN MAMOULIAN 1897 – 1987

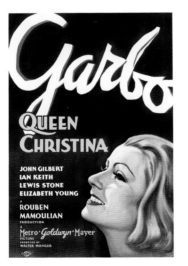

▲ Cinematographer William Daniels captured Greta Garbo's beauty in close-ups.

▼ The title is eclipsed by Garbo's star billing.

Swedish actress Greta Garbo was the brightest star in the MGM firmament but she was spoiled and demanding: the studio bosses lived in constant fear that she might lose interest in her film career. Her contract with MGM had run out in 1932 after which she spent months on holiday in Sweden. The chance to play Queen Christina of Sweden—in a movie project she helped initiate—persuaded her to return to Hollywood.

It is a measure of Garbo's immense power during this period that she determined the choice of leading man and approved the director. MGM had considered Laurence Olivier to play the role of her lover but after he and Garbo failed to gel in rehearsals Garbo suggested John Gilbert, her former lover and her costar in silent movies such as *Flesh and the Devil* (1926). A big star in the silent era, Gilbert brought an easy charm to his role as Spanish envoy Antonio.

Queen Christina is widely recognized as Garbo's finest screen performance. She brings hauteur, mischief and intense glamour to her role as the Swedish queen, caught up in the maelstrom of the Thirty Years' War and trying to balance her romantic yearnings with the political demands of her role. Rouben Mamoulian directs with great flair and visual panache what might otherwise have been a stolid historical epic. The crowd scenes and the intimate moments between Garbo and Gilbert are equally confidently handled. Despite the enthusiastic critical response, Garbo expressed reservations. "I tried to be Swedish but it's difficult in Hollywood to be allowed to try anything. It's all a terrible compromise," she later observed. **GM**

👁 KEY SCENES

1 THE LOVERS TOGETHER
After Christina and Antonio meet at a country inn, Christina moves around the room in a carefully choreographed sequence, touching objects and sighing, "I have been memorizing this room. In the future, in my memory, I shall live a great deal in this room."

4 ANTONIO'S DYING SWOON
Christina goes to find Antonio but discovers him wounded from a duel with his rival, the jealous Count Magnus (Ian Keith). She cradles her mortally injured lover in her arms and promises to return him to Spain. When he dies, her grief and disbelief are manifest.

🕐 STAR PROFILE: GRETA GARBO

1905–25
Born Greta Lovisa Gustafsson in Stockholm, Sweden, Garbo left school at thirteen, and worked first in a barber shop, then as a clerk in a department store, where she modeled for the store's film advertisements. From 1922 to 1924 she studied at Stockholm's Royal Dramatic Theatre School. One of her teachers was the director Mauritz Stiller (1883–1928), who changed her name to Garbo and gave her a significant role in *Gösta Berlings saga* (*The Atonement of Gösta Berling*, 1924). She starred alongside Asta Nielsen and Werner Krauss in *Die freudlose Gasse* (*Joyless Street*, 1925).

2 "MY FATHER DIED FOR SWEDEN AND I LIVE FOR HER"
The mob surrounds the palace, up in arms about the queen's intimacy with a Spaniard. Showing magnificent arrogance, the steely Christina faces them down alone. She calms the angry crowd and reminds them of her regal authority.

1926–29
Stiller and Garbo were invited to Hollywood by Louis B. Mayer and put under contract to MGM. To Stiller's disappointment, Garbo's first US film, *The Torrent*, was directed by Monta Bell (1891–1958). Stiller directed his protégée in only one film, *The Temptress*, before falling afoul of Mayer; he returned to Sweden and died soon afterward. Garbo meanwhile became one of Metro's top female stars in films that showcased her mysterious looks and frank sensuality, notably *Flesh and the Devil* (1926), *Love* (*Anna Karenina*, 1927), *A Woman of Affairs* (1928), and *The Kiss* (1929). Her frequent costar was John Gilbert; they became lovers, but Garbo shied away from marriage.

1930–41
Despite the studio's misgivings, Garbo's Swedish accent came across well in her first sound film, *Anna Christie*. Increasingly known for her aloofness and dislike of interviews, she lent her mystique to a dozen more films, many of them period pieces. Deciding she should play comedy, the studio put her in *Ninotchka* (1939) and *Two-Faced Woman* (1941). Appalled by the latter's bad press, Garbo abruptly retired from the screen.

3 CHRISTINA'S ATTEMPTED ABDICATION
Christina tells her noblemen that she has chosen love over duty and will therefore have to relinquish the emblems of power. When they refuse to accept her abdication, she removes her crown and robes before bidding a tearful farewell.

1942–90
Garbo became a recluse. Occasional talk of a comeback led to nothing. In 1954 she was awarded an Honorary Oscar, but failed to show up to collect it. She died in New York in 1990.

FRENCH POETIC REALISM

1 One of the early triumphs of sound cinema, René Clair's satire *A nous la liberté* draws parallels between working in a factory and life in prison.

2 Marcel Pagnol's *César* features stage entertainer Raimu as a strong-willed cafe owner trying to reunite his family.

3 Sacha Guitry stars as a lovable scoundrel, The Cheat, in the entertaining comedy, *Le roman d'un tricheur*.

F rench cinema in the 1930s is particularly associated with the iconic figure of star Jean Gabin and the Poetic Realist films made later in the decade. The origin of these films can be traced back to the chaos engendered by the introduction of talkies in 1929. At that time, French filmmaking was known principally for its visual and formal innovation. The guiding principle of its outstanding films was the Romantic idea of the artist-author as a talented genius. In Paris the largely Surrealist-inspired avant-garde created a climate in which the narrative norms of Hollywood did not hold sway. At first the French industry took protectionist measures, believing that synchronized dialogue would make English-speaking Hollywood uncompetitive. However, the two once-dominant French studios, Pathé and Gaumont, had become weak conglomerates, in no position to exploit the situation with an economic depression now in full swing. When in 1930 a US-German cartel deal was struck, Paramount was quick to equip its Joinville studio to crank out "canned theater"—French-language copies of Hollywood successes.

Among the first to film in sound was René Clair (1898–1981). His fluid use of sound and image made the silent to sound transition look easy. Clair filled his elaborate, hugely successful films with images that mask or comment obliquely on the sound source, and song sequences that could be mimed. The prestige productions *Sous les toits de Paris* (*Under the Roofs of Paris*, 1930), *Le million* (1931), *A nous la liberté* (*Freedom for Us*, 1931, above), and *Quatorze*

KEY EVENTS

1930	1931	1931	1933	1933	1934
Paramount floods the market with French-language versions of Hollywood movies. The German studio UFA does the same with its films.	René Clair makes two hugely successful films set in Paris, *Le million* and *A nous la liberté*, at German company Tobis-Klangfilm's new studio at Epinay.	Post-synchronized dubbing renders remaking films in French unnecessary. Paramount converts Joinville studio into a dubbing center.	Marcel Pagnol's *Jofroi* (*Ways of Love*) features a largely amateur cast.	Hitler comes to power in Germany, sparking an exodus of German creative talent to Hollywood, London, and Paris.	Successful playwright Marcel Pagnol becomes an advocate of cinema. He builds his own studio in Marseilles, which he uses and leases out.

118 1930–39

Juillet (*Bastille Day*, 1933) are light-hearted films that create an imaginary old Paris of great charm, which fed French audiences' hunger for fun-filled nostalgia and brought Clair international fame.

With approximately 4,000, mostly individually owned, cinemas to reequip at great expense, France took longer to convert to sound than the Netherlands, Germany, and Britain, and French cinema owners were vulnerable to Hollywood distributors' exclusive deals. Soon, a quarter of films shown in French either originated from or had been made abroad. Caught in a vice between Hollywood and Germany's principal film studio UFA, French producers had to invent, at speed, a new national cinema with popular appeal. Their solution was to import theater and vaudeville stars, and the playwrights and directors with whom they worked, and make farces, melodramas, and military comedies that had the advantage of already being well loved as plays. By the second half of the decade, a mere ten directors were responsible for more than a quarter of the French films released from 1936 to 1938. Even more than directorial influence, it was the personae of comic singers Fernandel, Georges Milton, and Charles-Joseph "Bach" Pasquier, of popular actors including Raimu, Arletty, Harry Baur, Jules Berry, Michel Simon, and Louis Jouvet, and of young actresses such as Michèle Morgan and Annabella that set the tone of French cinema.

Playwright Marcel Pagnol (1895–1974) was an early convert and in 1934 built his own studio in his home city of Marseilles. Initially he wrote screenplays of his stage hits, although he did both write and direct the final part of his Marseilles trilogy, *César* (1936, right), which capitalized on the success of his play *Marius* (1929). The best films he directed were derived from the novels of Jean Giono and were at least partly shot on location, a radical move at the time. Pagnol even built the village of Aubignane for *Regain* (*Harvest*, 1937). Sacha Guitry (1885–1957), an equally famous dramatist, had written some silent shorts in the 1920s but it was in 1936—when he conceived his own form of "filmed theater"—that his career as a director took off. From then on he made light, humorous films starring himself and featuring taut dialogue, such as *Le roman d'un tricheur* (*The Cheat*, 1936, right), *Faisons un rêve* (*Let Us Do a Dream*, 1936), *Désiré* (1937), and *Quadrille* (1938).

Jean Vigo (1905–34) was more of a cinephile maverick. He made highly personal films, such as his documentary *A propos de Nice* (1930) that depicts a city haunted by images of death. Shot while he was already ill with the tuberculosis that would kill him, his *Zéro de conduite: Jeunes diables au collège* (1933) is a satirical portrait of a boarding school, and was banned. Neither film lasts an hour, but Vigo made one feature, *L'Atalante* (1934, see p. 122), which depicts the honeymoon of a newlywed couple on a barge and became a landmark in cinema by establishing the Poetic Realism school.

Vigo was already dead and Guitry's film career hardly begun when French cinema hit a mid-decade low. Pathé and Gaumont almost collapsed and

1934	1935	1936	1937	1938	1939
Fascist gangs riot in Paris. The uniquely poetic work of Jean Vigo reaches its apogee—and its end—with *L'Atalante* (see p. 122).	The virtual collapse of Pathé and Gaumont leaves the French film industry fragmented.	The socialist Popular Front alliance comes to power but is soon undermined, and relinquishes control of the French government a year later.	*Pépé le Moko* by Julien Duvivier cements Jean Gabin's image as a doomed Everyman.	Jean Renoir's *La bête humaine* and Marcel Carné's *Le quai des brumes* establish the creative dominance of the Poetic Realists.	Hitler's troops invade Poland, and France declares war on Germany in response.

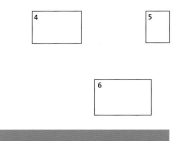

4 The shadowy menace of *Pépé le Moko*
combines Poetic Realism with gangster
thriller and established Jean Gabin as
the ideal tragic hero.

5 The pacifist Jean Renoir's *La grande
illusion* is a powerful antiwar film that
proved so successful it was banned by
the Nazis.

6 Louis Jouvet excels as interfering snoop
Archibald Soper in the Marcel Carné and
Jacques Prévert collaboration *Drôle de
drame ou L'étrange aventure du Docteur
Molyneux*, a bizarre black comedy
satirizing the middle classes.

Paramount's French production activities were wound up. Overnight, French
production became a fly-by-night cottage industry, even more dependent
on coproductions. Hitler's rise to power in Germany in 1933 did not stop, for
instance, the anti-Fascist Jean Grémillon (1898–1959)—whose flop *La petite Lise*
(*Little Lise*, 1930) was arguably a forerunner of Poetic Realism—from working
in Berlin. In fact, with a few exceptions, French cinema in the 1930s largely
ignored the political struggles that broke out on the streets of Paris with the
Fascist riots of February 1934 and the happier Bastille Day demonstration in
1935 that cemented the socialist Popular Front alliance.

Hitler's racist policies saw the German industry lose much of the native
talent that had produced its recent flowering with films such as *Die 3-Groschen
Oper* (*The Threepenny Opera*, 1931) by G. W. Pabst (1885–1967), *M* (1931, see p.
82) by Fritz Lang (1890–1976), and *Liebelei* (*Flirtation*, 1933) by Max Ophüls
(1902–57). Many of the best German directors—including Pabst, Lang, Ophüls,
Douglas Sirk (1900–87), Robert Siodmak (1900–73), and Billy Wilder (1906–
2002)—had émigré sojourns in France, which may have been crucial to French
cinema's upturn in quality from the middle of the decade onward. German
cinematographers Eugen Schüfftan and Curt Courant, in particular, helped
Marcel Carné (1906–96) move cinema into the shadowy streets.

The Poetic Realist school of gritty nocturnal dramas of doomed romance
set in a working-class milieu—that perhaps began with *La petite Lise*—was
developed by Belgian-born Pierre Chenal (1904–90) in *La rue sans nom* (*Street
Without a Name*, 1934). However, it was another Belgian-born director, veteran
Jacques Feyder (1885–1948), assisted by the young Carné, who first set the new
standard of quality in *Le grand jeu* (1934), a romantic drama about a man (Pierre
Richard-Willm) who joins the French Foreign Legion and becomes obsessed
with a woman (Marie Bell) who looks identical to the girl he left behind.

Actor Jean Gabin came to represent the tragic face of Poetic Realism.
He first found fame in three films by Julien Duvivier (1896–1967). In *La bandera*
(*Escape from Yesterday*, 1935) Gabin plays a murderer who joins the Spanish
Foreign Legion. In *La belle équipe* (*They Were Five*, 1936) he is one of a cartel of
unemployed workers who buy a winning lottery ticket and open a restaurant
together with uneasy results. In *Pépé le Moko* (1937, above) Gabin plays a
gangster hiding in Algiers's kasbah, lured to his doom by the love of a tourist
from Paris (Mireille Balin). Duvivier carried this sense of foreboding into two
later films about regret. *Un carnet de bal* (*Christine*, 1937) again stars Bell as a

widow seeking out former lovers, and *La fin du jour* (*The End of the Day*, 1939), which is set in a retired actors' home. The fatalism of these films matched the mood of a country that saw the Popular Front win power in 1936, only to lose it again a year later.

Jean Renoir (1894–1979), a veteran of silent films, was a humanist with Communist leanings. He found success with *La chienne* (*Isn't Life a Bitch?*, 1931), in which Michel Simon's bank cashier kills his whore lover (Janie Marèze) and lets her pimp (Georges Flamant) take the rap. However, it was Renoir's films made later in the decade that established his reputation. In *Le crime de Monsieur Lange* (*The Crime of Monsieur Lange*, 1936), scripted by Leftist poet Jacques Prévert, a publishing collective is threatened by the return of its scoundrel owner, who is then murdered. *La grande illusion* (*Grand Illusion*, 1937, right) stars Gabin and Erich von Stroheim and critiques World War I through the relationship between three French prisoners of war and their German prison camp commander. *La bête humaine* (*Judas Was a Woman*, 1938) is based on an Emile Zola novel about a crime of passion and once more stars Gabin as the fated individual. All three films mark Renoir as a master, although it is *La règle du jeu* (*The Rules of the Game*, 1939, see p. 124), describing a weekend's frolics among the bourgeois rich and their servants, that marks the summit of his achievement in that decade.

The finest exponent of Poetic Realism was Carné. He formed a firm bond with Prévert on *Drôle de drame ou L'étrange aventure du Docteur Molyneux* (*Bizarre, Bizarre*, 1937, below), an excellent actors piece starring Louis Jouvet as an interfering bishop, but their collaboration coalesced with *Le quai des brumes* (*Port of Shadows*, 1938). Gabin plays opposite Michèle Morgan, as an army deserter who falls for a seventeen-year-old orphan in a misty dockside location and then pays for his moment of happiness, in an atmosphere saturated with defeatism. The equally doom-laden romance in poverty drama *Hôtel du Nord* (1938) was made without Prévert and is less convincing. However, *Le jour se lève* (*Daybreak*, 1939) is perhaps the supreme example of Poetic Realism. Here Gabin plays a foundry worker goaded into jealousy and murder by a vile seducer, reflecting on his fate in his dingy room while the police wait below. The murderer and seducer that was Nazi Germany would soon be at France's door, but the legacy of the nation's classic cinema would survive it and produce Carné's transcendent *Les enfants du paradis* (*Children of Paradise*, 1945). **NJ**

JEAN GABIN
PIERRE FRESNAY
ERIC VON STROHEIM

LA GRANDE ILLUSION

JEAN RENOIR

L'Atalante 1934

JEAN VIGO 1905 – 34

▲ Lovers on an unconventional honeymoon.
▼ Bargeman Père Jules appears on the poster.

Jean Vigo's first and only full-length feature is widely considered one of cinema's masterpieces. It is an earthy, tactile, and ravishingly romantic inquiry into that vital period of emotional ripening that occurs directly after marriage. The story is simple but throbs with texture and detail: Dita Parlo's doe-eyed, small-town Juliette has (somewhat hurriedly, it appears) taken Jean Dasté's angular barge skipper Jean as her husband, and in doing so has agreed to join him and his lovably eccentric first mate Père Jules (Michel Simon) on their battered barge *L'Atalante*, bound for Le Havre via Paris.

Jean and Juliette's relationship initially stutters as neither seems quite certain of the conventions of cohabitation. The presence of Père Jules is fundamental in helping the lovers to assuage their initial doubts. His cabin is filled with trinkets from his travels (including a human hand in a jar) and his body is daubed with tattoos: he represents the simplicity, experience, humor, and worldliness that Jean and Juliette unknowingly crave.

L'Atalante movingly suggests that love should not only embrace the physical being, but also should include the acceptance of a person's whole world, even if that world happens to be a canal barge populated by stray cats and a sage old seadog. Vigo was a director who had total faith in the lyricism of his images, and his sensual use of montage, editing, camera movement, framing, performance, and the occasional special effect allowed him to realize on film his passionate notions of love, expression, and independence. Vigo died from tuberculosis shortly after the film's completion in 1934, at only twenty-nine. **DJ**

1 THE FEAR OF THE NEW

Juliette does not have the radiant smile of a new bride; instead she shows fear and self-doubt. The wedding procession, which Vigo films with everyone wearing black and looking serious, represents bourgeois society as opposed to the more eccentric life on the barge.

4 DANCE DANCE DANCE

During shore leave the lovers visit a club where Juliette is dragged onto the dance floor by a traveling salesman. It marks the couple's first major falling-out, but it also reveals Jean's protectiveness of his bride and Juliette's inexperience in publicly expressing affection.

2 THE LIFE AND TIMES OF PÈRE JULES

Juliette visits the cluttered cabin of Père Jules for a tour of his trinkets. His body etched with crude tattoos, Jules represents the sexuality and freedom found outside conventional society. His selflessness and humor eventually rub off on the couple.

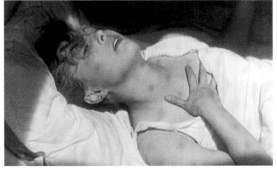

5 CABIN FEVER

In what is arguably one of the most erotically charged scenes ever filmed, the separated pair realize their love in a night of illusory passion. Their orgasmic dreams of reconciliation are vividly realized in a series of crosscut shots as they writhe in their separate beds.

3 GOOD FORTUNE

Père Jules visits a palm reader and finds good fortune (and a lot more besides). Meanwhile, Jean and Juliette are each trying to see an image of the other while under water, the suggestion being that their mutual love would be confirmed.

🕑 DIRECTOR PROFILE

1905–29

Jean Vigo was born in an attic in Paris, the son of Spanish anarchist Eugène Bonaventura de Vigo i Salles (also known as Miguel Almereyda). Colored by his father's politics, Vigo's artistic sensibility often espoused upheaval and individualism.

1930–32

In 1930 Vigo made *A propos de Nice* with a secondhand camera given to him by his father-in-law. The film is a witty and vaguely surreal assemblage of footage capturing the cultural divide between the rich and poor of the Riviera resort. He profiled the French swimming champion Jean Taris in a short documentary film, *Taris, roi de l'eau* (1931).

1933–34

Vigo courted the ire of French censors with his bawdy comedy about the joys of anarchism, *Zéro de conduite: Jeunes diables au collège*. He died just after completing *L'Atalante* in 1934 and remains one of the great "what ifs?" of world cinema.

La règle du jeu 1939
The Rules of the Game   JEAN RENOIR 1894 – 1979

▲ Jealousies simmer below stairs in Renoir's dissection of the French class system.

▼ The poster illustrates the theatrical turn of events at the château.

At first glance, Jean Renoir's *La règle du jeu* appears to be a frothy divertissement—a light, formal comedy of romantic misunderstanding. However, gradually the froth blows away to reveal a bitter panorama of moral instability, as France heads toward war: a portrait, Renoir said, of "a society dancing on a volcano."

The film is mostly set at the château of Marquis Robert de la Chesnaye (Marcel Dalio), who throws a house party with his wife, Christine (Nora Gregor). The guests include intrepid aviator Jurieux (Roland Toutain)—who is hopelessly in love with Christine—and his friend Octave, a failed musician, played by Renoir himself. Marceau (Julien Carette), a poacher newly hired as a servant, takes a fancy to Christine's maid Lisette (Paulette Dubost), to the fury of her jealous gamekeeper husband, Schumacher (Gaston Modot).

In this formally complex film, elegant camerawork and manic choreography turn the château's corridors into both a labyrinth and a vaudeville stage, while dense sound recording offsets the often overt theatricality, creating a disorienting effect of overlapping dialogue. The famous hunting party sequence, with its long takes and quasi-documentary feel, reveals the brutality and callousness at work beneath the elegant surface.

Badly received on release, the film was banned by the French government for its supposedly demoralizing effect. Cut radically, it was not rediscovered in its original version until the late 1950s. Revered by the French Nouvelle Vague (see p. 248) directors, it remains a subtly perplexing, endlessly watchable film. **JR**

👁 KEY SCENES

1 HOMECOMING HERO
The film opens at Le Bourget airport with crowds greeting Jurieux (Toutain), who has made an heroic solo transatlantic flight. Jurieux is oblivious to the attention, only noticing that his beloved Christine is not present. He is pleased to see his old friend Octave (Renoir).

2 FARCE AND FESTIVITIES
The marquis holds a costume play at his château, with all the guests taking part. Octave, trapped in a bear costume, is at the heart of the surrounding chaos. What begins in a mood of poised good humor escalates into a dangerous farce.

3 THE PARTY IS OVER
Jurieux is accidentally shot dead by Schumacher. The accident is shocking because it is swept calmly under the carpet as society closes ranks. The aristocrats troop back indoors but their shadows on the château wall suggest the ghosts of a society that has had its day.

🕐 DIRECTOR PROFILE

1894–31
Jean Renoir was born in Paris, the son of the painter Pierre-Auguste Renoir. He directed his first silent film in 1924. The scatological farce *On purge bébé* (1931) was his first sound film. His muse in these early years was his first wife Catherine Hessling, who became Pierre-Auguste Renoir's favorite model in his later years.

1932–38
He directed a corrosive satire of the follies of the bourgeoisie, *Boudu sauvé des eaux* (*Boudu Saved from Drowning*, 1932). Films such as *Madame Bovary* (1933) revealed his skill at literary adaptation. *Le crime de Monsieur Lange* (*The Crime of Monsieur Lange*, 1936) is an ensemble piece about a working-class community that reflected his left-wing political allegiances. *La grande illusion* (1937) remains one of cinema's most subtly provocative antiwar statements.

1939–45
After the negative reception of *La règle du jeu*, Renoir went to Italy to work on a version of *Tosca*. When Germany invaded France, he left for the United States. His projects there included the anti-Nazi film *This Land Is Mine* (1943).

1946–79
Renoir shot his first color film, *The River* (1951), in India. In his final period he made small-scale films, culminating in television movie *Le petit théâtre de Jean Renoir* (*The Little Theater of Jean Renoir*, 1969). Jacques Rivette (b. 1928) interviewed him in 1966 for the documentary *Jean Renoir, le patron*.

MORAL COMEDIES

La règle du jeu set the benchmark for a tradition of moral comedies and ensemble dramas. With its country-house setting and tangle of amorous games between servants and aristocrats, it was later a model for the British-set *Gosford Park* (2001, below), directed by Robert Altman (1925–2006) from an Academy Award–winning script by Julian Fellowes. Renoir's moral comedies have been much emulated in the United States, notably by Woody Allen (b. 1935), and more recently by such independent directors as Nicole Holofcener (b. 1960) and Lisa Cholodenko (b. 1964). His influence also shows in the work of Indian director Satyajit Ray (1921–92) in films such as *Days and Nights*

in the Forest (1970). Renoir was revered by the French Nouvelle Vague (see p. 248). His real heir in that group, however, was its least typical member, Eric Rohmer (1920–2010), notably in his "Six Moral Tales."

SCREEN COMICS EMBRACE SOUND

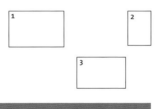

1 Groucho Marx plays Professor Quincy Adams Wagstaff in *Horse Feathers*. The plot of the film centers on an intercollegiate football game.

2 *It's a Gift* was one of several films W. C. Fields made for Paramount with the child actor Baby LeRoy.

3 The Three Stooges provide some memorable slapstick hospital moments in *Dizzy Doctors*.

As "talkies" replaced silent cinema in the 1930s, screen comics took radical action in adapting to the new possibilities. The Mack Sennett (1880–1960) tradition of slapstick and physical comedy was transformed into verbal choreography in which one actor played the "straight man" and the other delivered the punchlines. Jimmy Durante delighted in splitting infinitives and W. C. Fields—who improvised much of his own dialogue—constantly explored double meanings in films such as *It's a Gift* (1934, opposite above).

Hearing screen comics speak was a bizarre and novel experience; some were more suited to the new medium than others. Bucking the trend for talkies, Charlie Chaplin (1889–1977) released the silent film *City Lights* (1931); he did not make his first talking picture until *The Great Dictator* (1940, see p. 158). Laurel and Hardy adapted instantly to talkies, but other comics did not have such an easy transition. Hampered by studio pressure and restrictions, Buster Keaton (1895–1966) was pushed away from the artistic flourishes of his silent work and into compromised sound films such as *Speak Easily* (1932). Harold Lloyd's career faltered, and Harry Langdon soon vanished into limbo.

With the addition of sound and recorded dialogue, comedy films moved into the realm of surrealism. Comedic moments verged on the absurd, with Oliver Hardy's neck elongating impossibly in *Way Out West* (1937) and Harpo Marx producing a candle burning at both ends in *Horse Feathers* (1932, above). Such fantastical happenings prefigured the logic-defying world of Looney Tunes.

KEY EVENTS

1931	1932	1932	1933	1934	1935
The Stolen Jools stars a who's who of comedy stars, including Laurel and Hardy, Buster Keaton, Our Gang, Jack Hill, Dorothy Lee, and Jack Oakie.	Laurel and Hardy's *The Music Box* (see p. 128) wins the first ever Academy Award for Best Short Subject (Comedy).	In the twilight of his career, Roscoe "Fatty" Arbuckle stars in his first film for Warner Bros, *Hey, Pop!* He dies penniless the following year.	Moe, Larry, and Curly star together for the first time as part of "Ted Healy and His Stooges" in *Nertsery Rhymes*. It is less than twenty minutes long.	The first Three Stooges feature, *Woman Haters*, is released.	The Marx Brothers star in their first film for Metro-Goldwyn-Mayer, *A Night at the Opera*. It lacks the trademark anarchy of their earlier films for Paramount.

Many comics of the 1930s came from vaudeville backgrounds and had honed their skills on stage before making the leap to the screen. W. C. Fields's pool table routine in *Six of a Kind* (1934) was created during his days treading the boards; Jack Benny was already an accomplished violinist and Jimmy Durante a jazz pianist and they worked these talents into their performances. Calling on the perfectionism developed in stage rehearsals, Stan Laurel and Oliver Hardy worked tirelessly on the two-minute dance sequence in *Way Out West*. Some of these comics created distinctive personas, defined by trademarks, popular roles or particular features, such as Jimmy Durante's big nose or the spindly Stan in contrast with the rotund Ollie. These two reached their creative peak during the 1930s, appearing in classics such as *The Music Box* (1932, see p. 128).

Perhaps the most brilliant comic creation was the Marx Brothers. Of the three, Groucho was the most iconic with his glasses, cigar, and endless supply of sharp one-liners. The Marx Brothers brought their anarchic slapstick stylings from the stage to the screen and combined them with dialogue too intricate for them to have used in their vaudeville days. In films such as *Duck Soup* (1933, see p. 130) they defined the art of the wisecrack and their influence on comedians such as Woody Allen (b. 1935) is evident in the movie *Love and Death* (1975), for example.

As the Marx Brothers redefined comedy films, their fellow New Yorkers The Three Stooges emerged and became a staple of US lowbrow comedy. Curly, Larry, and Moe had a hugely prolific career together, starring (with some later changes of personnel) in more than two hundred short and feature films. The Stooges are best remembered for their violent brand of slapstick, usually perpetrated against each other, in movies such as *Dizzy Doctors* (1937, below). **SW**

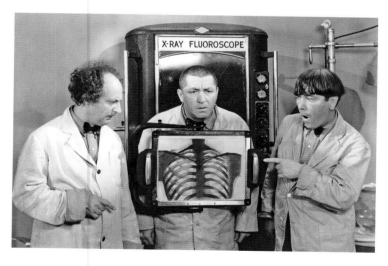

1936	1936	1937	1937	1938	1938
Charlie Chaplin "speaks" on screen for the first time in *Modern Times*—but only to sing a song in gibberish.	Harold Lloyd and veteran director Leo McCarey (1898–1969) team up on screwball comedy *The Milky Way*. It is a critical and commercial success.	British comedic actor Will Hay creates his most iconic character in *Oh, Mr Porter!*, directed by Marcel Varnel (1894–1947).	Director and slapstick film pioneer Mack Sennett is presented with an honorary Academy Award for his lifelong contribution to comedy.	The old king of comedy W. C. Fields passes the torch to the pretender to the throne, Bob Hope, in *The Big Broadcast of 1938*.	The final short in the sixteen-year-old *Our Gang* series, *Hide and Shriek*, is released. It is made by comedy veteran Hal Roach (1892–1992).

The Music Box 1932
JAMES PARROTT 1897 – 1939

▲ Laurel and Hardy appear as accident-prone men in a universe of hostile objects.

▼ The film won an Oscar for Best Short Subject.

A typical scenario in Laurel and Hardy's short comedies involves Stan and Ollie as blue-collar workers trying ineptly but with dogged dedication to perform a simple task. In *The Music Box* their mission is to deliver a mechanical player piano, a woman's present to her husband, one Professor von Schwarzenhoffen. Unfortunately, their destination is at the top of a steep flight of steps, but Stan and Ollie determine to do whatever it takes to deliver their burden—even if it keeps dragging them back down the steps. The ordeal does not end when they reach the top: they still have to get the piano into the house, which involves hauling it in through the upstairs window, in the process wrecking the premises. One of the peculiarities of *The Music Box*, giving it a curiously realistic and melancholic feel, is the use of long shots down the staircase, framing Stan and Ollie as pathetically distant, yet heroic figures.

The film, directed by the duo's regular collaborator James Parrott, involves Stan and Ollie in various spats with people they encounter—a nursemaid, a patrolling cop, and finally the explosive Professor (Billy Gilbert). Where Charlie Chaplin tended to taunt and creatively transform a world that was slower than he was, and Buster Keaton displayed heroic virtuosity in stopping an unstable world from collapsing around him, Laurel and Hardy were simple souls at war—sometimes with each other, but more generally with inanimate objects and unfailingly belligerent individuals. Their opponents were sometimes their wives, sometimes authority figures, but most often impotently enraged men—played memorably in many of their films by James Finlayson. **JR**

👁 KEY SCENES

1 AT WAR IN EVERYDAY LIFE
Stan and Ollie meet a nurse with a baby buggy coming down the stairs while they are trying to get up. The situation escalates into hostility. Cue a choice bit of (Hays Code era) innuendo, as the woman complains, "He kicked me . . . right in the middle of my daily duties."

2 THE BURDEN OF LOGIC
A postman tells Stan and Ollie that they need not have dragged the piano up the stairs, as they could have driven their truck up the hill. Ollie huffs—and with impeccably perverse logic, the two drag the piano all the way down again in order to bring it up in the truck.

3 THE HATS ROUTINE
Stan and Ollie's hats—symbols of their decorum and professionalism—get mixed up. Stan converts Ollie's over-sized bowler into a Homburg. Ollie, like the viewer, reacts with surprise because it is a shock to see Stan without his signature headgear.

🕐 STAR PROFILE: LAUREL AND HARDY

1890–1918
Stan Laurel was born Arthur Stanley Jefferson in Ulverston, Lancashire, in 1890. He emigrated to the United States in 1912 and made his first film in 1917. Oliver Hardy (born Norvell Hardy in Harlem, Georgia, 1892) made his first film in 1914 and became a support player to comics Larry Semon and Charley Chase.

1919–30
Laurel and Hardy appeared separately in *The Lucky Dog* (1919). They debuted as a team in *Putting Pants on Philip* (1927), before establishing their familiar characters in more than one hundred films—most of their output for producer Hal Roach.

1931–40
Their first feature, *Pardon Us*, was released in 1931. Later films included *Sons of the Desert* (1933), the uncharacteristic fairy-tale musical *Babes in Toyland* (1934), the cowboy parody *Way Out West* (1937)—featuring the well-known song "The Trail of the Lonesome Pine"—and *A Chump at Oxford* (1940).

1941–50
After ending their relationship with Hal Roach in 1941, Laurel and Hardy worked at Twentieth Century Fox and MGM, although their features there were little liked by admirers.

1951–65
Their final feature, *Atoll K* (a.k.a. *Robinson Crusoeland* in the United Kingdom and *Utopia* in the United States) in 1951, showed both comedians in physical decline. Hardy died in 1957; Laurel died in 1965, after becoming mentor to a new generation of comedians, including Jerry Lewis.

THE DOUBLE ACT

Among comedy acts, Stan Laurel and Oliver Hardy remain the prototypical yin-and-yang duo. Yet their dual persona was far more subtle and adaptable than a mere fat and thin or clown and straight man pairing. Laurel's traits were his effete, contemplative delicacy and a profound stupidity that occasionally revealed glimpses of bizarre brilliance. Ollie, meanwhile, was clumsy and overbearing but with pretensions to gallant touches, seen in his coy habit of flicking his tie. Much of the pair's genius lay in their grasp of absurd formality: the calm slowness of the double takes that punctuated the

routines; Ollie's frustrated appeals to camera; and the carefully phased encounters in their ongoing wars with constant foil James Finlayson, in which they would watch his infuriated outbursts before they retaliated, always after a solemn, mutual nod.

Duck Soup 1933
LEO McCAREY 1898 – 1969

▲ The mute Harpo takes a telephone call.
▼ *Duck Soup* was the last of the Marx Brothers' films to feature Zeppo.

Rufus T. Firefly (Groucho Marx), President of Freedonia, tells pixieish spy Pinky (Harpo Marx), "You're a brave man. Go and break through the lines, and remember while you're out there risking life and limb through shot and shell, we'll be in here thinking what a sucker you are." After a run of stage-derived vehicles in which the Marx Brothers invade country house parties, stow away on ocean liners, or go to college, Paramount set them loose on the entire world by making Groucho the leader of an armed nation. *Duck Soup* was a commercial disappointment and marked the end of the Marx Brothers' most creative period. The mood of the times—the hardships of the Great Depression at home and the real war in Europe—did not dispose anyone to laugh at trench warfare without the sentiment that Charlie Chaplin, for instance, brought to comedy, but these elements of social satire made *Duck Soup* a modern classic when it was revived in the 1960s.

The Marx Brothers' method was always to attack the powerless and the pompous alike—bullying a struggling street vendor and snippy ambassador of a rival country with equal glee. Here they deploy vicious satire as well as harmless, near-surreal lunacy. The premise is that the European nation of Freedonia has been subsidized so heavily by Mrs. Teasdale (Margaret Dumont) that she can insist her obviously maniacal candidate be appointed Head of State. The film benefits from having, in Leo McCarey, a director who provides a solid frame for the hilarious hysteria. *Duck Soup* is now regarded as a classic on a par with political comedies such as *Dr. Strangelove* (1964, see p. 276). **KN**

👁 KEY SCENES

1 FEUD

Spies Chico and Harpo, posing as street traders, get into a feud with a lemonade seller (Edgar Kennedy), whose business and hat come to a bad end. "I'll teach you to kick me," says Kennedy. "You don't have to teach me. I know how," retorts Chico.

2 THE MIRROR ROUTINE

Harpo pretends to be Groucho's reflection, with impossible skill—even though the brothers exchange places during the skit. It is one of the best-remembered sequences in film comedy, and often imitated (actually the brothers stole it from Raymond Griffith).

3 "THIS MEANS WAR!"

The ultimate insanity of an ultimately insane film—the brothers go to war with a song ("All God's Chillun Got Guns"), Harpo strides through a battlefield with a recruiting poster ("Join the Army and See the Navy"), and Groucho heroically mows down his own troops.

🕐 STAR PROFILE: THE MARX BROTHERS

1887–1928

The five Marx Brothers—Chico (Leonard, 1887–1961), Harpo (Adolph/Arthur, 1888–1964), Groucho (Julius, 1890–1977), Gummo (Milton, 1893–1977), and Zeppo (Herbert, 1901–79)—rose from vaudeville troupe to Broadway headliners. Gummo later became an agent.

1929–33

At Paramount, the four Marx Brothers made a series of hilarious, innovative, subversive, and sometimes nightmarish comedies: *The Cocoanuts* (1929), *Animal Crackers* (1930), *Monkey Business* (1931), *Horse Feathers* (1932), and *Duck Soup*.

1934–41

After moving to MGM, without Zeppo, the three brothers were packaged by studio head Irving Thalberg into a more commercially acceptable form, from *A Night at the Opera* (1935) and *A Day at the Races* (1937) to *The Big Store* (1941). Their brand of anarchy was toned down, pre-Hays Code naughtiness was dropped (Harpo became childish rather than satyrlike), and tedious love interest subplots were added.

1942–79

Although the team reunited, purportedly because of Chico's money troubles, for *A Night in Casablanca* (1946) and *Love Happy* (1949), the Marx Brothers pursued individual careers (they appeared separately in *The Story of Mankind*, 1957). Groucho became a quiz show host and television personality, enjoying great success from 1947 to 1961 as the host of *You Bet Your Life*, later renamed *The Groucho Show*.

STRAIGHT MEN (AND WOMEN)

It has been said that Margaret Dumont (below) brought more to the Marx Brothers team than Zeppo. Dumont's blithe indifference to the antics around her is precious because her simple refusal to notice how lunatic the brothers are makes her as insane as they are. Edgar Kennedy offers another kind of comic foil: he is funny in himself because he cannot shrug off what Harpo and Chico do, and responds with slow-burning anger to their ridiculous assaults (James Finlayson, frequent foil for Laurel and Hardy, takes the same route). In the Marxist utopia of *Duck Soup*, pompous uniformed fools (Louis Calhern, Leonid Kinskey) insist

on acting as if this were a serious movie—paving the way for a whole style of comedy in *Airplane!* (1980), where hitherto terribly stiff actors (Leslie Nielsen, Robert Stack, Lloyd Bridges) keep a straight face as they churn out patent absurdities or double entendres.

DEPRESSION-ERA MUSICALS

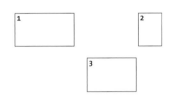

1 Director Lloyd Bacon (1889–1955) gave Busby Berkeley full rein to develop his choreographic ideas in *42nd Street*.

2 The poster for *Footlight Parade*, which starred James Cagney in his first big singing and dancing musical role as an unemployed yet enterprising Broadway theatrical producer.

3 Fred Astaire and Ginger Rogers star as lovers who find success on the dance floor and in the casino in *Swing Time*.

The Wall Street crash of October 1929 ushered in an era of desperation and mounting unemployment in the United States. By 1933, it was estimated that as many as fourteen million Americans of working age were without jobs. Thirties musicals captured the recklessness and febrile energy that people evinced in the face of the Great Depression.

"The long-lost dollar has come back to the fold / With silver you can turn your dreams to gold," runs the lyric in the "We're in the Money'" sequence choreographed by Busby Berkeley in *Gold Diggers of 1933* (1933, see p. 134). Money is celebrated because many people have so little of it. The cheeriness of the coin-clad chorus girls seems forced and the elision of sex with money is obvious. Yet it would be a mistake to think that 1930s musicals were only about opulence, sex, and escapism. In such a grim climate, dancing was a gesture of defiance. In *42nd Street* (1933, above) Berkeley's end sequence shows cops, gangsters, and shopkeepers all dancing, as if to keep the social problems of the day at bay. Backstage musicals of the era, among them *42nd Street* and *Footlight Parade* (1933, opposite above), were predicated on the idea that rehearsals demanded "grind and blood and sweat." There would always be a martinet showman demanding more and an ingenuous young hero or heroine would knuckle down and become star of the show. The relentless optimism of the showman and his cast would always be rewarded eventually.

There was a divide in 1930s musicals between the Warner Bros. films featuring Berkeley's wildly expressionistic choreography and the movies in which the stars did the dancing. As Fred Astaire famously said, "Either the

KEY EVENTS

1929	1929	1930	1933	1933	1935
The stock market crash starts a decade-long slump in the US economy and provides a fertile environment for Hollywood musicals to flourish.	MGM releases *The Broadway Melody*, the first "All Talking—All Singing—All Dancing" feature film.	Busby Berkeley's career as a Hollywood choreographer begins with the musical *Whoopee!*, produced by Sam Goldwyn and Florenz Ziegfeld.	*Flying Down to Rio* brings Fred Astaire and Ginger Rogers together on the screen for the first time.	Warner Bros. makes *42nd Street* and *Gold Diggers of 1933* (see p. 134). Two of the year's top-grossing films, they revitalize the musical as a genre.	Jeanette MacDonald and Nelson Eddy have their first hit with the MGM operetta *Naughty Marietta*.

camera dances or I do." In Astaire movies, the star tended to be shown full frame and in long takes so that audiences could appreciate his movements. In Berkeley sequences, the dancers were part of extremely elaborate geometric patterns that the choreographer contrived on screen. The camera would swoop around them, over them and, sometimes, even between their legs. Audiences did not know whether the performers could really dance. There were no such doubts about Astaire, whose legs were insured for a reported $1 million and who even prevailed on technicians to design equipment to film him dancing.

Astaire's routines look effortless. In films such as *Top Hat* (1935, see p. 136) he always has a cheery smile on his face while Ginger Rogers looks radiant, as if they are dancing spontaneously. Depression-era audiences could lose themselves in musical sequences that appeared utterly carefree—but the routines were nothing of the sort. Astaire was ferociously tough on himself and almost as tough on Rogers. He was reckoned to have worn out at least one thousand pairs of dancing shoes during his career. While making *Swing Time* (1936, below), this arch perfectionist pushed Rogers to rehearse a difficult sequence so many times that her feet bled into her satin slippers.

Another difference between Astaire musicals and the films featuring Berkeley's army of chorus girls is that the former are rooted in individualism, while the latter celebrate collectivism. Scholars have suggested that Berkeley was either a New Deal idealist, who extolled the merits of the group, or a dirty old satyr whose camera was like a leering eye, peeking at the voluptuous chorus girls from every available angle. **GM**

1936	1936	1938	1938	1939	1940
Top Hat (see p. 136) is nominated for four Academy Awards, including Best Picture and Best Dance Direction.	Fred Astaire and Ginger Rogers star in *Swing Time*, one of the greatest of their ten movie collaborations.	Choreographer Hermes Pan wins the last Academy Award given for Best Dance Direction, for *A Damsel in Distress* (1937).	*Carefree* becomes well known as the film in which Fred Astaire and Ginger Rogers share their first proper on-screen kiss.	Busby Berkeley directs his first straight film solo, the thriller *They Made Me a Criminal*, starring John Garfield.	Gene Kelly begins his march to stardom when he wins the lead role in the Broadway production of *Pal Joey*.

Gold Diggers of 1933 1933

MERVYN LEROY 1900 – 87

▲ The "We're in the Money" sequence choreographed by Busby Berkeley.

▼ The original Art Deco–style film poster.

Avery Hopwood's play *The Gold Diggers* (1919) reversed the cliché of the wealthy roué and the naive chorus girl to present a new stereotype: the smart, mercenary showgirl who targets wealthy men. It was filmed in 1923 and then again as the talkie *Gold Diggers of Broadway* (1929); *Gold Diggers of 1933* updates a Roaring Twenties fable for the Great Depression, stressing the divide between struggling show folk and the old-money types they target. There is still a comic bootlegger in the house, and although impresario Barney Hopkins (Ned Sparks), who vows to put on a show about "The gay side, the hard-boiled side, the cynical and funny side of the Depression," is shoved aside when the plot gets sidetracked in farcical romance, the film's closing number "Remember My Forgotten Man" is a rare fusion of social realism and musical spectacular.

The breezy "We're in the Money" is cut short as the sheriff's men arrive to strip the coins off the chorus girls' costumes because Barney has not paid his bills. Then Brad Roberts (Dick Powell), a scion of wealth whose older brother Lawrence Bradford (Warren William) disapproves of his showbiz ambitions, romances prim Polly Parker (Ruby Keeler), while Lawrence goes for sexy Carol King (Joan Blondell). Directed by Mervyn LeRoy, the film moves along at a clip, and Busby Berkeley's brilliant direction of the big numbers, which range from riotous fantasias of libidinous surrealism ("Pettin' in the Park") to an ambitious panorama of postwar social decline, makes them the high points. **KN**

👁 KEY SCENES

1 "WE'RE IN THE MONEY"
This ironic anti-Depression sequence is fabulously and deliberately vulgar, with lines such as "We never see a headline 'bout a breadline today." It combines beautiful girls, over-sized coins and Ginger Rogers singing in Pig Latin, "Ereway inhay the oneymay."

4 "REMEMBER MY FORGOTTEN MAN"
Berkeley features war veterans who are down on their luck in this hard-hitting sequence. Women pine for the men who fought in World War I and joined bread lines in the 1930s: "Remember my forgotten man? / You put a rifle in his hand."

2 OVERHEAD SHOT
In the "Pettin' in the Park" number, Berkeley demonstrates a signature overhead shot as chorus girls heft giant snowballs in a circle, creating movement via the cinematic means of his innovative camerawork rather than solely by choreography.

🕐 CHOREOGRAPHER PROFILE

1895–1929
Born into a family of vaudeville performers in Palm Springs, California, William "Busby" Berkeley Enos made his stage debut at the age of five. As a soldier in World War I, he staged military parades and marching drills, and then served as an aerial observer. This training may have influenced his penchant for geometric patterns in choreography and later trademark use of overhead shots. He began work as a choreographer in 1919 and went on to stage the dances for a total of seventeen Broadway productions, including *A Connecticut Yankee* (1927).

1930–32
Samuel Goldwyn produced a series of vehicles for comedian Eddie Cantor, mostly based on successful stage shows; he brought Berkeley, who devised production numbers for the Broadway versions, to Hollywood to re-create them for the cinema in *Whoopee!* (1930) and *The Kid from Spain* (1932).

1933–38
Berkeley found a niche at Warner Bros., creating increasingly elaborate and purely cinematic musical numbers for *42nd Street* (1933), *Gold Diggers of 1933*, *Footlight Parade* (1933), and *Dames* (1934), gaining greater creative control over filming than was customary for a choreographer. He made his codirectorial debut with the drama *She Had to Say Yes* (1933).

3 SHADOWPLAY
Late in the "Pettin' in the Park" sequence, there is an exercise in pre-Code titillation as a sudden downpour prompts the chorus girls to retreat behind transparent screens. They are seen undressing in silhouette in what was a very risqué scene for the time.

1939–43
He left Warner Bros. for MGM, Hollywood's premier studio for musicals, where he directed Judy Garland and Mickey Rooney in their first musical, *Babes in Arms* (1939), and Gene Kelly in his screen debut *For Me and My Gal* (1942). In 1943 Berkeley went back to Warner Bros. before returning to Broadway.

1944–76
Berkeley made a few films throughout the 1950s and his last movie was the retro *Billy Rose's Jumbo* (1962) for MGM. He returned to Broadway in 1971 to direct a revival of the 1920s hit *No, No, Nanette*, starring Ruby Keeler. He died at eighty.

Top Hat 1935
MARK SANDRICH 1900 − 45

▲ Monochrome magic: a dapper
Fred Astaire performs the title song.

▼ Tunes, tap, and top hat for the poster.

This film is the fourth, and by general consent the finest, of the nine musicals that Fred Astaire and Ginger Rogers made together for RKO. The plot, as always, is forgettable—some inane fluff about mistaken identities, dragged out to quasi-interminable length—but the other elements meld seamlessly. There is a support cast of veteran farceurs: Edward Everett Horton, dithering and double-taking to near manic levels; Erik Rhodes as a peacocking comedic Italian; and Helen Broderick, blithely unflappable as Horton's wife. Van Nest Polglase's stunning white Art Deco sets are a delight to the eye, as Irving Berlin's songs are to the ear. Above all there are Fred and Ginger, superbly choreographed by Hermes Pan, their terpsichorean chemistry by this stage dissolved into the quintessential expression of movement as rapture.

Of course, nothing could really be as perfect as all this appears. There were script problems: Astaire felt he was being portrayed as "an objectionable young man without charm or sympathy or humor" and demanded rewrites. His perfectionism wore Rogers down, not for the first time, and he was enraged by the blue ostrich-feather dress she designed for the "Cheek to Cheek" number. Feathers flew everywhere, into his mouth and nose, while the dress (he claimed) made Rogers look like "a chicken being attacked by a coyote."

However, not a hint of these disruptions appears on screen. Astaire, as ever, makes it all look effortless. The perfect pairing of Fred and Ginger ("He gives her class, she gives him sex," Katharine Hepburn noted) had by now made them box-office gold. *Top Hat* gave RKO its biggest moneymaker of the decade. **PK**

👁 KEY SCENES

1 "NO STRINGS (I'M FANCY FREE)"
The first solo number by Jerry Travers (Fred Astaire) sees him perform a noisy routine in Horton's London hotel suite. His tap-dancing disturbs Dale Tremont (Ginger Rogers), who is trying to sleep in the room below. She heads upstairs to complain—and captivates him.

2 RAIN DANCE
Disguised as a cab driver, Travers drives Tremont to her riding lesson in a park. Sheltering in a bandstand from a shower, the two dance together to Berlin's "Isn't This a Lovely Day to Be Caught in the Rain?" and she gradually mellows toward him.

3 AN AMERICAN IN PARIS
Set against a backdrop of a Parisian street scene, Astaire's only ensemble number of the film *Top Hat* may well be his most famous routine. It is the first time that he works with a cane as a prop and at the end of the sequence he uses it to gun down his chorus line.

4 POLGLASE'S VENETIAN WONDERLAND
In this scene we see Van Nest Polglase's Venice—a pure Art Deco fantasy. The waters were dyed black so as to show up more dramatically against the pure white background of the set—which was the largest built in RKO's history to that date.

5 "CHEEK TO CHEEK"
The big romantic number came complete with ostrich feathers. Astaire apologized for his reaction to the feathers and gave Rogers a gold feather charm; he also parodied the dance with Judy Garland in *Easter Parade* (1948). "Feathers" became Rogers's nickname.

⏱ STAR PROFILE: GINGER ROGERS AND FRED ASTAIRE

1899–1932
Fred Astaire was born in 1899. He began dancing professionally with his sister Adele in 1906. From 1918 he starred in hit musicals on Broadway and in London. Ginger Rogers (b. 1911) made her stage debut in 1925 as a vaudeville dancer and her screen debut in *Young Man of Manhattan* (1930).

1933–95
Astaire and Rogers were first paired in RKO's *Flying Down to Rio* (1933). Astaire continued in musicals, notably *The Band Wagon* (1953) and *Funny Face* (1957). His last film with Rogers was *The Barkleys of Broadway* (1949). Rogers largely left musicals for straight roles (*Kitty Foyle*, 1940; *Roxie Hart*, 1942; *Monkey Business*, 1952). She made her last film in 1965 and died in 1995. Astaire moved into straight roles in 1959. His films include *The Towering Inferno* (1974, see p. 362). He died in 1987.

NAZI AND SOVIET CINEMA

1 The poster was a vital tool of Soviet and Nazi film propaganda. From left, *Zemlya*, *Der ewige Jude*, and *Grunya Kornakova*.

2 Critics have seen beyond the propaganda of Leni Riefenstahl's work and admired the aesthetics of films such as *Olympiad*.

3 *Chapayev* tells the story of the legendary Red Army commander. The film won accolades in Europe and the United States.

C an an oppressive society produce good art? This question continues to overshadow the ability to assess dispassionately the films that came out of Nazi Germany and the Soviet Union. For many it would be offensive to consider that films such as *Olympiad* (*Olympia*, 1938, opposite above) and *Triumph des Willens* (*Triumph of the Will*, 1935, see p. 140) could be enjoyed as entertainment. However, the common belief, as stated by cultural historian Jeffrey Richards, that "the one notable exception to the large-scale absence of talent in the Nazi cinema is Leni Riefenstahl" is surely mistaken. Consider the exquisite *Rembrandt* (1942), directed by a card-carrying Nazi, Hans Steinhoff (1882–1945).

Both Adolf Hitler and Joseph Stalin were insatiable film enthusiasts. This was a mixed blessing, as they saw the medium as a conduit for propaganda and had little patience with notions of subtlety or even-handedness. Yet the priority given to production in color by both Joseph Goebbels and Stalin demonstrates that their taste for grandeur went far beyond the needs of propaganda and their desire to show that they could hold their own with Hollywood.

The handling of day-to-day film production in Germany during the 1930s was delegated to the loyal Goebbels, whose passion for film far surpassed even that of the Führer. It is thanks to him that overt Nazi propaganda on German screens was confined largely to the newsreels. However, as the campaign of officially sanctioned harassment gathered momentum after Kristallnacht in 1938, Goebbels oversaw the production of a quartet of anti-Semitic feature films—culminating in 1940 with *Jud Süss* and the vile "documentary" *Der ewige Jude* (*The Eternal Jew*, above). Usually, however, Goebbels was concerned at

KEY EVENTS

1930	1931	1933	1934	1936	1937
The Soviet film industry is centralized under the state film trust, Soyuzkino, headed by Boris Shumyatsky.	The first Soviet sound film, *Putyovka v zhizn* (*Road to Life*) by Nikolai Ekk (1902–76), examines the problem of children displaced as a result of World War I.	Goebbels bans *Das Testament des Dr. Mabuse* (*The Testament of Dr. Mabuse*) directed by Fritz Lang (1890–1976).	The satirical comedy *Poruchik Kizhe* (*Lieutenant Kijé*), the first film to carry a score by composer Sergei Prokofiev, is released.	The Olympic Games are catalogued by Leni Riefenstahl (1902–2003) in *Olympiad*. The first Soviet color film is *Grunya Kornakova* (*Nightingale*, above).	Boris Shumyatsky discontinues Sergei Eisenstein's *Bezhin lug* (*Bezhin Meadow*) after a troubled two-year production.

least as much with the artistic quality of German films as with their worth as propaganda. For the industry, one of his most alarming actions was banning, in 1934, two minor comedies simply for not being good enough, although they had already been passed by the censor.

The pioneering figure of Soviet cinema Sergei Eisenstein (1898–1948) was influential for his use of montage. After his acclaimed *Bronenosets Potyomkin* (*Battleship Potemkin*, 1925, see p. 58), the Soviet director went on to direct *Oktyabre* (*October* or *Ten Days that Shook the World*, 1927), a dramatization to celebrate the tenth anniversary of the revolution in 1917. Yet Eisenstein found himself continually thwarted by the state-run film trust and criticized for his innovative techniques, which were deemed ideologically unsound. *Alexander Nevsky* (1938, see p. 142) was the first film he managed to complete in nearly ten years.

The conventional view, as voiced by writer Ephraim Katz, was that the "postwar years represented the low point in the history of the Soviet cinema." However, these films were not at the time routinely mocked abroad the way they are today. Roger Manvell wrote in 1950: "The style in which these films are made is as closely realistic as that of a documentary, while the characterization continuously emphasizes the human element. It is only to be expected that . . . these films glorify the Soviet social and political point of view, but not without humor or humanity." Nor are they dull. The phenomenal success of *Chapayev* (1935, below right) directed by brothers Georgi (1899–1946) and Sergei (1900–59) Vasilyev—described by film historian Georges Sadoul as "among the ten masterpieces of the Soviet cinema"—had set in motion a long run of war stories built around the inspiration provided by a single great leader. By the time novelist Graham Greene reviewed *Lenin v oktyabre* (*Lenin in October*, 1937), directed by Mikhail Romm (1901–71), he had come to the view that "It is to be all 'Heroes and Hero-Worship' now . . . . The USSR is to produce Fascist films from now on." Yet he acknowledged "the excitement of melodrama handled with the right shabby realism," and called *Lenin v oktyabre* "one of the best entertainments we have seen in a cinema for a long while."

As the heroic aura of "our gallant Russian allies" has faded and the brutal reality of a regime that hounded filmmakers Eisenstein and Alexander Dovzhenko (1894–1956)—director of *Zemlya* (*Earth*, 1930, opposite)—into early graves has come into sharper focus, so the standing of the films produced in Stalin's Russia has plummeted. Yet Russian art director Leon Barsacq's comment that "Stalinist pageants of the ilk of *Unforgettable Year* [1952] and *Fall of Berlin* now seem to belong to the category of grotesque pop art iconography" evokes precisely the vivid comic-strip approach that makes a film such as *Padeniye Berlina* (*The Fall of Berlin*, 1949) such hypnotic viewing. Or, at least, it does so now long after the Kafkaesque nightmare that spawned these baubles has passed, so that the films can be appreciated without the audience feeling the need to glance fearfully over their shoulders to see who else is watching. **RMC**

1937	1938	1939	1941	1942	1943
Stalin orders director Mikhail Romm to glorify the Soviet Union's first leader with *Lenin v oktyabre*. It is an artistic and commercial success.	Boris Shumyatsky is executed following a purge of the Soviet film industry. Leni Riefenstahl's *Olympiad* is released in Germany.	Alexander Dovzhenko's *Shchors* is released. A biography of the partisan Bolshevik leader Nikolai Shchors, it is commissioned by Stalin.	Hans Steinhoff's anti-British film *Ohm Krüger* (*Uncle Kruger*), on the Boer War, is released. It is the first winner of the Film of the Nation Award in 1944.	Goebbels continues to micromanage German films such as the historical epic *Der grosse König* (*The Great King*) by Veit Harlan (1899–1964).	The lavish fantasy *Münchhausen* by Josef von Báky (1902–66) is released. On Goebbels's orders it offers no propaganda, only escapist relief from the war.

Triumph des Willens 1935
Triumph of the Will   LENI RIEFENSTAHL 1902 — 2003

▲ Fascism on an epic scale: the year after Hitler came to power more than thirty thousand followers line up at Nuremberg.

▼ The Nazi eagle dominates the film's poster, rendered in the style of a woodcut.

Along with Leni Riefenstahl's subsequent *Olympiad* (*Olympia*, 1938), *Triumph des Willens* remains one of the few film titles to emerge from Nazi Germany that most people would be able to name today. The opening titles boast that it was "Produced by Order of the Führer," and Riefenstahl consequently had at her disposal unprecedented facilities, including a production staff of more than 170, to produce an imposing—and intimidating—record of the Nuremberg Rally of September 5–10, 1934. Critic David Shipman noted that "a peculiar mystique" surrounds the film, while in the 2011 edition of *Leonard Maltin's Movie Guide*, it rates four stars and elicits the accolade of being "rightly regarded as the greatest propaganda film of all time."

Most people, however, will know the film only from highlights included in other documentaries, rather than from having watched all two hours of it. As long ago as 1969, author David Stewart Hull expressed the opinion that it "was probably slightly too long, for after a while the scenes of marching men become tiresome to most audiences." Other dissenting voices included writer Brian Winston, who stated in 1998: "All this rubbish about her genius really ought to stop . . . . Of course, pointing a camera at hundreds of thousands of men in close formation yields images fascinating to the fascist in all of us; but from the filmmaking point of view it really isn't that hard at all. In fact, how could you fail?" Despite such criticisms there is no denying the power of the film, capturing as it did the force of feeling in prewar Germany. Riefenstahl's legacy and the film's significance as an historical document are indisputable. **RMC**

⊚ KEY SCENES

1 THE FÜHRER ARRIVES
Described by film writer Steven Bach as "one of the most elaborate star entrances in film history," Adolf Hitler's arrival by airplane and progress by motorcade through Nuremberg to his hotel occupies a full one-tenth of the film's running time.

2 LABOR SERVICE RECRUITS
During a drill for the Reichsarbeitsdienst (Labor Service), thousands of fit young men from every corner of the Fatherland march in uniforms—green in real life—carrying spades as if they were rifles. The militarism inherent in the sequence is inescapable.

3 CEREMONY TO HONOR THE WAR DEAD
Flanked by the heads of the SA and SS, Hitler marches through massive blocks of tens of thousands of uniformed party members in a ceremony plainly designed to make visual sense only through a camera lens mounted high in the air.

⊕ DIRECTOR PROFILE

1902–32

Leni Riefenstahl was born in 1902. Initially a dancer, her first starring role was in *Der heilige Berg* (*The Holy Mountain*, 1926), followed by athletic leading roles in "mountain films" such as *Die weiße Hölle vom Piz Palü* (*White Hell of Pitz Palu*, 1929) and *Das blaue Licht* (*The Blue Light*, 1932), which she also directed and which won a silver medal at the Venice Film Festival. The film prompted Hitler to approach Riefenstahl to make films for the Nazi party; she became a devoted admirer.

1933–45

She was Hitler's director of choice to make documentary records of the Nuremberg Rallies of 1933—*Sieg des Glaubens* (*Victory of Faith*)—and 1934, and of the Berlin Olympics in 1936. *Triumph des Willens* was pilloried by many in the West, but established Riefenstahl as the world's foremost female director. Her next feature, *Tiefland* (*Lowlands*), however, remained unfinished at the end of the war and was not completed and released until 1954. It was denied admittance to the Cannes Film Festival that year.

1946–2003

Riefenstahl's longevity and combative nature maintained her public profile during the five decades that followed Germany's defeat and allowed no letup in the controversy that dogged her for the remainder of her 101 years. Her only postwar film project to see completion, the documentary *Impressionen unter Wasser* (*Underwater Impressions*, 2002), received its television premiere a week before her hundredth birthday.

NUREMBERG REVISITED

Triumph des Willens provides a poignant record of Nuremberg before it was largely reduced to rubble by Allied planes on January 2, 1945. Later that year, many of the stars of Riefenstahl's film were reunited for what was, for most of them, to be their final appearance. Held in the International Palace of Justice, the eleven-month war trial (below) was a largely tedious affair. One of its most dramatic moments came with the screening of an hour-long documentary directed by George Stevens (1904–75) called *Nazi Concentration Camps*, which stunned everyone in the courtroom. It set a precedent for the use of film as courtroom evidence.

Alexander Nevsky 1938

SERGEI EISENSTEIN 1898 – 1948

▲ Nevsky—a leader, a man whose qualities all Soviets could aspire to and be inspired by.

▼ The film's propaganda calls for a strong and unified home front.

Sergei Eisenstein only completed his first sound feature in 1938. He had returned to Russia after the fiasco of his trip abroad where ¡Que Viva Mexico! had collapsed, and Bezhin lug (Bezhin Meadow) was aborted. As a Soviet artist dependent on the approval of those in power, he made Alexander Nevsky just at the right moment: this thirteenth-century story of Russia defeating Teutonic forces was supported officially for the warning it gave to the Germans that the Soviets would destroy any who invaded their land. A year later the German–Soviet pact scuttled that message, and the film was suppressed—but revived to great acclaim after Germany invaded the USSR in 1941.

Photographed, as was all Eisenstein's work, by the great Eduard Tissé, Alexander Nevsky, like its successors, showed the director retaining all his compositional genius; but a grander, more operatic tone replaced the early energy and the powerful montage effects of his silent masterpieces.

Especially impressive is the magnificent blend of sound and visuals. Eisenstein's composer was Sergei Prokofiev, in whom Eisenstein felt that he and Tissé had "found the third companion in our crusade for the kind of sound cinema we had been dreaming of." The composer's score for Alexander Nevsky is crucial to the film's impact. It yielded a cantata for performance in the concert hall, where the contralto solo in "The Field of the Dead" is more poignant than in the film—since the film's propaganda element lays stress not on the battle's desolation but on its heroic survivors. Eisenstein's art triumphed over the propaganda required of him, but it remained a limitation. **MS**

1 ALEXANDER THE GREAT
Even on his first appearance, Nikolai Cherkassov's Alexander Nevsky is clearly an iconic figure: imposing, authoritative, wise. He is a leader without thought for himself and fully conscious of the need for everyone, himself included, to serve the interests of the nation.

3 BATTLE ON THE ICE
The film's big set piece is a long sequence in which Nevsky and his soldiers put the enemy to flight. The power is built up less from individual compositions than from the movement and vigor within shots. The drama is further aided by the editing.

2 ROMANTIC SUBPLOT
Two friends become rivals for the love of a girl named Olga. As befits the propaganda of the piece, she decides to marry whichever man is the braver in battle. However, the call to fight is not for men only and it is a woman, Vasilisa, who is proclaimed the bravest of all.

4 THE MESSAGE
In a work of propaganda the message is rarely muted. At the film's climax 1242 and 1938 become one when all potential aggressors are told that "he who comes sword in hand by the sword shall perish." For good measure, the words of the speech appear on-screen.

PROKOFIEV AND FILM

Although Dmitri Shostakovich produced many more film scores, the oeuvre of Sergei Prokofiev (right) includes some of the best-known film music ever written. His suite from his score for *Poruchik Kizhe* (*Lieutenant Kijé*, 1934) has outstripped the fame of the film by Alexander Fainzimmer (1906–82). Prokofiev's relationship with Eisenstein was marked by mutual respect. The composer described the director as "a man of fine musical understanding," whereas Eisenstein had such regard for his collaborator's music that he would sometimes shoot material to fit passages that Prokofiev had already written. His music, Eisenstein noted, "never becomes mere illustration. It shows in an amazing way the inward progress of events, their dynamic structure."

EARLY ANIMATED FILM

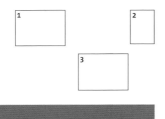

1 Lotte Reiniger's *Die Abenteuer des Prinzen Achmed* is based on stories from *1001 Nights*, and was made under the auspices of the Weimar Republic.

2 *Steamboat Willie* was the first Mickey film released and the third produced following *Plane Crazy* and *The Gallopin' Gaucho* (both 1928).

3 The Fleischer Studios' *Gulliver's Travels* used a live-action performance by actor Sam Parker as a reference for their animation of Gulliver.

In 1908 *Fantasmagorie* by Emile Cohl (1857–1938) mesmerized audiences, showing the possibilities of animation. The German silhouette animator Lotte Reiniger (1899–1981) had great success in 1926 with what is now the world's oldest surviving animated feature film, *Die Abenteuer des Prinzen Achmed* (*The Adventures of Prince Achmed*, above). In 1928 animation's most famous son was born. He is an icon, recognizable the world over, having appeared in hundreds of shorts and films. Mickey Mouse first appeared in 1928 and the best known of the early Mickey cartoons is that year's *Steamboat Willie* (opposite above). The magic of Disney Studio's animation is evident in this early example, with catchy music and anthropomorphic characters. For decades, artists have convinced viewers that, despite looking almost identical to Mickey, Minnie is female, simply by putting her in a dress and placing a bow on her head.

In the golden age of Disney, Walt Disney and his "Nine Old Men" (key animators) worked tirelessly at producing animation for the masses and creating what would become the template in Western cinema for animated feature films. Between 1937 and 1942 they released *Snow White and the Seven Dwarfs* (1937, see p. 146), *Pinocchio* (1940), *Fantasia* (1940), *Dumbo* (1941), and *Bambi* (1942). Each film is a cultural milestone and each is pioneering in its own way—*Fantasia*'s combination of animation and stereophonic sound recording, for example, or the balance of emotional peaks and grave darkness in *Pinocchio* and *Bambi*.

Concurrently, Fleischer Studios, MGM, and Warner Bros. were crafting world-class animation of their own. Fleischer created the legendary Betty Boop,

see p. 146

KEY EVENTS

1929	1930	1932	1932	1932	1935
Warner Bros. launches Looney Tunes cartoons into movie theaters. These early shorts precede Bugs Bunny, featuring Bosko and Buddy instead.	*Le roman de renard* (*The Story of the Fox*), by Wladyslaw Starevich (1882–1965), is one of stop-motion animation's finest achievements.	One of the forgotten greats of animation, Quirino Cristiani, makes *Peludopolis*—the first animated feature film to use synchronized sound.	In *Betty Boop's Bamboo Isle*, the titular character showcases her blend of wide-eyed promiscuity.	*Flowers and Trees*—part of Disney's *Silly Symphonies* series—wins the first ever Academy Award for Best Short Subject: Cartoons.	The Hays Act is passed, "cleaning up" offending media and transforming characters such as Betty Boop into more wholesome figures.

whose mixture of innocence and provocation would prove controversial, while her figure and Brooklyn-accented gangster's moll persona have been endlessly parodied. If Betty was the queen of Fleischer Studios, then Popeye was its king. Marking his arrival in *Popeye the Sailor* (1933), the squint-eyed, supernaturally strong man has an adoring sweetheart, displays a macho tattoo, and spends his time smoking and getting into fights. Fleischer also produced the United States's second full-length animated feature film: *Gulliver's Travels* (1939, below) was a critical and commercial success but could not save the studio from an untimely demise.

MGM established its legacy with the appearance of Tom and Jerry in 1940 in *Puss Gets the Boot*. Warner Bros., meanwhile, had its own brand of animation with Looney Tunes and Merrie Melodies. These anarchic shorts were a world apart from the selective focus composition and sentimental style of Disney. Animators Chuck Jones and Friz Freleng were able to experiment and, voiced by the incomparable Mel Blanc, the screwball characters of Bugs Bunny and Daffy Duck provided an alternative to the traditional, Everyman heroes of Mickey Mouse and Popeye. Animation is limited only by imagination, and audiences young and old alike have been awed and entertained for more than a century by animated films. As critic C. A. Lejeune remarked in her review of *Snow White and the Seven Dwarfs* at the time of its release: "Sometimes it is, frankly, badly drawn. But I think it will give more people more pleasure of a simple kind than any other film of its generation." **SW**

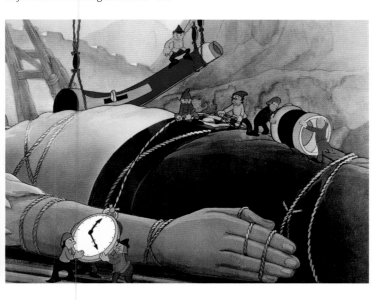

1935	1935	1936	1937	1940	1941
Len Lye (1901–80) releases *A Colour Box*. It is a milestone in direct animation—a process in which images are created directly on film stock.	Oskar Fischinger (1900–67) creates the groundbreaking experiment in visual music *Allegretto*.	The Soviet Union established Soyuzmultfilm—a studio that used traditional animation but developed a more experimental style.	*Snow White and the Seven Dwarfs* (see p. 146), made by Disney, is released.	In the midst of a classic run of shorts, *A Wild Hare* is released, featuring the first appearance of Bugs Bunny.	China creates its first animated feature film, *Princess Iron Fan*, made in difficult economic and artistic conditions during World War II.

Snow White and the Seven Dwarfs 1937
DAVID HAND, WILLIAM COTTRELL, WILFRED JACKSON, ET AL.

▲ Snow White meets Dopey, Sneezy, Happy, Grumpy, Doc, Bashful, and Sleepy.

▼ The iconic Walt Disney castle can be seen in the background of the poster.

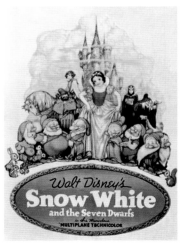

They called it "Disney's folly"—Walt Disney's attempt to prove that animation was fit for more than just short films and supporting features, and could challenge live action as a forum for great feature storytelling, real emotions, and artistic expression. It seems obvious now, but back in the 1930s Disney's ambitions were dismissed as foolhardy. Cinema was still an adult art form and movies made exclusively for children were relatively rare. *Snow White and the Seven Dwarfs* was the first animated feature film to be produced in Hollywood, and the first to be distributed globally.

What is remarkable about the film is not that it was the Walt Disney Company's first animated feature, but that it remains perhaps their best. Everything audiences now associate with Disney's animated output is present and correct: flawless heroes and blushing heroines, terrifying villains, breathtaking visuals, moral lessons, cute anthropomorphic animals, fairy-tale storytelling, and mildly irritating songs. The film may lack ambiguity or great character depth— although the dwarfs are physically well-rounded, they remain caricatures—but its enduring popularity proves the success of Disney's endeavors.

It also contains some of the most beautiful and, at times, terrifying images ever created for the screen: the wicked queen's transformation sequence is enough to give grown men nightmares. Like all great fairy tales, *Snow White and the Seven Dwarfs* addresses our most primal fears—parental abandonment, betrayal, loneliness—in a safe environment, then dispels them with wit, charm, humor, and a good, old-fashioned, romantic Hollywood ending. **TH**

👁 KEY SCENES

1 "I'M WISHING . . . ."
Audiences got their first hint of how breathtakingly original animation could be in this early sequence. With the "camera" positioned beneath the water, Snow White sings into the wishing well and her echoing voice creates ripples on the water's surface.

4 THE WICKED WITCH
One of Disney's strengths has always been to counterbalance cozy comedy with real terror: here, the wicked queen/witch disguises herself as an old crone in an attempt to sell Snow White a deadly poisoned apple.

2 INTO THE WOODS
Inspired by German Expressionist cinema and Surrealist painting, Disney's animators depicted Snow White's flight from the huntsman as a nightmarish world, with the trees coming to life and trying to take hold of her.

5 "SOMEDAY MY PRINCE WILL COME"
After Snow White is poisoned by the apple, the dwarfs lay her in a golden casket, where she remains until she is brought back to life by the kiss of her true love. It may be a happy-ever-after, Hollywood schmaltzy ending, but Depression-era audiences loved it.

3 "HEIGH-HO!"
Catchy songs have been a staple of the Disney repertoire since the very beginning, and this memorable marching tune, with its repetitive lyrics, simplistic melody, and whistled refrain, has been sung by children around the world for three-quarters of a century.

🕐 STUDIO PROFILE: WALT DISNEY

1923–67
In 1923 Walt Disney and his older brother Roy founded Disney Brothers Cartoon Studios, later Walt Disney Productions. In 1939 they were awarded an honorary Oscar for *Snow White and the Seven Dwarfs*: one full-sized statuette and seven miniature "dwarf" Oscars. Disney released a classic run of hits, including *Pinocchio* (1940), *Dumbo* (1941), *Bambi* (1942), *Cinderella* (1950), *Peter Pan* (1953), and *Sleeping Beauty* (1959). Walt died in 1966, after producing *The Jungle Book* (1967).

1968–88
Disney's animated output became erratic. The failure of *Tron* (1982) and *Return to Oz* (1985) put a strain on their finances.

1989–present
The Little Mermaid (1989), *Beauty and the Beast* (1991), *Aladdin* (1992), and *The Lion King* (1994) all broke box-office records. The studio collaborated successfully with Pixar and Walden Media.

THE SCREWBALL COMEDY

I t is fitting that the most American of genres should derive its title from the game of baseball. The screwball comedy genre consists of a cluster of fast-moving, irreverent comedies—it reached its apogee in the 1930s and 1940s. More precise definitions tend to differ in emphasis: in his book *Screwball: Hollywood's Madcap Romantic Comedies* (1989), Ed Sikov writes that "a whole genre developed around the perverse idea that love could only be enhanced by aggravation." The genre flourished from 1934—the year that produced *Twentieth Century*, *It Happened One Night* (above), and *The Thin Man*—to 1952 with the last of the classic screwball comedies—*Monkey Business*—directed by Howard Hawks (1896–1977). The essential themes of screwball—randomness, reverse snobbery, and the clash between romance and economic reality—made these films resonate with cinemagoers in the period following the Wall Street crash.

1 Clark Gable lectures Claudette Colbert on hitchhiking techniques in Frank Capra's *It Happened One Night*. The mismatched couple is a typical feature of screwball.

2 William Powell's butler and Carole Lombard's socialite make an elegant pair on the poster of *My Man Godfrey*.

3 In *The Philadelphia Story* the marriage plans of Tracy Lord Haven (Katharine Hepburn) go awry with the arrival of *Spy* magazine reporter (James Stewart).

Screwball comedies may incorporate elements from other types of movies: for example, detective (*The Thin Man*), gangster (*Ball of Fire*, 1941), and black comedy (*Arsenic and Old Lace*, 1944). They may temper romance with economic survival (*Palm Beach Story*, 1942) or delve into populist politics (*Mr. Smith Goes to Washington*, 1939). They may be heartless and cynical (*Nothing Sacred*, 1937) or relatively well behaved (*The Philadelphia Story*, 1940, opposite below).

Twentieth Century, based on a Broadway hit by Ben Hecht and Charles MacArthur and directed by Hawks, provides one of the classic templates for the screwball comedy. Irreverent, acerbic, and fast-paced, it features

KEY EVENTS

1929	1933	1935	1935	1936	1937
Wall Street crashes on October 29, heralding the start of the Great Depression. Screwball films were to reflect the economic times in which they were made.	Franklin D. Roosevelt becomes President of the United States. The First New Deal to create jobs and enable economic recovery commences.	Carole Lombard and Fred MacMurray star in Paramount's *Hands Across the Table*, directed by Mitchell Leisen (1898–1972).	Gregory La Cava directs *She Married Her Boss*. The story features a trademark theme of the screwball genre—marriage.	Frank Capra wins his second Academy Award—for directing *Mr. Deeds Goes to Town*.	Leo McCarey (1898–1969) directs Cary Grant and Irene Dunne in *The Awful Truth*. Grant perfects the light comedy touch at which he will excel.

John Barrymore as a monstrously egotistical Broadway producer trying to manipulate his one-time protégée, played by Carole Lombard, to sign up with him once more during a transcontinental train journey. The climax of the film is a resumption of creative hostility rather than romantic resolution. Clashing egos also feature in Hawks's *His Girl Friday* (1940), a version of Hecht and MacArthur's play *The Front Page* (1928), which employs a similar narrative line, with an editor trying to finagle his star reporter into working for him again. In the Hawks version, the reporter Hildy Johnson is recast as a woman, bringing sexual tension to the professional sparring.

Screwball comedy often takes the form of an unsentimental education. In *It Happened One Night*—directed by Frank Capra (1897–1991)—Claudette Colbert's pampered heiress learns about life and about her own feelings from Clark Gable's hard-bitten journalist. In *My Man Godfrey* (1936, right) by Gregory La Cava (1892–1952), William Powell plays a tramp hired by Carole Lombard's scatterbrained socialite as the family butler. She falls in love with him and he saves her father's business from ruin. That Godfrey is, in reality, a blue-blood and that his life in the lower depths has been his own choice effectively blunts any class criticism. In *The Philadelphia Story*, directed by George Cukor (1899–1983), Cary Grant helps his ex-wife Katharine Hepburn understand the limits of her own brittle perfectionism, while in *Ninotchka* (1939), Melvyn Douglas's Parisian man about town instructs Greta Garbo's unbending Soviet official in the virtues of love and frivolity. The gender roles are reversed in many of the films. Hepburn's eccentric free spirit jolts nervous paleontologist Grant out of his stultifyingly cautious existence in Hawks's exemplary *Bringing Up Baby* (1938, see p. 150); Barbara Stanwyck's sassy con artist sets out to fleece (and then teaches a lesson to) a rich, woman-shy reptile expert (Henry Fonda) in *The Lady Eve* (1941, see p. 152).

Capra directed two uncharacteristic exercises in populist optimism within the genre. In *Mr. Deeds Goes to Town* (1936) Gary Cooper's Longfellow Deeds struggles to use his inherited fortune to help dispossessed farmers, and three years later in *Mr. Smith Goes to Washington*, James Stewart takes to the floor of the US Senate in an idealistic filibuster against political corruption. In both movies, Jean Arthur is on hand to provide the romantic interest while giving the innocent heroes clear-eyed practical support. Capra's films are exceptions to the rule, however. For the most part screwball comedies eschew lessons in democracy or public spiritedness. The most profound message in all screwball comedy comes in an elegant demonstration of the true nature of the comic muse in *Ninotchka*, directed by Ernst Lubitsch (1892–1947). Sitting in a cafe with Garbo's unsmiling Soviet envoy, Melvyn Douglas's boulevardier tries to amuse her with a series of long-winded jokes. Distracted by her stony response, he leans back in his chair, which collapses under him and sends him sprawling on the floor—and Garbo suddenly dissolves into beatific laughter. **DP**

1937	1938	1938	1939	1940	1941
William Wellman (1896–1975) directs *Nothing Sacred*. It is the first screwball comedy to be filmed in color.	Howard Hawks's madcap caper *Bringing Up Baby* (see p. 150) fails at the box office but later becomes a much-loved classic of the genre.	Frank Capra's *You Can't Take It With You* is released. It features the fast, witty dialogue characteristic of screwball comedy.	Claudette Colbert and James Stewart star in *It's a Wonderful World*.	Cary Grant and Rosalind Russell exchange quick-fire repartee in Howard Hawks's *His Girl Friday*.	Alfred Hitchcock (1899–1980) directs *Mr. and Mrs. Smith*, an untypical foray for the director into the screwball genre.

Bringing Up Baby 1938
HOWARD HAWKS 1896 – 1977

▲ Hepburn's kooky character uses her fast-talking charm to win the attention of the stuffy paleontologist played by Grant.

▼ Despite a roster of big names, *Bringing Up Baby* bombed at the box office and is considered to have been ahead of its time.

With *Bringing Up Baby*, Howard Hawks perfected the screwball comedy. All the key elements of the genre are present: the rapid-fire, overlapping, cross-purposes dialogue; the uptight respectable citizen in the shape of Cary Grant's academic paleontologist, who is disrupted, disconcerted, and discombobulated by a free-spirited intruder of the opposite sex in the form of Katharine Hepburn as a ditsy socialite; the supporting cast of voluble eccentrics, each one allowed his or her moment of glory with an opinionated, borderline-nutcase monologue; the Hays Code–teasing sexual innuendo; and the set piece incidents of mounting absurdity. All these elements are at the service of a zany plot, clinging on to a fragile thread of narrative logic while constantly shooting off at unexpected angles.

Hawks had noted the chemistry between Grant and Hepburn in *Holiday* (1938), where it was Grant's character that represented the disruptive force, but that film was a more decorous affair, involving less slapstick and indignity. In *Bringing Up Baby* highlights include Grant's desperate attempts to disentangle himself from Hepburn's deranged logic and resume his game of golf with a potential donor to his dinosaur project: "I'll be with you in minute, Mr. Peabody!"; Grant and Hepburn trying to coax her pet leopard "Baby" down from a roof with their off-key rendering of "I Can't Give You Anything but Love, Baby"; and Hepburn bamboozling the local constable (Walter Catlett) with her hammy impersonation of a Brooklyn gun moll. Although *Bringing Up Baby* was a flop on its release, it has since been recognized as one of the peaks of 1930s Hollywood comedy. **PK**

👁 KEY SCENES

1 "LEFT FOOT FIRST"
Dr. David Huxley (Grant) inadvertently rips Susan Vance's (Hepburn) dress, leaving her underwear exposed. To conceal this, he moves in close behind her and they exit in fast lock-step, provoking much hilarity among the onlookers.

2 TAKING BABY FOR A WALK
Yet again trying to extricate himself from Susan's madcap schemes, David heads off along the street, unaware that she has let loose her pet leopard, Baby, which has taken a liking to David and is close on his heels. The leopard symbolizes the free spirit of his owner, Susan.

3 "YOU LOOK SO SILLY!"
David and Susan hunt in the woods for Baby and Susan's pet terrier, George, who has buried one of David's dinosaur bones. David slips and falls down a bank. Susan does too, and the butterfly net she is carrying falls over David's head: the huntress has captured her prey.

4 DOWNFALL OF THE BRONTOSAURUS
Susan tracks down David at his lab to give him the lost bone and he retreats up the steps beside his prized brontosaurus skeleton. Susan climbs a ladder, loses her balance, and then scrambles onto the brontosaurus, which falls over, thus destroying David's ossified world.

🕐 DIRECTOR PROFILE

1896–1923
Born in Goshen, Indiana, into a well-off family, Howard Hawks studied mechanical engineering at Cornell University. During the summers of 1916 and 1917, he worked on some early movies while working as an intern at the Famous Players–Lasky Studio in Hollywood. After graduation he joined the United States Army Air Service.

1924–29
Hawks returned to Hollywood to work as a props man at the Mary Pickford Company, moving to the editing department and then the script department. He wrote and directed his first feature, *The Road to Glory* (1926), for Fox Film Corporation. After his Fox contract ended in 1929, he never signed a long-term contract with a single studio again.

1930–40
He directed for various studios in a wide variety of genres: war movie (*The Dawn Patrol*, 1930), prison movie (*The Criminal Code*, 1931), gangster (*Scarface*, 1932), period drama (*Barbary Coast*, 1935), adventure (*Only Angels Have Wings*, 1939), and, supremely, screwball comedy (*Twentieth Century*, 1934, *Bringing Up Baby*, and *His Girl Friday*, 1940).

1941–53
Hawks received an Oscar nomination for Best Director in 1942 for the war film *Sergeant York* (1941). He continued to genre hop, almost always with success: war movie (*Air Force*, 1943); screwball (*Ball of Fire*, 1941, *I Was a Male War Bride*, 1949, *Monkey Business*, 1952); adventure (*To Have and Have Not*, 1944); private eye (*The Big Sleep*, 1946); his first Western, *Red River* (1948), starring John Wayne; and even a successful musical comedy, *Gentlemen Prefer Blondes* (1953).

1954–77
The director had some failures, including the creaky period drama *Land of the Pharaohs* (1955). During his waning years he produced a trio of relaxed, confident Westerns starring Wayne: *Rio Bravo* (1959), *El Dorado* (1967), and *Rio Lobo* (1970). He received his only Oscar, an Honorary Award, in 1975.

The Lady Eve 1941

PRESTON STURGES 1898 – 1959

▲ The apple echoes the Garden of Eden.

▼ The poster highlights the scientist's predicament: "Bewitched and Bewildered."

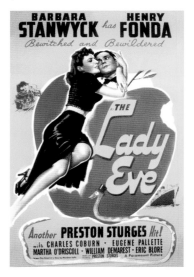

The success of *The Lady Eve*, Preston Sturges's third film for Paramount, set the seal on his reputation as the United States's premier comedy writer-director. Henry Fonda's Charles Pike is an emotionally repressed ophiologist (snake scientist), heir to a brewing fortune that allows him to indulge his interest in reptiles. His shipboard romance with Barbara Stanwyck's Jean Harrington—an adventuress who intends to deceive him, but learns to love him—brings out his emotional depth. When he rejects her after finding out the truth about her past, he loses his newly won emotional wisdom and his innocence becomes priggishness, which sets him up for punishment in a movie that draws on the biblical story of the Garden of Eden.

The Lady Eve shifts effortlessly from farce to feeling. Fonda shows the passionate heart beating beneath the stuffed shirt, mixing naivety, dignity, and vulnerability; Stanwyck shimmers between mercenary manipulator and starry-eyed romantic with an added turn as a fruity English aristocrat. William Demarest, as Pike's crude valet Muggsy, heads up a list of regular Sturges players (Arthur Hoyt, Harry Rosenthal, Al Bridge, Victor Potel), who give the Sturges signature to a variety of background roles. Nobody is what they seem in *The Lady Eve*. The dishonest people carry themselves with class: "Let us be crooked but never common," intones Jean's cardsharp father, "Colonel" Harrington (Charles Coburn); while Pike's father's (Eugene Pallette) buffoonish exterior hides wisdom and sensitivity. At the heart of Sturges's comedy is the quasi-Shakespearean notion that disguise is the surest key to the true self. **DP**

👁 KEY SCENES

1 EDEN

Returning from an Amazonian expedition, Charles Pike boards an Atlantic liner. As the heir to a brewing fortune, he is the unwitting subject of attention. Beautiful con artist Jean Harrington sets out to fleece the naive scientist, who is shy of women, but falls for him.

2 THE FALL

Learning who Jean really is, Charles rejects her and returns to his family estate in Connecticut. Planning revenge, Jean infiltrates the Pike mansion in the guise of Lady Eve Sidwich, an eccentric English woman. Oblivious to the deception, Charles falls in love with her.

3 PARADISE REGAINED

Having endured Lady Eve's revenge, Pike once more boards a liner to South America, where Jean awaits him. They meet "accidentally" and fall into a passionate embrace. The temptress triumphs as they forgive each other and acknowledge their mutual love.

🕐 DIRECTOR PROFILE

1898–1939

Preston Sturges was born in Chicago. His first play, *The Guinea Pig*, transferred to Broadway in 1929. His second, *Strictly Dishonorable* (1929), ran for sixteen months on Broadway. Its success attracted the attention of Hollywood and he began writing for Paramount. Throughout the 1930s he worked as a screenwriter for MGM, Universal, and Columbia.

1940–44

Sturges sold his screenplay *The Great McGinty* for $10 on the condition that he directed it; he made his directorial debut in 1940. He won the Academy Award for Best Original Screenplay for the film and became one of Hollywood's first star writer-directors. A sequence of comic masterpieces followed: *Christmas in July* (1940), *The Lady Eve, Sullivan's Travels* (1941), *The Palm Beach Story* (1942), *The Miracle of Morgan's Creek* (1944), and *Hail the Conquering Hero* (1944).

1945–59

Seeking independence, Sturges formed California Pictures with Howard Hughes (1905–76). They produced one film, *The Sin of Harold Diddlebock* (1947) starring Harold Lloyd, but Hughes took the film away from Sturges and released it recut as *Mad Wednesday* (1950). After the partnership was dissolved, Sturges had a return to form with *Unfaithfully Yours* (1948), but his *The Beautiful Blonde from Bashful Bend* (1949) was a failure. He moved to Europe and directed one more film, *Les carnets du Major Thompson* (*The Diary of Major Thompson*, 1955). He died at the Algonquin Hotel in New York.

MOTHER AND SON

If Preston Sturges's life and career seem like a series of brilliant improvisations, he was only following in the footsteps of his mother, Mary Dempsey. She went with her infant son to Paris, where she became friends with the dancer Isadora Duncan. After returning to Chicago, Mary married wealthy stockbroker Solomon Sturges, who adopted Preston. Soon Mary went back to Europe and became infatuated with the occultist Aleister Crowley (below). The relationship between Crowley and Preston was one of mutual loathing. Solomon was the opposite of Mary, reliable where

she was capricious. After their divorce he supported and encouraged Preston, who repaid his kindness with love. In *The Lady Eve* there is a hint of Mary in impulsive adventuress Jean Harrington, and of Solomon in the wisdom of Charles Pike's father.

UNDER THE SHADOW OF WAR

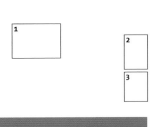

1 *All Quiet on the Western Front*—a highly powerful antiwar polemic—depicts the futility of war through the experiences of ordinary soldiers.

2 The poster for *The Man Who Reclaimed His Head* reflects Universal's plugging of the film as a horror thriller.

3 Francis Lederer plays a German-American Bundist in *Confessions of a Nazi Spy*. Hollywood's first anti-Nazi film, it was daringly released six months before war was declared in Europe.

I n 1930 *All Quiet on the Western Front* (above), a humanitarian World War I drama directed by Lewis Milestone (1895–1980) and based on the best-selling novel by Erich Maria Remarque, reflected the feelings of a generation of Americans who agreed with the words of the song "I Didn't Raise My Son to Be a Soldier." The film shows the conflict from the German side, and its villains are the politicians and civilians who use patriotism as an excuse to send young men to the front to die pointlessly. The film appealed to the sentiments of people who remembered the horrors of the "war to end all wars." Star Lew Ayres became so personally committed to pacifism that his career was later hampered by the revelation that he remained a conscientious objector during World War II when the national mood had changed. For much of the 1930s, despite—or because of—news from Europe and Asia, films such as *The Man Who Reclaimed His Head* (1934, opposite above) depicted world war as an evil fostered by crooked politicians, corrupt armaments dealers, and small-minded bigots.

The rise of Nazism disturbed many in Hollywood. Ironically, predominantly Jewish studio heads had a personal style that might have disposed them to admire Fascism—Columbia's Harry Cohn modeled his office after Benito Mussolini's—if it were not for the anti-Semitism that came along with it. Producers such as Cohn, Walt Disney (a rare Gentile in the industry), and Louis B. Mayer would have been—and, in the 1950s, were—much happier battling Communists, whom they saw as a personal threat (via the rise of screen unions), than the Fascists. Hollywood also hoped to secure the earnings of

KEY EVENTS

1931	1936	1937	1938	1938	1939
Lewis Milestone's *All Quiet on the Western Front* wins the Academy Award for Best Picture.	In the film serial *Flash Gordon* the hero fights Ming the Merciless, dictator of the Planet Mongo, and inspires the locals to overthrow his Fascist regime.	*The Road Back*, sequel to *All Quiet on the Western Front*, is released; it charts Germany's postwar experience.	Alfred Hitchcock's spy thriller *The Lady Vanishes* features sinister Teutonic-accented villains, never actually identified as Nazis.	William Dieterle (1893–1972) directs *Blockade*, an anti-Fascist film about the Spanish Civil War. It is tagged as "Romance under Fire!"	Michael Powell (1905–90) and Emeric Pressburger (1902–88) collaborate on *The Spy in Black*; it warns of the coming conflict.

their films in Europe. Intellectual and inflammatory anti-Hollywood rhetoric from left and right was not untinged with anti-Semitism in the 1930s, and the studio heads mostly wanted to keep quiet about politics and religion. When Warner Bros. courageously made *The Life of Emile Zola* (1937), which chronicles the French writer's involvement in the Dreyfus case, Dreyfus's Jewishness was barely mentioned. However, the popularity of *All Quiet on the Western Front* ironically forced Hollywood to make more films addressing the current state of Germany in the hope of reproducing the success of the original. *The Road Back* (1937), *Three Comrades* (1938), and *The Mortal Storm* (1940) are all official or unofficial follow-ups to *All Quiet on the Western Front* and show postwar Germany turning violently to the political right. *The Mortal Storm* hits on a key image for romantic Hollywood anti-Fascism, as idealized young lovers are hemmed in and persecuted by aggressors shown as a forest of stiff, raised arms.

Warner Bros. was the most anti-Nazi Hollywood studio, shutting down its Berlin operation—reputedly because anti-Semitic thugs murdered their German representative. In 1939 the studio produced the incendiary *Confessions of a Nazi Spy* (below right), a based-on-fact exposé of German spy activity in the United States that takes a swipe at the Nazi leanings of the German-American Bund. Another world war seemed inevitable, and the movie industry responded with films about it: *Idiot's Delight* (1939), based on Robert Sherwood's play, is about Americans caught in Europe at the outbreak of war, and was in theaters only months before the situation it depicts came to pass. The intimation is that US involvement in the conflict is inevitable. US isolationists were highly critical of the way Hollywood weighed in on the British side in the early days of the war, especially when British directors such as Charlie Chaplin (1889–1977, *The Great Dictator*, 1940, see p. 158) and Alfred Hitchcock (1899–1980, *Foreign Correspondent*, 1940, see p. 156) were concerned. Sensitive to these complaints that Hollywood was producing prowar, anti-Nazi propaganda, Metro-Goldwyn-Mayer backed one implicitly pro-Axis movie— *Florian* (1940), an allegorical drama about the training of Austria's Lipizzaner horses, in which a loving disciplinarian brings together disparate animals and whips the stable into shape, defused by Robert Young as a scarcely credible Hitler stand-in.

By 1941, Hollywood was arguably on a better footing to fight a war than the US military or any defense-related industry. Resigned to the loss of European markets, in line with President Roosevelt's "Good Neighbor Policy," the industry would make attempts as varied as the doomed, unfinished *It's All True* (1943) by Orson Welles (1915–85) and Twentieth Century Fox's Carmen Miranda musicals to court South and Central American markets. Even before the entry of the United States into the war, Hollywood was in production on a number of propagandist efforts. Within weeks of Pearl Harbor, Hollywood would be making patriotic war movies. **KN**

Foreign Correspondent 1940
ALFRED HITCHCOCK 1899 – 1980

▲ An assassin strikes, on rainswept steps.

▼ Smiling faces for the poster, although the film's epilogue was altogether more stark.

When the United States was still neutral and isolationists complained that Hollywood let foreign nationals make British propaganda, *Foreign Correspondent* was a controversial film—although it cut most of the political material from Vincent Sheean's source memoir and suggests World War II was started by shadowy Mabuse types masquerading as a peace league. In Alfred Hitchcock's usual style, the master villain (Herbert Marshall) is a dignified character who sacrifices himself (in a rough draft of *Notorious*, 1946) for the sake of his honest, patriotic English daughter (Laraine Day).

It opens in August 1939, at the headquarters of the (fictional) *Daily Globe*, with an editor frustrated by useless reports dribbling in from his drunken expert (Robert Benchley) in Europe. He decides to assign a no-nonsense crime reporter, Johnny Jones (Joel McCrea), to the whole continent, renaming him "Huntley Haverstock" to give him a more credible byline. Although the real-world background should make it more serious than such British thrillers as *The 39 Steps* (1935) or *The Lady Vanishes* (1938) in which villains are spies for no named country, Hitchcock delivers the same type of highly wrought entertainment.

A plot straggles from London to Holland and back as Jones gets into and out of scrapes, aided by a sardonic, covertly patriotic British journalist (George Sanders) and resisting the obvious deduction that the woman he loves is intimately involved with the conspiracy. Only a coda, added months after production, turns this into a propaganda piece, as Jones issues a call to arms to a not-yet-convinced United States (with the "Star-Spangled Banner" playing over the end title). **KN**

⊚ KEY SCENES

1 THE ASSASSINATION IN THE RAIN
A sea of umbrellas is agitated as a hitman flees through the crowd after apparently killing Dutch diplomat Mr. Van Meer in Amsterdam. Disguised as a press photographer, the assassin used a gun hidden by his camera.

2 THE CLUE OF THE WINDMILLS
Jones, Carol Fisher (Laraine Day), and reporter Ffolliott (George Sanders) drive into the countryside after the killer. But in a landscape full of windmills, which structure houses the enemy spies? Could it be the one whose sails are turning the wrong way, against the wind?

3 THE PLANE CRASH
From inside a nose-diving plane, the sea gets closer. It is, in fact, a back projection (on rice paper) of footage previously shot. When the plane "crashes," real water is poured through the paper and onto the cast—an innovative use of optical and physical effects.

4 THE PATRIOTIC BROADCAST
This stirring afterthought has the US hero, now thoroughly devoted to the anti-Fascist cause, broadcasting an urgent tribute to the heroism of blitzed Britain as sirens wail and bombs fall on London. "This is a big story," he says, "and you're part of it."

⊙ DIRECTOR PROFILE

1899–1928

Alfred Hitchcock was born in London. In 1920 he entered the British film industry, designing title cards. He directed the unsuccessful Anglo-German coproductions *The Pleasure Garden* (1925) and *The Mountain Eagle* (1926). He made his first "Hitchcockian" film, the suspense thriller *The Lodger* (1927). After its success, he made a variety of comedies and dramas.

1929–33

Hitchcock directed Britain's first "talkie," the thriller *Blackmail* (1929). *Murder!* (1930) and *Number Seventeen* (1932) followed, as did stiff adaptations of middlebrow plays (*Juno and the Paycock*, 1930; *The Skin Game*, 1931).

1934–39

After a musical (*Waltzes From Vienna*, 1934), Hitchcock worked with producer Michael Balcon on a series of light-hearted, ingenious, fast British thrillers with a surreal, black-comic edge (*The Man Who Knew Too Much*, 1934; *The 39 Steps*, 1935; *Young and Innocent*, 1937; *The Lady Vanishes*, 1938).

1940–50

Producer David O. Selznick imported Hitchcock to Hollywood. They had a fractious relationship on *Rebecca* (1940) and *Spellbound* (1945). He made more personal, even experimental films, on loan, or while Selznick was distracted: *Suspicion* (1941), *Shadow of a Doubt* (1943), *Lifeboat* (1944), and *Notorious* (1946).

1951–59

Hitchcock came into his own with *Strangers on a Train* (1951) and turned out the classics *Rear Window* (1954), *The Trouble With Harry* (1955), *Vertigo* (1958), and *North By Northwest* (1959). He also hosted and sometimes directed the television show *Alfred Hitchcock Presents*.

1960–80

In 1960 he made a modest horror film, *Psycho* (see p. 296), that reinvented the screen shocker. He tried to mould Tippi Hedren into a star in *The Birds* (1963) and *Marnie* (1964). Hitchcock directed his last film, *Family Plot*, in 1976 and died in 1980.

The Great Dictator 1940
CHARLIE CHAPLIN 1889 – 1977

▲ *The Great Dictator* proved to be Charlie Chaplin's biggest box-office hit.

▼ The film was its star's first talking picture.

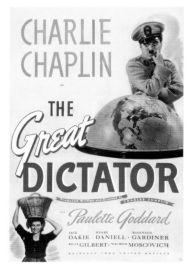

It seems inevitable that Charlie Chaplin would play Adolf Hitler on screen; they were born within days of each other and shared a certain facial characteristic. As critic and filmmaker Basil Wright said, "Hitler's mistake of wearing Charlie's moustache left Chaplin no choice but to seize on this one gorgeous opportunity." *The Great Dictator* has not worn well compared with its anti-Nazi contemporaries *Pastor Hall* and *The Mortal Storm* (both 1940), but the simple fact of the film's existence and the stills of Chaplin in costume exert a fascination far beyond that of the film Chaplin actually made.

The film cost Chaplin "$2,000,000 of my own money and two years' work" in the face of threatening letters and pressure from the Hays Office and United Artists to abandon the film. By the time it opened, on October 15, 1940, a major event was anticipated, as it showcased the talking-film debut of one of the screen's few artists viewed at the time as equal to the task of challenging Hitler. Outstanding among the cast is Henry Daniell's supercilious Garbitsch (alias Goebbels). Despite (or perhaps because of) friction with Chaplin on the set, his scenes carry a menace lacking elsewhere in the film, for example, when he declares, "You've got to rouse the people's anger. At this time violence against the Jews might take the public's mind off its stomach." Later Chaplin admitted, "Had I known of the actual horrors of the German concentration camps I could not have made *The Great Dictator*; I could not have made fun of the homicidal insanity of the Nazis." Naturally, the film was banned in Germany, but Hitler himself watched it twice, alone. His opinion of it was not recorded. **RMC**

1 "DEMOCRAZIE SCHTONK! LIBERTIE SCHTONK! FREESPRACHEN SCHTONK!"
Our introduction to Adenoid Hynkel (Charlie Chaplin) is a speech delivered in gibberish German that, in retrospect, turns out to be a counterweight to the speech given by his substitute at the film's conclusion.

3 NAPALONI ARRIVES
Jack Oakie's brash Bacterian dictator, Napaloni (modeled on Benito Mussolini), and Hynkel spend much of the film arguing over the fate of Osterlich (Austria) and ceaselessly compete to upstage each other. This culminates in a duel played out on dentists' chairs.

2 HYNKEL DANCES WITH THE GLOBE
To the accompaniment of the Prelude to Act 1 of *Lohengrin*, Chaplin reveals the balletic grace of the Chaplin of old. There was such a globe in the Berlin Chancellery, pictures of which were studied for the film. Ironically, after the war it was one of the few items there left intact.

4 FINAL SPEECH
This six-minute speech took Chaplin two months to write. "It really is a tremendous speech," enthused George Orwell, "a sort of version of Lincoln's Gettysburg Address done into Hollywood English, one of the strongest pieces of propaganda I have heard for a long time."

HITLER AND HOLLYWOOD

Although Hitler has made countless "guest" appearances in war movies since *The Great Dictator*, Hollywood has to date attempted only two films charting the Führer's rise to power. John Farrow's *The Hitler Gang* (1944, right) starred Bobby Watson, who was already familiar to audiences as wartime Hollywood's incarnation of what one of *Variety*'s reviewers termed "the world's number one rat," in hokum such as *The Devil with Hitler* in 1942. In *The Hitler Gang*, Watson rose to the challenge of carrying a straight feature film in what proved an unsensational précis of Hitler's career to date. Stuart Heisler's long-forgotten *Hitler* (1962) starred Richard Basehart in a film described by Denis Gifford as "virtually a remake of *The Hitler Gang* but with the accent on sexual perversion."

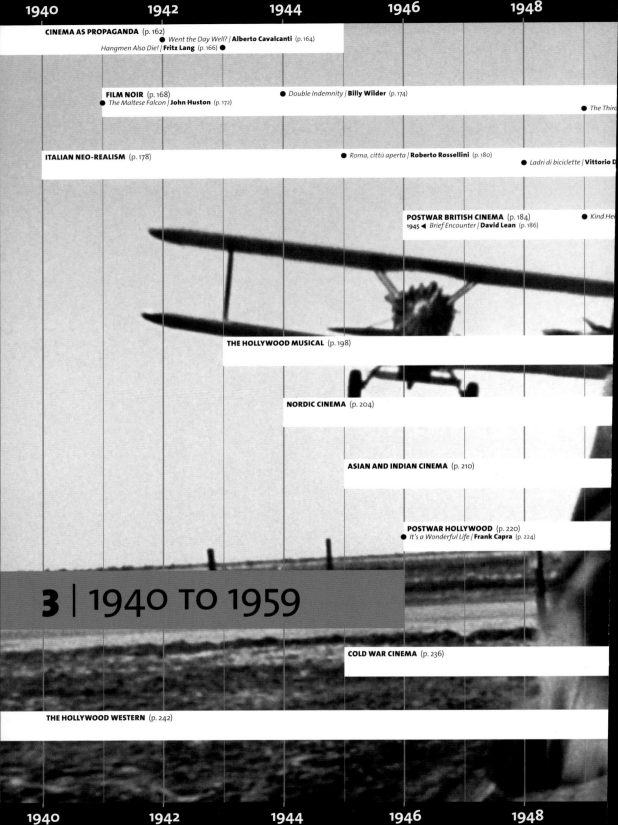

CINEMA AS PROPAGANDA (p. 162)
● *Went the Day Well?* | **Alberto Cavalcanti** (p. 164)
Hangmen Also Die! | **Fritz Lang** (p. 166) ●

FILM NOIR (p. 168)
● *Double Indemnity* | **Billy Wilder** (p. 174)
● *The Maltese Falcon* | **John Huston** (p. 172)
● *The Third*

ITALIAN NEO-REALISM (p. 178)
● *Roma, città aperta* | **Roberto Rossellini** (p. 180)
● *Ladri di biciclette* | **Vittorio D**

POSTWAR BRITISH CINEMA (p. 184)
1945 ◀ *Brief Encounter* | **David Lean** (p. 186)
● *Kind He*

THE HOLLYWOOD MUSICAL (p. 198)

NORDIC CINEMA (p. 204)

ASIAN AND INDIAN CINEMA (p. 210)

POSTWAR HOLLYWOOD (p. 220)
● *It's a Wonderful Life* | **Frank Capra** (p. 224)

3 | 1940 TO 1959

COLD WAR CINEMA (p. 236)

THE HOLLYWOOD WESTERN (p. 242)

(p. 176)

Robert Hamer (p. 188)

FRENCH CINEMA (p. 190) ● *Le salaire de la peur* / **Henri-Georges Clouzot** (p. 196)
                            ● *Casque d'or* / **Jacques Becker** (p. 194)

● *Singin' in the Rain* / **Gene Kelly, Stanley Donen** (p. 202)

● *Ordet* / **Carl Theodor Dreyer** (p. 206)
                            ● *Det sjunde inseglet* / **Ingmar Bergman** (p. 208)

● *Tokyo monogatari* / **Ozu Yasujiro** (p. 214)
            ● *Shichinin no samurai* / **Kurosawa Akira** (p. 216)
                    ● The *Apu* Trilogy / **Satyajit Ray** (p. 218)

Ben-Hur / **William Wyler** (p. 226) ●
Some Like It Hot / **Billy Wilder** (p. 228) ●

REBELLIOUS YOUTH (p. 230)   ● *Rebel Without a Cause* / **Nicholas Ray** (p. 234)
                    ● *The Wild One* / **Laslo Benedek** (p. 232)

● *Pickup on South Street* / **Samuel Fuller** (p. 238)   ● *Invasion of the Body Snatchers* / **Don Siegel** (p. 240)

● *The Searchers* / **John Ford** (p. 246)

NOUVELLE VAGUE (p. 248)   *Les quatre cents coups* / **François Truffaut** (p. 252) ●
                               A bout de souffle / **Jean-Luc Godard** (p. 254) ●

CINEMA AS PROPAGANDA

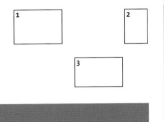

1 Noël Coward's fatherly Captain Edward V. Kinross in *In Which We Serve* was inspired by Captain Lord Louis Mountbatten, who was commander of the destroyer HMS *Kelly* when it was sunk during the Battle of Crete in May 1941.

2 *Thirty Seconds Over Tokyo* tells the true story of a daring US bomb attack on Japan from an aircraft carrier in 1942.

3 In *Why We Fight* Frank Capra took original enemy footage and propaganda, edited it and then put a narration over the top to expose the Axis powers as a force of evil using their own material.

In June 1942 Lieutenant Commander John Ford USNR (1894–1973) was wounded by shrapnel while standing on an atoll in the Pacific with a 16mm hand-held camera filming Japanese planes attacking. His footage became part of the documentary short *The Battle of Midway* (1942). Ford claimed that his role was to bring news of the war to the home front: "It's for the mothers of America. It is to let them know that we're in this war and that we've been getting the shit kicked out of us for five months, and now we're starting to hit back."

During World War II many of cinema's talents were involved in the war effort, and the best films raised wartime propaganda to the level of popular art. In Britain Humphrey Jennings (1907–50) brought poetry to the documentary with his vision of life on the home front, *Listen to Britain* (1942). The debut feature *In Which We Serve* (1942, above) by David Lean (1908–91) and codirected with Noël Coward (1899–1973), is the fictionalized account of a ship told through the memories of its shipwrecked crew. *Went the Day Well?* (1942, see p. 164) by Alberto Cavalcanti (1897–1982) shows a sleepy English hamlet transformed into a bloodbath when its villagers take up arms and turn on their Nazi captors.

In Germany much of the propaganda meant demonization. *Jud Süss* (1940), commissioned by Joseph Goebbels and directed by Veit Harlan (1899–1964), took Lion Feuchtwanger's novel of 1925 and Wilhelm Hauff's novella of 1827 and twisted them into virulent anti-Semitic propaganda. *Feldzug in Polen* (*Campaign in Poland*, 1940) by Fritz Hippler (1909–2002), a documentary made after the invasion of Poland, was designed to show Poles as aggressors against Germany.

KEY EVENTS

1939	1939	1940	1940	1940	1941
Confessions of a Nazi Spy by Anatole Litvak (1902–74), about a real-life spy trial, is the first explicitly anti-Nazi film from Hollywood.	Germany invades Poland on September 1. Two days later France and Britain declare war on Germany.	In April Hollywood learns that several Polish film exhibitors who showed *Confessions of a Nazi Spy* have been hanged in their cinemas.	*L'assedio dell'Alcazar* is released in August in Italy and wins the Mussolini Cup for Best Italian Film at the Venice Film Festival.	*Jud Süss* is released on September 24 in Berlin and becomes the most popular film of the year in the Third Reich, seen by more than twenty million people.	The United States enters the war after the Japanese attack Pearl Harbor in Hawaii on December 7.

In 1940 Italy and Spain coproduced *L'assedio dell Alcazar* (*The Siege of the Alcazar*), directed by Augusto Genina (1892–1957), a feature created to show the heroism of Francisco Franco's soldiers through a fictionalized account of the siege of Alcazar by Republican forces. The great exponent of postwar Neo-Realism (see p.178), Roberto Rossellini (1906–77), made a trilogy to help the Italian war effort between 1941 and 1943: *La nave bianca* (*The White Ship*), a drama sponsored by the propaganda arm of the Italian Navy; *Un pilota ritorna* (*A Pilot Returns*) about an Italian pilot interned in a British prison; and *L'uomo dalla croce* (*Man with a Cross*), about Italy's efforts on the Eastern Front in 1942.

The United States joined the war in 1941, but many films prior to that criticized isolationism, and *Foreign Correspondent* (1940, see p. 156) by Alfred Hitchcock (1899–1980) sent an emotional message from bombed London to the then neutral United States. After Pearl Harbor, Hollywood waded into the Axis powers with gusto in such films as *Hangmen Also Die!* (1943, see p. 166) and *Thirty Seconds Over Tokyo* (1944, right). Frank Capra (1897–1991) made *Why We Fight* (1943–45, below), a series of documentaries explaining war policy to the troops that was also released to the public. The documentary short about the Italian campaign, *San Pietro* (1945) by John Huston (1906–87) was so realistic that initially the authorities blocked its release. When Russia became an ally against the Axis powers, Hollywood was pressurized to make pro-Soviet movies. *Mission to Moscow* (1943) by Michael Curtiz (1886–1962) is notorious for its sympathetic depiction of Joseph Stalin. *The North Star* (1943), directed by Lewis Milestone (1895–1980), features Russian partisans singing lyrics by Ira Gershwin. Yet, by the end of the war Russia was the enemy and both films came under scrutiny by the House Un-American Activities Committee. **DP**

1942	1942	1943	1943	1945	1945
Cary Grant and Ginger Rogers mock the Nazis in *Once Upon a Honeymoon* directed by Leo McCarey (1898–1969)	President Franklin D. Roosevelt sees the first documentary in Frank Capra's *Why We Fight* series and orders it to be released for viewing by the public.	John Ford's short, *The Battle of Midway*, wins an Academy Award for Best Documentary.	Warner Bros makes *Mission to Moscow* at President Roosevelt's request to help garner support for the Soviet Union.	*San Pietro*, John Huston's unflinching depiction of the Battle of San Pietro Infine in 1943, is regarded as an antiwar movie.	Germany surrenders in May. In August atomic bombs are dropped on Hiroshima and Nagasaki and Japan surrenders.

Went the Day Well? 1942
ALBERTO CAVALCANTI 1897 – 1982

▲ The villagers are held captive in a church.

▼ "Went the day well?" was a familiar phrase used in epitaphs to those fallen in battle.

There is a populism about Ealing Studios' war films that sets them apart from other World War II British movies, with none of the deference to the officer class that is shown to Noël Coward's naval captain in *In Which We Serve* (1942). In Ealing's offerings, anyone with a posh accent is generally careless, incompetent, or worse. *Went the Day Well?* is no exception. It shows the danger of social forelock-tugging with a touch of dark humor. A platoon of soldiers arrives in a sleepy English village. They are welcomed and given billets. The lady of the manor invites their commanding officer, a well-spoken major, to dinner. However, the soldiers are Germans, come to disrupt communications in advance of a planned invasion. Once they reveal themselves, instinctively the terrified villagers look to the squire for leadership. But he is a quisling, in league with the invaders, and their trust in him nearly proves fatal. Only once they take their destiny into their own hands and fight back are the Germans routed.

Director Alberto Cavalcanti brought his documentary background to the texture of this suspenseful film along with a realistic tough-mindedness. The English villagers are vividly characterized. At first cozy and complacent, they finish by retaliating with as much ruthlessness as their erstwhile captors. Given that it was made in 1942, the film's unquestioning optimism is striking. Events are told in flashback, with a prologue and epilogue by the churchwarden (Mervyn Johns). He reveals the mass grave of the German soldiers and adds that the incident was hushed up "until after the war was over and old Hitler got what was coming to him." **PK**

👁 KEY SCENES

1 THE ENEMY CONFERS
The audience is let in on the secret identity of the platoon of "Royal Engineers" when Kommandant Orlter, alias Major Hammond (Basil Sydney), meets the squire, Oliver Wilsford (Leslie Banks), and it is revealed that one is a German officer, the other a pro-Nazi traitor.

2 THE FIRST KILLING
The aged Vicar Ashton (C. V. France) goes to raise the alarm by ringing the church bell, but he is thwarted and gunned down by the German major. Wilkie Cooper's moody cinematography accentuates the brutality of the film's first shocking moment.

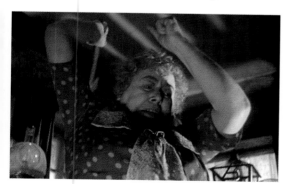

3 THE POSTMISTRESS STRIKES
The motherly, elderly postmistress, Mrs Collins (Muriel George), is the first villager to hit back against the invaders—and with unexpected violence. She throws pepper in the eyes of her German lodger and then buries an axe in his head with ferocious force.

4 BATTLE OF THE MANOR HOUSE
Land Army girls Peggy Pryde (Elizabeth Allan) and Ivy Dawking (Thora Hird) find they rather enjoy "potting Jerries." Their courage served as rousing propaganda when an invasion was a possibility and contemporary audiences were being encouraged to be vigilant.

🕐 DIRECTOR PROFILE

1897–1933
Alberto de Almeida Cavalcanti was born in Rio de Janeiro. He studied law in Rio and then left Brazil to study architecture and interior design in Geneva. He moved to Paris and worked as a set designer on films for avant-garde director Marcel L'Herbier (1890–1979). Cavalcanti directed his first film in 1926, the city symphony *Rien que les heures* (*Nothing But Time*).

1934–39
Cavalcanti left Paris when John Grierson (1898–1972) invited him to join the General Post Office Film Unit, working on shorts, including the satire *Pett and Pott: A Fairy Story of the Suburbs* (1934), the experimental *Coal Face* (1935), and critically acclaimed *Night Mail* (1936). When Grierson left the unit in 1937, Cavalcanti took over as head. When World War II broke out, as a foreign national Cavalcanti was obliged to quit what became the Ministry of Information's Crown Film Unit.

1940–48
Cavalcanti joined Ealing Studios as an associate producer and director. There he directed the features *Went the Day Well?*, the musical *Champagne Charlie* (1944), the segments of the portmanteau *Dead of Night* (1945), and an adaptation, *The Life and Adventures of Nicholas Nickleby* (1947), before leaving to become an independent director. He made three more movies in the United Kingdom, including the gritty Film Noir (see p.168) *They Made Me a Fugitive* (1947).

1949–53
He returned to his native country and co-founded the Brazilian Film Institute. Cavalcanti directed three films in Brazil, most notably *O canto do mar* (*Song of the Sea*, 1952), about migrant life in the drought areas of northeastern Brazil, which won a Grand Prize nomination at the Cannes Film Festival.

1954–82
As his left-wing views caused problems with the Brazilian authorities, Cavalcanti went back to Europe and eventually settled in France, making films in East Germany, France, the United Kingdom, Romania, and Israel. He died in Paris in 1982.

Hangmen Also Die! 1943
FRITZ LANG 1890 – 1976

▲ Svoboda (Brian Donlevy) desperately tries to dodge the authorities.

▼ The film's anti-Nazi propaganda message was dressed up in the guise of a contemporary wartime thriller.

Fritz Lang's *Hangmen Also Die!* was inspired by the assassination of SS general and Reichsprotektor of Bohemia and Moravia, Reinhard Heydrich, in Prague in 1942, and the savage Nazi reprisals that followed. The film's screenplay was cowritten by John Wexley, Lang, and fellow German refugee Bertolt Brecht, who had moved to the United States in 1941. Hampered by miscast leads and a proliferation of US accents that render its depiction of Prague vaguely comical, Lang's film remains an absorbing thriller, atmospherically photographed by James Wong Howe and scored by Hanns Eisler, who was nominated for an Academy Award.

Heydrich himself, the "Hangman" of the title, appears only in a brief prologue; he is played as a mincing bully by German émigré Hans Heinrich von Twardowski. His assassination takes place off screen. Lang instead concentrates on the machinations of the underground Resistance as they attempt to spirit away the assassin and of the Gestapo as they try to find him and, when they fail, exact bloody revenge. At its best the film recalls *M* (1931, see p. 82) in both its look and its deployment of parallel narratives: it juxtaposes the Nazis with the Resistance as *M* juxtaposes the police investigation with the trawl conducted by Berlin's underworld. Lang plainly relished creating a gallery of grotesque cartoon Nazis—most of them played by recent German refugees— among whom Gestapo Inspector Alois Gruber (Alexander Granach), in his waistcoat, bow tie, and bowler hat, provides Brian Donlevy's stolid Dr. Franticek Svoboda with an adversary equal to *M*'s Inspector Karl Lohmann. **RMC**

1 HEYDRICH'S INSTRUCTIONS TO THE CZECH PEOPLE
In a chilling scene, the furious commander outlines his vision and demands. He pronounces the Czech armaments workers to be "stinking swine" and that production will henceforth be managed by the Gestapo, who can sort out what he calls a "putrid mess."

3 AND G STANDS FOR GESTAPO
Under suspicion by the Nazis, Professor Stephen Novotny (Walter Brennan) instructs his daughter Nasha (Anna Lee) in the perils of careless talk. Lang cited the scene as one only Brecht could have written, in a film that is Brecht's only Hollywood screen credit.

2 CZECHOSLOVAKIA CELEBRATES
While Czech patriot and assassin, surgeon Dr. Svoboda, lies low in a cinema, word that the "Hangman" has been shot sweeps the audience, which erupts into spontaneous applause. A Nazi soldier stops the film and demands to know who started the clapping.

4 "NO SURRENDER!"
Pescaček (James Bush) is taken away to his death. He is one of four hundred Czech civilians taken hostage by the Nazis and held until the killer surrenders. His countrymen see him off by singing his poem, now set to music, in a very Brechtian show of mass defiance.

REINHARD HEYDRICH ON FILM

Heydrich's assassination on the streets of Prague denied him greater notoriety as a war criminal for years. In *Hangmen Also Die!* he appears in a brief prologue, but both Lang's film and *Hitler's Madman* (1943) by Douglas Sirk (1900–87) were more concerned with the aftermath: the slaughter of an entire village. The assassination itself was re-created in the original location in *Atentát* (1965) and *Operation: Daybreak* (1975). The Wannsee Conference of January 20, 1942, which set the agenda for the "final solution to the Jewish question," was a closely guarded secret at the time—along with Heydrich's role as chairman—but the conference has since been re-created for television in *Die Wannseekonferenz* (1984) and *Conspiracy* (2001, right).

FILM NOIR

1 Consummate noir actor Robert Mitchum elicits a smoldering glance from *Out of the Past* costar Jane Greer.

2 The poster for Alfred Hitchcock's Oscar-nominated *Shadow of a Doubt*.

3 Richard Conte and Shelley Winters, a couple on the lam in Robert Siodmak's *Cry of the City*.

ilm Noir is a slippery concept to define. Is it a genre, a style, an atmosphere, a mood, or a look? Must a Film Noir be shot in black and white? Must it have an urban setting? Must it involve violent crime? Must it end unhappily? Were true noir films made only in the United States during the classic period—from 1941 to 1958? Should films made elsewhere, or after this watershed, be classified as neo-noir, retro-noir, or even noir pastiche?

Film historians have argued about these and related issues for years without ever arriving at a consensus. Some have cast their net startlingly wide: British critic Raymond Durgnat, always provocative, included the original *King Kong* (1933) and *2001: A Space Odyssey* (1968, see p. 292) in his noir pantheon, which may be diluting the concept beyond reason. Most critics, however, would accept that noir Westerns (*Pursued*, 1947), noir costume dramas (*The Black Book*, 1949), and even the occasional British noir film (*Night and the City*, 1950—the archetypal noir title) can be legitimately admitted to the canon.

Deciding when Hollywood noir started is equally problematic. Its origins are traced back to the shadowy, angled, paranoid world of German Expressionism, and certainly such refugees from Nazism as Fritz Lang (1890–1976), Karl Freund (1890–1969), and Robert Siodmak (1900–73) brought with them visual and thematic elements that fed into, and darkened, the Hollywood mainstream. This generation of European filmmakers recognized the medium's potential to create complex psychological effects while exploiting controversial subject matter— something already intrinsic to the work of directors such as Alfred Hitchcock

KEY EVENTS

1941	1942	1943	1944	1945	1946
John Huston's version of *The Maltese Falcon* (see p. 172) is released. It is now recognized as the first definitive Film Noir.	In *Casablanca*, Rick (Humphrey Bogart) chooses sides, marking the end of US isolationism, both on and off screen.	Alfred Hitchcock's first noir film is *Shadow of a Doubt*. *Ossessione*, directed by Luchino Visconti (1906–76), premieres.	Five classic noir films are released: *Double Indemnity* (see p. 174), *Laura*, *Murder My Sweet*, *Phantom Lady*, and *The Woman in the Window*.	This year's noir films include *To Have and Have Not* (Humphrey Bogart and Lauren Bacall), and the female-oriented *Mildred Pierce*.	Hollywood films are shown in Paris and termed "Film Noir." *The Blue Dahlia* and *The Postman Always Rings Twice* premiere, as does *The Big Sleep*.

(1899–1980), who produced his debut noir, *Shadow of a Doubt* (above right) in 1943. Fritz Lang's *M* (1931, see p. 82), about a serial child killer, is among one of the earliest crime films to marry a noirish visual style with a noir-type plot. The German thriller starred the archetypal noir actor Peter Lorre in an insidiously disturbing performance; it also featured a voice-over narration, a device that was to become a hallmark of the genre. Another of Lang's films, *You Only Live Once* (1937), with its doomed young couple (Henry Fonda and Sylvia Sidney) on the run from fate and the law, also seems to prefigure aspects of Film Noir. Yet neither of these works conveys the sense of existential claustrophobia, of all-enveloping duplicity, that distinguishes the quintessential noir.

Another candidate sometimes proposed as the first Hollywood Film Noir is *Stranger on the Third Floor* (1940), a twisty, atmospheric thriller, again starring the middle-European expatriate Peter Lorre. Yet *Stranger on the Third Floor* was only a sixty-four-minute B movie, directed by the little-known Boris Ingster (1903–78); despite being photographed by Nicholas Musuraca, one of noir's finest cinematographers, it exerted little influence at the time. The film with the strongest claim to having kicked off the Hollywood noir cycle is the crime thriller *The Maltese Falcon* (1941, see p. 172), although its makers had no intention of starting a trend, let alone inaugurating one of the most analyzed, admired, and influential cycles in the history of cinema.

The elusiveness of the genre can be traced partly to the fact that it became known as noir only after the event. The concept is an ex post facto historical construct, akin to expressions such as "the Middle Ages." Filmmakers who created Westerns, or swashbucklers, or biopics knew exactly what conventions they were working in; few, if any, of the people who made noir films would have referred to their work as such. The concept "Film Noir" was devised by French movie critics who, noting a new trend emerging in the US movies that reached France en masse after the German occupation in World War II, named it after the popular *policièr* imprint known as Série noire. The term was coined to denote a dark and downbeat underworld of crime and corruption; French critic Nino Frank first used the term in 1946. However, outside France, the words "Film Noir" did not enter popular parlance until the 1960s.

Noir heroes are rarely nice guys. Cynical, ruthless, looking to take advantage and lacking in sentimentality, they are typically insecure, disillusioned loners, unsure of themselves and apathetic about the future. They were often played by actors such as Humphrey Bogart or Robert Mitchum (star of cornerstone noir flick *Out of the Past*, 1947, opposite), who could tap into the dark side of their screen personas. In the world of noir, even if the hero is lucky enough to survive the last reel, he rarely gets the girl. Film Noir is typified by mistrust between the characters, a loss of innocence, a forbidding urban setting (as in *Cry of the City*, 1948, right) and a sense of despair—often offset by a determinedly grim humor that keeps the audience just the right side of bleakness. The genre served as a riposte to contemporary Hollywood musicals and romantic comedies. As the mainstream proudly presented its clean-cut heroes and sugar-pie heroines, Film Noir conjured up an army of antiheroes and femmes fatales.

1947	1949	1953	1954	1955	1957
A boom year for Film Noir sees *Dead Reckoning*, *Fear in the Night*, and *Out of the Past* debut. *The Naked City* and *Sorry, Wrong Number* follow in 1948.	*The Third Man* (see p. 176), set in postwar Vienna, opens; *The Asphalt Jungle* and *Sunset Boulevard* follow in 1950.	Actress Ida Lupino is the first woman to direct a noir film, *The Hitch-Hiker*.	*Crime Wave*, *Human Desire*, and *Witness to Murder* all premiere.	Robert Mitchum stars as a psychotic villain in *Night of the Hunter*. It is a character style that will become one of his trademarks.	*Sweet Smell of Success*, starring Burt Lancaster and Tony Curtis, is released. In 1958 Orson Welles's *Touch of Evil* is widely seen as the last classic Film Noir movie.

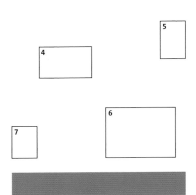

4 *The Blue Dahlia* was based on a novel by Raymond Chandler. Its stars Alan Ladd and Veronica Lake became a popular noir couple.

5 *Crossfire*'s musical score and minimal lighting conveyed a sense of claustrophobia and pent-up violence that gripped the audience and stayed with them as they left the auditorium.

6 Having discovered that she is being poisoned by her husband and his mother, Alicia (Ingrid Bergman) collapses in Alfred Hitchcock's *Notorious*.

7 In 1946 real-life husband and wife Bacall and Bogart starred in the movie version of Raymond Chandler's noir novel of 1939. It was the first to feature hard-boiled private eye Philip Marlowe.

The classic period of Hollywood Film Noir coincides with the war years and the postwar anti-Communist witch hunt. Noir, with its pervasive atmosphere of fear and paranoia and sense of hopeless fatalism, presents an oblique response to the political climate of the time. In many noir films, it is possible to detect an anxiety about the conflict engulfing Europe, which would eventually draw in the United States—or, in later years, about the Cold War claustrophobia choking the whole country as well as the threat of nuclear annihilation. John Huston (1906–87) made *The Maltese Falcon* before the United States entered World War II; yet within it can be detected, submerged beneath the private-eye conventions, an apprehension of events in Europe. *The Third Man* (1949, see p. 176), directed by Carol Reed (1906–76) and set and filmed in postwar Vienna, is steeped in the messy aftermath of World War II and reflects the prevailing ambience of anxiety, pessimism, and suspicion. Occupied Vienna is ruled by four different military powers, while a black-market drugs racket plagues the devastated city. Urban landscapes often provided the setting for Film Noir. The shadowy wet streets of the metropolis provided the perfect setting for the nightmarish events and uneasy atmosphere of noir.

Favorite noir techniques included low-key "chiaroscuro" lighting, odd camera angles, the use of flashbacks, first-person voice-over narration, sharp wisecracking dialogue, and nonlinear plotlines. Cinematographers of the era, such as Nicholas Musuraca, John F. Seitz, and John Alton, used expressionistic lighting to create mood and heighten tension. Arthur Edeson in particular is credited with creating the classic noir look. He shot his first feature in 1914 and went on to film several of Douglas Fairbanks's swashbucklers and the early sound movie *All Quiet on the Western Front* (1930). Also in the 1930s he photographed classic Universal horror films directed by James Whale (1889–1957): *Frankenstein* (1931, see p. 92), *The Old Dark House* (1932), and *The Invisible Man* (1933), whose combination of German Expressionism with shadowy gothic mood and tongue-in-cheek melodrama was to establish the template for horror movies. In 1941 Edeson was director of photography on *The Maltese Falcon*.

The plots and themes of Film Noir have their roots in the US hard-boiled pulp novels and crime fiction of the period, whose tone carried over to the resulting dialogue. *Double Indemnity* (1944, see p. 174), another noir classic, was adapted by director Billy Wilder (1906–2002) and author Raymond Chandler from the novel by James M. Cain. Chandler's writing inspired several major noirs, including *The Big Sleep* (1946, left). In *Double Indemnity* Walter Neff (Fred

MacMurray) opens his narration with the line "How could I have known that murder can sometimes smell like honeysuckle?" Neff becomes embroiled in a murder plot by the scheming Phyllis Dietrichson (Barbara Stanwyck). Noir females are archetypes: either dutiful, loving women or femmes fatales—gorgeous, mysterious, double-crossing, and ready to do anything to stay on top.

During the 1940s and 1950s, the tone of Film Noir deepened. The shadows grew gloomier and more encroaching, the highlights brasher and more hysterical, and the camera angles more vertiginous, while the sense of fatalism intensified and became ever more internalized. "Fate or some mysterious force," muses the hero of *Detour* (1945), "can put the finger on you or me for no good reason at all." Other traumas of the period clouded the texture: anti-Communist paranoia, disorientation, and the postwar mood of emptiness. *Crossfire* (1947, right) flags up the potential for violence in demobbed veterans; the lingering specter of Nazism emerges in *Notorious* (1946, below); a nagging worry about what wives and girlfriends got up to on the home front festers in *The Blue Dahlia* (1946, opposite above); and alcoholism, an increasing problem in postwar America, all but wipes out the hero of *The Lost Weekend* (1945).

The audacious *Touch of Evil* (1958) by Orson Welles (1915–85) marks the end of the US Film Noir cycle. A lurid tale of corruption in a sleazy border town, it features Charlton Heston as an honorable Mexican narcotics agent, Marlene Dietrich as a cigar-smoking bordello madam, and Welles as a degenerate US cop. The film is famed for its three-minute unbroken opening shot and its final chase, featuring extravagant visual and experimental sound effects.

As the United States slipped deeper into the neuroses of the Cold War, noir's downbeat, doom-laden visions seemed like a riposte, a disenchanted flipside to the optimism and flag-waving piety of much of Hollywood's output. Those patriotic parades on Main Street had their sardonic counterpart in the mean streets; the brighter the lights and the louder the drums, the darker the shadows and the more hollow the echoes. As film historian Colin McArthur commented, "The meanings spoken by Film Noir are not social, relating to the problems . . . of a particular society, but metaphysical, having to do with angst and loneliness as essential elements of the human condition." **PK**

The Maltese Falcon 1941
JOHN HUSTON 1906 – 87

▲ Sam Spade (Humphrey Bogart) holds the "black bird." Dramatic lighting helped to create the film's chilling atmosphere.

▼ The original film poster betrays the novel's pulp origins.

A film version of Dashiell Hammett's *The Maltese Falcon* was John Huston's directorial debut and it made both him and Humphrey Bogart household names. It established the perennial Huston theme of the doomed quest: a group of people in pursuit of an objective that, in the end, proves unattainable or illusory. Acting as his own screenwriter, he interfered as little as possible with Hammett's original text, creating a style and mood that was simply a response to the material.

Huston assembled a peerless cast for his tale of greed, corruption, and murder, including Bogart, who is ideally cast as gumshoe Sam Spade. The role defined his iconic screen persona as the cool, cynical character disillusioned by a lifetime of hard-learned lessons and broken dreams. The film boasts a rich gallery of villains: Mary Astor is a seductive and duplicitous femme fatale; Sydney Greenstreet plays orotund arch-villain Kasper Gutman; perennial fall guy Elisha Cook Jr. is Gutman's twitchy, near-psychotic sidekick; and Peter Lorre appears as the avaricious, effeminate Joel Cairo.

Another shrewd decision was to hire Arthur Edeson as cinematographer. Edeson's high-contrast lighting and dramatically skewed angles create an edgy, downbeat atmosphere. Huston made his masterpiece despite a shooting schedule of just six weeks and a modest budget. He chose to shoot the entire film in sequence, creating a realistic sense of continuity. Filming began at a relatively leisurely pace, with the tension expertly building as the speed increased, a device that is enhanced by Adolph Deutsch's atmospheric score. **PK**

⊙ KEY SCENES

1 SETTING UP THE MYSTERY
The titular falcon enters the plot. Sam Spade is temporarily at the mercy of Joel Cairo, who, having offered Spade $5,000 to find a jewel-encrusted statue of a falcon, pulls a gun on him. Spade overcomes Cairo, knocks him out, and searches his belongings.

2 ENTER THE FEMME FATALE
Having lied to Brigid O'Shaughnessy (Mary Astor) by telling her the apartment is under surveillance, Spade skeptically questions her. Brigid is elusive, spinning various tales before pulling him to her for a long kiss. Aroused but unimpressed, he demands the truth.

3 THE DENOUEMENT
Spade presents Cairo, Brigid, and Kasper Gutman with the Maltese Falcon. It proves to be a leaden replica, devoid of jewels. Concluding that the two statues were switched in Constantinople, Gutman asks the others to help him search for the real statue; only Cairo agrees.

⊙ DIRECTOR PROFILE

1906–41
John Huston was born in Nevada, Missouri. He initially trained as a scriptwriter for Warner Bros. His directorial debut, *The Maltese Falcon*, was instantly hailed a classic. It also established the obsessive quest as a recurring theme in his films.

1942–46
He served in the US army and made powerful wartime documentaries, including *Let There Be Light* (1946), a highly realistic portrayal of the treatment meted out to shell-shocked soldiers. The film was banned as potentially bad for morale.

1947–52
He won an Oscar for *The Treasure of the Sierra Madre* (1948) and went on to direct some of his finest movies, such as *The Asphalt Jungle* (1950) and *The African Queen* (1951).

1953–69
While movies such as *Moby Dick* (1956) and *The Misfits* (1961)—the latter starring Clark Gable and Marilyn Monroe—made an impression, Huston's critical standing slumped during the 1960s.

1970–87
Huston returned to his classic form in the 1970s with the boxing drama *Fat City* (1972), the Rudyard Kipling–inspired *The Man Who Would Be King* (1975), and the black comedy *Prizzi's Honor* (1985), for which the director received an Oscar nomination. His last film was the James Joyce adaptation *The Dead* (1987). He died at eighty-one while on location taking a small part in *Mr. North*, the directorial debut of his son, Danny.

PAGE TO SCREEN

The limited success of two earlier film versions of *The Maltese Falcon* led John Huston to take what appeared to be a radical, perhaps even foolhardy, step when he wrote the screenplay of Dashiell Hammett's novel "to follow the book rather than depart from it." Published in 1930, *The Maltese Falcon* had established Hammett as the United States's leading detective novelist and his character Sam Spade was appreciated as the epitome of the cynical, hard-boiled detective. The authenticity of Hammett's character was hard-won, the fruit of the author's experiences as a career detective. Recognizing the cinematic values of Hammett's tight narrative and terse, laconic dialogue, Huston transferred the book to the silver screen with the lightest of touches. It is a tribute to Huston's sensitivity to the high quality of Hammett's work that he produced not only one of the finest detective movies but also the definitive film version of the novel. In 1989, the Library of Congress saw the movie as "culturally, historically, or aesthetically significant" and voted to preserve it.

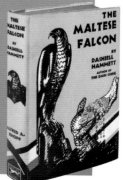

Double Indemnity 1944
BILLY WILDER 1906 – 2002

▲ Walter Neff, gun in his hand, looks over the deceased Phyllis.

▼ A splendidly noir tagline. Edward G. Robinson looks on disapprovingly.

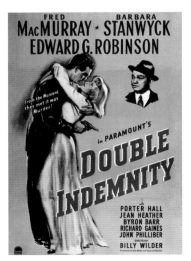

It is when Walter Neff (Fred MacMurray) spots Phyllis Dietrichson (Barbara Stanwyck) wrapped in a towel on the stairs that the temperature in *Double Indemnity* really begins to rise. Neff is an insurance salesman who has pushed his way into a house in the hills of Los Angeles in a bid to sell a renewal on a motor insurance policy. "Is there anything I can do?" Phyllis purrs.

There is an open eroticism in Billy Wilder's film that had rarely been seen in earlier Hollywood thrillers. The setting is sunny California but this is a very dark film. Adapted by Raymond Chandler from the James M. Cain novel of 1936, it starts with lust and hurtles toward murder. Ensnared by Phyllis, Neff agrees to murder her husband (Tom Powers) for his insurance money. He knows, though, that his boss (Edward G. Robinson) has a knack of spotting false insurance claims. The entire story is told in flashback by Neff, speaking into a dictaphone. Wilder and Chandler realized that the voice-over is an expressive tool in its own right and the use of which should not be restricted to communicating plot points.

Stanwyck was reluctant initially to play the femme fatale; Wilder taunted her into it, asking if she was scared to take on the role. MacMurray too was unsure about playing the part of a philanderer, but Wilder talked him into it. It helped that the film's backers, Paramount, knew the clean-cut actor was soon to decamp to another studio, and hoped that *Double Indemnity* would ruin his reputation.

The feeling in Hollywood was that the film was an unsavory endeavor. In the event, Wilder and Chandler received an Oscar nomination for screenwriting and the movie ushered in a franker, more adult approach toward thrillers. **GM**

👁 KEY SCENES

1 THE WOMAN ON THE STAIRCASE
Neff is bewitched at this first, fateful glimpse of Phyllis in her towel. The fake-looking wig was Wilder's idea. Reportedly, he only realized how awful it looked a month into filming, but later stated that it had been a deliberate attempt to convey the character's tackiness.

2 COOKING UP MURDER IN THE SUPERMARKET
Neff and Phyllis meet in the aisles of Jerry's supermarket to plot the demise of her husband. The heavily stocked shelves reference burgeoning consumer culture and the promises of the American dream—which, like many other noir movies, the film undermines.

3 THE DOOR OPENING OUTWARD
Neff's boss, Barton Keyes (Robinson), leaves Neff's apartment, unaware that Phyllis is there too. In real life, doors should open inward—and almost always do. Wilder, though, used poetic license to increase the dramatic tension of the scene.

🕐 DIRECTOR PROFILE

1906–38
Billy Wilder was born in Vienna. His first writing credit was for *Hell of a Reporter* (1929). He worked with Fred Zinnemann (1907–97) and Robert Siodmak on *Menschen am Sonntag* (*People on Sunday*, 1929). As Hitler rose to power, Wilder moved to Hollywood and became a screenwriter.

1939–44
He was Oscar-nominated for his work on the screenplay of the Greta Garbo comedy *Ninotchka* (1939). *The Major and the Minor* (1942) was his first film as a director in Hollywood.

1945–59
He worked as editor on the US army documentary film *Death Mills*, about the recently liberated Nazi death camps, followed by the bittersweet comedy *A Foreign Affair* (1948). He won Oscars for *The Lost Weekend* and *Sunset Boulevard* (both 1950) and directed comedies *The Seven Year Itch* (1955) and *Some Like It Hot* (1959, see p.228), both featuring Marilyn Monroe.

1960–68
The Apartment (1960) started the new decade promisingly, picking up three more Oscars, and was followed by *Irma La Douce* (1963). Subsequent offering *Kiss Me, Stupid* (1964) was less well received, although *The Fortune Cookie* (1966) garnered Walter Matthau an Oscar for Best Actor in a Supporting Role.

1969–2002
The Private Life of Sherlock Holmes (1970) was heavily cut. *Fedora* (1978) won acclaim, but his swan song, *Buddy Buddy* (1981), flopped and his career waned. He died of pneumonia in 2002.

PAGE TO SCREEN

According to movie lore (largely corroborated by their own accounts), Billy Wilder and Raymond Chandler heartily loathed each other. Wilder had hired Chandler to work on the adaptation of James M. Cain's novel because he admired Chandler's *The Big Sleep* (and also because his regular writing collaborator, Charles Brackett, turned down the project as being "too grim"). However, the two men soon discovered they were temperamentally incompatible. Wilder relished Chandler's dialogue and descriptions but later told Cameron Crowe that the novelist could not "construct." He also claimed that Chandler gave him "more aggravation than any writer I ever worked with." Chandler for his part wrote to his publisher that working with Wilder on *Double Indemnity* was "an agonizing experience and has probably shortened my life." The two men never collaborated again. However, Chandler acknowledged that he learned "as much about screenwriting as I am capable of learning" from Wilder.

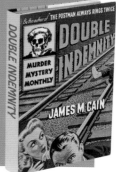

The Third Man 1949
CAROL REED 1906 – 76

▲ Reed had the cobbled streets sprayed with water to pick out reflected light.

▼ The climactic chase scene is highlighted on the theatrical release poster.

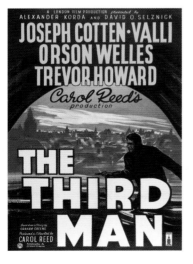

Written for the screen by Graham Greene, *The Third Man* takes the urban paranoia of Hollywood Film Noir and relocates it to Europe, exploring the shattered postwar city of Vienna, divided between four military powers and plagued by black-marketeering scoundrels. Greene was an unacknowledged key figure in noir, providing the source stories for *This Gun for Hire* (1942) and *Ministry of Fear* (1944).

Into this world comes American innocent Holly Martins (Joseph Cotten), a pulp Western writer. Holly is shocked to learn that his boyhood friend, the shady Harry Lime (Orson Welles), has died recently in suspicious circumstances. He meets one of Harry's girlfriends, Anna (Alida Valli), and a succession of sinister eccentrics as he seeks the "third man" at the scene of Lime's fatal accident. Harry turns out to have faked his own death in order to evade a military policeman (Trevor Howard) and is still peddling black market penicillin. Will Holly join his old friend, a twinkling boyish Mephistopheles, or will he help book him?

A rare British film that is as accomplished technically as the best of classic Hollywood, this is a cracking mix of political thriller, weird romance, gothic mystery, and black-and-white poetry; Anton Karas's unforgettable zither theme was a chart hit. The film's most famous speech (the "cuckoo clock" anecdote) was written by Welles on the spur of the moment as an addition to Greene's script to fill out the character. It is a perfectly acted film, with wonderful work from Cotten (whose own history with Welles informs their scenes together) as the bewildered, disillusioned protagonist. **KN**

KEY SCENES

1 THE BOOK CLUB
Holly addresses a literary group who do not realize that he writes Westerns. The event does not go well. The panel assumes he is joking when he cites Zane Grey as his greatest influence, and Holly struggles to give his thoughts on James Joyce.

2 THE RESURRECTION OF HARRY LIME
A cat nestles against familiar legs in a doorway. An overhead light comes on. Holly catches sight of Harry Lime, alive after all, flashing a mischievous, almost flirtatious look as his theme strikes up. One of cinema's greatest villainous charmers makes his entrance.

3 THE CUCKOO CLOCK SPEECH
The two friends are reunited and, in one of cinema's best-known speeches, Harry outlines his view of the world. His conclusion? "In Switzerland they had five hundred years of democracy and peace, and what did that produce? The cuckoo clock."

4 CHASE BENEATH THE CITY
Harry is pursued through the sewers of Vienna, and finally trapped and killed. The scenes were shot in two locations: on site in the Viennese sewer system and at Shepperton Studios, England. Welles's late arrival in Vienna forced Reed to use body doubles for him.

5 AT THE FUNERAL
With neat symmetry, the film both opens and closes with a funeral for Harry, although only the closing ceremony is genuine. Holly waits after the funeral to speak with Anna but she refuses to acknowledge him, shunning the man who betrayed Harry Lime.

DIRECTOR PROFILE

1906–32
Carol Reed was born in 1906. He started out in theater before working on film adaptations. He acted in *The Flying Squad* (1929).

1933–46
Reed became a leading British film director with *Bank Holiday* (1938), *The Stars Look Down* and *Night Train to Munich* (both 1940), *Kipps* (1941), *The Young Mr. Pitt* (1942), and *The Way Ahead* (1944).

1947–61
The Fallen Idol (1948) and *The Third Man* teamed Reed with Graham Greene. They reunited for *Our Man in Havana* (1959), a return to form for the director.

1962–76
After quitting *Mutiny on the Bounty* (1962), Reed made two "big" films—*The Agony and the Ecstasy* (1965) and the Oscar-winning *Oliver!* (1968)—but wound down with two "small" ones, *The Last Warrior* (1970) and *Follow Me!* (1972).

ITALIAN NEO-REALISM

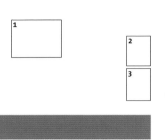

1 Clara Calamai and Massimo Girotti
  as doomed lovers in Luchino Visconti's
  shocking tale of lust, *Ossessione*.

2 Roberto Rossellini's *Germania anno
  zero* tells the tragic story of a young
  boy attempting to survive in postwar
  Berlin. It shows that although the war
  was over, its effects were still felt
  by survivors.

3 An Italian poster for *Stromboli* starring
  Ingrid Bergman emphasizes the
  harshness of the life her character
  encounters when she goes to live
  on the volcanic island.

The term "Neo-Realism" was first coined by Italian critics in the early 1940s. Screenwriter Cesare Zavattini was one of the key writers of the Neo-Realist movement and one of its main theorists. He called on filmmakers to take to the streets, get onto buses and trams and to "steal" their stories from the everyday, writing in his wartime diary, *Sequences from a Cinematic Life*: "Set up a camera in the street, in a room, see with insatiable patience, train ourselves in the contemplation of our fellow man in his elementary actions." Zavattini went on to script such films as *Ladri di biciclette* (*The Bicycle Thief*, 1948, see p. 182), *Umberto D.* (1952), and *Miracolo a Milano* (*Miracle In Milan*, 1951) all of which focus on the hardships ordinary people encounter in contemporary Italy. Italian cinema of the Neo-Realist period is full of stories of people trying to solve everyday problems. This was a reaction to the style of the *Telefono Bianco* (White Telephone) movies of the 1930s that emulated Hollywood films and focused on bourgeois society. Neo-Realist films often used nonprofessional actors and were filmed on location in poor areas, depicting people performing mundane daily activities, with the emphasis on gritty realism and a sense of rough energy.

Ossessione (1943, above), directed by Luchino Visconti (1906–76), is sometimes cited as the first Neo-Realist film, although it is a movie with strong noirish elements. Its screenplay is based on James M. Cain's crime novel *The Postman Always Rings Twice* (1934). Visconti worked on it with fellow writers and filmmakers from the magazine *Cinema*, among them Giuseppe De Santis.

KEY EVENTS

1940	1942	1943	1944	1945	1947
Federico Fellini (1920–93) begins working as a screenwriter in Rome.	De Sica collaborates with Zavattini for the first time on the screenplay for *I bambini ci guardano* (*The Children Are Watching Us*, 1944).	Regarded as one of the first Neo-Realist films, *Ossessione* falls foul of censors in Fascist Italy, who destroy the film's negative, but Visconti saves a print.	Federico Fellini meets Roberto Rossellini, who enlists him to provide dialogue for *Roma, città aperta*.	Roberto Rossellini makes the first film in his trilogy about the war, *Roma, città aperta*.	Michelangelo Antonioni (1912–2007) cowrites the screenplay for De Santis's *Caccia tragica*, about an agricultural co-op.

It is a seamy tale set in provincial Italy about a tramp who has an affair with the wife of a restaurant owner; the lovers plot to kill the husband. Visconti faced censorship problems with the film, which was banned in Fascist Italy.

Neo-Realist protagonists range from the very young to the very old. *Umberto D.*, directed by Vittorio De Sica (1902–74) is about an elderly man (Carlo Battisti) reduced to poverty but clinging desperately to his dignity. He potters around Rome with his one loyal companion, his dog. By contrast, children have prominent roles in *Ladri di biciclette* and *Miracolo a Milano*. However, Neo-Realist directors did not always take a documentary-style approach to material. For example, De Sica's *Miracolo a Milano*, concerning a homeless group living in a shanty town on the outskirts of postwar Milan, might well be described as "magical realist." Alongside its digs at greedy landowners and venal squatters, the film has a strong fantasy element. Nor did all Neo-Realist films use nonprofessional actors. *Roma, città aperta* (*Rome, Open City*, 1945, see p. 180), by Roberto Rossellini (1906–77), features Anna Magnani, one of Italian cinema's biggest postwar stars, and the actor, writer, and director Aldo Fabrizi (1905–90).

Roma, città aperta won the Grand Prix at the Cannes Film Festival and had an immediate impact. Movie myth suggests that the director made it with "short ends"—scraps of film stock given to him by camera-wielding US soldiers who had liberated Rome in World War II. His shooting style was determined by the constraints under which he was working. Scenes were shot rapidly with abrupt cutting. Rossellini was inspired by his own experiences hiding from Nazi patrols out to force young Italians into fighting for the Fascists. The idea that he made the movie without planning is exaggerated. Nonetheless, it has a roughness and energy that have come to be seen as Neo-Realist hallmarks.

Rossellini went on to make *Paisà* (1946), a sprawling war film about the end of the war in Italy. This was followed by the brutal *Germania anno zero* (*Germany Year Zero*, 1948, above right) set in rubble-strewn, burned-out Berlin and detailing the plight of a boy struggling to survive in the wake of the Nazi defeat. There is a big difference between the films in Rossellini's war trilogy and his work with Ingrid Bergman in *Stromboli* (1950, right). This is a strange and eerie story about a young Lithuanian emigrée who marries an Italian fisherman to escape a displaced person's camp at the end of the war. She goes to live with him on a remote island and finds herself bewildered and oppressed by the patriarchal society she encounters.

By the early 1950s, Neo-Realist cinema in Italy no longer had the urgency that characterized the movement in the immediate postwar years. Conditions had changed; Italian society was more affluent and filmmakers were less concerned about portraying those on the margins. Yet Neo-Realism's influence was wide, and Cinema Novo in Brazil, Free Cinema in Britain, the French Nouvelle Vague (see p. 248) and the *cinéma-vérité* movement in documentary were all indebted to the work of directors such as De Sica and Rossellini in the 1940s. **GM**

1948	1948	1949	1949	1950	1953
Luchino Visconti makes *La Terra Trema* (*The Earth Trembles*). Its style is close to what is defined today as Neo-Realism.	De Sica's *Ladri di biciclette* (see p. 182) is released. It is regarded as a Neo-Realist classic and wins an Honorary Academy Award in 1950.	De Santis makes Silvana Mangano a star and sex symbol when he casts her as a voluptuous peasant in the then-shocking *Riso amaro* (*Bitter Rice*).	The "Andreotti Law" offers subsidies to Italian filmmakers if their work meets with government approval and does not blemish Italy's image.	A married Bergman provokes a scandal by leaving Hollywood to star in Rossellini's *Stromboli* and subsequently begins an affair with him.	*I vitelloni*, Fellini's film about young delinquents stuck in a small town, is released and later wins the Silver Lion at the Venice Film Festival.

Roma, città aperta 1945
Rome, Open City   ROBERTO ROSSELLINI   1906 – 77

▲ After witnessing their priest's death, the boys return to Rome along the via Trianfole.

▼ A faceless Fascist bears down on Don Pietro and Pina in the emotive poster.

Roberto Rossellini took a famously improvisatory approach to *Roma, città aperta*, shot on the streets of newly liberated Rome. Much of the material was shot silent, with sound elements added later. The editing is brisk, because the director had no spare film. "Usually the film ran out before the scene was over," griped Aldo Fabrizi, who played a priest in the anti-Nazi Resistance.

The director drew on his own experiences hiding from Nazi patrols looking for young Italians to force into fighting for the Fascists. He originally planned to make a documentary; when he turned to fiction, it was with a documentarist's eye. "I try to capture reality," he once said, "nothing else." The torture scenes seem oddly topical in today's era of Guantánamo and Abu Ghraib. We see a Resistance fighter flayed, whipped, and burned as Don Pietro (Fabrizi) sits next door.

As critics have pointed out, *Roma, città aperta* is not the straightforward Neo-Realist movie it first appears to be. Alongside the newsreel-style footage, there are elements that would not be out of place in a Hollywood melodrama. There is a courageous housewife (Anna Magnani) who seems like an Italian Mrs. Miniver, heroic street children, and a priest with a strong resemblance to Father Brown. In one chilling scene, the young actress who betrayed the Resistance faints when she realizes the suffering she has caused. She has been bribed with a fur coat. As she collapses, it is taken from her to coax someone else into betrayal. No one could film a death scene better than Rossellini: the shooting of Magnani as she runs down a street and the execution of the priest in front of a crowd of children are staged with maximum pathos and drama. **GM**

1 A ROOFTOP ESCAPE
As German soldiers beat at the door, Resistance fighter Giorgio Manfredi (Marcello Pagliero) escapes across the roofs. This may be a Neo-Realist film dealing with the Nazi occupation of Rome, but for a moment Giorgio looks as dashing as a Douglas Fairbanks hero.

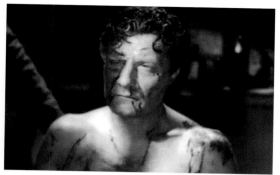

4 THE TORTURE SCENE
The priest Don Pietro Pellegrini sits helplessly as he hears the terrible cries of the tortured Resistance fighter Giorgio in the next room. A few minutes later, viewers see the fighter's bloodied and scarred body.

2 THE RAID ON THE APARTMENT BLOCK
A Nazi patrol orders all the occupants of an apartment block, including those who are sick, to assemble outside in the courtyard. Don Pietro arrives just in time to conceal weapons belonging to the Resistance under an old man's bed.

5 THE SHOOTING OF THE PRIEST
A group of boys look on, grief-stricken and horrified, as their beloved priest is shot by the Nazis. To show solidarity, and give him courage in his final moments, they whistle to him. Afterward, in the film's understated but hopeful closing shot, they walk back to the city.

◷ DIRECTOR PROFILE

1906–53

Roberto Rossellini was born in Rome. His father was an architect who reportedly built the city's first cinema. Having worked as a movie technician, and directed documentaries, in 1942 Rossellini made his first feature, *La nave bianca* (*The White Ship*). He also shot covert footage of anti-Fascist Resistance fighters. His famed "war trilogy" began with *Roma, città aperta*, continuing with *Paisà* (1946) and *Germania anno zero* (*Germany Year Zero*, 1948).

1954–77

Viaggio in Italia (*Voyage to Italy*, 1954), starring his then wife Ingrid Bergman, was not a box-office hit at the time, but is now widely regarded as his masterpiece. *La prise de pouvoir de Louis XIV* (*The Rise to Power of Louis XIV*, 1966) was one of a series of biopics of notable historical figures that Rossellini made. He died of a heart attack at seventy-one. His last film was *Il messia* (*The Messiah*, 1975).

3 THE SHOOTING OF PINA
When her fiancé Francesco is rounded up by the Nazis and taken away in a truck, Pina (Magnani) runs after him. In footage that looks as though it has been taken directly from a newsreel, she is shot dead on the road. Her devastated son throws himself on her body.

Ladri di biciclette 1948
The Bicycle Thief   VITTORIO DE SICA   1902 – 74

▲ Nonactors Maggiorani and Staiola gave touching but unsentimental performances.

▼ A poignant poster for the film that picked up an Honorary Oscar in 1950.

If the measure of a film is the admiration it elicits, Vittorio De Sica's *Ladri di biciclette* must be of the highest rank. Directors from René Clair (1898–1981) and Jacques Becker (1906–60) to Robert Bresson (1901–99) rhapsodized about De Sica's Neo-Realist fable and its simplicity. An unemployed man (Lamberto Maggiorani) in postwar Rome is offered a job sticking up posters—on condition that he has a bicycle. He procures one, but when it is stolen, his life threatens to unravel. De Sica and his screenwriters realized the immense drama that can be present in an everyday story. The struggles of Antonio and his son as they try to recover the bicycle prove no less absorbing than those of a hero in an action movie. A crowded city makes as dramatic a backdrop as a battlefield.

The director pitched the film to Hollywood producer David O. Selznick, who proposed Cary Grant to play the unemployed man; De Sica countered that Henry Fonda might be a better choice. In the end, De Sica cast Maggiorani, "a simple workman of Breda who left his work for two months to lend his face to me." Whatever his lack of experience, the actor was strikingly handsome and dapper.

Certain sequences are highly stylized. When Antonio is looking for his missing bicycle, De Sica throws in shots of bike after bike. There is something nightmarish about his quest—as if the whole city is against him. De Sica also captures much of the natural drama of the streets. The child (Enzo Staiola) is not a doe-eyed, dimple-chinned Disney infant; Staiola was the son of refugees and has a toughness and resourcefulness about him. This, though, only adds to the pathos. As De Sica put it, "He is the most lovable child in the world." **GM**

👁 KEY SCENES

1 THE THEFT OF THE BICYCLE
Antonio (Maggiorani) is on a ladder sticking up a poster when a young delinquent in a military cap makes off with his bicycle. He gives pursuit but it is already too late. Antonio's bicycle has disappeared and, with it, his livelihood.

4 THE VICTIM TURNS THIEF
With all his other options exhausted, Antonio tries to steal a bicycle himself. Inevitably, however, he is caught. His distraught son picks up his hat. On seeing the child, the bicycle's owner relents and decides not to press charges. Antonio and Bruno return home.

2 A SIMPLE MEAL
The father may be broke but he still takes his son, Bruno (Staiola), for a pizza. For a few moments, at least, they can forget their plight. Bruno spots a family feasting on pasta. "To eat like that you need a million lira a month at least," his dejected father tells him.

🕐 DIRECTOR PROFILE

1902–45
Vittorio De Sica was born in Sora, near Rome. He became a leading actor in Italian silent movies; his acting work ran in parallel with his directing throughout his career. *Maddalena, zero in condotta* (1940) was his first solo outing as a director. His fourth, *I bambini ci guardano* (*The Children Are Watching Us*, 1944), marked his first collaboration with the great screenwriter Cesare Zavattini. Together, they were key figures in the emergence of Neo-Realism, taking the camera away from the "papier-mâché" of the studio and "into life."

1946–50
He made *Sciuscià* (*Shoeshine*) in 1946. De Sica often featured children as protagonists. Here, he told the story of two kids eking out an existence on the streets of Rome by shining shoes; they get into trouble when they try to buy a horse. *Ladri di biciclette*, De Sica's best-known film, received an extraordinarily warm response worldwide and, in 1950, won a special Oscar.

1951–52
In *Miracolo a Milano* (*Miracle in Milan*, 1951) De Sica and Zavattini pushed at the limits of Neo-Realism with a film that, for all its strong political undertone, also has fantasy elements. *Umberto D.* (1952) is a moving film about an impoverished old man trying to survive (and maintain his dignity) in postwar Italy.

1953–64
In his Neo-Realist prime, De Sica often worked with unknown actors. However, in the Oscar-nominated romantic comedy *Matrimonio all'italiana* (*Marriage Italian Style*, 1964) his collaborators were two of Italian cinema's biggest stars— Marcello Mastroianni and Sophia Loren.

1965–74
Il giardino dei Finzi Contini (*The Garden of the Finzi-Continis*, 1970), a Golden Bear winner at the Berlin Film Festival and an Oscar winner too, explored the impact of Fascism and anti-Semitism on a wealthy Jewish family in late 1930s Italy. De Sica died in Neuilly-sur-Seine, France, in 1974.

3 MAKING THE ACCUSATION
Antonio spots the man he is sure stole his bicycle. He accuses him on a crowded street but the man collapses and the crowd turns against Antonio instead. He has no real evidence of the man's guilt, so the police advise him to drop the matter.

POSTWAR BRITISH CINEMA

1 Martin Scorsese (b. 1942) has often praised *The Red Shoes*, which he says "weaves a mystery of creativity and obsession."

2 Richard Attenborough is Pinkie in *Brighton Rock*, directed by John Boulting (1913–85). A remake of the film released in 2011 transports the setting to the swinging sixties.

3 Peter Cushing takes on a rare villainous role in *The Curse of Frankenstein*.

The British film industry emerged from World War II with confidence. Cinema attendances peaked in 1945 and remained above their prewar levels for the next decade. And the quality of British films—hitherto regarded as lacking either the artistic value of European (particularly French) cinema or the populist appeal of Hollywood—was recognized as having hit a new level of cultural maturity. Many of the new talents who had emerged during the war years reached their peak in the postwar period. After collaborating with Noël Coward (1899–1973) on *In Which We Serve* (1942), *This Happy Breed* (1944), and *Brief Encounter* (1945, see p. 186), David Lean (1908–91) made two moody and expressionist Dickensian adaptations—*Great Expectations* (1946) and *Oliver Twist* (1948). Carol Reed (1906–76) emerged as a major filmmaker with *Odd Man Out* (1947), *The Fallen Idol* (1948), and *The Third Man* (1949, see p. 176)—the last two marking a fruitful collaboration with novelist Graham Greene, whose *Brighton Rock* (opposite above) was filmed in 1947. The Anglo-Hungarian team of Michael Powell (1905–90) and Emeric Pressburger (1902–88) extended their wartime collaboration on films such as *The Life and Death of Colonel Blimp* (1943) into a cycle of Technicolor fantasies that included the charming *A Matter of Life and Death* (1946), the exotic melodrama *Black Narcissus* (1947), and the bravura dance spectacle *The Red Shoes* (1948, above). Most of these films were produced by the J. Arthur Rank Organization, which

(see p. 186)

KEY EVENTS

1946	1948	1948	1949	1950	1951
A Matter of Life and Death is chosen as the first Royal Film Performance.	*Odd Man Out* is voted Best British Film by the British Film Academy, the first of three consecutive wins for Carol Reed.	The Laurence Olivier adaptation of *Hamlet* wins Academy Awards for Best Actor and Best Picture.	A trio of classic Ealing comedies—*Passport to Pimlico*, *Whisky Galore!* and *Kind Hearts and Coronets* (see p. 188)— is released.	Ealing's *The Blue Lamp* introduces (and kills off) the character of George Dixon. He is resurrected for the BBC TV series *Dixon of Dock Green* (1955–76).	The British Board of Film Censors introduces the "X" certificate (which prohibits exhibition viewers under sixteen years old).

emerged during the war as the dominant producer-distributor in Britain. Rank, at this time, was prepared to take economic and aesthetic risks in order to bring prestige to the British film industry: David Lean averred that under Rank's aegis filmmakers "can make any subject we wish, with as much money as we think that subject should have spent on it." Several British hit films, notably *The Red Shoes* and the Laurence Olivier (1907–89) production of *Hamlet* in 1948, also succeeded in the United States. This propelled the British film industry into one of its periodic attempts to compete with Hollywood on its own terms. Unfortunately, for every major success there was an even bigger flop, such as *Caesar and Cleopatra* (1945) and *Bonnie Prince Charlie* (1948).

The failure of Rank's attempt to rival Hollywood brought about a policy of economic retrenchment and a more conservative approach to filmmaking in the 1950s. Postwar British cinema came to be recognized not so much for its auteurs as for its genres. Gainsborough Pictures had already shown that low-budget production based on popular genres could reap rewards in the home market with its costume melodramas *The Wicked Lady* (1945), *Caravan* (1946), and *The Magic Bow* (1946); *The Wicked Lady* became the most popular British film of the 1940s. It was Ealing Studios, however, that most caught the postwar zeitgeist with its cycle of acclaimed comedies, including *Passport to Pimlico* (1949), *Whisky Galore!* (1949), *Kind Hearts and Coronets* (1949, see p. 188), *The Lavender Hill Mob* (1951), and *The Man in the White Suit* (1951). These are evocative of the films of Frank Capra (1897–1991) in taking the side of the "little man" in his fight against the system, although the Ealing films focus on the community rather than the individual. Their quirky, eccentric characters and whimsical stories were the fulfillment of studio head Michael Balcon's belief in a genuinely British cinema that did not need to compete with Hollywood.

In the 1950s British cinema became culturally and aesthetically more conservative. The biggest hits of the decade were either middle-class comedies such as the "Doctor" films—beginning with *Doctor in the House* in 1954—or war films shot in a sober semidocumentary style, such as *The Cruel Sea* (1953) and *The Dam Busters* (1955). Ealing declined as a creative force, its last film of note being the black comedy *The Ladykillers* (1955). As cinema attendances declined from the mid-1950s producers had to find new formulas. Hammer Film Productions, a small independent studio, recognized the potential of exploitation fare with *The Quatermass Xperiment* (1955) and horror with *The Curse of Frankenstein* (1957, right). This first classic "Hammer horror" features groundbreaking use of bright, scarlet blood. Both films embraced the recently introduced "X" certificate. Away from such gleefully morbid entertainment, adult themes were explored in a variety of modes throughout the 1950s and into the 1960s: juvenile delinquency (*Cosh Boy*, 1953), sexual perversion (*Peeping Tom*, 1960), and homosexuality (*Victim*, 1961). All this helped to pave the way for the emergence of the British New Wave (see p. 258). **JC**

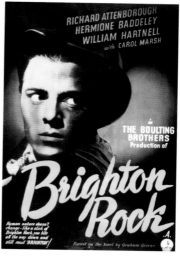

1953	1955	1956	1957	1958	1960
The coronation of Queen Elizabeth II is commemorated in *A Queen Is Crowned*.	*The Dam Busters*, the most successful British film of the 1950s, is released.	John Osborne's *Look Back in Anger* is performed at the Royal Court Theatre.	The first British horror film shot in color—Hammer's *The Curse of Frankenstein*—is released.	The first "Carry On" film, *Carry On Sergeant*, appears. David Lean's *The Bridge on the River Kwai* wins seven Academy Awards including Best Picture.	Total cinema admissions in Britain fall to 500 million: this is less than half the level of only four years previously.

Brief Encounter 1945
DAVID LEAN 1908 – 91

▲ Behind their formal restraint, Laura and Alec share moments of great tenderness.

▼ The poster with the key railway station.

The finest of the four Noël Coward adaptations that launched David Lean's directorial career is often praised (and almost as often mocked) as the classic cinematic statement of British emotional repression. Shot in the final months of World War II (although the war is never even obliquely referred to), *Brief Encounter* can seem hopelessly dated: not only for its flat, upper-middle-class vowels, but also for the idea that two people who are passionately attracted to one other should hesitate (let alone agonize with guilt) before falling into bed together. Yet in terms of its period, the film is ruthlessly accurate: this is how people of this time and social class would have behaved.

For all its tormented self-denial, this is a film about passion and the violence of passion—the way it can rip into placid ordinary lives and lacerate them. "I didn't think such violent things could happen to ordinary people," muses Laura Jesson (Celia Johnson) in her retrospective voice-over that carries the film, the anguished monologue she mentally addresses to her kindly, dull husband but can never utter out loud. Trevor Howard is convincing as the doctor she falls for but it is Johnson's voice that guides the audience through the film, and the subtlety of her acting is supreme. At one point she sits at her dressing table, smilingly talking to her husband; then as he turns away she sees herself in the mirror and her face registers the realization that, for the first time ever, she has lied to him—and that the lie has torn her world apart. Rachmaninov's bittersweet Piano Concerto no. 2, thundering and yearning on the soundtrack, provides the ideal emotional counterpoint. **PK**

1 FIRST MEETING
In the station café at Milford Junction, Laura Jesson (Celia Johnson) encounters Dr. Alec Harvey (Trevor Howard) when he removes grit from her eye. The unglamorous railway station provides the backdrop to nearly all of the pair's meetings over the next seven weeks.

2 "YOU KNOW WHAT'S HAPPENED, DON'T YOU?"
In a boathouse after a minor boating mishap, Laura and Alec begin to acknowledge openly their feelings for each other. The gloomy mood of the settings of all their meetings mirrors the doomed nature of their unfulfilled relationship.

3 SUICIDAL THOUGHTS
After saying good-bye to Alec forever, an emotionally fraught Laura considers throwing herself under a train. This scene marks the peak of the melodrama. Alec represented passionate love and an escape from humdrum life, but Laura chooses convention over romance.

4 "THANK YOU FOR COMING BACK TO ME"
Laura's husband Fred (Cyril Raymond) tactfully intimates he has some inkling of what has been happening. Laura briefly rebelled against the limitations of her ordinary life, but in the end sticks with it. She behaves with the restraint typical of women of her era.

DIRECTOR PROFILE

1908–41

David Lean was born in Croydon, south London, to strict Quaker parents who forbade him to attend the cinema. As a teenager he watched films secretly and was captivated. In 1928, despite parental disapproval, he became a teaboy at the Gaumont-British studios in London, and worked his way up from clapper boy to senior editor. He edited films by Anthony Asquith (1902–68), such as *Pygmalion* (1938), and Michael Powell and Emeric Pressburger, such as *49th Parallel* (1941).

1942–54

In 1942 Noël Coward gave Lean the opportunity to co-direct the naval war drama *In Which We Serve*. Lean directed three more adaptations of Coward's plays—*This Happy Breed* (1944), *Blithe Spirit* (1945), and *Brief Encounter*. He also directed two celebrated adaptations of Charles Dickens—*Great Expectations* (1946) and *Oliver Twist* (1948). The latter films starred Alec Guinness, whom Lean frequently cast. Lean became rated as one of Britain's foremost directors, but *The Passionate Friends* (1949) and *Madeleine* (1950), both starring his then-wife Ann Todd, were not well received. He cast Todd again in aviation drama *The Sound Barrier* (1952), and Charles Laughton in the classic Lancashire comedy *Hobson's Choice* (1954).

1955–91

Lean moved in a new direction in 1955 when he entered his international phase with Venice-set romance *Summer Madness*, which starred Katharine Hepburn as a middle-aged American who has a romance while on holiday in Venice. Five big-budget films—considered overblown and impersonal by some critics—rounded off his career: *The Bridge on the River Kwai* (1957), *Lawrence of Arabia* (1962), *Doctor Zhivago* (1965), *Ryan's Daughter* (1970), and *A Passage to India* (1984). During the final months of his life, Lean was in pre-production to make a film of Joseph Conrad's *Nostromo*, for which he had assembled an all-star cast, including Marlon Brando. He was six weeks away from starting filming when he died of throat cancer in 1991.

Kind Hearts and Coronets 1949

ROBERT HAMER 1911 – 63

▲ Mazzini: behind bars, but not yet defeated.

▼ The poster bears the telling tagline: "A hilarious study in the gentle art of murder."

A hilarious study in the gentle art of MURDER

Although categorized as an Ealing comedy, *Kind Hearts and Coronets* deviates startlingly from the typical format. Ealing comedies are cozy, even complacent, whereas Robert Hamer's darkly comic tale of a social-climbing serial killer is callous and amoral. The humor of Ealing comedy is good-natured and folksy, but *Kind Hearts and Coronets* is cool, ironic, and witty. Ealing comedy tends to move toward consensus, with opposing sides reaching a compromise for the general good, and sex is avoided or treated with embarrassed jocularity. However, *Kind Hearts and Coronets* thrives on confrontation and several scenes carry a potent erotic charge. In Ealing comedies the criminals pay for their crimes, while in the final reel of this classic film the calculating Louis Mazzini stands a good chance of getting off scot-free.

Ealing's maverick director, Robert Hamer, set out to make a film that "paid no regard whatever to established, although not practiced, moral convention, in which a whole family is picked off by a mass murderer." With his cowriter, John Dighton, Hamer brought sparkle to the dialogue, especially to the cool detachment of Louis's voice-over. Alec Guinness's depiction of the entire D'Ascoyne clan established him as a comic actor of rare versatility. He is matched by Dennis Price, whose Byronic Louis anchors the whole story, and by Joan Greenwood, who is toe-curlingly delicious as his purring, manipulative mistress, Sibella. In his short career, Hamer made some intriguingly offbeat films, although none of them approaches the sustained poise and Wildean wit of *Kind Hearts and Coronets*, the finest black comedy British cinema has yet produced. **PK**

👁 KEY SCENES

1 THE FIRST VICTIM
As the punt with his first D'Ascoyne victim and a girl he brought for an illicit weekend tips over the weir, Louis says, "I was sorry about the girl, but found some relief in the reflection that she had presumably during the weekend already undergone a fate worse than death."

3 THE DESCENT OF LADY AGATHA
Lady Agatha D'Ascoyne, a passionate suffragette, makes a balloon ascent to scatter pamphlets over London. Louis brings her down with a bow and arrow: "I shot an arrow in the air; she came to earth in Berkeley Square." The film is full of word play and literary references.

2 THE D'ASCOYNES ASSEMBLED
After his latest murder, Louis attends the funeral service and gets a chance to see all the D'Ascoynes who stand between him and the dukedom. Alec Guinness's tour-de-force portrayal of the entire family set him up as a first-rate comic actor.

4 LOUIS ON TRIAL
Through the treachery of his mistress, Sibella, Louis, having now succeeded to the dukedom, is tried for a murder he did not commit—that of Sibella's husband, Lionel. The film's morally ambiguous ending caused US censors to request changes.

PAGE TO SCREEN

Kind Hearts and Coronets was based on the novel *Israel Rank: The Autobiography of a Criminal,* by Roy Horniman, which was originally published in 1907. The book is light, witty, and entertaining, written in an aphoristic sub-Wildean style. Above all—and this is undoubtedly what appealed most to director Robert Hamer—it expresses an amused disdain for conventional morality. Horniman's hero is half-Jewish (his Jewish father having married a daughter of the aristocratic Gascoyne family), and the author pokes quiet fun at the casual racism of Edwardian England. Following so soon after World War II, a comedy about a Jewish serial killer would scarcely have been acceptable, and therefore in the film version the character of Israel Rank became the half-Italian Louis Mazzini. *Kind Hearts and Coronets* retains the essential plot of the novel, as well as most of its characters, and for once a filmed adaptation improves enormously on the original book. The plotting is more varied and inventive—and whereas in the book Israel is arrested for the bungled murder of his final victim, Earl Gascoyne, the film introduces the delicious irony of having Louis convicted for the one murder he did not commit.

FRENCH CINEMA

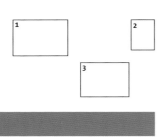

1 Simone Signoret and Anton Walbrook
in *La ronde*. The source drama, *Reigen*,
inspired David Hare's play *The Blue Room*.

2 Edith Scob, in a human mask, dominates
the poster for Georges Franju's dark
cult movie *Les yeux sans visage*.

3 Murder in mind. Véra Clouzot stars
as Christina in *Les diaboliques*. *Psycho*
author Robert Bloch declared it his
favorite horror film.

The 1950s was a period of convulsion in the French film industry, with
an Oedipal struggle between a new generation of filmmakers and their
forebears. The standard-bearer for change was François Truffaut (1932–84),
writing in *Cahiers du cinéma*, the magazine launched in April 1951 by film critics
André Bazin, Jacques Doniol-Valcroze, and Joseph-Marie Lo Duca. Truffaut read the
early editions of *Cahiers* in military prison in early 1952. By 1953 he was writing
for the magazine. In 1954 he contributed an invitation to storm the barricades.
"A Certain Tendency in French Cinema" was a polemical broadside against what
he dismissed as "le cinéma de papa." The young critic railed at filmmakers who
specialized in tasteful literary adaptations. There was more to his revolt than
dismay at the hidebound style of moviemaking he considered epitomized by the
work of Jean Aurenche and Pierre Bost, the era's leading screenwriting team, and
of directors such as Claude Autant-Lara (1901–2000) and Yves Allégret (1907–87).
"A great many of the producers of the time had collaborated with the Germans
during the war," filmmaker Marcel Ophüls (b.1927) later noted of Truffaut's essay,
"and so there were all sorts of reasons to try to eliminate their stranglehold
and, incidentally, the stranglehold of the unions on French filmmaking."

Truffaut extolled US B movies at the expense of stolid "quality" French
filmmaking. He argued passionately for a more personal style of filmmaking,
one in which directors would take risks and leave their thumbprints on their
work. This was the creed known as "la politique des auteurs."

KEY EVENTS

1951	1952	1953	1953	1954	1955
Bresson's *Journal d'un curé de campagne* is the first of three 1950s classics, with *Un condamné à mort s'est échappé* (1956) and *Pickpocket* (1959).	Rene Clément's *Jeux interdits* wins the Golden Lion at the Venice Film Festival.	*Le salaire de la peur* (see p. 196) wins the Palme d'Or at the Cannes Film Festival and the Golden Bear at the Berlin Film Festival.	A new French state film fund is created, with the requirement that films it backs should have a certain artistic quality.	"A Certain Tendency in French Cinema," François Truffaut's polemic against the old guard, appears in *Cahiers du cinéma*.	*Du rififi chez les hommes*, Jules Dassin's heist movie, marks the beginnings of a new spate of French crime films.

However, French cinema of the 1950s boasts many films that counter the image of the decade as staid and middlebrow. *Le salaire de la peur* (*The Wages of Fear*, 1953, see p. 196), by Henri-Georges Clouzot (1907–77), about truck drivers negotiating potholed South American roads with a cargo of nitroglycerine, was riveting and sweaty action fare. His *Les diaboliques* (*The Fiends*, 1955, below) was a supremely creepy thriller with a plot secreting more twists than a sackload of corkscrews. It was based on a novel by cult writers Pierre Boileau and Thomas Narcejac, who also furnished the story for *Vertigo* (1958) by Alfred Hitchcock (1899–1980) and the screenplay for the surrealistic horror thriller *Les yeux sans visage* (*Eyes Without a Face*, 1960, right) by Georges Franju (1912–87). Elsewhere, Max Ophüls's Vienna-set (but French-made) Schnitzler adaptation *La ronde* (1950, opposite) was a stagy, sophisticated, and caustic account of the love lives of a group of characters who are ultimately all interlinked.

In truth, 1950s French cinema was far richer and more complex than Truffaut's polemics suggested. This was not simply a decade in which a group of young cinephiles watched Alfred Hitchcock and Howard Hawks (1896–1977) movies at the Cinémathèque, sneered at the older generation, then went on to launch their own filmmaking careers. Established directors such as Clouzot, Franju, Ophüls, Jean Renoir (1894–1979), René Clair (1898–1981), Robert Bresson (1901–99), Jacques Becker (1906–60), Jacques Tati (1907–82), and René Clément (1913–96) all made major films during what proved to be a transitional decade for French film history.

1956	1957	1958	1959	1959	1960
Brigitte Bardot becomes a star after her appearance in *Et dieu... créa la femme* (*...And God Created Woman*), directed by Roger Vadim (1928–2000).	Box-office records are broken, with 400 million visitors to French cinemas.	François Truffaut is banned from Cannes Film Festival for his attacks on the event.	François Truffaut wins the directing prize at Cannes Film Festival for *Les quatre cents coups* (*The 400 Blows*, see p. 252).	The first full-length film by Alain Resnais (b. 1922), *Hiroshima, mon amour* (*Hiroshima, My Love*), is released.	Godard's *A bout de souffle* (*Breathless*, see p. 254), *Le petit soldat*, and Truffaut's *Tirez sur le pianiste* (*Shoot the Piano Player*) are released.

Even before Truffaut, Jean-Luc Godard (b. 1930) and his *Cahiers* colleagues began to make their first features toward the end of the decade. Other directors were already chafing against the older generation. The debut feature from Agnès Varda (b. 1928), *La pointe courte* (which she described as "a bomb of nonconformity"), premiered in 1955. The twenty-five-year-old director, drawing inspiration from Brecht and from William Faulkner's Modernist novel *Wild Palms*, told two separate stories side by side—one about a couple with marital difficulties, the other about fishermen fighting for their rights. Unconventionally funded (the technicians and actors formed a co-op) and shot on a tiny budget, *La pointe courte* failed to make an impact at the box office but it showed a young filmmaker a long way removed from the "tradition of quality" that Truffaut so abhorred.

It is also a moot point whether the prolific and versatile Aurenche and Bost were quite such conventional writers as Truffaut had implied. "Truffaut misfired . . . . He should have attacked the directors, not the screenwriters," Bertrand Tavernier later wrote, defending the duo. "He missed the target. By attacking Aurenche, he attacked the person who was closest to the new wave—the person who was ready to experiment and was the most open." Tavernier enlisted Aurenche as screenwriter on several of his films of the 1970s, among them *L'horloger de St Paul* (*The Watchmaker of St. Paul*, 1974).

French cinema of the 1950s was in many ways characterized by its great technical masters, such as René Clément. His feature *Jeux interdits* (*Forbidden Games*, 1952), about two children using fantasy to cope with trauma and death during World War II, was attacked by some as mawkish but won a Golden Lion in Venice and an Oscar for Best Foreign Language film. Clément had worked with Jean Cocteau (1889–1963) on *La belle et la bête* (*Beauty and the Beast*, 1946) and directed a fine Resistance film, *La bataille du rail* (*The Battle of the Rails*, 1946), but it was his misfortune to be tarred as a "quality" filmmaker. Claude Autant-Lara suffered likewise. His best-known films of the decade included caustic comedy *L'auberge rouge* (*The Red Inn*, 1951) and an adaptation of Stendhal's *Le rouge et le noir* (*The Red and the Black*, 1954). Whatever harm Truffaut did to his reputation, it was nothing to the opprobrium Autant-Lara brought on himself with his forays late in life into right-wing politics and support of the National Front.

Following his return to Europe from Hollywood, Max Ophüls revisited thoroughly French concerns in a number of period films made in the 1950s. *Le plaisir* (1952) was adapted from three short stories by Guy de Maupassant.

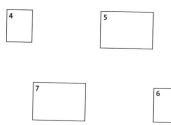

The mood of *Madame de...* (1953), set in Paris at the turn of the century and hinging on missing earrings and infidelity, is summed up when a man notes that his marriage is "only superficially superficial." The settings may be high-society drawing rooms and ballrooms but the suffering of the characters is very real.

After nearly fifteen years abroad Jean Renoir returned to his native country to make *French Cancan* (1954), set in Belle Epoque Montmartre. Like most of his later films it is lively and colorful but lacks the bite of his prewar work. Jacques Becker, an ex-colleague of Renoir, was well regarded by the *Cahiers* critics. His finest film was *Casque d'or* (*Golden Marie*, 1952, see p. 194), a richly romantic evocation of the Parisian underworld of the 1890s. Almost its equal was the crime movie *Touchez pas au grisbi* (*Honor Among Thieves*, 1954), which reinvigorated Jean Gabin's screen career. This film's influence on the postwar French crime film was wide—it can be seen in the cool minimalism of *Du rififi chez les hommes* (*Rififi*, 1955, opposite above) by Jules Dassin (1911–2008), a heist movie shot on location with a wonderfully laconic narrative style and a celebrated wordless safe-cracking sequence that runs for almost half an hour. A similarly downbeat mood pervaded *Bob le flambeur* (1956, opposite below) by Jean-Pierre Melville (1917–73), about an ageing gangster who plots to rob a casino. The French approach to Film Noir (see p. 168) had a melancholy lyricism that would influence later US crime movies.

With its plangent music and imagery of seaside pursuits, Jacques Tati's wryly escapist *Les vacances de M. Hulot* (*Monsieur Hulot's Holiday*, 1953, right) is a celebration of the French at leisure. In its gentle, slow-burning way, it is very funny. Nobody plays tennis quite like Tati. At the same time, there is an undertow of melancholy: Hulot is an incongruous figure who can never quite fit in. With its famous scene of travelers rushing between platforms to catch a train, the film also hints at the turmoil that goes hand in hand with leisure.

Robert Bresson, another director feted by the *Cahiers* gang, created an existential masterpiece in *Un condamné à mort s'est échappé* (*A Man Escaped*, 1956, above) about a French Resistance fighter imprisoned by the Nazis who spends his every moment plotting to escape. Truffaut greatly admired its lean, pared-down style. As he wrote, this was "one of those films which can be said not to contain a single useless shot or a scene that could be cut or shortened. It's the very opposite of those films that seem like a montage, a collection of images." As his remarks attest, French cinema of the 1950s was not quite as ossified as he himself had suggested in his notorious *Cahiers* broadside. **GM**

4 Time for a robbery? Jean Servais glowers in the poster for Jules Dassin's movie released in 1955.

5 French Resistance fighter Fontaine (François Leterrier, center left) in *Un condamné à mort s'est echappé*. The film was based on the real-life wartime experiences of André Devigny.

6 Service with a smile: the poster for Jacques Tati's (Oscar-nominated) debut as Monsieur Hulot.

7 Isabelle Corey exudes doe-eyed charm in gangster flick *Bob le flambeur*.

Casque d'or 1952
Golden Marie   JACQUES BECKER 1906 – 60

▲ Simone Signoret's ripe sensuality glows from the screen in *Casque d'or*. She won a British Academy Award for her performance.

▼ The central character Marie is known as "Casque d'Or" for her golden hair.

Jacques Becker was determined that *Casque d'or* should not be, in any conventional sense, a period film. "I wanted my actors to behave as though they were living at the period of the film," he explained, "not as if they were wearing costumes." His re-creation of Paris at the turn of the century is lovingly detailed and exact, and within it his cast move, speak, and hold themselves credibly as in their native habitat. Every character, no matter how briefly glimpsed, is precisely characterized, giving viewers the sense that—as Becker put it—they "go on living off-screen, between scenes, even before the film starts." This is a world seen whole, neither romanticized nor sensationalized, but presented as a complex, living community in its own right.

At the center of this world are the doomed lovers, Marie and Manda. Becker was a consummate director of actors, subtle, considerate, and responsive, and he drew from Simone Signoret and Serge Reggiani the performances of their careers. The chemistry between them is palpable—Reggiani tender and tenacious beneath an appearance of frail taciturnity, Signoret at once self-assured and vulnerable. Most of the film's action takes place in the streets and smoky estaminets of Paris but midway through the film Becker grants his lovers a brief riverine idyll, during which some of their most tender scenes take place.

The film was received coolly in France on its release but was later admired by future exponents of the Nouvelle Vague (see p. 248) for the way it evoked the past with (in the words of François Truffaut) "tenderness and violence." Tenderness and violence—Becker's masterpiece summed up in a phrase. **PK**

👁 KEY SCENES

1 MANDA MEETS MARIE
At a riverside café near Belle Epoque Paris, Manda, a reformed criminal turned carpenter, encounters Marie, a gangster's moll. The attraction between them is immediate. He asks her to dance, arousing the jealousy of her boyfriend, Roland (William Sabatier).

2 THE KNIFE FIGHT
Manda comes looking for Marie at a Montmartre estaminet. The rivalry with Roland leads to a knife fight in the backyard, presided over by gang boss Leca (Claude Dauphin), in which Manda kills Roland. The threat of violence hangs over many of the film's locations.

3 IDYLL BY THE RIVER
The couple spend their first night as lovers in the country. Manda hands Marie a bowl of coffee through an open window—rarely in cinema has the sweet transience of erotic passion been more vividly evoked. This interlude contrasts with the dark city scenes.

4 MANDA'S REVENGE
Having escaped from the police with Marie's help, Manda hunts down gang boss Leca, who has framed Manda's friend Raymond (Raymond Bussières) for the murder of Roland. He shoots Leca dead in a backyard before once again giving himself up to the police.

5 THE EXECUTION
Having killed Leca, Manda is executed by guillotine. Marie watches in horror from an attic overlooking the execution yard. The film's story is said to be based on real-life events that took place in the Parisian underworld in 1898.

🕐 DIRECTOR PROFILE

1906–41
Jacques Becker was born in Paris to a French father and a Scottish mother. He became assistant to Jean Renoir (1894–1979) during Renoir's finest period. After directing a couple of shorts, he was drafted into the army.

1942–51
He directed six films, including a thriller (*Dernier atout*, 1942), a murder mystery (*Goupi mains rouges*, 1943), a tragicomedy set in the Paris fashion world (*Falbalas*, 1945), and three light comedies. All show his sense of milieu and psychological insight.

1952–60
Becker directed two of his finest films, *Casque d'or* and *Touchez pas au grisbi* (*Honor Among Thieves*, 1954), a downbeat and highly influential crime thriller. *Le Trou* (*The Night Watch*, 1960), a prison-break movie filmed in sober, near-documentary style, was completed shortly before his death.

Le salaire de la peur 1953
The Wages of Fear   HENRI-GEORGES CLOUZOT 1907 – 77

▲ Mario (Yves Montand) strives to save Jo (Charles Vanel) from an oily death.

▼ Drama and the threat of disaster combine in the film's pulp-style poster.

According to filmmaker Basil Wright, *Le salaire de la peur* "has some claim to be the greatest suspense thriller of all time; it has the suspense, not of mystery but of Damocles's sword." It won the Palme d'Or at Cannes and the Golden Bear at Berlin, and became the first foreign-language production to play as a first feature on the British circuits.

A very long film (156 minutes) based on a very short novel by Georges Arnaud set in Guatemala—a location that the film never specifies—*Le salaire de la peur* offers viewers a classic of what would now be called "high concept" entertainment. An international crew of down-and-outs, Mario (Yves Montand), Jo (Charles Vanel), Bimba (Peter van Eyck), and Luigi (Folco Lulli), seize their chance to secure the airfare to get out of the South American hellhole of Las Piedras by taking on a virtual suicide mission, driving 200 gallons (910 liters) of nitroglycerine, needed to extinguish a blazing oil well, along a treacherous 300-mile (480-km) road. The fact that the Southern Oil Company sends two trucks shows their lack of confidence in all four drivers arriving safely ("at least one's got to get there").

"Dialogue, which played a major role in my first films, has diminished in importance," declared Clouzot at the time; "*Le salaire de la peur* is a visual film in which the dialogue is largely in the background." Critic Richard Mallett observed that Clouzot "holds the balance admirably between their behavior under stress and the essentially mechanical difficulties of the journey." Scenes depicting the casual indifference of the US-run Southern Oil Company to the lives of its employees were trimmed on its original US release. **RMC**

👁 KEY SCENES

1 SOUTHERN OIL'S OFFICE
Southern Oil boss Bill O'Brien (William Tubbs) graphically demonstrates what happens when nitroglycerine is spilled. A *New York Times* review seized on "the gingerly, breathless handling" of the nitroglycerine: "You sit there waiting for the theater to explode."

2 LUIGI AND BIMBA BLOW UP THE BOULDER
Problems pile up for the foursome. After they have negotiated a rotten wooden platform set precariously above a chasm, they find a boulder blocking their passage. Bimba rigs up a thermos full of nitroglycerine as a makeshift bomb to remove it.

3 JO IN THE OIL
Mario uses Jo as a human wheel grip to extricate their truck from an oil-filled crater. The attempt is successful, but Jo is left severely wounded. Charles Vanel had the longest career of any French actor; he made his screen debut in 1912.

🕐 DIRECTOR PROFILE

1907–41
Henri-Georges Clouzot was born in 1907. He entered the film industry as an assistant director and spent ten years as a scriptwriter. His work included *Un soir de rafle* (*Dragnet Night*, 1931) and *Les inconnus dans la maison* (*Strangers in the House*, 1942). He spent several years in sanatoriums from the mid 1930s.

1942–56
His first feature as director (*L'assassin habite au 21*, 1942) was an immediate success. He followed it with several impressive studies in lowlifes, including *Le corbeau* (*The Raven*, 1943), *Quai des orfèvres* (*Quay of the Goldsmiths*, 1947), and *Manon* (1949). He then enjoyed phenomenal international success with *Le salaire de la peur* and *Les diaboliques* (1955), the latter based on the novel *Celle qui n'était plus*, which was purchased by Clouzot much to the chagrin of Alfred Hitchcock, who was looking to mount his own version. His first film in color was the highly original and acclaimed documentary *Le mystère Picasso* (*The Mystery of Picasso*, 1956).

1957–77
Clouzot was plagued by poor health; his work was criticized by many of the French Nouvelle Vague (see p. 248) filmmakers. His later films such as *Les espions* (1957), *La vérité* (1960), the unfinished *L'enfer* (1964), and *La prisonnière* (*Woman in Chains*, 1968) were less successful. Clouzot's first wife, Véra Gibson-Amado, whom he married in 1950, starred in three of his films (*Le salaire de la peur*, *Les diaboliques*, *Les espions*) and collaborated on the screenplay of a fourth (*La vérité*). Clouzot died in Paris.

TRUCKING IN THE MOVIES

With its restless combination of wheels, landscape, and machismo, trucking provided a rugged backdrop to melodramas such as *They Drive by Night* (1940) by Raoul Walsh (1887–1980) and Jules Dassin's *Thieves' Highway* (1949). The international success of *Le salaire de la peur* led to variations in more exotic settings: the Sahara in *Ice Cold in Alex* (1958) and the Ivory Coast in *The Big Gamble* (1961). The intimidating size of the average truck inspired not only raucous 1970s comedies such as *Smokey and the Bandit* (1977) and *Convoy* (1978) but also the sparse debut feature film *Duel* (1971, left) by Steven

Spielberg (b. 1946), in which it dawns on Dennis Weaver's urban Everyman that an unseen trucker is out to kill him. In *Roadgames* (1981) by Richard Franklin (1948–2007), amiable trucker Stacy Keach realizes that he has attracted the attention of a maniac.

THE HOLLYWOOD MUSICAL

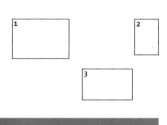

1 After the attack on Pearl Harbor, *Yankee Doodle Dandy*'s cast and crew decided to make the film patriotic and uplifting.

2 *Meet Me in St. Louis* tells the story of a family living in St. Louis at the time of the World's Fair in 1904.

3 Three sailors on shore leave in 1944 have twenty-four hours to explore the Big Apple in *On the Town*.

In the 1940s Hollywood musicals adopted a bright, brassy, militant tone. *Yankee Doodle Dandy* (1942, above) by Michael Curtiz (1886–1962) matched the mood of a nation entering World War II being patriotic, sentimental, aggressive, and as much a deification of President Franklin D. Roosevelt as of its ostensible subject, song-and-dance man George M. Cohan (James Cagney). The closure of war-torn European markets forced Hollywood to look to Latin America for overseas revenues, prompting a mini boom in Latin American musicals such as *Down Argentine Way* (1940), starring Carmen Miranda. The prevailing tone was of gung-ho gaiety in the all-star cast of *Thank Your Lucky Stars* (1943). In contrast, *Meet Me in St. Louis* (1944, opposite above), by Vincente Minnelli (1903–86) and starring Judy Garland, was a nostalgic, bittersweet confection built around extant songs, looking back at a turn-of-the-century childhood.

After the war, biopics continued to be built around the lives and back catalogue songs of performers such as Al Jolson (Larry Parks) in *The Jolson Story* (1946), or songwriters such as Cole Porter (Cary Grant) in *Night and Day* (1946). Heavily fictionalized and contrived, this cycle traded in relishable cliché such as the ironic or apt counterpoint of an artist's private life with his or her biggest hit song or the "genius of creation" scene as the hero struggles with a tune, making a few false starts ("Day and night . . . hmm") before the recognizable standard emerges. Fred Astaire and Ginger Rogers, the great musical stars of

KEY EVENTS

1943	1949	1952	1952	1953	1954
Oklahoma!, by Richard Rodgers and Oscar Hammerstein II, opens on Broadway, to run for an unprecedented 2,212 performances.	*On the Town*, directed by Gene Kelly and Stanley Donen, is released. It wins the Oscar for Best Music, Scoring of a Musical Picture in 1950.	Vincente Minnelli's *An American in Paris*, built around the music of George Gershwin and starring Gene Kelly, takes the Oscar for Best Picture.	Donen and Gene Kelly make *Singin' in the Rain* (see p. 202) for producer Arthur Freed's unit at MGM when the studio is at its creative peak.	Vincente Minnelli and Fred Astaire respond to *Singin' in the Rain* by producing their own backstage musical, *The Band Wagon*.	Donen's *Seven Brides for Seven Brothers* highlights the unusual choreography of Michael Kidd with a dance number around raising a barn.

198   1940–59

the 1930s, reunited for a final, weak film, *The Barkleys of Broadway* (1949), but Astaire was better served by teaming with crooner Bing Crosby in such films as *Holiday Inn* (1942). His position as the movies' premier male musical star was challenged by the younger, more obviously athletic Gene Kelly (1912–96), who made his screen debut in *For Me and My Gal* (1942) and was soon delivering innovative efforts such as *Anchors Aweigh* (1945), in which he dances with MGM's animated star Jerry Mouse, and *Cover Girl* (1944), in which he partners his own reflection.

Minnelli worked with Astaire in *Yolanda and the Thief* (1945) and with Kelly in *The Pirate* (1948), opting for fantasy and stylization in film musicals. These talents, mostly working under Arthur Freed at MGM, became the powerhouses for a musical boom in the 1950s. *Anchors Aweigh*, about sailors on leave desperate to make it to a concert at the Hollywood Bowl, and the sports-themed *Take Me Out to the Ball Game* (1949), the last solo directorial credit for Busby Berkeley (1895–1976), are both precedents for *On the Town* (1949, below). Directed by Kelly and Stanley Donen (b. 1924) and based on a Leonard Bernstein Broadway show of 1944, Bernstein's book-and-lyrics team Adolph Green and Betty Comden worked with Roger Edens on new numbers for the film. Three sailors (Kelly, Frank Sinatra, Jules Munshin) have one day to see New York and meet three girls (Vera-Ellen, Betty Garrett, Ann Miller) along the way. In its exhilarating opening, shot on location, the film escapes from the soundstage artificiality of all previous screen musicals, although some of its highlights are as fantastical, set bound, and balletic as anything from Minnelli. For the rest of the decade, Minnelli, Donen, Kelly, and Astaire played a game of one-upmanship, advancing the film musical by elegant leaps and bounds.

1955	1956	1956	1957	1959	1961
Oklahoma! finally arrives on the big screen, directed by Fred Zinnemann, and goes on to scoop two Oscars a year later.	Frank Sinatra and Bing Crosby team up in *High Society* with Grace Kelly. A big hit, it grosses more than $13 million.	Henry King (1886–1982) directs Rodgers and Hammerstein's *Carousel*. The musical is innovative for its tragic plot.	Frank Sinatra stars opposite Kim Novak and Rita Hayworth in George Sidney's *Pal Joey*.	Vincente Minnelli's *Gigi*, the last of the great MGM musicals under producer Arthur Freed, takes the Academy Award for Best Picture.	*West Side Story* is released. A year later it wins ten Academy Awards—more than any other musical film.

Kelly worked with Minnelli on the Oscar-winning *An American in Paris* (1951), built around the George Gershwin catalogue, but rejoined Donen for *Singin' in the Rain* (1952, see p. 202). Both films were huge hits and much admired. However, a small distinction was made between Minnelli's faintly foreign artistic pretensions (a lengthy ballet built around the specific looks of different French painters) and Donen's more down-to-earth self-mockery; for example, the cut from smug movie star Kelly's motto of "Dignity, always dignity" to the slapstick vaudeville capers of his earlier days. Amusingly, this became the subject of Minnelli's retaliatory film, the innovative, scurrilous, divinely inventive backstage musical *The Band Wagon* (1953). Astaire, whose contribution to gimmick dances had been hoofing on the ceiling in *Royal Wedding* (1951), plays musical comedy star Tony Hunter, who takes jokes about his age in good part and teams with a ballet dancer played by Cyd Charisse, in the first of her run of spectacular, pliable performances.

Without Kelly, Donen directed *Seven Brides for Seven Brothers* (1954), an outdoorsy Western musical conceived for the screen, starring macho baritone Howard Keel and highlighting the energetic choreography of Michael Kidd. With Kelly, Donen delivered *It's Always Fair Weather* (1955), a disenchanted yet interesting follow-up to *On the Town* about three wartime comrades who find they have little in common when they meet up in peacetime. Charisse provides a match for Kelly—like Astaire, Kelly often found himself dancing alone because it was a rare costar who could keep up with him. Donen then worked with Astaire on *Funny Face* (1957) and teamed with George Abbott (1887–1995) to direct transfers of recent stage successes, such as *The Pajama Game* (1957). Minnelli did less well with Broadway transplants, directing Kelly in *Brigadoon* (1954) and Keel in *Kismet* (1955) to rather stuffy effect. Minnelli guided Leslie Caron through the Oscar-winning *Gigi* (1958, opposite above), the last great effort from Freed's MGM unit. Based on a novella by Colette and featuring music by Frederick Loewe and lyrics by Alan Jay Lerner, the story centers on a courtesan in training (Caron) in turn-of-the-century Paris. Although coming to the end of his dance career, Astaire remained in the game, taking a victory tour with *Daddy Long Legs* (1955) opposite Caron, *Funny Face* opposite Audrey Hepburn, and *Silk Stockings* (1957) opposite Charisse. Kelly solo directed the experimental curio *Invitation to the Dance* (1956), but stayed in touch commercially with *Les Girls* (1957) by George Cukor (1899–1983).

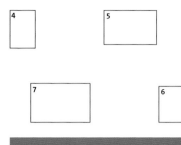

Broadway hit *Oklahoma!* (1943) was the defining musical of its era, but did not arrive on-screen until 1955, directed by Fred Zinnemann (1907–97). Its long run encouraged Western musicals outside the singing cowboy rut but its importance was in confirming a direct feed between Broadway and Hollywood that kept up a flow of stage to film productions throughout the decade, including *Show Boat* (1951), *Carmen Jones* (1954), *Guys and Dolls* (1955), *The King and I* (1956), *South Pacific* (1958, below right), and *Porgy and Bess* (1959). A few of these allowed film and recording stars such as Doris Day and Sinatra to tackle established roles and great songs; others allowed stage performers such as Yul Brynner to repeat their star-making turns, and some bewilderingly cast Rossano Brazzi as a Frenchman or nonsinging Marlon Brando as a musical lead. *Kiss Me Kate* (1953) by George Sidney (1916–2002) has cinematic attack and all have the benefit of proven scores, but they are not such lasting achievements as the musicals of Donen, Kelly, and Minnelli. Although production-line musical programmers tailed off, big-ticket superproductions carried on in the 1960s with *West Side Story* (1961), *My Fair Lady* (1964), and *The Sound of Music* (1965).

The 1950s offered old-fashioned showcases for talents such as Marilyn Monroe and Jane Russell in *Gentlemen Prefer Blondes* (1953) by Howard Hawks (1896–1977) or Crosby and Danny Kaye in Curtiz's *White Christmas* (1954, opposite). Crosby teamed with Sinatra and Grace Kelly in *High Society* (1956, opposite above), a remake of *The Philadelphia Story* (1940), gifted with a Cole Porter score and directed by Charles Walters (1911–82). "Old groaner" Crosby is still the romantic lead, but Sinatra demonstrates the blue-eyed cool that was making him the definitive male singer for a hipster generation, and that would carry on into the semi-musical "rat pack" romps of the 1960s.

The real changes in the musical, and in music generally, were aimed at the teenyboppers who succeeded the bobby-soxers who had been Sinatra fans when he first emerged as a heartthrob singer. In 1956 Elvis Presley made his screen debut in *Love Me Tender*. Ensuing musicals were built around his surly, sexualized presence, but his potential was sabotaged by poor management— "Colonel" Tom Parker turned down *West Side Story* on his behalf. *The Girl Can't Help It* (1956) by Frank Tashlin (1913–72), the first great pop musical, features youth-appeal performers Eddie Cochran, Little Richard, and Fats Domino. However, Richard Lester (b. 1932) was to change the game with *A Hard Day's Night* (1964). Setting imaginative montages to songs rather than enshrining performance, Lester set in motion a process whereby the movie musical was to be superseded by the pop video as an adjunct to a chart career. **KN**

4 Mike Connor (Frank Sinatra) helps ice maiden Tracy Lord (Grace Kelly) discover her human side in *High Society*.

5 Gaston (Louis Jordan) dances with Madame Alvarez (Hermione Gingold) while Gigi (Leslie Caron) indulges in a little champagne.

6 Mitzi Gaynor and Rossano Brazzi in *South Pacific*. Brazzi's character's singing voice was dubbed by opera star Giorgio Tozzi.

7 Crosby, Kaye, Vera-Ellen, and Rosemary Clooney in suitably festive mood for the finale of *White Christmas*.

Singin' in the Rain 1952
GENE KELLY 1912 – 96 STANLEY DONEN b. 1924

▲ The iconic scene where Kelly dances, sings the title song, and twirls an umbrella.

▼ MGM made this musical at its height.

Singin' in the Rain is a nostalgia movie, claiming the late 1920s as a halcyon era, affectionately ridiculing fashions, personalities, and musical tastes of the period while telling an insider story about a film industry in upheaval. Arthur Freed, head of the musicals unit at MGM, wanted to build a film around a clutch of nearly forgotten songs he and Nacio Herb Brown had written in the 1920s and 1930s for a string of forgotten movies. When he assigned Betty Comden and Adolph Green to the project, they went on strike because they wanted to use their own songs or those by Cole Porter, Irving Berlin, or Richard Rodgers and Oscar Hammerstein II. Contractually obliged to complete the script, they drew on Hollywood memories of the momentous arrival of talking pictures.

Gene Kelly, Debbie Reynolds, and Donald O'Connor are the genial leads, but the plot is propelled by Jean Hagen, as the silent star whose hideous voice dooms her in talkies. Kelly, who codirected with Stanley Donen, hurries through the story in comic sketches with music, saving sheer genius for the dance. Every dance number is a winner: O'Connor risking serious injury with athletic slapstick in "Make 'Em Laugh"; wordplay in an elocution lesson in "Moses Supposes"; the trio toppling furniture in "Good Morning"; Kelly's solo in a downpour in "Singin' in the Rain"; and an amazing fantasy diversion, "Broadway Rhythm Ballet," that matches Kelly's moves with the long legs of vamp Cyd Charisse. *Singin' in the Rain* has since become a nostalgia object in itself but a first viewing remains a revelation. **KN**

1 "GOOD MORNING"
Having hit on the idea of rescuing Don's (Kelly) movie by turning it into a musical, Don, Kathy (Reynolds), and Cosmo (O'Connor) celebrate with an exuberant dance. Reynolds was unused to dancing and her feet bled from the performance.

3 BROADWAY VAMP
The spectacular "Broadway Rhythm Ballet" fantasy routine lasts fourteen minutes. A young ingenue (Kelly) arrives in New York with an urge to perform: "Gotta dance!" He becomes ensnared by the inhumanly long, shapely legs of a Broadway siren (Charisse).

2 "SINGIN' IN THE RAIN"
In love with Kathy, the euphoric Don splashes through puddles and gets soaked "singin' in the rain." The actor's amazing solo performance became legendary. He danced in water mixed with milk, so that the puddles and raindrops would be visible on film.

4 CURTAIN UP
At the premiere of Don's film, *The Dancing Cavalier*, the audience wants its star Lina (Hagen) to sing live. Don hauls the curtains apart to reveal that Kathy is hidden behind them singing the song Lina is miming. Don introduces Kathy as the real star of his movie.

HOLLYWOOD ON HOLLYWOOD

The cinema has been turning the camera on itself since the silent era (*Merton of the Movies*, 1924). A potent mix of gossip, glamour, showbiz tragedy, and sly self-promotion informs the likes of *What Price Hollywood?* (1932) and *A Star Is Born* (1937, 1954). A later cycle dealt with sacred monsters in California gothic hell-houses, from the pessimistic *Sunset Boulevard* (1950) to *What Ever Happened to Baby Jane?* (1962). Specific segments of the film industry are examined in *Ed Wood* (1994, right) and *Gods and Monsters* (1998). Voyeurism, power, and the darker aspects of filmmaking have been explored in such films as *Peeping Tom* (1960), which features a serial-killing cameraman, and *The Stunt Man* (1980), starring Peter O'Toole as a Mephistophelean director.

NORDIC CINEMA

1 Henrik (Birger Malmsten) and Marie (Maj-Britt Nilsson) in Ingmar Bergman's *Sommarlek*.

2 Anita Björk plays an aristocrat amorously involved with a servant on her estate in *Fröken Julie*, Alf Sjöberg's adaptation of an August Strindberg play.

3 A gentle, folk-style poster for Hasse Ekman's moving *Flicka och hyacinter*, one of the masterpieces of Swedish cinema.

The 1950s saw a renaissance in Nordic cinema, which had been at the forefront of cinematic achievement during the silent era. In the late 1910s and early 1920s, the best films of Victor Sjöström (1879–1960), Mauritz Stiller (1883–1928), and Carl Theodor Dreyer (1889–1968) achieved an almost unequaled delicacy and naturalism. However, with the coming of sound and the growing dominance of Hollywood, the sparsely populated Nordic countries became linguistically and culturally isolated.

By the late 1940s, though, Scandinavia—especially Sweden—was again making creative films; film historian Peter Cowie has claimed: "Probably no other nation of comparative population has matched the artistic success of Sweden in the cinema." Central to that success was the photogenic beauty of its rural and urban landscapes and the contrast between its austere Lutheran traditions and its twentieth-century evolution into a pacific, secular social democracy.

These concerns found expression during the 1950s in the work of Ingmar Bergman (1918–2007). His finest early films, *Sommarlek* (*Summer Interlude*, 1951, above) and *Sommaren med Monika* (*Summer with Monika*, 1953), were melancholy romances, set against the backdrop of the Stockholm archipelago, the wild and temporary seasonal beauty of which reflected the transience of love. Such films were in a traditional Swedish vein, also typified by *Hon dansade*

KEY EVENTS

1944	1946	1949	1950	1951	1952
In Sweden, Alf Sjöberg makes *Hets* from an Ingmar Bergman script; its international success heralds the revival of Swedish film.	Ingmar Bergman makes his directorial debut with *Kris* (*Crisis*).	Norwegian directors Edith Carlmar and Arne Skouen make their first films with *Døden er et kjærtegn* and *Gategutter* (*Street Boys*) respectively.	Bergman films tragic romance *Sommarlek* (1951), which typifies his early style. Other notable Swedish films include Hasse Ekman's *Flicka och hyacinter*.	Arne Mattsson makes the tragic romance *Hon dansade en sommar*, which goes on to scoop the Golden Bear at Berlin. Sjöberg makes *Fröken Julie*.	Bergman shoots *Sommaren med Monika* (1953). Erik Blomberg makes *Valkoinen peura* in Finland.

en sommar (*One Summer of Happiness*, 1951) by Arne Mattsson (1919–95), another tragic love story set against a rural backdrop. Bergman then moved toward allegory and existentialism in *Det sjunde inseglet* (*The Seventh Seal*, 1957, see p. 208). Despite the medieval setting and fantasy premise, it addressed the very twentieth-century dilemma of the man without faith seeking meaning in life. In *Jungfrukällan* (*The Virgin Spring*, 1960) Bergman revisited medieval times, exploring Scandinavia's dual heritage of paganism and Christianity. *Smultronstället* (*Wild Strawberries*, 1957) was a gentler, more realistic account of an old man taking stock of his life, prefiguring the more psychological emphasis of Bergman's 1960s work.

Alf Sjöberg (1903–80) has been unjustly overshadowed by the two outstanding Swedish artists with whom he was associated. His best-known film abroad, *Hets* (*Frenzy*, 1944), was scripted by Bergman, who has taken the credit for its bleak psychological undercurrents, although the claustrophobic atmosphere is surely down to its director. During the 1950s, Sjöberg adapted works by Sweden's greatest playwright, August Strindberg, realizing a memorable version of *Fröken Julie* (*Miss Julie*, 1951, right) and an innovative, rather playful historical film in *Karin Månsdotter* (1954), based on Strindberg's *Erik XIV*. Little known outside Sweden, Hasse Ekman (1915–2004) deserves greater fame for *Flicka och hyacinter* (*Girl with Hyacinths*, 1950, below right), a haunting story about an investigation into a girl's suicide. The film showed the unusual sexual frankness of postwar Swedish cinema, while subtly probing the compromises made by Sweden to remain neutral during World War II. Also notable was the work of Arne Sucksdorff (1917–2001) who creatively melded fiction and documentary.

Denmark's greatest director, Carl Theodor Dreyer, made only one film during the 1950s. *Ordet* (*The Word*, 1955, see p. 206) was, however, a masterpiece, an austere yet humane parable whose miraculous elements were beautifully undercut by the subtle realism of the performances and settings. The decade also saw the emergence of Gabriel Axel (b. 1918), later to achieve fame with *Babettes gæstebud* (*Babette's Feast*, 1987). His feature debut, *Altid Ballade* (*Nothing but Trouble*, 1955), was a charming realist account of a working-class family.

Norway's most talented filmmaker was Arne Skouen (1913–2003), whose *Ni liv* (*Nine Lives*, 1957) won international acclaim and an Oscar nomination. It is a tense and skillfully crafted account of the wartime flight of a Resistance fighter to neutral Sweden. Debuting with the chilling *Døden er et kjærtegn* (*Death Is a Caress*, 1949), Norway's first female director, Edith Carlmar (1911–2003), sustained a career through the 1950s. Her final film, the rites of passage story *Ung flukt* (*The Wayward Girl*, 1959), marked the first appearance of actress Liv Ullmann.

Notable Finnish works included *Valkoinen peura* (*The White Reindeer*, 1952), a Lapp folk tale adapted for cinema by Erik Blomberg, which made impressive use of the Nordic scenery, and the war film *Tuntematon sotilas* (*The Unknown Soldier*, 1955) by Edvin Laine (1905–89), which remains the highest-grossing Finnish film. **AJ**

1953	1954	1955	1957	1959	1960
Bergman's *Gycklarnas afton* (*Sawdust and Tinsel*) is a haunting study of humiliation, set against a circus background.	Arne Mattsson's *Salka Valka* and *Fortroll ad vandrig* (*Enchanted Journey*) are released.	Carl Dreyer's *Ordet* (see p. 206) is probably the greatest Danish film of the 1950s. Edvin Laine's *Tuntematon sotilas* is released—Finnish cinema's biggest hit.	Bergman makes *Det sjunde inseglet* (see p. 208) and *Smultronstället*. Arne Skouen's *Ni liv* wins international attention for Norwegian cinema.	Edith Carlmar's last film, *Ung flukt*, is released in Norway.	*Jungfrukällan* marks the end of the overtly allegorical phase of Bergman's career.

Ordet 1955
The Word CARL THEODOR DREYER 1889 – 1968

▲ Inger's "death" helps to reconcile the two families to Anne and Anders's romance.

▼ The stark poster depicts Johannes (Preben Lerdorff Rye) in the role of preacher.

Morten Borgen (Henrik Malberg) is an old farmer widely respected for his piety. His wife has died. His youngest son, Anders (Cay Kristiansen), wants to marry Anne (Gerda Nielsen), but her father comes from a sect whose beliefs Morten abhors. Mikkel (Emil Hass Christensen), the eldest son, is not religious. His wife Inger (Birgitte Federspiel) cannot inspire him with her faith. The other son, Johannes, a theology student, is a gimlet-eyed religious madman.

Dreyer's restraint makes the final reel "miracle" all the more overwhelming. *Time* noted the intense and sincere way the film wrestles with issues of religious faith. "The story is told with the luminous sincerity that haloes most of what Dreyer does," *Time*'s reviewer noted. "He has a deeper sympathy with the burgher virtues, a higher sense of the prosperous interior than almost any artist since the Flemish Renaissance; his frame imparts the spiritual light of common things."

Ordet often seems harsh but the film ends on a redemptive note. Johannes, the crackpot visionary, turns out to have a spiritual purity that helps resolve the doubts and disputes that afflict the others' lives. When Inger "dies" in childbirth, he is able to bring her back to life because a child believes in him. With her faith, he has the strength to beg God for "the word" that will resurrect the dead mother.

With its slow tracking shots, close-ups of the actors' faces ("a land one can never tire of exploring," as the director called them) and its subtle use of sound, Dreyer's adaptation of Kaj Munk's play is very finely crafted. Other films dealing with religious faith and doubt often seem phony. By contrast, *Ordet* invites us to take that leap and "believe." **GM**

1 "WOE UNTO YOU, HYPOCRITES!"
Driven to distraction by immersion in the works of Kierkegaard, and now in the throes of a Messiah complex, Johannes seems mad as he stands at the start of the film on a windswept hill, holding forth like an Old Testament prophet.

3 "HE'S LYING IN THE TUB IN FOUR PIECES"
Mikkel gives a brutal summary of the stillbirth. When Inger miscarries, it becomes harder than ever for the family to keep the faith. The doctor (Henrik Skjær) debates with Morten about the relative strengths of science and religious belief.

2 "YOU SEEM AS IF GOD HAS ABANDONED YOU"
The old farmer Morten is close to despair. He is physically frail and is tormented by his sons, who are letting him down. God has not heard his prayers and he blames himself. Grudgingly, he has come to accept that miracles just do not happen.

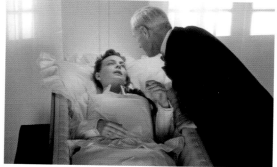

4 THE MESSAGE
Just as the coffin lid is about to shut on Inger, Mikkel's daughter Maren (Ann Elisabeth Groth) tugs on Johannes's sleeve, imploring him to save the dead woman. The child's faith galvanizes him and the miracle is accomplished.

PAGE TO SCREEN

Dreyer had seen Kaj Munk's play *I Begyndelsen var Ordet* in the early 1930s and had been deeply moved by it. The play was originally written in 1925, but was not performed until seven years later. The fate of Munk, a Danish playwright and pastor who was killed by the Nazis in 1944, lent a special poignancy to this film, which was shot in West Jutland, where Munk had been a pastor. He had written the part of Borgen, the patriarchal old farmer, for actor Henrik Malberg. Malberg had not been able to play the role on stage, but Dreyer gave him the chance to portray the farmer on-screen. On its release, the film was immediately hailed as a masterpiece, becoming a commercial and critical success. Despite Dreyer's faithfulness to the original text, *Ordet* makes one important change to the play. As described by Munk, the miracle is ambiguous. He leaves the possibility that Inger was not really dead. In Dreyer's film, her resurrection is a genuine miracle. The play had been filmed previously in 1943 by Gustaf Molander (1888–1973). This Swedish adaptation did not premiere until after World War II and did not garner the same acclaim as Dreyer's version.

KAJ MUNK

ORDET

NYT NORDISK FORLAG · ARNOLD BUSCK
KØBENHAVN · MCMXXII

Det sjunde inseglet 1957
The Seventh Seal   INGMAR BERGMAN 1918 – 2007

▲ Bengt Ekerot's white-faced, black-caped Death became an archetype in cinema.

▼ The poster visually references the chess game that is central to the film's story.

Ingmar Bergman's *Det sjunde inseglet* may now be regarded as the epitome of brooding, introspective Scandinavian cinema, but it owed its existence to a romantic comedy. The success of Bergman's *Sommarnattens leende* (*Smiles of a Summer Night*, 1955) prompted backers Svensk to take the leap of faith with a project they initially regarded with great foreboding.

A disillusioned knight (Max von Sydow) is on his way home from the Crusades. Violence, disease, and death are all around him. The country is being ravaged by the Black Death; an artist is working on a fresco of the Dance of Death in a church; and the hooded, white-faced Death (Bengt Ekerot) is waiting to collect his dues from the knight. The film had its origins in a short play called *Wood Painting* by Bergman that was broadcast on the radio in 1954, with Bergman as narrator. Bergman's own eschatological musings were lent fresh urgency by what was going on in the world at the time. It was the height of the Cold War, when many feared the world might face nuclear annihilation.

The film provided a series of unforgettable images that would be imitated and parodied, most notably the knight's chess game with Death on the beach and the dancing characters led away over the brow of the hill by the Grim Reaper. Bergman acknowledged various influences on the film from Albrecht Dürer's woodcuts and Victor Sjöström's *Körkarlen* (*The Phantom Carriage*, 1921) to Carl Orff's choral work, *Carmina Burana*. For many artists and filmmakers who followed Bergman, *Det sjunde inseglet* was one of the first points of reference when it came to discussing and exploring death. **GM**

👁 KEY SCENES

1 CHESS ON THE BEACH
The black-caped Death appears before the knight. "I have long walked at your side," he tells him. Not ready to be taken away, the knight talks his nemesis into playing chess. Bergman had seen an image of this scene many years earlier in a church in Uppland.

4 THE DANCE OF DEATH
In the final scene of the film Jof, the actor who has second sight, sees a vision of Death, with his scythe and hourglass, leading the knight and his other victims in a solemn Dance of Death over the distant brow of a hill.

⏲ DIRECTOR PROFILE

1918–45
Ingmar Bergman was born the son of a Lutheran priest in Uppsala, Sweden. His script for *Hets* (*Frenzy*, 1944) offered an early glimpse of many of his later preoccupations as a director: young love, sexual jealousy, resentment of authority. Bergman directed some scenes in the film.

1946–54
Bergman made his directorial debut with the melodrama *Kris* (*Crisis*, 1946), but the director regarded *Sommarlek* (*Summer Interlude*, 1951) as his first fully realized film.

1955–60
His romantic comedy *Sommarnattens leende* (*Smiles of a Summer Night*, 1955) was rapturously received at the Cannes Film Festival in 1956. It established Bergman as an international name and paved the way for him to make his masterpiece *Det sjunde inseglet*.

2 DEATH THE CONFESSOR
The knight is desperate to pour out his anguish to his deathly shadow. "I want to confess as honestly as I can but my heart is empty," he laments. "I see myself and am seized by disgust and fear. Through my indifference to people, I've been placed outside their society."

1961–75
Bergman's "faith trilogy" began with *Såsom i en spegel* (*Through a Glass Darkly*, 1961), followed by *Nattvardsgästerna* (*Winter Light*, 1963), and *Tystnaden* (*The Silence*, 1963). *Persona* (1966) was his rawest and formally most experimental work from this period and starred Norwegian actress Liv Ullmann, who became Bergman's muse, playing the lead in nine of his films. The pair had a daughter together in 1966.

1976–2002
Bergman was arrested for tax evasion in 1976 and vowed he would never work in Sweden again. He went into exile in Germany. He returned to Sweden to make *Fanny och Alexander* (*Fanny and Alexander*, 1982), then announced he was retiring from film directing. He continued to direct for theater and television, and to write.

2003–7
Bergman's last film, *Saraband* (2003), was made for television and was distributed theatrically in many territories. He died not long after his eighty-ninth birthday on the remote island of Fårö, where he had lived for many years.

3 DANCING ON FIRE
The traveling performer Jof is forced to gambol like a dancing bear on a burning table in a packed inn. This is an example of one of many scenes in which actors were humiliated in symbolic fashion in Bergman's work.

ASIAN AND INDIAN CINEMA

1 The truth surrounding a duel to the death between a samurai and a bandit forms the crux of the story of *Rashomon*.

2 Masayuki Mori and Machiko Kyo star in a masterpiece of the golden age of Japanese cinema, *Ugetsu monogatari*.

3 Tatsuya Nakadai delivers a raw and unforgettable performance as the idealistic protagonist of *Ningen no joken*.

Films have been in production in Asia ever since the silent era. Japan was retelling kabuki stories on film as early as the first decade of the twentieth century, while the first Indian feature film, *Raja Harishchandra*, dates from 1913. Japanese cinema enjoyed its first golden age in the 1930s, with directors such as Mizoguchi Kenji (1898–1956), Ozu Yasujiro (1903–63), and Shimizu Hiroshi (1903–66) all producing outstanding films in a distinctively Japanese style and idiom. In China in the same decade, work emerged from the Shanghai film industry, where directors such as Yu Sun (1900–90) opted for a style of realist melodrama to examine the problems of a vast but weak nation, beset by foreign threats and undermined by disunity at home.

Until the 1950s, however, Asian cinema remained largely unknown in the West. A handful of Japanese films had been screened in Europe and North America before World War II, as were a couple of Indian-made silents under the direction of the German Franz Osten (1876–1956). However, it was the screening of *Rashomon* (1950, above) by Kurosawa Akira (1910–98) at the Venice Film Festival in 1951, where it won the Golden Lion, that alerted international audiences to the richness of Japanese cinema, setting in motion a process that would lead to wider acclaim for Asian cinema in the West. Kurosawa was a fitting ambassador for Japanese film. A liberal humanist, he tackled

KEY EVENTS

1945	1948	1949	1950	1951	1952
During the US occupation of Japan, a code of censorship is imposed on Japanese cinema, designed to inculcate liberal and democratic values.	*Xiao cheng zhi chun* (*Spring in a Small Town*) is one of the finest films produced in postwar Shanghai.	Zheng Junli directs *Wuya yu maque* in Shanghai. Chairman Mao nationalizes China's film industry.	The Korean War begins. Kurosawa Akira directs *Rashomon*; it wins the Golden Lion the following year.	Raj Kapoor makes *Awaara* in Bollywood. Kinoshita Keisuke makes Japan's first color film, *Karumen kokyo ni kaeru*.	The US occupation of Japan ends. Mizoguchi Kenji makes *Saikaku ichidai onna. Aan*, by Mehboob Khan (1907–64), is released in India.

what appeared to be universal themes, exploring the inaccessibility of truth in *Rashomon*, and depicting a man's response to mortality in *Ikiru* (1952). An admirer of Western culture, he adapted the literature of its authors for cinema, transplanting Russia's Dostoyevsky to Hokkaido in *Hakuchi* (*The Idiot*, 1951), and fusing Jacobean and Japanese theatrical traditions in his samurai Macbeth, *Kumonosu-jo* (*Throne of Blood*, 1957). Given this Western influence, it was no surprise that his work won such admiration abroad, nor that his acclaimed samurai films, *Shichinin no samurai* (*Seven Samurai*, 1954, see p. 216) and *Yojimbo* (1961), were themselves remade as Westerns.

Kurosawa's triumph at Venice helped draw international praise for other Japanese directors, many of whom had been making films since the silent era. The serene late period films of Mizoguchi Kenji, preeminently *Saikaku ichidai onna* (*The Life of Oharu*, 1952), *Ugetsu monogatari* (1953, right), and *Sansho dayu* (*Sansho the Bailiff*, 1954), combined a profound humanity with an extraordinary stylistic beauty. Mizoguchi's use of the moving camera was unmatched for its delicacy and precision, yet the style was never merely decorative; rather, it always served to give visual expression to the emotions and circumstances of his characters. By contrast, the other master of postwar Japanese cinema, Ozu Yasujiro, hardly ever moved his camera, opting for an austerely quietist style to narrate his subtle stories of the Japanese family. In films such as *Banshun* (*Late Spring*, 1949), *Bakushu* (*Early Summer*, 1951), and *Tokyo monogatari* (*Tokyo Story*, 1953, see p. 214), Ozu explored the troubled relations between parents and children with compassion and a resigned wisdom.

These great directors were only the finest of many distinguished filmmakers working in the productive postwar Japanese film industry. Among them were Gosho Heinosuke (1902–81), a subtle and versatile dramatist whose films capture an intriguing mixture of moods; Ichikawa Kon (1915–2008), a barbed social critic whose best films drolly satirized postwar society; Kinoshita Keisuke (1912–98), maker of subdued but sentimental melodramas, uniquely Japanese in flavor; Naruse Mikio (1905–69), author of downbeat stories of strong women in adversity; Yoshimura Kozaburo (1911–2000), director of understated dramas again focused on female characters; and Kobayashi Masaki (1916–96), humanist director of the epic war trilogy *Ningen no joken* (*The Human Condition*, 1959–61, right). In a more action-oriented vein, filmmakers such as Hiroshi Inagaki (1905–80) realized stylish samurai films that, at their best, combined immaculately choreographed violence with criticism of the feudal values that had held sway in Japan for many centuries. This variety of content and profundity of theme were combined with popularity: in its heyday, the Japanese studio system achieved consistent commercial success, and by the end of the 1950s was producing some five hundred films a year. Only in the 1960s, as Japanese audiences turned their attention to foreign films or stayed at home to watch television, did the film industry enter a period of decline.

1955	1956	1957	1958	1959	1961
Naruse Mikio makes the tragic melodrama *Ukigumo*, considered by critics to be his masterpiece.	Singhalese director Lester James Peries makes his debut with *Rekava*, a film centered on rural life in Ceylon.	Mehboob Khan directs the Bollywood epic *Bharat Mata* (*Mother India*). It recounts the history of India through the life story of one woman.	Satyajit Ray directs *Jalsaghar* (*The Music Room*), the haunting tragedy of a landowner fallen on hard times.	Japanese New Wave director Oshima Nagisa (b. 1932) makes his debut with *Ai to kibo no machi* (*A Town of Love and Hope*).	In South Korea, Yu Hyun-mok makes *Obaltan*, widely considered by critics to be the finest Korean film.

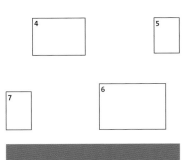

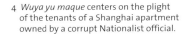

4 *Wuya yu maque* centers on the plight
   of the tenants of a Shanghai apartment
   owned by a corrupt Nationalist official.

5 Hindi film *Kaagaz ke Phool* was a box-office
   flop on its release. It was revived as an
   international cult classic in the 1980s.

6 The lavish romantic melodramas of
   Hindi cinema's golden era in the 1950s
   featured imposing large-scale sets, such
   as those used for Raj Kapoor's *Awaara*.

7 The poster for the South Korean film
   Jayu buin, a romantic melodrama that
   charts the extramarital activities of a
   professor and his wife.

The success of postwar Japanese cinema was in part a consequence of the country's political stability during those years. The contemporaneous output of the other East Asian film industries suffered more from the impact of history. China, as the old Confucian curse has it, was going through interesting times. In the immediate postwar years, directors such as Zheng Junli (1911–69) had crafted probing, socially critical films and developed an inventive visual style. Junli made *Wuya yu maque* (1949, above) when Chiang Kai-shek's Nationalist government was about to fall before the Communist takeover, and the film was not released until after the Chinese civil war. Many of these directors were left leaning, but, ironically, a lot of them suffered after Chairman Mao's Communists took full power. The severe criticism leveled at Yu Sun's *Wu Xun zhuan* (1950)—which told the story of nineteenth-century cultural hero Wu Xun—initiated a period of stringent state intervention in the Chinese film industry. Nationalization, and rigorous dictates regarding acceptable subject matter, largely stifled creative filmmaking in the 1950s. A tentative liberalization later in the decade allowed a handful of remarkable films to emerge up until the mid-1960s, of which the most internationally famous is perhaps the melodrama *Wutai jiemei* (1964) by Xie Jin (1923–2008). The onset of the Cultural Revolution in 1966, however, led to a temporary cessation of all filmmaking in China.

The development of postwar Korean cinema was also impeded by politics. The Korean War ended in the division of the peninsula into two separate countries, ruled respectively by authoritarian left- and right-wing regimes, both of which imposed strict censorship. Nevertheless, in the 1950s, South Korea produced some significant films based on popular novels, such as *Jayu buin* (*Madame Freedom*, 1956, left) by Han Hyeong-mo (1917–99), a story of adultery that became a major commercial success. By the end of the decade, a number of important South Korean directors had emerged, including Yu Hyun-mok (1925–2009), and in 1959 more than one hundred films were produced in the country. The interval between the fall of Syngman Rhee's regime in 1960 and the rise of Park Chung-hee's military dictatorship the following year allowed Yu to make *Obaltan* (*The Stray Bullet*, 1961), a bleak, brooding account of shanty town life, ranked by some critics as the finest film ever made in Korea.

Farther west, the thriving film industry of India began to win international acclaim in the postwar era for the work of its greatest director, the Bengali Satyajit Ray (1921–92), who captured attention with *Pather panchali* (1955) and the two subsequent films that together formed the *Apu* trilogy (see p. 218). These works followed a child from a rural background in his journey from boyhood to manhood, using his personal experience to create a microcosm of Indian life. Ray continued to produce outstanding films, such as *Charulata* (1964), a profound study of the loneliness of a married woman, in the following decade and beyond. A more direct political engagement was visible in the work of another Bengali filmmaker, Ritwik Ghatak (1925–76), whose naturalistic *Nagarik* (*The Citizen*, 1952) predated *Pather panchali* but failed to achieve a commercial release. He went on to make his masterpiece *Meghe dhaka tara* (*The Cloud-Capped Star*, 1960), about the tragic experience of a female refugee in Calcutta.

Ray and Ghatak's contribution to Bengali-language films represents one pole of the Indian cinema. The other pole was represented by the Hindi-language popular movie, the product of the Mumbai-based industry known as Bollywood (see p. 542), purveyor of melodramatic entertainments that combined action, romance, and song and dance. Subsequent emigration from the Indian subcontinent has made Bollywood fare familiar in the West, but in the 1950s, few of these films were distributed internationally. However, *Awaara* (1951, below) directed by Raj Kapoor (1924–88) was nominated for the Grand Prize at Cannes. Also making distinguished films in a popular idiom was the actor-director Guru Dutt (1925–64), most celebrated for *Kaagaz ke Phool* (1959, right), a tragic account of the failing career and marriage of a film director.

In Ceylon (Sri Lanka), Lester James Peries (b. 1919), generally considered his country's finest filmmaker, made his debut in 1956 with *Rekava*. Singhalese cinema, like Bollywood, had been dominated by stylized melodrama; Peries's film brought to it a new realism. In its story of the mistreatment of a boy believed to have magic powers, it voiced a subtle criticism of traditional beliefs. Active film industries also existed in the Philippines, Malaysia, Indonesia, Thailand, Pakistan, Iran, and Soviet Central Asia. The work of these industries since World War II is still little known internationally, but there may well be gems to discover. After all, few in the West in 1945 would have guessed that the then-unknown Asian cinema might include directors of the stature of Mizoguchi Kenji or Satyajit Ray. **AJ**

Tokyo monogatari 1953
Tokyo Story   OZU YASUJIRO 1903 – 63

▲ Shukichi (Ryu Chishu) and Tomi (Higashiyama Chieko) opt to end their trip.

▼ Ozu's film captured Japanese traditions and family ties at a time of deep change.

Ozu Yasujiro, claims writer Donald Richie, "had but one major subject, the Japanese family, and but one major theme, its dissolution." In *Tokyo monogatari*, Ozu gave that theme its most far-reaching expression, showing how changes in postwar Japanese society created divisions in the family. *Tokyo monogatari* is far from a mere historical document, and although Ozu has been called "the most Japanese of Japanese directors," the relevance of his work transcends the specific lineaments of Japanese culture.

The film centers on an elderly couple, resident in the port town of Onomichi in western Japan, who go to visit their adult children in the capital. Preoccupied with their own lives, the children neglect their parents' needs. Only their widowed daughter-in-law, Noriko, offers them the affection and commitment that they might have expected from their blood relatives. From this simple story, Ozu fashions a profound account of a country in the throes of a rapid and troubled process of modernization, where traditional mores are giving way to liberal individualism and industrial capitalism. However, this story of a particular time and place is also a description of the human condition.

Ozu's uniquely understated style largely eschews camera movement and builds the drama out of the subtleties of facial expression, gesture, and tone of voice. The performances of Ryu Chishu and Higashiyama Chieko as the parents are entirely convincing, despite the fact that Ryu plays a character some twenty years older than his real age. Hara Setsuko's performance as the kindly Noriko imbues this largely melancholy film with a redeeming note of hope. **AJ**

1 "WILL I STILL BE HERE?"
While the father Shukichi observes from inside the house, his wife, Tomi, walks with her little grandson, Minoru, on a grassy bank. "What are you going to be when you grow up?" Tomi asks him. "A doctor, like your father? By the time you're a doctor, will I still be here?"

2 "THEN YOU HAD AS MUCH TROUBLE AS I DID"
After a bus tour around Tokyo, Shukichi and Tomi go to the house of their widowed daughter-in-law Noriko. They inspect a photograph of their late son. Over a glass of sake, Tomi asserts that her husband used to drink too much; Noriko admits that their son was the same.

3 "LET'S GO HOME"
After a sleepless night at the lively beach resort of Atami, the elderly couple sit on a sea wall and decide to cut their trip short. As she tries to get up, Tomi suffers a dizzy spell, which Shukichi ascribes to sleeplessness. They then walk together along the sea wall.

🕐 DIRECTOR PROFILE

1903–30
Ozu Yasujiro was born in Tokyo. After debuting with what turned out to be his only period film, *Zange no yaiba (Sword of Penitence*, 1927), Ozu specialized in light comedy at one of Japan's major studios, Shochiku.

1931–36
An increasing seriousness is detectable in films such as *Tokyo no korasu (Tokyo Chorus*, 1931) and *Otona no miru ehon—Umarete wa mita keredo (I Was Born, But...*, 1932), which helped to establish the familial concerns and bittersweet tone of Shochiku and Ozu's speciality, the so-called *shomin-geki* (see panel below). Ozu's first sound film, *Hitori musuko (The Only Son*, 1936), established his austere mature style, with understated narrative and camera movement.

1937–48
Military service interrupted Ozu's career and his output was also affected by the limitations placed on filmmakers under Japan's militarist regime. He made only two films between 1937 and 1947, resuming during the US occupation with *Nagaya shinshiroku (Record of a Tenement Gentleman*, 1947).

1949–63
Banshun (Late Spring, 1949), an understated study of a father-daughter relationship, set the template for the humanity and resignation of Ozu's post-war work. With *Bakushu (Early Summer*, 1951) and *Tokyo monogatari*, it forms a loose trilogy examining Japanese family life. His later films reworked earlier plots and themes. He died in Tokyo on his sixtieth birthday.

SHOCHIKU AND *SHOMIN-GEKI*

Ozu Yasujiro was a distinguished representative of the Japanese studio system, which released more than three hundred films in 1953. Actors such as Hara Setsuko (below) were major stars, with recognized personae and a huge fan base. Ozu's dramas were some of the most outstanding of the Japanese *shomin-geki* genre (films about the lower middle classes), in which his studio, Shochiku, specialized. Its hallmarks were understated melodrama and a mix of humor and melancholy. Directors such as Shimizu Hiroshi and Kinoshita Keisuke also contributed to this genre, which became one of the most characteristic traditions of Japanese film art.

Shichinin no samurai 1954
Seven Samurai KUROSAWA AKIRA 1910 – 98

▲ The grandeur of the action scenes is unparalleled in Japanese cinema.

▼ Kurosawa's classic is set during the 1580s, during the Warring States Period.

The samurai film holds a position in Japanese cinema equivalent to that of the Western in Hollywood (see p. 242), providing an arena in which Japanese filmmakers and audiences can identify with their history and cultural heritage. Like the Western, it was one of the most popular genres in its country of origin; in the late 1950s, about a third of all Japanese films were set in the past, and most of these focused on the samurai.

Kurosawa Akira was to win fame as a master of the genre even though, before *Shichinin no samurai*, the bulk of his films were set in the present. Yet Kurosawa proved immediately in tune with the genre, which suited his taste for epic narrative. The movie took a year to film, and Kurosawa's perfectionism disturbed its studio, Toho, who threatened to cancel the project. However, on release the film proved a huge commercial hit.

Although Kurosawa's film remains the best-known example of its genre for Western audiences, it is not a conventional samurai movie. It does not draw, like most of its ilk, on figures of Japanese history or folklore. Rather, its story of a group of ronin (masterless samurai) helping the inhabitants of a poor village to fend off a group of bandits owes much to the American Western, and especially to John Ford (1894–1973), whose *Stagecoach* (1939) was the favorite film of screenwriter Shinobu Hashimoto. Kurosawa is also indebted to Ford for his imagery. It is appropriate that the film was remade in Hollywood in 1960 as *The Magnificent Seven*—the same title that was given to Kurosawa's film when it was first distributed in the United States in a severely cut print. **AJ**

👁 KEY SCENES

1 THE THREAT
Bandits consider raiding a village but, because they took its rice the previous autumn, there is nothing worth taking; they decide to return after the barley harvest. Kurosawa's opening shot of the riders in silhouette against a lowering sky pays tribute to director John Ford.

2 NOW WE ARE SEVEN
The villagers hire samurai, whom they fear, to protect them. Having raised a false alarm, Kikuchiyo (left) upbraids the villagers for running to the samurai, whom they had previously rejected, for help. Leader Kanbei (right) invites him to become the seventh samurai.

3 THE FARMER'S SON
The angry samurai find armor and weapons looted from samurai killed by the farmers. Kyuzo says he would like to kill every farmer, to which Kikuchiyo demands, "Who made animals of the farmers? You samurai did!" Kanbei asks, "You're a farmer's son, aren't you?"

4 THE FINAL BATTLE
After a tense period of waiting, the bandits launch their final attack on the village. Mounted on horseback, they ride into the village; the samurai and villagers resist fiercely. The final battle unfolds in the pouring rain, with the combat churning the ground to mud.

🕐 DIRECTOR PROFILE

1910–49
Kurosawa Akira was born in Tokyo. He trained as a painter but made his directorial debut with a martial arts film, *Sugata Sanshiro* (1943). Initially obliged to make wartime propaganda, he compensated during the occupation with *Waga seishun ni kuinashi* (*No Regrets for Our Youth*, 1946), about the persecution of prewar liberals. He also made two outstanding urban thrillers: *Yoidore tenshi* (*Drunken Angel*, 1948)—his first film with actor Toshiro Mifune—and *Nora inu* (*Stray Dog*, 1949).

1950–65
Rashomon won the Golden Lion at Venice and established Kurosawa's international reputation. Kurosawa followed up with some of his most distinctive and widely distributed films: the humanist *Ikiru* (1952), *Shichinin no samurai*, and the samurai version of Shakespeare's *Macbeth*, *Kumonosu-jo* (*Throne of Blood*, 1957). The cynical period films *Yojinbo* (1961) and *Tsubaki Sanjuro* (1962) proved major commercial hits, but after *Akahige* (*Red Beard*, 1965)—his last of fifteen films with Mifune—Kurosawa found funding unobtainable in Japan.

1966–74
Kurosawa was set to direct the Japanese segment of Twentieth Century Fox's *Tora! Tora! Tora!* in 1968 but he struggled to work in a Hollywood production and was fired. He made an unsuccessful attempt to establish independent production with *Dodes'kaden* (1970). Unable to secure future funding for film work and suffering with health problems, the director tried to commit suicide in December 1971.

1975–98
Kurosawa gained foreign funding to make the Siberian-set *Dersu Uzala* (1975) and the samurai films *Kagemusha* (1980) and *Ran* (1985). *Ran* was partly based on Shakespeare's *King Lear*. Fan Francis Ford Coppola (b. 1939) was a coproducer on *Kagemusha*, which was a commercial and critical success, winning the Palme d'Or at Cannes Film Festival. His later films were less acclaimed. *Madadayo* (1993) was his last film before he died.

The Apu Trilogy 1955–59
SATYAJIT RAY 1921–92

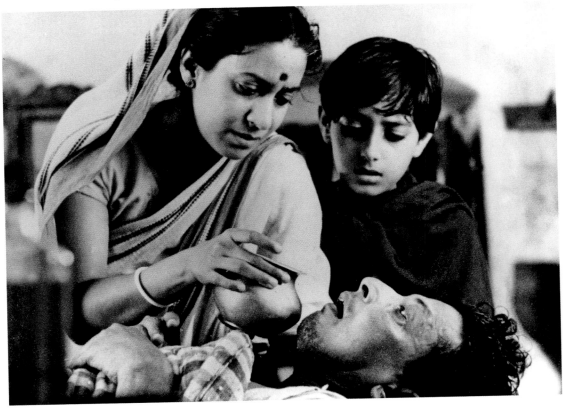

▲ Subir Banerjee was cast as the young Apu after Ray's wife saw him in the street.

▼ The films are the story of Apu's life.

When Satyajit Ray's *Pather panchali* (1955) was screened at the Cannes Festival in 1956, it caused a sensation. For the first time in the half century of its existence, the Indian film industry had produced a film that could bear comparison with the work of cinema's finest directors. That it was made in Bengal, far from the Indian movie capital of Bombay (now Mumbai), by a first-time director with unknown actors and a derisory budget, made it all the more astonishing. When Ray followed up with two sequels— *Aparajito* (1956) and *Apur sansar* (*The World of Apu*, 1959), it was clear that one of the great masters of humanist cinema had declared himself.

In *Pather panchali* young Apu grows up in a small Bengali village while his mother, Sarbojaya, struggles to support him and his sister, Durga, in the frequent absences of her husband Harihar, an ineffectual Brahmin priest. After Durga's death from pneumonia the family leaves for Benares. In *Aparajito* Harihar earns his living on the banks of the Ganges, but when he dies of fever, Sarbojaya takes Apu back to the country. A bright lad, he wins a scholarship to study in Calcutta. Left alone, Sarbojaya weakens and dies. *Apur sansar* finds Apu unwillingly pressed into marriage. Yet the union is a joyful success—until his wife dies in childbirth. Refusing to see his infant son, Apu flees into the wilderness, but finally returns to claim the boy and re-engage with the world.

Ray would go on to make more complex and sophisticated films, but the warmth, compassion, humor, emotional directness, eye for detail, and natural skill with actors evinced by the *Apu* trilogy give it lasting appeal. **PK**

KEY SCENES

1 PATHER PANCHALI

Apu and his sister, Durga, are wandering through a field of fluffy white *kaash* plants when they hear the sound of a train. Apu runs toward the plume of smoke on the horizon—and there before his wondering eyes is a visitation from the mysterious outside world.

2 APARAJITO

After the death of his father in Benares, Apu is taken by his mother back to the countryside. He is now all she has in the world—but slowly, inexorably, he will grow away from her, even as her need for him becomes more urgent.

3 APUR SANSAR

Having lost his young wife, Apu wanders for years, desolate and bitter, but finally returns to claim the son he has never seen. At first the boy rejects him but finally, as Apu leaves, runs after him. Apu, his son riding on his shoulders, sets out for the city and the world.

DIRECTOR PROFILE

1921–55

Satyajit Ray was born in Calcutta into a middle-class family. He studied at Rabindranath Tagore's "world university" at Santiniketan. He joined a British advertising agency as an art director and founded Calcutta's first film society. His first film, *Pather Panchali*, won international acclaim.

1956–63

He completed the *Apu* trilogy and was hailed as one of the great masters of humanist cinema. He steadily widened his scope with such films as *Jalsaghar* (*The Music Room*, 1958), *Devi* (*The Goddess*, 1960), his first color film, *Kanchenjungha*, made in 1962, and *Mahanagar* (*The Big City*, 1963).

1964–69

Two of his finest films—*Charulata* (1964) and *Aranyer din ratri* (*Days and Nights in the Forest*, 1970)—bookended a variable period in his career. But it included the first of his films for children, the lively fantasy *Goopy Gyne Bagha Byne* (*The Adventures of Goopy and Bagha*, 1968).

1970–81

Entering a more political phase, Ray examined social protest, industrial machinations, and British imperial misgovernment in *Pratidwandi* (*The Adversary*, 1971), *Seemabaddha* (*Company Limited*, 1971), and *Shatranj ke khilari* (*The Chess Players*, 1977).

1982–92

Illness slowed his output in his later years, but he achieved a final valedictory flourish in *Agantuk* (*The Visitor*, 1991). He received an honorary Oscar weeks before his death on April 23.

PAGE TO SCREEN

Pather panchali, the first novel of Bibhutibhushan Banerji (1894–1950) and one of the best-loved works in twentieth-century Bengali literature, was first published in 1929. Banerji subsequently wrote two sequels, *Aparajito* and *Kajal*, but they never attained the same popularity. Ray's *Pather panchali* covers roughly the first two-thirds of Banerji's novel, up to the point where the family leaves for Benares. Despite never using a complete script, Ray remained close to his source material, with the same five main characters and most of the same key events, conveying much of Banerji's sense of pantheistic wonder. *Aparajito* uses the rest of the first novel and the first half of its sequel, but dispenses with some major episodes and shifts the main emphasis to Apu's relationship with his mother. *Apur sansar* adapts a further chunk of the sequel, but with a toughening and darkening of the tone. The last hundred pages of Banerji's *Aparajito*, and the whole of *Kajal*, play no part in Ray's trilogy. *Pather panchali* is rightly regarded as the author's masterpiece.

POSTWAR HOLLYWOOD

Hollywood profited greatly from World War II. In addition to showing their effectiveness as propaganda machines, the major studios successfully exported their product to allied countries, where film budgets were limited because of the war effort. The popularity of Hollywood films abroad during World War II was expected to continue into the postwar years. However, economic, cultural, social, and political circumstances, as well as the specter of a new entertainment format—television—all played their part in curtailing the power and growth of one of the most profitable US industries.

Hollywood still looked healthy in the immediate aftermath of the war: 1946 was to become the most successful year in terms of cinema attendance, beating the record set in 1939. The most successful film of the year was Disney's *Song of the South*, but arguably the most important release was *The Best Years of Our Lives* by William Wyler (1902–81). A drama about the return of three servicemen from combat, the film grapples with the complexities of the men's lives, the memories of combat that haunt them and the challenges their families and loved ones face. The film ends on a relatively upbeat note, but there is no escaping the struggle that lies ahead for each of the characters, reflecting the state of unease that pervaded much of the United States.

This ambivalence marked even the postwar classic *It's a Wonderful Life* (1946, see p. 224) by Frank Capra (1897–1991). The ending may superficially

1 James Stewart as wheelchair-bound photographer L. B. Jeffries in *Rear Window*, the second of four films the actor made with Alfred Hitchcock.

2 Elia Kazan's drama *On the Waterfront* won four Academy Awards, including Best Actor and Best Film.

3 Marilyn Monroe at her most iconic in *The Seven Year Itch*.

(1946, see p. 224)

KEY EVENTS

1946	1947	1947	1947	1948	1949
Audiences flock to cinemas in greater numbers than ever before. *The Best Years of Our Lives* dominates the Oscars and the Golden Globes.	HUAC arrives in Los Angeles. The Hollywood Ten condemn McCarthyism and the Hollywood Blacklist.	Marilyn Monroe makes her film debut in *Dangerous Years*.	The Hollywood Antitrust Case (United States v. Paramount Pictures, Inc, 334 US 131) begins.	Vincente Minnelli (1903—86) directs *The Pirate*. The year is retrospectively regarded as the end of Hollywood's golden age.	Raoul Walsh (1887—1980) directs *White Heat*, which marks the end of the classic gangster genre.

smack of the sentimentality that marred too many of the director's films, but there is no mistaking the dark tone that pervades the whole film, particularly in James Stewart's browbeaten performance. After serving in the US Air Force, Stewart had to be persuaded to return to acting. His wartime experience had affected him deeply, which was reflected in the darker roles he played. This shift in his persona would be explored by Alfred Hitchcock (1899–1980) in *Rear Window* (1954, opposite) and *Vertigo* (1958), and by Anthony Mann (1906–67), for whom he excelled in playing a variety of morally compromised characters.

The mixture of light and dark in actors, characters, and films was exemplified in the work of Billy Wilder (1906–2002). One of cinema's most versatile directors, he proved prolific in the 1940s and 1950s, as he switched between the drama of *The Lost Weekend* (1945), the pitch-black *Sunset Boulevard* (1950), and making an icon out of Marilyn Monroe in *The Seven Year Itch* (1955, below right) and *Some Like It Hot* (1959, see p. 228). Hollywood's move toward darker territory had begun earlier with the arrival of the House Un-American Activities Committee (HUAC) in 1947. The committee was charged with investigating the infiltration of Communist sympathizers among the entertainment elite and, as a result, more than 250 members of the Hollywood community were blacklisted, while a significant number were forced to identify Communist sympathizers. One of the most prominent of these was Elia Kazan (1909–2003), whose film *On the Waterfront* (1954, above right), seen as a riposte to his critics, has as its lead character a mob informer (played by Marlon Brando). In contrast to Kazan, Ring Lardner Jr., one of the many writers blacklisted and charged with contempt at a hearing in 1947, famously informed the committee, "I could answer...but if I did, I would hate myself in the morning." The writer Lillian Hellman was more scathing. In 1948 she wrote, "Naturally, men scared to make pictures about the American Negro, men who only in the last year allowed the word 'Jew' to be spoken in a picture, who took more than ten years to make an anti-Fascist picture, these are frightened men and you pick frightened men to frighten first. Judas goats, they'll lead the others to slaughter for you."

Hollywood was terrified by the investigations, which cast a shadow over the industry. In a knee-jerk response, a number of studios produced anti-Communist features, including *My Son John* (1952) and *Pickup on South Street* (1953, see p. 238). Even children's films, such as the Dr. Seuss adaptation *The 5,000 Fingers of Dr. T* (1953), were seen to contain red-baiting connotations. The trend passed, but the damage caused by the investigations, along with the increased strain on each studio's purse, the impact of television, and an increasingly diverse audience less interested in what studios were offering, marked the end of the golden age of the Hollywood studio system.

Although audiences had flocked to the cinema in the immediate postwar period, attendance began to flag in the late 1940s. During the war, many

1950	1951	1952	1956	1957	1959
Two of Hollywood's bleakest, most self-reflective films are released—Billy Wilder's *Sunset Boulevard* and *In a Lonely Place* by Nicholas Ray (1911–79).	Vincente Minnelli directs *An American in Paris*. Billy Wilder's *Ace in the Hole* presents a scathing take on celebrity culture.	The Supreme Court allows filmmakers to challenge censors over their First Amendment rights.	*Rock Around the Clock* lures teenagers into cinemas, where they dance in the aisles and slash the seats.	*Sweet Smell of Success* by Alexander Mackendrick (1912—93) once again debunks the myth of stardom and celebrity in US showbiz.	The record-breaking Oscar winner *Ben-Hur* (see p.226) marks the apotheosis of the epic film. *Rawhide*, starring Clint Eastwood, premieres on CBS.

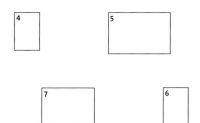

people remaining at home had more free time on their hands and going to the cinema was an effective, entertaining, and low-cost way of occupying it. However, with the return of service personnel, people became more settled into domestic life. The growth of the suburbs, the routine of finding work, and starting and supporting families took precedence. In many cases, because of the postwar economic dip and a scarcity of employment, a cinema ticket was no longer affordable. Television was a much cheaper form of entertainment. In 1940 there were 3,785 television sets in the United States. By 1960 nine out of every ten households had televisions. After the initial outlay, television enabled families to enjoy endless hours of entertainment. Acknowledging their audiences' love of cinema, the television companies began to compete with the studios, offering series that replicated cinema's most popular genres. Their success came so quickly that smaller studios faced bankruptcy and the networks bought up their lots and used them to film their own entertainment for the masses.

In response, the Hollywood studios moved into areas where television could not compete. The epic thus came into vogue for the first time since the days of silent cinema. *Quo vadis* (1951), *The Robe* and *Salome* (both 1953), *The Ten Commandments* (1956), *Alexander the Great* (1956), and *Ben-Hur* (1959, see p. 226) offered audiences spectacle on a grand scale. CinemaScope was developed and cinemas were modified to accommodate larger screens. Other tricks, from 3D to sensory devices that wafted smells into the auditorium or sent a small jolt of electricity through cinema seats, were also employed.

More traditional domestic genres were combined to satisfy audiences by offering something new. Thus the family drama was blended with elements of the frontier Western for *Giant* (1956, below), a portrait of family life on the Texan oilfields directed by George Stevens (1904–75). Douglas Sirk (1900–87) followed suit. With their Expressionist use of color, employed to great effect in *Magnificent Obsession* (1954), *All That Heaven Allows* (1955, above left), and *Imitation of Life* (1959), and by skirting the fringes of what was permissible in terms of sexual content for cinema at that time, his films offered a contrast to the duller tones of television dramas. However, such trends captivated audiences only for a limited period, whereas ongoing serials could guarantee long-term audiences. Television rapidly became the dominant form of entertainment for the US populace. Hollywood's demise was hastened by legal changes in the studio system and activities by filmmakers abroad.

4 Rock Hudson and Jane Wyman in a typically romantic and melodramatic poster for *All That Heaven Allows*.

5 Lee J. Cobb re-enacts the scene of the murder a little too vehemently in *Twelve Angry Men*. Unmoved, Henry Fonda stands over him as Juror No. 8.

6 The poster for Alfred Hitchcock's *North by Northwest*. This espionage thriller was the closest the director ever came to making an action-adventure film.

7 Jett Rink (James Dean) and Leslie Benedict (Elizabeth Taylor) in the epic *Giant*. It was the last of Dean's films before his death and earned him an Academy Award.

The Hollywood Antitrust Case of 1948—United States v. Paramount Pictures, Inc, 334 US 131—ended years of vertical integration whereby studios could own the theaters in which their films were shown. The ruling also limited block booking of a studio's films and the fixing of admission prices. The impact of the law sent shockwaves through Hollywood, undermining a system that had dominated Tinseltown for three decades. The ruling caused significant damage to Hollywood's increasingly beleaguered coffers. In addition there was bad news from abroad. Countries affected by the war saw in cinema a way to rebuild national pride, and countries such as France, Italy, and Britain began to produce their own films and moderate a deluge of US imports by imposing tariffs and quotas.

On a more positive note, a decline in motion picture censorship allowed filmmakers greater freedom of speech in the United States. In 1952 the Supreme Court overturned a decision made in 1915, finally allowing films the protection of freedom of speech as guaranteed in the First Amendment. The ruling also allowed individuals to challenge decisions made by boards of censors, which was what Otto Preminger (1905–86) did in 1953 when attempts were made to ban his film, *The Moon is Blue*, in Kansas, Ohio, and Maryland for its audacious use of the word "virgin." Questions about responsibility and social rights were also asked in *Twelve Angry Men* (1957, above) directed by Sidney Lumet (b. 1924). As well as being a superbly tight and well-acted drama, the film confronted prejudice and pricked the collective conscience three years before a new era of social revolution was ushered in.

The world and the world of cinema were about to change. The rebellious teenagers from the 1950s became the easy riders of the 1960s; the dapper hero of many a screwball comedy (see p. 148), Cary Grant, was on the run for his life in *North by Northwest* (1959, right); pretty boy Tony Curtis subverted his image in 1957 to play press agent Sidney Falco in the noirish *Sweet Smell of Success*; US directors were beginning to be influenced by the French auteurs; and in reaction to social and political upheaval, a new era of on-screen violence and liberal-minded filmmaking was about to take hold. The golden age of Hollywood was over and cinema was now looking toward a brave but unknown future. **IHS**

It's a Wonderful Life 1946

FRANK CAPRA 1897 – 1991

▲ *It's a Wonderful Life* has one of the most intense of all happy endings in cinema.

▼ Frank Capra produced, financed, directed, and co-wrote the film.

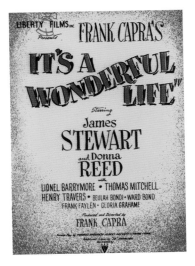

Small-town banker George Bailey (James Stewart), his life seemingly in ruins and his bank on the point of collapse thanks to the machinations of local fat cat Mr. Potter (Lionel Barrymore), contemplates suicide at Christmas. Wingless guardian angel Clarence (Henry Travers) shows him what his home town of Bedford Falls would be like if he had never been born.

Only George's idealism and self-sacrifice in staying in this backwater has kept the community such a wholesome, if stuffy, place—with friendly people, folksy drug stores, and *The Bells of St. Mary's* playing at the local cinema. If he were not there, the town would be a noirish hellhole in which friendly Violet (Gloria Grahame) is dragged away by the vice cops and Main Street is a riot of neon and raucousness; the cinema would be a burlesque house. Convinced that his life is worth living after all, George fixates on a pressed flower given him by a daughter he has thoughtlessly wished out of existence. He returns to his proper reality for a tearful family reunion—the bank is saved by small investors, the angel gains his wings and George sobs "Merry Christmas" to all and sundry. It is such a powerful, upbeat scene that the film can leave its major quandary unresolved—Potter still has the bank's stolen money and remains malign.

Frank Capra's fable became a Christmas television staple when the rights lapsed in 1974. It has grown in reputation since then, thanks to a daring mix of fantasy and archetypal Americana, and its grappling with postwar disillusion. Often mislabeled as an epitome of schmaltz, it is actually a complex film with as much unresolved tragedy as faith in the triumph of the human spirit. **KN**

KEY SCENES

1 "LASSO THE MOON"
Young George discusses his future with sweetheart Mary and promises her everything: "You want the moon? Just say the word and I'll throw a lasso around it and pull it down." The idealistic youthful George contrasts starkly with the older, disillusioned man.

2 ON THE BRIDGE
Having reached his lowest ebb, George crashes in a snowstorm and staggers to a bridge, intent on suicide. His guardian angel, Clarence, manifests to save his life. Capra developed a new type of film snow to shoot the Christmas-set film, which was made during a heatwave.

3 "AN AWFUL HOLE"
Without George Bailey, Bedford Falls has become Potterville, an ugly travesty of its true self. Clarence teaches George an important lesson: "Strange, isn't it? Each man's life touches so many other lives. When he isn't around he leaves an awful hole, doesn't he?"

4 HAPPY REUNION
George is reunited with his family, his friends and his life—and a bell confirms that Clarence has got his wings. An ending with a religious tone was mooted first then dismissed, but the emotional impact of family and friends coming to George's rescue endured.

DIRECTOR PROFILE

1897–1927
Born in Sicily, Frank Capra arrived in the United States with his family in 1903. After studying chemical engineering and serving in World War I, Capra entered the film industry, working as a gag writer for producer Mack Sennett. He took over as director of the Harry Langdon vehicle *The Strong Man* (1926), only to be dismissed from *Long Pants* (1927).

1928–33
Capra became Columbia's leading director, making a range of comedies and dramas, featuring such stars as Jean Harlow and Barbara Stanwyck—*Submarine* (1928), *Platinum Blonde* (1931), *American Madness* (1932), and *The Bitter Tea of General Yen* (1933).

1934–41
It Happened One Night (1934) swept the Oscars, establishing Capra as the best-known director in the United States. He followed up with a run of films (in collaboration with screenwriter Robert Riskin) that created a brand—nicknamed "Capra-corn"—of socially relevant screwball comedy, built around canny-naive, all-American heroes played by Gary Cooper or James Stewart. This included *Mr. Deeds Goes to Town* (1936), *You Can't Take It With You* (1938), *Mr. Smith Goes to Washington* (1939, without Riskin), and *Meet John Doe* (1941). The popular fantasy *Lost Horizon* (1937) was similarly thoughtful about the state of the world.

1942–45
He abandoned Hollywood to make wartime propaganda films, including the *Why We Fight* series. His only commercial release was *Arsenic and Old Lace* (1944).

1946–91
It's a Wonderful Life was nominated for five Oscars including Best Director. An independent production, it was not a box-office hit. Capra made a few more minor films—*Riding High* (1950) and *A Hole in the Head* (1959)—and educational films—*Our Mr. Sun* (1956) and *Hemo the Magnificent* (1957) both for television. His last feature film, *Pocketful of Miracles* (1961), was a remake of his earlier *Lady for a Day* (1933).

Ben-Hur 1959

WILLIAM WYLER 1902 – 81

▲ The famous chariot race required 15,000 extras and took five weeks to film.

▼ The poster has an aptly monumental look.

A remake of the silent epic released in 1925, *Ben-Hur* was one of a series of spectaculars that were huge successes at the box office in the 1950s. Following *Quo vadis* (1951), *The Robe* (1953), and *The Ten Commandments* (1956), *Ben-Hur* was perceived as the most epic of all epic films. However, it is also remembered for a snide review ("Loved Ben...Hated Hur") as well as its achievements. The key to the criticism is director William Wyler's adoption of the Cecil B. DeMille (1881–1959) theory that audiences for biblical films feel permitted to enjoy orgiastic sex and violence only because the wrath of God descends upon the unrighteous at the end.

A more sophisticated filmmaker than DeMille, Wyler thought that it was not enough to bring the temple down on the evil characters. So the strong, simple story of Judah Ben-Hur (Charlton Heston), the Jewish nobleman betrayed and enslaved by his treacherous Roman friend Messala (Stephen Boyd), fluctuates between crowd-pleasing action set pieces and "inspiring" encounters with Christ that allow Heston to wrestle with religious matters. The best scenes take place in the first half of the film; the post-chariot race section lingers too long in the leper colony. Subsequent sword-and-sandal epics, from *Spartacus* (1960) to *Gladiator* (2000), played down sermonizing and played up the violence, suggesting a lesson learned. Still, as Heston and Boyd glare over their chariot reins, audiences cannot help but love *Ben-Hur*. The movie was the top-grossing film of the year and scored an Academy Award tally unequalled until *Titanic* (1997). **KN**

KEY SCENES

1 FRIENDS FOREVER
Judah and Messala reaffirm their boyhood bond. Legend has it that Heston resisted the suggestion, put forward by Gore Vidal in an early draft, that the antagonists be former lovers, but Heston claimed he was aware of the subtext, which Boyd especially plays up.

2 GALLEY SLAVE
The calculating Messala turns against Judah and condemns him to slavery on a Roman galley ship. After being forced to serve in the galleys, Ben-Hur encounters the ship's new commander, Consul Quintus Arrius (Jack Hawkins).

3 THE SEA BATTLE
During a clash with Macedonian pirates, Quintus Arrius's galley is attacked and ultimately sunk, but Judah saves his life and the lives of fellow rowers. On his return to Rome, Arrius petitions for Judah's freedom and adopts him as his son.

4 IN THE ARENA
The chariot race set piece (directed by Andrew Marton and Yakima Canutt) was conceived to be more impressive than the scene from the silent version. Heston is in the thick of the action but he did have a stunt double for parts of the race—Joe Canutt, son of Yakima.

5 MIRACLE IN THE LEPER COLONY
After the Crucifixion, a shower washes the blood of Christ into the leper colony, where Judah Ben-Hur's mother and sister are cured. This further motivates the hero to dedicate himself to the new Christian faith.

DIRECTOR PROFILE

1902–35
Alsace-born William Wyler became one of Universal's A-list directors with *Hell's Heroes* (1929).

1936–41
He left Universal to work for independent producer Samuel Goldwyn on projects that included *Wuthering Heights* (1939).

1942–54
Having made war documentaries, Wyler returned to Goldwyn for the key postwar film *The Best Years of Our Lives* (1946).

1955–59
After crime dramas (*Detective Story*, 1951) and super-Westerns (*The Big Country*, 1958), Wyler's career peaked with *Ben-Hur*.

1960–81
Wyler tried to keep up in the "new Hollywood" with films such as *The Liberation of L. B. Jones* (1970). His final big hit was the resolutely old-fashioned *Funny Girl* (1968).

Some Like It Hot 1959

BILLY WILDER 1906 – 2002

▲ Marilyn and a bewigged Tony Curtis.

▼ Monroe takes star billing on the poster, along with some gentle innuendo.

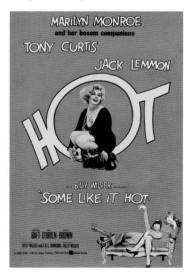

It is easy to forget what a risky proposition *Some Like It Hot* once seemed. This was a gender-bending comedy drama set against one of the most violent events in US gangland history: the St. Valentine's Day Massacre in 1929. Its star, Marilyn Monroe, was notoriously unreliable. There was much doubt as to whether a general audience would warm to a film that combined jokes about cross-dressing with scenes of mass murder. As Billy Wilder later told interviewer Cameron Crowe, legendary producer David O. Selznick had predicted, "They're going to crucify you. They're going to walk out in droves."

Wilder, however, guessed correctly that audiences would enjoy subject matter that deliberately flouted notions of good taste. Despite his tribulations in working with Monroe on *The Seven Year Itch* (1955), he also knew that if he persevered, she would be "amazing" on screen. "And she was, believe it or not, an excellent dialogue actress," he told Crowe. "She knew where the laugh was."

The plot, partially borrowed from an old German movie, is straightforward. Jack Lemmon and Tony Curtis play two musicians who inadvertently witness a gangland massacre in Chicago. To get out of town quick, they disguise themselves as women musicians and take jobs in a traveling all-female jazz band.

In Britain, the *Manchester Guardian* tutted over the "harsh and even repellent cynicism" that ran through Wilder's work. *Time* magazine carped that Monroe had been "trimmer, slimmer, and sexier" in earlier movies. However, *Some Like It Hot* yielded so many pleasurable moments that the public was won over, and the film has nestled at the top of audiences' all-time favorite lists ever since. **GM**

👁 KEY SCENES

1 THE WRONG PLACE AT THE WRONG TIME
"Hands up! Face the wall." It is Chicago 1929. Musicians Joe (Tony Curtis) and Jerry (Jack Lemmon) hide as Spats (George Raft) orders a rival gang's massacre in a city car park. They are spotted escaping, however, and machine-gun bullets rake Jerry's double bass.

2 "I WANNA BE LOVED BY YOU!"
Sugar Kane Kowalczyk (Marilyn Monroe) at her most alluring as she performs an old musical standard in a Florida nightspot. *Time* magazine's comments on the actress's weight were accurate, if unkind: Monroe was actually pregnant at the time.

3 WHAT'S IN THE CAKE?
The gangsters have come to Florida under the cover of attending a convention for Italian opera lovers. Security for the event is ultra-strict, but when a gunman pops out of an enormous cake, Spats finally gets his comeuppance.

4 "NOBODY'S PERFECT!"
Jerry, still in drag, tries to deflect the attentions of millionaire Osgood (Joe E. Brown). He runs through a long list of excuses, all dismissed by Osgood. Finally Jerry reveals, "I'm a man!" "Well," Osgood replies, beatific smile still on his face, "nobody's perfect!"

🕐 STAR PROFILE: MARILYN MONROE

1926–41
Marilyn Monroe was born Norma Jeane Mortenson—her surname was later changed to Baker. Her mother Gladys was mentally unstable. Norma had a troubled childhood that included spells in foster homes and state institutions.

1942–45
At only sixteen, she married James Dougherty in what many regard as a marriage of convenience to escape the influence of her mother. With her husband overseas on military duty, she began to work as a model.

1946–50
Having been spotted by a talent scout, she signed a studio contract with Fox and changed her name to Marilyn Monroe; she was divorced in 1946. Her Fox contract was not renewed and a subsequent contract with Columbia, signed in 1948, also quickly lapsed. But she began to pick up roles in some notable films, among them *The Asphalt Jungle* and *All About Eve* (both 1950). In 1949 she worked briefly as a nude model.

1951–54
After winning a seven-year contract at Fox, she established herself as one of the studio's biggest stars in films such as *Gentlemen Prefer Blondes* and *How To Marry a Millionaire* (both 1953). In 1954 she married baseball star Joe DiMaggio. They divorced later that year.

1955–62
Monroe studied at Lee Strasberg's Actors' Studio and dated playwright Arthur Miller; they married in 1956. She attracted critical plaudits for *Bus Stop* (1956). After *The Prince and the Showgirl* (1957), directed by Laurence Olivier, she withdrew from film work for a year; *Some Like It Hot* (1959) marked her comeback. She and Miller were divorced in 1961 and her final completed film was *The Misfits* (1961). In 1962 she sang a famously sensual version of "Happy Birthday" in public to President John F. Kennedy. Later that year she was found dead in her apartment, at the age of thirty-six.

REBELLIOUS YOUTH

1 Cal (James Dean) suffers at the hands of a brothel bodyguard (Timothy Carey) in the Cain and Abel tale *East of Eden*.

2 Elvis Presley in *Jailhouse Rock*—subversive for its time. Presley's dance routine won plaudits from Gene Kelly.

3 Richard Dadier (Glenn Ford) confronts a teenage firebrand (a youthful Sidney Poitier) in *Blackboard Jungle*.

B etween the release of *The Wild One* (1953, see p. 232) and *Easy Rider* (1969) Hollywood engaged in an extended on-off romance with American youth, explaining, indulging, and exploiting the phenomenon of the teenager. Although significant at the time, such youth-oriented films are by their very nature ephemeral and only a few of them managed to make the issue of mid-century generational conflict feel universal. *The Wild One*, directed by Laslo Benedek (1905–92), is often seen as having kick-started the cycle, although it is only marginally a youth-oriented film; the bikers in the movie seem more like Western outlaws than troubled teens. Marlon Brando was nearly thirty years old when he made the film, but his inarticulate grace, along with the sunglasses, leather jacket, and air of unspecific defiance, made him briefly the poster boy of discontented youth.

James Dean replaced Brando's simmering intensity with hurt introspection. In his first major feature film, *East of Eden* (1955, above) directed by Elia Kazan (1909–2003), Dean's depiction of the wayward son vying for the love of his father resonated strongly with young audiences in the mid 1950s. Released later the same year, urban drama *Rebel Without a Cause* (see p. 234), directed by Nicholas Ray (1911–79), took the world of juvenile delinquency out of the streets and into a prosperous middle-class neighborhood. It also gave Dean the

KEY EVENTS

1952	1953	1954	1955	1956	1956
Marlon Brando's method acting earns him an Oscar nomination for his performance as Stanley Kowalski in *A Streetcar Named Desire*.	*The Wild One* (see p. 232) immortalizes Marlon Brando as a leather-jacketed rebel.	Elvis Presley makes his first recordings for the Sun label in Memphis.	*East of Eden* and *Rebel Without a Cause* (see p. 234) are released. James Dean dies in a car crash, at the age of twenty-four.	Dean's final film, *Giant*, directed by George Stevens (1904–75), is released posthumously. Elvis Presley makes his film debut with *Love Me Tender*.	Elvis Presley releases his first number one hit "Heartbreak Hotel" and makes his first appearance on national television.

role with which he is most identified. His Jim Stark is in a state of not so much rebellion as incomprehension with regard to the world around him.

In *Blackboard Jungle* (1955, below) Richard Brooks (1912—92) puts juvenile delinquency back in the inner-city school system. As a slice of well-intentioned social comment, with Glenn Ford as a teacher forced to confront his delinquent students, the film was hijacked by the inclusion of Bill Haley's "Rock Around the Clock." It was the first big Hollywood movie to feature rock 'n' roll on its soundtrack, and in British cinemas teddy boys regularly rioted at screenings of the film. In the 1950s rock 'n' roll, not cinema, was the truest expression of teenage experience, with the young Elvis Presley as its charismatic avatar. Presley's career in cinema began with dramatic roles; *Jailhouse Rock* (1957, right) was one of the few films to capture the rawness of his early years. After his army service, however, his film career declined into a series of nice-guy starring roles in increasingly bland musicals.

Too amorphous to be a genre, these films of the 1950s seem today to be as much about Hollywood trying to understand and exploit the new generation as about the discontents of youth. The brief career of James Dean produced the one defining representation of the troubled generation of mid-century America. His death before the release of *Rebel Without a Cause* fixed his image forever in a rictus of adolescent angst. By the mid 1960s the emergent counter-culture had changed the course of youth-oriented films. In 1966 Roger Corman (b. 1926) directed biker movie *The Wild Angels*. Featuring a gang rape and a biker funeral with a coffin draped in a Nazi flag, *The Wild Angels* is far more confrontational than *The Wild One*. **DP**

1957	1957	1958	1958	1958	1964
American International Pictures releases *I Was a Teenage Werewolf*, starring Michael Landon as a juvenile delinquent.	*Jailhouse Rock* confirms Elvis Presley's talent as an actor, although subsequent films see his potential squandered.	Elvis Presley joins the US army. Erstwhile outsider icons Marlon Brando and Montgomery Clift appear in *The Young Lions*.	Jack Arnold (1916—92) makes *High School Confidential* ("A teachers' nightmare! A teen-age jungle!"). It features a Jerry Lee Lewis title song.	Steve McQueen stars as a high school student in *The Blob*, one of a string of low-budget B-movies made in the late 1950s.	The Beatles' first tour of the United States helps initiate a swing away from the United States toward British youth culture.

The Wild One 1953
LASLO BENEDEK 1905 – 92

▲ The Black Rebels Motorcycle Club line-up. Sales of leather jackets soared after the film.

▼ Sex, violence, and Brando's brooding presence are played up on the poster.

In 1947 the Hell's Angels Motorcycle Club—then composed mostly of World War II veterans who carried over the nicknames and colors of their military units—rode into the small town of Hollister, California, and annoyed residents with their high-spirited antics. The incident, sensationalized in a *Harper's Magazine* article "The Cyclists' Raid," inspired Stanley Kramer, known for liberal-leaning "social problem" pictures, to produce this once-controversial drama. It was banned in Britain until 1968, for fear that Vespa-riding hoodlums would imitate the reckless driving and irresponsible behavior of the Black Rebels gang (many of whom ride British Triumph bikes) who terrorize Wrightsville over a holiday weekend.

Johnny (Marlon Brando) followed up star-making roles ("That 'Streetcar' man has a new desire!" fizzed one tagline) with this exercise in social comment as exploitation. Less convincingly grungy than Harley-riding villain Chino (Lee Marvin), he is credibly soulful enough to reform after he has fallen for a nice local girl (Mary Murphy). The film wavers between trashy and preachy, but has classic moments as motorcycles roar along the quiet roads and a complaint of "What are you rebelling against?" is greeted with the classic snarl "Whattaya got?"

There is still a frisson today in this motorized update of the Western outlaw story as troublemakers move into the sort of 1950s small town seen as the backbone of the United States and act like an army of occupying barbarians. As an exposé of juvenile delinquency, it is less on-the-nose than *Blackboard Jungle* (1955) or *Rebel Without a Cause* (1955, see p. 234)—for a start, the bikers are all more grown-up than the script suggests—but it triggered a drive-in subgenre. **KN**

1 BIKE GANG

In the pre-credits opening shot, the censorious words "This is a shocking story....It is a public challenge not to let it happen again" flash up. On an open road, a gang of bikers appears. They roar into the foreground as the titles come up.

3 ENTER CHINO

Johnny and his gang are about to quit the town when up roars his nemesis. Chino (Lee Marvin, with a permanent sneer clamped around his stogie), an ex-Black Rebel, is now leader of rival gang The Beetles. Marvin taught himself to ride a motorcycle for the part.

2 THE REBELLIOUS LOOK

Marlon Brando wears biker leathers, a sneer on his lips. A poster icon of rebellion, non-conformity, and—thanks to artist Tom of Finland and the biker in the Village People—gay sexuality. After this film, a leather jacket was as much a threat as a fashion statement.

4 WOUNDED ANGEL

Having abandoned his gang for the love of a good girl, Johnny is alone when the townsfolk attack. Like many sensitive troublemakers of the 1950s, and several other Brando martyrs, from Zapata to the whipped cowboy of *One-Eyed Jacks* (1961), he suffers beautifully.

BIKER MOVIES

There were B-picture follow-ups to *The Wild One* in the 1950s, such as *Motorcycle Gang* (1957), and biker iconography informs *Scorpio Rising* (1964) directed by Kenneth Anger (b. 1927). However, the biker movie did not emerge as a subgenre until Roger Corman's hit *The Wild Angels* (1966). Variations highlighted girl gangs (*The Mini-Skirt Mob*, 1968) and bikers in Vietnam (*Nam's Angels*, 1970); there was also the self-explanatory *Werewolves on Wheels* (1971). *The Wild Angels* inspired *Easy Rider* (1969), a more arty take that fed into a range of 1970s road movies, including one with an anti-biker, the motorcycle cop of *Electra Glide in Blue* (1973). Biker movies continue as a nostalgia item; the form also led to the television series *Sons of Anarchy* (2008–).

Rebel Without a Cause 1955

NICHOLAS RAY 1911 – 79

▲ Jim Stark stands apart in his red jacket.

▼ A sensationalist poster for a genuinely powerful film with emotive performances.

Early in *Rebel Without a Cause*, Jim Stark (James Dean) lets loose a feral cry, "You're tearing me apart!" as his parents fret around him in an LA police station, where he has been taken for public drunkenness. Dean is the epitome of the angst-ridden teen rebel—a type that had not been seen on screen in quite such intense focus before—but he is nothing like the punkish kids seen in films such as *Dead End* (1937) or *Angels With Dirty Faces* (1938). This is not a kid from the wrong side of the tracks. He is a 1950s American teenager, affluent and good-looking. European audiences, living in relative austerity, were startled to see that all the wild young adults in the film had their own cars.

At the time, Warner Bros already had rights to a non-fiction book, called *Rebel Without a Cause*, about a criminal delinquent. Nicholas Ray had come up with a story idea called "The Blind Run," about troubled youngsters. Ray did not base his tale of disaffected youth only on the opinions of educational theorists and psychologists. He spoke directly to the kids too. LA teen gangster Frank Mazzola (later to become a successful film editor) had a small role in the film and advised Ray on gang culture. However, this was not gritty realism. Sleekly shot in color and CinemaScope, it had a fablelike quality.

Dean is a compelling screen presence, but the strength of his performance blinds audiences to the other story that the film tells—that of the middle-aged parents so sadly estranged from their own children. Jim Backus (the voice of cartoon figure Mr. Magoo) brings touching pathos to the role of Jim's henpecked father, an emasculated figure no less at odds with the times than his son. **GM**

👁 KEY SCENES

1 "YOU'RE TEARING ME APART!"
This famous howl of anguish leaves Jim's parents open-mouthed and bewildered. They give him love, so why is he so set against them? Jim is the core of a group of three alienated teenagers in the film, the others being Judy (Natalie Wood) and Plato (Sal Mineo).

2 THE FIGHT AT THE PLANETARIUM
Buzz (Corey Allen) and Jim go into hand-to-hand knife combat at the Griffith Observatory; Los Angeles acts as a panoramic backdrop. By beating him on his own terms, Jim not only proves he is no coward but also threatens to prize away Buzz's girl, Judy.

3 BUZZ'S DEMISE
Buzz and Jim drive stolen cars toward a cliff in a game of "chickie run," but Buzz's leather jacket becomes caught on the door handle, preventing his escape, and he dies when his vehicle hurtles over the precipice. His gang, and the police, are now after Jim, Judy, and Plato.

4 THE DEATH OF PLATO
Jim's devoted friend Plato talks with Judy moments before he is shot dead by the police. He is wearing Jim's red jacket and has an unloaded gun in his hand. His death is so devastating that it helps bring Jim and his father together.

🕐 DIRECTOR PROFILE

1911–45
Nicholas Ray studied architecture with Frank Lloyd Wright. In the 1930s he joined federal theater projects, part of Franklin D. Roosevelt's New Deal culture program. He worked as a director's assistant on *A Tree Grows in Brooklyn* (1945).

1946–49
In 1946 Ray directed his only Broadway musical, *Beggar's Holiday*. Three years later came his debut as a movie director, the noir *They Live by Night*. The film, which revolves around young criminal lovers, shows both Ray's affinity for outsiders and his flair for telling stories about young characters.

1950–52
With *In a Lonely Place* (1950) Ray elicited one of Humphrey Bogart's bravest, least characteristic performances, as a Hollywood screenwriter charged with murder.

1953–54
Ray turned the Western on its head with *Johnny Guitar* (1954) starring Joan Crawford, his baroque foray into the genre. Unusually for a Western, strong female characters drive the film's narrative.

1955–60
Rebel Without a Cause became Ray's greatest success. His *The True Story of Jesse James* (1957) was reputedly to have starred James Dean, but the role passed to Robert Wagner.

1961–79
Ray moved to Europe and made large-scale, sweeping epics, *King of Kings* (1961)—mauled by the critics at the time—and *55 Days at Peking* (1963). Ray's reputation went into decline, his health deteriorated and he struggled to get further projects off the ground, although a chance meeting with Dennis Hopper at a Grateful Dead concert led to his teaching filmmaking. He taught at the Lee Strasberg Institute and New York University. In 1979 he collaborated with Wim Wenders (b. 1945) on a documentary, *Lightning Over Water* (1980), about his own death. He died of lung cancer in 1979.

COLD WAR CINEMA

1 The eyes have it: aliens take human hosts in *It Came from Outer Space*.

2 The poster for *I Was a Communist for the FBI*—a film that inverts the threat of Communist infiltration by presenting a US agent as a fifth columnist instead.

3 Concern about the relatively new nuclear age—and basic human vulnerability—emerges in *The Incredible Shrinking Man*, starring Grant Williams.

Images of panic from another time: a man runs into the oncoming traffic screaming, "They're after you! They're after all of us!" An old woman gives a sweating Communist spy permission to put her out of her misery. A young woman guns down her co-conspirator for a chance to open a metal box and set loose the hissing snakes of nuclear destruction. These sequences from three movies of the mid fifties (*Pickup on South Street*, 1953, see p. 238; *Kiss Me Deadly*, 1955; *Invasion of the Body Snatchers*, 1956, see p. 240) show US cinema at its most visceral, capturing the psychological undercurrents of the nation in the era of the Cold War and McCarthyism. The arrival of the House Un-American Activities Committee (HUAC) in Hollywood in September 1947 had the studio heads running scared. At a secret meeting at New York's Waldorf-Astoria Hotel that November, they adopted a policy of co-operation.

Often cited as the first Cold War film, *The Iron Curtain* (1948), directed by William Wellman (1896–1975), is a relatively sober account, based on real events, of a spy ring in Canada. The crudeness of the politics of many of the films that followed is reflected in titles such as *The Red Menace* (1949) directed by R. G. Springsteen (1904–89), in which an ex-GI is sucked into a Communist ring, or *I Was a Communist for the FBI* (1951, opposite above) by Gordon Douglas (1907–93), about an undercover agent infiltrating the Communist Party. Made cheaply and without big stars, the studios' propaganda efforts seem almost apologetic.

KEY EVENTS

1945	1947	1948	1950	1951	1953
Under the presidency of Harry S. Truman, atomic bombs are dropped on Hiroshima and Nagasaki.	The alleged discovery of alien corpses and wreckage in New Mexico is dubbed the Roswell Incident. HUAC arrives in Hollywood.	The Hollywood Ten—writers and directors who would not testify to HUAC—are jailed; the Soviet Union blocks Allied access to Berlin in the Berlin Blockade.	Senator Joe McCarthy claims that the State Department is "infested with Communists." The Korean War begins.	The second wave of HUAC investigations in Hollywood begins.	The Korean War ends. *It Came from Outer Space* is released.

The Woman on Pier B (1949), which was first titled *I Married a Communist* until the studio changed it, directed by Robert Stevenson (1905–86), was offered by Howard Hughes to various directors as a loyalty test. The absurdities of its script are counterbalanced by the noirish cinematography of Nicholas Musuraca and a strong cast headed by Robert Ryan. John Wayne starred in *Big Jim McLain* (1952) directed by Edward Ludwig (1898–1982), as a two-fisted investigator for HUAC who exposes a nest of Commies in Hawaii (poster strapline: "He's a Go-Get-'Em Guy for the USA on a Treason-Trail that leads Half-a-World Away!").

The films that truly reflected their age did not rely on simplistic propaganda. Director Samuel Fuller (1912–97) was no apologist for McCarthyism. In his *Pickup on South Street*, Communist spies are loose in New York, trying to steal government microfilm, but the film's morality resides in its petty criminals. J. Edgar Hoover loathed it. *Kiss Me Deadly* (1955) by Robert Aldrich (1918–93) reinvents Mickey Spillane's right-wing avenger Mike Hammer as a narcissistic thug, out of his depth in search of "the Great Whatsit," a metal box that houses nuclear annihilation.

In the summer of 1947 newspapers reported that unidentified debris had been found in New Mexico, bringing with it the first stirrings of UFO paranoia. The alien invasion plots in science fiction films echoed Cold War anxieties. *The Thing from Another World* (1951), directed by Christian Nyby (1913–93) but bearing the stamp of its producer Howard Hawks, features a blood-drinking alien unwittingly brought into an Arctic research post. Its closing line, "Watch the skies, everywhere!" could be read as a wake-up call to the nation. *It Came from Outer Space* (1953, opposite) is more ambiguous; while the aliens are relatively benign, they take up temporary residence in human bodies. *Invasion of the Body Snatchers*, with its alien pods replicating their human hosts, could be read as a metaphor for the menace of Communism or for the creeping conformity of the United States under McCarthyism. *Invaders from Mars* (1953) was less ambiguous: a small boy sees his parents turned into robot-voiced zombies by the evil little green (read: "Red") parasites; the aliens are routed by the full righteous force of the US army.

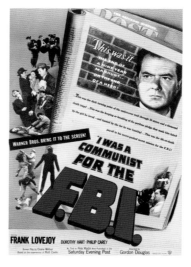

The Incredible Shrinking Man (1957, right) by Jack Arnold (1916–92) provides the most poignant metaphor for the fears of mid-century America. An LA businessman notices that he is beginning to shrink—the irreversible consequence of chance nuclear contamination. On his journey to nothingness, he is reduced to living in a doll's house that replicates his own suburban home, and faces his final struggle for survival alone in his cellar, a speck among the detritus of US life.

In the 1960s it seemed possible that some of the political ghosts could be exorcized. *The Manchurian Candidate* (1962) by John Frankenheimer (1930–2002) showed a McCarthy-clone senator as a buffoon used to front a Communist takeover in the United States and *Point of Order* (1964) by Emile de Antonio (1920–89) used TV footage of the Army-McCarthy hearings to reveal the truth about McCarthyism. By then the Cuban Missile Crisis and the Kennedy assassination meant that the fears of the 1950s had morphed into a different shape. **DP**

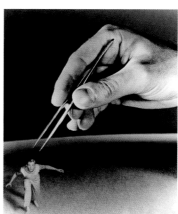

1954	1955	1957	1961	1962	1963
The Army-McCarthy hearings take place, to address claims of favoritism toward a McCarthy associate.	*Kiss Me Deadly*, directed by Robert Aldrich, is released.	Joseph McCarthy dies. Jack Arnold's *The Incredible Shrinking Man* is released.	The abortive Bay of Pigs invasion of Cuba attempts to unseat Fidel Castro.	The construction of missile bases on Cuba, with Soviet aid, sparks the Cuban Missile Crisis. *The Manchurian Candidate* is released.	John F. Kennedy is assassinated.

Pickup on South Street 1953

SAMUEL FULLER 1912 – 97

▲ The trampy, misused Candy and cocky McCoy are thrown together by chance.

▼ Jean Peters beat Marilyn Monroe and Ava Gardner to the female lead of Candy.

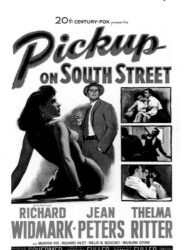

20th CENTURY-FOX presents

Pickup ON SOUTH STREET

STARRING
RICHARD JEAN THELMA WIDMARK·PETERS RITTER

with MURVYN VYE · RICHARD KILEY · WILLIS B. BOUCHEY · MILBURN STONE

JULES SCHERMER SAMUEL FULLER SAMUEL FULLER DWIGHT TAYLOR

Ex-newspaperman Samuel Fuller had already received a rap on the knuckles from the FBI for his blunt depiction of the realities of war in *The Steel Helmet* (1951). According to his autobiography, the writer-director earned an interview with J. Edgar Hoover for the "problematic" content in the brutal noir thriller *Pickup on South Street*. This was in part due to the film's suggestion that federal agents would use bribes to secure information, but chiefly because it showed a US citizen ready to "play footsie" with Communist conspirators. It would be easy to view the film—as did Hoover—as a pulpy, paranoid product of the "reds under the bed" era, but that would be to miss Fuller's point entirely. The film is not about Communists; it is about moral bankruptcy.

It stars Richard Widmark as Skip McCoy, a sharp-suited rapscallion with a toothy grin and charisma to burn. He is a subway grifter who courts trouble when he filches a valuable microfilm that is on its way to a cadre of "scheming Commies." The hapless girl delivering the film is Candy (Jean Peters), an unwitting envoy between the disparate factions, who spends much of the film being battered and bruised. Although the ever-darkening intrigues of its story offer the film's most obvious pleasures, Fuller's crackling, street-savvy dialogue—informed by his time as a "yellow" crime journalist in New York—and his pulsating, skillfully co-ordinated direction—his use of camera movement to enhance emotion is particularly noteworthy, echoed now in the work of Martin Scorsese (b. 1942) and Quentin Tarantino (b. 1963)—ensures the film's position as a crime classic. **DJ**

👁 KEY SCENES

1 THE GRIFT

The taut, fluidly choreographed opening jump-starts the narrative, as McCoy inadvertently takes a microfilm from Candy's purse. Both are being watched by an FBI agent. Fuller's use of close-ups and tight angles frames the act from the three different perspectives.

2 A POISONED KISS

The crossover of conflicting motives is clear in McCoy and Candy's close-up embrace. Behind the facade of passion, she thinks she is buttering him up to buy the film back from him cheaply; he is waiting for an offer to see just how important his prize really is.

3 MOE'S EXECUTION

World-weary police snitch Moe (Thelma Ritter) is shot in the head by Communist stooge Joey (Richard Kiley), after delivering a moving, lightly existential final monologue. As the shot rings out, Fuller pans to a gramophone record that has reached its end.

4 BLOOD ON THE TRACKS

In an echo of the film's opening shot, Skip picks Joey's pocket, but then they exit the train and engage in a protracted punch-up in the ticket hall. The violence spills on to the tracks, a deadly progression underscoring the pair's nihilistic attitudes toward life.

🕐 DIRECTOR PROFILE

1912–36

Samuel Fuller was born in Massachusetts to Jewish-Russian immigrants. He began his career in journalism as a copy boy for the *New York Journal* in 1924 before becoming a fully fledged crime reporter for the *New York Evening Graphic*.

1937–45

From the mid 1930s Fuller wrote pulp novels and screenplays (the first two being for *Hats Off*, 1936, and *It Happened in Hollywood*, 1937). In 1941 he was assigned to the 1st Infantry Division (known as The Big Red One) as a rifleman and toured Africa, Sicily, and mainland Europe.

1946–50

Fuller directed his first three movies with independent producer Robert Lippert, the most notable being his debut, *I Shot Jesse James* (1949).

1951–57

Despite his insistence on dealing with controversial subjects, Fuller was given a contract with Twentieth Century Fox, where he produced some of his best work, including *Fixed Bayonets!* (1951) and *Pickup on South Street*.

1958–64

Two independent, low-budget films from this period perfectly sum up the primitive, deliciously hysterical Fuller style—*Shock Corridor* (1963) and *The Naked Kiss* (1964).

1965–66

Fuller made an iconic cameo appearance in *Pierrot le fou* (1965) by Jean-Luc Godard (b. 1930), in which he sums up cinema in a single, effortlessly cool quip: "A film is like a battleground... love, hate, action, violence, death. In one word: emotion."

1967–97

He made his long-cherished, grunt's-eye-view war epic *The Big Red One* (1980), but it failed to set the box office alight. Fuller moved to Paris (he was more appreciated in Europe than in the United States) after the wave of controversy sparked by his anti-racism film *White Dog* (1982). He died in 1997.

Invasion of the Body Snatchers 1956

DON SIEGEL 1912 — 91

▲ The survivors spot the pods—danger in seemingly innocuous packaging.

▼ An alarmist and eye-catching poster.

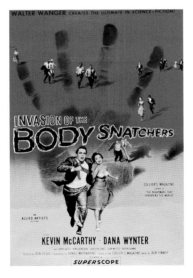

No other film has captured the malaise of the middle of the twentieth century quite as emphatically as Don Siegel's *Invasion of the Body Snatchers*. The script, by Daniel Mainwaring, based on a magazine serial by Jack Finney, predicates a nightmare of creeping conformism that has been variously interpreted as a metaphor for McCarthyism and an exercise in Cold War paranoia. However it has been interpreted, the film's paranoid intensity transcends its era.

Dr. Miles Bennell (Kevin McCarthy) is summoned from a medical conference to his practice in the apparently normal Californian town of Santa Mira, which is in the grip of a contagious delusion: people have taken to denying vehemently that close family members are who they say they are. What seems at first to be a form of mass hysteria is revealed as part of an extra-terrestrial takeover of humanity when seed pods that have the power to replicate their human hosts are discovered. What the invasion offers is a life without the messy complications of emotion; as one of the pod people says, "Love, desire, ambition, faith—without them, life's so simple."

McCarthy is ideal as the last man holding out against the invasion, his once bland features twisted into revulsion as he uses a pitchfork to destroy his embryonic shadow self. The original ending ("You're next!") was deemed too bleak by the studio, and a framing device was imposed that suggested the world could be alerted to the threat in time. However, the atmosphere of hysteria is so great that no audience can really believe that humanity has a chance. **DP**

👁 KEY SCENES

1 "I'M NOT CRAZY!"

The movie is bookended by scenes featuring the hero in a frantic, desperate state. The film begins in a hospital ward, where a doctor is summoned to treat an hysterical patient, Dr. Miles Bennell, who is screaming warnings at anyone who will listen.

2 "HE'S GOT THE CRAZY IDEA THAT SHE ISN'T HIS MOTHER"

The bulk of the film takes place in flashback. In this scene Miles meets people who claim that their closest relatives are not the same. He also meets his high-school sweetheart, Becky Driscoll, and as they become close the town begins to change around them.

3 "IT'S A MALIGNANT DISEASE"

Realizing that the town is gradually being taken over by the alien pods, Miles and Becky hide out in the doctor's office, medicating themselves to keep awake through the night. In the morning they see trucks being loaded with pods to be taken to other towns.

4 "I NEVER KNEW FEAR UNTIL I KISSED BECKY"

Miles and Becky are pursued by the townspeople. Hiding in an abandoned mine, they know that if either of them falls asleep, when they awaken they will no longer be themselves. To Miles's horror, Becky falls asleep and is altered instantly.

🕐 DIRECTOR PROFILE

1912–42

Don Siegel was born on October 26, 1912 in Chicago. He was educated at Cambridge in England. He worked for Warner Bros in the montage department and directed the montage for *Casablanca* (1942).

1943–54

His first feature film, *The Verdict* (1946), starred Sidney Greenstreet and Peter Lorre. After this he directed low-budget films in a variety of genres: Film Noir (*The Big Steal*, 1949; *Private Hell 36*, 1954), prison movie (*Riot in Cell Block 11*, 1954), and Western (*Duel at Silver Creek*, 1952).

1955–64

After the success of *Invasion of the Body Snatchers* his most notable films were the taut Film Noir (see p. 168) *The Line-Up* (1958), the war film *Hell Is for Heroes* (1962), the Elvis Presley Western *Flaming Star* (1960), and *The Killers* (1964), a version of the Ernest Hemingway short story.

1965–73

Coogan's Bluff (1968) marked the beginning of his association with Clint Eastwood (b. 1930). Siegel featured Eastwood in four further films, including *Two Mules for Sister Sarah* (1970), *The Beguiled* (1971), and their most famous creation, the crime thriller *Dirty Harry* (1971). He also directed the gritty cop movie *Madigan* (1968) and the crime drama *Charlie Varrick* (1973).

1974–91

After *Charlie Varrick* his output became more erratic, but included two late masterpieces: the autumnal Western *The Shootist* (1976), starring John Wayne, and the spare prison drama *Escape from Alcatraz* (1979), which was the director's last pairing with Eastwood. He also featured in a cameo role when Philip Kaufman (b. 1936) successfully remade *Invasion of the Body Snatchers* in 1978. Siegel died in California on April 29, 1991. As a footnote, Clint Eastwood's Academy Award-winning paean to the old West, *Unforgiven* (1992), features a dedication to "Sergio and Don," Eastwood's two greatest influences—Sergio Leone (1929–89) and Don Siegel.

THE HOLLYWOOD WESTERN

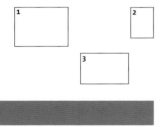

1 Marshall Will Kane (Gary Cooper) in
High Noon. The role had been turned
down by Gregory Peck, Marlon Brando,
and Kirk Douglas, among others.

2 Poster for *Lonely Are the Brave* —Kirk
Douglas's pick of his own films.

3 Howard Hawks's *Red River* took as its
subject the first cattle drive from ranches
in Texas to the railroad terminus in
Kansas, along the Chisholm Trail.

The Western has been a staple of Hollywood cinema from the earliest
days. It is undoubtedly the most American of genres, but not always
the most highly regarded. Perhaps because they could be made fast
and cheaply—the landscape was there ready-made, and real cowboys were
available as extras—Westerns were often dismissed as "program filler." During
the silent era, pioneers such as Allan Dwan (1885–1981) and Raoul Walsh
(1887–1980) often churned out one a week, from scripting to final cut. By 1909
the Bison company had arrived in California; by 1910 Broncho Billy Anderson had
become the first Western star; and according to film historian Ed Buscombe's
calculations, 213 out of the 1001 US pictures made that year were Westerns.
With the coming of sound the genre's popularity dipped somewhat, although
the number of Westerns made hardly decreased until the 1960s: Hollywood
made more than 800 of them in the 1950s.

Stagecoach (1939) by John Ford (1894–1973) marks the beginning of a
period in which Westerns were directed by major filmmakers such as Ford
himself (returning to the genre after more than ten years' absence), Michael
Curtiz (1886–1962), Fritz Lang (1890–1976), and Howard Hawks (1896–1977),
who created well-known classics including *Red River* (opposite, 1948) and *Rio
Bravo* (1959). After World War II, a developing critical interest in Hollywood
focused initially on directors such as Ford but later on the Western genre itself,

KEY EVENTS

1939	1943	1946	1947	1948	1950
Stagecoach, Jesse James, Dodge City, and *Destry Rides Again* herald the revival of the 'A' Western.	Howard Hughes and Jane Russell bring sex to the Western: *The Outlaw* is released after two years of censorship negotiations.	*My Darling Clementine* is one of many films retelling Wyatt Earp's story. Producer David Selznick's over-heated *Duel in the Sun* is a box-office triumph.	Robert Mitchum and Teresa Wright star in *Pursued*, one of a handful of "noir Westerns."	John Wayne stars in *Fort Apache*, the first in John Ford's "7th Cavalry" trilogy.	James Stewart takes half of the profits for *Winchester '73* and plays a Civil War veteran who marries an Apache in *Broken Arrow*.

which came to be seen in terms of a US myth, an imaginary space for the battle between outlaw and lawman, wilderness and civilization.

The Western is the most easily recognizable of Hollywood genres. The James gang in *The Assassination of Jesse James by the Coward Robert Ford* (2007) and the bandits in *The Great Train Robbery* (1903, see p. 22) wear different hats but their appearance and actions clearly identify them as belonging to the same genre. Westerns are commonly associated with a particular geographical and historical location: west of the Mississippi, south of the 49th parallel, north of the Rio Grande and some time between 1865 (the end of the American Civil War) and 1890 (when a US Census Report stated that The Frontier no longer existed). That is too neat. There are contemporary Westerns (*Lonely Are the Brave*, 1962, right), Canadian Westerns (*The Far Country*, 1954), Mexican Westerns (*Vera Cruz*, 1954), and Eastern Westerns (*Drums Along the Mohawk*, 1939). For some, the Western is a narrative that can take place in Texas, Vietnam, or outer space; *Outland* (1981) relocates *High Noon* (opposite, 1952) to one of Jupiter's moons. Yet a set of historical events, characters, and places remains at its core.

The Western both celebrates and rewrites US history. John Ford, the best known director of Westerns, claimed that his depiction of the gunfight at the OK Corral in Tombstone, Arizona, in *My Darling Clementine* (1946) drew directly on what he was told by Wyatt Earp himself. This account—like those of many other Westerns said to be based on fact—has been much debated; it has been said that Westerns are not so much about the West as about other Westerns. Given the hold that the myth of The Frontier has over the American psyche,

LIFE CAN NEVER CAGE A MAN LIKE THIS!

KIRK DOUGLAS

GENA ROWLANDS
WALTER MATTHAU

MICHAEL KANE

CARROLL O'CONNOR
WILLIAM SCHALLERT

"Lonely are the Brave"

1952	1956	1958	1959	1960	1960
Gary Cooper's marshal confronts the Miller gang without help from the Hadleyville townspeople in (and at) *High Noon*.	John Ford's *The Searchers* (see p. 246) is released. Although a commercial success, the film receives no Academy Award nominations.	Republic, one-time producer of more than thirty Westerns a year, ceases production.	Robert Ryan confronts Burl Ives in *Day of the Outlaw*; Randolph Scott tracks down Lee Van Cleef in *Ride Lonesome*.	*Shichinin no samurai* (*Seven Samurai*, 1954, see p. 216) by Kurosawa Akira (1910–98) inspires Hollywood's *The Magnificent Seven*.	Anthony Mann (1906–67) directs his last Western film, *Cimarron*, starring Glen Ford and Maria Schell.

such revisionism is only to be expected. Occasionally this process has itself become the subject of Hollywood Westerns, whether in iconoclastic films such as *Buffalo Bill and the Indians, or Sitting Bull's History Lesson* (1976) by Robert Altman (1925–2006), or Ford's *The Man Who Shot Liberty Valance* (1962), famous for the line: "This is the West, sir. When the legend becomes fact, print the legend."

Like Altman, Ford was aware that the Western was manufactured legend, but unlike him he saw this in generally positive terms: only in *The Searchers* (1956, see p. 246) did he properly explore the darker side of the Western hero. In the late 1930s and early 1940s, the Western's dominant tone was one of affirmation tinged with nostalgia. *Jesse James* (1939)—and its sequel, Fritz Lang's *The Return of Frank James* (1940)—presented the notorious outlaw brothers as the champions of rural values against the encroachments of Northern banks. In *They Died with their Boots On* (1941) Raoul Walsh gave a romanticized picture of General Custer, and *Buffalo Bill* (1944) by William Wellman (1896–1975) did a similar job.

Ford's *My Darling Clementine* sees Wyatt Earp (Henry Fonda) arrive in Tombstone and leave a town in which cattle rustlers and drunken Indians have been replaced by the church and the school. *Shane* (1953) provided a more self-conscious variation on the story of the arrival of the gunman with a past who rids the town of villainy before returning to the wilderness. These two films best encapsulate the classic Hollywood Western. Both use their settings as a space for a showdown between opposing forces: in *My Darling Clementine*, between the law-abiding and the lawless; in *Shane*, between homesteaders and cattle barons. Both look to a positive future, if not one in which the hero necessarily belongs.

Less affirmative Westerns were a feature of the 1940s and, in particular, the 1950s. Written by the soon to be blacklisted Carl Foreman, *High Noon* was recognized at the time not only for the skill with which the suspense builds toward the midday deadline at the heart of the film, but also as an allegory of the way fear in the Hollywood community was preventing effective resistance to contemporary anti-Communist investigations (although the film is equally open to more conservative readings). Other blacklisted writers who worked on Westerns included Albert Maltz and Ben Maddow, who penned *Broken Arrow* (1950) and *Johnny Guitar* (below, 1954) respectively. *Broken Arrow* is an

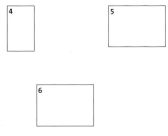

early example of a more sympathetic portrayal of Native Americans as also evidenced in *Apache* (1954), *The Last Hunt* (1956), and *Run of the Arrow* (1957). *Johnny Guitar* (a particular favorite of French New Wave directors, see p. 248) starred Sterling Hayden and Joan Crawford. Hayden had named names at the House Un-American Activities Committee hearings in 1951; a character is forced to do the same in the film.

The "psychological Western" became another marked trend of the post-war period. Raoul Walsh's *Pursued* (1947) has Robert Mitchum haunted by his past in a shadowy noir landscape, Paul Newman was an unbalanced Billy the Kid in *The Left Handed Gun* (opposite above, 1958), and in *The Gunfighter* (1950) Gregory Peck played a man haunted by his own reputation as "the fastest draw," knowing some young pretender would emerge to gun him down. Spencer Tracy played a one-armed war veteran in the modern-day Western *Bad Day at Black Rock* (1955) by John Sturges (1910–92), come to ferret out a guilty secret from smalltown folk. Even John Wayne played troubled characters in *Red River* and *The Searchers*, although he was more relaxed in *Rio Bravo* (above, 1959), Howard Hawks's self-proclaimed reply to *High Noon*.

Two actor-director collaborations of the period stand out. Between 1956 and 1960 Budd Boetticher (1916–2001) made a series of low-budget films with Randolph Scott (and screenwriter Burt Kennedy) that were quietly downbeat and remarkably spare in terms of narrative and characterization. James Stewart played the obsessive lead in five Anthony Mann (1906–67) Westerns: *Winchester '73* (1950), *Bend of the River* (1952), *The Naked Spur* (1953), *The Far Country* (1954), and *The Man from Laramie* (1955).

The Hollywood Western lived on into and beyond the 1960s, driven by a new generation of directors who had moved from television into the film industry, including Robert Altman, Arthur Penn (1922–2010), and Sam Peckinpah (1925–84). Peckinpah was particularly important, revising Western conventions affectionately in *Ride the High Country* (1962) and more violently in *The Wild Bunch* (1969) and *Pat Garrett and Billy the Kid* (1973). The genre even survived the box-office disaster of *Heaven's Gate* (1980). Hollywood paused, but went on to make teen Westerns (*Young Guns*, 1988), boy-meets-boy Westerns (*Brokeback Mountain*, 2005), and in 2007 to remake *3:10 to Yuma* (1957), the sort of efficient, character-based combination of lawlessness and landscape that had been a regular feature of its movies in the 1950s. **GB**

4 Paul Newman as the vengeful Billy the Kid in *The Left Handed Gun*.

5 *Rio Bravo* memorably paired John Wayne with Dean Martin. The film anticipated *El Dorado* (1967) and *Rio Lobo* (1970)—both also directed by Hawks and starring Wayne—and *Assault on Precinct 13* (1976) by John Carpenter (b. 1948).

6 The poster for *Johnny Guitar*. As suggested by Joan Crawford's prominent image, the movie's narrative was driven by powerful female characters.

The Searchers 1956

JOHN FORD 1894 – 1973

▲ Martin (Jeffrey Hunter) and Ethan (John Wayne) continue their hunt in a blizzard.

▼ The film's tagline echoes the search: "he had to find her...he had to find her..."

John Ford's *The Searchers* is regarded as his greatest film, as well as that of its star, John Wayne. Certainly it is their most complex. Wayne's towering portrayal of Ethan Edwards subverted the mythic image of the Western hero. Ethan and Martin Pawley (Jeffrey Hunter), his adopted one-eighth Cherokee nephew, undertake a five-year quest in the south-western wilderness to avenge the Comanches' slaughter of Ethan's brother's family and to rescue his niece Debbie (played by sisters Lana and Natalie Wood) from them, but Ethan gradually resolves to kill her for the "crime" of miscegenation. The early 1950s ushered in a cluster of adult Westerns and Ford showed he was aware of the break with traditionalism when he conceived *The Searchers* as "a psychological epic." Finding the body of his sister-in-law, Martha (Dorothy Jordan), raped and mutilated by Chief Cicatriz, or Scar (Henry Brandon), Ethan goes insane because he loved Martha, and Scar's violation of her mirrors his own sexual need.

Frank Nugent adapted the screenplay from Alan Le May's novel of 1954, which was inspired by a teamster who ransomed his captured wife and children from the Comanches in 1865. Visually, the film ranges from the narrowly expressionistic to the sweepingly majestic, thanks to the VistaVision cinematography of Winton C. Hoch, who made the sandstone buttes and pinnacles of Monument Valley surreally alienating. Max Steiner's score strikes a range of moods from melancholy to threatening. Hunter, Brandon, Vera Miles (as Martin's girlfriend, Laurie Jorgensen), and Ward Bond (as Reverend Captain Samuel Johnston Clayton) excel amid the supporting cast. **GF**

1 FORBIDDEN FEELINGS
After the American Civil War, veteran Ethan returns to the ranch where his brother Aaron (Walter Coy) lives with his wife Martha and children. The illicit love between Ethan and Martha is observed tacitly by Reverend Captain Samuel Clayton of the Texas Rangers.

3 DRIVEN MAD
Ethan and Martin are shown white women rescued from the Comanche by the 7th Cavalry Regiment. After years held in captivity, all of the women have gone insane. Ethan looks at them with bitter hatred, saying: "They ain't white anymore. They're Comanche."

2 HORRIFIC DISCOVERY
Off screen, Ethan buries the mutilated body of Lucy Edwards (Pippa Scott). Angered by the gruesome sight, Ethan stabs the ground with his knife. He does not tell Martin and Lucy's beau, Brad Jorgensen (Harry Carey Jr.), what he has seen but is spurred on to find Debbie.

4 FOUND AT LAST
Years later, Ethan and Martin are guided to the camp of the Comanche chief, Scar, in Mexico. They realize that Debbie is one of Scar's four wives. Martin shoots Scar and Ethan captures his reluctant niece in his arms and says tenderly, "Let's go home."

JOHN FORD AND RACISM

Ford became sympathetic toward Native Americans and African Americans in the twilight of his career, but he always had to defend himself against charges of racism. Ethan is not the only racist in *The Searchers* (right). Laurie, desperate for Martin to abandon the quest to fetch Debbie home, is equally virulent: "Fetch what home? The leavings a Comanche buck sold time and again to the highest bidder, with savage brats of her own?" Because he is part Cherokee, Martin is seemingly more tolerant of interracial kinship. Yet when his Native American bride (Beulah Archuletta) lies down next to him, he kicks her away. The sorrow Martin expresses when she is found murdered by cavalrymen barely mitigates his—and Ford's—ugly treatment of her.

NOUVELLE VAGUE

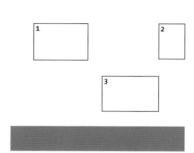

1 Nana (Anna Karina) turns to prostitution in *Vivre sa vie*. Director Godard tells Nana's tragic story in twelve episodes, each punctuated with intertitles.

2 The poster for Claude Chabrol's *Le beau Serge*—a film widely regarded as the first of the Nouvelle Vague movement.

3 Jacques Rivette's camera delights in expansive views of the French capital in his debut feature *Paris nous appartient*.

Few movements in cinema have been as influential as the French New Wave, or Nouvelle Vague. What began as a gathering of aspiring young critics working on a cinema journal developed into a collection of filmmakers whose work redefined modern cinema. The genesis of the movement lay in the guiding presence of two unique individuals, film archivist Henri Langlois and critic André Bazin. The latter was one of the founders in 1950 of the journal *Cahiers du cinéma*; Langlois was a co-founder of the Cinémathèque Française, a film archive giving regular screenings in Paris. Many of the future members of the Nouvelle Vague knew Langlois personally and would attend the Cinémathèque with an almost religious fervor, often debating over what they had watched well into the early hours. The cineastes who later wrote for *Cahiers du cinéma* included François Truffaut (1932–84), Jean-Luc Godard (b. 1930), Jacques Rivette (b. 1928), and Eric Rohmer (1920–2010).

The journal dismissed the conservative French cinema of the time and instead championed US directors and the development of the auteur theory. The discernible signature of a director—the personal stamp that defined a filmmaker's work—was viewed as a sign of greatness. The critics at *Cahiers* joined other Cinémathèque regulars in wanting to make their own films. Although immature, the early films of Godard, Rivette, and Rohmer highlighted a marked shift in aesthetics, moving the action from the studio to real locations. This was possible because of the advances in technology, with cheap, high-quality portable cameras and faster film stock now available that allowed access to almost anywhere and filming without the aid of lighting.

KEY EVENTS

1952	1954	1955	1957	1958	1959
Jean-Luc Godard, Eric Rohmer, and Jacques Rivette begin writing for *Cahiers du cinéma*.	François Truffaut sparks debate with his article on the quality of French cinema, "A Certain Tendency in French Cinema."	Agnès Varda directs *La pointe courte*, which now looks like an early dalliance with the Nouvelle Vague style.	François Truffaut directs the short film *Les mistons* (The Brats), the themes of which are further developed in his feature debut in 1959.	Louis Malle directs *Ascenseur pour l'échafaud* (Lift to the Scaffold) and *Les amants*.	*Hiroshima mon amour*, directed by Alain Resnais, is feted at the Cannes Film Festival. Eric Rohmer directs *Le signe du lion*.

The Nouvelle Vague began officially with *Le beau Serge* (1958, right), directed by Claude Chabrol (1930–2010), although it was Truffaut's *Les quatre cents coups* (*The 400 Blows*, 1959, see p. 252) and Godard's *A bout de souffle* (*Breathless*, 1960, see p. 254) that made the biggest waves. Having been banned from Cannes in 1958 for his critical stance toward French cinema, Truffaut was the triumph of the following year's festival. Partly autobiographical and shot where Truffaut grew up, *Les quatre cents coups* featured Jean-Pierre Léaud as Antoine Doinel, whose life and loves the director would document across five films over the next twenty years.

By turns witty, playful, wild, and brash, *A bout de souffle* has come to be seen as the defining film of the Nouvelle Vague. It was based on a story by Truffaut and featured all the elements that underpinned the style of this movement. Godard threw in literary and movie references, even casting Jean-Pierre Melville (1917–73)—one of the French directors *Cahiers du cinéma* did admire—as a character in the film. According to some sources, it was Melville who suggested Godard cut the film so that scenes jumped straight to the action, creating the jump cut, which disrupted the flow of conventional "invisible" editing. The story itself was disposable, mirroring a comment made by a character in Godard's third feature, *Vivre sa vie* (*My Life to Live*, 1962, opposite), who says of a book she is reading, "The story's dumb but it's very well written."

Eric Rohmer's *Le signe du lion* (1959) was less rapturously received, but with its location shooting and literary references it aligned him with his colleagues. Jacques Rivette's *Paris nous appartient* (*Paris Belongs to Us*, 1961, below) was the longest of the early Nouvelle Vague features, but its exploration of Paris makes

1960	1961	1962	1963	1964	1965
Jean-Luc Godard breaks all the rules with *A bout de souffle* (see p. 254). Claude Chabrol returns with *Les bonnes femmes*.	Anna Karina stars in her first Godard film, *Une femme est une femme*. Alain Resnais intrigues audiences with his *L'année dernière à Marienbad*.	François Truffaut's *Jules et Jim* is released. His *Antoine et Colette* sees the return of an older Antoine Doinel. Agnès Varda plays with real time in *Cléo de 5 à 7*.	Jean-Luc Godard releases three impressive films in one year: *Le petit soldat*, *Les carabiniers* (*The Soldiers*), and *Le mépris* (*Contempt*).	*Les parapluies de Cherbourg* (*The Umbrellas of Cherbourg*), directed by Jacques Demy (1931–90), draws on the movement's style.	The Nouvelle Vague enjoys a last hurrah with Jean-Luc Godard's *Alphaville* and *Pierrot le fou*.

it one of the most beautiful, even if it lacks the wild abandon of Godard's and Truffaut's films. Claude Chabrol, arguably more than any other director of the Nouvelle Vague, remained fascinated by one genre, the thriller, and found it a rich vein to mine in his exploration of human foibles. After his debut, *Le beau Serge*, a simple profile of provincial French life, *Les cousins* (1959) provided a template for the films that followed. In the same year, *A double tour* (*Web of Passion*) successfully recombined the movement's elements into more mainstream fare. Chabrol continued on this track, developing a distinctive body of work.

Films by other directors that fall under the umbrella of the Nouvelle Vague include *Cléo de 5 à 7* (*Cleo 5–7*, 1962, below left), which featured a cameo by Godard in a short film within a film, and the beguiling *Le bonheur* (1965), whose portrait of a patriarchal society and the quiet suffering of a cuckolded wife positioned it in sharp contrast to other more male-centric films. Both films were directed by Agnès Varda (b. 1928), whose feature debut in 1955, *La pointe courte*, merged a fictional story of an unhappy marriage with documentary footage of a fishing village caught in the grip of an economic downturn. The film was unique at the time in both its narrative structure and the way it was filmed, and is now recognized as a work of contemporary relevance from one of France's greatest filmmakers.

Alain Resnais (b. 1922) is another director whose early work is aligned with the Nouvelle Vague. *L'année dernière à Marienbad* (*Last Year in Marienbad*, 1961, above) is arguably the most enigmatic. It was written by Alain Robbe-Grillet, a member of the avant-garde literary movement—Nouveau Roman—whose creative path crossed with that of Nouvelle Vague. The film concerns itself— like much of Resnais's subsequent work—with memory and identity. With its fluid camerawork, accompanied by the soft tones of Giorgio Albertazzi's narration, the film is cinema as a dream. Although it was more middlebrow fare, *Un homme et une femme* (*A Man and a Woman*), directed by Claude Lelouch (b. 1937) in 1966, drew inspiration from the Nouvelle Vague in the way it rewrote the cinematic romance, playfully shifting between color and black and white, as well as counterpointing interior monologues with dialogue.

Truffaut's *Jules et Jim* (1962, below) became one of the defining films of the French New Wave. The film, which centers on a love triangle set before, during and after World War I, makes use of many of the techniques and elements that hallmarked the new style, such as the incorporation of newsreel footage, freeze frames, dolly shots, and a voice-over narration. It also features a classic soundtrack, scored by Georges Delerue. The film stars Jeanne Moreau, who typified the Nouvelle Vague actress as described by critic Ginette Vincendeau: "Beautiful, but in a kind of natural way; sexy, but intellectual at the same time." Moreau also appeared in *Les amants* (*The Lovers*, 1958) directed by Louis Malle (1932–95), which exhibited an amorality and casual approach to sex—another trope of many Nouvelle Vague films. With later films, such as *Fahrenheit 451* (1966), Truffaut moved toward a more conventional style. However, as he showed by his actions at the Cannes Film Festival in 1968, where he demonstrated in support of the student movement, he remained a vocal activist in French cinema.

Godard was the most prolific of the movement's filmmakers, and he continued to play with genre, displaying his love of literature, cinema, and philosophy with films including *Une femme est une femme* (*A Woman Is a Woman*, 1961) and *Bande à part* (*Band of Outsiders*, 1964, right). Godard's films, like many others of the Nouvelle Vague, are littered with references to US cinema—the crooks in both *A bout de souffle* and *Bande à part* are ardent fans of Hollywood B-movies. Godard continues to influence younger generations of filmmakers and when Quentin Tarantino (b. 1963) named his production company A Band Apart, he paid tribute to the legendary French director. *Pierrot le fou* (1965) would begin the overt politicization of Godard's work, which increased throughout the decade.

Later on, the close *confrérie* of the Nouvelle Vague would be riven by feuds and arguments. By the end of the 1960s Truffaut and Godard were scarcely on speaking terms. But in the early days the members of the group often collaborated and helped each other out. The group did not consist only of directors. Among the actors strongly associated with the Nouvelle Vague can be counted Jeanne Moreau, Anna Karina, Michel Bouquet, Jean-Paul Belmondo, Jean-Claude Brialy, Stéphane Audran, and, of course, Truffaut's on-screen alter ego Jean-Pierre Léaud. Behind the cameras was another group of frequent collaborators, including cinematographers Henri Decaë, Sacha Vierny, Nicholas Hayer, Nestor Almendros, and Raoul Coutard, and editors Lila Herman, Cécile Decugis, Claudine Bouché, and Agnès Guillemot, as well as composers Georges Delerue and Michel Legrand. **IHS**

4

5

7

6

4 In this ambiguous still from *L'année dernière à Marienbad* the figures standing in the grounds of the chateau cast shadows while the trees do not.

5 The striking poster for *Bande à part* uses a montage of scenes from the film—one of Jean-Luc Godard's most playful.

6 Catherine (Jeanne Moreau), Jim (Henri Serre), and Jules (Oscar Werner) enjoy happy times in Truffaut's classic of the Nouvelle Vague, *Jules et Jim*.

7 Agnès Varda's *Cléo de 5 à 7* charts two hours in the life of a French singer who thinks she is dying.

Les quatre cents coups 1959
The 400 Blows   FRANÇOIS TRUFFAUT 1932 – 84

▲ Antoine's passion for cinema is one of the few bright lights in his unhappy life.

▼ The character of Antoine Doinel came to be regarded as Truffaut's alter ego.

Film critic turned director François Truffaut incorporated autobiographical elements into his debut feature about a thirteen-year-old Parisian boy whose unhappy home life puts him on the path to delinquency. The character Antoine Doinel (played by Jean-Pierre Léaud) shared with Truffaut a troubled childhood, a defiant attitude and an early love for the movies. The film took the world by storm and made the Nouvelle Vague—the New Wave of young French filmmakers—the most discussed cinematic theme of the day. Yet when Jean-Luc Godard's *A bout de souffle* (*Breathless*, 1960, see p. 254) arrived the following year, the diversity within the Nouvelle Vague was revealed. Godard's film was truly innovative in its techniques, while *Les quatre cents coups* is in many ways a French rediscovery of the Italian Neo-Realism (see p. 178) of the 1940s.

In echoing the everyday reality of *Ladri di biciclette* (*Bicycle Thieves*, 1948, see p. 182) and its location shooting, Truffaut's film presents an emotionally intense portrait of childhood. With this film Truffaut also rewrote the rules of CinemaScope, proving that Hollywood's timidity about camera movement and fast editing in that medium had been out of place. Shot by Henri Decaë in black and white and DyaliScope (the French equivalent of CinemaScope), it is a film that would lose its character in color and that gains immeasurably from being seen in the cinema. Truffaut's later films became increasingly conventional, not so far from the "cinéma de papa" that the iconoclastic young critic had excoriated in the pages of *Cahiers du cinéma*. Yet *Les quatre cents coups* still retains all the fierce energy and joy of discovery characteristic of the Nouvelle Vague. **MS**

👁 KEY SCENES

1 PARIS

The panning shots behind the credit titles establish the fact that in Antoine's story Paris is less a backdrop than a character weaving its way through the narrative. The city is part of the texture of this boy's world, the air he breathes yet also the sea in which he may drown.

4 WHO IS RESPONSIBLE?

Antoine escapes and reaches a beach but has nowhere left to run. In a breathtaking solution to the problem of a tale with no clear-cut ending, Truffaut freezes this final shot as Antoine turns to face the audience with a questioning and accusing stare.

2 MOMENTS OF INSIGHT

Antoine sees his mother kiss a stranger. This highlights his growing awareness that his home life lacks real meaning. It confirms that the woman who is not the mother he would like is also a bad wife, deceiving the husband who treats him, a bastard, as one of the family.

3 THE DELINQUENT

Antoine is caught after he steals a typewriter and he is sent to a juvenile detention center. Face to face with a psychologist, Antoine expresses himself more fully than ever before. The power of this scene stems from its being shot with live sound and no script.

🕐 DIRECTOR PROFILE

1932–58

François Truffaut was born in Paris out of wedlock and never knew his biological father. During his unhappy childhood, cinema was his one great solace. In 1953 he began writing as a critic for the journal *Cahiers du cinéma*. In 1957 he turned to filmmaking. His acclaimed short film *Les mistons* (*The Brats*) focuses on a group of young boys in provincial France who are infatuated with a beautiful woman.

1959–62

He gained instant fame with his first feature *Les quatre cents coups*—the film that heralded the arrival of the Nouvelle Vague movement. He also provided fellow French New Wave filmmaker Jean-Luc Godard with a story, which became *A bout de souffle*. Truffaut's second feature *Tirez sur le pianiste* (*Shoot the Piano Player*, 1960) was more controversial, but in 1962 *Jules et Jim* proved another triumph.

1963–79

In 1967 Truffaut published his book-length interview with Alfred Hitchcock (1899–1990), which remains an acclaimed classic. Aside from the initially undervalued *Fahrenheit 451* (1966), made in England, and a Hollywood acting role in *Close Encounters of the Third Kind* (1977), directed by Steven Spielberg (b. 1946), Truffaut remained in France and directed a run of popular films including two in which he acted—*L'enfant sauvage* (*The Wild Boy*, 1970), and *La chambre verte* (*The Vanishing Fiancée*, 1978). Léaud's Antoine Doinel (of *Le quatre cents coups*) featured again in subsequent films but to diminishing returns. *La nuit américaine* (*Day for Night*, 1973)—a film about filmmaking—became the director's most acclaimed movie of the 1970s.

1980–84

Although *Le dernier métro* (*The Last Metro*, 1980) was popular, his last films arguably showed a falling-off. Truffaut died of a brain tumor in 1984, at fifty-two. He was five films short of his personal goal of thirty and still had many films in preparation. He is buried in Paris's Montmartre cemetery.

A bout de souffle 1960
Breathless   JEAN-LUC GODARD b. 1930

▲ One of the Nouvelle Vague's definitive couples. In 1960 there were none more French and none more cool.

▼ The classic poster that has adorned the walls of students' rooms the world over.

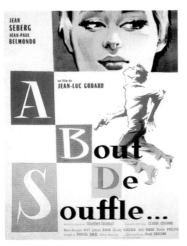

Based on a true-crime treatment by François Truffaut, Jean-Luc Godard's first film is dedicated to Monogram Pictures, the US B-movie factory that turned out endless Bela Lugosi and East Side Kids pictures and one existentialist masterpiece, *Detour* (1945) directed by Edgar G. Ulmer (1904–72). An iconic picture, *A bout de souffle* is minimally plotted and kept from rambling only by jagged editing that cuts the ordinary business of getting from one place to another. Accompanied by ominous yet cool piano jazz, the characters in the film seem to dash about as if their lives were on fast-forward.

Michel Poiccard (Jean-Paul Belmondo) is a vicious hoodlum, growling sexual predator, and casual killer—he shoots a cop in an offhand, almost absurd fashion—who exhales clouds of smoke from an ever-present cigarette. Wearing a Bogartian fedora, he constantly rubs a thumb over his upper lip in imitation of his US screen idol. A casual exploiter of women, who deftly robs an old girlfriend for petty cash, Michel is mixed up with Patricia Franchini (Jean Seberg), a cool blonde American—at once a Hitchcockian heroine and a Film Noir untrustworthy dame—who is experimenting with her feelings. A row-cum-flirtation-cum-role-play game in her tiny, messy apartment lasts for a third of the brief movie, a chunk of claustrophobia in the middle of a piece that is otherwise always on the move, thanks to Godard's innovative jump cuts.

In the end, similarly experimentally, Franchini reveals Poiccard's whereabouts to the cops and they shoot him down. As he lies dead, she takes on his persona and rubs her thumb across her upper lip. She has left him, breathless. **KN**

👁 KEY SCENES

1 THE LOOK

After a profane introduction, Michel lowers his newspaper to look out from under the brim of his 1940s hat. With unparalleled shifty insolence, he exhales a plume of cigarette smoke. This breakthrough role made Belmondo a leading light of the Nouvelle Vague.

4 GUNNED DOWN

Betrayed by Patricia, Michel is shot in the back by the cops and runs down the street, a bloodstain spreading across his back, then falls, still puffing smoke, to die. She looks on in horror but then callously accepts his dying words ("You're a real louse").

2 OUT OF THE STUDIO

Michel and Patricia meet on the Champs-Elysées. He is a petty thug acting like a B-movie hood from the 1940s; she is an American gamine of the moment. Shot on location, the film records the sights and sounds of Paris with great immediacy and spontaneity.

3 "BOGEY!"

Michel studies the cinema publicity for *The Harder They Fall* (1956). Michel's poses and attitudes are borrowed from film — he models himself on Bogart's screen persona. A fan of US cinema, Godard incorporates quotations from other films in *A bout de souffle*.

🕐 DIRECTOR PROFILE

1930–59

Jean-Luc Godard was born in Paris to Swiss parents. He spent World War II in Switzerland, returning to Paris after his parents' divorce in 1948. He studied ethnology at the Sorbonne and began attending the ciné-clubs of Paris's Latin Quarter, where he met André Bazin, co-founder of influential film magazine *Cahiers du cinéma*. During this period he also met the other filmmakers and theorists who would give birth to the Nouvelle Vague. From 1952 he wrote criticism for *Cahiers du cinéma*, often under the pseudonym "Hans Lucas." Godard frequently championed vital US B-movies over the supposedly stuffy French "cinéma de papa." He directed several short films, including *Charlotte et son Jules* (1958), which featured Jean-Paul Belmondo.

1960–67

Following his iconic feature debut, *A bout de souffle*, Godard directed a series of films that are among the masterworks of the French Nouvelle Vague — *Vivre sa vie* (*My Life to Live*, 1962), *Le mépris* (*Contempt*, 1963), *Bande à part* (*Band of Outsiders*, 1964), *Alphaville* (1965), *Pierrot le fou* (1965), and *Weekend* (1967). In 1960 he married actress Anna Karina; four years later they established their own production company, Anouchka Films.

1968–79

Following *les évenements de 68*, Godard joined Jean-Pierre Gorin (b. 1943) in the Dziga-Vertov Group and made films increasingly at odds with conventional cinema, informed by his embrace of Maoist politics (*Le vent d'est*, 1970; *Tout va bien*, 1972; *Numéro deux*, 1975). To explain his highly charged opinions, he produced a number of "ciné-tracts."

1980–present

Godard returned to fiction film with *Sauve qui peut (la vie)* (*Slow Motion*, 1980), *Je vous salue, Marie* (*Hail Mary*, 1985), *Détective* (1985), and *King Lear* (1987) among others. He continues to make films, including impressionist documentaries about cinema, culture, and politics.

4 | 1960 TO 1969

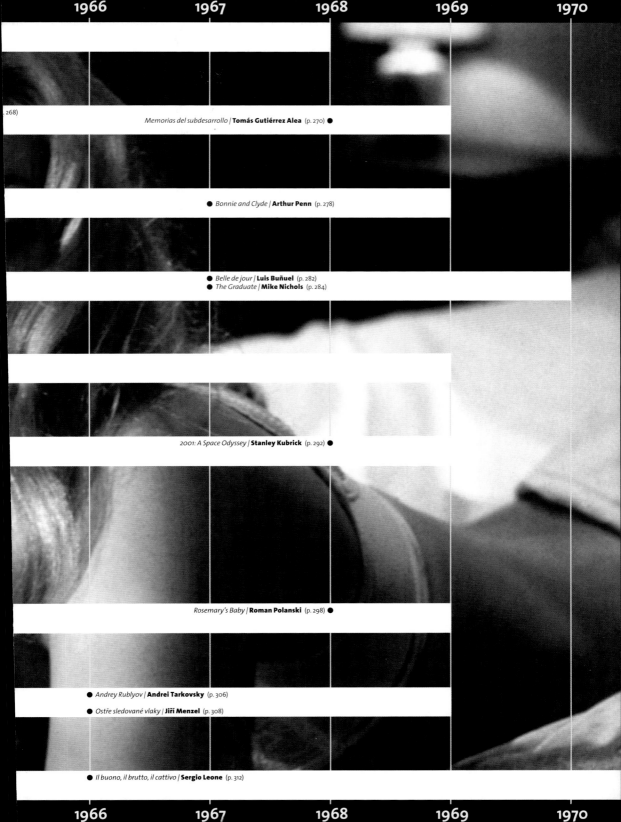

BRITISH NEW WAVE

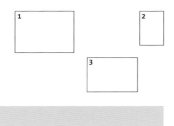

1 Reformatory boy Colin Smith (Tom Courtenay) escapes the bleakness of his life through running, in *The Loneliness of the Long Distance Runner*.

2 *A Kind of Loving*: the girl's eyes brim with hope, but significantly the expression of her lover (played by Alan Bates) is hidden.

2 Dirk Bogarde and Julie Christie tangle in *Darling*, a satire on mid-1960s Britain.

Flashback to 1956. A series of short, low-budget British documentaries is screened in London. As one newspaper puts it, "every beard and duffel coat in London, every urchin-cut and pair of jeans seemed to converge" on the South Bank to see the "Free Cinema" films. The documentaries are honest explorations of subjects such as amusement parks, dance halls, or youth clubs. Compared to British cinema of the era, such work was groundbreaking. To filmmaker and critic Lindsay Anderson (1923–94), the 1950s was an era of complacency and "tepid humanism" in British cinema. It was the epoch of John Mills war films and stiff-upper-lipped dramas in which "chaps" like Jack Hawkins smoked pipes.

The British New Wave movement was driven by a group of critics turned filmmakers who had been closely associated with Oxford University's film magazine *Sequence* in the late 1940s, and had then gone on to write for *Sight and Sound*. Key figures included Anderson, Karel Reisz (1926–2002), Tony Richardson (1928–91), and Gavin Lambert (1924–2005). When the group went on to make feature films, its focus was firmly on the northern industrial heartland of Britain. Yet the film generally credited with kick-starting the British New Wave was made by a director unassociated with the *Sequence* group, Jack Clayton (1921–95). *Room at the Top* (1958), with its northern, working-class hero and unprecedented frank treatment of sex and class, set a template that was followed by Reisz's *Saturday Night and Sunday Morning* (1960, see p. 260), Richardson's *The Loneliness of the Long Distance Runner* (1962, opposite) and Anderson's *This Sporting Life* (1963, see p. 262). John Schlesinger (1926–2003), like Clayton, stood slightly apart from the key group, but his *A Kind of Loving* (1962, right), starring Alan Bates, follows the same pattern. These were all films made, as Richardson later wrote, with "a minimum of equipment, real locations, and a natural, unmade-up look."

Most of the British New Wave films were adapted from novels or plays, such as Richardson's film versions of John Osborne's play *Look Back in Anger* (1959) and Shelagh Delaney's play *A Taste of Honey* (1961). The latter was unusual in having a female protagonist, played by newcomer Rita Tushingham. Given the Oxbridge backgrounds of the directors, some critics were skeptical about the authenticity of the British New Wave films. An article in the *Guardian* derided the way these southern, middle-class filmmakers gazed northward, seeking "the tougher living and richer accents which suit their sociological tastes."

Inevitably the energy of the British New Wave soon dissipated. Tony Richardson put out the period romp *Tom Jones* (1963) before leaving for Hollywood. After *Billy Liar* (1963) Schlesinger turned his attention back down south with *Darling* (1965, below). Anderson, never prolific, made no more films until *If...* (1968). Even so, the spirit of the New Wave had lastingly transformed British cinema. Its influence can be seen in the films of Ken Loach (b. 1936), Mike Leigh (b. 1943), and Terence Davies (b. 1945) and more recently in the work of Andrea Arnold (b. 1961), Lynne Ramsay (b. 1969), and Paweł Pawlikowski (b. 1957). **GM**

Saturday Night and Sunday Morning 1960

KAREL REISZ 1926 – 2002

▲ Arthur in his element: with styled hair, dressed in a suit, and sipping of ale.

▼ The film was rated "X" for its frank portrayal of sex, alluded to in the poster.

"'SATURDAY NIGHT AND SUNDAY MORNING' IS IN...

Saturday night you have your fling at life... and Sunday morning you face up to it!

ABSOLUTELY STAGGERING!"

"SATURDAY NIGHT AND SUNDAY MORNING

"Easily the best British movie since 'Room At The Top'!"

starring ALBERT FINNEY

SHIRLEY ANNE FIELD RACHEL ROBERTS and introducing HYLDA BAKER

The film opens with Arthur Seaton (Albert Finney) at his factory lathe. "Don't let the bastards grind you down," he growls. Shot from below with a cigarette dangling from his mouth and a look of arrogant defiance on his face, Finney is far removed from the placidity and cheeriness of most British leading men of the era.

Saturday Night and Sunday Morning, adapted from Alan Sillitoe's novel, touches on boozing, adultery, violence, and abortion, but that is not what made the film subversive. Its real edge comes from its celebration of a hero who is a natural-born rebel, unashamedly interested in his own pleasures. Arthur, as played by Finney, is not given to remorse. Nor is he agitating for revolution. As he puts it: "What I'm out for is a good time. All the rest is propaganda."

"A lot of people were outraged when the film came out . . . . They thought that the world was going to come to an end because it looked like I had been in bed with a married woman who was not my wife," Finney recalled, in an interview in 1982, of the scenes showing Arthur with his married mistress Brenda (Rachel Roberts). He joked about the elaborate conventions for showing sex on screen in British movies. "You had to have one foot on the floor, like in snooker."

This was "lad" cinema par excellence. Reisz and Sillitoe were celebrating the aggression and humor of the film's abrasive hero without judging him. What they realized, though, was that the "bastards" would find a way of grinding down even a reckless figure like Arthur Seaton. Arthur—for all his rebelliousness—may end up like his parents, passively watching his new television. **GM**

KEY SCENES

1 "DON'T LET THE BASTARDS GRIND YOU DOWN"
Early in the film, Arthur is shown working in a factory. He is obviously both very good at his job and very bored. The scene signals his defiance. His voice-over makes it clear that he is already bucking the system.

2 THE FAIRGROUND FIGHT
Arthur has been having a fling with Brenda, a married woman who is pregnant by him. At the fairground, he is beaten up by her husband's soldier brother. This is the first sign that Arthur is not as much in control of his life as he likes to imagine.

3 A BRAVE NEW LIFE?
Arthur and Doreen (Shirley Anne Field) walk down the grassy slope toward their future. He always vowed he would not settle down and that he still has some fight left in him but she wants a new house "with a bathroom and everything." It is his duty to provide it.

DIRECTOR PROFILE

1926–47
Karel Reisz was born in Czechoslovakia. In 1938 he came to the United Kingdom as a refugee from the Nazis. His clear perspective on British class and changing social mores is attributable to his outsider's eyes. In 1947 he was cofounder of the influential British film magazine *Sequence*.

1948–59
Reisz was part of the Free Cinema Documentary Movement. In 1955 he codirected the short documentary *Momma Don't Allow*, based around an evening in a Wood Green jazz club. He also directed *We Are the Lambeth Boys* (1958), about a group of rebellious, working-class teenagers.

1960–70
Having directed *Saturday Night and Sunday Morning*, Reisz produced two key films of the 1960s, *This Sporting Life* (1963, see p. 262) and *Morgan: A Suitable Case for Treatment* (1966). His film *Isadora* (1968) received a hostile reception, however.

1971–81
After a hiatus in his filmmaking career, Reisz directed *The Gambler* (1974), an updating of the Dostoevsky novella, starring James Caan, and *Dog Soldiers* (1978), a post-Vietnam film with Nick Nolte. He enjoyed critical success with his Harold Pinter–scripted John Fowles adaptation, *The French Lieutenant's Woman* (1981).

1982–2002
His notable projects included *Sweet Dreams* (1985) and the Arthur Miller–scripted *Everybody Wins* (1990). Reisz died in 2002.

PAGE TO SCREEN

Alan Sillitoe's novel *Saturday Night and Sunday Morning* is full of autobiographical elements. Sillitoe grew up in a tough, working-class background in Nottingham and left school with no degree at fourteen. Like Arthur he worked in factories. The book was turned down by several publishers, discomfited by its bleak view of working-class life. When it was published in 1958, the film rights were snapped up by Harry Saltzman, later to produce the James Bond movies. Sillitoe, who wrote the screenplay for director Karel Reisz, was feted for a portrayal of working-class life that combined defiance and lyricism. Reisz's film captured the restlessness and irreverence of Arthur as conceived by Sillitoe. But as Reisz later commented, "I think in Alan's book, Arthur is more simply a hero, a spokesman—Alan's heart goes with him. The film has that element but it also sees him as part of his landscape and tries to see him as a product of the way he has to make his living . . . It sees the victim side of his predicament."

This Sporting Life 1963
LINDSAY ANDERSON 1923 – 94

▲ Machin (Harris) and Margaret (Roberts) develop an intense but futile relationship.

▼ The film was based on David Storey's novel; he also wrote the screenplay.

Lindsay Anderson's *This Sporting Life* boasts an in-your-face physicality rarely seen in British films of the era. "It has a blow like a fist. I've never seen an English picture, which gave such expression to the violence and capacity for pain that there is in the English character," noted critic Penelope Gilliat. Richard Harris was ideal casting for the role of Frank Machin, the working-class coal miner turned rugby league star. Not only was Harris a proficient rugby player, who looked at home alongside the real-life professionals from Yorkshire's Wakefield Trinity club, but he had a brooding, introspective quality that led critics to compare him with Marlon Brando.

Anderson—the standard-bearer for Free Cinema and one of the most outspoken polemicists of British film culture in the 1950s—was making his film debut at the mature age of forty. His interest in David Storey's novel was less in the northern settings and rugby subculture than in the character of Machin. What intrigued him was that this macho brute of a man also "had a great innate sensitivity and a need for love of which he is hardly aware." Critic and screenwriter Gavin Lambert later claimed that Anderson's films had a hidden homoerotic element. In *This Sporting Life*, Lambert suggested, the director was reacting strongly (albeit indirectly) to "the physicality of the footballer and his world, the tussles on the field and the emotional steam in the locker room."

However, the film is as much a love story as a drama about a restless and rebellious sporting star. Anderson throws tenderness and lyricism into a story that is outwardly brutal in the extreme. **GM**

👁 KEY SCENES

1 THE DENTIST'S CHAIR
Frank Machin (Harris) has his teeth smashed on the rugby field and ends up in a dentist's chair. Under the gas, he has a series of flashbacks of past events. Anderson and editor Peter Taylor use an innovative cutting style for the film's flashback-based narrative.

2 RELATIONSHIP WITH MRS. HAMMOND
Machin lodges with the emotionally cold Margaret Hammond (Roberts), whose husband has died recently. As she obsessively polishes her late husband's shoes, she begins to share her feelings. A fraught sexual relationship develops between the pair.

3 KING OF THE WORLD
When Machin scores a spectacular try in front of a packed crowd, he is on top of the world. Off the field, the aggressive Machin is less successful. He becomes a celebrity in the rugby world but this begins to affect him and his relationship with Margaret.

4 "YOU'RE A MAN. YOU'RE A BLEEDING MAN"
As Margaret makes the bed, Machin grabs her. At first, she resists him but then sends her daughter out to play and succumbs. In her grief Margaret is unable to show Machin affection. They are both cruel to one another, but Machin's emotions tip over into violence.

🕐 DIRECTOR PROFILE

1923–46
Lindsay Anderson was born in Bangalore, India, the son of a British army officer. He was educated at an English private school and Oxford. Despite his impeccable establishment credentials, he reacted fiercely against the snobbery and obsession with class in postwar Britain.

1947–62
First as a contributor to *Sequence*, which he co-founded in 1947, and then working for *Sight and Sound* and *The New Statesman*, Anderson developed into an outspoken polemicist and cultural theorist. He began to make documentaries with a strongly personal thrust and helped draw up the manifesto for the documentary film movement, Free Cinema. He was also closely involved with productions at the Royal Court Theatre in London.

1963–82
This Sporting Life, Anderson's directorial feature debut, was adapted from David Storey's novel originally published in 1960. In subsequent years, Anderson was to direct several of Storey's plays on the London stage. Anderson's informal "condition of Britain" filmic trilogy began with *If...* (1968), a subversive satire set in a British private school. It continued with *O Lucky Man!* (1973), about the misadventures of a coffee salesman in early seventies Britain, and ended with *Britannia Hospital* (1982), a scathing comedy about British society that used the National Health Service as a metaphor. The trilogy featured the character Mick Travis, who was played by Malcolm McDowell.

1983–94
A long-term champion of John Ford (1894–1973) and of his Westerns in particular, Anderson wrote a biography, *About John Ford* (1983), seen by many as a definitive study of the director. For his final feature in 1987, *The Whales of August*, he worked with Hollywood legends Bette Davis, Lillian Gish, and Vincent Price. Anderson died in France on August 30, 1994, at the age of seventy-one.

LATIN AMERICAN CINEMA

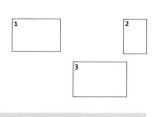

1 In Glauber Rocha's defining *O dragão da maldade contra o santo guerreiro*, killer Antônio das Mortes (Maurício do Valle) is hired to dispose of a *cangacieros* (guerilla leader) but comes to question his task.

2 Ruy Guerra's *Os fuzis* is a powerful tale of class division. It won the Silver Bear Extraordinary Jury Prize at the 14th Berlin International Film Festival.

3 In Nelson Pereira dos Santos's bleak and moving *Vidas secas*, cowhand Fabiano (Atila Iório) leads his family across Brazil's unforgiving *sertão* landscape, hoping to find work in the more urban south.

atin America is a vast and diverse region. Geographically, it encompasses an area stretching from the southern tip of South America to its border with California and the islands of the Caribbean. Politically, in the 1960s, it accommodated both the right-wing military government of Brazil and the Communism of Cuba. Cinematically, it housed countries that had established major commercial film industries before and during the 1960s, and others where film production was minimal.

Arguably the most significant national cinema in South America during the 1960s was that of Brazil, the continent's largest and most populous country, which was set apart from the rest of the region by its language—Portuguese—and by its distinct culture revealing African influences as well as those of European colonists and the indigenous peoples. By 1930, good work had emerged from the Brazilian cinema, but its real breakthrough came in the early 1960s with the burgeoning Cinema Novo movement, characterized by the slogan "an idea in the head and a camera in the hand." Its most important figure, both as theorist and critic, was writer-director Glauber Rocha (1939–81), whose best-known film, *O dragão da maldade contra o santo guerreiro* (*Antônio das Mortes*, 1969, above), is an account of a gunman hired to kill bandits who later becomes a revolutionary. Influenced by Italian Neo-Realism (see p. 178) and the French Nouvelle Vague (see p. 248), Rocha made his feature debut in 1962 with *Barravento* (*The Turning Wind*), and subsequently directed *Deus e o Diabo na terra do sol* (*Black God, White Devil*, 1964, see p. 268), a visually extraordinary study of rural life that used local legend and the music of J. S. Bach and Heitor

KEY EVENTS

1961	1962	1962	1963	1964	1964
Argentinian films include *La mano en la trampa* and *Piel de verano*, directed by Leopoldo Torre Nilsson.	In Brazil, Cinema Novo practitioner Glauber Rocha makes his debut with *Barravento*.	Anselmo Duarte's *O pagador de promessas* wins the Palme d'Or at Cannes. Luis Buñuel makes *El ángel exterminador* in Mexico.	Cinema Novo director Nelson Pereira dos Santos makes the grimly realistic *Vidas secas*.	Notable Brazilian Cinema Novo films include Ruy Guerra's *Os fuzis* and Rocha's *Deus e o Diabo na terra do sol* (see p. 268). Brazil suffers a military coup.	Soviet director Mikhail Kalatozov makes *Soy Cuba*.

Villa-Lobos to mount a sharp critique of conditions in the impoverished northeast and to explore the options of the rural poor. The military coup of 1964 led to increasing restrictions on the Brazilian film industry, but Rocha responded with the allegorical *Terra em transe* (*Entranced Earth*, 1967).

In contrast to the stylization of Rocha's films, other figures from the Cinema Novo opted for a greater realism of style. Former documentary director Nelson Pereira dos Santos (b. 1928) made *Vidas secas* (*Barren Lives*, 1963, below), a grueling account of rural poverty in the desolate landscape of the northeast. Ruy Guerra (b. 1931) made *Os fuzis* (*The Guns*, 1964, right), a powerful study of a group of soldiers protecting a warehouse from starving local peasants. Later in the decade, after the 1964 coup and a further coup in 1968, Joaquim Pedro de Andrade (1932–88) brought a contrasting approach to *Macunaíma* (1969), a wild comedy that explored questions of race, sexuality, and politics.

The 1960s also brought Brazilian cinema its most significant accolade at an international film festival, when *O pagador de promessas* (*The Given Word*, 1962) by Anselmo Duarte (1920–2009), the story of a landowner who vows to carry a cross to a far-off church if his ailing donkey recovers, scooped the Palme d'Or at Cannes and is to date the only Brazilian winner of the prestigious award. Duarte essayed similar religious themes with *Vereda da Salvação* (*The Obsessed of Catale*, 1964), about a man who believes he is Jesus. The socially critical aspects of these films led to his imprisonment as a suspected Communist, and he also endured criticism from the Cinema Novo filmmakers.

A parallel movement to the Cinema Novo evolved in Mexico, where a group of young critics established the magazine *Nuevo Cine* and leveled scathing criticism at the commercial Mexican film industry, with its dependence on safe genres, such as musicals and comedies. One member of the *Nuevo Cine* circle, J. M. García Ascot (1927–86), suggested alternative paths for the Mexican cinema with *En el balcón vacío* (*On the Empty Balcony*, 1961), based on his wife's memories of childhood during the Spanish Civil War and exile in Mexico, and described by critic John King as "a Proustian evocation of lost time." In 1965 and 1966 two key film adaptations of stories by the Colombian author Gabriel García Márquez were made, *En este pueblo no hay ladrones* (*In This Town There Are No Thieves*) by Alberto Isaac (1925–88) and *Tiempo de morir* (*Time to Die*) by Arturo Ripstein (b. 1943).

The most distinguished cinematic artist working in Mexico, however, was the émigré Spaniard Luis Buñuel (1900–83), who had left his native country at the time of the Civil War. He had sustained a distinguished career in the Mexican industry through the 1950s with films such as *Los olvidados* (*The Young and the Damned*, 1950), *El* (*Torments*, 1953), and *Nazarín* (1958), which combined social commentary and Surrealism. Among Buñuel's last Mexican films was the overtly Surrealist *El ángel exterminador* (*The Exterminating Angel*, 1962), a haunting parable about a group of people trapped at a dinner party that—inexplicably—nobody can leave. This account of the discreet charm of the bourgeoisie set the tone for the last fifteen years of Buñuel's career, but apart from the satirical film *Simón del desierto* (*Simon of the Desert*, 1965, opposite above), he was to make all his subsequent films in Europe.

Elsewhere in Latin America, the most notable film industry was that of Argentina. In the late 1950s, Leopoldo Torre Nilsson (1924–78) had already won international acclaim for his melodramatic accounts of the effete upper class, most notably *La casa del ángel* (*The House of the Angel*, 1957), which was shown, and won praise, at Cannes. This film was co-scripted and based on a novel by Beatriz Guido, who was to become Torre Nilsson's regular screenwriter and his wife. She adapted *La mano en la trampa* (*The Hand in the Trap*, 1961) and *Piel de verano* (*Summerskin*, 1961) from her own novels. With *El ojo de la cerradura* (*The Eavesdropper*, 1966), Torre Nilsson tackled South American politics more directly, recounting the story of a right-wing revolutionary. By the early 1960s, Torre Nilsson's success had helped to usher in an Argentinian New Wave, influenced in part by the French one. Notable films included *Tres veces*

4 *Soy Cuba* is epic Soviet and Cuban propaganda. Maria (Luz María Collazo) meets an American at a club and sleeps with him. He leaves her money for her time, but also for her crucifix, which he takes.

5 Simón (Claudio Brook) lives atop a pillar as a sign of his faith, which is repeatedly tested in Luis Buñuel's *Simón del desierto*, based on the story of St. Simeon Stylites.

6 Octavio Getino and Fernando Solanas's *La hora de los hornos: Notas y testimonios sobre el neocolonialismo, la violencia y la liberación* is an exercise in "Third Cinema."

Ana (*Three Times Anna*, 1961) by David José Kohon (1919–2004), which told three stories of sexuality, each starring María Vaner as a different woman named Anna, and *Crónica de un niño solo* (*Chronicle of a Boy Alone*, 1965), by Leonardo Favio (b. 1938), the story of a shantytown boy in an orphanage.

However, the most significant film movement in 1960s Argentina was a conscious attempt to move away from foreign models. Fernando Solanas (b. 1936) and Octavio Getino (b. 1935) collaborated on *La hora de los hornos: Notas y testimonios sobre el neocolonialismo, la violencia y la liberación* (*The Hour of the Furnaces*, 1968, below right). A didactic account of Argentinian history and politics, it became a model for "Third Cinema": a distinctive style of filmmaking for the Third World that would present an alternative to the "first cinema," patterned on Hollywood, and the "second cinema" of the new waves.

The Chilean film industry found its form in the late 1960s. Avant-garde filmmaker Raúl Ruiz (b. 1941) made his first feature with *Tres tristes tigres* (*Three Sad Tigers*, 1968), which established the intellectual game-playing that would characterize his oeuvre. Most of his career, however, was to be spent abroad, mainly in France. More realistic in style was *El chacal de Nahueltoro* (*The Jackal of Nahueltoro*, 1969) by Miguel Littín (b. 1942), a rough-edged but extremely powerful documentary-style depiction of a murderer, which uses his experiences to dramatize the desperate living conditions of Chile's poor. After the victory of the Marxist Salvador Allende in the elections in 1970, Littín was briefly to head the state-run Chile Films, but resigned even before Allende's deposition was followed by exile for both him and Ruiz.

None of the other Spanish-speaking countries of mainland South America—Bolivia, Colombia, Ecuador, Peru, Venezuela, Paraguay, and Uruguay—maintained extensive film production during the 1960s; in some of these countries only shorts or documentaries were made. However, many of the most remarkable Latin American films of the decade were produced outside the South American continent, on the Caribbean island of Cuba, where the revolution of 1959 changed the face of what had hitherto been a minor commercial industry. In 1961, after Cuban leader Fidel Castro nationalized local industries and established ties with the Soviet Union, the United States severed diplomatic relations and Castro's regime moved securely into the Soviet orbit. This new alignment found cinematic expression when Mikhail Kalatozov (1903–73), the Georgian-born director of the Soviet classic *Letyat zhuravli* (*The Cranes Are Flying*, 1957), came to the island to make *Soy Cuba* (*I Am Cuba*, 1964, opposite). This visually astonishing work of propaganda charted the nation's course from prerevolutionary oppression to an idealized and celebratory present.

Native Cuban filmmaker Tomás Gutiérrez Alea (1928–96) made one of the first post-revolutionary films, the Neo-Realist war movie *Historias de la revolución* (*Stories of the Revolution*, 1960). His later work displayed a developing dialectic of social criticism: *La muerte de un burócrata* (*Death of a Bureaucrat*, 1966) was a startling satire on the convolutions of socialist bureaucracy, whereas *Memorias del subdesarrollo* (*Memories of Underdevelopment*, 1968, see p. 270) was a somber account of post-revolutionary life that displayed a sceptical intelligence remarkable in a film produced under a totalitarian regime. In the same year Humberto Solás (1941–2008) made *Lucía*, a powerful account of female experience during three different periods of Cuban history, notable for its dramatic intensity and its immaculate period reconstruction.

Circumstances in Cuba, the only country in Latin America to have implemented a successful and lasting left-wing revolution, were unique. However, as the overt social criticism that characterized the finest films made in Brazil, Argentina, and Mexico demonstrates, the trend toward politically engaged cinema was not. Latin America in the 1960s was a region where cinema could not afford not to be political. **AJ**

Deus e o Diabo na terra do sol 1964
Black God, White Devil   GLAUBER ROCHA 1939 – 81

▲ Messianic priest Sebastião (Lídio Silva) leads his flock in search of a promised land.

▼ Bandit leader Corisco adorns the poster.

copacabana filmes apresenta **deus e o diabo**
yoná magalhães **na terra do sol**
geraldo d'el rey
othon bastos   um filme de glauber rocha
mauricio do valle   produção·luiz augusto mendes

History and politics collide with myth and religion in Glauber Rocha's *Deus e o Diabo na terra do sol*, a stark drama about a peasant family transformed by poverty and degradation into radicals fighting landowners and the church. Steeped in folkloric allusions that are mostly incomprehensible to an international audience, the film nevertheless succeeds because of the clarity of its overriding message. As Rocha commented, "The feast of metaphors, allegories, and symbols is no carnival of subjectivity; it is the refusal to analyze rationally a reality that has been stifled by European culture and American imperialism. I am making films which resist the classification of colonial anthropology." The movie is a remarkable achievement for a directorial debut, particularly from someone so young—Rocha was twenty-two when he made it. The story, about a young couple in the 1940s who turn to a radical preacher and then a bandit after society has deemed them unworthy of fair treatment and respectability, arose from the filmmaker's reaction to the iniquities of Brazil's political elite.

Deus e o Diabo na terra do sol eschews conventional characterization, instead employing each character as a cipher in order to distill an ideology that either opposed or represented the state and its colonial mindset. At the same time, Rocha understood the mechanics of film, creating sequences that simmer with tension. The film is celebrated for its score, which features music by folk singer Sérgio Ricardo, and is stunningly shot by Waldemar Lima, who captures the scorched earth in which the main characters forge an existence. **IHS**

👁 KEY SCENES

1 BREAKING THE LAW

Manuel's (Geraldo Del Rey) journey to radicalization begins with his murder of a rancher. With this scene, Rocha clearly positions every character either with the corrupt rulers or with those who suffer under them.

2 THE MEEK SHALL INHERIT THE EARTH

Christianity and socialism are inextricably entwined in a priest's sermon on a mountain, which transforms into a revolutionary call to arms. In the scenes that follow, the cross and the gun become twin symbols in the peasant revolt.

3 THE MODERN SISYPHUS

Mirroring Albert Camus's argument that "all great deeds and all great thoughts have a ridiculous beginning," Rocha plays on the Sisyphus myth with a sequence where Manuel carries a rock on an unending road. It is both a penance and the path to enlightenment.

4 THE FINAL SHOOTOUT

The climactic gun battle between Antonio das Mortes and Corisco (Othon Bastos) prefigures the unconventional Spaghetti Western (see p. 310) style, with its jump cuts showing the director's reluctance to play by the rules of the conventional Hollywood shootout.

🕐 DIRECTOR PROFILE

1939–59
Glauber Rocha was born in Brazil on March 14, 1939. In addition to showing an interest in theater and politics, while living in Salvador he worked as a freelance film reviewer for a local newspaper. In 1959 he attended law school, where he directed his first short, *Pátio*, followed by *A cruz na praça* in the same year.

1960–63
Following the positive response to his short films, Rocha gave up his studies to become a filmmaker. His first feature film was *Barravento* (*The Turning Wind*, 1962).

1964–70
Deus e o Diabo na terra do sol was nominated for the Palme d'Or at the Cannes Film Festival. The first part of a trilogy, it was followed by *Terra em transe* (*Entranced Earth*, 1967) and perhaps his most famous film *O dragão da maldade contra o santo guerreiro* (*Antônio das Mortes*, 1969). In 1965 Rocha was imprisoned for demonstrating against a meeting of the Organization of American States. His last Brazilian film, before going into self-imposed exile in countries such as Spain, Chile, and Portugal, was *Cabezas cortadas* (*Cutting Heads*, 1970).

1971–78
During his exile, Rocha directed a series of films dominated by allegory and symbolism, including *Der leone have sept cabeças* (1971), *Câncer* (1972), and *Claro* (1975). He returned to Brazil in 1978 to stand for election in the Bahia region.

1979–80
Rocha's last feature was *A idade da terra* (*The Age of the Earth*, 1980). An avant-garde rallying cry against colonialism, the sixteen reels of which are intended to be shown in any order, it has been hailed by Michelangelo Antonioni (1912–2007) as "a lesson in how modern cinema should be made."

1981
Rocha contracted a serious lung infection and returned to Brazil. He died in Rio de Janeiro at forty-three, on August 22.

Memorias del subdesarrollo 1968
Memories of Underdevelopment   TOMÁS GUTIÉRREZ ALEA 1928 – 96

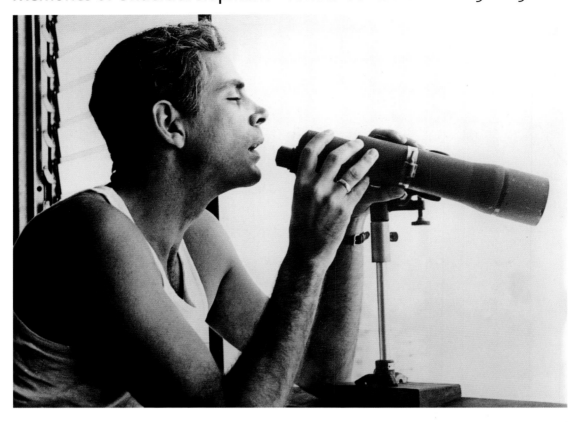

▲ Sergio looks through his telescope at the events unfolding on Havana's streets.

▼ An enigmatic sketch adorns the poster.

Tomás Gutiérrez Alea is Cuba's most celebrated director and *Memorias del subdesarrollo* is his masterpiece. A sophisticated film about the role of the intellectual in society, its narrative flits between reality and fiction, support for the Cuban Revolution and a critical eye. It has inspired generations of socially minded directors. Based on Edmundo Desnoes's novel, it is set in Havana in the time between the failed Bay of Pigs invasion in 1961 and the Cuban missile crisis in 1962. Opening with the exodus of the middle classes (who prospered under the Batista regime) to the United States, it focuses on one of their number who has stayed behind.

Sergio (Sergio Corrieri) is a bourgeois adrift, scornful of his own class, yet also of the masses represented by the revolution, whose lack of culture appalls him. His desire to write a novel is hampered by inertia: Sergio spends his time looking through his telescope at the battle-scarred city, wandering its streets and seducing young women. As Elena (Daisy Granados), a working-class girl whom Sergio tries to mold into his idealized Western image, says: "You're neither revolutionary, nor counter-revolutionary . . . . You're nothing." This intelligent but painfully detached man makes an intriguing prism through which to consider the fault lines in a new society hindered by US hostility and its own underdevelopment.

Alea began as a documentary filmmaker much influenced by Italian Neo-Realism (see p. 178). Here, he skillfully merges documentary-style shooting, archive newsreel, and still images from the Batista period, with Sergio as the glue between them. The result is brilliant dialectical filmmaking. **DM**

👁 KEY SCENES

1 EXODUS

Havana, 1961. Many people are leaving the country for the United States. Sergio bids farewell to his family and his wife; when they have gone, he seems extremely relieved. One would assume this to be archive footage were actors not in the middle of the action.

2 BAY OF PIGS

A sequence of newsreels, archive interviews, and still images assesses the trial of the Bay of Pigs conspirators, the atrocities of the Batista regime, and the bourgeois elite who flourished under the dictator. A voice-over likens the would-be invaders to that bourgeoisie.

3 SEDUCTION

Sergio seduces Elena, a young would-be actress. Having taken her to a film studio, where they watch a montage of sexual scenes cut by prerevolution censors, they return to his apartment. She puts on one of his wife's dresses before they embrace, then make love.

4 MISSILE CRISIS

The Cuban missile crisis puts the whole island on alert. Castro is seen on television, refusing to give in to US threats of nuclear attack. A fearful Sergio paces inside his apartment and walks alone on the seafront. He describes Castro's defiance as "an expensive dignity."

🕐 DIRECTOR PROFILE

1928–58

Tomás Gutiérrez Alea was born in Havana. After graduating with a degree in law from Havana University, he trained at the Centro Sperimentale in Rome, engaging with Italian Neo-Realism. He returned to Cuba in 1953 and aligned himself with Castro's fight against the Batista dictatorship. With Julio García Espinosa (b. 1926), Alea codirected *El mégano* (*The Charcoal Worker*, 1955), a short documentary about exploited workers, which was later confiscated by the Batista government.

1959–60

After the Cuban revolution, Alea cofounded the Cuban Film Institute with Santiago Alvarez (1919–98). His first feature, *Historias de la revolución* (*Stories from the Revolution*, 1960), is a Neo-Realist account of the armed struggle against Batista.

1961–73

La muerte de un burócrata (*Death of a Bureaucrat*, 1966) pays homage to Charlie Chaplin, Harold Lloyd, and Laurel and Hardy, while providing a satirical swipe at the heavy hand of bureaucracy. Alea's fifth film, *Memorias del subdesarrollo*, earned him international recognition, and was the first Cuban film to receive widespread distribution in the United States since the days of the revolution.

1974–93

In 1974 Alea was unable to obtain a US visa to enter the country to collect a Best Film award for *Memorias del subdesarrollo* at the National Society of Film Critics Awards. Costume drama *La última cena* (*The Last Supper*, 1976), set in eighteenth-century Cuba, tells of a slave owner who tries to practice more humane treatment of his slaves.

1994–96

Fresa y chocolate (*Strawberry and Chocolate*, 1994) questions the Communist Party's treatment of homosexuals. It became the first Cuban film to receive an Oscar nomination as Best Foreign Language Film. Alea directed his last film, *Guantanamera* (1995), the year before he died.

THE NEW HOLLYWOOD

1 Jack Lemmon as the mild-mannered office schnook "Bud" Baxter in Billy Wilder's *The Apartment*.

2 *Breakfast at Tiffany's* gave Audrey Hepburn the defining role of her career and immortality as a style icon.

3 *Who's Afraid of Virginia Woolf?* was largely faithful to Edward Albee's play, which appears prominently on the poster.

In the 1950s, the old studio system, and even the notion that Hollywood was the world center of filmmaking, had been dismantled. In the next decade, Hollywood—like US society generally—was in a state of upheaval. The court-enforced separation of the production and distribution setups of the main studios was followed by a growth in "runaway" productions—big US movies shot overseas either to use box-office takings trapped in countries whose laws insisted money made there should be spent there, or to take advantage of resources such as cheaper labor for extras. Yet the old studio lots remained as Hollywood succeeded New York as the main hub of television production.

Looking at lists of box-office returns and industry awards, however, it would be easy to think that little had changed. Big roadshow musicals and historical spectacles dominated in the 1960s, although upstart genres such as the technically British James Bond franchise and the Spaghetti Western (see p. 310) muscled in on the action. The 007 movies grew out of a climate of hipster paranoia that yielded US movies such as *The Manchurian Candidate* (1962). Spaghetti Westerns turned *Rawhide's* Clint Eastwood into a lasting Hollywood icon but they were all-Italian productions. Hollywood did get in on the act, but James Coburn's agent Derek Flint did not quite match the cool of Sean Connery's Bond. In addition, *Butch Cassidy and the Sundance Kid* and *The Wild Bunch* (both 1969) built in different ways on Italy's reinvention of the Western.

KEY EVENTS

1960	1961	1962	1963	1964	1965
Alfred Hitchcock (1899–1980) compels audiences to see *Psycho* (see p. 296) from the beginning by enforcing a "no late admission" policy.	*The Misfits* features the final screen appearances of Clark Gable and Marilyn Monroe.	Marilyn Monroe dies. The runaway production of *Cleopatra* drags on and on. John Ford directs *The Man Who Shot Liberty Valance*.	For the second year running, the Best Picture Oscar goes to British-international rather than Hollywood products (*Tom Jones*, *Lawrence of Arabia*).	After a hard-fought battle with the censor, *The Pawnbroker*, directed by Sidney Lumet (b. 1924), is released. It features naked breasts.	*The Sound of Music* bests *Gone with the Wind* (1939) at the box office and reinvigorates the roadshow musical.

This was also an era of crisis in the old ways of doing things. The excess of *Cleopatra* (1963) came close to closing down Twentieth Century Fox and brought an end to the epic film. Similarly, films such as *Dr. Dolittle* (1967) demonstrated that the big musical blockbuster—in many ways the success story of the 1960s—was not infallible. The notion that a studio should devote the bulk of its resources to one or two spectaculars took a series of hits in the decade. Aging studio executives at Universal and Columbia, who saw the profits coming in from movies stemming from the sixties counterculture, such as *Easy Rider* (1969), did not understand their appeal, so younger movers such as Robert Evans (at Paramount) rose to power in the new Hollywood.

There were still last hurrahs to come from many long-serving industry greats, including Billy Wilder (1906–2002). His bittersweet comedy drama *The Apartment* (1960, opposite) starred Wilder favorite Jack Lemmon, who played a lonely insurance executive currying favor with his senior managers by allowing them to use his apartment to conduct their extramarital trysts. Following the enormously popular *Some Like it Hot* (1959, see p. 228), *The Apartment* was a big commercial and critical success (winning five Oscars including Best Director and Best Picture), although its theme of adultery drew disapproval from some quarters.

New, younger directors became established—often, after work in television—and were as open to influence from the new Europe as from old Hollywood. They included Arthur Penn (1922–2010), Norman Jewison (b. 1926), Mike Nichols (b. 1931), and Sydney Pollack (1934–2008). Blake Edwards (b. 1922) had started to make a name for himself with his comedies, particularly the popular *Pink Panther* series. He also directed Audrey Hepburn in one of her most iconic roles, as quirky, party girl Holly Golightly in *Breakfast at Tiffany's* (1961, above right). Adapted from a Truman Capote novella, the film lightened up the book's darker tones and Edwards's comedic touch made it one of the most memorable romantic comedies of the decade.

At the beginning of the 1960s, lists of films stars were dominated by actors such as Cary Grant, Elizabeth Taylor, Frank Sinatra, and John Wayne. By the end of the decade, there was a new pantheon, among them Paul Newman, Warren Beatty, Faye Dunaway, Robert Redford, Dustin Hoffman, Sidney Poitier, Jane Fonda, and Barbra Streisand. It was not all about being young and pretty, however: long-serving bit-part thugs played by Charles Bronson and Lee Marvin were bumped up to action movie leads, while the top-grossing US film of 1966 featured one of the old guard, Elizabeth Taylor, in Mike Nichols's *Who's Afraid of Virginia Woolf?* (right). It was adapted from Edward Albee's four-character stage play and saw Taylor uttering obscenities and Richard Burton taking all the punishment. The casting of the noted beauty as the frumpy, older Martha raised eyebrows but her strong performance, together with those of costars Burton, George Segal, and Sandy Dennis, received high praise.

ELIZABETH TAYLOR
RICHARD BURTON

IN ERNEST LEHMAN'S PRODUCTION OF

EDWARD ALBEE'S

WHO'S
AFRAID OF
VIRGINIA
WOOLF?

1966	1967	1967	1968	1969	1969
Who's Afraid of Virginia Woolf? is the last picture to win an Academy Award for Black and White Cinematography.	*The Graduate* (see p. 284) and *Bonnie and Clyde* (see p. 278) represent a new youth-oriented brand of studio picture.	John Boorman brings Nouvelle Vague–inspired cutting and existential angst to the US crime movie in *Point Blank*.	In a year of widespread revolt around the globe, *Oliver!* and *Funny Girl* are nevertheless the major success stories.	Westerns return, but in revisionist mode: *Midnight Cowboy* takes the Best Picture Oscar but John Wayne beats Jon Voight to Best Actor with *True Grit*.	*Butch Cassidy and the Sundance Kid*, *The Wild Bunch*, and *Easy Rider* all travel West and end with their free-spirited heroes dead in the dust.

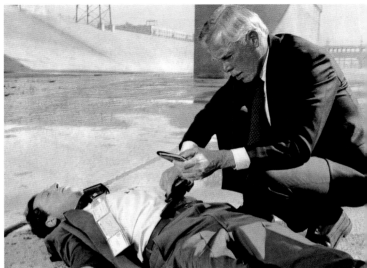

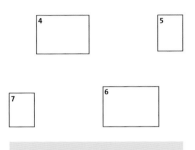

4 Lee Marvin as the iron-faced Walker in the neo-noir *Point Blank*. Eschewing the murky tones of traditional noir, John Boorman shot the film in bright daylight.

5 *Bullitt* established the character of the rebellious, verging-on-insubordinate police officer as seen in later movies such as *Dirty Harry* (1971).

6 An unlikely friendship grows between the two marginalized drifters in *Midnight Cowboy*, John Schlesinger's study of the underbelly of US society.

7 *In the Heat of the Night* was radical for featuring a nonwhite actor in a lead role. It courted further controversy because Sidney Poitier's character, Tibbs, reacted to being hit by a white man by slapping him back.

In New York, John Cassavetes (1929–89)—who maintained a career as a movie star to support his work as an auteur—experimented with free-form, improvisational cinema, whereas Andy Warhol (1928–87) pointed his camera at junkies, hustlers, dropouts, and transvestites to turn them into "superstars." Some US directors, such as Stanley Kubrick (1928–99) and Richard Lester (b. 1932) preferred to work in Britain, which had experienced its own new wave (see p. 258) One of Kubrick's key films of the decade was the black comedy *Dr. Strangelove or: How I Learned to Stop Worrying and Love the Bomb* (1964, see p. 276).

Foreign imports to the United States, such as John Schlesinger (1926–2003), John Boorman (b. 1933), and Roman Polanski (b. 1933), took a fresh look at America and made important, unsettling pictures. Boorman's stylish revenge thriller *Point Blank* (1967, above) was adapted from a classic pulp novel and starred Lee Marvin, who requested that the Englishman take the director's chair. Marvin plays a lone gunman battling a big, impersonal corporation hiding behind a veneer of respectability. The film's striking visuals and frenetic pace show the influence of the Nouvelle Vague (see p. 248). *Point Blank* proved more interesting to filmmakers than to contemporary audiences, although its standing has increased steadily. Fellow incomer Schlesinger produced one of the strongest films of the decade's close. *Midnight Cowboy* (1969, opposite) shone a light on the United States's underclass and the taboo subject of male prostitution. The drama made the career of unknown actor Jon Voight, featured a hauntingly plaintive theme song by Harry Nilsson, and earned three Academy Awards (including Best Picture and Best Director).

The story of Hollywood films in the 1960s can also be seen in terms of changing censorship standards and political-social attitudes. This was an era that ran from the Rat Pack to Woodstock, from the idealism of JFK's Camelot to the anger of the protest movement fighting for civil rights and against the war in Vietnam. The old Hays Code was on the way out, and new ratings had to take account of the more blatant treatment of sex, violence, and profanity in the movies. By the end of the decade, aboveground films were willing to show and say things that had once been confined to grindhouse or drive-in outsiders like Russ Meyer (1922–2004). In the anything-goes late 1960s, Meyer was asked to make a blockbuster at Twentieth Century Fox—*Beyond the Valley of the Dolls* (1970). New levels of screen violence were seen in the bullet-riddled finales of Arthur Penn's *Bonnie and Clyde* (1967, see p. 278) and *The Wild Bunch*

(1969) by Sam Peckinpah (1925–84). Glossy, teasing Rock Hudson and Doris Day comedies, which trod carefully around sexual issues, made way for neurotic, cynical, zeitgeist-riding essays on modern mores such as *The Graduate* (1967, see p. 284). Liberal attitudes set in: Spencer Tracy was forced to tolerate Sidney Poitier as a prospective son-in-law in *Guess Who's Coming to Dinner?* (1967), although black audiences preferred Poitier demanding respect from Rod Steiger in *In the Heat of the Night* (1967, opposite below). Norman Jewison's film centered on an African American detective investigating a murder in a racist Mississippi town and mirrored the edgy mood of the civil rights era.

John Wayne remained a top box-office draw—thanks to working with John Ford (1894–1973) and Howard Hawks (1896–1977) on late masterpieces, finally snagging an Oscar for *True Grit* (1969). The cowboy hero of younger audiences was Eastwood and they liked even their cop heroes—such as Steve McQueen in *Bullitt* (1968, right)—to be alienated, cool and antiestablishment. Directed by another expat Englishman, Peter Yates (b. 1929), *Bullitt* remains famous for its lengthy car chase through the streets of San Francisco, groundbreaking in cinema history, for which editor Frank P. Keller won an Oscar.

Even in traditionally safe Hollywood Oscar-winning genres, there were signs of changing times: *A Man for All Seasons* (1966), a historical pageant, features an antiauthoritarian rebel cut down by the establishment just like the bikers blasted by rednecks in *Easy Rider*; *Oliver!* (1968), a tuneful musical, it must not be forgotten, is about crooks, murderers, child abusers, and whores who could match Joe Buck and Ratso Rizzo from *Midnight Cowboy*. The first Best Picture Oscar winner of the decade, *The Apartment*, is about disenchantment with the gray-flannel American dream; the last, Schlesinger's *Midnight Cowboy*, is about life among dropouts and castoffs who could not aspire to even the desperate position of Billy Wilder's corporate drone protagonist. The times would keep changing. Soon, exploitation producer Roger Corman was to institute a policy of giving young, exciting talent work experience and opportunity. This would lead to emerging talents such as Francis Ford Coppola (b. 1939) and Martin Scorsese (b. 1942) writing and directing their own, game-changing films. And in 1969, barely out of their teens, Steven Spielberg (b. 1946) directed Joan Crawford in a segment of the television pilot *Night Gallery* while George Lucas (b. 1944) was working on his feature debut *THX 1138*. **KN**

Dr. Strangelove 1964

STANLEY KUBRICK 1928 – 99

▲ The War Room. Set designer Ken Adam had previously worked on *Dr. No* (1962).

▼ French illustrator Tomi Ungerer created the original film poster.

While adapting an edge-of-doom novel—*Red Alert*, by Peter George—into *Dr. Strangelove or: How I Learned to Stop Worrying and Love the Bomb*, Stanley Kubrick mused that such an immense, absurd subject should be tackled as a "nightmare comedy" and brought in satirist Terry Southern to add tartness to the richly quotable dialogue. Even so, much of the insanity was lifted from official research materials.

Panicked by fluoridation, which he sees as a Communist plot against "our precious bodily fluids," impotent Strategic Air Command General Jack D. Ripper (Sterling Hayden) starts World War III. Peter Sellers produces his best screen work, playing three roles: the RAF group captain who tries selflessly to reason with Ripper; the liberal president who has to cope not only with a drunken and upset Soviet premier on the hotline, but also with his own turbulent staff ("Gentlemen, you can't fight in here—this is the War Room!"); and the ex-Nazi apocalypse expert Strangelove, whose artificial arm uncontrollably "heils" at embarrassing moments. Also memorable are George C. Scott as General Buck Turgidson, unable to conceal his almost sexual enthusiasm for nuclear holocaust, and Slim Pickens as the pilot who winds up going down with his nuke. In the final scene, pay attention to Peter Bull, who is marvelously glowering as the Soviet ambassador: while Sellers's Strangelove is wrestling with his wheelchair, the stone-faced Bull is visibly on the point of exploding with laughter. In Kubrick's vision, the sexual inadequacy of middle-aged men in the power elites of East and West leads to the end of the world. **KN**

⊙ KEY SCENES

1 "TRY A LITTLE TENDERNESS"
The in-flight refueling of a bomber is scored with a romantic tune, transforming stock air force footage into a bizarre midair copulation. Later, the end of the movie joltingly employs Vera Lynn's "We'll Meet Again" to accompany footage of nuclear mushroom clouds.

2 THE HOTLINE
President Merkin Muffley (Peter Sellers) tries to explain to the Russian premier, who is drunk, that there is about to be an accidental attack on his country. "I'm talking about the bomb, Dmitri . . . the hydrogen bomb."

3 RODEO DIVE
Major T. J. "King" Kong (Slim Pickens) rides a nuclear bomb like a bucking bronco as it drops on Russia. Sellers was earmarked for this role too, but was unable to take it on. The part was offered to John Wayne and *Bonanza* star Dan Blocker before passing to Pickens.

4 "MEIN FÜHRER, I CAN WALK!"
Dr. Strangelove explains his vision for the post-nuclear future—with high-ranking politicians and generals and fertile young women preserving the US way of life in deep underground shelters—as his recalcitrant metal arm tries to give a Nazi salute.

⊙ DIRECTOR PROFILE

1928–55
Stanley Kubrick was born in Manhattan, New York. Originally a still photographer, he made a few documentary shorts (*Flying Padre, Day of the Fight*, both 1951) before raising finance for his debut feature *Fear and Desire* (1953); he later suppressed the film, calling it "bumbling" and "amateur." It was followed by *Killer's Kiss* (1955), on which Kubrick was writer, director, producer, and cinematographer.

1956–61
After the impressive noir heist film *The Killing* (1956), Kubrick was hired by Kirk Douglas for *Paths of Glory* (1957) and *Spartacus* (1960). Fraught experiences with Douglas on the latter, and during his brief tenure as original director of Marlon Brando's *One-Eyed Jacks* (1961), persuaded Kubrick to relocate to England.

1962–79
Kubrick became his own producer on a series of large-scale pictures (mostly novel based), on which he exercised his famed perfectionism. *Lolita* (1962) marked his first collaboration with Peter Sellers, and was followed by *Dr. Strangelove or: How I Learned to Stop Worrying and Love the Bomb*. Kubrick cowrote the screenplay for enigmatic sci-fi epic *2001: A Space Odyssey* (1968, see p. 292) with author Arthur C. Clarke. *A Clockwork Orange* (1971) was notorious for its extreme violence and sexual scenes. Kubrick himself halted the UK distribution of the film, on police advice; it remained effectively banned for twenty-seven years. *Barry Lyndon* (1975) won four Academy Awards, more than any other of his films.

1980–99
Despite mixed reviews, *The Shining* (1980) proved popular with audiences and became a cult horror classic; it was followed by Vietnam movie *Full Metal Jacket* (1987). Kubrick's final film was *Eyes Wide Shut* (1999), a dark examination of human sexuality; the director died four days after a private screening of the final cut. Famously reclusive and obsessive, he worked extensively on several unrealized projects, including a science fiction script that Steven Spielberg filmed as *A.I.: Artificial Intelligence* (2001).

Bonnie and Clyde 1967

ARTHUR PENN 1922 – 2010

▲ Beatty and Dunaway make a pretty pair.

▼ Publicity for the film boasted, "They're young, they're in love, and they kill people."

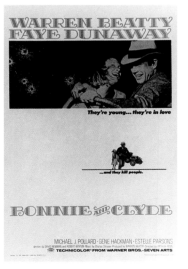

Conceived by writers David Newman and Robert Benton as a US Nouvelle Vague (see p. 248) film, this project was shepherded by producer-star Warren Beatty. He got Warner Bros. to back him because its corporate memory recalled the profits it made with gangster films in the decade when the real Bonnie and Clyde were making headlines. In the 1930s Warner Bros. had to incorporate censor-appeasing scenes of official disapproval to indicate that the hoodlums of movies such as *Scarface* (1932) were not heroes. In tune with the counterculture mood of the 1960s, the sharp-suited, grinning Beatty and chic Faye Dunaway are unashamedly beautiful rebels sticking it to the humorless establishment. Clyde talks up his Robin Hood reputation as an enemy of the banks who have foreclosed on poor folks and Bonnie sends a romanticized poem about their lives (and deaths) to the newspapers. However, director Arthur Penn leavens the couple's gorgeousness with nonstop bickering in their extended gang and casual violence, which inevitably leads to bloody demises all around.

Beatty plays Clyde as sexually troubled, although he and Bonnie finally sleep together before the fatal ambush, while Dunaway is haunted even when they are riding high. The Barrow gang is completed by goonish C. W. (Michael J. Pollard), Clyde's blowhard brother Buck (Gene Hackman), who was jealous that he did not receive title billing, and Buck's prissy, complaining wife (Estelle Parsons). It is an exhilarating, fresh, and funny film—as shocking in its series of bungled robberies as in its outbursts of loud, fast-cut, blood-spurting violence. **KN**

👁 KEY SCENES

1 MESSY ROBBERY
Bonnie and Clyde make a messy escape from a bungled robbery—
they are delayed by C. W.'s insistence on parking the car properly.
The comedy comes to a shocking end when a bank official is shot
in the face. Fast-picking banjo music accompanies the getaway.

2 EUGENE AND VELMA
The gang members abduct a terrified yet excited young couple—
Eugene (Gene Wilder) and Velma (Evans Evans)—stoking the sense
of their growing celebrity. When they find out what Eugene does for
a living (he is an undertaker), Clyde is spooked and stops having fun.

3 LEGEND IN THE MAKING
Bonnie reads a poem she has sent to the newspapers (as did the
real Bonnie Parker) about their exploits: "Some day they'll go down
together / They'll bury them side by side / To a few, it'll be grief /
To the law, a relief / But it's death for Bonnie and Clyde."

4 FAMILY REUNION
Bonnie and Clyde enjoy a convivial reunion with Bonnie's family but
Bonnie's mother casts a pall when she says her good-bye is for the
last time. The scene is filmed in the soft hue of a lazy summer day,
but the whole gang is dressed in funereal black.

5 THE DEATH SET PIECE
Penn turns graphic violence into art in the finale. The outlaws are
caught in an ambush and gunned down in an orgy of bullets that
pepper their car and beautiful bodies with holes. Only moments
before, the couple had reached their sexual climax.

🕐 DIRECTOR PROFILE

1922–57
Arthur Penn was born in Philadelphia. From 1951 he worked
in live television, directing productions for Playhouse 90.

1958–67
He directed films based on television dramas, *The Left-Handed
Gun* (1958) and *The Miracle Worker* (1962). His career took a
slide with *Mickey One* (1965) and *The Chase* (1966), before he
directed *Bonnie and Clyde* in 1967.

1968–81
Penn directed the counterculture-themed *Alice's Restaurant*
(1969) and the revisionist Western *Little Big Man* (1970). Even
failures such as *The Missouri Breaks* (1976) are interesting.

1982–2010
He directed several films including *Target* (1985) and *Dead of
Winter* (1987) but worked mostly in television. He died in 2010,
the day after he turned eighty-eight.

SEX AND THE CINEMA

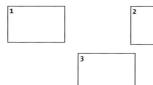

1 *Jag är nyfiken—gul* documented Swedish society during the sexual revolution through the experiences of a rebellious young woman. It features scenes of nudity and staged sexual intercourse.

2 The hip fashion photographer is shown at work in the poster for *Blow-Up*. The portrayal of the photographer is said to be partly based on David Bailey.

3 Jane Fonda as the highly sexual Barbarella. Her character memorably experiences (and burns out) the pleasure-inducing Excessive Machine.

The swinging sixties brought with them a new attitude toward sex, youth, drugs, and personal freedom that impacted on the arts, pushing censorship to its limits. Early in the decade, British New Wave (see p. 258) director Tony Richardson (1928—91) cast aside social realism in favor of farcical comedy for *Tom Jones* (1963), his adaptation of Henry Fielding's eighteenth-century novel. With its knowing winks and risqué content, it follows the sexual adventures of the young Tom, played with gusto by Albert Finney. To twenty-first-century viewers, *Tom Jones* appears coy in its portrayal of Tom's amorous encounters, but the film was racy for the time. When Jones and Mrs. Waters have dinner together, Richardson depicts the pair's lustful desires with innuendo as they sup on oysters, tear at chicken legs, and smother their mouths with juicy pears.

Cinema's reassessment of social mores was not confined to Western society. In Japan, directors such as Shohei Imamura (1926—2006) showed the changing role of women and uninhibited sexuality in films such as *Nippon konchuki* (*The Insect Woman*, 1963), which tells the story of a peasant girl turned geisha, who is sexually abused by her stepfather and damned for her "carnal desire." The film charts the history of pre- and postwar Japan in the twentieth century as tradition gave way to a liberal, industrial society.

As the decade progressed, cinema became more open to tackling taboo subjects and mirroring the events taking place in an increasingly liberal society. *Blow-Up* (1966, opposite above), directed by Michelangelo Antonioni (1912—2007), was a hit thanks partly to its explicit sex scenes and take on the drug-taking

KEY EVENTS

1960	1961	1964	1966	1967	1968
The American Food and Drug Administration approves the first oral contraceptive, which becomes known as "the pill."	British film *A Taste of Honey* challenges the censors with its taboo subjects (illegitimacy, homosexuality, and mixed-race relationships).	*Nippon konchuki* is nominated for the Golden Bear at the Berlin Film Festival. Sachiko Hidari wins the Silver Bear for Best Actress.	Michelangelo Antonioni is nominated for a Best Director Oscar for *Blow-Up* and wins the Palme d'Or at Cannes the following year.	Luis Buñuel (1900—83) directs *Belle de jour* (see p. 282). The film wins the Golden Lion at the Venice Film Festival.	In the United States, the Motion Picture Production Code is abandoned in favor of the Motion Picture Association of America film-rating system.

excesses of contemporary fashionable London. *Belle de jour* (1967, see p. 282) shocked audiences with its story of a Parisian housewife, played by Catherine Deneuve, who becomes a prostitute by day in order to fulfill her sadomasochistic fantasies. Vilgot Sjöman (1924–2006) caused outrage with his frank depictions of sex and violence in his story of a promiscuous young woman, *Jag är nyfiken—gul* (*I Am Curious (Yellow)*, 1967, opposite). Mike Nichols (b. 1931) perfectly captured US society teetering on the brink of the sexual revolution in *The Graduate* (1967, see p. 284), a study of sex across the age divide. Most US cinema up to then had been conventional but *The Graduate* bridges the old and new worlds, pointing to the more experimental cinema that was to come in the 1970s.

As the 1960s drew to a close and censorship laws were relaxed, films began to shock for the sake of it. Kitsch sci-fi movie *Barbarella* (1968, below) stars Jane Fonda as a fortieth-century astronaut who goes to the planet Tau Ceti to find lost scientist Durand-Durand. With Fonda's inexplicable costume changes from one see-through outfit to another, lesbian undertones when the lascivious Great Tyrant (Anita Pallenberg) meets Barbarella, and the scenes of fetishistic bondage gear, this camp cult film has a sadomasochistic edge.

At the decade's end, Dennis Hopper cowrote and starred in the road movie *Easy Rider* (1969) with Peter Fonda. They play hippies who ride their motorbikes from Los Angeles to New Orleans. Their drug-fueled romps with naked women are first innocent and later scary, but never explicit. Hopper used the new freedom available to filmmakers to ask questions nagging at the nation's youth. The revolution was no longer about sex, but ideas. **CK**

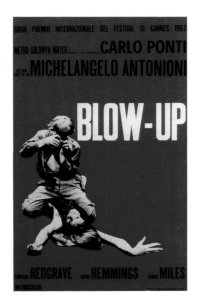

1968	1968	1968	1969	1969	1970
The Graduate (see p. 284) gains seven Academy Award nominations and Mike Nichols wins an Oscar for Best Director.	The stage musical *Hair* causes controversy for its depiction of drug use, nudity, and sexuality. The film version does not appear until 1979.	Strikes started by students in Paris lead to a two-week general strike that nearly brings down the French government.	*Jag är nyfiken—gul* is banned in Massachusetts for being pornographic. A legal case ensues and the film is found not to be obscene.	An estimated 400,000 people attend the Woodstock Festival near the village of Bethel, New York state. It is the largest rock concert of the decade.	Classic road movie *Easy Rider* wins two Oscar nominations.

Belle de jour 1967
LUIS BUÑUEL 1900 – 83

▲ Catherine Deneuve brings emotional distance to the part of housewife Séverine.

▼ Séverine stares out from the film's poster. It is the most famous image of what is arguably Deneuve's defining role.

It is hard to imagine *Belle de jour* being made during any decade but the 1960s. Based on a novel published in 1928, the film's challenging sexual themes and disruption of the suburban norm fitted the prevailing mood of the sixties. However, this is no straightforward plea for liberation. French housewife turned prostitute Séverine (Catherine Deneuve) is punished for her transgression in most interpretations of the film's ending. She appears submissive, only aroused by cruel, aggressive, or dangerous men. She rarely smiles—one memorable moment of bliss crosses her face when she lies on the bed, spent, after an encounter with a client who makes the other prostitutes nervous. Is Séverine a masochist seeking illicit thrills she dare not ask her husband for? In part, perhaps, but *Belle de jour* is more complex than that. Deneuve's haunting performance, combined with Luis Buñuel's stark, economic direction, suggests deep-seated socio-psychological issues that may not be cured by Séverine's attempts to live out her fantasies. Perhaps she is misguided in believing the brothel will satisfy her needs. But does Buñuel—who changed the book's ending—mean to say that Séverine should have turned to her husband to fulfill her fantasies, or that she should have denied them altogether?

Belle de jour aroused considerable controversy when first released, but most complaints involved the risqué subject matter. Buñuel is restrained in his depiction of actual sex acts: this is a scrubbed-up view of prostitution, complete with designer wardrobes and flowing champagne. Whether this is Séverine's fantasy or Buñuel's remains one of the film's many mysteries. **AS**

👁 KEY SCENES

1 SÉVERINE'S DREAM
The film opens to the jingling of coach bells, arguably a signal that Séverine is dreaming. She is in a horse-drawn carriage with her husband, who chastises her for being cold with him. He commands his coachmen to stop in the forest, where he has Séverine whipped.

2 THE BROTHEL
Séverine climbs the stairs to the brothel, amid flashbacks to her childhood. The welcoming but businesslike Madame Anaïs quickly understands her purpose. Séverine agrees to return that afternoon. Anaïs names her "Belle de Jour" as she will work only during the day.

3 WHAT'S IN THE BOX?
A client shows a prostitute a box containing an unseen item that buzzes. She refuses to work with him, but Séverine agrees. He rings a bell and Séverine smiles, perhaps reminded of the coach bells in her fantasy. The mystery of the box is tantalizing to the viewer.

4 PIERRE: DEAD OR ALIVE?
Mr. Husson arrives and says he will tell Séverine's invalid husband Pierre the truth. Husson departs; Pierre's lifeless hand implies he is dead. Suddenly, he jumps up and converses with Séverine, who hears bells and looks out of the window. Is this her new dream?

⏱ STAR PROFILE: CATHERINE DENEUVE

1943–63
Catherine Fabienne Dorléac was born in Paris to actors Maurice Dorléac and Renée Deneuve. She made her debut in *Les collégiennes* (*The Twilight Girls*, 1957). Taking her mother's maiden name, she made many films with director Roger Vadim (1928–2000), with whom she had a child in 1963.

1964–79
The musical *Les parapluies de Cherbourg* (*The Umbrellas of Cherbourg*, 1964) by Jacques Demy (1931–90) made her famous. *Repulsion* (1965), directed by Roman Polanski (b. 1933), further established her stardom before *Belle de jour* made her an international sex symbol. Her role as an emotionally distant beautiful woman in this film earned her nickname the "ice maiden." Deneuve married photographer David Bailey in 1965; they divorced seven years later. She had a second child, Chiara, by actor Marcello Mastroianni, with whom she made four films. She continued to film in Europe with occasional roles in US films, including *Hustle* (1975). Deneuve became the face of Chanel No. 5 in the 1970s, causing US sales of the perfume to soar.

1980–98
Deneuve won a César award for Best Actress for *Le dernier métro* (*The Last Metro*, 1980) by François Truffaut (1932–84) and gained a further cult following for her turn as a bisexual vampire in *The Hunger* (1983), directed by Tony Scott (b. 1944) and also starring David Bowie and Susan Sarandon. *Indochine* (1992) landed her a second César and she and Mastroianni worked together for the last time in *Les cent et une nuits de Simon Cinéma* (*A Hundred and One Nights of Simon Cinema*, 1995). In 1994 Deneuve was appointed UNESCO Goodwill Ambassador for the Safeguarding of Film Heritage.

1999–present
Controversy surrounded her role in *Dancer in the Dark* in 2000. Deneuve continues to work in both Hollywood and Europe, with acclaimed films including *The Girl on the Train* (2009).

The Graduate 1967

MIKE NICHOLS b. 1931

▲ Benjamin tries to inject meaning into his emotionally empty affair with Mrs. Robinson.

▼ Mrs. Robinson's leg dominates the poster.

JOSEPH E. LEVINE
MIKE NICHOLS
LAWRENCE TURMAN

This is Benjamin. He's a little worried about his future.

THE GRADUATE

ANNE BANCROFT .. DUSTIN HOFFMAN · KATHARINE ROSS
CALDER WILLINGHAM .. BUCK HENRY PAUL SIMON
SIMON .. GARFUNKEL LAWRENCE TURMAN
MIKE NICHOLS TECHNICOLOR® PANAVISION®

United Artists

With a style that borrowed from European art cinema, a deft sense of comic timing, flashes of risqué material, and a popular soundtrack, *The Graduate* brought a young audience back to the cinema. It also announced the arrival of the "Hollywood renaissance." The US film industry's brief flirtation with youthful rebellion and a director-led cinema did not last, but *The Graduate* has proved remarkably enduring, a film of its time that remains fresh and disarmingly ambiguous.

Buck Henry (who plays the hotel clerk) and Calder Willingham's screenplay kept relatively close to Charles Webb's novel: Webb wrote it in 1963, not long after graduating himself. The film's story, in which a bored young graduate drifts into an affair with an older, married woman, mirrors the decade's changing social and sexual mores. The closest it gets to reflecting on contemporary student unrest is when Benjamin Braddock (Dustin Hoffman) is asked by his Berkeley landlord if he is "one of those agitators." Still, Benjamin's journey from apathy to action clearly struck a chord with contemporary young audiences uneasy with established values. The film also modified the stylistic norms of the time. Veteran cinematographer Robert Surtees made full use of the width of the frame (and frames within frames) to convey a sense of alienation, while the skillful and innovative use of editing and sound moves the story smoothly forward while establishing Benjamin's disorientation as he conducts the affair. In his skillful playing of the role, Hoffman opened up new possibilities to the kind of leading man Hollywood would accept. **GB**

KEY SCENES

1 WHAT ARE YOU GOING TO DO NOW?
Newly graduated Benjamin Braddock returns to Los Angeles and to a party in his honor. His parents' friends pester him with questions and advice about his future ("Just one word . . . . Plastics," says one). Burdened by expectations, Benjamin escapes to his room.

2 MRS. ROBINSON
Having initially rejected Mrs. Robinson's advances, Benjamin meets her at the Taft Hotel and their affair begins. Mrs. Robinson is almost businesslike in her seduction of the naive Benjamin. Anne Bancroft brought just the right mix of indifference and intimidation to the role.

3 LATE FOR THE WEDDING
Benjamin learns that Elaine Robinson (Katharine Ross) is getting married and races to the church. He arrives to see the groom kiss the bride, but he attracts Elaine's attention and they fend off those who try to stop them leaving. They catch a bus to an uncertain future.

DIRECTOR PROFILE

1931–71
Mike Nichols was born Michael Igorevitch Peschkowsky in Berlin, Germany. He and his Jewish family moved to the United States in 1939. He attended the University of Chicago where he began to work in improvisational comedy. Nichols directed Neil Simon's *Barefoot in the Park* on Broadway in 1963. It was massively successful and he fell in love with directing. His first two films, *Who's Afraid of Virginia Woolf?* (1966) and *The Graduate*, were box-office triumphs. Not so *Catch-22* (1970), but the place of *Carnal Knowledge* (1971) in the sexual revolution was assured when the US Supreme Court overturned earlier rulings that had declared it obscene.

1972–82
Neither *Day of the Dolphin* (1973) nor *The Fortune* (1975) attracted much attention in the 1970s, and it appeared that Nichols's Hollywood career was coming to an end.

1983–97
Nichols returned successfully as a mainstream director (and producer) with *Silkwood* (1983). The stylistic flourishes of earlier films gave way to more solidly crafted dramas and comedies of the sexes, such as *Working Girl* (1988).

1998–present
Nichols returned to collaboration with Elaine May in *Primary Colors* (1998), and continued the gentle political satire in *Charlie Wilson's War* (2007). He directed *Wit* (2001) and *Angels in America* (2003) for HBO, television work that is as significant as anything he has done since his early films.

SOUNDTRACK AND SCREEN

Having asked Paul Simon to write material for the film, Mike Nichols decided to use songs from two earlier Simon & Garfunkel albums, some of the then-unfinished "Mrs. Robinson" (below) plus music by Dave Grusin. Both the film and music industries profited from this use of popular material. The soundtrack was central to the film's success, and the eventual album topped the charts until it was replaced by *Bookends*, the album containing a complete version of "Mrs. Robinson" and other songs written for but not used in the film. How music was used was also distinctive. "The Sounds (later "Sound") of Silence" is sung at the beginning, the end, and during the montage sequence intercutting Benjamin idling at home during his affair with Mrs. Robinson. The lyrics,  starting with "Hello darkness, my old friend," suggest Benjamin's inner thoughts, although they never directly connect with the narrative, and the bleak words are offset by the upbeat delivery.

SPY FILMS

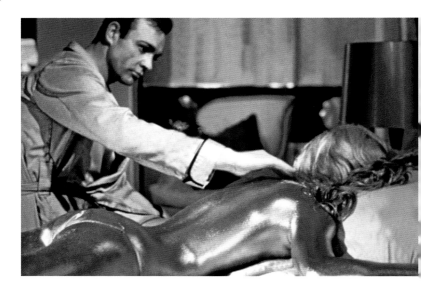

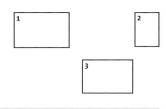

1 Sean Connery as James Bond in
Goldfinger. This classic scene of the
woman painted gold was later homaged
in Daniel Craig's second outing as Bond,
Quantum of Solace (2008).

2 The moody poster for Martin Ritt's
adaptation of John Le Carré's *The Spy
Who Came in from the Cold*.

3 Michael Caine as the insubordinate
"anti-Bond" Harry Palmer, in espionage
thriller *Funeral in Berlin*.

The spy film has always been split into two types. The first group consisted of sensational thrillers with narratives built around chase and pursuit. The Bulldog Drummond films and two Alfred Hitchcock (1899–1980) adventures, *Foreign Correspondent* (1940, see p. 156) and *Saboteur* (1942), exemplified this type. The second group encompassed more existential thrillers, often adapted from writers such as Eric Ambler and Graham Greene, for example, *Journey into Fear* (1942) and *Ministry of Fear* (1943). This type of spy film featured "ordinary" protagonists rather than professional secret agents and was characterized by its noirish, Expressionist-influenced style.

The heyday of the spy film came during the Cold War, when the genre became a vehicle for the geopolitical and ideological conflict between the free democratic West and the totalitarian Communist bloc. Early Cold War films such as *I Was a Communist for the FBI* (1951) were crude products of McCarthyite paranoia but as the "Red Scare" faded filmmakers were able to turn a more critical eye on the spying game. Hitchcock's *North by Northwest* (1959) touches upon the moral ambiguity of the Cold War, and the John Frankenheimer (1930–2002) thriller *The Manchurian Candidate* (1962) exploited anxieties about brainwashing (a characteristic Cold War theme) with a plot that uncannily anticipated the assassination of President Kennedy in 1963.

Spy films of the 1960s responded to events such as the building of the Berlin Wall (1961) and the Cuban missile crisis (1962). The sensational spy thriller was represented preeminently by the James Bond films, based on the

KEY EVENTS

1959	1962	1963	1964	1964	1965
Alfred Hitchcock's *North by Northwest*, a landmark of the genre and a major influence on the early Bond movies, is released.	United Artists releases two of the most influential spy films: *The Manchurian Candidate* and *Dr. No* (the first of the Bond films).	John F. Kennedy is assassinated. His death gives rise to a host of conspiracy theories.	On television, *The Man from U.N.C.L.E.* series begins, introducing the world to Napoleon Solo and Illya Kuryakin.	*Goldfinger* is the third Bond film and the one that establishes the formula.	"Bondmania" reaches its peak with *Thunderball*, while "anti-Bonds" emerge in *The Spy Who Came in from the Cold* and *The Ipcress File*.

novels by Ian Fleming, and beginning with *Dr. No* in 1962, followed in 1963 by *From Russia with Love* (see p. 288). The Bond films differed fundamentally from the books in that the filmmakers dispensed with Fleming's Soviet villains and replaced them with a supranational criminal syndicate, thus detaching the screen Bond from the ideological context of the Cold War. The Bond films combine visual spectacle (exotic locations, action sequences) with images of conspicuous consumption and permissive sexuality. It proved a winning formula at the box office and the series has remained in near-continuous production ever since. *Goldfinger* (1964, opposite) and *Thunderball* (1965) marked the height of "Bondmania," and, although later films in the series have become formulaic, Bond remains the archetypal secret agent action hero and the model for other franchises such as the *Mission Impossible* and Jason Bourne films.

A counter-cycle of "anti-Bond" films in the mid 1960s adopted a more cynical and ambiguous perspective. Martin Ritt (1914–90) directed the faithful adaptation of John Le Carré's *The Spy Who Came in from the Cold* (1965, right), which was the antithesis of the Bond movies with its shabby antihero, austere black-and-white cinematography and bleak wintry locations. Its mood of suspicion and moral ambiguity is closer to the existential anxiety of Film Noir (see p. 168) than to the fantasy world of James Bond. Michael Caine played Cockney spy Harry Palmer in three films based on the novels by Len Deighton: *The Ipcress File* (1965), *Funeral in Berlin* (1966, below), and *Billion Dollar Brain* (1967). With their moles and double agents, these films reflected the reality of espionage in the wake of the cases of the Cambridge spy ring that included Guy Burgess, Donald Maclean, and Kim Philby. **JC**

1966	1966	1966	1966	1967	1969
US "Spoof Bonds" appear in the shape of James Coburn's Derek Flint (*Our Man Flint*) and Dean Martin's Matt Helm (*The Silencers*).	Another John Le Carré adaptation, *The Deadly Affair*, stars James Mason and Harry Andrews.	Ian Fleming publishes the last of his Bond adventures: *Octopussy* and *The Living Daylights*.	Alfred Hitchcock revisits the world of espionage with *Torn Curtain*, starring Paul Newman and Julie Andrews.	James Coburn appears again in a more satirical, freewheeling take on the spy movie, *The President's Analyst*.	Mankind first sets foot on the moon, ending the space race and adding a sense of adventure to the mood of Cold War paranoia.

From Russia with Love 1963
TERENCE YOUNG 1915 – 94

▲ Sean Connery in his definitive role.

▼ The film was a box-office hit, scooping more than $70 million.

The second James Bond film, *From Russia with Love*, reunited star Sean Connery, director Terence Young, and screenwriter Richard Maibaum. It benefited from a budget that was twice its predecessor's relatively modest $950,000, and from a superlative supporting cast, including Robert Shaw as taciturn assassin Grant and Lotte Lenya as the memorably toadlike villainess Rosa Klebb. It was also the film that featured the first of Bond's many ingenious gadgets: his attaché case equipped with knives and tear gas is employed to deadly effect during the brutal fight on the Orient Express.

Later films in the Bond series would prove the adage that bigger is not necessarily better, but *From Russia with Love* is a fine, taut spy adventure that remains within the bounds of plausibility. In many respects it is a throwback to spy novels of the 1930s rather than anticipating the technological spectacle of later films. Instead of taking on a megalomaniac supervillain who plots to subjugate the world, Bond's mission is to capture a Russian decoding machine, unaware that he is actually a pawn in a gambit by SPECTRE (Special Executive for Counter-intelligence, Terrorism, Revenge, and Extortion) to pit the British and Russians against each other. The film eschews the high-tech trappings of most Bond films and instead focuses on characterization and mood.

The Bond producers, Cubby Broccoli and Harry Saltzman, were now so confident in the success of their series that they were able to proclaim in the end credits: "James Bond will return in the next Ian Fleming thriller *Goldfinger.*" And so he did, and in a further twenty films. **JC**

👁 KEY SCENES

1 THE PRE-TITLE SEQUENCE
An atmospheric two-minute "teaser," in which Grant (Shaw) stalks a Bond lookalike through ornamental gardens, establishes how deadly Grant is. From the outset the audience knows the very real threat that Bond will face.

3 THE ORIENT EXPRESS
Bond and Tatiana (Daniela Bianchi) escape from Istanbul, traveling in luxury on the Orient Express. Bond's innate snobbery proves useful. He realizes Grant is an enemy agent when the Russian makes the haute-culinary mistake of ordering red wine with fish.

2 THE GYPSY CAMP
Bond and Kerim Bey's (Pedro Armendariz) evening entertainment includes a catfight between two Gypsy girls who are rivals for the chief's son. Bond is warned not to intervene. Such erotic spectacles are part of the Bond films' appeal.

4 THE DENOUEMENT
Villainess Rosa Klebb (Lenya) makes a final effort to kill James Bond, attacking him with the poison-tipped spikes in her shoes. Tatiana demonstrates whose side she is on when she shoots Klebb. "She's had her kicks," Bond remarks wryly—a classic Bond quip.

PAGE TO SCREEN

While later Bond movies would come to bear less and less resemblance to Ian Fleming's novels, the early films, *From Russia with Love* in particular, are closer to their source material. Richard Maibaum's screenplay maintained the structure of the book, where the reader/viewer is introduced to the enemy conspiracy before Bond becomes aware of it. The characters of Tatiana, Kerim, Grant, and Klebb are maintained from the book, as well as several key scenes such as the attack on the Gypsy camp and the journey on the Orient Express. However, Maibaum made two important changes. He "opened up" the last quarter of the film with more spectacular action sequences: the motorboat chase and the helicopter attack—which was borrowed from Alfred Hitchcock's espionage thriller *North by Northwest* (1959). He also switched Fleming's Soviet enemy SMERSH for the international terrorist organization SPECTRE—seen as a move to "depoliticize" the Bond films by separating them from the Cold War. The book was published in 1957 and was the fifth written by Fleming. Initially not a success, it was only when John F. Kennedy announced his admiration for it that the book became a best seller.

SCIENCE FICTION

1 Rod Taylor prepares for time travel in *The Time Machine*. A plaque on the machine's indicator panel reading "Manufactured by H. George Wells" is clearly visible in several of the film's scenes.

2 *Alphaville* blended dystopian science fiction with Film Noir, signified by the attire of the main figure in the poster.

3 *Planet of the Apes* was groundbreaking for its prosthetic makeup techniques, mastered by John Chambers.

Science fiction films of the 1960s belong to a broad genre. Although the 1950s was dubbed a golden age of sci-fi movies—characterized by noirish Cold War paranoia in films such as *The Thing from Another World* (1951)—it was during the 1960s that science fiction became its own beast. Fifties-style space invasions and monster rampages continued to be made, but science fiction also manifested in forms as varied as political speculation (*The Manchurian Candidate*, 1962), nightmare horror (*Seconds*, 1966), and tongue-in-cheek space opera (*Barbarella*, 1968).

Films that in the 1950s would have been made in black and white took on color. In *King Kong vs. Godzilla* (1963), titans of earlier eras returned in eye-pleasing colors and took a more child-friendly course that would see the fearsome Godzilla reformed as a defender and friend to small children. Similar family-friendly adventure was offered in *The Time Machine* (1960, above), in which director George Pal (1908—80) toned down the bitter pessimism of H. G. Wells's novel, first published in 1895. If science fiction in the 1950s was all about fear of the unknown, then in the 1960s—owing to a fascination with all things "space age" resulting from the Soviet and US space race—science fiction embraced opportunity. The moon explorations sparked interest in outer space adventures, and encouraged special effects advances (specifically model work and mattes) that made it possible to realize convincingly the gadget-

KEY EVENTS

1961	1961	1962	1963	1964	1965
Yuri Gagarin, the first man in space, returns as hero of the Soviet Union. Historic events help to fuel cinema's creative imagination.	Directed by Joseph Losey (1909–84), *The Damned* (released in the United States in 1963) weds 1950s nuclear paranoia to 1960s rebellion.	Soviet film *The Amphibian Man* combines seafaring adventure with science-fiction fantasy.	*The Day of the Triffids* is released. It is based on John Wyndham's post-apocalyptic novel written in 1951.	Michael Moorcock becomes editor of British sci-fi magazine *New Worlds*; it champions new wave writers (J. G. Ballard and Harlan Ellison).	Directed by Peter Watkins (b. 1935), *The War Game* gets theatrical release and wins an Academy Award for Best Documentary Feature in 1966.

290 **1960–69**

laden future of *2001: A Space Odyssey* (1968, see p. 292). Released in the same year, *Planet of the Apes* (below) saw an astronaut crew crash on a planet in the future where apes have evolved into the dominant species and humans are enslaved. The memorable image of the broken Statue of Liberty at the film's end symbolizes perfectly the prevailing anxieties of nuclear war and its radioactive, rubble-strewn aftermath spurred by the Cuban missile crisis.

A populist pulp form in Britain, the United States, and Japan, science fiction began to resonate in other cultures—and essays in serious (if satirical) futurism came from art-house auteurs such as François Truffaut (1932–84) in *Fahrenheit 451* (1966) and Jean-Luc Godard (b. 1930) in *Alphaville* (1965, right). In the latter American Eddie Constantine plays a character—secret agent Lemmy Caution—who would not look out of place in a noirish thriller of the 1940s. Although set in a dystopian future, *Alphaville* was filmed in actual Parisian locations of the period.

Oddly, with a few exceptions, including Ray Bradbury (*Fahrenheit 451*) and John Wyndham (*The Day of the Triffids*, 1963), there was a reluctance in the 1960s to adapt the works of living writers: Philip K. Dick would not become a frequently filmed author until after *Blade Runner* (1982).

Although many sci-fi films of the era were big hits, such as the *Planet of the Apes* franchise, the masterpiece of the decade was *2001: A Space Odyssey* directed by Stanley Kubrick (1928–99). Blessed with still unmatched special effects, it tuned into the space craze of the time. Audiences questioned what it might mean but were still mesmerized by its transcendental vision. Hailed and reviled, *2001* dared to be as much art movie as Buck Rogers fare, but its influence on subsequent filmed science fiction is impossible to overestimate. **KN**

1965	1967	1967	1968	1968	1969
Jean-Luc Godard's *Alphaville* finds the future in corporate corners of Paris.	Hammer studios releases the conceptually ambitious *Quatermass and the Pit*, directed by Roy Ward Baker (1916–2010).	The first successful heart transplant is performed. It inspires films such as *Frankenstein Must Be Destroyed* and *Change of Mind* (both 1969).	*Planet of the Apes*—at once Swiftian satire and Flash Gordon adventure—sets a precedent for science fiction franchises to come.	*2001: A Space Odyssey* (see p. 292) is released. Kubrick's collaboration with writer Arthur C. Clarke, it is conceived as the ultimate science fiction film.	Some speculate that science fiction is rendered obsolete by Neil Armstrong's "one small step" on the moon.

2001: A Space Odyssey 1968
STANLEY KUBRICK 1928 – 99

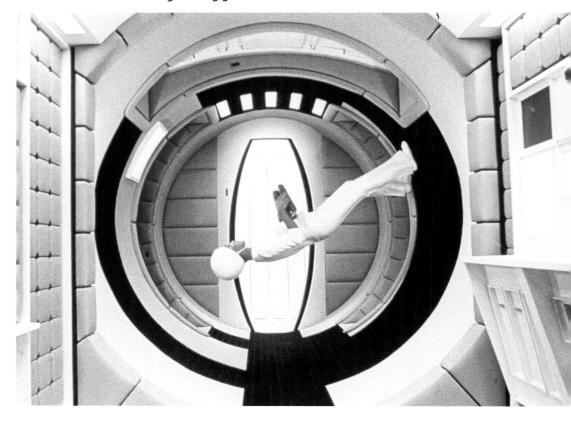

▲ A steward appears to defy gravity as a result of groundbreaking special effects.

▼ The poster accentuates the vast, unforgiving nature of space.

An epic drama of adventure and exploration

When Stanley Kubrick had the notion to make the ultimate science fiction film, he asked for "the best science fiction writer in the world" as a collaborator. At that time, most experts would have suggested Ray Bradbury, but Kubrick was seeking a visionary with a grounding in the actual science of the space race. He formed an unlikely partnership with the English author Arthur C. Clarke, who specialized in big ideas and practical science, but was a workmanlike novelist.

The seed of the script was Clarke's "The Sentinel," a magazine story about an alien artifact placed on the moon as a measure of humankind—when the human race attains a level of technology that enables it to reach the Earth's satellite, a signal is sent to the extraterrestrial civilization that the new species is worth contacting. In the film this vision of progress is combined with Frankensteinian drama as HAL, the ship's computer, turns against its masters and tries to murder the crew; however, the true business of the film is transcendence. It takes its epic voyages as slowly as a European art movie, and lets its meticulous visuals overwhelm the viewer even as the on-screen characters rarely trouble to look out of the windows. The narrative is attenuated, ambiguous. The viewer becomes aware that an unknowable alien race, represented by black monoliths, has tinkered with human evolution since the Stone Age—teaching a proto-hominid how to use a tool, then leaving a message on the moon that inspires a manned mission to Jupiter. It is from here that astronaut Bowman (Keir Dullea) will finally discover man's destiny. **KN**

◉ KEY SCENES

1 THE DAWN OF MAN
The black monolith appears to Moonwatcher, one of a tribe of proto-hominids who live on the African plains. Richard Strauss's soundtrack "Also sprach Zarathustra" signifies the beginnings of civilization and warfare.

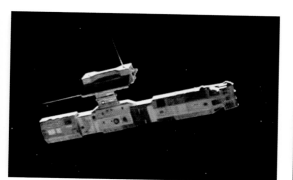

2 MATCH CUT
The flung bone becomes an orbital weapons platform in a match cut that spans the millennia. Often celebrated as one of the best cuts in film history, the rhythm is timed perfectly and the message is clear. It is human evolution condensed to a matter of seconds.

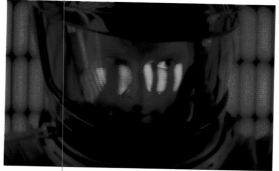

3 HAL IS DESTROYED
In a tense, sweaty, claustrophobic sequence, Bowman dismantles the rebel computer HAL from the inside. The dying of the artificial intelligence is conveyed by the machine's halting attempt to sing a music-hall song: "Daisy, Daisy . . . ."

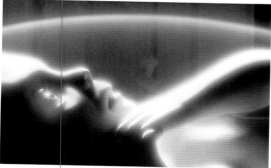

4 STAR CHILD
Bowman goes "beyond the infinite," passing through an alien-maintained hotel before being reborn and renewed. Floating in eternity, the wide-eyed Star Child, the being that was once Bowman, regards the Earth.

THE PREEXISTING SCORE

Alex North, who composed the music for *Spartacus* (1960), was hired to provide a score for *2001*. Kubrick put preexisting music to his rough cut as a temporary track to guide North in writing something similar, but then decided to use his temporary track selections (Richard Strauss, György Ligeti, etc.) on the finished film. Richard Strauss's "Also sprach Zarathustra" (right) became well known, and was used by the BBC as a theme for Apollo mission coverage. North recycled portions of his *2001* score in *The Shoes of the Fisherman* (1968), *Shanks* (1974), and *Dragonslayer* (1981). *2001* was a pioneer in the use of the collage score, causing others—Martin Scorsese (b. 942), Quentin Tarantino (b. 1963)—to use tracks from their record collections in their films.

"Also sprach Zarathustra
Tondichtung
(frei nach Friedr. Nietzsche)
FÜR GROSSES ORCHESTER
von
Richard Strauss
OP 30

HORROR MOVIES

Far from being just a string of shocks and scares, horror movies in the 1960s often used the genre as a device to explore wider themes. *Village of the Damned* (1960, above) imagines a scenario in which society has been subverted from within by a force that has infiltrated the minds of its children; *Night of the Eagle* (1962) fuses witchcraft with questions of belief and superstition; and in *Vargtimmen* (*Hour of the Wolf*, 1968) Ingmar Bergman (1918–2007) considers the role of art and the artist within the framework of a relationship film with horror elements. Even exploitation master Roger Corman (b. 1926) took time out during the decadence and theatricality of *The Masque of the Red Death* (1964) to debate the nature of religious faith.

Perhaps the most interesting discussions that took place were in the films that commented on contemporary society. There are clear antibourgeois swipes in the grotesque revelries of the affluent depicted in Corman's Poe cycle and in the Roger Vadim (1928–2000) segment of *Histoires extraordinaires* (*Tales of Mystery and Imagination*, 1968), as well as with the cackling, Upper West Side Manhattan witches' coven of *Rosemary's Baby* (1968, see p. 298). This could be interpreted as a sixties condemnation of the greedy, in the spirit of postwar freedom, equality, and civil liberties.

KEY EVENTS

1960	1960	1960	1961	1962	1962
Alfred Hitchcock's *Psycho* (see p. 296) alters film forever with its depiction of violence and sexuality and a never-bettered use of the MacGuffin.	One of the first in the "demonic children" subgenre, *Village of the Damned* is a faithful adaptation of John Wyndham's novel *The Midwich Cuckoos*.	Due to its violent content, *La maschera del demonio* (*The Mask of the Vampire*), by Mario Bava (1914–80), is banned in the United Kingdom.	Influenced by *Psycho*, William Castle (1914–77) releases *Homicidal*. This early slasher film has a "fright break" for those too scared to watch.	*An Occurrence at Owl Creek Bridge* wins the Academy Award for Best Short Film. It will later influence *Jacob's Ladder* (1990) and *Donnie Darko* (2001).	Joan Crawford and Bette Davies exploit their famed rivalry in a brutal portrayal of the perils of fame, *What Ever Happened to Baby Jane?*

Witchfinder General (1968) is a potent reminder of historical atrocities as well as a brutal metaphor for Senator McCarthy's Communist witch hunts of the 1950s. Low-budget horror came to the fore and films such as *Night of the Living Dead* (1968, right), by George A. Romero (b. 1940), represented a new wave that questioned whether the world is good and morally just. With intense close-ups, skewed camerawork, and well-developed characters, it marked the arrival of a maverick director and alerted audiences to new concerns. The zombies (revived by radiation) can be seen as referencing racism and war and, in contrast to many other horror films, the danger is nationwide, maybe even worldwide.

As well as the supernatural malevolence of *The Haunting* (1963) and the alien invaders of *The Day of the Triffids* (1962), horror was also given a human face. The danger could be anyone and the terror was real, as seen in *Peeping Tom* (1960) and *Psycho* (1960, see p. 296). Following *Psycho* with *The Birds* (1963, opposite below), Alfred Hitchcock (1899–1980) once again subverted what audiences expect from a heroine. The classic female lead in a horror film is fair, virginal, dressed in white, and acts as a moral compass: the good-hearted Mina survives Dracula, while we see what having sex does to Mia Farrow in *Rosemary's Baby*. Unlike the vast majority of female horror leads, Tippi Hedren's Melanie in *The Birds* is not a shrinking violet but a confident woman who pursues a man all the way to his front door. With this female characters now had far more scope than just looking terrified.

Horror was popular not only in the United States, but in Europe and Asia too. The supernatural horror of *Onibaba* (1964) and *Kwaidan* (*Ghost Stories*, 1964) signaled a "J-horror" invasion thirty years before *Ringu* (*Ring*, 1998). *Giallo* films emerged, offering a career in horror movies for many European directors including Dario Argento (b. 1940). French horror movies made little impact, despite the chilling *Les yeux sans visage* (*Eyes Without a Face*, 1960) by Georges Franju (1912–87), but a French parentage can be attributed to those films influenced by the Grand Guignol movement, such as the stylized horror (and more specifically Grande Dame Guignol) of *What Ever Happened to Baby Jane?* (1962) and the lushness of Hammer's output. With a core trio of director Terence Fisher (1904–80) and stars Christopher Lee and Peter Cushing, Hammer became the dominant studio in Britain, churning out such colorful entries as *Dracula: Prince of Darkness* (1966) and *Frankenstein Must Be Destroyed* (1969), and reaching its peak in 1968 with the Richard Matheson-scripted *The Devil Rides Out*.

Particularly in Western cinemas, the 1960s represented a time when horror movies were respected as art. Yet it was also the decade when the genre began to lose its focus. Studios realized they could churn out endless sequels and schlocky imitators. Horror films became a cheap commodity; drive-in theaters made the switch to exploitation fare. Nonetheless, for a time, horror movies in the 1960s provided a range and imaginative scope that flourished before the arrival and saturation of the teen slasher market. **SW**

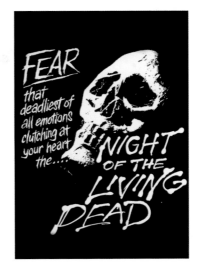

1 The sinister children in *Village of the Damned* all have pale blond hair, striking eyes, and telepathic powers that they use to protect themselves.

2 With *Night of the Living Dead*, director George A. Romero created an urgent, daring blend of horror and social commentary that signaled a new wave in the horror genre.

3 The climactic scene of *The Birds* took seven days to shoot. The birds were attached to Tippi Hedren's clothes by nylon threads. The actress has described it as "the worst week of my life."

1963	1963	1963	1968	1968	1969
The Haunting is the definitive haunted house tale. Martin Scorsese (b. 1942) calls it his favorite horror film. It influences *Shutter Island* (2010).	Exploitation and splatter cinema announces its arrival with the release of *Blood Feast*, directed by Herschell Gordon Lewis (b. 1929).	Mario Bava releases what is considered the first *giallo* film, *La ragazza che sapeva troppo* (*The Evil Eye*)— a nod to Hitchcock.	The Motion Picture Production Code becomes redundant. The MPAA film rating system classifies films as General, Mature, Restricted, and X-rated.	Horror in disguise? *Chitty Chitty Bang Bang* features the nightmarish Child Catcher, played effectively by Robert Helpmann.	*The Oblong Box* unites horror giants Vincent Price and Christopher Lee. It is the last of the Edgar Allan Poe adaptations from American International.

Psycho 1960
ALFRED HITCHCOCK 1899 – 1980

▲ Norman Bates stands ominously outside his house as Marion arrives at the motel.

▼ A half-clad Janet Leigh adorns the poster.

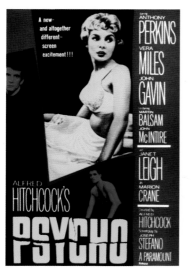

Alfred Hitchcock liked to claim that his sole aim as a filmmaker was "to put the audience through it." By this criterion, *Psycho* must rank as his supreme cinematic achievement. Plenty of Hitchcock films had the audience on the edge of its seats, but *Psycho* was surely the first to have viewers hiding under their seats, screaming.

Even for those who have seen the film countless times, *Psycho* is still one of the scariest movies ever made. All the elements cohere: Bernard Herrmann's trenchant strings-only score, jabbing and tearing like a flock of ruthless beaks; Josef Stefano's laconic boiling down of Robert Bloch's pulp novel; director of photography John L. Russell's encroaching shadows in every corner; Janet Leigh's touchingly vulnerable portrayal of Marion Crane; Anthony Perkins, in the role that made and ruined his career; and above all Hitchcock at the top of his form, using pure technique to manipulate and terrify viewers, audaciously killing off his heroine forty minutes into the film. The director then pulls his cruelest trick, shifting the audience's identification with Marion to Norman. Only gradually do viewers realize that they have switched allegiance to a psychotic killer.

Psycho was the biggest hit of Hitchcock's career. Shot fast and cheaply in black and white, using his pared-down television team, it grossed $15 million on its US release alone. "It's tremendously satisfying," Hitchcock told François Truffaut (1932–84), "to be able to use the cinematic art to achieve something of a mass emotion. It wasn't a message that stirred the audience, nor was it a great performance or their enjoyment of the novel. They were aroused by pure film." **PK**

◉ KEY SCENES

1 THE SUSPICIOUS COP
Having stolen $40,000 from her boss's client, Marion Crane (Leigh) flees, heading for the town where her boyfriend lives. Sleeping in her car by the roadside she is awakened by a traffic cop. Her agitated behavior betrays her guilt and confusion.

2 "MOTHER'S NOT QUITE HERSELF TODAY"
At the Bates Motel, Norman (Perkins) apologizes for his mother's jealous outburst and offers Marion a snack supper in his "parlor" behind the motel office. Norman Bates became the defining role of Perkins's career, typecasting him as a killer.

3 THE SHOWER SCENE
Marion is stabbed to death in the shower. The scene is a famous feat of editing—thirty-six shots in just thirty seconds. Viewers do not see the knife entering Marion's flesh, but feel as though they do through sleight of hand, sound effects, and the score's shrieking violins.

4 THE KILLING OF ARBOGAST
A private detective hired by Marion's employer, Milton Arbogast (Martin Balsam), comes to investigate the Bates's house. As he climbs the stairs, the gray-haired figure seen in the shower scene rushes out wielding a huge knife.

5 MEET MOTHER
Exploring the Bates's house to find out what became of her sister, Lila Crane (Vera Miles) encounters a gray-haired figure sitting in the cellar. But when the chair swings around it reveals the mummified remains of Norman's mother.

◷ COMPOSER PROFILE

1911–55
Born in New York, Bernard Herrmann studied at Juilliard before joining CBS in 1934. He composed scores for *Citizen Kane* (1941) and *The Magnificent Ambersons* (1942). His other notable scores include *The Devil and Daniel Webster* (1941), which won him an Oscar, *Jane Eyre* (1943), *Hangover Square* (1945), and *The Day the Earth Stood Still* (1951).

1955–75
Herrmann composed scores for nine Hitchcock films, including *Vertigo* (1958), *North by Northwest* (1959), *Psycho*, and *The Birds* (1963). The two parted company when the director rejected the score for *Torn Curtain* (1966). He then worked with François Truffaut on *Fahrenheit 451* (1966) and *La mariée était en noir* (*The Bride Wore Black*, 1968). Herrmann died in California after writing the highly acclaimed, somber score for *Taxi Driver* (1976, see p. 358).

Rosemary's Baby 1968
ROMAN POLANSKI b. 1933

▲ In the film's dramatic climax, Rosemary finally learns the truth about her child.

▼ A moody meditation on the issue at the heart of the film provides the poster image.

Having directed impressive films in Poland—*Nóz w wodzie* (*Knife in the Water*, 1962)—and England—*Repulsion* (1965)—Roman Polanski made his US debut working with contrasting powerhouse producers Robert Evans and William Castle, who had secured the rights to Ira Levin's best-selling novel. One of the great paranoid horror films, *Rosemary's Baby* weds Polanski's skill with visions of unease to solid Hollywood storytelling.

It starts with quiet ominousness. Fragile Rosemary Woodhouse (Mia Farrow) and her ambitious actor husband (John Cassavetes) move into a fabulous apartment in a desirable New York brownstone. The heroine then either drifts into madness during a difficult pregnancy or becomes the target of a conspiracy between her husband and her devil-worshipping neighbors to bring the Antichrist into the world. Levin's story offers a feminist view of marriage as a trap and conventional society as a conspiracy to sacrifice a woman's independence to bring about a cozy dystopia. Yet the demonic trimmings, influential on *The Exorcist* (1973, see p. 336), rather than the social criticism, linger longest in the film. Farrow, with her haunted face and pixie haircut, is ambiguously beleaguered throughout her ordeal, and the supporting cast collaborate with creepy deference.

Polanski teases out the sinister side of the glitzy Manhattanite world, while Levin's clever plot bites deeper as it grinds on, bringing the film to a climax that is at once momentously horrific and subtly sentimental ("he has his father's eyes"). Christopher Komeda's eerie lullaby score is especially memorable. **KN**

👁 KEY SCENES

1 A FIRST OMEN
Rosemary smells the herb (the fictional "tannis root") her neighbors insist their protegée (Angela Dorian) wear in a chalice around her neck. The film's early scenes show Farrow wearing a wig, which is soon discarded to reveal her iconic Vidal Sassoon haircut.

3 ANOTHER BETRAYAL
Rosemary turns to her old doctor for help, but he calls in the senior physician who is part of the cult and she is returned to the satanists. Farrow's waiflike, vulnerable appearance served her well for playing Rosemary, whose health deteriorates as her pregnancy progresses.

2 NIGHTMARE CONCEPTION
After eating a drugged dessert prepared by her neighbor Minnie (Ruth Gordon), Rosemary has a disturbing dream, in which she is held down by the coven, painted with mystic symbols and raped by a demonic presence. This scene is one of the film's most terrifying.

4 ANTI-PIETÀ
Encouraged by the coven to be a true mother to the Antichrist, the devastated Rosemary approaches the cradle and sees what her baby looks like. Polanski, faithful to Levin's novel, creates a chilling ending, as Rosemary starts to gently rock her son's cradle.

SATANIC CINEMA

The Devil starred early in cinematic history. In *Le manoir du diable* (1896) director Georges Méliès (1861–1938) played Mephistopheles. The best straight version of the Faust legend is still *Faust* (1926) by F. W. Murnau (1888–1931) but pacts with the Devil have featured in films from *All That Money Can Buy* (1941) to *The Devil's Advocate* (1997). Many dramas, including *Wall Street* (1987) and *The Devil Wears Prada* (2006), boil down to the Faust story, dressed up in the specific concerns of their decades. Devil worship crept into the movies mostly as a threat, as in *The Seventh Victim* (1943), whose Manhattan coven prefigures Ira Levin's, and Hammer's rip-roaring *The Devil Rides Out* (1967). Among cinema's best devils is Robert De Niro in *Angel Heart* (1987, right).

EUROPEAN CINEMA

1 An ominous darkness surrounds the lovers Piero (Alain Delon) and Vittoria (Monica Vitti) in Antonioni's *L'eclisse*.

2 The poster for Jacques Tati's *Play Time* accentuates how anonymous modern architecture dwarfs the individual.

3 Geneviève (Deneuve) with her widowed mother (Anne Vernon) at their umbrella shop in Jacques Demy's wildly colorful romance, *Les parapluies de Cherbourg*.

European cinema in the 1960s represented a rich cavalcade of personal vision, stylistic revisionism, and intimate engagement with the shifting political landscape. It was a decade of reaction, revolution, and maturity in which filmmakers twisted the traditional grammar of narrative cinema and even sometimes rebelled against the movements with which they had become associated. Many films of the decade reshaped timeworn templates to fresh and sometimes alienating effect, a charge that was led by the progenitors of the French Nouvelle Vague (see p. 248). Indeed, in this period the work of key directors subscribed closely to the dictates of the auteur theory—the director as artist—that was formulated in the late 1950s.

Aside from the Nouvelle Vague and the associated Rive Gauche (Left Bank) movement that included Chris Marker (b. 1921) and Agnès Varda (b. 1928), there were other important talents whose work was rooted in shared ideals. Jacques Demy (1931–90) was married to Varda, and his films were—like the Nouvelle Vague—inspired by Hollywood pulp movies. Instead of the hard-edged Film Noir (see p. 168) lynchpins of Edgar G. Ulmer (1904–72) and Fritz Lang (1890–1976), Demy made movies born out of the bruised romanticism of directors such as Douglas Sirk (1900–87) and Stanley Donen (b. 1924). His superlative debut feature *Lola* (1961) concerned a pouting, basque-sporting

(see p. 248)

KEY EVENTS

1960	1960	1961	1962	1962	1962
Luchino Visconti (1906–76) directs *Rocco e i suoi fratelli* (*Rocco and his Brothers*).	*L'avventura* is booed by the audience at Cannes Film Festival but wins the Jury Prize in recognition of the way it reinvents the visual language of cinema.	*La dolce vita* (see p. 304) is released in the United States and becomes a box-office sensation.	Attracted by Europe's openness to maverick directors, Orson Welles decamps from the United States to Paris to make *Le procès*.	Roman Polanski makes his feature debut with *Nóz w wodzie*, which is nominated for an Oscar for Best Foreign Language Film in 1964.	Andrei Tarkovsky makes his feature debut, *Ivanovo detstvo* (*Ivan's Childhood*), setting out to become one of the major artists of the period.

cabaret dancer (Anouk Aimée) holding out with her young son until her lover returns to sweep her away from squalor. Demy's vibrant films often involve people who had put their lives on hold, and are usually about the emotional strains of packing up and moving forward. His celebrated soap operetta *Les parapluies de Cherbourg* (*The Umbrellas of Cherbourg*, 1964, below right) is a stylized slice of provincial melancholia in which star-crossed lovers, Geneviève Emery (Catherine Deneuve) and Guy Foucher (Nino Castelnuovo), must dream of what could have been when he is drafted into the Algerian War.

One of the decade's most glorious French follies is *Play Time* (1967, right) by Jacques Tati (1907–82). Considered something of a "never to be repeated masterpiece," the film's production has gone down in filmmaking lore as the very definition of auteurist perfectionism gone haywire. Tati put up his entire cinematic back catalogue as financial collateral, mostly to fund construction of an elaborate set on the outskirts of Paris—dubbed Tativille—through which his spring-heeled interloper Monsieur Hulot could haplessly navigate. Rejecting an overarching story, Tati constructed a film comprising a series of sketches involving Hulot's diffident courtship of a US tourist set against a backdrop of silvery glass-and-steel edifices and futuristic abodes stuffed with crackpot utilitarian appliances. Making most directors seem blind to the possibilities of space and depth within the frame, Tati's micro-comic choreography—what he called "the democratization of comedy"—also magnifies concerns of previous films such as *Mon oncle* (1958), in particular the alienating effects of the modern age. When *Play Time* failed Tati went bankrupt.

Although Italian director Michelangelo Antonioni (1912–2007) caused a stir at the Cannes Film Festival in 1960 with his courageous parable of lingering ennui among a group of jaded jet-setters in *L'avventura* (*The Adventure*), he also made stylistic advances in the way buildings and landscape are used to inform mood on-screen. Initially the film proposes a basic mystery. Anna (Lea Massari) goes missing during a boat trip in the Mediterranean and her lover, Sandro (Gabriele Ferzetti) and best friend, Claudia (Monica Vitti), embark on an epic journey to find her. It then gradually subverts expectation by focusing on the existential misery of the couple as their feelings for one another are stifled by the ghost of their lost friend. Antonioni's radical use of mise-en-scène presents the couple as being trapped in open spaces, up towers and, in one memorable scene, surrounded in the street by a group of leering men. The film is the first part of a seminal trilogy about alienation that also comprises *La notte* (*The Night*, 1961), which follows the fortunes of an estranged couple, and *L'eclisse* (*The Eclipse*, 1962, opposite), which examines a doomed love affair.

Where Antonioni made open space seem suffocating, Polish director Roman Polanski (b. 1933) pulled off a similar trick with interiors. Following an accomplished career making film shorts, Polanski's debut feature was the taut

un film de jacques tati

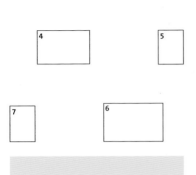

4 In Fellini's *8½* heart throb Mastroianni played the exhausted director Guido, adding gray streaks in his hair and wearing a black hat, black suit, and black-rimmed glasses.

5 A quasi-documentary technique in *La battaglia di Algeri* depicts the grisly horrors of war.

6 Anthony Perkins as the hunted and confused Josef, destined to meet a bad end in the dreamlike *Le procès*.

7 The poster for the thriller *Nóz w wodzie* reflects the film's tight composition and sense of desolation.

three-hander *Nóz w wodzie* (*Knife in the Water*, 1962, below left) in which coiled erotic tensions between a man (Leon Niemczyk), his wife (Jolanta Umecka), and a mysterious hitchhiker (Zygmunt Malanowicz) reach tipping point on a small sailing boat. The film forces the prejudices of idealistic, prosperous characters into the open as they confront a third party trying to invade their lives.

The travails of the idle rich were a prominent feature of European cinema in the 1960s, nowhere more so than in the social satire *La dolce vita* (1960, see p. 304) by Federico Fellini (1920–93). Featuring a surfeit of romantic iconographic images, the film charts the moral decline of glamorous Eurotrash as they allow thrill-seeking to cloud the realities of a Rome emerging from postwar stagnation. *La dolce vita* was a turning point in Fellini's career, as he embraced more self-consciously artful concerns following his Neo-Realist films of the 1950s. Fellini continued to explore baroque fantasy with his autobiographical masterpiece, *8½* (1963, above), about the inner turmoil of a jaded film director, Guido Anselmi (Marcello Mastroianni), when he hits a creative block while working on a science fiction movie. A movie about the creative process of filmmaking and the alienation of modern living, in *8½* Fellini incorporates dream sequences and flashbacks as Anselmi reflects on his life and his relationships with women.

Italian director Gillo Pontecorvo (1919–2006) built on the foundations of Neo-Realism (see p. 178) with his chronicle of urban guerilla warfare, *La battaglia di Algeri* (*The Battle of Algiers*, 1966, opposite above), commissioned by the Algerian government. Shot on location in Algiers's labyrinthine kasbah, the film has a dual-pronged narrative tracing the violent actions of a guerilla cell rebelling against French colonialist rule and the questionable counter-insurgency that follows. Based on the memoirs of freedom fighter Saadi Yacef (who played one of the principal roles and was a producer), the film elicits an emotional immediacy through its newsreel-like photography and dramatic scenes of cafe bombings and prisoner torture, but its subjective depiction of history goads the viewer into assuming a moral standpoint.

The cluster of films that make up the Czech New Wave of the mid- to late 1960s use allegory and subtext to cloak their political disquiet about the Communist regime prior to the Prague Spring of 1968. *Ostře sledované vlaky* (*Closely Observed Trains*, 1966, see p. 308) by Jiří Menzel (b. 1938) masks its ire in the bawdy tale of a young railway station worker desperate to lose his virginity as World War II rumbles on around him. It is an amusing and sweet-natured picture, yet it broaches serious issues, most notably the chasm between the intentions of political legislation and the wants and desires of normal people. *Horí, má panenko* (*The Fireman's Ball*, 1967) was the breakthrough film from Miloš Forman (b. 1932), and its depiction of roistering, sexed-up firemen and their inept attempts to organize a party in their headquarters planted similar barbs about the problems of exerting leadership over an unyielding and independently minded populace. Just as funny, but markedly more audacious in its use of framing, editing, and performance, is *Sedmikrásky* (*Daisies*, 1966) by Věra Chytilová (b. 1929), a madcap essay on anarchy in which two scantily clad women called Marie let their destructive impulses run wild.

The 1960s saw a relaxing of strict censorship laws in the Soviet Union, and the period of state-monitored Socialist Realist filmmaking under Joseph Stalin was on the wane. Directed by Andrei Tarkovsky (1932–86), *Andrey Rublyov* (*Andrei Rublev*, 1966, see p. 306) is a spiritual biopic of a fifteenth-century icon painter, who took a vow of silence because of the widespread suffering he witnessed. Its religious and political content still attracted the attention of the state censors. Elsewhere in the Communist bloc, Ukraine-based director Kira Muratova (b. 1934) was making films that engaged openly with the politics of the moment. *Korotkie vstrechi* (*Brief Encounters*, 1967, not released until 1988) offers a quietly startling depiction of life in the Soviet Union and the failures of Communism. Muratova herself plays a housing officer, Valentina Ivanovna, who is involved in a love triangle that includes her wandering geologist husband, Maksim (Vladimir Vysotsky), and her housemaid, Nadya (Nina Ruslanova). Tensions arise when country girl Nadya moves to town in pursuit of Maksim after their affair ends.

Europe became a hive of idiosyncratic cinematic invention during the decade, so it is no surprise that US actor and director Orson Welles (1915–85) was drawn there. His *Le procès* (*The Trial*, 1962, below), is an expressionistic and highly personalized take on Franz Kafka's novel about Josef K (played in the film by Anthony Perkins), a bureaucrat condemned for an unnamed crime in an unnamed country. It is shot in Zagreb, Dubrovnik, Rome, Milan, and Paris. Welles was unable to film in Prague but improvised by using Paris's abandoned, cathedral-like Gare d'Orsay as the headquarters of the nameless totalitarian state. Although *Le procès* puzzled critics at the time, Welles considered it among his most accomplished films. The movie's reputation has since grown because of its surrealistic depiction of a nightmarish situation. **DJ**

La dolce vita 1960
FEDERICO FELLINI 1920 – 93

▲ Reporter Rubini (Mastroianni) succumbs to the voluptuous starlet Sylvia (Ekberg).

▼ The poster shows the hapless Rubini surrounded by the women in his life.

Federico Fellini became an art-house favorite with *La strada* (1954) but it was *La dolce vita* that catapulted him to international fame. Almost overnight the film's title became shorthand for stylish decadence and its star, Marcello Mastroianni, in his midnight shades, an icon of cool. Half-attracted, half-repelled, Fellini's movie charts the activities of Rome's cafe-haunting, celebrity-obsessed, tirelessly partying fashionistas. Mastroianni plays Marcello Rubini, a serious writer turned gossip columnist, who despises what he has become and the people he mixes with, yet is unable to resist the glitzy lifestyle, money, and easy sex. His colleague, the photographer Paparazzo (Walter Santesso), would lend his name to a tribe of intrusive snappers.

With *La dolce vita* Fellini bade farewell to the Neo-Realism (see p. 178) of his cinematic roots. Spurred on by the excesses he was chronicling, Fellini's visual imagination went into overdrive and baroque imagery runs riot. In the opening sequence a huge statue of Christ, its arms wide, is helicoptered across Rome. Later, Anita Ekberg's brainless, bosomy starlet Sylvia cavorts, nearly naked, in the Trevi Fountain, and a hysterical media circus descends on the site of a bogus miracle engineered by three young kids on the make. Rubini is torn between the attractions of a neurotic heiress, Maddalena (Anouk Aimée), and his girlfriend, Emma (Yvonne Furneaux); while the one man he respects, the writer Steiner (Alain Cuny), shoots his children and himself in despair. *La dolce vita* records the spiritual and moral decay of a generation, but like all the best satires, it cannot tear its fascinated gaze away from what it deplores. **PK**

KEY SCENES

1 CHRIST OVER ROME
In the prologue, a huge statue of Christ is flown over the Eternal City's skyline to St. Peter's Square in the Vatican, while Marcello and Paparazzo follow in a helicopter. The men are distracted by the sight of some bikini-clad women sunbathing on a rooftop.

2 ARRIVAL OF THE STAR
Marcello is sent to Rome airport to report on the arrival of a glamorous Swedish-American movie star, Sylvia. Her appearance causes a feeding frenzy among the reporters. Marcello is enamored by the actress and invites her to tour St. Peter's.

3 THE TREVI FOUNTAIN
After a hedonistic night on the town with Marcello, Sylvia wades drunkenly into Rome's most famous fountain. Infatuated, the tuxedo-clad Marcello follows her. The depiction of the couple's sensual abandon has become one of cinema's iconic scenes.

4 NOCTURNAL PROCESSION
Marcello attends a decadent party at a countryside castle, where a crowd of international aristocrats parade around the grounds in exotic costumes. Maddalena asks Marcello to marry her, but she is toying with him, and he is then seduced by another woman.

5 UNHEARD MESSAGE
Walking by the sea after another orgiastic party, Marcello sees an angelic girl, Paola (Valeria Ciangottini), he has met before in a cafe. She tries to tell him something, but the sound of the waves drowns her out and Marcello returns to join the partygoers.

DIRECTOR PROFILE

1920–51
Federico Fellini was born in Rimini. He went to Rome in 1939 to study law but began writing stories and drawing cartoons, eventually writing gags for movies and radio shows. He cowrote the script with Roberto Rossellini (1906–77) for the Neo-Realist *Roma, città aperta* (*Rome, Open City*, 1945, see p. 180), which won an Oscar for Best Screenplay.

1952–59
He made his solo directorial debut with *Lo sceicco bianco* (*The White Sheik*, 1952) and established an international reputation with *I vitelloni* (1953). In 1957 *La strada* became the first of four of his films to win an Oscar for Best Foreign Language Film.

1960–93
La dolce vita won the Palme d'Or at the Cannes Film Festival. After *8½* (1963) Fellini's films became highly stylized and fantastical but he remained a force in world cinema.

Andrey Rublyov 1966
Andrei Rublev ANDREI TARKOVSKY 1932 – 86

▲ The peasant girl, Durochka (Irma Raush), and her savior, Rublyov (Solonitsyn).

▼ The film's poster incorporates a painting of Christ by Andrey Rublyov from 1420.

Seven psychologically momentous fragments in the lifetime of the nomadic fifteenth-century Russian monk and icon painter Andrey Rublyov (Anatoli Solonitsyn) are lightly fictionalized and abrasively rendered in this breathtaking monochrome epic of principles lost and found from the master of metaphysical inquiry, Andrei Tarkovsky. Medieval Russia is scrupulously composed as a rolling medley of dank, fog-glazed quagmires and dismal, deprived townships flooded with braying peasants, who are susceptible to violent attacks from bands of Tartar pillagers ravaging the country.

Like many contemporary biographical filmmakers, Tarkovsky approached his subject by fleshing out identity-shaping chapters in Rublyov's life, such as his presence at the sacking of the town of Vladimir after which he took a vow of silence and his observation of the forging of a church bell. Tarkovsky does not attempt to contrive a convenient narrative arc from the tumult of events, rather, drama is omnipresent and filtered through the subjective consciousness. Tarkovsky invites viewers to experience this savage world through the melancholic eyes of its subject, with the miasma of sound and imagery serving as the stimulus for Rublyov's interior torment. In so doing, the film offers penetrating reflections on the prerogative of the artist, the human value of spirituality, and the mysteries of blind faith. Made for Mosfilm with a modest budget of one million rubles, the film was cut from 205 to 186 minutes by Soviet censors, who were wary of its religious themes, political ambiguity, and violent scenes, and delayed its general release until 1971. **DJ**

👁 KEY SCENES

1 THE BALLOON
The prologue assumes the perspective of a brave peasant, Efim (Nikolai Glazkov), as he takes to the skies roped beneath a hot-air balloon in an effort to avoid a crowd of attackers. He soars through the sky and over a lake, only to crash beside another baying mob.

2 THE WITCH
Rublyov is spotted spying on nude revelers at a pagan feast; he is captured and tied to a cross. A naked maiden, Marfa (Nelly Snegina), releases him. The next day Rublyov sees Marfa being manhandled by soldiers, but he ignores her plight and looks away.

3 THE SACRIFICE
Following the bloody Tartar raid on Vladimir, Rublyov kills an attacker who is trying to rape an idiot peasant girl. He transcends his role of objective artist and engages with the course of history. To absolve himself, he gives up painting and takes a vow of silence.

4 THE FORGING OF THE BELL
Boriska (Nikolai Burlyayev) claims to hold his dead father's secret of making bell bronze. The scene portrays the minute processes of medieval bell casting right through to its unveiling, only to have the tearful but relieved boy reveal that he was lying about his claim.

5 LIFE AND ART
The film segues from crisp, high-contrast black and white into rich color for its short epilogue, where Tarkovsky slowly pans across sixteen of Rublyov's icons and frescoes, their magnificence enhanced by Vyacheslav Ovchinnikov's dense choral soundtrack.

🕐 DIRECTOR PROFILE

1932–61
Andrei Tarkovsky was born in the village of Zavrazhye in western Russia. From 1954 he studied film directing at Moscow's All-Union State Institute of Cinematography.

1962–71
He won the Golden Lion at the Venice Film Festival for his feature debut, the wartime drama *Ivanovo detstvo* (*Ivan's Childhood*, 1962). His second film, *Andrey Rublyov*, was awarded the FIPRESCI Prize at the Cannes Film Festival in 1969.

1972–86
Tarkovsky produced a cycle of films that examine the function of memory, starting with the science fiction movie *Solyaris* (*Solaris*, 1972). His most abstract work, *Zerkalo* (*The Mirror*, 1975), draws on episodes from his childhood, and *Stalker* (1979) is a philosophical puzzle about notions of utopia. His last film, *Offret* (*The Sacrifice*, 1986), offers a vision of the apocalypse.

Ostře sledované vlaky 1966
Closely Observed Trains   JIŘÍ MENZEL b. 1938

▲ The closely observed trains of the title are World War II German military transport.

▼ The film shows how adolescence continues in the face of shocking historical events.

Based on Bohumil Hrabal's novel, *Ostře sledované vlaky* was part of the Czech New Wave that flourished briefly in the mid-1960s before being crushed along with the liberal Dubček regime when Soviet tanks rolled into Prague in August 1968. The pre-credit sequence of Jiří Menzel's film shows Nazi tanks entering Czechoslovakia in 1939 as the protagonist, Miloš, poignantly narrates a potted history of his family and, by extension, his country. The story of Miloš's grandfather, killed while trying to hypnotize German troops into leaving Czechoslovakia, establishes the film's unsettling blend of moods. Much of the film is farcical but, as Menzel has said, "The true poetry of this movie lies not in the absurd situations themselves, but in their juxtaposition with obscenity and tragedy."

The film is set in wartime at a provincial railway station, where the young Miloš has his first job. At first, the war impinges on the drama as an ominous backdrop, but the station signalman, Hubička, is a partisan and eventually enlists Miloš's aid in the anti-Nazi struggle. Much of the film, however, is concerned less with politics than with Miloš's sexual frustrations — it is premature ejaculation that spurs Miloš to an unsuccessful suicide attempt.

Menzel directs with consistent wit and invention, displaying an informality of composition that adds to the film's improvisational feel. Given its lightness of touch the ending comes as a shock, but it speaks volumes about the tragic national experience of central Europe in the twentieth century — a tragedy that links the 1940s, when the film is set, with the 1960s, when it was made. **AJ**

1 THE INTERRUPTED KISS
As a train pulls into the station, Miloš is hailed by the guard Masa. She leans down to kiss him, but Hubička blows the whistle and the train carries her away. Miloš is left standing with closed eyes until Hubička slips the whistle between his parted lips.

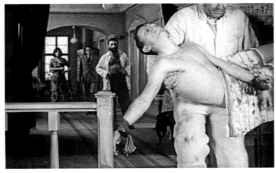

2 THE SUICIDE ATTEMPT
Depressed by his sexual failures, Miloš rents a room in a seedy hotel and cuts his wrists. A workman chiseling at the wall in the adjacent hallway accidentally breaks through the bathroom wall, finds the unconscious Miloš, and carries him out of the hotel.

3 THE STAMP SCENE
At night in the station office, Hubička snoozes in his chair; his female colleague, Zdenka, topples him to the floor. He chases her, then they stretch out together along the table. As the clock strikes twelve, he kisses her, and then rubber stamps her leg and buttock.

🕐 DIRECTOR PROFILE

1938–69
Jiří Menzel was born in Prague. He studied at the Prague Film School (FAMU) and served as assistant to Věra Chytilová (b. 1929). He directed a segment of her anthology film *Perlicky na dne* (*Pearls of the Deep*, 1966), based on stories by Czech author Bohumil Hrabal. He drew on Hrabal again with his debut feature, *Ostře sledované vlaky*, and made the highly regarded *Rozmarné léto* (*Capricious Summer*, 1968). However, *Skrivánci na niti* (*Larks on a String*, 1969, released 1990), also based on Hrabal, was banned for its criticism of Communism.

1970–89
Obliged to recant, Menzel was unable to realize another feature until 1974, and his 1970s work is considered minor. He made something of a return to form with another Hrabal adaptation, *Postřižiny* (*Cutting It Short*, 1981), and the popular comedy *Vesničko má středisková* (*My Sweet Little Village*, 1985). In 1989, with the fall of Communism in Czechoslovakia, he became head of the direction department at FAMU.

1990–present
In 1990 Menzel filmed his own stage production of Vaclav Havel's *The Beggar's Opera*. After the 1993 breakup of Czechoslovakia, he made the Russian-language film *Život a neobyčejná dobrodružstvi vojaká Ivana Čonkina* (*The Life and Extraordinary Adventures of Private Ivan Chonkin*, 1994), a satiric take on World War II, and directed another Hrabal adaptation, *Obsluhoval jsem anglického krále* (*I Served the King of England*, 2006).

THE CZECH NEW WAVE

The Czech New Wave filmmakers produced what Mira and Antonin Liehm have called "a merciless portrait of the whole fabric of society, the like of which Czechoslovak film had never produced before." The deceptively light, witty satires of Miloš Forman (below) and Ivan Passer (b. 1933) used personal drama to criticize political issues. Other directors joined Menzel in dramatizing its wartime experience. For example, *...A páty jezdec je Strach* (*The Fifth Horseman Is Fear*, 1965), by Zbyněk Brynych (1927–95), depicted the totalitarianism of the past to comment obliquely on that of the present. The Czech

New Wave came to a halt in 1968 when the USSR invaded. Forman and Passer left for the United States and other directors found they were unable to work. Many of the finest films of the 1960s were "banned forever," emerging only with the fall of Communism.

THE SPAGHETTI WESTERN

The Hollywood Western (see p. 242) had entered its twilight years by the late 1950s. The enemy of communities forging a new life on the great frontier was no longer the black-clad gunslinger or marauding "injun," but the specter of television, offering audiences cheaply produced series such as *Gunsmoke* and *Bonanza*. The genre had yet to breathe its last gasp, however. Its savior would be that most un-Western of places—Europe.

Film production in Europe had gained momentum in the decade after World War II and Hollywood was the obvious model for producers to emulate. Hammer Film Production's Michael Carreras (1927–94) made the first Spaghetti Western, *Tierra brutal* (*The Savage Guns*, 1961), an English-language coproduction with Spain. However, with the exception of the English-speaking actors who sometimes appeared in these films, the language of choice for the new genre was Italian.

A desire to reinvent the American West and a Japanese samurai film influenced the first major Spaghetti Western. Sergio Leone (1929–89) loosely based *Per un pugno di dollari* (*A Fistful of Dollars*, 1964) on *Yojinbo* (1961), directed by Kurosawa Akira (1910–98). In terms of morality, setting, and style, the film stands in stark contrast to traditional Westerns. There are no good characters: the hero, played by Clint Eastwood (star of television show *Rawhide*) is a gunslinger motivated by personal gain, with only momentary flashes of conscience. Native Americans no longer played a role, not even in *C'era una volta il West* (*Once Upon a Time in the West*, 1968, above), with its play on the archetypal Western scenario of the east's expansion westward and the

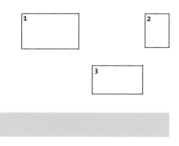

1 Henry Fonda plays (against type) the vindictive killer Frank in Sergio Leone's epic *C'era una volta il West*.

2 The poster for *Django*—the film's harsh violence contributes to the apocalyptic feel of the film.

3 Away from his work in Sergio Leone's epics, Lee Van Cleef took on another career-defining role as *Sabata*'s morally gray hero.

KEY EVENTS

1961	1962	1964	1964	1965	1966
Tierra brutal marks the arrival of a new genre—the Spaghetti Western. It is filmed in Almería, later a favorite Spanish location.	Harald Reini (1908–86) directs *Der Schatz im Silbersee* (*Treasure of Silver Lake*), adapted from author Karl May's Winnetou series.	Sergio Leone's *Per un pugno di dollari* is released. It remains the definitive Spaghetti Western.	*Cavalca e uccidi* (*Ride and Kill*) is one of the first Spaghetti Western comedies.	*Una pistola per Ringo* (*A Pistol for Ringo*) introduces the first franchise of the genre; the charismatic hero is played by Giuliano Gemma.	*Il buono, il brutto, il cattivo* (see p. 312) confirms Clint Eastwood's iconic status as the "Man with No Name."

310   1960–69

dangers this entailed. Instead, most of the action unfolded in the southern states, with Mexico and a Latin population playing a signifiant role.

Leone's world was a violent one, driven by Ennio Morricone's memorable scores. The director's next film, *Per qualche dollaro in più* (*For a Few Dollars More*, 1965), teamed Lee Van Cleef with Eastwood, as a young upstart who gains some degree of moral guidance from an old-timer with revenge on his mind. Leone was once again aided by Morricone's score, with a central theme that highlighted the composer's gift for subtlety and added emotional heft to the film's climactic shootout. *Il buono, il brutto, il cattivo* (*The Good, the Bad and the Ugly*, 1966, see p. 312) cemented Leone's reputation as a master of the genre and Morricone as every Spaghetti director's composer of choice.

Other directors' careers would be defined by their work on Spaghetti Westerns. Sergio Corbucci (1926–90) will be remembered for the brutal—even by the genre's standards—*Django* (1966, right). In contrast to Leone's arid backdrops, Franco Nero's eponymous antihero stalked his prey through a muddied, rain-drenched landscape, dragging a coffin containing his weapon of choice, a machine gun. Gianfranco Parolini (b. 1930) found success with the *Sabata* trilogy (1969–71, below), which featured mainstays of Western cinema Lee Van Cleef and Yul Brynner (in the title role). The films, all blackmail and rifle play, are accompanied by Marcello Giombini's stirring scores.

Although *Lo chiamavano Trinità* (*They Call Me Trinity*, 1970) by Enzo Barboni (1922–2002) remains a fine film, the comedy betrayed the Spaghetti Western as having passed its prime and being ripe for parody. The genre came to an end with *Keoma* (1976) but the spirit and style of the Spaghetti Western has since held sway over two generations of filmmakers, from Clint Eastwood (b. 1930) and Sam Raimi (b. 1959) to Quentin Tarantino (b. 1963) and Robert Rodriguez (b. 1968). **IHS**

DJANGO
FRANCO NERO | SERGIO CORBUCCI
LOREDANA NUSCIAK | EASTMANCOLOR · WIDESCREEN

1967	1968	1968	1970	1971	1973
Giulio Petroni (1917–2010) remakes *Per qualche dollaro in più* as *Da uomo a uomo* (*Death Rides a Horse*), with Lee Van Cleef reprising his role.	*C'era una volta il West* legitimizes the genre among critics and has since been regarded by many as Sergio Leone's best film.	Sergio Corbucci's *Il grande silenzio* (*The Great Silence*) is released. It stars Klaus Kinski as a bounty hunter.	The genre is parodied by Enzo Barboni's entertaining *Lo chiamavano Trinità*.	Sergio Leone's last Spaghetti Western, *Giù la testa* (*A Fistful of Dynamite*), is more political and less impressive than his earlier films.	*Il mio nome è Nessuno* (*My Name Is Nobody*), the last quality film of the genre, is released. It is directed by Tonino Valerii (b. 1934) from Sergio Leone's idea.

Il buono, il brutto, il cattivo 1966
The Good, the Bad and the Ugly   SERGIO LEONE 1929 – 89

▲ Clint Eastwood in classic pose, complete with cigar, poncho, and slit-eyed stare.

▼ Star Van Cleef also appeared in *Per qualche dollaro in più* as a different character.

Although critically overshadowed two years later by *C'era una volta il West*'s (*Once Upon a Time in the West*) celebrated deconstruction of the Western myth, *Il buono, il brutto, il cattivo* remains arguably Sergio Leone's greatest film. The third of the *Dollars* trilogy of Westerns that defied the conventions of the genre, it deployed the amorality of the earlier films against the historical backdrop of the American Civil War.

Clint Eastwood returned, in his last role for Leone, to play another antihero, Blondie. He is pitted against Lee Van Cleef's gun for hire and Eli Wallach's Mexican bandit, Tuco. The latter provides the emotional journey in the film. He represents the downtrodden and the abused, from the petty thieves to the noncommissioned soldiers of the Civil War; pawns in a game, the strategies of which are overseen by men willing to place at risk the lives of others, but never their own. Even Blondie acknowledges this disparity: he destroys a strategically vital bridge to ensure there will be no more casualties in the fighting over it, and offers his coat to a young, dying soldier. There is no nobility in death, either in war or in any of the many shootouts that punctuate the film.

Leone cut much of *Il buono, il brutto, il cattivo* to Ennio Morricone's score, which remains one of the composer's best. From the chart-topping theme song and the elegiac "Story of a Soldier" to "The Ecstasy of Gold," and "The Trio"—a breathtaking climax accompanying a sequence of long shots, close-ups, and swirling camera movement—Morricone's music and Sergio Leone's stark and brutal style ensured that the Western would never be the same. **IHS**

👁 KEY SCENES

1 HUNTING TUCO
After a long prologue that feels like a warm-up for the opening of the film, an unkempt Tuco jumps through a window after despatching three gunfighters. His entrance to the film is in marked contrast to those of the other main characters.

2 BROTHERS REUNITED
Tuco awaits the return of his brother at the monastery where Blondie is convalescing. Blondie witnesses their reunion, but soon they come to blows because Tuco is resentful that his brother left him with no choice but to pursue a criminal career.

3 BLOWING UP THE BRIDGE
Acknowledged as Leone's homage to *The General* (1926, see p. 66), the destruction of the bridge is one of the film's emotional high points. Blondie and Tuco destroy the bridge in order to get to the other side of the river, and to fulfill the wish of a dying officer.

4 THE FINAL SHOOTOUT
The Sad Hill cemetery was built in Carazo near Salas de los Infantes, in northern Spain. Intercutting extreme close-ups with long shots, the climax, accompanied by Ennio Morricone's thrilling score, is among the most suspenseful sequences the director created.

🕐 DIRECTOR PROFILE

1929–63
Sergio Leone was born in Rome. He began as assistant director and second unit director on a range of Italian productions, from uncredited work on *Ladri di biciclette* (*The Bicycle Thief*, 1948, see p. 182) and *Quo vadis* (1951) to *Ben-Hur* and *Gli ultimi giorni di Pompei* (*The Last Days of Pompeii*) in 1959. He completed the latter, which he also wrote, when director Mario Bonnard (1889–1965) fell ill. His directorial debut was *Il Colosso di Rodi* (*The Colossus of Rhodes*, 1961).

1964–67
Per un pugno di dollari (*A Fistful of Dollars*, 1964) cemented Leone's reputation, defined Clint Eastwood's screen persona, and redefined the Western. Its bleak, nihilistic worldview was expanded in the sequel *Per qualche dollaro in più* (*For a Few Dollars More*, 1965) and to even greater critical and financial success in *Il buono, il brutto, il cattivo*.

1968–70
C'era una volta il West (*Once Upon a Time in the West*, 1968) remains the definitive anti-Western, a critique of the United States's expanding frontier and the power of market forces. Leone also contemplated adapting Miguel Cervantes's *Don Quixote*. This retelling would have featured Clint Eastwood as the hero and Eli Wallach as his sidekick, Sancho Panza.

1971–89
Leone's *Giù la testa* (*A Fistful of Dynamite*, 1971) is a flawed, politically strident Mexican Western starring Rod Steiger and James Coburn. He was producer and codirector on *Il mio nome è Nessuno* (*My Name Is Nobody*, 1973) and *Un genio, due compari, un pollo* (*A Genius, Two Partners, and a Dupe*, 1975). Leone's last film was the epic US gangster drama, *Once Upon a Time in America* (1984), starring Robert De Niro, James Woods, and Jennifer Connelly in her debut role. The film's running time is more than three hours and the director battled the studio over the final cut. At the time of his death from a heart attack in 1989, Leone was planning a film about the siege of Leningrad, starring De Niro.

5 | 1970 TO 1989

WEST EUROPEAN CINEMA

1 A meal to die for? Jean Yanne serves Stéphane Audran in Claude Chabrol's thriller *Le boucher*.

2 An appropriately surreal poster image for Luis Buñuel's Oscar-winning *Le charme discret de la bourgeoisie*.

3 Dirk Bogarde as the ailing composer, Von Aschenbach, who falls for an ethereal youth in Luchino Visconti's *Morte a Venezia*.

I n the 1970s the pantheon of established masters who had set the tone of West European filmmaking in the postwar years began to find themselves edged aside by a new generation of up-and-coming filmmakers with ideas and attitudes of their own. In German cinema (see p. 326), this happened relatively smoothly because at the start of the decade there were few senior figures of any stature. Elsewhere the transition was less orderly, because some of the old masters—such as Luis Buñuel (1900–83), Robert Bresson (1901–99), and Ingmar Bergman (1918–2007)—were still going strong. All three had a good decade. Bergman's work included *Viskningar och rop* (*Cries and Whispers*, 1972, see p. 324), perhaps the most psychologically harrowing of all his films, and *Trollflöjten* (*The Magic Flute*, 1975), the piece regarded by many as the best example of opera on film. Bresson widened his range with the Dostoevsky adaptation *Quatre nuits d'un rêveur* (*Four Nights of a Dreamer*, 1971) and the pitiless moral fable *Le diable probablement* (*The Devil, Probably*, 1977). Buñuel was as teasing and provocative as ever with his final films, including *Le charme discret de la bourgeoisie* (*The Discreet Charm of the Bourgeoisie*, 1972, opposite above) and *Cet obscur objet du désir* (*That Obscure Object of Desire*, 1977).

Others, however, were flagging. *Professione: reporter* (*The Passenger*, 1975) would prove to be the last major film by Michelangelo Antonioni (1912–2007). The same might be said for Mihalis Kakogiannis (b. 1922), whose *Iphigenia* (1976)

KEY EVENTS

1970	1972	1972	1973	1973	1974
Luis Buñuel's *Tristana* is released, starring Catherine Deneuve and Franco Nero.	Sex, butter, and Brando: Bertolucci's *Ultimo tango a Parigi* provokes more international headlines than any previous non-English-language movie.	Concern over corruption in Italy fuels Francesco Rosi's Cannes prizewinner *Il caso Mattei*, starring the great Gian Maria Volonté.	A major new talent is revealed when Spain's Victor Erice makes his first feature, *El espíritu de la colmena*.	In *Amarcord* Federico Fellini briefly recaptures some of his old magic.	With his prize-winning debut *L'horloger de Saint-Paul*, based on a Georges Simenon novel, Bertrand Tavernier becomes a director to watch.

rounded off his "Ancient Greek" trilogy. *Parade* (1974), the final work by Jacques Tati (1907–82), made for television, disappointed, even if *Trafic* (1971) showed moments of his erstwhile genius and the last film by Jean-Pierre Melville (1917–73), the crime drama *Un flic* (1972), felt weary. By the end of the decade several major figures had departed, leaving their final films. Italian cinema in particular lost some of its icons: Roberto Rossellini (1906–77), Vittorio De Sica (1901–74), Pier Paolo Pasolini (1922–75), and Luchino Visconti (1906–76), the latter near peak form with *Morte a Venezia* (*Death in Venice*, 1971, below right) and *Gruppo di famiglia in un interno* (*Conversation Piece*, 1974).

In France the former lions of the Nouvelle Vague (see p. 248) continued to develop their distinctive styles. Claude Chabrol (1930–2010) began a prolific decade with one of his best films, the Hitchcockian *Le boucher* (*The Butcher*, 1970, opposite), and François Truffaut (1932–84) had a box-office hit with the movie about moviemaking *La nuit américaine* (*Day for Night*, 1973). However, for consistent quality they were outshone by their *Cahiers du cinéma* associate Eric Rohmer (1920–2010), who rounded off his "Six Moral Tales" with *Le genou de Claire* (*Claire's Knee*, 1970, see p. 320) and *L'amour l'après-midi* (*Chloe in the Afternoon*, 1972). Before embarking on his series of "Comédies et Proverbes" in the eighties, Chabrol diverged into two literary adaptations, *Die Marquise von O...* (1976) and *Perceval le Gallois* (1978). The only truly commercial work in this period by Jean-Luc Godard (b. 1930) was *Tout va bien* (*Everything's All Right*, 1972)—featuring Yves Montand and Jane Fonda—while Jacques Rivette (b. 1928) was at his most playfully experimental in *Celine et Julie vont en bateau* (*Celine and Julie Go Boating*, 1974).

The sad decline of Jacques Demy (1931–90) continued with his would-be Cocteau-esque fairy tale *Peau d'ane* (*Once Upon a Time*, 1970). His wife Agnès Varda (b. 1928) produced little in the decade but *L'une chante, l'autre pas* (*One Sings, the Other Doesn't*, 1977) offered a warmly romantic view of the upheavals of feminism. In *Stavisky* (1974), Alain Resnais (b. 1922) created a chillingly elegant account of a French political scandal in the 1930s, while *Providence* (1977), his first English-language film, took a fantasy-haunted journey through the mind of a dying writer.

Other filmmakers tackled issues of social, political, and historical concern. *O thiasos* (*The Traveling Players*, 1975) made the name of Theo Angelopoulos (b. 1935), who was internationally known for complex films rooted in Greek history. Sympathy for the poor linked to social concerns permeates such Italian films as *L'albero degli zoccoli* (*The Tree of Wooden Clogs*, 1978) by Ermanno Olmi (b. 1931) and *Padre padrone* (*My Father, My Master*, 1977) by the Taviani brothers, Paolo (b. 1931) and Vittorio (b. 1929), while *Il caso Mattei* (*The Mattei Affair*, 1972), by Francesco Rosi (b. 1922), scathingly investigated corruption in politics. One director who built a career on films dealing with cases of state-sponsored injustice was the Greek-born Costa-Gavras (b. 1933), who took French

SERGE SILBERMAN presenta

le charme discret de la bourgeoisie

avec par ordre d'entrée en scène
FERNANDO REY
PAUL FRANKEUR
DELPHINE SEYRIG
BULLE OGIER
STÉPHANE AUDRAN
JEAN-PIERRE CASSEL
JULIEN BERTHEAU
MILENA VUKOTIC
MARIA GABRIELLA LA MAIONE
CLAUDE PIÉPLU
MUNI
FRANÇOIS MAISTRE
PIERRE MAGUELON
MAXENCE MAILFORT

scénario de
LUIS BUÑUEL
en collaboration avec
JEAN-CLAUDE CARRIÈRE

UN FILM DE LUIS BUÑUEL

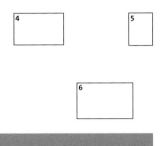

4 Public events, including dancing, a bonfire, a parade, and a car race, recur in Federico Fellini's bittersweet *Amarcord*, based on his memories of prewar Rimini.

5 The original Spanish poster for *El espíritu de la colmena*, the story of how a young girl's life is dramatically altered when she watches the classic horror film *Frankenstein* (1931, see p. 92).

6 Pier Paolo Pasolini's *Salò o le 120 giornate di Sodoma* is a violent, sexually graphic examination of the moral depths inherent in human nature, set against a background of Fascism.

nationality. In the 1970s he directed *L'aveu* (*The Confession*, 1970), criticizing the Communists in Prague in 1951, *Etat de siège* (*State of Siege*, 1972), targeting CIA involvement in Uruguay, and *Section spéciale* (1975), dealing with France's wartime Vichy government.

Eclectic as ever, Louis Malle (1932–95) moved easily from political and historical themes to intimate family dramas. In *Lacombe Lucien* (1974), he confronted the edgy subject of homegrown French Fascism during the occupation, while with *Le souffle au coeur* (*Dearest Love* or *Murmur of the Heart*, 1971) he shocked the French establishment with his sympathetic treatment of mother-son incest. On a similar note, *Amarcord* (*I Remember*, 1973, above), a stylized evocation by Federico Fellini (1920–93) of his Fascist-era home town, was masterful.

For some filmmakers the personal was political. Marco Ferreri (1928–97) alarmed the censors with his allegories of capitalist greed—the sex and gluttony splurge of *La grande bouffe* (*Blow-Out*, 1973) and the even more overwrought *L'ultima donna* (*The Last Woman*, 1976). Yet the scandal these films aroused was nothing compared with the furor over *Ultimo tango a Parigi* (*Last Tango in Paris*, 1972), by Bernardo Bertolucci (b. 1940). Branded as obscene by the Italian courts, it provided a field day for the press thanks to the presence of Marlon Brando. Bertolucci's career went international, although admirers of the far subtler *Il conformista* (*The Conformist*, 1970, see p. 322) and *Strategia del ragno* (*The Spider's Strategem*, 1970) may have regrets about that. The last film by Pier Paolo Pasolini—*Salò o le 120 giornate di Sodoma* (*Salò, or the 120 Days of Sodom*, 1975, opposite below), which relocated the excesses of De Sade to Mussolini's short-lived north Italian republic of 1944—almost rivaled Bertolucci's film in notoriety. Another director with a talent for unsettling audiences was Jean Eustache (1938–81), with his dispassionate studies of sexuality, such as *La maman et la putain* (*The Mother and the Whore*, 1973) and *Une sale histoire* (*A Dirty Story*, 1977).

Many of these films were responding, either openly or by implication, to the rise of feminism. More considered responses emerged in the work of a number of West European female directors in the 1970s. Norway's Anja Breien (b. 1940) scored a success with the good-humored feminism of *Hustruer* (*Wives*, 1975). The melodrama of Italian films such as *Il portiere di notte* (*The Night Porter*, 1974) by Liliana Cavani (b. 1933) and *Travolti da un insolito destino nell'azzurro mare d'agosto* (*Swept Away*, 1974) by Lina Wertmüller (b. 1926) contrasted with the minimalism of French playwright Marguerite Duras

(1914–96) in such films as *India Song* (1975). Minimalism also informed *Jeanne Dielman 23 Quai du Commerce, 1080 Bruxelles* (1975), a study of bourgeois prostitution by Chantal Akerman (b. 1950). Several actresses turned to directing, including Gunnel Lindblom (b. 1931) with her study of a dysfunctional Swedish family in the ironically titled *Summer Paradise* (1976).

Elsewhere in Spain Carlos Saura (b. 1932), a feature director since 1960, continued his oblique comments on his country's Fascist regime, the cruel fable of *Cria cuervos* (*Raise Ravens*, 1976) being his most memorable of the decade. The rural-set drama *Furtivos* (*Poachers*, 1975), directed by José Luis Borau (b. 1929) and released only weeks before the death of Franco, offered an allegory of life under the aging dictator. The first full-length feature by Victor Erice (b. 1940), *El espíritu de la colmena* (*The Spirit of the Beehive*, 1973, right), created much debate. Featuring the remarkable child actress Ana Torrent but susceptible to many levels of interpretation beyond being a childhood study, this debut established Erice as a director equaled only by Terrence Malick (b. 1943) in achieving such high esteem for such a limited oeuvre.

Not all the young European directors of the 1970s were reacting against the work of their elders; some wanted to extend and develop a tradition. Two French filmmakers who had learned their craft working with the Nouvelle Vague made their feature debuts. Claude Miller (b. 1942) directed *La meilleure façon de marcher* (*The Best Way to Walk*, 1976), a drama about troubled adolescents at a holiday camp that showed the influence of Truffaut, followed by the Chabrolian psychological thriller *Dites-lui que je l'aime* (*This Sweet Sickness*, 1977). Meanwhile, Bertrand Tavernier (b. 1941) launched a distinguished career with a subtle adaptation of Georges Simenon's *L'horloger de Saint-Paul* (*The Watchmaker of St. Paul*, 1974), going on to show a versatility reminiscent of Malle in two very different period dramas, *Que la fête commence...* (*Let Joy Reign Supreme*, 1975) and *Le juge et l'assassin* (*The Judge and the Assassin*, 1976).

Some filmmakers, however, were simply too unique to be pigeonholed into any overall tendency. Maurice Pialat (1925–2003), who would give Isabelle Huppert and Gérard Depardieu fine roles in *Loulou* (1980), established himself as a maker of tough, abrasive films such as the queasily autobiographical *Nous ne vieillirons pas ensemble* (*Break-Up*, 1972). His films were uncomfortable to watch and, reputedly, equally uncomfortable to make, but they matched the spirit of a troubled decade. **MS**

Una producción Elías Querejeta

EL ESPIRITU DE LA COLMENA

interpretada por Fernando Fernán Gómez, Teresa Gimpera y las niñas Isabel Tellería y Ana Torrent. Fotografía de Luis Cuadrado. Música compuesta por Luis de Pablo. Director: Victor Erice.

Le genou de Claire 1970

Claire's Knee   ERIC ROHMER 1920 – 2010

▲ Aurora (Aurora Cornu) inspects the finger Claire hurt playing volleyball. Aurora's talks with Jérôme give a wry overview of events.

▼ The temptation of Jérôme: a voyeur's-eye view for the film's poster.

The six films that make up Eric Rohmer's cycle of "Moral Tales" (released between 1963 and 1972) are all concerned with the ways that desire can unbalance the moral equilibrium. Ruthlessly literate, deviously erotic, and modest in scale, they consist of subtle variations on an almost identical conceit, which Rohmer has admitted was inspired by *Sunrise* (1927, see p. 70) by F. W. Murnau (1888–1931): boy has girl, boy meets another girl, boy considers straying with second girl, boy ends up returning to the original girl but with reservations. This setup allowed Rohmer to investigate the intricacies of milieu—time, place, environment—and the ways in which it subverts, invites, and impedes romance.

Le genou de Claire—the fifth of the Moral Tales—is a wry, discursive work that, like a previous film, *La collectioneuse* (*The Collector*, 1967), takes place in the course of a single holiday. Jérôme (Jean-Claude Brialy), a frisky diplomat who is soon to be married, has returned to Lake Annecy to sell a property, but is confronted with sexual temptation in the form of two coquettish teenage half sisters, Laura (Béatrice Romand) and Claire (Laurence de Monaghan). In the case of Claire, he develops a near fetishistic fixation with her knee.

Far from focusing exclusively on Jérôme's anxieties and amusingly haughty methods of self-justification, Rohmer constructs a complex and ambiguous story comparing the flowery expressiveness of language to the reality of inner feeling. When Jérôme does manage to lay his hand on Claire's knee, the release of coiled sexual tension is immense, although audiences can choose whether to buy in to his sweetly perverse misadventure. **DJ**

👁 KEY SCENES

1 LAKE ANNECY
Rohmer's trusted cinematographer Néstor Almendros captures the idyll of Annecy with admirable restraint, without overemphasizing its prettiness. Jérôme's trip by motorboat stresses how the secluded riverside properties are ripe for clandestine romance.

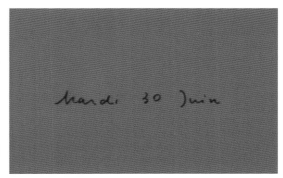

2 TIME
Rohmer regularly inserts title cards showing the day and the date. On a dramatic level, this gives the film its basic structure and puts a time limit on Jérôme's exploits, forcing him to live out his fantasies before the opportunity fades away.

3 THE KISS
Flirting with the teenage Laura, Jérôme tries to steal a kiss while they are trekking in the mountains. She initially plays along, and then pulls away. "Can't we play anymore?" asks Jérôme. "No," she replies, "I'd like love to be for real."

4 A TOUCH
Jérôme sees Claire's boyfriend being intimate with another girl. As he tells her about her boyfriend's duplicity, he places his hand on Claire's knee. The audience later learns that he judged the boyfriend by his own dubious morals: the boy was actually consoling the girl.

🕐 DIRECTOR PROFILE

1920–49
Born in Tulle, France, as Maurice Henri Joseph Schérer, he later changed his name (which combines those of director Erich von Stroheim and author Sax Rohmer). He moved to Paris as a teenager and started work as a teacher of literature, news reporter, and novelist. Rohmer published his only novel, *Elizabeth*, in 1946, under the pseudonym Gilbert Cordier.

1950–62
Rohmer began to work as a film critic and wrote for revolutionary journal *Cahiers du cinéma* under editor André Bazin. As an editor of the magazine himself between 1956 and 1963, he helped devise the auteur theory, and had made five short films by 1958, the first being *Journal d'un scélérat* in 1950. He made his debut feature film, *Le signe du lion* (*The Sign of Leo*), in 1959, becoming one of the founding fathers of the Nouvelle Vague (see p. 248).

(see p. 248)

1963–73
While working in television, Rohmer made his first series of films, the male-focused "Six Moral Tales"—starting with *La boulangère de Monceau* (*The Bakery Girl of Monceau*, 1963) and ending with *L'amour l'après-midi* (*Chloe in the Afternoon*, 1972). It was with *Ma nuit chez Maud* (*My Night at Maud's*, 1969), which secured two Academy Award nominations, that his reputation was established.

1974–87
Rohmer made his second series of films, the "Comédies et Proverbes" (1981–87), which focused more closely on female characters. Highlights include *Pauline à la plage* (*Pauline at the Beach*, 1983) and *Le rayon vert* (*The Green Ray*, 1986).

1988–2010
In his last two decades he made a film quartet based on the four seasons, a historical drama with green-screen technology—*L'anglaise et le duc* (*The Lady and the Duke*, 2001)—a political thriller, *Triple Agent* (2004), and an eccentric pastoral—*Les amours d'Astrée et de Céladon* (*The Romance of Astrea and Celadon*, 2007). Rohmer died in Paris, at eighty-nine.

Il conformista 1970

The Conformist BERNARDO BERTOLUCCI b. 1940

▲ Marcello Clerici—a man wracked with contradictions—goes to visit his fiancée.

▼ Violence, sexuality, and Marcello's innate conservativism drive the film's narrative.

Bernardo Bertolucci's *Il conformista* is part intellectual thriller, part neo-noir a free adaptation of Alberto Moravia's 1930s-set novel about a well-to-do but deeply self-divided Italian bureaucrat, Marcello Clerici, who volunteers to be an assassin for the Fascists. It was the director's most visually dazzling, precisely layered, and intellectually demanding contribution to the formally experimental, overtly political cinema of the period.

The film was an early successful exercise in international coproduction for Bertolucci, set in Paris and Rome, with a French and Italian cast. Gaston Moschin brought an element of dangerous buffoonery to his portrayal of blackshirt Manganiello, Clerici's minder, and Dominique Sanda exuded an air of seductive eroticism and emotional vulnerability in her role as Anna, wife of Clerici's ex-professor Quadri, the intended target. Jean-Louis Trintignant, with his suavity, unostentatious intelligence and air of hidden emotions, made a perfect Clerici, embodying the delusions of a man alienated from normal life by his country's divided and violent history, his own homicidal and sexual guilt and the dubious privileges of his wealthy background and disturbed parents.

Abandoning the chronological order of Moravia's novel, Bertolucci used an elaborate flashback structure to add psychological depth, dreamlike interpretation, and fractured symbolism to his depiction of Fascism. He added a wealth of literary and cinematic reference, quotation, and allusion to widen his enquiry into an examination of his country's Fascist past, its contemporary legacy, and the complex motivations underlying political engagement. **WH**

👁 KEY SCENES

1 SHADOW OF A GUNMAN
Clerici waits outside Paris's Hotel D'Orsay for his Fascist co-conspirator Manganiello. His intended victim, exiled anti-Fascist agitator Quadri (Enzo Tarascio), has escaped. In pursuit, Clerici recalls in flashback the key moments of his troubled past.

2 FATHER FIGURE
Having tracked down Quadri in Paris, Clerici repeats to his ex-tutor Plato's myth of the cavern, an allegory of reality versus illusion. Quadri, impressed, tells Clerici that he does not talk like a convinced Fascist and resolves to regain the faith he once held in his ex-student.

3 "ET TU, BRUTE?"
Clerici and Manganiello catch up with Quadri in a remote, wintry forest. Quadri is stabbed by multiple assailants, recalling the assassination of Shakespeare's Julius Caesar. Anna runs to Clerici's car for help, but he offers none and she, too, is murdered.

🕐 DIRECTOR PROFILE

1940–63
Bernardo Bertolucci was born in Parma. He was introduced by his critic father to director and fellow Marxist Pier Paolo Pasolini, who hired him to work on *Accatone* (1961) and wrote the screenplay for Bertolucci's debut *La commare secca* (1962).

1964–70
He pursued his leftist, radical concerns and Freudian obsessions with the Oscar-nominated *Prima della rivoluzione* (1964), *Partner* (1968), *Strategia del ragno* (*The Spider's Stratagem*; 1970), and *Il conformista*, all of which increased his international critical standing.

1971–77
Ultimo tango a Parigi (*Last Tango in Paris*, 1972) brought him both commercial and critical success—and worldwide notoriety for his candid approach to sex. *Novecento* (1900, 1976), his move into bigger-budget, epic cinema, was a commercial disappointment.

1978–93
Having worked with British screenwriter Clare Peploe on *La luna* (1979), Bertolucci collaborated with her brother Mark and producer Jeremy Thomas on the Oscar-winning *The Last Emperor* (1987) and the two other parts of his "Eastern" trilogy, *The Sheltering Sky* (1990) and *Little Buddha* (1993).

1994–present
He turned to less commercially risky but still individual projects, including his Tuscan-set romance *Stealing Beauty* (1996) and his tribute to 1968, *The Dreamers* (2003).

BLUE MOVIE

With *Il conformista* Bertolucci began a long association with a number of collaborators, including director of photography Vittorio Storaro (below), with whom he was to make eight films. His discussions with Storaro focused on light, color, and composition. Bertolucci has said that he chooses the lens, the camera movements, and the relationship between the camera and the characters; "everything else is the cinematographer's creation." The film gave Storaro "the chance to discover the vibration, the emotion of the color blue." The cold textures and associations of that color pervade the

movie. It helps to contrast the red warmth of the Paris-shot scenes with the forbidding monumentality of the Fascist-built "sets" located in the Italian town of Sabaudia, and evoke visual echoes of the *stile fascista* in 1930s Italy.

Viskningar och rop 1972
Cries and Whispers   INGMAR BERGMAN 1918 – 2007

▲ Back home to look after her dying sister, Maria (Liv Ullmann) thinks about the past.

▼ The film poster illustrates the sisters—all in white—in happier times.

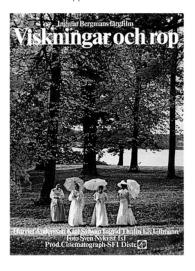

Ingmar Bergman's *Viskningar och rop* picks precisely through the bones of his favorite themes: the futility of love, the near impossibility of true communication, the inaccessibility of faith. It recalls Russian writer Anton Chekhov's tale of three sisters and the films of Japanese director Ozu Yasujiro (1903–63) in its stillness and familial disconnection. Yet *Viskningar och rop* marks a period of reinvention and reinvigoration in Bergman's career—the fluid flashbacks, sensual close-ups, and sumptuous, suffocating color fashioning a psychodrama that is both rich and rigorous.

The director said he could imagine all of his films in black and white except for this one, and here the seductive style informs the content. Regular cinematographer Sven Nykvist experimented for three weeks to capture the many shades of red—the color of blood, passion, and (for Bergman) the soul—of the furnishings. The ghostly, enigmatic women drift through proceedings in gowns and nightdresses of startling white.

Karin (Ingrid Thulin) and Maria (Liv Ullmann) tend to their dying younger sister Agnes (Harriet Andersson) but it is the maid, Anna (Kari Sylwan), who brings her comfort. *Viskningar och rop* portrays a world in the grip of pain—physical, emotional, spiritual. Dream sequences and flashbacks establish how past and present overlap, while offering explanation for the emotional paralysis on display. Yet Bergman rarely envisaged a world without hope and the film ends on a grace note. Anna reads a joyful passage from Agnes's diary and the action flashes back to capture the sisters' blissful stroll in a blazing autumnal park. **JG**

KEY SCENES

1 SETTING THE SCENE
The film opens with a series of slow pans introducing a gallery of ticking, chiming clocks. Time is one of the film's themes. Maria sleeps in a red room while Agnes is sprawled on her bed, grimacing in pain. The first human utterance is an agonized gasp.

3 BACK FROM THE DEAD
Agnes dies but is resurrected in a dream sequence. Maria runs screaming from the room when Agnes kisses her. An uncharacteristic zoom close-up frames the face of Agnes as tears seep from her eyes. "I'm dead, you see. But I can't go to sleep," she says.

2 KARIN'S DREAM
Traumatized by her loveless marriage, Karin has a dream. Dressed for bed, she inserts a shard of glass between her legs, enters her husband's room and pulls up her soaked nightdress. She completes the horror by smearing her mouth with blood.

4 AN ODE TO JOY
Anna reads an extract from Agnes's journal that recalls her sisters' arrival, before she was incapacitated by illness: "We even went for a short walk. It was such an event . . . . All my pain was gone. The people I'm most fond of were with me . . . . I thought: This really is happiness."

WORKING WITH SVEN NYKVIST

Swedish cinematographer Sven Nykvist (far right) shared camera credits with Hilding Bladh on Ingmar Bergman's *Gycklarnas afton* (*Sawdust and Tinsel*) in 1953 before going on to become the director's favored director of photography. The pair collaborated on more than twenty films, including *Såsom i en spegel* (*Through a Glass Darkly*, 1961), *Persona* (1966), *Scener ur ett äktenskap* (*Scenes from a Marriage*, 1973), and *Fanny och Alexander* (*Fanny and Alexander*, 1982). Nykvist revolutionized the close-up and eschewed the hard-edged compositions of Bergman's early work in favor of simple, natural lighting. He won Academy Awards for his lush color photography on *Viskningar och rop* and *Fanny och Alexander*.

NEW GERMAN CINEMA

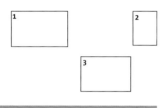

The cinema of the German Federal Republic of the 1970s saw the most exciting revival in German filmmaking since the 1920s. It had its origins in 1962, when the so-called Young German Cinema movement emerged, following the signing of the Oberhausen Manifesto that year by such directors as Edgar Reitz (b. 1932) and Alexander Kluge (b. 1932). By the late 1970s, a group of German directors—among them Hans-Jürgen Syberberg (b. 1935), Volker Schlöndorff (b. 1939), Werner Herzog (b. 1942), Rainer Werner Fassbinder (1945–82), and Wim Wenders (b. 1945)—had garnered acceptance and international celebrity for themselves and established the New German Cinema (a term first used at the New York Film Festival in 1967) as a major dynamic and influential force on the world stage.

Film critics generally ascribe the New German Cinema with four defining characteristics. Many of its leading practitioners were young and new to filmmaking during the 1970s. It conformed to the post-French Nouvelle Vague movement in its emphasis on the director's overall control of his or her movie and in its adoption of new, more mobile technologies and smaller crews. It was influenced, positively and negatively, by US cinema, both classic and new. Finally, the radical cinema it represented was a reaction against the old, discredited, Nazi-tainted "commercial" works of the previous generation of filmmakers (so-called "Papa's cinema")—typically nostalgic "Heimat" films, stale Westerns, Edgar Wallace–style crime thrillers, escapist romances, comedies, and soft pornography.

1 Going for gold: Lope de Aguirre (Klaus Kinksi) seeks the lost city of El Dorado in Werner Herzog's *Aguirre, der Zorn Gottes*.

2 The specter of terrorism—and the way its coverage in the media can generate public alarm—pervades *Die verlorene Ehre der Katharina Blum*.

3 The first part of a road-movie trilogy, Wim Wenders's *Alice in den Städten* sees journalist Phil Winter (Rüdiger Vogler) unwittingly drawn into helping young Alice (Yella Rottländer) to trace her grandmother.

KEY EVENTS

1969	1970	1971	1972	1973	1974
Volker Schlöndorff's *Michael Kohlhaas—Der Rebell* is entered at Cannes. Rainer Werner Fassbinder's debut *Liebe ist kälter als der Tod* premieres.	The Berlin Film Festival collapses over *O.K.*, a Michael Verhoeven (b. 1938) film offering a controversial depiction of US atrocities in the Vietnam War.	Werner Herzog's *Fata Morgana* and *Land des Schweigens und der Dunkelheit* are released. The Filmverlag der Autoren is founded.	The Filmverlag's first releases include Wim Wenders's *Die Angst des Tormanns beim Elfmeter* (*The Goalkeeper's Fear of the Penalty*).	Thomas Mauch wins the Cinematography Award at the German Film Awards for *Aguirre, der Zorn Gottes*.	Wim Wenders releases *Alice in den Städten*. The Film and Television Agreement ushers in a new era of TV-produced German movies.

This rebellious status of the 1970s New German Cinema has been much debated by critics, who cite the apolitical and metaphysical nature of Herzog's films such as *Aguirre, der Zorn Gottes* (*Aguirre, Wrath of God*, 1972, opposite); the criticism of an invasive media in *Die verlorene Ehre der Katharina Blum* (*The Lost Honor of Katharina Blum*, 1975, right); or the avoidance of direct condemnation of Nazi collaboration in such films as *Deutschland bleiche Mutter* (*Germany, Pale Mother*, 1980). Early 1970s West German films still betrayed the influence of the previous decade, when filmmakers had been forced to adapt to the parlous, intellectually moribund condition of the German film industry. This industry was still recovering from World War II, and from a reconstruction made under the influence, and in the commercial interests, of the US-dominated Allied powers. It was also weakened by an historic low (reached in 1963) in domestic cinema attendances, and by the early popularity of television in West Germany.

At least until the Film and Television Agreement (1974), many young filmmakers worked with student productions or short films; movies were self-produced or federal- or state-subsidized, low-budget, independent, mostly black and white, and often formally experimental. Works included Wim Wenders's first collaboration with cinematographer Robby Müller in their 16mm Munich Filmschool graduation film *Summer in the City* (1970), a seductive road movie dominated by rock and pop music (The Kinks, The Lovin' Spoonful). With its existential meanderings, sense of dislocation, US cineaste tastes, and deeply felt evocations of place and time, it prefigured the thematic obsessions of his subsequent work, such as *Alice in den Städten* (*Alice in the Cities*, 1974, below).

1975	1976	1977	1978	1979	1980
Fassbinder's *Faustrecht der Freiheit* (*Fox and His Friends*) and *Die verlorene Ehre der Katharina Blum* by Margarethe von Trotta are released.	Wim Wenders's *Im Lauf der Zeit* (*Kings of the Road*) is released.	Baader-Meinhof group members die in Stammheim. Federal states' funding is increased. Wenders's *Der amerikanische Freund* is released.	Release of Hans-Jürgen Syberberg's *Hitler: ein Film aus Deutschland*; Fassbinder's French coproduction *Despair* is his first film with an international crew.	Sixty German filmmakers sign the Hamburg Declaration, trumpeting "a new German cinema." Herzog's *Nosferatu: Phantom der Nacht* has a cool reception.	Helma Sanders-Brahms (b. 1940) releases *Deutschland bleiche Mutter*. *Die Blechtrommel* wins the Oscar for Best Foreign Film.

The early self-produced movies by Werner Herzog included his anarchic depiction of a rebellion by a community of small people, in *Auch Zwerge haben klein angefangen* (*Even Dwarfs Started Small*, 1970), and a deeply moving documentary about a fifty-six-year-old deaf-blind woman Fini Straubinger, *Land des Schweigens und der Dunkelheit* (*Land of Silence and Darkness*, 1971). Rainer Werner Fassbinder made a notable debut with *Liebe ist kälter als der Tod* (*Love Is Colder Than Death*, 1969), a somber foray into the world of the US B movie, followed by the movie-reference-laden account of a returned Vietnam veteran, *Der amerikanische Soldat* (*The American Soldier*, 1970), and his first color film—*Warum läuft Herr R. Amok?* (*Why Does Herr R. Run Amok?*, 1970)—in which Kurt Raab's ostensibly placid draftsman resorts to murder and then suicide.

This sector was widely criticized—among other things for its restriction of authorial control and its increasing censoriousness, a reaction to what the various subsidy bodies saw, post 1968, as an unacceptable antiestablishment position on the part of the filmmakers that would peak in the later 1970s. In response, Wenders, Herzog, Fassbinder, Kluge, and others formed their own production, distribution and marketing organization, the Filmverlag der Autoren, in 1971. Many of their finest films were made under this banner, including Herzog's *Aguirre, der Zorn Gottes* and *Jeder für sich und Gott gegen alle* (*The Enigma of Kaspar Hauser*, 1974; see p. 332), Kluge's *In Gefahr und größter Not bringt der Mittelweg den Tod* (*The Middle of the Road Is a Very Dead End*, 1974), Wenders's *Alice in den Städten* and *Der amerikanische Freund* (*The American Friend*, 1977), and Fassbinder's *Die bitteren Tränen der Petra von Kant* (*The Bitter Tears of Petra von Kant*, 1972; see p. 330).

As the 1970s progressed, the tasks that West German filmmakers had set themselves—to describe the realities faced by contemporary Germans—took on either a more focused or a more internationalist dimension. The position of foreign workers, for instance, was addressed in a number of Fassbinder's films, notably and compassionately in *Angst essen Seele auf* (*Fear Eats the Soul*, 1974), a reworking of the melodrama *All That Heaven Allows* (1955), directed by Douglas Sirk (1900–87). The role of women is analyzed in films such as *Die allseitig reduzierte Persönlichkeit* (*The All-Round Reduced Personality*, 1978) by Helke Sander (b. 1937) and *Das zweite Erwachen der Christa Klages* (*The Second Awakening of Christa Klages*, 1978) by Margarethe von Trotta (b. 1942). The relationship between urban terrorism and increased police presence comes under scrutiny in von Trotta's Heinrich Böll adaptation *Die verlorene Ehre der Katharina Blum*, *Messer im Kopf* (*Knife in the Head*, 1978) by Reinhard Hauff (b. 1939) and Fassbinder's *Die dritte Generation* (*The Third Generation*, 1979).

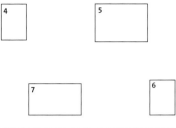

Finally, the debate on the Nazi inheritance was expanded by Hans-Jürgen Syberberg in his very lengthy essay-film-cum-Brechtian-operatic-spectacle *Hitler: ein Film aus Deutschland* (*Hitler: A Film from Germany*, 1978).

The year 1977 was a key one, both for the West German state and for New German Cinema. It saw the abduction and murder of industrialist Hanns-Martin Schleyer, and the suicide of Gudrin Ensslin and the death of other members of the Red Army Faction/Baader-Meinhof group in Stammheim prison—events that are generally seen as marking the end of Germany's so-called "decade of terror." In the omnibus film *Deutschland im Herbst* (*Germany in Autumn*, 1978, opposite above), directors including Fassbinder, Reitz, and Schlöndorff offered an immediate response to these events.

The New German Cinema gained its highest level of recognition during this period. *Palermo oder Wolfsburg* (*Palermo or Wolfsburg*, 1980) by Werner Schroeter (1945–2010) took the Berlin Film Festival's Golden Bear the year after Fassbinder's *Die Ehe der Maria Braun* (*The Marriage of Maria Braun*, 1979; opposite below) took the Silver; Schlöndorff's Gunter Grass adaptation *Die Blechtrommel* (*The Tin Drum*, 1979, above) was awarded the Oscar for Best Foreign Film in 1980; and the following year, a version of Lothar Buchheim's submarine novel *Das Boot* (*The Boat*, 1981, right) by Wolfgang Petersen (b. 1941) achieved phenomenal domestic and international success. Yet this was just when the most critical and dissident voices that had so recently helped to define the New German Cinema were being marginalized, its formal experimentation halted, and its filmmakers encouraged or forced into "acceptable" projects likely to enhance or "culturally legitimize" the international image of German cinema. Some acceded to the demands of foreign investors; others, like Wenders and Herzog, moved abroad to continue making movies.

However, this is to discount the continuity of the rich and enduring collaboration in Germany between television and film. In 1980 Fassbinder, arguably the most original, prolific, and influential of all the New German Cinema directors, made his masterpiece: a deeply felt literary adaptation of his lifelong love—Alfred Döblin's magnum opus *Berlin Alexanderplatz* (1929)—shot in Bavaria for airing on the public broadcast service ADR. Fassbinder died in 1982, a date that can be taken to mark—if slightly belatedly—the end of a period that included the audacious flowering of German cinema in the 1970s and the decline in the country's filmmaking immediately following it. **WH**

4 A poster for *Deutschland im Herbst*, featuring pieces from several renowned directors. In 1977, the year filming began, over half of all German film production emanated from directors connected to the New German Cinema.

5 Oskar Matzerath (David Bennent)— a boy who opts never to grow up—with his most beloved possession, in Volker Schlöndorff's *Die Blechtrommel*.

6 Drama below the waves: the brooding poster for Wolfgang Petersen's acclaimed submarine movie *Das Boot*.

7 Maria (Hanna Schygulla) confronts her love Hermann (Klaus Löwitsch) on his return from Canada in Rainer Werner Fassbinder's tangled tale of love triangles *Die Ehe der Maria Braun*.

Die bitteren Tränen der Petra von Kant 1972
The Bitter Tears of Petra von Kant   RAINER W. FASSBINDER 1945 – 82

▲ Petra and Sidonie discuss relationships in front of the huge reproduction of a Nicolas Poussin painting in Petra's lavish bedroom.

▼ The film, one of Fassbinder's most powerful, explores the dynamics between desire and power in Petra's relationships.

Rainer Werner Fassbinder, who allegedly wrote the script for *Die bitteren Tränen der Petra von Kant* on a plane journey, first allowed it to be staged as a theater piece. The story takes place inside an apartment and has many lengthy dialogue scenes, yet the film is among the most vitally cinematic of its creator's career. Informed by Douglas Sirk's melodramas, its glamorous, terrifying imagery references a range of cinema styles—as if an austere anxiety merchant, such as Carl Theodor Dreyer (1889–1968) or Ingmar Bergman (1918–2007), were to collaborate with Michael Powell (1905–90) or Vincente Minnelli (1903–86).

Fashion designer Petra von Kant (Margit Carstensen) is a stand-in character for Fassbinder himself and the story allegorizes his circle (transforming a mostly gay male crowd into an all-woman cast). The divalike Petra mistreats her silent, adoring assistant Marlene (Irm Hermann) as she enters into a relationship with would-be model Karin (Hanna Schygulla). Karin exploits and rejects her, prompting a despair that drives Petra to alienate her mother, daughter and sister, and finally prompts even Marlene to pack up and leave.

The story is stylized but ferocious depths of feeling are conveyed in the heightened performances—Petra's tendency to monologize balances Marlene's silence—and highly colored, often vampirish imagery. Stressing Petra's despair, the camera sinks to floor level in the final section: objects (mannequins, a bed headboard) often break up the frame, while insistent sounds (Marlene's angry typing, 78 rpm "records from my youth") accompany flirtations, arguments, and emotional meltdowns. **KN**

👁 KEY SCENES

1 MARLENE'S TEAR
Petra talks to Sidonie (Katrin Schaake) about her failed marriage and fusses with her makeup as the camera zooms in on the face of Marlene to register a glistening tear. Fassbinder dedicated the film to his assistant Peer Raben: "To the one who became Marlene here."

2 FEMME FATALE
Fassbinder gives Karin a full-on Hollywood femme fatale introductory shot, in which the ruthless aspiring model wears an ostrich-feather collar and is lit by the slats of a Venetian blind. Karin exploits Petra as much as the latter does Marlene.

3 "RECORDS FROM MY YOUTH"
In a deep focus shot, Petra, dressed as Theda Bara, talks about "records from my youth" and how they make her feel. Karin dances alluringly to the Walker Brothers in the foreground, and Marlene turns from her typing to glare from the back of the shot.

4 LIE TO ME
Upset when Karin deliberately fantasizes out loud about having sex with "a big black man with a big black cock," the devastated Petra, wearing an orange wig, asks her girlfriend to lie to her as a single tear mars her face.

🕐 DIRECTOR PROFILE

1945–68
Rainer Werner Fassbinder was born the son of an actress, Liselotte Pempiet. He entered the theater as a teenager and worked extensively in all capacities, from writing and directing through acting to stage management and publicity.

1969–71
Fassbinder made ten films, mostly extensions of his theater work, from *Liebe ist kälter als der Tod* (*Love Is Colder Than Death*, 1969)—booed at the Berlin Film Festival—to *Warnung vor einer heiligen Nutte* (*Beware of a Holy Whore*, 1971). *Katzelmacher* (1969) presaged the subject of the alienated outsider in a hostile environment, a theme that was to recur throughout his work. In 1971 he received acclaim for *Händler der vier Jahreszeiten* (*The Merchant of Four Seasons*).

1972–75
A leading director in the New German Cinema movement, Fassbinder made innovative, personal, transgressive films influenced by Hollywood melodrama, with a repertory cast of actors who weave in and out of his films (and personal life). Among them are *Die bitteren Tränen der Petra von Kant*, *Angst essen Seele auf* (*Fear Eats the Soul*, 1974), *Martha* (1974), *Effi Briest* (1974), *Fox* (1975), and *Mutter Küsters Fahrt zum Himmel* (*Mother Küster's Trip to Heaven*, 1975).

1976–82
During this period Fassbinder maintained a fast-paced work schedule. His films moved beyond his personal concerns with often epic productions looking at contemporary Germany and the country's troubled recent past. These included *In einem Jahr mit 13 Monden* (*In a Year of 13 Moons*, 1978), *Die Ehe der Maria Braun* (*The Marriage of Maria Braun*, 1979)—which proved to be his greatest success—*Despair* (1978), *Lili Marleen* (1981), *Lola* (1981), *Die Sehnsucht der Veronika Voss* (*Veronika Voss*, 1982), and *Querelle* (*Querelle: A Film about Jean Genet's "Querelle de Brest,"* 1982). He died at thirty-seven of heart failure, precipitated by drug use. He was working on a film about the life of Rosa Luxemburg.

Jeder für sich und Gott gegen alle 1974
The Enigma of Kaspar Hauser   WERNER HERZOG b. 1942

▲ Werner Herzog also cast Bruno S. as the lead role in *Stroszek* (1977).

▼ The film's original title translates as: "Every man for himself and God against them all."

Werner Herzog's second mainstream film, *Jeder für sich und Gott gegen alle*, established him as one of the great idiosyncratic visionaries of modern cinema. In the film Herzog combined two of his perennial interests: the use of detailed historical or documentary sources—here the famous and tragic case of the eponymous foundling who, in 1828, arrives in a small Bavarian town after a lifetime locked in a dark cellar without human contact—and a concern for their metaphysical implications and what they may reveal about the human condition.

His success rested on three factors. In describing, in moving domestic detail, the five brief years of Kaspar's "freedom," Herzog shows his confident handling of, and respect for, precise historical detail. Secondly, his inspired, possibly risky, casting of a nonprofessional in the main role—the formerly institutionalized forty-one-year-old street singer Bruno S.—set against the contained, highly disciplined work of the other professional cast members created an intensity of performance, and opened up channels of expression that were as unorthodox as they were communicative and emotionally involving. Lastly, Herzog's adventurous approach—his audacious use of classical music, flickering dream sequences, and the horror movie inflections of cinematographer Jörg Schmidt-Reitwein's framings—made for a less didactic relationship between film and viewer than is usual in "classical" cinema. Everything, from Herzog's humorous musings on the blinkered pursuit of self-interest to the pathos of Kaspar's situation, and the mystery of individual destiny, was able to emerge. **WH**

1 MAKING CONTACT
The horrific, cloaked figure of Kaspar's unnamed guard and future assassin (Hans Musäus) enters the cell where the boy has spent his whole life chained and incarcerated without human contact, with only bread and water for a diet and a wooden horse for company.

2 THE FOUNDLING, FOUND
On May 26, 1828, Kaspar is found alone in the streets of Nuremberg. Unable to stand properly or speak—save the sentence, "I want to be a gallant rider, like my father before me"—he is taken to the tower for the criminal and the insane.

3 "MOTHER, I AM SO FAR AWAY FROM EVERYTHING"
Kaspar cradles the daughter of the compassionate Nuremberg jailor (Volker Prechtel). He is later put on display in a circus of curiosities before attracting the sponsorships of kindly Professor Daumer (Walter Ladengast) and effete Lord Stanhope (Michael Kroecher).

4 A DEATH FORETOLD
Kaspar, mortally wounded by the mysterious assailant "M. L. O." (Hans Musäus), rushes to embrace his custodians Daumer and Kathe (Brigitte Mira). Kaspar's autopsy satisfies medical science by revealing a deformation of the liver and left cranial hemisphere.

⏱ DIRECTOR PROFILE

1942–67
Werner Herzog was born in Munich. He expressed his wanderlust and self-taught individualism by extensive solo travels in Europe and North America and by making several self-produced short films and documentaries.

1968–71
Encouraged by fellow New German Cinema mavericks, including Rainer Werner Fassbinder, Herzog made a series of impressive, little-distributed, low-budget features, including *Lebenszeichen* (*Signs of Life*, 1968), *Auch Zwerge haben klein angefangen* (*Even Dwarfs Started Small*, 1970), *Fata Morgana* and *Land des Schweigens und der Dunkelheit* (*Land of Silence and Darkness*, both 1971), all sharing a darkly compassionate, quasi-metaphysical view of outsiderdom.

1972–79
Herzog established collaborations with two unusual lead actors, Klaus Kinski and Bruno S., garnering international notice with Kinski's extraordinary portrayal of a crazed Spanish conquistador in *Aguirre, der Zorn Gottes* (*Aguirre, the Wrath of God*, 1972) and winning the Jury Prize at Cannes for *Jeder für sich und Gott gegen alle*. He went on to direct, among others, his masterpiece, *Nosferatu: Phantom der Nacht* (1979) and his searing Büchner adaptation *Woyzeck* (1979).

1980–87
Fitzcarraldo (1982), his second arduous South American–set period epic—and penultimate Kinski collaboration—won him the Best Director Award at the Cannes Film Festival, but it proved the highest point of his feature film ambitions and self-admitted "monomania." *Cobra Verde* (1987), his last collaboration with Kinski, met with lukewarm critical and commercial response and proved a watershed in his career.

1988–present
After two decades dedicated to documentary work, Herzog made a surprise return to narrative features with the cop thriller *Bad Lieutenant: Port of Call New Orleans* (2009) and *My Son, My Son, What Have Ye Done?* (2009).

THE NEW HORROR

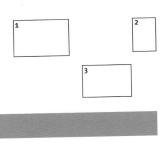

1 The psychotic killer in John Carpenter's stylistic horror movie *Halloween* remains masked until the final climactic scene.

2 Blood is a powerful visual metaphor for the prom queen with telekinetic powers in Brian De Palma's *Carrie*.

3 The ghosts of the murdered Grady twins appear repeatedly throughout *The Shining*, providing some of the film's most haunting images.

I n terms of quantity (certainly) and quality (arguably), the 1970s mark the blood meridian of the horror genre. Subversive, nihilistic, and shockingly immediate with its *vérité* camerawork, apocalyptic zombie movie *Night of the Living Dead* (1968) by George A. Romero (b. 1940) suggested there was something very wrong with the United States, and a new generation of filmmakers did not so much pass the torch as burn everything to the ground. "You watch these movies and you know you're in the hands of a maniac," said John Landis (b. 1950), referring to the distinctive, dangerous output of Wes Craven (b. 1939), Brian De Palma (b. 1940), David Cronenberg (b. 1943), David Lynch (b. 1946), and John Carpenter (b. 1948). This was a new breed of auteur, influenced by films such as *Psycho* (1960, see p. 296) and *Rosemary's Baby* (1968, see p. 298), as well as the French Nouvelle Vague (see p. 248) and the social, political, and economic environment of the time. "It's all about bad karma—it's got to go somewhere," said Wes Craven, referring to Vietnam, the Civil Rights movement, feminism, the sexual revolution, the Kent State shootings, and the oil embargo. Where it went was into a glut of do-it-yourself exploitation movies obliterating the myth of the nuclear family and lingering on the diseased and dispossessed.

Even Britain joined in, fusty Hammer coughing up some pleasingly bleak surprises (*Demons of the Mind*, 1972) in its protracted demise before the light went out, and the fall of the houses of Tigon and Amicus ushering in the sadistic pictures of ex-porn director Pete Walker (b. 1939; *House of Whipcord*, 1974).

KEY EVENTS

1970	1971	1972	1973	1974	1976
Dario Argento (b. 1940) begins a career-long obsession with killing women beautifully in *L'uccello dalle piume di cristallo* (*The Bird with the Crystal Plumage*).	Vincent Price appears in camp horror *The Abominable Dr. Phibes* as a man exacting revenge on the doctors behind his wife's botched surgery.	Wes Craven's *The Last House on the Left* sticks the knife into flower power and raises the bar on screen savagery.	Brian De Palma's first foray into voyeuristic horror, *Sisters*, employs Hitchcock's split-screen effect.	Proto-slasher *Black Christmas* comes with killer point-of-view shots. Tobe Hooper (b. 1943) ups the ante with *The Texas Chainsaw Massacre*.	*Carrie* launches trends for teenage heroines, telekinetic or psychic protagonists, and adaptations of horror books by writer Stephen King.

Meanwhile, an amazing double bill in 1973 offered up *Don't Look Now*, a shattering study of grief and superstition by Nicolas Roeg (b. 1928), and *The Wicker Man* (see p. 338), an eerily erotic pagan nightmare set on a Scottish island.

Rosemary's Baby paved the way for a slew of religious shockers. The most famous of these, *The Exorcist* (1973, see p. 336) and *The Omen* (1976), are also examples of the trend for studio horror films boasting big budgets and star names. *Jaws* (1975, see p. 364) and *Alien* (1979) pumped new blood into the monster movie, while *The Shining* (1980, below) featured stunning sets, opulent production design, immaculate technique, and a major star and director in Jack Nicholson (b. 1937) and Stanley Kubrick (1928–99). Brian De Palma made a watershed horror film (and the best adaptation yet of a Stephen King novel) in *Carrie* (1976, right). This was prestige horror for audiences who would sooner eat their own foot than watch gut-churning cannibal movies or lurid *gialli* out of Italy.

Blockbuster horror continued well into the 1980s, with studios seeking to widen the genre's appeal more by softening the scares and adding humor, special effects, and fun. The result was family-friendly scare fare such as *Poltergeist* (1982) and *Ghostbusters* (1984), pictures that proved a welcome alternative to the formulaic slasher movies stalking cinemas in the wake of John Carpenter's superior suspense vehicle *Halloween* (1978, opposite). Elsewhere, the advances in prosthetic effects made by the likes of Rick Baker (*An American Werewolf in London*, 1981) and Rob Bottin (*The Thing*, 1982) meant splatter mattered. A handful of intelligent, subversive horror films also emerged, Cronenberg's *The Fly* (see p. 430) in 1986 (seen by many as a comment on fear of AIDS) and sadomasochistic fantasy *Hellraiser* (1987) by Clive Barker (b. 1952) among them. **JG**

The Exorcist 1973

WILLIAM FRIEDKIN b. 1935

▲ Good in the dark, evil in the light: Father Merrin confronts the possessed Regan.

▼ The stark poster employs noir-esque chiaroscuro to create a sense of foreboding.

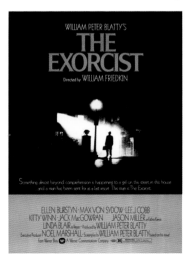

William Peter Blatty, hitherto a comedy screenwriter (*A Shot in the Dark*, 1964), based his best-selling novel on accounts of an incident of possession and exorcism that took place in the United States in 1949. Although a familiar enough horror story—an innocent is threatened by a monster, which is defeated at great cost by religious figures—*The Exorcist* is mounted as a more serious picture than, say, *Dracula: Prince of Darkness* (1966). Controversy has raged for decades between director William Friedkin, screenwriter Blatty, and Warner Bros. as to the final form of the film and its precise theological meaning, but 1970s viewers were less likely to come away pondering the existence of God and the purpose of evil in the great design than thoroughly scared by an expert succession of cutting-edge shocks.

Regan (Linda Blair), daughter of a movie star (Ellen Burstyn), displays symptoms (including profanity, urinating on the carpet, projectile vomiting, speaking in tongues, and self-abuse with a crucifix) that might betoken an extremely disturbed adolescence or actual possession by the devil (or the Assyrian wind demon, Pazuzu). After medical and psychiatric avenues are exhausted, the Catholic Church is called in, represented by doubting priest Father Karras (Jason Miller) and seasoned exorcist Father Merrin (Max von Sydow). The unruly teenager is tied to a bed (which occasionally levitates) and chanted over by the priests, in a scene that resonates as more horrific after decades of clerical pedophilia scandals than it did when the stakes simply seemed to be her soul and the great battle between Good and Evil. **KN**

👁 KEY SCENES

1 PAZUZU
Near the ruins of the ancient city of Nineveh (Iraq), archaeologist Father Lankester Merrin comes across a stone carving of what seems to be the face of a grinning demon. He goes on to find a statue of the demon king Pazuzu, the face of which resembles the carving.

2 CRUCIFIX
Regan is brought home from a clinic, where she has undergone tests. Her mother puts her to bed and notices a crucifix under the pillow. This leads to one of the film's most shocking scenes, as Regan masturbates bloodily with a crucifix—a symbolic loss of virginity.

3 THE EXORCIST CALLS
Father Merrin approaches the Georgetown house, looking up at the lit window. The image, used for the film's poster, is as powerful for what is not tangible—objects are indistinct, areas of light are overwhelmed by darkness and shadow—as for what is revealed.

4 SACRIFICE
After an intense battle between the possessed Regan, Merrin, and Karras, Father Karras takes the demon into himself and then deliberately throws himself out of the window, saving the girl's soul at the price of his own life.

🕒 DIRECTOR PROFILE

1935–70
Born in Chicago, the son of a merchant seaman, William Friedkin joined WGN TV on graduating from high school. He directed for television (one of the last episodes of *The Alfred Hitchcock Hour* in 1965), made his big-screen debut with a Sonny and Cher vehicle (*Good Times*, 1967), and directed art-house films based on plays (*The Birthday Party*, 1968; *The Boys in the Band*, 1970). His sole commercial studio film, the period musical comedy *The Night They Raided Minsky's* (1968), was a flop.

1971–73
Crime thriller *The French Connection* (1971) picked up five Academy Awards, including a Best Director gong for Friedkin. Both this and *The Exorcist* (1973—nominated for ten Academy Awards) were enormous commercial and critical successes, and influential in introducing an intense, hard-hitting, free-form style to their respective genres. Friedkin was now regarded as one of the leading young directors of the "New Hollywood," along with figures such as Francis Ford Coppola (b. 1939) and Peter Bogdanovich (b. 1939).

1974–80
Sorcerer (1977), a remake of *Le salaire de la peur* (1953, see p. 196), ended Friedkin's winning streak—although the director himself considers it his best work. Crime comedy *The Brink's Job* (1978), based on the Great Brink's robbery in Boston in 1950, was also unsuccessful at the box office. He courted much controversy with the gay-themed serial killer picture *Cruising* (1980), starring Al Pacino.

1981–present
Although he made the occasional decent cinema film, notably steely cop thriller *To Live and Die in L.A.* (1985) and the creepy theatrical adaptation *Bug* (2006), Friedkin worked mostly with uncongenial material (*The Guardian*, 1990; *Jade*, 1995; *Rules of Engagement*, 2000) or in television (*C.A.T. Squad*; *CSI*). *The Exorcist* was re-released in 2000 and became a massive hit all over again.

The Wicker Man 1973

ROBIN HARDY b. 1939

▲ An all-female early morning fertility ritual on Summerisle.

▼ The film's shocking climax is prefigured in the arresting poster image.

This is a movie that takes religion seriously—a rare enough event in British cinema. *The Wicker Man* pits dour, Scots-Presbyterian Christianity against exuberant paganism, and exposes the flaws in both of them. Witty, irreverent, reveling in the cut and thrust of doctrinal combat, Anthony Shaffer's script hits its peak in the clash between Edward Woodward's uptight mainland cop Sergeant Howie and Christopher Lee's urbane Lord Summerisle. "And what of the true God? What of Him?" protests Howie, appalled that pagan eroticism is the island's official creed. "He's dead," responds Summerisle cheerfully. "He can't complain. He had his chance and—in modern parlance—blew it."

Made at the weary end of the British horror cycle, *The Wicker Man* shrugs off the gothic fangs and capery of the Hammer stable in favor of the limpid sunlight and blossom of a Hebridean spring. Pious policeman Howie, the fool-king-virgin, is led by the nose by all the islanders: the hunted leading the hunters.

The film's greatest asset—besides Lee's performance—is Shaffer's coolly intelligent script. The island's religion, founded (we are told) by the present lord's grandfather, offers the kind of loopy mishmash you would expect from a solemn Victorian freethinker: a hodgepodge of ancient lore, druidical mumbo, and chunks from James Frazer's *The Golden Bough*. Even better, this is a movie with the courage of its convictions. As the flames crackle, and Howie's desperate howls of "The Lord is my shepherd" are met by the islanders' joyous chant of "Summer Is Icumen In," the viewer waits for the filmmakers to chicken out, for the Highland Seventh Cavalry to come thundering over the hill. But no. The sacrifice is consummated. **PK**

KEY SCENES

1 THE LANDLORD'S DAUGHTER
Arrived on Summerisle to investigate a report of a missing girl, Howie is shocked by the bawdiness in the island's pub, as the locals sing in explicit praise of the attractions of Willow (Britt Ekland), the landlord's daughter.

2 "HERE THE OLD GODS AREN'T DEAD"
Increasingly bewildered and dismayed by the attitudes and sights he encounters on Summerisle, Howie confronts the island's lord, Lord Summerisle. The sergeant learns that Christianity has been banished on the island in favor of paganism.

3 THE TEMPTING OF SERGEANT HOWIE
The pagans play fair. Howie, chastely saving himself for his marriage bed, has temptation thrust at him in the comely shape of Willow, gyrating naked outside his bedroom. Had he succumbed and lost his virginity, he would no longer have been acceptable as a sacrifice.

4 THE SACRIFICE
Trapped inside the giant wicker frame, along with assorted livestock, Howie is burned to death as a gift to the sun god. The words of May Morrison (Irene Sunter) have proved eerily prophetic: "You'll simply never understand the true nature of sacrifice."

⏱ STAR PROFILE: CHRISTOPHER LEE

1922–56
Christopher Lee was born in London to a British father and an Italian mother. After wartime service with the RAF, he took up acting, making his screen debut in *Corridor of Mirrors* (1948) by Terence Young (1915–94). He went on to play a small role in *Hamlet* (1948) directed by Laurence Olivier (1907–89). Lee acted in around thirty films before signing up with the Hammer studio.

1957–69
Lee played the monster in *The Curse of Frankenstein* (1957) and the title role in *Dracula* (1958); he went on to play the Count six more times for Hammer. He also played the title roles in *The Mummy* (1959), *Rasputin, the Mad Monk* (1966), and *The Face of Fu Manchu* (1965, plus three sequels).

1970–74
Moving away from the horror roles that made his name, Lee played the part of Holmes's brother Mycroft in *The Private Life of Sherlock Holmes* (1970) by Billy Wilder (1906–2002), and a Bond villain, Scaramanga, in *The Man with the Golden Gun* (1974). (Ian Fleming, his step-cousin, had suggested him for the title role in the first Bond film, *Dr. No* (1962), but the part went to Joseph Wiseman.) In 1973 he appeared in *The Wicker Man* (which he later warmly described as "a brilliant film").

1975–present
After some questionable choices, such as *Police Academy: Mission to Moscow* (1994), Lee had a resurgence toward the end of the century. He appeared in a number of high-profile films, including *Sleepy Hollow* (1999) and *Charlie and the Chocolate Factory* (2005). Among his most notable later roles are Saruman in the *Lord of the Rings* trilogy (2001–03, see p. 530), Count Dooku in two episodes of the *Star Wars* series (2002, 2005) and the title role in *Jinnah* (1998) as the founder of modern Pakistan, a part that he described as "the best thing I've ever done, by a long, long way." Lee received a CBE in 2001 and was knighted eight years later. He continues to act in several films a year; to date he has appeared in more than 260 movies. He returned to Hammer Films for *The Resident* (2011).

HOLLYWOOD CRIME MOVIES

The seventies opened with the trial of Charles Manson for murders that struck at the Hollywood elite. The break-in at the Watergate building permanently tainted the highest office in the land and an unpopular war in Vietnam ended with the ignominious evacuation of US forces from Saigon. Like the era to which they belonged, crime movies were characterized by disillusionment, distrust of authority, and paranoia.

Three of the period's classic films perceive the nation's moral bankruptcy through the lens of history. Francis Ford Coppola (b. 1939) gave the world *The Godfather* (1972, see p. 342) and its sequel *The Godfather Part II* (1974) and, by doing so, reinvented the gangster movie as grand opera. Both films place the Mafia immovably at the heart of US life, coincidentally giving a new meaning to that most American of concepts, "the family." *Chinatown* (1974, see p. 344) directed by Roman Polanski (b. 1933) also investigates the criminal foundations of US society, its tale of murder and incest played out against the backdrop of the corruption endemic in the growth of Los Angeles.

Lack of faith in the law is the theme of many of the decade's policiers. *Dirty Harry* (1971, above), from director Don Siegel (1912–91), features Clint Eastwood's Detective Harry Callahan going rogue on the streets of San Francisco in pursuit of a sadistic serial killer. *Dirty Harry* is not an endorsement of vigilantism (as its liberal critics claimed); its subject is the destructive synergy between cop and psychopath. In *The French Connection* (opposite below), director William

1 In *Dirty Harry*, Clint Eastwood hoists his weapon of choice, a .44 Magnum, "the most powerful handgun in the world."

2 Richard Roundtree as *Shaft*—the archetypal cool cat. Isaac Hayes's "Theme from Shaft" went on to win a Grammy Award and an Academy Award for Best Original Song.

3 *The French Connection* was a critical and commercial hit, winning five Academy Awards, including for Best Film, Screenplay, and Best Actor for Gene Hackman's portrayal of Popeye Doyle.

KEY EVENTS

1970	1971	1971	1972	1973	1974
The trial of Charles Manson begins. The National Guard gun down four students at Kent State University.	William Friedkin directs *The French Connection*, which wins four Oscars including Best Actor for Gene Hackman and Best Director.	Charles Manson and his codefendants are found guilty on all counts. *Dirty Harry* and *Klute* are released.	Five men are arrested for breaking into the Watergate complex. J. Edgar Hoover dies. Richard Nixon is reelected with a landslide victory.	The Watergate burglars are tried and convicted. Vice President Agnew resigns amid charges of bribery, tax evasion, and money laundering.	Nixon resigns on August 9. His successor, Gerald Ford, issues him a pardon. Patty Hearst is kidnapped by the Symbionese Liberation Army.

Friedkin (b. 1935) presents the law as a charmless, foul-mouthed cop called Popeye Doyle, a marked contrast to the urbane, aristocratic drug kingpin he is trying to bring down. Based on actual events, it shows police and criminals operating on a basis of moral equivalency.

In *The Long Goodbye* (1973) by Robert Altman (1925–2006) Raymond Chandler's knight-errant private eye Philip Marlowe is reimagined for the seventies. Elliott Gould's Marlowe is a man out of his time, chain-smoking his way through a Hollywood where a gangster's preferred method of extracting information is to stage an impromptu nude encounter group. Scriptwriter Leigh Brackett worked on an earlier Chandler adaptation, *The Big Sleep* (1946), and her script for Altman captures the cadences of the 1970s cult of the self.

In his essay "The 'Me' Decade and the Third Great Awakening" (1976), Tom Wolfe defined the solipsism of the age. He could have been writing about the Los Angeles of *The Long Goodbye*. Clint Eastwood (b. 1930) made his directorial debut with *Play Misty for Me* (1971), a film that plugs into the mores of the "Me" decade, transforming his screen persona from action hero to a preening late-night disc jockey. His character is a mellow jazz lothario, bewildered when the fan he carelessly beds turns into a homicidal stalker.

The evolution of black consciousness in the 1970s was reflected in the "blaxploitation" phenomenon, with films targeting black audiences. The tone for the genre was set by *Shaft* (1971, right) directed by the African American filmmaker Gordon Parks (1912–2006) and featuring a charismatic soul-brother private eye, and the more ambiguous *Super Fly* (1972), directed by Parks's son Gordon Parks Jr. (1934–79), with a ghetto drug dealer as hero. Both films feature the genre's signature of groundbreaking scores that are as successful as the films themselves—*Shaft*'s by Isaac Hayes and *Super Fly*'s by Curtis Mayfield.

In a decade that opened with the Manson trial and featured the mass suicide of the Jim Jones cult, it was possible to believe that the Devil was on the loose, a mood best captured in the Jack Starrett (1936–89) occult road movie *Race with the Devil* (1975). In this exercise in post-Manson paranoia, two couples holidaying in a recreational vehicle witness a human sacrifice and are pursued by devil-worshipping cult members. It presents the Southwest of the United States in the grip of a satanic conspiracy.

Although both the 1960s and the 1980s produced some excellent crime movies, the profusion of original works capturing an era's zeitgeist makes the 1970s a golden age for the genre. Despite the trend in recent years for remaking crime classics (*Shaft* in 2000, *Assault on Precinct 13* in 2005, *The Taking of Pelham 123* in 2009), occasionally the DNA of seventies crime movies has been used to create superior original thrillers, such as *Jackie Brown* (1997) by Quentin Tarantino (b. 1963), *Zodiac* (2007) directed by David Fincher (b. 1962), and *The Town* (2010) by Ben Affleck (b. 1972). These films prove that the attitude and morality of seventies crime dramas are still as relevant today. **DP**

The mob wanted Harlem back. They got Shaft... up to here.

SHAFT

SHAFT's his name. SHAFT's his game.

1975	1976	1977	1978	1979	1981
The fall of Saigon. Neo-noir thriller *Farewell My Lovely* is released.	Tom Wolfe coins the term "the 'Me' decade" in *New York* magazine.	*The Gauntlet*, Clint Eastwood's sixth film as director, is released. Jimmy Carter succeeds Gerald Ford as president.	Cult leader Jim Jones orders the mass suicide of nine hundred cult members in the commune of Jonestown.	Patty Hearst is released from prison at the behest of Jimmy Carter.	*Cutter's Way* directed by Ivan Passer (b. 1933), a leading figure of the Prague Spring, is released.

The Godfather 1972
FRANCIS FORD COPPOLA b. 1939

▲ Marlon Brando received an Oscar for his performance as Don Vito Corleone.

▼ The poster shows Brando's profile but the film's strong ensemble cast is also listed.

Francis Ford Coppola's film of Mario Puzo's best seller, at once an art movie and a commercial blockbuster, marks the end of a classical Hollywood era and the dawn of the age of the megamovie. Marlon Brando's magisterial, operatic patriarch stands for everything about old Hollywood that the movie brat Coppola aspired to, and the younger generation of Corleones are played by the new A-list (Al Pacino, James Caan, Robert Duvall, Diane Keaton; in the sequel, Robert De Niro). Appropriately, the film follows a similar transition in organized crime, as the gentlemanly if sinister world of patriarch Don Vito Corleone (Brando) is eclipsed by the more brutal, expedient, and political organization represented by the doomed Sonny (Caan) and the calculating Michael (Pacino).

The film was a critical and commercial success, creating a legacy and seeping into popular culture with such catchphrases as "Luca Brasi sleeps with the fishes" and "Make him an offer he can't refuse." Perhaps because it already has a period setting, evoked by Gordon Willis's amber-tinted photography and Nino Rota's elegantly decadent score, *The Godfather* dates less than many early 1970s films, even if its take on corrupt corporate America is aimed as much at the Nixon era as the period in which it is set. Coppola dares to take a complex story at a deliberate, art-film pace, making its moments of action and horror more telling for the leisurely paths woven between them. Coppola extended the Corleone saga in *The Godfather Part II* (1974), *The Godfather Part III* (1990) and various television or DVD reedits and rearrangements. **KN**

👁 KEY SCENES

1 "I BELIEVE IN AMERICA"
The film opens in the office of Don Vito Corleone. He strokes his cat and listens to the appeal of the undertaker. These shady dealings are contrasted with the wedding celebration outside, highlighting the two adjacent worlds of family and business.

2 WAKE-UP CALL
Having turned down a softly spoken appeal by Tom Hagen (Robert Duvall) to cast Johnny Fontane (Al Martino) in his new war movie, horse-loving producer Jack Woltz (John Marley) wakes up with a horse's head in his bed. He proceeds to cast Fontane in the movie.

3 ASSASSINATION
En route to visiting his bruised and beaten sister, Connie (Talia Shire), Sonny arrives at a toll booth. Mob rivals are waiting and he is gunned down, his car and body riddled with bullets. Killing off a lead character in such violent fashion shocks the audience.

4 DON VITO'S DEATH
Out of hospital and convalescing, Don Vito begins to retreat from the world of crime. Playing with his grandson in the garden, he puts in orange-peel teeth and chases the boy through the tomato vines, before succumbing to a heart attack.

5 BAPTISM AND MASSACRE
While Michael stands godfather to his niece (played by the infant Sofia Coppola) at her baptism, pledging to "renounce Satan and all his works," the family's enemies are gunned down on his orders. Coppola intercuts the two events.

6 SHADOWS GATHER
Michael has taken up residence in his late father's office. The former idealist becomes the new godfather and the film ends in the same place it started. Kay (Keaton) watches as mysterious figures pay their respects to Don Corleone. As she looks on, the door is closed.

Chinatown 1974

ROMAN POLANSKI b. 1933

▲ Gittes (Jack Nicholson) picks up the scent.

▼ The poster plays on Film Noir tropes, such as the gumshoe and the femme fatale.

Set in Los Angeles in 1937 but overshadowed by crimes dating back to the founding of the town, this is the archetypal, retro-chic, private eye movie. *Chinatown* re-creates the world of Raymond Chandler, complete with clean-lined cars and snappy suits, but adds an ironic awareness of genre conventions and a Watergate-era cynicism about a conspiracy-laden society. Despite its noirish feel, it is a sunstruck piece—although it finds its darkness in the mythical, monumental corruption of the topsy-turvy district evoked in the title.

J. J. (Jake) Gittes (Jack Nicholson), a smart but sleazy private eye who comes across more like an upmarket Mike Hammer than an authentic Philip Marlowe, investigates the supposed adultery of a city official, only to uncover both a massive confidence scheme to make a profit out of bringing water to the desert city and a tangled web of incest and violence emanating from robber baron Noah Cross (John Huston). Cross, one of the great villains of 1970s cinema, has abused his daughter Evelyn (Faye Dunaway), and now wants to further enslave the thirsty city by cornering its water supply.

A multilayered masterpiece, perhaps the perfect synthesis of an auteur (director Roman Polanski) and a high-class script and star (writer Robert Towne, star Jack Nicholson), this film takes the private eye genre to its ultimate conclusion. The trench-coated knight errant is demystified, powerless against a social and spiritual evil from which he only barely abstains. Whereas traditional Warner Bros. private eye movies were fast-paced and punchy, *Chinatown* is serpentine and languorous, its complex plot filled with potent shocks. **KN**

KEY SCENES

1 SATISFYING THE CLIENT
Jake Gittes survives on sleazy day-to-day work as a detective in a morally gray world. In this scene he coldly hands over photographs to a cuckolded husband and watches the client's response to seeing his wife having sex with another man.

2 NOSY FELLOW
An undersized thug (Polanski) slits Gittes's nose to warn him off further investigations. "You're a very nosy fellow, kitty cat, huh? You know what happens to nosy fellows, huh? No? Wanna guess? Huh? No? Okay—they lose their noses!"

3 REVELATIONS
Jake confronts Evelyn and demands she tell the truth about the case. Evelyn claims that Katherine (Belinda Palmer) is her daughter, and is slapped by Jake; she then claims the girl is her sister and is slapped again. She finally admits, "She's my sister and my daughter."

4 "FORGET IT, JAKE. IT'S CHINATOWN"
Evelyn attempts to escape with Katherine. The police open fire, shooting Evelyn in the head. Her evil father-abuser makes off with the hysterical Katherine. Jake's partner leads him away and, as Jake looks back a final time, tells him to forget it.

DIRECTOR PROFILE

1933–63
Roman Polanski was born in Paris to Polish parents. He entered films as an actor in *Pokolenie* (*A Generation*, 1954), by Andrzej Wajda (b. 1926), and directed several shorts himself while also acting in other directors' features.

1964–67
He moved to England, where he made his first English-language productions, *Repulsion* (1965), *Cul-de-Sac* (1966), and *Dance of the Vampires* (1967).

1968–78
Polanski based himself in the United States, where he enjoyed great acclaim for his thrillers *Rosemary's Baby* (1968, see p. 298) and *Chinatown*. In 1969 he suffered the appalling death of his pregnant actress wife Sharon Tate at the hands of the Manson family. He also made *Macbeth* (1971) in Britain, *¿Que?* (*What?*, 1972) in Rome, and *Le locataire* (*The Tenant*, 1976) in Paris, before a charge of sex with an underage girl obliged him to move to Europe.

1979–2001
Now largely based in Paris, where he played Mozart on stage in *Amadeus* in 1980, Polanski published his autobiography in 1984 and married actress Emmanuelle Seigner in 1989. In Europe, he made *Tess* (1979), *Pirates* (1986), *Frantic* (1988), *Bitter Moon* (1992), *Death and the Maiden* (1994), and *The Ninth Gate* (1999).

2002–present
His World War II film *The Pianist* (2002) about a Jewish-Polish musician won him an Academy Award for Best Director and snagged Adrien Brody a Best Actor Award. Polanski followed *The Pianist* with *Oliver Twist* (2005), *To Each His Own Cinema* (2007), and mystery thriller *The Ghost* (2010), which he edited under house arrest in Switzerland. In 2010 the Swiss authorities rejected the United States' request for extradition and Polanski was declared a free man. He began work later that year on an adaptation of the award-winning play *God of Carnage* by Yasmina Reza.

HOLLYWOOD PARANOIA

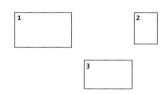

1 *Soylent Green*, directed by Richard Fleischer (1916–2006), depicts the dark forces of corporate America at work in a future where food scarcity causes riots.

2 The film poster for Alan J. Pakula's *The Parallax View* references themes of anonymity and patriotism.

3 Laurence Olivier and Dustin Hoffman star in an uncomfortable central scene from *Marathon Man*, in which Olivier's character is revealed as a torturer.

Hollywood's run of political and psychological thrillers in the 1970s is generally interpreted as a paranoid reaction to the Watergate scandal and the fallout from the Communist witch hunt of the 1950s. Other contributing factors included the specter of the Vietnam War and the feeling among liberals that although everyone hated the war it continued because of government intractability. There was also a growing sense that Hollywood did not understand its audience. All of this combined to make Hollywood uncertain and the nation introspective.

The prototype for the Hollywood conspiracy thriller is *The Manchurian Candidate* (1962), directed by John Frankenheimer (1930–2002). Ostensibly about a Communist plot against the US government, the film reveals that the conspiracy is the work of native politicians and military leaders. Throughout the 1960s and early 1970s, films depicting authority figures as shady and corrupt became common. However, Hollywood paranoia came to a head with the Watergate scandal in 1972.

A definite feeling of unease was visible across many Hollywood genres: in Westerns such as *Pat Garrett and Billy the Kid* (1973), political dramas such as *The Candidate* (1972), gangster thrillers such as *The Godfather: Part II* (1974), and science fiction movies such as *Soylent Green* (1973, above). In each the forces of US power and politics are depicted as untrustworthy, exploiting ordinary people for personal or corporate gain. *Soylent Green* presents the

KEY EVENTS

1970	1971	1971	1971	1972	1972
Antiestablishment films such as *Catch-22*, *The Strawberry Statement*, and *WUSA* are released.	Alan J. Pakula eases into his "paranoia trilogy" with *Klute*; it establishes themes that become essential to the conspiracy thriller genre.	The publication of the Pentagon Papers reveals government obfuscation over US political and military involvement in Vietnam.	Directed by Sidney Lumet (b. 1924), *The Anderson Tapes* features the prevalence of electronic surveillance as a major theme.	The Watergate burglaries take place on May 28 and June 17 at the Democratic National Committee headquarters in Washington, DC.	*The Candidate* is released and takes a cynical view of US party politics, emphasizing its pointlessness.

bleakest view, portraying New York in 2022 as a dystopia in which people are unknowingly living as cannibals and corrupt officials are complicit in the cover-up.

The iconic film of the period is *The Parallax View* (1974, right), a brooding thriller directed by Alan J. Pakula (1928–98) in which Warren Beatty's hippie reporter investigates the Kennedy-like assassination of a crusading US senator and stumbles across a plot that touches the highest levels of business and government. The film set the stylistic template for the conspiracy movie: a labyrinthine narrative, booming sound effects and overlapping dialogue, brutalist steel-and-glass architecture, and a sparing use of soundtrack music. *The Conversation* (1974, see p. 348) directed by Francis Ford Coppola (b. 1939) and *Night Moves* (1975) directed by Arthur Penn (1922–2010) adopt a similarly cold modernist style but tell more intimate stories; both films star Gene Hackman as a private detective coming up against forces far beyond his control, and losing his identity in the process. In these films the doomed hero, despite being intelligent and committed, does not simply fall prey to powerful outside influences, but is also the victim of his own emotional weakness, instability, and obsessive nature. The only film to tackle the Watergate scandal directly was *All the President's Men* (1976, see p. 350). Despite its narrative complexity and fact-filled script, the film was a hit with audiences desperate to put the Nixon era behind them. After *All the President's Men*, with Nixon ousted and the Vietnam War over, the paranoia began to give way to the more optimistic likes of *Star Wars* (1977, see p. 366). Vestiges remained in films such as *Marathon Man* (1976, below) directed by John Schlesinger (1926–2003), although the force of corruption in that film is not a government organization but an individual, in the shape of a Nazi war criminal. **TH**

As American as apple pie.

Paramount Pictures Presents
AN ALAN J. PAKULA PRODUCTION
WARREN BEATTY
THE PARALLAX VIEW
HUME CRONYN WILLIAM DANIELS and PAULA PRENTISS
Director of Photography GORDON WILLIS · Music Scored by MICHAEL SMALL
Executive Producer GABRIEL KATZKA Screenplay by DAVID GILER and LORENZO SEMPLE, Jr.
Produced and Directed by ALAN J. PAKULA PANAVISION® TECHNICOLOR® A Paramount Picture

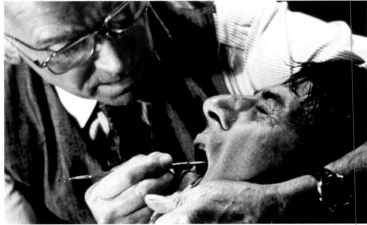

1973	1974	1975	1976	1977	1978
The Watergate conspiracy deepens. Films such as *Soylent Green* explore themes of moral decline and the widespread abuse of power.	Nixon resigns his presidency. *Chinatown* (see p. 344), *The Conversation* (see p. 348), and *The Parallax View* examine conspiracy themes.	*Night Moves* and *Nashville* present more intimate, personal takes on ideas of surveillance, criminality, and assassination.	*All the President's Men* (see p. 350) lays the ghost of Nixon and the Watergate scandal to rest. *Marathon Man* and *Network* are released.	*Star Wars* opens and reveals a public appetite for a simpler mainstream cinema.	*Coma*, like *Capricorn One* (1977), uses the iconography of paranoia to tell an escapist tale.

The Conversation 1974

FRANCIS FORD COPPOLA b. 1939

▲ Harry Caul doing what he does best.

▼ The film's poster plays on the interception of dialogue and lines of communication.

Harry Caul is an invader of privacy. The best in the business. He can record any conversation between two people anywhere.

So far, three people are dead because of him.

The Directors Company presents
GENE HACKMAN
"THE CONVERSATION"

Co-starring JOHN CAZALE · ALLEN GARFIELD · CINDY WILLIAMS · FREDERIC FORREST
DAVID SHIRE · FRED ROOS · FRANCIS FORD COPPOLA

Between the first two parts of the *Godfather* epic (1972 and 1974), Francis Ford Coppola directed this smaller-scale paranoia movie that addresses the world of Watergate, the Kennedy and King assassinations, Jimmy Hoffa, and Howard Hughes. Catholic surveillance expert Harry Caul (Gene Hackman), working for a sinister corporate director (Robert Duvall), records a conversation in a busy San Francisco square. From a few phrases passed between his employer's wife (Cindy Williams) and her lover (Frederic Forrest), Harry suspects that they are in danger of being murdered. After much conscience wringing, and dogged by shadowy persuaders (a sleek young Harrison Ford, bearing cookies and threats), he opts to intervene—only to find that he has misjudged the situation by fatally missing the stresses in a crucial sentence that tell a different horrible story. Meanwhile, the isolated genius is gnawed by a set of phobias that paint him into an existential corner. He holds himself above the hustlers of his profession (Allen Garfield, John Cazale), who bug him and play back a private conversation at a surveillance convention, and alienates his girlfriend (Teri Garr) by treating her like a prostitute—only to be betrayed by a casual pickup (Elizabeth MacRae) with her own agenda.

The film grew partly out of Coppola's increasing involvement in technical wizardry. In time, he would come to direct, like Harry, from inside a gadget-filled trailer—arguably remote from his cast and prone to similar misunderstandings. Appropriately, the film is also a showcase for Coppola's sound editor, Walter Murch, who supplies a textured, dark soundtrack—worth a listen with your eyes shut. **KN**

1 "HE'D KILL US!"
Ann (Williams) and Mark (Forrest) have a conversation as they walk in San Francisco's Union Square. There are many background noises and distractions, but Harry manages to tape and edit the dialogue so the words can be distinguished, although their meaning is unclear.

3 OUR LADY
Harry is shocked to discover that he is now under surveillance himself, although he is unsure how he is being bugged. Having dismantled everything else in his apartment looking for a listening device, he investigates his statue of the Madonna.

2 THE BLOODY TRUTH
Concerned for Ann and Mark's welfare, Harry rents a room next to theirs in a hotel and listens in on them. Hearing a disturbance, he races to their room. Blood wells out of the toilet. Harry finally understands the snatch of conversation he has been listening to.

4 SAXOPHONE SOLO
By the end of the movie, Harry has reduced his flat to a ruin—even tearing apart the fabric of the walls in his attempt to find a bug—a metaphor, perhaps, for the way he has destroyed his life. Afterward, he sits and plays his tenor saxophone in the wreckage.

SIGHTS AND SOUNDS

One inspiration for *The Conversation* is *Blow-Up* (1966, right) by Michelangelo Antonioni (1912–2007). It is based on a Julio Cortázar story, in which a photographer poring over prints believes he may have discerned the grainy evidence that a murder has been committed. In turn, *The Conversation* and *Blow-Up* influenced *Blow Out* (1981) by Brian De Palma (b. 1940), in which a sound man recording eerie noises for a low-budget horror movie accidentally tapes a suspicious car crash. These are films that could be made only by people who grew up with sound cinema and are as interested in the technical processes (which become part of the plot) as the story. The directors of these three movies have displayed a fascination with gadgets, new technologies, and elaborate camerawork.

All the President's Men 1976

ALAN J. PAKULA 1928 – 98

▲ The *Post*'s team watch the latest political developments unfold on television.

▼ A bold—but justifiable—claim for the tagline of the film's poster.

Two guys sitting in a newspaper office typing, or making telephone calls is not the most visually exciting material, yet this is what the viewer gets for about half of *All the President's Men*. It is a tribute to Alan J. Pakula's direction, William Goldman's scripting, and the skill of the cast that the tension is kept up and the mundane, repetitive business of asking questions, following leads, getting rebuffed and persisting—the plodding job of the investigative reporter—remains absorbing. It helps that the ultimate quarry is the big one: the US president, forced to resign only two years before the film's release.

Pakula had directed a key "paranoid movie" of the 1970s, *The Parallax View* (1974), so the true story of how two determined *Washington Post* reporters, Bob Woodward and Carl Bernstein, exposed a complex web of corruption linked to the Watergate break-in found him on home territory. As sleuths, Robert Redford and Dustin Hoffman shrewdly play their contrasting screen images off against each other, while Hal Holbrook brings sardonic relish to the role of Woodward's White House informant, Deep Throat. As *Post* editor Ben Bradlee, Jason Robards coolly walks off with all his scenes (and an Oscar for Best Supporting Actor).

The film's lighting scheme, courtesy of ace director of photography Gordon Willis, counterpoints the brightly lit *Post* offices with the murky shadows of Washington's public buildings where the reporters ferret out the truth. The filmmakers focus on the story, resisting any temptation to "add the human angle" by digressing into its characters' personal lives; if these two have women in their lives the audience sees nothing of them, and the film is all the stronger for it. **PK**

👁 KEY SCENES

1 THE BREAK-IN
On June 17, 1972 police officers catch five men breaking into the Democrat campaign headquarters in the Watergate building in Washington, DC. The greatest corruption scandal ever to hit the United States is up and running.

4 DEATH THREATS
Fearing that his apartment is bugged, after a tip-off from Deep Throat, Woodward turns up some background classical music and he and Bernstein (Hoffman) proceed to type notes to each other.

2 DEEP THROAT
Woodward (Redford) meets his chief insider informant, Deep Throat (named after the notorious blue movie), in an underground garage at night. During the film, the character's face is shot in half shadow, metaphorically echoing the tenebrous, secretive nature of his role.

5 HAIL AND FAREWELL
On the TV screen Nixon is being sworn in for a second term, while in the background Woodward and Bernstein are busy typing the story that will bring him down. Nixon's resignation speech is heard at the end of the film, over a shot of a teletype relaying the news.

🕐 DIRECTOR PROFILE

1928–62
Alan J. Pakula was born in the Bronx. He joined MGM, then Paramount. His first film as producer, *Fear Strikes Out* (1957), was directed by Robert Mulligan (1925–2008).

1963–68
Pakula formed an independent production company with Mulligan. Their first production, *To Kill a Mockingbird* (1962), won three Oscars.

1969–81
He made his directorial debut with *The Sterile Cuckoo* (1969). The follow-up, *Klute* (1971), was a critical and box-office hit. He went on to direct intelligent, politically aware films, *The Parallax View* (1974), *All the President's Men,* and *Rollover* (1981).

1982–98
Sophie's Choice (1982) was Pakula's last big hit; his final film was *The Devil's Own* (1997). He was killed in a road accident in 1998.

3 THE GO-AHEAD
The duo gets the go-ahead to break the big story—that US Attorney-General John Mitchell is running the Republican "dirty tricks department." The *Post*'s offices were painstakingly reproduced, for the film, even down to the colors of the desks.

US DRAMA

The first critics and commentators to take popular cinema seriously tended to valorize a so-called golden age of the Hollywood studio system of the 1930s and 1940s, with 1939 somewhat arbitrarily tagged as "the movies' greatest year." That orthodoxy has been superseded by the argument that the 1970s were the greatest years of US cinema—although a simplification of the story holds that a domination of the industry by groundbreaking, important movies was ended by the rise of big, comic book–style blockbusters from Steven Spielberg (b. 1946) and George Lucas (b. 1944). At the start of the decade, a leading man was likely to be someone as complicated as Robert Eroica Dupea (Jack Nicholson) in *Five Easy Pieces* (1970); at the end, he was more likely to be as two-dimensional as Clark Kent (Christopher Reeve) in *Superman* (1978).

However, it should be remembered that, even before Spielberg's *Jaws* (1975, see p. 364) and Lucas's *Star Wars* (1977, see p. 366), the major studios were happy to ride any profitable trend. Critical and award-winning successes, such as *The French Connection* (1971), by William Friedkin (b. 1935), and *The Sting* (1973, opposite above), by George Roy Hill (1921–2002), inspired tough cop-car chase films and nostalgic male-buddy comedy dramas; *Freebie and the Bean* (1974) combined both these formulas and was one of a run of mismatched buddy cop pictures and television shows (black/white, male/female, gay/straight, human/alien) that would carry over into the 1980s and beyond. *Paper Moon* (1973, opposite below) offered another lopsided pairing, in the wiseacre young orphan (Tatum O'Neal) and the father figure con man (Ryan O'Neal).

1 George C. Scott salutes the US flag in the title role of *Patton*.

2 The poster for Depression-era, con trick movie *The Sting*. Stars Robert Redford and Paul Newman had teamed up four years previously in buddy movie *Butch Cassidy and the Sundance Kid*, also directed by George Roy Hill.

3 Real-life daughter and father Tatum and Ryan O'Neal in Peter Bogdanovich's *Paper Moon*. Tatum, who was nine at the time of filming, learned her lines from a tape recorder rather than a script.

KEY EVENTS

1970	1971	1972	1972	1973	1975
A wave of challenging movies—widely seen and acclaimed, even at the Oscars—starts with *Five Easy Pieces* and *MASH*.	*The Godfather* replaces *The Sound of Music* (1965) as the highest-grossing film of all time and also picks up the Best Picture Oscar.	*Deep Throat* makes pornography briefly fashionable and incredibly profitable.	*The King of Marvin Gardens* and *The Candidate* are released.	The standard opening day of a film moves from Wednesday to Friday, with greater emphasis on the now all-important "first weekend" takings.	*Jaws* (see p. 364), a summer release, bests *The Godfather*'s (see p. 342) box-office take and is widely credited as the first blockbuster.

Youth audiences responded well to the anarchic antics of Donald Sutherland and Elliot Gould in *MASH* (1970) by Robert Altman (1925–2006), the offbeat romantic team of Bud Cort and Ruth Gordon in *Harold and Maude* (1971) by Hal Ashby (1929–88), and Jack Nicholson's Oscar-winning turn as McMurphy in *One Flew Over the Cuckoo's Nest* (1975, see p. 356). More conservative audiences were equally enthusiastic about old-fashioned heroes, such as rogue cop Harry Callahan (Clint Eastwood) in *Dirty Harry* (1971), Sheriff Buford Pusser (Joe Don Baker) in *Walking Tall* (1973), and vigilante Paul Kersey (Charles Bronson) in *Death Wish* (1974). The divisions in society assessed from different angles in these films resonated in a series of movies about the culture clash within the United States, exacerbated by differing opinions over the Vietnam War. Paranoid Vietnam veteran Travis Bickle (Robert De Niro) in *Taxi Driver* (1976, see p. 358) by Martin Scorsese (b. 1942), who fails as a political assassin and instead becomes a vigilante hailed as a hero, represents one view of the war.

Bonnie and Clyde (1967, see p. 278), *The Graduate* (1967, see p. 284), *Night of the Living Dead* (1968), *Easy Rider* (1969), *The Wild Bunch* (1969), and *Medium Cool* (1969) were made in the late 1960s but it was in the 1970s that their commercial and artistic lessons were applied. The enormous flowering of creativity may have been down to the fact that audiences had made hits out of films that middle-aged or geriatric studio heads simply did not understand, so they greenlit projects that baffled them, on the grounds that maybe audiences would like something else as bewildering as the bone that turns into a spaceship in *2001: A Space Odyssey* (1968, see p. 292) or David Hemmings making photographic enlargements in *Blow-Up* (1966). This gave rise to a great many films that have become accepted classics: not only films that flopped on release but later became cult masterpieces, such as *Two-Lane Blacktop* (1971) or *Willy Wonka and the Chocolate Factory* (1971), but also instant-hit Oscar winners. Making *The Godfather* (1972, see p. 342) in the 1970s was not a particularly radical decision because gangster pictures had been a Hollywood mainstay since the 1930s. However, entrusting the project to an inexperienced director whose last studio project had been *Finian's Rainbow* (1968) just because he was Italian-American was a move born of inspired desperation.

One complaint heard from top US political and military brass after the loss of Vietnam was that—*The Green Berets* (1968) aside—Hollywood let the side down by not mobilizing the gung-ho propaganda machine the way it had in World War II. Instead of *Yankee Doodle Dandy* (1942), young people went to see *Woodstock* (1970); instead of Betty Grable showing her legs and Duke Wayne taking Iwo Jima, Jane Fonda supported the enemy and Donald Sutherland looked stoned. The best the movies could do for anyone's war effort was *Patton* (1970, opposite) by Franklin J. Schaffner (1920–89), which was either a celebration of a great US military hero or a subversive depiction of an Establishment figure as a dangerous madman, depending on your politics.

PAUL NEWMAN · ROBERT REDFORD
ROBERT SHAW

THE STING

...all it takes is a little Confidence.

DAVID S. WARD · GEORGE ROY HILL · TONY BILL, MICHAEL and JULIA PHILLIPS

1975	1976	1976	1977	1977	1979
Michael Ovitz founds Creative Artist Agency. Power shifts from studios to packagers, who put together and place projects with one of the majors.	Paramount is the first major studio to authorize the release of its film catalogue on video; VHS begins its ascendancy over the rival Betamax system.	Martin Scorsese's *Taxi Driver* (see p. 358)—often voted Best Film of the Decade—is released.	*Star Wars* makes more money than *Jaws*. A super-produced Flash Gordon serial, it encourages studios to prioritize action films over adult drama.	The Oscar for Best Picture goes not to George Lucas's *Star Wars* but to Woody Allen's *Annie Hall*.	Six directors, including Francis Ford Coppola and Martin Scorsese, are cited as the new power brokers in the book *The Movie Brats*.

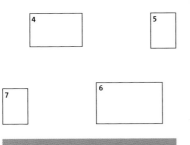

4 At the climax of *Rocky*, the "Italian stallion" (Sylvester Stallone) meets Apollo Creed (Carl Weathers) in a New Year's Day boxing match.

5 Ted (Dustin Hoffman) and his son Billy (Justin Henry), just before Billy runs off to spend the rest of the day with his estranged mother Joanna (Meryl Streep), in the moving *Kramer vs. Kramer*.

6 In perhaps the most enduring shot from *Manhattan*, Isaac (Woody Allen) and Mary (Diane Keaton) sit talking until daybreak close to New York's Queensboro Bridge.

7 The poster for Terrence Malick's second film, *Days of Heaven*. The film itself was influenced by the haunting quality of the work of painters such as Andrew Wyeth and Edward Hopper.

(It was Richard Nixon's favorite film, which appalled its makers.) There were even films, from *Alice's Restaurant* (1969) to *Big Wednesday* (1978), in which the heroes were draft dodgers and the US military were at best clowns and at worst the forces of evil. In its early days, Hollywood had been run by immigrant moguls who felt a desperate need to show off their patriotism, to the extent of supporting President Franklin Roosevelt, whose policies they privately hated and feared. They had enough stake in what was going on in Europe to take World War II so personally that films made between 1942 and 1946 seem more pro-government than actual government-sponsored propaganda. In the 1970s, major Hollywood studios backed *The Parallax View* (1974) and *All the President's Men* (1976, see p. 350), paranoid visions of government conspiracy. By the time Hollywood started making films about Vietnam, few were guaranteed to please John Wayne: witness *Coming Home* (1978), *The Deer Hunter* (1978), and *Apocalypse Now* (1979, see p. 394).

It may be that the most important US filmmaker of the decade was a man who had directed nearly all his films before 1971 (after which he mainly produced exploitation quickies): Roger Corman (b. 1926). While the studios were still trying to follow up *The Sound of Music* (1965), Corman was giving jobs to Monte Hellman (b. 1932), Robert Towne (b. 1934), Paul Bartel (1938–2000), Francis Ford Coppola (b. 1939), Peter Bogdanovich (b. 1939), Jonathan Demme (b. 1944), Joe Dante (b. 1946), Martin Scorsese, Robert De Niro, and Jack Nicholson. Without Corman's approach—keep the camera moving, include nudity, leaven clichés with humor, use music that is not yet in fashion (i.e., cheap) but soon will be, and be sure there is a smidgen of social comment for the college crowd— there would not have existed *American Graffiti* (1973), *Mean Streets* (1973), *The Conversation* (1974, see p. 348), *Chinatown* (1974, see p. 344), or *Shampoo* (1975).

Corman's business plan also impressed other independents working in genre movies away from studio interference. Seventies drive-ins and college cinemas were full of crazes and movies that embraced multifarious genres. There were black action films (*Shaft*, 1971; *Blacula*, 1972), soft and hardcore sex (*The Student Nurses*, 1970; *Deep Throat*, 1972) and road movies (*Electra Glide in Blue*, 1973; *Badlands*, 1973). John Carpenter (b. 1948) created spare genre pictures (*Dark Star*, 1974; *Assault on Precinct 13*, 1976). Clint Eastwood (b. 1930) transformed himself from star to star-director (*Play Misty for Me*, 1971; *The Outlaw Josey Wales*, 1976). Terrence Malick crafted experimental, symbolic narratives (*Days of Heaven*, 1978, left). Then there were the "early, funny movies" of Woody Allen (b. 1935), which led to *Annie Hall* (1977)—the point when he decided just being funny was not enough—and romantic comedy-cum-love letter to New York *Manhattan* (1979, below). There was still room for an intense, emotive drama such as *Kramer vs. Kramer* (1979, right)—witness its five Academy Awards.

From a collection of young filmmakers came the blockbuster summer event movie—*Jaws*. The film was not without precedent: Hollywood at first viewed Spielberg's shark movie simply as a continuation of the disaster cycle of *The Poseidon Adventure* (1972) or *The Towering Inferno* (1974, see p. 362). It was only when *Jaws* became as successful as *The Godfather* that anyone saw how significant the film was, and viewed it as a "high concept" horror picture. Another significant, influential studio hit in this field was *Westworld* (1973). Thereafter, studio resources were allotted to directors such as Spielberg, Lucas, Brian De Palma (b. 1940), John Milius (b. 1944), John Landis (b. 1950), and even their Italian godfather Francis Ford Coppola. It has been argued that *Star Wars* ended the run of creativity with a detour into commercially exploitable childishness, but Lucas was seeking a sense of wonder as genuinely as Nicolas Roeg (b. 1928) in *The Man Who Fell to Earth* (1976) or Spielberg in *Close Encounters of the Third Kind* (1977). *Star Wars* is even in tune with the politics of the era: its heroes are bad-hair-day rebels against established order, and the Grand Moff Tarkin and Darth Vader could easily stand in for President Nixon and Lieutenant Calley.

It may be that the long-term effects of *Star Wars* brought about the closing down of the opportunities that benefited 1970s Hollywood. From *Jaws* and *Star Wars*—along with films from John Carpenter, Walter Hill (b. 1942), and others— came a sense of the rediscovery of classic Hollywood modes, which prompted US filmmakers to draw as much on John Ford (1894–1973), Howard Hawks (1896–1977), and Alfred Hitchcock (1899–1980) as Michelangelo Antonioni (1912–2007), Ingmar Bergman (1918–2007), and Jean-Luc Godard (b. 1930). It is possible to see zero-to-hero boxing movie *Rocky*, (1976, opposite above) in this light too, although the original film proved more intriguing than its many sequels. This brought back an energy and sense of fun to a cinema that had been in peril of generating too many slow, joyless films, and attracted a huge audience that had, by and large, stayed away from pictures later to be viewed as significant. **KN**

One Flew Over the Cuckoo's Nest 1975

MILOŠ FORMAN b. 1932

▲ McMurphy is restrained. Filming took place at the Oregon State Hospital in Salem, the setting of Kesey's source novel.

▼ Nicholson's work gained him an Oscar.

Ken Kesey's novel, an allegory of repression and rebellion set in a 1960s mental hospital, was adapted by Miloš Forman into a comedy drama with an unassuming, near-documentary look. Jack Nicholson excels in his role as antihero Randle P. McMurphy, who unwisely cons his way out of prison into a mental institution without realizing he has switched from serving a sentence with a release date to being committed until adjudged sane by the same people he is challenging on a daily basis. McMurphy is smug in his belief that he has duped the authorities into sending him to the asylum but it becomes apparent that he really is cracking up, for only a madman would dare to clash with forces who can legally electrocute and lobotomize him. Louise Fletcher's soft-spoken sadist Nurse Ratched represents the worst type of matronly authoritarianism and opposes Randle at every turn. On its release, the film seemed the story of a heroic rebel against an oppressive system; actually, McMurphy is, in his cooler way, on as much of a power trip as his archenemy, although his example does spur defiance from some inmates.

Forman cast unknown, funny-looking actors to mingle with real mental patients, and many who were unknown at the time went on to become prolific character actors, including Danny DeVito, Christopher Lloyd, and Brad Dourif. Unlike many Best Picture Oscar winners, the film deals with profound subject matter without seeming self-important: Forman's approach and the all-around great acting make it play as a small character story as well as a big statement about the human condition. **KN**

👁 KEY SCENES

1 GROUP THERAPY
McMurphy incites the other patients to resist the tyrannical regime of Nurse Ratched, by using the group therapy sessions—Ratched's subtle method of humiliating the inmates by getting them to turn on each other—to voice complaints and show unity.

2 ROAD TRIP
McMurphy takes his fellow inmates out on a chaotic, morale-boosting sea fishing trip that does more for their mental health than any of the treatment offered in the institution. This scene is in sharp relief to all the others, which were filmed at the hospital.

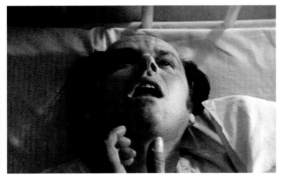

3 MERCY KILLING
Fellow inmate Chief Bromden (Will Sampson) discovers that McMurphy has been lobotomized. Not wanting to let him live in such a diminished state, the Chief smothers him with a pillow. McMurphy gives the Chief the courage to attempt an escape.

4 FREEDOM
The Chief, carrying out the escape plan masterminded by McMurphy, pulls out a hydrotherapy console, tosses it through a window, climbs through it, and runs off into the distance. The broken window later causes the other patients to celebrate.

🕐 DIRECTOR PROFILE

1932–70
Miloš Forman was born Jan Tomas Forman in Cáslav, Czechoslovakia. Both his parents died while in the Nazi concentration camp at Auschwitz. He studied at the School of Cinema in Prague before directing a series of bittersweet comedy dramas with a satirical, antiauthoritarian edge: *Konkurs* (*Talent Competition*, 1964), *Cerný Petr* (*Peter and Pavla*, 1964), *Lásky jedné plavovlásky* (*Loves of a Blonde*, 1965), and *Horí, má panenko* (*The Firemen's Ball*, 1967). After the Prague Spring of 1968, Forman went into exile in New York, where he later was appointed professor of film studies at Columbia University.

1971–90
He directed films exploring the US experience with the same degree of critical engagement he had brought to the films he made under Communism: *Taking Off* (1971), *One Flew Over the Cuckoo's Nest*—for which he won an Oscar for direction, one of five Academy Awards the film picked up—*Hair* (1979), and *Ragtime* (1981). In 1977 Forman became a naturalized citizen of the United States. He made international "prestige" pictures, including *Amadeus* (1984)—which surpassed the success of *One Flew Over the Cuckoo's Nest*, gaining a total of eight Oscars—and *Valmont* (1989) among them. Forman remains one of only three directors alive to have won two Best Picture Academy Awards, the others being Francis Ford Coppola and Clint Eastwood.

1991–2006
Forman received another Academy Award nomination for Best Director for *The People vs. Larry Flynt* (1996) and won a Golden Globe. Other films during this period include *Goya's Ghosts* (2006) and *Man on the Moon* (1999), the latter a biopic of US comedian Andy Kaufman. In 2000 Forman costarred with Edward Norton in his directorial debut *Keeping the Faith*.

2007–present
In 2009 he made his first film back in the Czech Republic, *Dobre placená procházka* (*A Walk Worthwhile*).

Taxi Driver 1976
MARTIN SCORSESE b. 1942

▲ "Here is a man who would not take it anymore." Travis Bickle practices his gunplay.

▼ The antihero stands alone in the city.

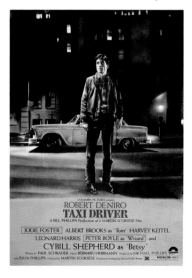

Of all the "movie brats" associated with the New Hollywood of the 1970s, Martin Scorsese was arguably the most challenging. While Francis Ford Coppola enhanced the mainstream, and Steven Spielberg and George Lucas rebranded it, Scorsese courageously strode off into his own territory. *Mean Streets* (1973) had already introduced many of the director's traits: his vibrant use of New York locations; a fluid, energetic visual style; a fascination with criminal subculture and disturbed male protagonists; and graphic violence. In *Taxi Driver* these were accompanied by a topical and incendiary script, written by a troubled Paul Schrader in just ten days, to "exorcize the evil I felt within me."

Robert De Niro is mesmerizing as Travis Bickle, the disturbed Vietnam veteran turned cabbie, whose search for a purpose segues from political assassination to the "salvation" of a teenage prostitute (played by thirteen-year-old Jodie Foster). The action is seen almost entirely from Travis's perspective, including a daringly expletive-riddled voice-over as his taxi glides through the rain and steam of Manhattan's streets. De Niro's nuanced character study is complemented by Bernard Herrmann's last great score (completed barely hours before the composer died)—its abrupt shifts between jazzy melancholy and the foreboding combination of snare drum and horns suggest the potential for violence that underpins Travis's loneliness and romantic self-delusion.

Taxi Driver was nominated for four Oscars and won the Palme d'Or in Cannes. In 1981, John Hinckley Jr. infamously cited his obsession with the film—and Foster in particular—as a catalyst for his attempted assassination of Ronald Reagan. **DM**

KEY SCENES

1 TRAVIS'S WORLDVIEW
Vietnam veteran Travis Bickle, in New York after an honorable discharge, starts work as a taxi driver. As he drives his cab through Manhattan's streets, his voice-over reveals his loathing for what he sees: "Some time a real rain will come and wash away all the scum."

2 BAD DATE
Travis takes Betsy (Cybill Shepherd) on a disastrous date, his choice of a Swedish porn movie revealing his naiveté and inexperience of social exchange. Just as the date had offered a slim hope of social integration, Betsy's rejection is the fuse that ignites his rage.

3 "YOU TALKING TO ME?"
Planning his assassination of presidential candidate Charles Palantine, Bickle conducts an imaginary conversation in front of a mirror, ending with his drawing a gun. Improvised by De Niro, the scene reflects his character's isolation and longing for significance.

4 BLOODBATH
After his failed attempt to kill Palantine, Bickle transfers his sense of purpose to the child prostitute Iris. Driving to the hotel where she works, he shoots dead her pimp, her current client, and the hotel manager. The police enter the blood-spattered crime scene.

DIRECTOR PROFILE

1942–72
Martin Scorsese was born in New York City. He graduated from NYU's film school, gaining attention with his short films, including *It's Not Just You, Murray!* (1964). He directed his first feature, *I Call First* (1967), was assistant director and coeditor on *Woodstock* (1970), and directed *Boxcar Bertha* (1972) for exploitation movie producer Roger Corman.

1973–82
Forging one of cinema's most acclaimed director-actor partnerships, Scorsese and Robert De Niro made the first of eight films together: *Mean Streets* (1973). In 1980 they made *Raging Bull*, a biopic of boxer Jake La Motta, featuring lush black-and-white photography and a tour de force in method acting from De Niro. Scorsese also made *New York, New York* (1977), a musical starring Liza Minnelli and De Niro, and *The Last Waltz* (1978), a film of The Band's farewell concert.

1983–89
Scorsese found the rest of the decade less sympathetic to originality. Now well regarded, *The King of Comedy* (1982) flopped. *The Last Temptation of Christ* (1988) was critically well received but marred by controversy, drawing vehement protests from religious groups and being banned in some countries.

1990–2001
A reunion with De Niro produced the consummate Mafia movie *Goodfellas* (1990), a lurid remake of *Cape Fear* (1991), and *Casino* (1995). In 1990, the director established The Film Foundation, dedicated to film preservation. He directed the beautiful *Kundun* in 1997, a biopic of the Dalai Lama.

2002–present
Gangs of New York (2002) signaled a new collaboration with Leonardo DiCaprio, which includes *The Aviator* (2004) and *The Departed* (2006), the latter gaining Scorsese a belated Oscar. The Grammy-winning *No Direction Home* (2005) and *Shine a Light* (2008) continued his career-long involvement with music documentary, celebrating the work of Bob Dylan and The Rolling Stones respectively.

THE HOLLYWOOD BLOCKBUSTER

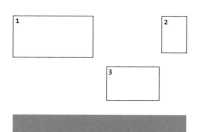

1 A climactic scene from Steven Spielberg's *Close Encounters of the Third Kind*.

2 The poster for *The Poseidon Adventure* sums up this watery disaster movie— "Hell, Upside Down."

3 Christopher Reeve takes to the skies in *Superman*. "You'll believe a man can fly" boasted the tagline for the film.

In the 1970s, as the world got smaller through increased communication and travel, Hollywood conversely made it larger than life. The arrival of the modern blockbuster was a reminder that cinema can be the ultimate form of escapism as well as an expressive art form. The blockbuster is perhaps best defined as a film that uses a narrow set of generic parameters—science fiction, horror, comedy, fantasy, disaster, or action—to attract the largest possible audience. Yet the concept behind the blockbuster is also important. What if your best friend is an alien (*ET: The Extra-Terrestrial*, 1982)? What happens when a commercial airplane is caught in a snowstorm with a bomb on board (*Airport*, 1970)? These ideas were compelling enough to persuade Hollywood producers to invest in them and for big audiences to pay to see them.

   The blockbuster's huge scale and technical skills typically invite awe. The mothership sequence in *Close Encounters of the Third Kind* (1977, above) is wondrous in the same way that movies such as *The Poseidon Adventure* (1972, opposite above) are thrilling. Hollywood blockbusters merge spectacle with the real world. Movies such as *The Towering Inferno* (1974, see p. 362) filter potential real-world catastrophes through a Hollywood lens. This is life but on a grand, glossy, fantastical scale. The blockbuster cranks up the drama with bigger, better sound and special effects. These add to the audience's sense of terror or wonder as good triumphs over evil or humanity survives against the odds.

KEY EVENTS

1970	1972	1975	1978	1980	1980
Airport mixes soap, catastrophe, and terrorism with a bomb-on-the-plane plot. *Airport 1975* (1974) and *Airport '79: The Concorde* (1979) follow.	Irwin Allen (1916–91) produces and codirects *The Poseidon Adventure*, and becomes the "master of disaster" for the 1970s.	The first "event" movie, *Jaws* (see p. 364) sets the standard for the modern blockbuster.	*Superman* gives birth to the superhero movie. *Jaws 2* is the first in a wave of inferior sequels to Steven Spielberg's classic of 1975.	*Airplane!* spoofs the disaster movie. Such ridicule prompts filmmakers to abandon the format. A lesser sequel appears two years later.	*The Empire Strikes Back* and *Superman II* prove that a good sequel can also hit big.

Jaws (1975, see p. 364) is the first film that fully fits the description of Hollywood blockbuster and it was also an experiment in the wide release. Its success partly reflected a change in distribution and marketing practices. Since the early days of cinema, films had been distributed city by city: from Los Angeles and New York, then out to smaller towns. Moviegoers across the United States saw Jaws at the same time, making it a national word-of-mouth event.

With Star Wars (1977, see p. 366) the balance between great character moments and pure excitement began to shift. Characters such as Han Solo (Harrison Ford) and Obi-Wan Kenobi (Alec Guinness) are still important—the film would not work if the audience did not care about the figures on the screen—but they are never allowed to stand in the way of the thrills. Steven Spielberg (b. 1946) brought things back down to Earth with a perfect blend of emotional truth and epic vision in Close Encounters of the Third Kind, but the character-focused blockbuster he championed became increasingly sidelined.

The Superman series (below) is the first example of a studio planning beyond a single installment. Large parts of the sequel were made concurrently with the first film's production. Both movies were extremely successful. Audiences still responded to good sci-fi, as proven by the success of Alien (1979) and Star Wars sequel The Empire Strikes Back (1980). It was a hard formula to repeat, however: several attempts to jump on the Star Wars bandwagon—notably Star Trek: The Motion Picture (1979)—failed. Spielberg had a golden touch but for every smash such as Ghostbusters (1984) there is a flop. The studios know, however, that one big hit will pay for all the disappointed hopefuls. And for better or worse, Hollywood's affair with the blockbuster shows no sign of abating. **TH**

1982	1983	1984	1984	1985	1989
Despite its modest scale, *ET: The Extra-Terrestrial* shatters box-office records and becomes the most successful film of its time.	*Return of the Jedi* completes the *Star Wars* (see p. 366) trilogy. *The Right Stuff* tries to fuse sci-fi and popular history—and flops at the box office.	Ivan Reitman (b. 1946) directs *Ghostbusters*. It fuses comedy and special effects to great success.	The Spielberg-produced black comedy *Gremlins* is released to mixed reviews but pulls in crowds at the box office.	*Back to the Future* defines cozy Reagan-era blockbuster cinema. The more infantile likes of *The Goonies* and *Return to Oz* do not find favor.	*Batman* updates the superhero blockbuster—and becomes the first movie to bank $100 million in its opening ten days.

The Towering Inferno 1974

IRWIN ALLEN 1916 – 91, JOHN GUILLERMIN b. 1925

▲ Newman faces the flames. McQueen had been approached for Newman's role, but opted for that of the fire chief.

▼ The theatrical release poster: a head-to-head between two Hollywood A-listers.

The acme of the disaster movie genre, *The Towering Inferno* was released following the fires that took place at the Andraus and Joelma Buildings in São Paulo, Brazil, events that inspired the novels behind the movie. As the makers of disaster movies in the 1970s were competing to outdo one another, Irwin Allen combined projects from two studios — Warner Bros. and Twentieth Century Fox — which were developing films based on books with similar premises: Richard Martin Stern's *The Tower* and Frank M. Robinson and Thomas N. Scortia's *The Glass Inferno*. With a complicated billing and plenty of script rewrites to balance the alpha-male roles of superstars Paul Newman (the architect who built the tallest building in the world) and Steve McQueen (the fire chief who has to cope with the fire that breaks out), the resulting film is every inch a machine-made picture. John Guillermin directed the arguments and soap operas — most of the trouble is down to developer William Holden's no-good, cost-cutting son-in-law (Richard Chamberlain), who used inferior materials on the faulty wiring — while Allen took charge of the action scenes, which predominate as the blaze spreads.

The film seems to suggest that all the well-dressed, absurdly wealthy partygoers deserve to suffer horrible fates while the firemen (to whom the film is dedicated) and rescue workers count the cost. However, the film is still capable of seducing even the most resistant viewer with its unashamed heroes and flair for cunningly contrived suspense scenes. *The Towering Inferno* is undeniably clichéd yet overwhelmingly entertaining. **KN**

1 GIRL ON FIRE

Lorrie (Susan Flannery), a personal assistant who is having an affair with publicity director Bigelow (Robert Wagner), dramatically catches fire and jumps out of the window. In total, the movie used nearly eighty stunt coordinators and stand-ins for the stars.

4 CAT RESCUED BY O.J.

Security chief Harry Jernigan (O.J. Simpson) tells con man Harlee Claiborne (Fred Astaire) that his love interest Liselotte (Jennifer Jones) has died after falling from the scenic elevator. He has, however, saved her cat, Elkie, whom he reverentially hands over.

2 CHILD RESCUED

Architect Doug Roberts (Newman) negotiates several storys of twisted metal that used to be a staircase before the gas explosion, with a cute but terrified little girl clinging to his neck. Newman carried out most of his own stunts in the film.

5 AND THE MORAL IS . . .

Exhausted, O'Hallorhan states that they are lucky that more people did not die. He warns that a worse catastrophe is possible, and the architect and fire chief agree that from now on they should consult with each other to avoid similar disasters.

🕐 PRODUCER — DIRECTOR PROFILE

1916–59

Irwin Allen was born in New York City. He began his career with the Oscar-winning documentary *The Sea Around Us* (1953), then specialized in cut-rate spectacles with odd premises (*The Story of Mankind*, 1957; *The Big Circus*, 1959).

1960–71

Allen carried his love of effects first into ramshackle sci-fi films *The Lost World* (1960) and *Voyage to the Bottom of the Sea* (1961), then into a run of popular, if schlocky, television series including *Lost in Space*, *The Time Tunnel*, and *Land of the Giants*.

1972–91

The Poseidon Adventure (1972) and *The Towering Inferno* (1974) rode the disaster wave. The formula soon palled, although three big losers have since attracted a camp following: *The Swarm* (1978), *Beyond the Poseidon Adventure* (1979), and *When Time Ran Out* (1980). Allen died from a heart attack in 1991.

3 FIREMAN RESCUED

Fire chief O'Hallorhan (McQueen) hangs on to a dangling comrade during a helicopter rescue of women and children trapped in a scenic elevator. He finally has to let the man drop, but by then they are safely near the ground and there is a blanket to catch him.

Jaws 1975
STEVEN SPIELBERG b. 1946

▲ A brief but memorable appearance from Chrissie (Susan Backlinie) opens the film.

▼ The iconic poster, by Tony Seiniger.

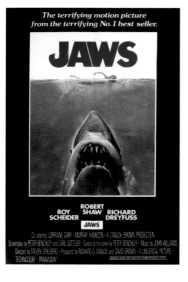

The terrifying motion picture from the terrifying No.1 best seller.

JAWS

ROY SCHEIDER · ROBERT SHAW · RICHARD DREYFUSS

JAWS

Co-starring LORRAINE GARY · MURRAY HAMILTON · A ZANUCK-BROWN PRODUCTION Screenplay by PETER BENCHLEY and CARL GOTTLIEB · Based on the novel by PETER BENCHLEY · Music by JOHN WILLIAMS Directed by STEVEN SPIELBERG · Produced by RICHARD D. ZANUCK and DAVID BROWN · A UNIVERSAL PICTURE · TECHNICOLOR® PANAVISION®

The film that invented the "summer blockbuster"—and the first to break the famed $100 million mark at the box office—was a genuine phenomenon. In the summer of 1975, everyone was talking about *Jaws*. The movie destroyed the swimming habits of a generation and propelled the career of a gifted young director into the stratosphere.

The shoot was infamously troubled, prolonged by the difficulties of working at sea and the malfunctions of the mechanical shark. Yet *Jaws* is a classic piece of storytelling, combining horror, adventure, and the character-driven tale of an outsider hero who must combat the community and his own fear of water. The narrative concerns the disruption of lives and livelihoods on the island resort of Amity, after a great white shark sets up camp in its waters. After it takes a bite out of the Fourth of July, police chief Martin Brody (Roy Scheider) sets out to sea on board the *Orca*, with its ferocious Captain Quint (Robert Shaw) and the oceanographer Matt Hooper (Richard Dreyfuss), to kill Amity's tormentor.

Jaws held early signs of Spielberg's pure cinematic instinct, from the use of the animal's point of view to heighten suspense, to the "forward-tracking, zoom out" shot when Brody realizes it has eaten a boy in front of his eyes. However, the film's success would be unthinkable without John Williams's soundtrack, founded on an ominous two-note motif for the shark, Verna Fields's editing, and the actors' performances. Robert Shaw's Ahab-like fisherman is the most memorable, although it was a Roy Scheider improvisation that gave *Jaws* its best line: "You're gonna need a bigger boat." **DM**

👁 KEY SCENES

1 NIGHT FEEDING
Chrissie leaves a beach party with a boy for a moonlight swim. He fumbles with his clothes while she heads out to sea. Suddenly she is tugged beneath the water, then dragged across the surface, screaming, before being pulled under. A heart-stopping opening.

2 THE FOURTH OF JULY
Amity's mayor opens the beaches for the Fourth of July holiday. There is a false alarm, panicking hundreds of swimmers. Meanwhile, the shark enters the "pond" where Brody's son Michael and his friends are boating. The shark kills a man who tries to help them.

3 THE *INDIANAPOLIS*
Quint relates his formative experience in World War II, when the USS *Indianapolis* was torpedoed and sunk. He describes days spent in the water, as sharks feasted on his shipmates. It is Spielberg's favorite scene; the author of its final draft is debated.

4 KILLING THE SHARK
Brody is alone on the sinking boat as the shark, having killed Quint, attacks again. He throws an air tank into its mouth, then climbs onto the mast with a rifle and fires at the tank. It explodes, blowing the animal to pieces. Hooper surfaces and the two men swim to shore.

🕐 DIRECTOR PROFILE

1946–69
Steven Spielberg was born in 1946. After failing to get into the University of Southern California, he enrolled at Long Beach's California State University. He worked as an unpaid intern at Universal Studios. He directed his first short film *Amblin'* in 1968. Its success led to a seven-year contract with Universal.

1970–74
He directed for US TV, including episodes of *Marcus Welby, MD* and *Columbo*, but most significantly the TV movie *Duel* (1971). He made his cinema debut with *The Sugarland Express* (1974).

1975–82
After *Jaws*, Spielberg consolidated his reputation with a pair of sci-fi classics—*Close Encounters of the Third Kind* (1977) and *ET: The Extra-Terrestrial* (1982). *Raiders of the Lost Ark* (1981), coproduced by George Lucas (b. 1944), was the first of a successful franchise. In 1981 Spielberg founded production company Amblin Entertainment.

1983–92
A relatively dry period for Spielberg saw *Indiana Jones* sequels and poorly received attempts at serious fare, such as *The Color Purple* (1985). He enjoyed commercial success as producer of *Back to the Future* (1985) and *Who Framed Roger Rabbit* (1988).

1993
While *Jurassic Park* spearheaded the use of CGI and made $900 million, Holocaust drama *Schindler's List* picked up seven Academy Awards, including Best Picture and Spielberg's first for Best Director.

1994–present
Spielberg established the Shoah Foundation, to record video testimonies of Holocaust survivors, and cofounded a new Hollywood studio, DreamWorks. *Saving Private Ryan* (1998) saw him pick up another Oscar for Best Director. He continued to alternate sci-fi and adventure with character-driven drama: *Minority Report* and *Catch Me If You Can* (both 2002), *War of the Worlds* and *Munich* (both 2005).

Star Wars 1977
GEORGE LUCAS b. 1944

▲ An X-fighter streaks along the surface of the Death Star in the finale of *Star Wars*.

▼ Admirably, this poster for *Star Wars* manages to cram in all the main characters.

Having preserved the rock 'n' roll and car culture of his adolescence in *American Graffiti* (1973), George Lucas turned to space adventure serials such as Flash Gordon and Buck Rogers for this confection, a seemingly throwaway picture that permanently changed the shape of the industry. Unable to secure the rights to *Flash Gordon*, Lucas cobbled together his own universe, which he would later rationalize into a Wagnerian epic. His inspiration was to make a film on the scale of something produced by David O. Selznick or directed by David Lean (1908–91), but with content they would barely recognize as children's entertainment: the monsters, spaceships, princesses, fights, and escapes found in the dozens of film serials turned out as fodder in Hollywood's golden age.

The feathery haircuts and wide-eyed stares of Mark Hamill and Harrison Ford suggest that the galactic rebels here are just a few years on from the drag racers of *American Graffiti*, with grown-ups Alec Guinness and Peter Cushing providing a touch of class, and funny robots pitched for children in the audience. As a nostalgic work, the script is glued together from the space adventure serials, *Sinbad* movies, samurai epics, Westerns, and World War II aviation films of Lucas's childhood. In this retro patchwork approach, the space vehicles are stand-ins for airplanes or battleships rather than proper rockets. Only John Williams's orchestral score is straight from golden-era Hollywood—the rest of the film is filtered through 1970s sensibilities, in everything from design to religion and politics to fashion. **KN**

KEY SCENES

1 THE OPENING CRAWL
After the serial-style story-so-far summation, the scene cuts to a star field and a huge spaceship looms up at the top of the screen—but it is only the forerunner of the even bigger Imperial cruiser that proceeds majestically to glide into view.

2 THE YEARNING FARM BOY
Luke (Hamill) returns to his uncle's farm. He is dissatisfied with his daily life and senses that there is a bigger universe out there as he looks up at the twin dimming suns and seems to hear an echo of John Williams's stirring theme.

3 THE HOLOGRAM
After Luke and his uncle buy R2-D2 and C-3PO from a trader, the young man begins to clean R2-D2. By accident, he activates a hologram of Princess Leia (Carrie Fisher), which conveys a desperate plea: "Help me, Obi-Wan Kenobi—you're my only hope."

4 THE SHOOTING OF GREEDO
In the Mos Eisley Cantina a bounty hunter called Greedo catches up with Han Solo (Ford), who owes money to Jabba the Hutt. Greedo plans to shoot the space pilot, but Han Solo retaliates. The question of who shot first has been much debated over the years.

5 LIGHTSABER DUEL
Obi-Wan Kenobi (Guinness) and his renegade pupil Darth Vader (Dave Prowse, voiced by James Earl Jones) meet in a final showdown in the bowels of the Death Star. Vader appears to triumph, but Obi-Wan becomes one with the pan-universal energy known as the Force.

6 "USE THE FORCE, LUKE"
As he strafes the Death Star in his fighter, Luke hears the words of his departed mentor and trusts his mystic instincts to guide his aim—the upshot is that the security is circumvented and the Empire's deadly weapon destroyed. It is a good time for the Rebellion.

AUSTRALIAN NEW WAVE

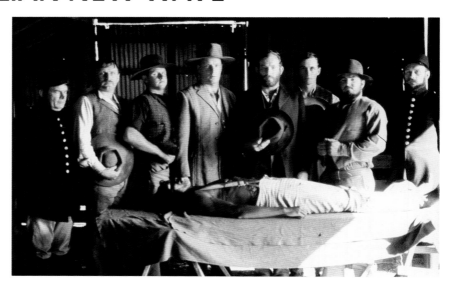

1 The exploited half-Aborigine Jimmie Blacksmith lies dead, having taken his violent revenge on white society.

2 A top-grossing film at the box office, *Mad Max* spawned two sequels and opened up the international market to Australian New Wave cinema.

3 *Crocodile Dundee* gave Aussie "Ocker" comic Paul Hogan his first acting role and earned him a Golden Globe.

ustralian cinema in the 1970s and early 1980s was an industry of two clearly separated halves. On one side, the prestige cinema of Fred Schepisi (b. 1939), Peter Weir (b. 1944), and Gillian Armstrong (b. 1950) told distinctively Australian stories: ornate, lovingly designed, rich with artistic integrity and quiet grace. On the other, the country's booming B-movie industry offered a parade of crude sex comedies, smash-and-grab action-adventures and inventive, bloody horror, collectively known as "Ozploitation."

In the late 1960s, aside from a few historical dramas, largely funded from abroad, the Australian film industry had produced very little cinema of its own. However, in the early 1970s a confluence of events changed all that. A new artistic counterculture was emerging, the increasingly popular homegrown television industry had been training directors, actors, and producers, and a series of government initiatives and tax loopholes meant that making movies was a far more economically attractive prospect. The result was a creative surge in the country's cinema, dubbed the "Australian New Wave" by the media.

The first successes were "Ocker" comedies, films about suburban living and sexual frustration that reflected the new cultural freedom, while simultaneously celebrating and mocking ideas of Australian masculinity and culture. Interestingly, the most important figure of the period, Peter Weir, began his career with a film that slotted neatly into neither the B movie nor the prestige group: *The Cars That Ate Paris* (1974) is an exploitation movie, but one almost entirely lacking in sex or gore, and clearly influenced by European

KEY EVENTS

1971	1971	1972	1974	1975	1976
Walkabout, directed by Nicolas Roeg (b. 1928), depicts the landscape of the Australian outback as a place of mystery and threat.	Low-budget sex comedy *Stork* becomes the country's first major homegrown hit.	The South Australian Film Commission is set up. Bruce Beresford (b. 1940) returns to Australia to direct the satirical *The Adventures of Barry Mackenzie*.	Peter Weir's *The Cars That Ate Paris* reveals a European influence. Biker drama *Stone* is a violent, macho take on the US B movie.	The Australian Film Commission is set up. Ken Hannam (1929–2004) adds to the Australian film renaissance with *Sunday Too Far Away*.	Bruce Beresford's *Don's Party* is released. Based on David Williamson's play of the same name, the story centers on the Australian federal election of 1969.

art-house cinema. His next film, *Picnic at Hanging Rock* (1975, see p. 370), however, came to define everything high-quality Australian cinema stood for: breathtaking landscapes, painstakingly re-created period settings, beauty, stillness, and a sense of lurking dread. The film both celebrates and questions aspects of Australian culture, specifically the still-powerful influence of the British, the unspoken dependence on class systems, and an Aboriginal culture that had been trampled underfoot by colonialism.

Taking their cue from *Picnic at Hanging Rock*, Australia's prestige filmmakers used cinema to further explore aspects of the country's colonial past. Fred Schepisi's *The Chant of Jimmie Blacksmith* (1978, opposite) evoked the wildness of the country's savage birth, portraying the forces of colonial progression as murderous thugs waging a war for dominance and tearing the native Aboriginal population apart in the process. Meanwhile, Gillian Armstrong's *My Brilliant Career* (1979, see p. 372) and Weir's *Gallipoli* (1981) investigated the country's attempts to survive the decline of the British Empire.

The B-movie industry was also finding its feet. Biker flick *Stone* (1974) took the template of producer Roger Corman's rebellious motorcycle epics and added explicit sex, violence, and a witty awareness of Australian identity, paving the way for the country's biggest worldwide smash, *Mad Max* (1979, right). The latter also introduced a new international star: Mel Gibson had the looks and rugged demeanor of a classic movie icon, but with an added toughness and emotional instability. His hugely successful decision to abandon Australia for Hollywood set a precedent for countless actors and directors. Aussie B movies often outshone their better funded US counterparts. The work of US-born screenwriter Everett De Roche in films such as eco-satire *The Long Weekend* (1978) fused low-budget B-movie thrills with witty dialogue and smart ideas about psychology, ecology, and landscape, filtered through an affectionate outsider's perspective on his adopted homeland.

Both the prestige and B-movie strands of Australian cinema began to falter in the mid-1980s, as government funding dried up and many key directors, such as Peter Weir, headed for Hollywood. (Fred Schepisi had been so disillusioned by the poor domestic reception for *The Chant of Jimmie Blacksmith* that he left Australia and did not return to make a film there for ten years.)

Australia's filmmaking culture is now little different from that of any small Western country: a wealth of modest dramatic pictures, a steady stream of talented writers, actors, and directors with their sights set on Hollywood and the occasional global smash, such as *Crocodile Dundee* (1986, right). Starring and written by the comedian Paul Hogan, *Crocodile Dundee* (and its sequel) set out to appeal to a mainstream US audience but struck a chord internationally. While it seems unlikely that filmmakers will recapture the spirit of boldness and experimentalism that defined the 1970s and 1980s, Australian cinema remains a byword for intelligent, well-crafted popular movies. **TH**

Picnic at Hanging Rock 1975

PETER WEIR b. 1944

▲ The rock looms over Miranda and her coterie just before their disappearance.

▼ The poster reflects the film's period feel.

Joan Lindsay's novel *Picnic at Hanging Rock* poses as reportage, to get around the inevitable complaint that a mystery with no solution is unsatisfying. This is carried over into Peter Weir's oneiric film adaptation, which opens with a caption giving dates and places in an effort to convince the audience that this is a true story.

It is Valentine's Day 1900, in the middle of an antipodean summer. The corseted, white-dressed nymphets of Mrs. Appleyard's School for Young Ladies are allowed an excursion to the local volcanic landmark—although the formidable headmistress (Rachel Roberts) keeps back an orphan, Sara (Margaret Nelson), against whom she has a grudge. Led by "Botticelli angel" Miranda (Anne Lambert), a quartet of girls break away to climb higher—but only one, Edith (Christine Schuler), dumpier and more earthly than her friends, returns. A spinster teacher disappears too, and all the forces of order—police, teachers, even an Aborigine tracker—fail to find the girls, until an English youth (Dominic Guard) finds Irma (Karen Robson), who has no memory of what happened but becomes a scapegoat for her classmates. Meanwhile, Sara—a passionate devotee of Miranda—suffers more ("It's for her terrible posture," a mistress shrieks when she is found tied to a board) and gothic shadows close over the school.

With Weir's *The Cars That Ate Paris* (1974) and *The Last Wave* (1977), the film forms a triptych about the mystic, primal haunting of a young country. It is also a study in seething eroticism, among repressed teachers and lighter-than-air pupils, which retains its mesmeric appeal decades on. **KN**

KEY SCENES

1 HANGING ROCK

In the opening scene Hanging Rock emerges fantastically out of the mists. The first words the audience hears are poet Edgar Allan Poe's "All that we see or seem / Is but a dream within a dream." Hanging Rock is a real geological formation northwest of Melbourne.

2 REFLECTIONS OF MIRANDA

The beautiful Miranda brushes her hair, regarding herself in several mirrors, and warns the girl who has a crush on her, "You must learn to love someone else apart from me, Sara. I won't be here much longer," suggesting a premonition of what is to come.

3 MYSTERY ON HANGING ROCK

In defiance of the headmistress's instructions, four of the girls decide to climb Hanging Rock. Three of them, including Miranda, wander trancelike into a cleft in the rock. The fourth girl, Edith, is left behind and runs back down the rock screaming.

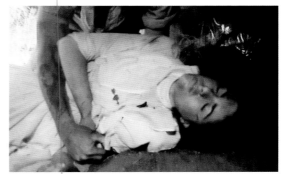

4 IRMA IS FOUND

The school picnic has been partly witnessed by another group at the rock, who later assist the search party. After rescuing Michael (Guard) and finding a scrap of lace in his hand, Albert (John Jarrett) finds Irma, alive but with no memory of the incident.

DIRECTOR PROFILE

1944–74

Peter Weir was born in Sydney, New South Wales. After working in television and on some short films, he made his directorial debut in 1974 with the surreal outback drama *The Cars That Ate Paris*.

1975–77

He became a leading Australian director with the landmark film *Picnic at Hanging Rock*. It kick-started the Australian New Wave as Australian films began to attract a new international audience. In 1977 Richard Chamberlain starred in *The Last Wave*, a darker film that picked up on some of the themes in *Picnic at Hanging Rock* and explored the relationship between Aboriginal and European cultures in Australia.

1978–84

In the early 1980s Weir directed a pair of Australian-inflected, but international historical-political epics: *Gallipoli* (1981), about the campaign during World War I that featured the first battle undertaken by the Australian and New Zealand Army Corps (ANZAC); and *The Year of Living Dangerously* (1982), set during the political turmoil surrounding President Sukarno's violent fall from power in Indonesia. The films launched Mel Gibson as an international star.

1985–2003

In the United States, the director worked with Harrison Ford (*Witness*, 1985; *The Mosquito Coast*, 1986); Ford was nominated for an Oscar for Best Actor in *Witness*. Weir's varied output included slightly pretentious drama (the overrated *Dead Poets Society*, 1989, and the underrated *Fearless*, 1993), romantic comedy (*Green Card*, 1990), science fiction satire (*The Truman Show*, 1998), and action-adventure (*Master and Commander: The Far Side of the World*, 2003).

2004–present

Despite his track record, Weir spent most of the decade on unrealized projects, but returned to filmmaking with *The Way Back* (2010), a fact-based story about a group of soldiers who escape from a Siberian gulag in 1940.

My Brilliant Career 1979

GILLIAN ARMSTRONG b. 1950

▲ The headstrong Sybylla (Judy Davis) dreams of a brilliant future as a writer.

▼ The poster emphasizes the romantic elements over the film's feminist themes.

Based on Miles Franklin's novel of the same name published in 1901, *My Brilliant Career* is the coming-of-age story of a young Australian woman, Sybylla Melvyn. It has become an Australian New Wave classic thanks to the sensual cinematography of Don McAlpine and strong performances by Judy Davis as Melvyn and Sam Neill as her wealthy beau, Harry Beecham.

Born to a poor family living on a cattle ranch in the bush, Melvyn struggles to find a role in life. She dreams of a career in the arts but her family have plans for her to work as a servant. She is saved temporarily from a life of drudgery by her grandmother, and moves to live with her and her aunt on their estate in Caddagat. However, the aunt explains that the reality of life is that a young woman can only hope to marry well, and that an independent woman of high spirits like Melvyn will pay for her ambition with a life of loneliness.

Gillian Armstrong's film tackles themes of adolescent yearning and the unselfishness that maturity can bring. She also shows the yawning gap between the hardship and poverty of life in the bush and the sophisticated gentility of middle-class families in communities that imitate the lifestyle of genteel Britain. The young country is forming its identity just as "misfit" Melvyn attempts to forge her own. *My Brilliant Career* is a vivid depiction of the position of women in the late nineteenth century and the lack of opportunities open to them, tackling issues from class to romance without sentimentality. The film's feminist themes resonate without ever stooping to didacticism or worthiness. It deservedly went on to earn a Palme d'Or nomination for Armstrong. **CK**

👁 KEY SCENES

1 MEN IN THE BUSH
Melvyn begins to write her novel. She is oblivious to her family in the sandstorm outside and does not consider fetching the washing from the line. This contrasts with her later maturity, indicated when she pegs washing at a farm where she goes to work as a governess.

2 BEAUTY TREATMENTS
Melvyn's aunt suggests that she undergo some beauty treatments—a face pack, soaking her hands in lemon rosewater, and brushing her unruly hair—to teach her how to "cultivate feminine vanity." She is seen as a creature to be tamed.

3 STANDING IN THE RAIN
Marriage prospects brighten when a family friend gives Melvyn a bunch of flowers. She later throws the flowers into a pond and as the flowers float it begins to rain. Melvyn becomes euphoric, standing in the rain, oblivious to her wet and ruined clothes.

4 PLAYING THE PIANO
Echoing an earlier scene in which her mother interrupts her playing to tell her she has "illusions of grandeur," here Melvyn's aunt tells her to stop playing "vulgar songs," which she has learned in a pub in the bush. She finds herself out of place in any environment.

5 THE PROPOSAL
Beecham returns to propose to Melvyn. Judy Davis communicates Melvyn's newfound maturity and sense of purpose, as well as the sad regret she feels in refusing Beecham. She realizes he is in love with her but she opts to be a writer rather than a wife.

🕐 DIRECTOR PROFILE

1950–79
Gillian Armstrong was born in Melbourne, Australia, and studied filmmaking and theatrical costume design before attending the newly founded Australian Film Television and Radio School. She made her directorial debut with the short *Old Man and Dog* (1970). When she directed *My Brilliant Career* in 1979, she became the first graduate from the Australian Film Television and Radio School to make a feature film and the first woman to direct a commercially released film in Australia since 1933.

1980–present
Her adaptation of Louisa May Alcott's *Little Women* (1994) brought Armstrong Hollywood success. She continued to exhibit a flair for literary adaptations with *Oscar and Lucinda* (1997) and *Charlotte Gray* (2001). In 2007 she released *Death Defying Acts*, a biopic thriller about Harry Houdini.

ASIAN AND INDIAN CINEMA

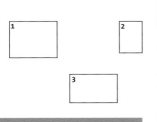

1 Oshima Nagisa's *Shonen*, the story of a ten-year-old boy whose family makes a living from staging hit-and-run accidents.

2 The psychedelic poster for the influential, action-packed *Ying chun ge zhi Fengbo*, by Hong Kong director King Hu.

3 The pleasure-loving Nawab Wajid Ali Shah (Amjad Khan, left) talks with his Prime Minister Ali Naqi Khan (Victor Banerjee, right) in *Shatranj ke khilari*.

For Asian cinema, the 1970s was the best of times and the worst of times. In Japan, the styles and genres that had been popular since before the Pacific War (1941–45) no longer drew or held audiences. Some studios went bankrupt; others depended on the repetition of successful formulas, such as Shochiku with the long-running Tora-san series—the bittersweet, humorous story of the rough-edged but basically decent Kuruma Torajiro (engagingly played by Atsumi Kiyoshi). Forty-eight installments emerged from 1969 to 1995, providing reliable nostalgic entertainment for the New Year and Obon summer holidays.

Less commercially oriented was the work of the Art Theatre Guild (ATG), which often tackled explicitly social and political themes in an avant-garde style. Some of Japan's finest art movies, by directors such as Kuroki Kazuo (1930–2006), Shinoda Masahiro (b. 1931), Terayama Shuji (1935–83), and Yoshida Yoshishige (b. 1933), were made with ATG funding. Especially admirable were the ATG films of Oshima Nagisa (b. 1932). *Shonen* (*Boy*, 1969, above) was the moving study of a boy forced by his parents to participate in a criminal scam; *Gishiki* (*The Ceremony*, 1971) was a masterly account of the Japanese postwar experience told through the story of one family. Still, Oshima had to look abroad to fund his most controversial film, the hardcore study of sexual obsession *Ai no corrida* (*In the Realm of the Senses*, 1976, see p. 378).

Mainland China, in the throes of the Cultural Revolution until 1976, produced very few films. Chinese-language cinema, however, flourished in

KEY EVENTS

1970	1971	1971	1972	1973	1973
Zhi qu wei hu shan (*Taking Tiger Mountain by Strategy*), by Xie Tieli (b. 1925), is the first Chinese film released since the start of the Cultural Revolution.	*Xia nu* (see p. 376), directed by King Hu, is released in Hong Kong. In Japan, Nikkatsu studio starts a "Roman Porno" line of soft-core pornographic films.	Art Theatre Guild produces *Gishiki* directed by Oshima Nagisa and *Shura* (*Pandemonium*) by Matsumoto Toshio (b. 1932).	Sinhalese director Lester James Peries (b. 1919) makes *Nidhanaya* (*The Treasure*), one of the finest achievements of Sri Lankan cinema.	Ritwik Ghatak (1925–76) makes *Titash ekti nadir naam* (*A River Called Titas*), one of the first films produced in the newly independent Bangladesh.	*Jingi naki tatakai* (*Battles Without Honor and Humanity*), by Fukasaku Kinji (1930–2003), initiates a series of Japanese yakuza movies.

Hong Kong and Taiwan, where the martial arts movie, especially as produced by Hong Kong–based studio Shaw Brothers, attracted international attention. Among the most famous of martial arts stars in the West was Bruce Lee, whose formidable combat skills and early death made him a legend. However, it was the films directed by Chia-Liang Liu (b. 1936) that elevated the kung fu genre. Films such as *Shao lin san shi liu fang* (*The 36th Chamber of Shaolin*, 1978) melded action, humor, and pathos. Also outstanding were the swordplay films of King Hu (1931–97), who released his masterpiece, *Xia nu* (*A Touch of Zen*, see p. 376), in 1971, followed by *Ying chun ge zhi Fengbo* (*The Fate of Lee Khan*, right) in 1973.

In India, Bollywood continued to stage song-and-dance extravaganzas, as well as, increasingly, action and gangster movies, and the "masala" movies, which combined many genres. Among the most famous Bollywood films of the decade were *Sholay* (1975), the "curry Western" directed by G. P. Sippy (1915–2007) that became the highest-grossing film in Indian history, and *Amar Akbar Anthony* (1977) by Manmohan Desai (1936–94), which examined India's cultural and religious diversity through its story of three brothers raised respectively as a Hindu, a Muslim, and a Christian. Meanwhile, in Bengal, Satyajit Ray (1921–92) continued to work in his precise, realist vein: *Shatranj ke khilari* (*The Chess Players*, 1977, below) won praise for its painstaking attention to historical detail. His films also acquired a more direct political emphasis: *Pratidwandi* (*The Adversary*, 1971) and *Jana Aranya* (*The Middleman*, 1975) focused on the problems of urban unemployment and the immoralities of capitalism, while the award-winning *Ashani sanket* (*Distant Thunder*, 1973) showed the effects of World War II on a Bengali village. Another Indian filmmaker dramatizing political and social concerns was Shyam Benegal (b. 1934) with the Indian New Wave feature *Ankur* (*The Seedling*, 1974). This film includes a level of violence and profanity unusual for Indian films of the time, and was nominated for the Golden Bear at the 24th Berlin International Film Festival. **AJ**

1975	1975	1976	1977	1979	1979
Directed by M. S. Sathyu (b. 1930), *Garam hawa* (*Hot Winds*) is a trenchant account of the problems faced by a Muslim family in Calcutta after partition.	G. P. Sippy makes the "curry Western" *Sholay*, destined to become Bollywood's, and India's, highest-grossing film.	Japanese New Wave master Oshima finds international funding to make his most controversial film, *Ai no corrida* (see p. 378).	Manmohan Desai makes the Bollywood classic *Amar Akhbar Anthony*. Satyajit Ray makes *Shatranj ke khilari*.	In South Korea, Im Kwon-Taek (b. 1936) makes his artistic breakthrough with *Jokbo* (*The Genealogy*).	After working on documentaries, Japan's Imamura Shohei (1926–2006) returns to fiction with *Fukushu suru wa ware ni ari* (*Vengeance Is Mine*).

Xia nu 1971
A Touch of Zen   KING HU 1931 – 97

▲ General Shih's logic-defying acrobatics help him evade the evil Hsu in *Xia nu*.

▼ This version of the poster attests to the lyricism of the film rather than its violence.

Critic Peter Rist has called King Hu "the least appreciated 'great director' in world film history," and "one of the most truly original filmmakers of the 1960s." Hu was the master of the *wuxia*, or martial arts, genre, a tradition that stretches back in Chinese cinema to the silent era, but which really took its modern form after Hu and some of his contemporaries imbued it with a new sophistication in the late 1960s.

Hu took three years to realize *Xia nu*, generally considered his masterpiece, in which he fused Chinese history and Buddhist theology with stylishly choreographed action and an elegant camera style. He directs with great flair, and his use of the camera, with elaborate tracking shots and dollies sometimes reminiscent of Mizoguchi Kenji (1898–1956), is ceaselessly inventive. Working in Taiwan rather than in Hong Kong—where he had made his first *wuxia* film, *Da zui xia* (*Come Drink with Me*, 1966)—he takes full advantage of the island's exquisite mountain landscapes, which provide a dramatic backdrop.

The action scenes are certainly memorable, but the film is notable too for its leisurely buildup, with the first third consisting of hints and foreshadowings rather than overt violence. There is also a dose of understated humor. Regrettably, the time and care that Hu lavished on the film were not repaid by immediate commercial success. Its length led to its being screened in two parts in Taiwan, and it was recut by its distributors in Hong Kong. In 1975 this final version won a special technical prize at Cannes, and by 2005 *Xia nu* was ninth in the Hong Kong Film Awards list of the best one hundred Chinese movies. **AJ**

KEY SCENES

1 SEARCHING FOR GHOSTS
At night, scholar Ku follows a mysterious figure into the grounds of an eerie, perhaps haunted fort. Bats scatter; lightning strikes; spiders loom from huge webs. The storm intensifies, and Ku finally catches up with a human figure, who turns out to be . . . his mother.

2 ENCOUNTER ON THE ROAD
The sinister Ou-Yang Yin meets an apparently blind man. When he addresses him as "General Shih," the man reacts and Ou-Yang knocks him down. But then Ku and his mother emerge from a side path, forcing Ou-Yang to hide. Ku and his mother help Shih to safety.

3 YIN AND YANG
After a night of love, Ku and Miss Yang are discovered by Ou-Yang Yin. He knocks Ku aside and draws his sword to attack Miss Yang, but she responds in kind. There follows the first of the film's long, athletic fight sequences. Ku follows them through the wood.

4 FIGHT IN THE FOREST
The heroes meet the red-uniformed guards of Mun Ta in a bamboo forest. They pursue them through the forest, then engage in close swordfighting. Bamboo is hacked to the ground and Miss Yang uses a bamboo shaft to vault into the air and dispatch her opponent.

DIRECTOR PROFILE

1931–64
King Hu was born in Beijing. After studying at art school, he left China for Hong Kong in 1949, working on sets for the art departments of various film studios. This was followed by a period of acting, writing, and directing at Hong Kong–based studio Shaw Brothers. He worked with Li Han-Hsiang (1926–96) on *Liang shan bo yu zhu ying tai* (*The Love Eterne*, 1963).

1965–71
He made his solo directorial debut with the war film *Da di er nu* (*Sons of Good Earth*, 1965), before achieving commercial success with the *wuxia* movie *Da zui xia*. Hu moved to Taiwan in 1967, set up his own studio, and made another major hit, *Long men kezhan* (*Dragon Inn*, 1967), which earned him backing for his most ambitious film, *Xia nu*. The bamboo fight scene in the latter inspired a similar duel in *Crouching Tiger, Hidden Dragon* (2000, see p. 500), directed by Ang Lee (b. 1954).

1972–89
Hu continued to make films on martial arts themes, including *Ying chun ge zhi Fengbo* (*The Fate of Lee Khan*, 1973) and *Zhong lie tu* (*The Valiant Ones*, 1975); however, like *Xia nu*, these were not commercially successful. *Shan zhong zhuan qi* (*Legend of the Mountain*, 1979) and *Kong shan ling yu* (*Raining in the Mountain*, 1979) were shot in Korea, but by the mid-1980s, Hu was unable to attract funding for further projects.

1990–97
Hu started to direct *Xiao ao jiang hu* (*Swordsman*, 1990), but disagreements with producer Tsui Hark led to his departure. His last completed film was *Hua pi zhi: Yin yang fa wang* (*Painted Skin*, 1993). When Hu died, of a stroke, he was seeking funding from Hollywood sources for *Wa gung huet lui si* (*The Battle of Ono*), a film about Chinese immigrants working on the railroads in Gold Rush–era California. He is remembered as a pioneer of *wuxia* whose idiosyncratic martial arts films drew on the rich traditions of Buddhism and Chinese opera.

Ai no corrida 1976
In the Realm of the Senses OSHIMA NAGISA b. 1932

▲ Erotic extremes: Sada Abe strangles her lover Kichizo Ishida, at his own insistence, as part of their lovemaking.

▼ The lovers, shown here on the poster, are played by Fuji Tatsuya and Matsuda Eiko.

Set in 1930s Japan, *Ai no corrida* details the bizarre affair between hotel owner Kichi-San and Sada, a maid employed at his hotel. Based on a true story, it is a thorough exploration of sex and togetherness: for much of the film the couple and the camera rarely leave the bedroom—a place devoted to their relationship in all its stifling glory.

Away from their heated proximity, the settings are sparsely populated with quiet, functional hallways and cold back alleys. The viewer glimpses the outside world: passing strangers and the great, smoking chimneys of industry. The main characters are set apart from others, inhabiting their own private world. Their affair is the last gasp of a more natural world before the oncoming changes that will engulf the imperially minded Japan.

Ai no corrida is well known for being the first nonpornographic film to show scenes of fellatio and an erect penis, and it implies that using such explicitness is the only way to tell this tale. By depicting sexual intimacy so graphically, director Oshima Nagisa is commenting on the liberalism and hypocrisy of contemporary Japanese culture, specifically the constraints on sexual imagery. Throughout history, and particularly in Japanese culture, sex and death are linked and Oshima illustrates this by contrasting Sada and Kichi's relationship with the fatalistic, unhesitating march of the soldiers. Sada looks almost in pain when she is close to Kichi, as if she can hardly bear their happiness. As they push themselves to extremes again and again, they and the audience know that their relationship can end only in one way. **SW**

◉ KEY SCENES

1 SADA AND KICHI'S FIRST MEETING
Sada is shy and polite but not cautious, whereas Kichi is intrigued and openly flirtatious. Both are captivated and it is not long before they meet again to further their relationship. New sexual experiences and new futures beckon.

2 A GEISHA LOOKS ON
Sada and Kichi often conduct their affair in full view of anybody who may be around: geishas, old ladies, or even a priest. These other characters are mesmerized by what they see. The director is forcing viewers to reflect on their own responses.

3 THE COUPLE CANNOT BEAR TO BE PARTED
In order to earn money Sada travels to a liaison with a teacher. On the train she wraps herself in Kichi's robe and breathes in his scent. She sleeps with the teacher as Kichi forces himself upon a geisha: they are further bonded by these simultaneous sexual experiences.

4 GOING TO EXTREMES
Sada and Kichi experiment sexually with food, seeing how far the other will go. The director and actors go to extreme lengths to show the intimate details of the couple's relationship, in which hunger has a lower priority than sexual exploration.

◷ DIRECTOR PROFILE

1932–61
Oshima Nagisa was born in Kyoto. Beginning as an apprentice in the Shochiku film studio in 1954, he moved swiftly through the ranks. *Ai to kibo no machi* (*A Town of Love and Hope*, 1959) was his debut feature film as director. In 1960 he released three films: *Seishun zankoku monogatari* (*Cruel Story of Youth*), *Taiyo no hakaba* (*The Sun's Burial*), and *Nihon no yoru to kiri* (*Night and Fog in Japan*). All are frank and controversial, particularly in the discussion of Japanese politics and the criticism of political reflection.

1962–75
Within a decade the prolific Oshima had completed sixteen films. These included *Amakusa shiro tokisada* (*The Rebel*, 1962), *Etsuraku* (*Pleasures of the Flesh*, 1965), *Ninja bugei-cho* (*Band of Ninja*, 1967), the Brechtian discussion of guilt *Koshikei* (*Death by Hanging*, 1968), the exploration of subjectivity *Shonen* (*Boy*, 1969), and *Natsu no imoto* (*Dear Summer Sister*, 1972).

1976–83
The controversial exploration of sex and Japanese culture, *Ai no corrida*, was released in 1976. In this joint French–Japanese production Oshima used freedoms impossible in Japan to create a graphic portrayal of sex and a deconstruction of stereotypical Japanese filmmaking. *Ai no borei* (*Empire of Passion*) followed in 1978 and the Japanese prisoner of war drama *Merry Christmas, Mr. Lawrence* was released in 1983.

1984–present
The "greatest ape romance since King Kong," Oshima's *Max mon amour* was released in 1986. It coolly and detachedly details the relationship between Charlotte Rampling's Margaret and a chimpanzee named Max. Oshima did not direct another film until 1999 and *Gohatto* (*Taboo*). The movie was a study of homosexuality and the last days of the samurai by the increasingly reclusive director; it garnered numerous awards and nominations.

A NEW ERA FOR MUSICALS

A musical love story.

Hollywood musicals (see p. 198) are closely associated with US cinema's golden age, but they did not so much die a death with the breakdown of the studio system, rather they changed form. The traditional musical could still be found, often slightly reimagined for a contemporary audience, but the genre was pushed into new areas, exploring contemporary issues and trends, as a platform for new music genres or in order to reevaluate the past.

The first two parts of *That's Entertainment!* (1974, 1976) were a reminder of the halcyon days of the Hollywood musical. There were also contemporary releases that differed little from musical productions of the fifties: *Scrooge* (1970) *Willy Wonka & the Chocolate Factory*, *Fiddler on the Roof* (both 1971), *Funny Lady* (1975), and *Annie* (1982) all adopted a classic shooting style and presented a perfect escape from reality. However, Norman Jewison (b. 1926) brought an inventive approach to *Jesus Christ Superstar* (1973), which boasted a score by musical theater's new wunderkinds, Andrew Lloyd Webber and Tim Rice. In the same year, another update on a biblical story, *Godspell: A Musical Based on the Gospel According to St. Matthew,* appeared. The countercultural movement that grew out of the 1960s was also represented by adaptations of stage shows: *Oh! Calcutta!* (1972) and *Hair* (1979, left). Although they adopted a conventional narrative structure, these films—like the shows on which they were based—were controversial for breaking taboos regarding nudity, sex, and politics.

KEY EVENTS

1972	1973	1973	1975	1977	1978
Norman Jewison's tale of a Jewish Russian peasant, *Fiddler on the Roof*, wins three Academy Awards, including one for Best Cinematography.	*Cabaret* (see p. 382) scoops eight Oscars, including Best Director, Best Actress for Liza Minnelli, and Best Actor in a Supporting Role for Joel Grey.	*Godspell* and *Jesus Christ Superstar* are released, both adaptations of successful stage musicals about the life of Christ.	*The Rocky Horror Picture Show* and *Tommy* highlight the popularity of the rock opera. Barbra Streisand returns as Fanny Brice in *Funny Lady*.	*Saturday Night Fever* and disco take on the world...and win. The album of the soundtrack becomes the best-selling soundtrack of all time.	*Grease* becomes one of the hits of the decade. The Bee Gees star in the flop *Sgt. Pepper's Lonely Hearts Club Band*, proving they are not infallible.

The dominant force of the US musical from the late 1960s was Bob Fosse (1927–87). Originally a choreographer, Fosse created a unique style, employing every limb to accentuate a dancer's movement. His *Cabaret* (1972, see p. 382) won eight Oscars, while *All That Jazz* (1979), a frank, semiautobiographical account of a director on the verge of collapse as he prepares for a new show, was awarded the Palme d'Or at the Cannes Film Festival.

Rock music dominated the majority of musicals from the 1970s. Alan Parker (b. 1944), who also directed *Bugsy Malone* (1976) and *Fame* (1980), directed *Pink Floyd The Wall* (1982). A more traditional style was evident in *Grease* (1978, opposite), which presents an affectionate take on high school rebellion and romance, and became one of that decade's biggest musical successes. *The Rocky Horror Picture Show* (1975) blends post-1960s sexual mores with a nod to 1940s horror films, all powered along by a series of skillfully produced song-and-dance numbers. Even the punk movement was represented—*The Great Rock 'n' Roll Swindle* (1980) introduced the Sex Pistols to the wider world.

The success of *Saturday Night Fever* (1977) virtually kick-started the disco phenomenon, thanks to the infectious soundtrack by the Bee Gees, and prompted a slew of dance films that grew in popularity throughout the 1980s. *Staying Alive* (1983) witnessed John Travolta's character, Tony Manero, attempt a career on Broadway, while in *Flashdance* (1983, below), Jennifer Beals's steelworker dreams of entering dance school. Conservatism came out against dance in two of the decade's most popular musicals, *Footloose* (1984) and *Dirty Dancing* (1987, right). Like all 1980s musicals, the music was prerecorded, often featuring tracks that were known to audiences, boosting their popularity. **IHS**

PATRICK SWAYZE · JENNIFER GREY

First dance.
first love.
The time of your life.

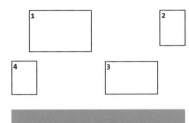

1 Travolta's energetic performance as gang leader of the T-Birds, Danny Zuko, in *Grease* made dancing look cool.

2 *Dirty Dancing* starred seasoned dancers Patrick Swayze and Jennifer Grey, and provided Swayze's breakthrough role.

3 In *Flashdance* Beals's welder, who wants to be a ballet dancer, works as a stripper by night after her confidence founders.

4 This poster design for *Hair* echoes the film's hippie counterculture concerns.

1980	1981	1983	1983	1984	1987
Bob Fosse's *All That Jazz* wins the Palme 'Or at the Cannes ilm Festival and our Academy Awards.	*Fame*, Alan Parker's story of a New York high school for students gifted in the performing arts, wins two Oscars.	*Flashdance*'s success marks the beginning of producers Jerry Bruckheimer and Don Simpson's domination of mainstream Hollywood movies.	Director Sylvester Stallone (b. 1946) has a commercial hit with *Staying Alive*.	Kevin Bacon struts his way to the top of the box office as a Chicago teenager in *Footloose*.	*Dirty Dancing* becomes one of the defining films of the 1980s.

Cabaret 1972
BOB FOSSE 1927 – 87

▲ Liza Minnelli with Joel Grey's demonic Master of Ceremonies.

▼ As the precocious and frail Sally, Minnelli gives the performance of her career.

Bob Fosse's masterpiece is a cynical critique of the decadent last days of the Weimar Republic and the rise of National Socialism, featuring catchy frivolous songs that belie the troubling developments in Europe Brian (Michael York) arrives in Berlin in 1931. He meets Sally Bowles (Liza Minnelli) and the two become lovers. She works in the Kit Kat Klub (note the three "K"s), an underground cabaret shut off from the world outside. Sally and Brian's fleeting love affair is thrown into perspective by the violent uprisings around them, which begin to destroy the liberties they so enjoy.

The glimpses of Nazi brutality go unnoticed by those who carouse at the cabaret. The songs bring the plot and characters vividly to life, driving the narrative onward as well as commenting on the events unfolding. "Maybe This Time" explains Sally's wide-eyed hopes; "If You Could See Her" is a terrifying allegory of the persecution rising against Berlin's Jewish population. The songs are performed on the stage of the Kit Kat Klub, and, aside from the expressionistic angles revealing the morally gray spectators, the routines are presented with realism. Fosse displays the performances from a distance using the glare of the lights to emphasize the small stage and the silhouetted heads of the audience members—conspirators in this dark world.

The final frames echo the opening scene, with blurred glass reflecting those who now populate the audience, identifiable only by armbands adorned with swastikas. A mirror is being held up to society and the figures in it are hazy and distorted with a common cruel outlook. **SW**

👁 KEY SCENES

1 "MEIN HERR"
The audience has just seen Sally at her lodgings, where she flaps around and talks incessantly. Here, in costume, on stage for her first performance, she is transformed. She commands the stage, channelling her naivety and excitement into allure and prowess.

2 "TOMORROW BELONGS TO ME"
What begins as a gentle pastoral tune transforms into a pounding celebration of Germans as the master race. The crowd of listeners becomes a chorus, passionately singing along. Leaving, Brian asks the old-money Maximilian, "You still think you can control them?"

3 LIFE IS A CABARET
Sally gives her greatest performance, believing in every word. It leaves the viewer with a feeling of optimism before the Master of Ceremonies gives his final, chilling speech. To the sound of a never-ending drum roll, the scene drifts into dark closing shots.

🕐 DIRECTOR PROFILE

1927–68
Robert Louis Fosse was born in Chicago. After regular work on stage and in film as an actor and dancer, he moved into choreography for the stage. His first choreographed musical was *The Pajama Game* in 1954, which was followed by *Damn Yankees* in 1955 and *New Girl in Town* in 1957. In 1959 he directed and choreographed *Redhead*, which won Tony awards for best musical and for Fosse's choreography.

1969–73
His debut as feature film director was *Sweet Charity* (1969)—a musical featuring Shirley Maclaine as an ever-hopeful dancer. Her optimism and ambition prefigured Liza Minnelli's Sally Bowles in *Cabaret*. At the Academy Awards in 1973, *Cabaret* was nominated for ten awards and went on to win eight, including Best Actress (Liza Minnelli), Best Supporting Actor (Joel Grey), and Best Director.

1974–87
Lenny (1974) is a frank biopic of controversial comedian Lenny Bruce, starring Dustin Hoffman. It was nominated for six Oscars. In 1975 Fosse wrote the lyrics and choreographed the original stage production of the hit musical *Chicago*. *All That Jazz* (1979) is a semiautobiographical film starring Roy Scheider and Jessica Lange that continued to explore Fosse's fascination with the dark side of fame. It won four Academy Awards, including Best Original Score. His last film was *Star 80* in 1983, a controversial biopic of a *Playboy* playmate. He died of a heart attack, at the age of sixty.

PAGE TO SCREEN

Christopher Isherwood's *Goodbye to Berlin* was published in 1939, the year that marked the start of World War II. It is a collection of vignettes inspired by Isherwood's own experiences in prewar Berlin. He witnessed firsthand the decadence and the pulsing life of the Weimar Republic, as well as the gathering storm heralded by the Third Reich. Isherwood was openly homosexual during a time when such openness was rare. He was accustomed to seeing different facets of society, of experiencing secret lives, and these hidden depths—a world of light and shadow—are crucial to his work. In the novel, Sally Bowles features in only one section of the book and she and Christopher (Brian in the film) never become lovers. *Goodbye to Berlin* was turned into a play, *I Am a Camera*, the title taken from a line in the book: "I am a camera with its shutter open, quite passive, recording, not thinking." The play was written by John van Druten in 1951, and made into a film in 1955 with Laurence Harvey and Shelley Winters in the lead roles. *Cabaret* is adapted from both novel and play.

AFRICAN CINEMA

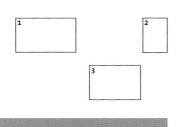

African cinema in the 1970s and 1980s witnessed an explosion of invention and creativity that rivaled any other cinematic renaissance in the world before or since. Its directors were fired by the opportunities, energy, and politics of the postcolonial era to create ever more distinctive and ambitious films. Yet compared with, for example, those of the French Nouvelle Vague (see p. 248) of the 1960s, the films are underappreciated today.

Often referred to as "the father of African film," the Senegalese author and director Ousmane Sembène (1923–2007) epitomized the new urgency of postcolonial Africa. In 1947 Sembène moved to France where he worked as a docker in Marseilles, joined the Communist party, and was a vocal trade unionist. His cinema displayed the same political and social engagement as he showed in life, and his inspirational debut *La noire de...* (*Black Girl*, 1966) was the first feature made by a black African to achieve international recognition.

Unique among emerging directors of the 1970s was the Senegalese Djibril Diop Mambéty (1945–98), whose debut feature *Touki Bouki* (*Journey of the Hyena*, 1973, opposite above) captured the voice of African youth and introduced a dizzying, experimental edge into African cinema. Author Manthia Diawara wrote that it "tears up the screen with fantasies of African modernity never before seen in film," and critic Mark Cousins has described it as "Africa's equivalent of *Easy Rider* or *A bout de souffle*." The film had a political edge, too; it follows a young couple who dream of leaving Senegal, and who embark on a series of adventures to raise the money needed, but decide at the last minute that they cannot leave their home country.

1 *Chronique des années de braise* charts the Algerian struggle for independence through the eyes of a peasant.

2 The poster for African road movie *Touki Bouki* shows cowherd Mory on his motorbike mounted with a cow's skull.

3 Haile Gerima's powerful film *Mirt sost shi amit* highlights the plight of an ordinary Ethiopian peasant family.

KEY EVENTS

1969	1970	1971	1973	1975	1975
The FESPACO festival is held for the first time in Ouagadougou, Burkina Faso. The biannual event is crucial to the future of African cinema.	Med Hondo's influential debut *Soleil O* marks a bold start to the new decade in African cinema.	Ousmane Sembène directs his third feature, *Emitai*, a visually rich drama set in the Diola society of rural Senegal.	Djibril Diop Mambéty's thrilling, experimental debut *Touki Bouki* wins the International Critics Award at the Cannes Film Festival.	Safi Faye becomes the first woman director from sub-Saharan Africa with her feature *Kaddu Beykat*.	The Federation Pan-Africain des Cinéastes (FEPACI) produces a charter calling for African films to address African problems.

Inspired by the example of Sembène and also by the founding of two vital African film festivals—Carthage in Tunisia in 1966 and FESPACO (the Pan-African Film and Television Festival) in Burkina Faso in 1969—by the dawn of the 1970s there was a palpable sense of promise about African cinema. Galvanized by writers such as Frantz Fanon, who in *Les damnés de la terre* (*The Wretched of the Earth*) argued that national liberation was only possible after the psychological liberation of individuals, the early 1970s saw trailblazing directors such as the Mauritania-born, Paris-based Med Hondo (b. 1936) move beyond simple imitations of Western films, to attain a cinema with a distinctively African voice that would address issues affecting African people.

In East Africa, the landmark film *Mirt sost shi amit* (*Harvest: 3,000 Years*, 1976, below) from Ethiopian-born Haile Gerima (b. 1946) was a furious, formally radical indictment of the oppression of Ethiopia's peasants by landowners, its characters symbolizing the relationship between Africa and the West. Meanwhile, in North Africa, filmmakers such as the Tunisian Abdellatif Ben Ammar (b. 1943) also produced challenging films, including the award-winning *Aziza* (1980). *Chronique des années de braise* (*Chronicle of the Years of Fire*, 1975, opposite) by Mohammed Lakhdar-Hamina (b. 1934) portrayed Algeria's struggle for independence from French colonial rule. The film created a new awareness of Algerian cinema, winning the Palme d'Or at the Cannes Festival.

If Western and Asian cinema have their roots in literature and the theater, then African directors began to look to the African oral storytelling tradition for inspiration. Films such as Hondo's documentary *Soleil O* (1973), about African

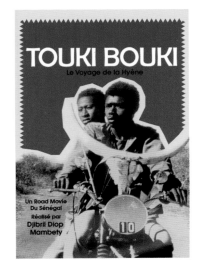

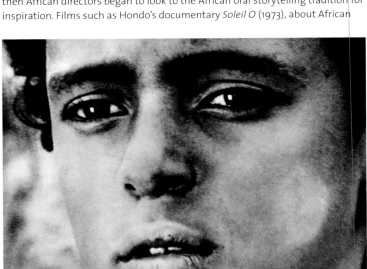

1982	1986	1986	1987	1988	1989
Gaston Kaboré makes the influential movie *Wend Kuuni*, set in the precolonial past. Souleymane Cissé's *Finyé* wins the top prize at FESPACO.	Burkinabé director Idrissa Ouedraogo directs *Yam daabo*.	Med Hondo's epic third feature *Sarraounia*, considered by some to be his masterpiece, wins the top prize at FESPACO.	Ousmane Sembène's *Camp de Thiaroye* exposes the poor treatment Senegalese veterans received from the French army after World War II.	Gaston Kaboré examines the rituals of the Mossi culture in *Zan Boko*.	Idrissa Ouedraogo releases his highly acclaimed second feature *Yaaba*. It wins the FIPRESCI prize at Cannes.

4 Aï Keïta in her first acting role, as the imposing African queen Sarraounia.

5 The poster for *Baara*. Set in a textile factory in contemporary Mali, the film critiques the African bourgeoisie.

6 Idrissa Ouedraogo beautifully captures the simple rhythms of African village life in his touching drama *Yaaba*.

émigrés in France, and Sembène's *Emitai* (1971) about the clash between the French army and Senegalese villagers at the end of World War II, employed key elements of the tradition, such as flashbacks and nonsequential narratives.

Following in Sembène and Hondo's wake were directors from across sub-Saharan Africa; people such as Ababacar Samb-Makharam (1934–87), director of *Kodou* (1970), or Safi Faye (b. 1943), also from Senegal, who became the first sub-Saharan African woman director with her feature *Kaddu Beykat* (*Letter from My Village*, 1975), a docudrama told through a letter narrated by Faye herself. The film is set in Faye's native village in Senegal and focuses on the daily life and customs of the inhabitants, while also telling the story of a young couple who wish to marry but cannot—because of a drought that has ruined his crops, the man cannot afford the bride price.

With independence still a recent memory, and postcolonial governments across Africa sliding into corruption, the focus of African cinema in the 1970s tended to be on the present. Films of the period covered a range of controversial and topical issues; Sembène's film *Xala* (1975, see p. 388) was cut by the Senegalese censors for its razor-sharp comment on the new post-independence elites, who had simply replaced the abuses of old colonial rulers with new ones of their own. His ambitious film *Ceddo* (1977), although set in the nineteenth century, had a clear message to impart about contemporary Africa in its story of African traditions under threat from outside; the lyrical film *Muna Moto* (1975) by Cameroonian Jean-Pierre Dikongué-Pipa (b. 1940) followed *Kaddu Beykat* in criticizing the bride price system; and a major new voice emerged in the Malian director Souleymane Cissé (b. 1940), who like Sembène had studied in Moscow. Cissé's second feature, *Baara* (*Work*, 1978, opposite above), explored the lives of everyday workers in a textile factory in Bamako and revealed Cissé's Marxist background in its depiction of an engineer who challenges the factory owners. The film won the top prize at FESPACO, as did his follow-up, *Finyé* (*The Wind*, 1982), which dealt with class and generational conflicts and showed students daring to challenge the authority of the military government.

If contemporary realities and subjects had dominated African cinema in the 1970s, then the 1980s saw African directors look to the precolonial past for inspiration. The move brought about a slower-paced cinema, one rooted more specifically in African myths than in the angry statements of the previous decade. The momentum for this came from the small West African country of Burkina Faso. Through its hosting of the FESPACO festival it had already had an impact on African cinema out of proportion to its status as one of the continent's poorest nations. However, in the early 1980s, and with the support of the nation's charismatic young leader Thomas Sankara, the country began to produce films that had a crucial impact on the development of African cinema.

Wend Kuuni (God's Gift, 1982) by Gaston Kaboré (b. 1951) was the breakthrough film. Set in the precolonial era, it centers on a mute young boy found alone in the bush who is adopted by villagers. Kaboré's next film, Zan Boko (1988), made implicit criticisms of the political situation in Burkina Faso at the time. Kaboré inspired other directors, including the Burkinabé Idrissa Ouedraogo (b. 1954), who made his own "village" films, including the highly regarded Yaaba (1989, below), in which a ten-year-old boy befriends an elderly woman who has become a social outcast.

The most celebrated African film of the 1980s also followed the example of Wend Kuuni. With the extraordinary Yeelen (1987, see p. 390), Souleymane Cissé left the contemporary realism of Baara and Finyé behind, instead telling a story of myth, magic, and ritual set in Mali in the thirteenth century, and derived directly from stories handed down through the oral tradition. The film is among the most beautifully photographed in world cinema.

Other remarkable African films of the decade include Med Hondo's epic Sarraounia (1986, opposite). In this historical drama Hondo immortalized one of the few African tribal leaders to oppose French expansionism—the Azna queen Sarraounia—who in 1899 fought off the militarily superior colonial forces in the Niger using guerrilla tactics. Hondo's film was critically acclaimed and won the top prize at FESPACO. The 1980s also saw the arrival of a new generation from across sub-Saharan Africa, among them another great Malian director, Cheick Oumar Sissoko (b. 1945), whose first feature Nyamanton (1986) depicts the lives of street children in Bamako. In Burkina Faso, S. Pierre Yaméogo (b. 1955) also appeared as a name to watch. Such talents ensured that African cinema remained a vital presence in international cinema into the 1990s, a time that also saw the flourishing of video film industries in the former British colonies of Ghana and Nigeria—countries where cinema had until then been hindered by a lack of financial and structural support such as that offered by France to its former colonies. **JB**

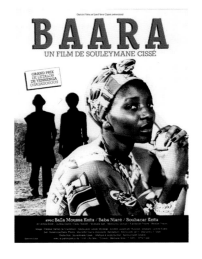

Xala 1975
OUSMANE SEMBÈNE 1923 – 2007

▲ In Sembène's satire the old colonial masters retain power behind the scenes.

▼ *Xala* won a special jury prize at the Karlovy Vary International Film Festival.

In his early films Ousmane Sembène had exposed the exploitation of the colonial system, but with *Xala*, which he adapted from his own novel of 1973, he turned his critical gaze on the ways in which Africa's postcolonial leaders had themselves begun to abuse their power, and ruthlessly castigated the new African bourgeoisie for its pretensions and arrogance.

The film opens on the day Senegal has won its independence, but the new African leaders are already accepting bribes from the former French colonialists, who remain influential and powerful. Among the new elite is El-Hadji Abdoukader Beye, a successful businessman, father, and husband to two women. To celebrate his new position in the Chamber of Commerce, El-Hadji decides to take a third wife. On his wedding night he discovers that he is suffering from the curse of impotence, or *xala*. His subsequent attempts to lift it only bring him financial ruin and humiliation.

Sembène uses El-Hadji's affliction as a metaphor for the failure of Senegal's new rulers to tackle the country's problems. The film is rich with the contradictions and cultural confusions of the postcolonial period. El-Hadji retains or drops African customs as it suits him. He is dismissive of African traditions, yet justifies his third marriage by declaring that polygamy is part of his religion. The clear message to Senegal's new rulers was too much for them to stomach, and *Xala* was cut heavily by the censors. However, that did not stop the film from becoming a hit both at home and abroad, and it is still regarded as one of Sembène's greatest achievements. **JB**

👁 KEY SCENES

1 INDEPENDENCE DAY
Senegal has gained independence, but after showing cheering crowds being pushed back by police, the country's new rulers accept briefcases of money from the former French colonialists, with whom they collude, and in whom the real power still resides.

2 EL-HADJI VISITS THE *MARABOUT*
Although skeptical of the old African ways, El-Hadji visits a *marabout* (holy man/healer) to be cured of his impotence. El-Hadji is a man who has abandoned his African traditions—as his first wife tells him, "You're neither fish nor fowl."

3 THE FINAL HUMILIATION
After losing his house, his job, and his status, El-Hadji discovers that the *xala* was placed on him by his half brother, whom he defrauded of his inheritance years before. His brother will lift the curse only if El-Hadji undergoes being spat on by a group of beggars and cripples.

🕐 DIRECTOR PROFILE

1923–59
Ousmane Sembène was born the son of a fisherman in Senegal. He spent his early years working in manual jobs, before being drafted to fight in World War II. He joined the Free French forces, remaining in France after demobilization. After working as a docker in Marseilles, he published his first novel in 1956. It was highly praised.

1960–71
Sembène returned to Senegal in 1960. Realizing that his books were reaching only a literate elite, he studied filmmaking at the Russian State Institute of Cinematography (VGIK) in Moscow in 1961, worked at the Gorki Studios, then returned to Senegal, where he made his first feature *La noire de...* (*Black Girl*, 1966). He directed the satire *Mandabi* (1968) and the anticolonial story *Emitai* (1971).

1972–87
Ceddo (1977) uses the story of a princess's kidnapping to explore the nineteenth-century clash between Muslim expansion and African tradition. *Camp de Thiaroye* (1987) attacked the treatment of Senegalese veterans by the French after World War II.

1988–2007
His last three films have been labeled a "trilogy of everyday heroism": *Guelwaar* (1992) focuses on a clash between a Christian and a Muslim community; *Faat Kiné* (2000) looks at the status of women in contemporary Senegal; and *Moolaadé* (2004) is a powerful story about a group of women who shelter girls from female circumcision.

PAGE TO SCREEN

Ousmane Sembène always maintained he preferred literature to film, but that he turned to cinema to better communicate his ideas to African people. He wrote nine novels and short story collections, starting with *Le docker noir* (*The Black Docker*, 1956), about an African docker who is executed for the accidental killing of a white woman. Sembène's early novels launched withering attacks on the evils of colonialism. His second novel *O pays, mon beau peuple!* (*Oh Country, My Good People!*, 1957) was an international success, but many critics consider the autobiographical *Les bouts de bois de Dieu* (*God's Bits of Wood*, 1960), which fictionalizes the railroad strike on the Dakar-Niger Line (1947–48), to be his masterpiece. Sembène's later novels, such as *Xala* (1973), turned their sights on the corruption he saw within Africa's new, postcolonial elites. His final full-length novel, *Le dernier de l'empire* (*The Last of the Empire*, 1981) explores how corruption leads to a military coup in a newly independent African nation.

Yeelen 1987
SOULEYMANE CISSÉ b. 1940

▲ Attu stands under a waterfall—images of water and light abound in the film.

▼ The blinding sun on the poster echoes the meaning of the film's title—"brightness."

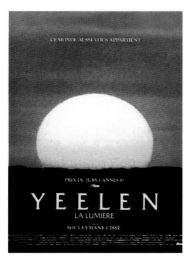

Souleymane Cissé made his international breakthrough with *Yeelen*. This innovative film, which won the Jury Prize at the Cannes Film Festival in 1987, was acclaimed around the world as among the finest African films ever made. A mythic fable set among the Bambara people in Mali in the thirteenth century, the film drew from stories passed down through the oral tradition.

Opening with a shot of a dazzling sun, the film follows the spiritual journey of Nianankoro, a young Bambara man who has grown up in fear of his evil father Soma, a sorcerer who abandoned him and his mother. The time has come for Nianankoro to confront his father, and he sets off to find his uncle, Soma's twin, who will provide him with the knowledge he will need. The film climaxes with the fatal confrontation between father and son.

With its historical setting, *Yeelen* marked a departure for Cissé, whose films up to that point had been largely realist dramas that examined contemporary Malian issues. Yet the film also makes less direct, allegorical comments about present-day Mali. The exploration of Bambara traditions was a process of rediscovery for Cissé himself, who described it as "an extraordinary lesson."

Despite a small budget and a series of problems during production that included bad weather and the death of a lead actor, Cissé succeeded brilliantly in evoking a mythical past ruled by magic. His vision was helped enormously by the lush cinematography of Jean-Michel Hummeau and Jean-Noel Ferragut, and by the music of Michel Portal and singer Salif Keita, which all combine to give the film its unique atmosphere. **JB**

👁 KEY SCENES

1 PARTING WAYS
Nianankoro's mother has protected him from his evil father throughout his childhood. Now he is a man and the time has come, he tells her, when he must leave her and face him. She gives him fetish objects that will protect him on his quest.

2 NIANANKORO MEETS ATTU
Nianankoro stops at a Peul village, where the local king asks him to use his magic to cure his infertile third wife, Attu. Nianankoro is overcome by desire and sleeps with her. The king forgives him and allows Nianankoro to take her as his wife. She later bears his son.

3 THE FINAL CONFRONTATION
The film climaxes when Nianankoro is brought face to face with his father Soma, who has sworn to kill him. Battling against each other with their magical powers, both are killed in a blinding flash of light. The ending mirrors the opening shot of the dazzling sun.

4 REBIRTH
Nianankoro's spirit lives on in an egg half-buried in the sand. The egg is dug up by Nianankoro's own son, in an act that represents the film's themes of creation, rebirth, and the passing of knowledge from generation to generation.

🕒 DIRECTOR PROFILE

1940–69
Souleymane Cissé was born in Bamako, Mali, and was raised as a Muslim in Dakar, where he attended secondary school. He returned to Mali after the country gained independence in 1960. During the 1960s, he studied at Moscow's VGIK film school, where he acquired the Marxist outlook on class and society that would shape his early feature films.

1970–73
After returning from Moscow, Cissé joined the Malian Ministry of Information as a cameraman, producing a number of documentaries and short films. In 1973 he produced his first medium-length film, *Cinq jours d'une vie* (*Five Days in a Life*). It tells the story of a young man who drops out of Islamic school and becomes a thief living on the streets.

1974–79
In this period Cissé made two films that dealt directly with working-class characters. *Den Muso* (*The Young Girl*, 1975) tells the story of a young mute girl who becomes pregnant after being raped and is rejected both by her family and by the child's father. The film was banned in Mali. *Baara* (*Work*, 1978) focuses on workers in a factory and received the top prize at the FESPACO festival in 1979.

1980–87
Cissé's film *Finyé* (*The Wind*, 1982) focuses on the clash between a group of modern students and their parents' generation and criticized military rule in Africa. Although mostly realist in style, the film has a number of fantasy sequences that anticipated his next feature, *Yeelen*, in 1987. *Finyé* earned Cissé his second top prize at FESPACO.

1988–present
Following the success of *Yeleen* at Cannes, Cissé spent many years working on his next film, *Waati* (1995). The film was nominated for the Palme d'Or at Cannes in 1995, although it failed to match the international acclaim that had greeted *Yeelen*. His film *Min Ye* (*Tell Me Who You Are*, 2009) received a special screening at the Cannes Film Festival.

THE LEGACY OF VIETNAM

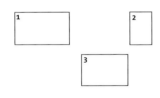

1 In *The Deer Hunter*, Michael (Robert De Niro) returns home from the war but struggles to settle in, believing his buddies to be dead in Vietnam.

2 *The Killing Fields* was based on the experiences of two journalists—a Cambodian and an American—and a British photographer during the Khmer Rouge's rise to power.

3 *Full Metal Jacket* follows young recruits through a dehumanizing process of military training and then on to the horrors of the Tet Offensive.

Vietnam was the first war of the television age, and produced lasting images of the harsh reality of warfare. In contrast to World War II, however, Hollywood showed a distinct lack of enthusiasm for making patriotic movies. Often cited as the only prowar feature made during the conflict, *The Green Berets* (1968) was critically derided for its simplistic stance. Hollywood films of the late 1960s and early 1970s often provided less direct reflections on the war. The brash antiauthoritarian tone of *MASH* (1970), directed by Robert Altman (1925–2006), was more relevant to Vietnam than to its nominal setting of the Korean War. *Ulzana's Raid* (1972), a mesmerizing Western by Robert Aldrich (1918–83), uses the story of a troop of cavalry on a doomed mission to recapture a group of Apaches as a brutal metaphor for an unwinnable war.

Actual dramatizations of the Vietnam War had to wait until the fighting was over. In 1978 *Coming Home*, by Hal Ashby (1929–88), criticized the war through the plight of a disabled veteran. Released the same year, *The Deer Hunter* (above), by Michael Cimino (b. 1939), was more ambiguous in its attitude. Although described as an antiwar film, it was attacked for its one-sidedly brutal picture of the North Vietnamese. The Russian roulette scene, in particular, attracted controversy because there was no evidence that the North Vietnamese had used the deadly game. It was *Apocalypse Now* (see p. 394), made by Francis Ford Coppola (b. 1939) the following year, that provided cinema's most powerful and enduring imagining of the Vietnam experience and set a benchmark by which all other Vietnam films have been judged.

see p. 394

KEY EVENTS

1971	1972	1973	1974	1976	1979
The Pentagon Papers about US policy in Vietnam are published by *The New York Times*. The US government's appeal to the Supreme Court to stop it fails.	Jane Fonda and Donald Sutherland tour US bases with the political revue "FTA" (Fuck the Army). Fonda causes a furor when she visits North Vietnam.	In a televised speech, President Nixon announces a plan to end the war in Vietnam.	*Hearts and Minds*, a film by Peter Davis (b. 1937) about the Vietnam War, is released. It wins the Oscar for Best Documentary in 1975.	The first Vietnamese "boat people" arrive in Australia. Refugees from the war risk traveling in dangerous, overcrowded boats.	*Apocalypse Now* (see p. 394) wins the Palme d'Or at Cannes Film Festival. It is also nominated for the Academy Award for Best Picture.

Films dealing with the emotional landscape of the United States in the wake of Vietnam provided an oblique comment on the war. *Who'll Stop the Rain* (1978) has a Vietnam veteran and his best friend's wife on the run with a consignment of Vietnamese heroin in California. The madness of the war is encapsulated in a line from the film: "You see, in a world where elephants are pursued by flying men, people are just naturally going to want to get high."

Oliver Stone (b. 1946) drew on his own experiences in Vietnam for *Platoon* (1986, see p. 396), the first film of a trilogy depicting different aspects of the war. The second film, *Born on the Fourth of July* (1989), was based on the memoir of a disabled war veteran, and the third, *Heaven & Earth* (1993), is the true story of a young Vietnamese woman who became the wife of a traumatized soldier. Stanley Kubrick (1928–99) created an intense vision of Vietnam when he rebuilt the battlefields of South East Asia in the East London marshes for *Full Metal Jacket* (1987, below). The conflict in Vietnam spilled over the border into Cambodia when the Americans pulled out in 1975. More than three million Cambodians were murdered by the Khmer Rouge regime, as is dramatized in the British film *The Killing Fields* (1984, right). It chronicles the barbaric events of "year zero," as experienced by two journalists—one local, Dith Pran (Haing S. Ngor) and one from New York, Sydney Schanberg (Sam Waterston)—including Pran's struggle to survive and ultimately escape from one of the tortuous labor camps.

In the twenty-first century, attitudes to Vietnam have reflected a new political context. Made in the first year of the Iraq war, *We Were Soldiers* (2002), starring Mel Gibson, offers a sympathetic view of US intervention. **DP**

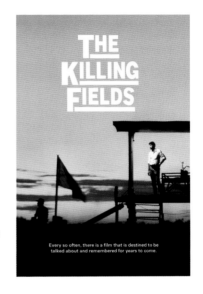

Every so often, there is a film that is destined to be talked about and remembered for years to come.

1979	1981	1982	1985	1987	1989
The Deer Hunter wins five Academy Awards, including Best Picture and Best Director.	In *Cutter's Way*, an obsessive, mutilated veteran symbolizes the damage wrought in Vietnam.	The Vietnam Veterans Memorial in Washington, DC, is completed. It is inscribed with the names of the 58,175 US servicemen killed.	Nonprofessional actor Haing S. Ngor wins an Academy Award for Best Actor in a Supporting Role for *The Killing Fields*.	Barry Levinson (b. 1942) directs *Good Morning, Vietnam*; it is based on the work of an armed forces radio presenter popular with troops serving in Vietnam.	*Casualties of War* is released. It focuses on the incident on Hill 192 in 1966, in which a Vietnamese girl is raped and beaten by US soldiers.

Apocalypse Now 1979
FRANCIS FORD COPPOLA b. 1939

▲ In a jarring image, a priest conducts Holy Communion on the battlefield.

▼ Marlon Brando's head—famously shaven for the part of Kurtz—dominates the dark, minimalistic poster.

At a Cannes press conference in 1979, Francis Ford Coppola said of the unfinished *Apocalypse Now*: "My film is not about Vietnam, it *is* Vietnam. It's what it was really like . . . and the way we made it was very much like the way the Americans were in Vietnam. We were in the jungle, we had access to too much money, too much equipment, and little by little we went insane."

George Lucas and John Milius (both b. 1944) had the idea of adapting Joseph Conrad's *Heart of Darkness* as a Vietnam movie, but it was taken up by their mentor Coppola. The epic film is structured as a series of set pieces along a river journey into hell: an air cavalry attack on a Vietcong village so Colonel Kilgore (Robert Duvall) can capture a surfing breakwater; the Playboy bunnies performing in a jungle amphitheater; the inadvertent massacre of a sampan full of peasants; Dennis Hopper's freaked-out photojournalist; and Marlon Brando's last-reel appearance as Kurtz, a tribal god in Cambodia awaiting his murderer. Coppola's masterpiece is visually stunning and his surrealist sequences, in particular, enhance the confusion and horror of the Vietnam conflict.

Apocalypse Now has entered the language: "Terminate with extreme prejudice"; "Charlie don't surf"; "I love the smell of napalm in the morning." As the documentary *Hearts of Darkness: A Filmmaker's Apocalypse* shows, the making of the movie—over budget, with Ferdinand Marcos taking back his choppers to fight rebels, Harvey Keitel fired and replaced by Martin Sheen (who nearly died of a heart attack), and Brando and Hopper improvising hours of nonsense as Coppola tried to make up his mind about the ending—is part of the legend. **KN**

👁 KEY SCENES

1 "THIS IS THE END"
Recorded in quintaphonic sound, the choppers sound as if they are actually flying overhead. Then the jungle erupts into surreal flames to the tune of The Doors' "The End." The scene fades from a burning jungle to Willard (Martin Sheen), going crazy in a hotel room.

2 "RIDE OF THE VALKYRIES"
Colonel Kilgore leads a helicopter attack against an enemy village, blaring out Wagner to spook the Vietcong; music played an integral part in the impact of *Apocalypse Now*. The film's innovative sound design, masterminded by Walter Murch, won an Oscar.

3 TIGER ATTACK
Chef (Frederic Forrest) and Willard get out of the boat to find mangoes but are terrified by the appearance of a tiger. "Never get out of the boat," muses Willard. "Unless you were going the whole way. Kurtz got off the boat. He split from the whole fucking program."

4 THE HOLLOW MAN
Kurtz rambles on philosophically, quoting T. S. Eliot and—in extremis—Joseph Conrad ("The horror, the horror"). Much of Brando's dialogue was improvised. His scenes were shot in heavy chiaroscuro, adding to the claustrophobia and drama of the performance.

🕐 DIRECTOR PROFILE

1939–63
Born in Detroit, Coppola grew up in New York. He entered the movie world as assistant to Roger Corman (b. 1926), doing odd jobs such as reediting Russian science fiction films and shooting nudie movies (*Tonight for Sure*, 1962). Coppola produced his debut feature, *Dementia 13*, in 1963.

1964–72
Coppola made a freewheeling, US New Wave movie (*You're a Big Boy Now*, 1966), experienced the hassle of working on a big studio runaway production (*Finian's Rainbow*, 1968) and renewed himself by going small and independent again (*The Rain People*, 1969). He was given the job of directing *The Godfather* mainly because of his Italian-American name.

1973–82
After making the ambitious sequel *The Godfather, Part II* (1974) and the smaller-scale *The Conversation* (1974, see p. 348), Coppola founded his own San Francisco–based studio Zoetrope, where he produced George Lucas's first films (*THX 1138*, 1971; *American Graffiti*, 1973) and an ambitious slate of projects. *Apocalypse Now* became a byword for excess but paid off on release, although Coppola tinkered with it for decades. A similarly scaled musical, *One from the Heart* (1982), sank Zoetrope.

1983–97
A contrite Coppola made low-budget youth films (*The Outsiders*, 1983; *Rumble Fish*, 1983) and a succession of well-behaved commercial properties (*Peggy Sue Got Married*, 1986; *Dracula*, 1992; *The Rainmaker*, 1997). His old habits returned in big, personal projects that did not quite click (*The Cotton Club*, 1984; *Tucker: The Man and His Dream*, 1988). Even *The Godfather, Part III* (1990) was not a surefire success.

1998–present
After a period away from cinema—during which his director daughter Sofia (b. 1971) and actor nephew Nicolas Cage, both of whom he once employed, became more bankable than he was—Coppola made smaller films again, including *Youth Without Youth* (2007) and *Tetro* (2009).

Platoon 1986
OLIVER STONE b. 1946

▲ New recruit Chris Taylor takes his bearings in Vietnam.

▼ A famous Art Greenspon photo from 1968 inspired the pose for the film's poster.

Writer-director Oliver Stone was the first Vietnam veteran to gain the Hollywood clout to make an autobiographical film about the conflict. *The Deer Hunter* (1978) and *Apocalypse Now* (1979, see p. 394) opened up the war as a film subject, but it was *Platoon* that brought home the reality of Vietnam to generations who came of age after the war was over.

Chris Taylor (Charlie Sheen), a stand-in for Stone, is an idealistic youth who has volunteered for a tour of duty with the infantry in Vietnam. He finds himself torn between two "fathers," the gentle and sensitive super-soldier Sergeant Elias (Willem Dafoe), who smokes dope and listens to soul music with black GIs, and the scar-faced and sadistic Staff Sergeant Barnes (Tom Berenger), who drinks booze and listens to country and western with rednecks. Chris follows the path of previous screen soldiers by "becoming a man," but while the recruits whipped into shape by John Wayne would always wind up saluting the flag, Chris ultimately loses his faith in America amid the blood and confusion.

Despite being overly schematic in its opposition of the two sergeants and their contrasted philosophies, *Platoon* is a powerful picture. Barnes, though terrifying, does teach Chris how to survive rather than become a martyr—the climax, unthinkable in earlier war films, consists of Chris making a last stand not by facing up to the enemy but by shooting a superior officer. As grueling and suspenseful as the film is, it is not untouched by nostalgia—the soundtrack consists of greatest hits from the 1960s and in one scene the soldiers sing along to "The Tracks of My Tears" by Smokey Robinson & The Miracles. **KN**

KEY SCENES

1 NEW RECRUIT
Chris arrives in Vietnam—clean-cut and idealistic, an all-American boy. The part had also been offered to Charlie Sheen's brother, Emilio Estevez, although he had to pass on it. Johnny Depp was approached for the role at one point, but was considered too young.

2 MASSACRE
A tense situation in a Vietnamese village gets out of hand and the jittery GIs perpetrate a war crime. The incident turns Chris, who was initially gravitating toward Barnes, toward Elias, who reports Barnes and another soldier for their part in the atrocity.

3 MARTYRDOM
Having been wounded by Barnes and deliberately left behind in the jungle, Elias is hunted and killed by the Vietcong. He assumes a cruciform pose as he is shot dead, watched despairingly by the rest of his platoon from an airborne helicopter.

4 OLD HAND
Now bloodied and disillusioned, Chris leaves Vietnam. He has undergone something of a rite of passage, and in his closing words speaks of the debt and duty those who survive owe to those who did not make it back from the conflict.

DIRECTOR PROFILE

1946–85
Oliver Stone was born in New York City, the son of a Wall Street banker. He later dropped out of Yale. After service with two different regiments in Vietnam (Stone was awarded a Purple Heart and Bronze Star for Gallantry), he began directing, making his debut with the short film *Last Year in Viet Nam* (1971). He went on to create low-budget horror films (*Seizure*, 1974; *The Hand*, 1981) and script higher-profile contemporary crime dramas (*Midnight Express*, 1978; *Scarface*, 1983; *Year of the Dragon*, 1985).

1986–87
Stone made his name as a director of films specifically concerned with US politics and mores, indicting contemporary US foreign policy (*Salvador*, 1986) and economic ethics (*Wall Street*, 1987) and returning to his Vietnam experience with the Oscar-winning autobiographical *Platoon*; Tom Berenger and Willem Dafoe were also nominated.

1988–95
He completed his "Vietnam trilogy" with *Born on the Fourth of July* (1989)—garnering another Best Director Oscar, and an Oscar nomination for lead Tom Cruise—and *Heaven & Earth* (1993), the latter told from a Vietnamese perspective. Stone picked over other US political and cultural scabs in *Talk Radio* (1988), *The Doors* (1991), *JFK* (1991)—Stone's favorite of his own movies—*Natural Born Killers* (1994), and *Nixon* (1995).

1996–2008
Having directed ten films in nine years, Stone slowed down his work rate. Sports movie *Any Given Sunday* (1999) was a box-office hit. He went on to make documentaries about US bêtes noires Fidel Castro (*Comandante*, 2003) and Hugo Chávez (*South of the Border*, 2009), together with ill-advised epic *Alexander* (2004). *World Trade Center* (2006) and the George W. Bush biography *W* (2008) addressed the state of the nation.

2009–present
In Stone's sequel *Wall Street: Money Never Sleeps* (2010) Michael Douglas reprised his memorable role of Gordon Gekko.

ACTION-ADVENTURE

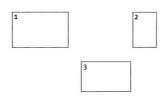

In the disenchanted mood of the late 1960s and early 1970s cinema tended to shun the simple shoot-'em-up thrills of chase, cowboy, or secret agent films. *Bullitt* (1968) and *The French Connection* (1971) may have offered set-piece car chases, but their settings involved cynicism, politicking, and antiestablishment heroes. *Dirty Harry* (1971) turned cowboy Clint Eastwood into Harry Callahan, the maverick cop archetype of the urban action film. Traditional Westerns and war films were replaced by lectures on the evils of violence, shown graphically in Sam Peckinpah (1925–84) films such as *The Wild Bunch* (1969) and *Straw Dogs* (1971).

The martial arts action film made an explosive entrance into mainstream Western cinema in the early 1970s, thanks to the iconic Bruce Lee. *Enter the Dragon* (1973, above) was the first Chinese martial arts film produced by a big Hollywood studio. Although Lee did not live to see the end result, his work influenced martial arts films all over the world for decades to come.

By the late 1970s, the mood had changed again. Directed by George Lucas (b. 1944), *Star Wars* (1977, see p. 366) is a return to the era of 1930s comic book heroes such as Flash Gordon, in which warfare in space is antiseptic—planets are blown up with no real sense of suffering—and bombing runs, a homestead massacre, and sword duels are not real felt events but references to scenes in earlier movies. Lucas and friend Steven Spielberg (b. 1946) continued to show their love for old-fashioned excitement in *Raiders of the Lost Ark* (1981, see p. 400).

Directed by Richard Donner (b. 1930), *Superman* (1978) made audiences "believe a man can fly"—and that Clark Kent (Christopher Reeve) was not an

1 *Enter the Dragon* saw Bruce Lee at the peak of his martial art powers prior to his tragically premature death in 1973.

2 Ellen Ripley (Sigourney Weaver) stands alongside Hollywood's best action heroes in the poster for *Aliens*.

3 John McClane (Bruce Willis) gets more than he bargained for when he drops in at his wife's office party in *Die Hard*.

KEY EVENTS

1971	1972	1974	1977	1979	1982
Sam Peckinpah takes violence to another level in *Straw Dogs*. It sparks controversy over the increase in violence on the big screen.	Steve McQueen and Ali McGraw go on the run after a botched heist in *The Getaway*.	Charles Bronson's architect turns vigilante in *Death Wish*. It reflects the growing mood in the United States as crime levels rise.	George Lucas's *Star Wars* revives the serial-style thrills of Flash Gordon and Buck Rogers for a new generation.	Former karate champion Chuck Norris stars in the martial arts film *A Force of One*.	Bodybuilder Arnold Schwarzenegger finds his first great screen role as *Conan the Barbarian*.

outdated character. Alex Raymond's comic book hero also got an update in *Flash Gordon* (1980), but despite its camp style and Queen soundtrack, the film did not do well at the box office. *Batman*, by Tim Burton (b. 1958), fared better in 1989, offering a darker, gothic superhero in withdrawn Bruce Wayne (Michael Keaton).

In the 1980s action-adventure films featured ever more muscular heroes. Arnold Schwarzenegger flexed pecs and snarled his few words as Conan and the Terminator. Sylvester Stallone transformed Rambo from a traumatized Vietnam veteran at war with his own country into a superhero out to even a score ("Do we get to win this time?") and Rocky from a washed-up slugger to a champion of America. Bruce Willis, then best known as Cybill Shepherd's wise-cracking costar in the television series *Moonlighting*, fought mock terrorists in a one-man crusade in *Die Hard* (1988, below) and its popular sequels. Such films were full of montages in which macho men train their bodies to sweat-sheened perfection or assemble a ridiculous amount of firepower in fetishized weaponry. *Commando* (1985) may be the most deliriously sado-erotic of these hulk-on-hulk spectacles, but *Predator* (1987) comes a close second, pitting Arnie against an alien. *The Killer* (1989), by Hong Kong's John Woo (b.1946), inspired a host of like-minded (violent) movies, including *Léon* (1994). Meanwhile, *Lethal Weapon*'s (1987) Mel Gibson and Danny Glover constituted only one of many mismatched cop teams in buddy cop movies such as *Stakeout* (1987).

The Bond franchise was reignited by Timothy Dalton in two grittier outings that prefigure later restarts with Pierce Brosnan and Daniel Craig. While with *Aliens* (1986, above right), James Cameron (b. 1954) followed up the original *Alien* (1979) with more direct action than horror—"This time, it's war"—for Sigourney Weaver's return as self-reliant, tough girl Ellen Ripley. **KN**

1984	1987	1988	1989	1989	1990
Arnold Schwarzenegger plays a killer robot from the future in the first *Terminator* (see p. 402) movie.	Timothy Dalton plays James Bond, 007, in *The Living Daylights*.	Bruce Willis dons a torn vest to play cop John McClane in *Die Hard*.	John Woo's *The Killer* attracts international attention. It is ironic, supercool, and has a body count that dwarfs any films emerging from the United States.	Tim Burton's *Batman* inaugurates a new generation of superhero films.	*Nikita*, by Luc Besson (b. 1959), mixes Hollywood and Eastern influences. Its assassin heroine is a style icon as much for her guns as her dress sense.

Raiders of the Lost Ark 1981
STEVEN SPIELBERG b. 1946

▲ In the opening scene, Indy takes a sacred gold idol—and nearly dies in the attempt.

▼ A retro look for the poster. Ford was Spielberg's first choice for the title role.

t is 1936. Indiana Jones (Harrison Ford), archaeology lecturer and treasure hunter, enters a booby-trapped South American tomb in search of a golden idol. He escapes with his life (just) but loses the prize to rival Bellocq (Paul Freeman). However, he gets to pit his wits against him again when the US government sends him to find the Ark of the Covenant (the vessel for the Ten Commandments) before the Nazis do. To complete the quest, Indy has to reunite with his fractious ex-girlfriend Marion (Karen Allen), battle countless foes, overcome his terror of snakes, and discover the meaning of ancient mysteries.

Star Wars grew out of producer-writer George Lucas's love of the Flash Gordon serials, whereas this collaboration with Steven Spielberg is rooted in the earthbound adventure serials of the 1930s and 1940s. Ford's Indy is as grumpy and battered as a 1970s movie hero, but endures the sort of perils faced by earlier heroes such as Buster Crabbe. Even the joke about his need to keep his fedora hat firmly on his head is rooted in the habit of serial heroes who did the same to conceal the fact that their more strenuous feats were performed by stunt doubles.

An enormously entertaining, confidently made romp, *Raiders of the Lost Ark* has an odd aspect—reversed in *Indiana Jones and the Temple of Doom* (1984) and *Indiana Jones and the Last Crusade* (1989)—the hero is sidelined as the film reaches its climax. Indy is tied to a post while the plot is resolved and justice meted out by a supernatural force. God beats the Nazis—irrespective of Indy's heroics—and the government consigns the holy relic to a huge warehouse straight out of *Citizen Kane* (1941, see p.110). **KN**

👁 KEY SCENES

1 THE SPIRIT OF ADVENTURE
The Paramount studio logo segues into a shot of a real mountain and the film begins. This device immediately gives the audience a flavor of the action, exoticism, and mystery in store—as well as being a neat visual trick.

4 THE GIANT SWORDSMAN
During a skirmish in Cairo, a formidable swordsman emerges from the crowd and demonstrates great dexterity with his blade. Rather than taking him on with his bullwhip, Indy pulls a pistol and casually shoots him. Harrison Ford suggested the end to this scene.

2 PERIL IN THE TEMPLE
The giant boulder, unleashed when Indy takes the idol from the altar, rolls after the adventurer as he runs across a booby-trapped chamber with poison darts coming from both sides. This hair-raising opening whets the audience's appetite for the thrills to come.

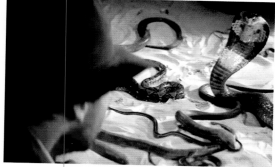

5 "WHY'D IT HAVE TO BE SNAKES?"
After being lowered into the pit, Indy comes face to face with his greatest fear, snakes. The scene was filmed with real snakes and a glass pane separating them from Harrison Ford. The cobra in front of him actually spat venom on to the glass during filming.

3 REUNION
Indy reappears in ex-lover Marion's life. He is recognizable by the shadow (particularly that of his trademark fedora) cast on the wall of her Nepalese bar. The distinctive silhouette of the hero appears repeatedly throughout the Indiana Jones franchise.

6 THE POWER OF GOD
The Ark of the Covenant is opened and the power of God smites the Nazis—Toht's face melts off his skull. Indy and Marion remain tied to the post and survive the conflagration because they keep their eyes shut and do not look at the Ark.

The Terminator 1984

JAMES CAMERON b. 1954

▲ Cyborg assassin the Terminator is a powerfully efficient killing machine.

▼ *The Terminator* fed the decade's thirst for action films with larger-than-life heroes.

In a future in which self-aware machines are at war with humanity, rebel leader John Connor is the key to the victory and ultimate survival of his people. In an attempt to prevent this happening, the SkyNet computer uses a time machine to transport a flesh-coated cyborg assassin (Arnold Schwarzenegger) to Los Angeles in 1984 to murder Connor's mother, Sarah (Linda Hamilton), before the hero is born. Connor retaliates by sending his trusted lieutenant, Kyle Reese (Michael Biehn), to keep his mother alive long enough to secure his future existence. Connor also has a hidden agenda, sending his friend back in time to become his father: he is also to die and thereby inspire Sarah to become the warrior woman he needs to raise him.

The Terminator is a great science fiction–action film that weds ideas from *The Outer Limits* and Philip K. Dick stories to the relentless, roller-coaster pacing of movies such as *Halloween* (1978). Although the Conan films had made him a muscleman hero, Schwarzenegger secured screen immortality with his one-time-only villain role (much better here than as the good guy robot in the sequels). The Terminator wipes out a club full of dancers and a police station full of cops in its single-minded search for Sarah Connor, gradually losing human shape to appear as a robo-skeleton for the final showdown.

James Cameron made his first big splash with this surprisingly intelligent B picture. Its themes—the hero who sacrifices himself to save an ideal woman, a paradoxical distrust of and fascination with technology and firepower—would recur more elaborately in his later films, such as *Avatar* (2009). **KN**

👁 KEY SCENES

1 "GIVE ME YOUR CLOTHES"
The deadly cyborg assassin, played by the pumped-up Schwarzenegger, makes his memorable entrance, completely naked. He soon approaches some street roughs and kills them for their clothing, before later donning his trademark leathers.

2 "COME WITH ME IF YOU WANT TO LIVE!"
Kyle Reese offers Sarah Connor a way out of danger at the club, but she has to trust him instantly. Sarah is a waitress who has no idea about her own importance as John Connor's mother. Her character is dramatically transformed during the course of the film and its sequel.

3 "I'LL BE BACK!"
The Terminator drives into a police station and slaughters dozens of cops in his pursuit of Sarah Connor. Schwarzenegger trained for weeks in handling guns before filming began. *Soldier of Fortune* magazine complimented him on his realistic handling of weapons.

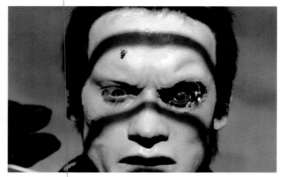

4 DO-IT-YOURSELF REPAIRS
While working on his injured eye, the Terminator is bothered by a motel manager. He scrolls down a menu of possible responses and selects the appropriate bon mot. Makeup artist Stan Winston was responsible for the film's visual effects.

🕐 DIRECTOR PROFILE

1954–83
James Cameron was born in Canada in 1954, but his family moved to the United States when he was seventeen. He quit his job as a truck driver after seeing *Star Wars* in 1977 and collaborated with Randall Frakes on an ambitious science fiction short, *Xenogenesis* (1978). He worked in effects and in technical capacities for Roger Corman (b.1926) and others, contributing to *Rock 'n' Roll High School* (1979), *Battle Beyond the Stars* (1980), *Escape from New York* (1981), *Galaxy of Terror* (1981), and *Android* (1982). His directorial debut was the troubled *Piranha 2: The Spawning* (1981), which was taken over by producer Ovidio Assonitis.

1984–89
Following the success of *The Terminator*, Cameron was sought after for studio sequels, scripting *Rambo: First Blood, Part II* (1985), and writing and directing *Aliens* (1986). A personal project, *The Abyss* (1989)—although technically innovative—was less successful and gained Cameron a reputation for perfectionism and self-indulgence.

1990–99
He revisited his breakthrough career point with *Terminator 2: Judgment Day* (1991), which modified the pessimism of the earlier film and featured pioneering CGI work. He produced and cowrote films (*Point Break*, 1991; *Strange Days*, 1995) for his then-wife Kathryn Bigelow (b. 1951) and delivered another hit with the comedy action film *True Lies* (1994), starring Arnold Schwarzenegger. *Titanic* (1997), a huge, troubled personal project, was released to enormous acclaim, box-office success, and an Oscar sweep.

2000–present
Cameron made underwater documentaries (*Ghosts of the Abyss*, 2003; *Aliens of the Deep*, 2005) and stayed away from commercial cinema for the best part of a decade. He returned triumphantly in 2009 with the 3-D science-fiction blockbuster *Avatar*, which won three Academy Awards. *Titanic* and *Avatar* remain the highest-grossing films to date.

EIGHTIES COMEDIES

When considering comedy films in the 1980s, one of the first phrase that springs to mind is "teen movie." This was the decade that saw Ferris Bueller skip school and take on the town, Joel Goodsen run amok in *Risky Business* (1983), and Marty McFly travel through time to drop in on his adolescent parents. Naughty but nice, these boys were fresh-faced teens on the cusp of adulthood, their cheeky charm and rebellious spirits thriving over the course of each riotous romp. Cockiness was applauded in the ambitious, career-minded 1980s: look at the entrepreneurial spirit of precocious young characters, a quality *Back to the Future* (1985) star Michael J. Fox also brought to *The Secret of My Success* (1987). They were often on the wrong side of authority figures who were routinely mocked, such as the teachers in *Ferris Bueller's Day Off* (1986, left) and *The Breakfast Club* (1985). There was a teen hero for every audience member, from nerds (*Revenge of the Nerds*, 1984) to losers in love (*Gregory's Girl*, 1981) and goofy duos (*Bill & Ted's Excellent Adventure*, 1989). For the young adventurers there was *The Goonies* (1985), while testosterone-fueled adolescents had *Porky's* (1982).

Porky's was a natural successor to the *National Lampoon* series launched in 1978, and a precursor to films such as *American Pie* (1999). These teen sex romps appeared with increasing regularity in the 1980s, as did farcical, extreme parodies such as *Airplane!* (1980, above) and *Top Secret!* (1984), which spoofed the disaster and spy movie genres respectively. A more sophisticated parody

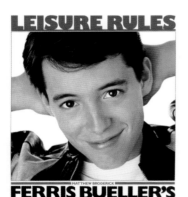

KEY EVENTS

1980	1980	1981	1982	1983	1983
Spoof *Airplane!* receives Golden Globe and BAFTA nominations, the latter a particularly rare accolade for a comedy.	*Saturday Night Live* stars Bill Murray and Chevy Chase appear in the wacky *Caddyshack*.	*Time Bandits* builds on the success of the Monty Python films and taps into the growing demand for family-friendly fantasy comedies.	The teen sex romp takes off with *Fast Times in Ridgemont High*, while *Airplane!* returns with *Airplane II: The Sequel*.	Race and class are explored in the life-swap comedy *Trading Places*, while Tom Cruise rises to fame in *Risky Business*.	Steve Martin cowrit and stars in *The Ma with Two Brains*, confirming his posi as a major comic contender.

came in the form of *This Is Spinal Tap* (1984, see p. 406), a hit spoof about a fictitious British heavy metal band that spawned the "mockumentary" genre.

Ambitious women were a source of fish-out-of-water comedy in *Nine to Five* (1980), *Private Benjamin* (1980), *Working Girl* (1988), and *Shirley Valentine* (1989). These movies reflected contemporary concerns about women's rights in both the workplace and the home, while losing no opportunity to laugh at the problems they faced and the hapless men in positions of authority. No longer content to be just the hero's love interest, feisty and forward-thinking actresses demanded their share of the action and the laughs: look at Kathleen Turner's Joan Wilder in *Romancing the Stone* (1984) or Jamie Lee Curtis in *A Fish Called Wanda* (1988), a film populated by hilariously foolish men. By the end of the decade, the sexes had found a way to coexist (by debating their differences) in *When Harry Met Sally* (1989, below). Drawing on Woody Allen and screwball comedy, and cementing the template for contemporary romantic comedies, *When Harry Met Sally* proved a high point in the careers of all involved.

Technological developments brought the possibility of walking, talking monsters and all the comical opportunities that came with them. *Gremlins* and *Ghostbusters* (both 1984) merged comedy horror with family fantasy to groundbreaking effect, while advances in animation enabled *Who Framed Roger Rabbit* (1988, see p. 408) to mix live action and cartoon characters with a result far more sophisticated than, say, *Bedknobs and Broomsticks* (1971). With their precocious teens and working women, the comedies of the 1980s reflected the changes of the decades, and generally found something to laugh at despite society's prevailing anxieties. **AS**

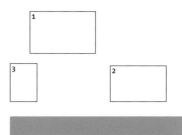

1 *Airplane!* was a spoof of disaster movies and a nonstop assault of wisecracks and visual gags.

2 Can men and women ever really be friends without sex getting in the way? *When Harry Met Sally* attempts to answer this question.

3 Matthew Broderick in *Ferris Bueller's Day Off*—just one of director John Hughes's many successful comedies in the 1980s.

1984	1985	1986	1987	1988	1989
Science-fiction horror comedies *Gremlins* and *Ghostbusters* are hits; as are police comedies *Beverly Hills Cop* and *Police Academy*.	Teen comedies cash in at the box office with *Back to the Future*, *The Breakfast Club*, *The Goonies*, and *Weird Science*.	*Ferris Bueller's Day Off* continues the teen trend, while new fish-out-of-water comedies include *Crocodile Dundee* and *Short Circuit*.	Director John Hughes aims at an older market with *Planes, Trains & Automobiles*, starring Steve Martin and John Candy.	Writers look to the skies with *Earth Girls Are Easy* and *My Stepmother Is an Alien*. Body-swap comedy *Big* has a more earthly supernatural twist.	*When Harry Met Sally* is to become one of the 1980s' most quoted romantic comedies ("I'll have what she's having").

This Is Spinal Tap 1984

ROB REINER b. 1947

▲ Grimacing rock god Nigel Tufnel puts his axe through its paces.

▼ The film's poster, in all its long-haired, leopard-skin, cowboy-booted glory.

Filmmaker Marty DiBergi (Rob Reiner) accompanies British band Spinal Tap—who have evolved from their Beatles knock-off early days into a heavy metal group "currently residing in the 'Where Are They Now?' file"—on an eventful, disastrous tour to promote their *Smell the Glove* album. When David St. Hubbins (Michael McKean) brings in his girlfriend Jeanine (June Chadwick) as manager to replace long-suffering Ian Faith (Tony Hendra), David's best friend Nigel Tufnel (Christopher Guest) quits. Is this the end for Spinal Tap?

The first feature from Reiner and cowritten (or made up on the spot) by the cast, this was—like *The Blues Brothers* (1980)—built around a parody band created for a television comedy (the one-off pilot *The T.V. Show*, 1979) and features some credibly over-the-top heavy metal songs ("Big Bottom," "Sex Farm") performed as befits "one of England's loudest bands." Influenced perhaps by the television movie *The Rutles: All You Need Is Cash* (1978), *This Is Spinal Tap* pokes fun at the reverential attitude of rock documentaries such as *Let It Be* (1970) and *The Last Waltz* (1978) and highlights the pretensions and absurdities of stadium rock—which has not stopped rock stars from behaving like Spinal Tap.

Among the freshest and most rewatchable comedies of the 1980s, this film is full of tiny, hilarious moments (Billy Crystal's "Mime is money") and perfectly pitched performances (Fran Drescher, Paul Shaffer). It is also canny enough to incorporate an emotional spine as the band nearly splits thanks to an interfering girlfriend but gets back together when boyhood friends David and Nigel realize they cannot live without (a) the music and (b) each other. **KN**

👁 KEY SCENES

1 THE *SMELL THE GLOVE* ALBUM COVER
Bobbi Flekman: "Ian, you put a greased, naked woman on all fours with a dog collar around her neck, and a leash, and a man's arm extended out up to here, holding on to the leash, and pushing a black glove in her face to sniff it. You don't find that offensive?"

3 THE STONEHENGE DEBACLE
Thanks to a mix-up between feet and inches on a rough diagram, a vital piece of stage scenery is too small. "I think that the problem may have been that there was a Stonehenge monument on the stage that was in danger of being crushed by a dwarf."

2 "WELL, IT'S ONE LOUDER, ISN'T IT?"
Nigel points out that all the amp numbers go up to eleven. Marty says, "Does that mean it's louder? Is it any louder?" to which Nigel replies, "Well, it's one louder, isn't it? It's not ten. You see, most blokes, you know, will be playing at ten . . . . Where can you go from there?"

4 NIGEL REJOINS THE BAND
Acting as an emissary for Ian, Nigel meets the band backstage prior to their farewell gig to announce that "Sex Farm" is a big hit in Japan and a tour is imminent. Later, he is watching from the wings when David summons him and Nigel joins in . . . to mild applause.

THE MOCK-DOC

In *Culloden* (1964), Peter Watkins (b. 1935) recreated history as documentary, with on-the-fly interviews, voice-over stats, and the rough-hewn look of news footage. *David Holzman's Diary* (1967), directed by Jim McBride (b. 1941), refined the mode, while in *Zelig* (1983), Woody Allen (b. 1935) explored its comic side. Christopher "Nigel Tufnel" Guest (b. 1948) continues to work the form (*Best in Show*, 2000, right; *A Mighty Wind*, 2003; *For Your Consideration*, 2006). *This Is Spinal Tap*'s influence can be seen in the rap-themed *Fear of a Black Hat* (1994) and the inside-Hollywood joke *The Disappearance of Kevin Johnson* (1996). The mock-doc has also become a horror film commonplace (*The Blair Witch Project*, 1999; *Diary of the Dead*, 2007; *Paranormal Activity*, 2007).

Who Framed Roger Rabbit 1988

ROBERT ZEMECKIS b. 1951

▲ Bob Hoskins with femme fatale Jessica Rabbit, huskily voiced by Kathleen Turner.

▼ The film reunited Zemeckis with his *Back to the Future* star Christopher Lloyd.

Hollywood, 1947: Roger Rabbit, costar of the successful Baby Herman cartoons, suspects his wife of being unfaithful. Private eye Eddie Valiant (Bob Hoskins) is hired by Roger's boss to obtain evidence that will convince Roger to file for divorce. Eddie photographs the voluptuous "toon" wife with gagmeister Marvin Acme and Roger goes wild. When Acme is found murdered, Roger becomes suspect number one and appeals to Eddie to clear his name. Shackled together, human and toon work the case, and are drawn to Toontown, the cartoon ghetto, where a fiendish conspiracy is being hatched.

Who Framed Roger Rabbit was a technical and logistical achievement: its seamless blend of human and animated action was masterful, and the resolution of the legal tussles required to secure cameo appearances by a horde of copyrighted cartoon characters from Disney, Warner Bros., and others was remarkable. Among the historic moments are the first teamings of Donald and Daffy Duck, and Mickey Mouse and Bugs Bunny. Unfortunately, Roger himself (voiced by Charles Fleischer) is too frenetic in his Tex Avery–style mugging to convince as someone with actual feelings, whereas Hoskins's hard-drinking burnout Eddie imports a touch of real pain that adds to the grit. Robert Zemeckis and animator Richard Williams mix animation and live action deftly, packing the frame with jokes worth revisiting (a cartoon cabbie driving a real car) and going wild when the human passes into the insanity of Toontown, where everything is alive and bumptious, pulling off the nightmare comedy stylings of Tex Avery, Chuck Jones, Friz Freleng, and Disney. **KN**

👁 KEY SCENES

1 THE REVEAL
The shooting of a 2-D cartoon is interrupted, and a human director interacts with 3-D toons. The floor falls out of a cartoon world in a manner that honors the old Warner Bros. conceit that Bugs, Daffy, and company all worked for the studio.

2 DAFFY AND DONALD SPAR
Daffy Duck expresses displeasure with his costar Donald Duck—"Thith ith the latht time I work with thomeone with a thpeech impediment"—in an astonishing, previously impossible crossover between the toon stables of Disney and Warner Bros.

3 JESSICA RABBIT
Roger's wife turns out not to be a cartoon rabbit but a curvy pinup in the mold of Rita Hayworth in *Gilda* (1946). Her "performance model" is Betsy Brantley, while Amy Irving provides the vocals to the sultry "Why Don't You Do Right? (Like Some Other Men Do)."

4 VISION OF DOOM
The villainous Judge Doom (Christopher Lloyd) offers a chilling picture of his idea of the future of Los Angeles: "I see a place where people get on and off the freeway. On and off, off and on all day, all night . . . . My God, it'll be beautiful."

🕐 DIRECTOR PROFILE

1951–80
Born in Chicago, Robert Zemeckis started out directing student short films (*The Lift*, 1972; *Field of Honor*, 1973). He teamed with fellow ex-University of Southern California film student Bob Gale to write an episode of cult television series *Kolchak: The Night Stalker*, as well as madcap folly *1941* (1979) for Steven Spielberg (b. 1946). Spielberg served as Zemeckis's mentor, also producing his first features as director (*I Wanna Hold Your Hand*, 1978, and *Used Cars*, 1980).

1981–93
He became an A-list Hollywood director with a run of hits that mixed big stars, effects savvy, and a scurrilous comic insight into US insanities. There was the Kathleen Turner and Michael Douglas comedy adventure *Romancing the Stone* (1984), the *Back to the Future* trilogy (1985, 1989, 1990), *Who Framed Roger Rabbit*, and the Goldie Hawn, Meryl Streep, and Bruce Willis vehicle *Death Becomes Her* (1992), which won an Academy Award for Best Visual Effects.

1994–2003
Following and including the Oscar-winning *Forrest Gump* (1994), Zemeckis's features became less openly comedic and more arch (*Contact*, 1997; *What Lies Beneath*, 2000; *Cast Away* 2000). He went on to produce horror films for Ernest Dickerson (b. 1951—*Tales from the Crypt: Demon Knight*, 1996—and Peter Jackson (b. 1961)—*The Frighteners*, 1996. Continuing in this vein, his Dark Castle production company created a run of mid-budget horrors (including *House on Haunted Hill*, 1999, and *Thir13en Ghosts*, 2001).

2004–present
Zemeckis abandoned live-action work in favor of CGI toons (latterly, with 3-D): *The Polar Express* (2004), *Beowulf* (2007), *A Christmas Carol* (2009), and a remake of The Beatles's *Yellow Submarine* (planned for 2012). In 2010 he announced work on *Timeless*, a return to live-action filmmaking and the theme of time travel (which he manipulated so memorably in *Back to the Future*).

BRITISH CINEMA

Filmmaking at its most potent can act as a mirror, forcing audiences to look at themselves. And no decade was more interested in looking at itself than the 1980s. During this fraught, filthy-rich, and poverty-stricken decade, Britain became a moviemaking powerhouse and its films were daring, unpredictable, ambitious, and divisive—mirroring the social and political state of the country.

Britain was competing on an international level. With *Chariots of Fire* (1981, above) and *Gandhi* (1982), its film industry was producing big films—ambitious stories that make money, win awards, and put studios on the map. As well as the landmark hits, cinema that discussed the current situation in Thatcherite Britain was alive and declaring itself. Films such as *My Beautiful Laundrette* (1985) commented on issues of identity, the youth of Britain, India's relationship to the United Kingdom, and homosexuality. Its portrait of a dark undercurrent in Britain contrasted with the excesses of the eighties, and the film's frank portrayal of gay culture was both timely and controversial. Cinema and politics became closely linked, with the government maintaining the pointed interest in British cinema that it had taken during the 1970s, provoking the suspicion of authority seen in *Defense of the Realm* (1985) and the frank anarchism of the work of Alex Cox (b. 1954), most famously *Sid and Nancy* (1986).

The changing times were likewise reflected in the rising British talent making waves in cinemas across the world. Helen Mirren was proving herself to be a remarkably individual and versatile leading lady in films as various as *The Long Good Friday* (1980), *Excalibur* (1981), *Pascali's Island* (1988), and

1 Harold Abrahams (Ben Cross) lags behind in the Trinity Great Court Run, but goes on to win the race—and the hundred meters at the 1924 Olympics—in *Chariots of Fire*.

2 *A Room with a View* paired Helena Bonham Carter with Julian Sands and marked a peak for production company Merchant Ivory, purveyors of well-acted, beautifully staged period drama.

3 Charles Crichton's directorial swan song, *A Fish Called Wanda*, offered up a memorable torture scene involving fries.

KEY EVENTS

1981	1981	1982	1982	1983	1983
Chariots of Fire wins Best Picture at both the Academy Awards and the BAFTAs, while composer Vangelis is also recognized for his iconic score.	For his supporting turn in the hit comedy *Arthur*, acting legend John Gielgud wins his first—and only—Academy Award.	FilmFour, a cornerstone of British film, releases its first production, *Walter*, directed by Stephen Frears (b. 1941).	*Gandhi*, an epic biopic by Richard Attenborough (b. 1923), is released. It will win eight Oscars, including Best Picture and Best Actor for Ben Kingsley.	Using an all-woman crew, Sally Potter (b. 1949) makes her director's debut with *The Gold Diggers*, a feminist drama starring Julie Christie.	The Director of Public Prosecutions issues a list of "video nasties." Thirty-two films are prosecuted, including *The Evil Dead* (1981) and *The Driller Killer* (1979).

The Cook, the Thief, His Wife and Her Lover (1989). The so-called "Brit Pack" emerged with stars Tim Roth, Colin Firth, and Gary Oldman all presenting themselves as antidotes to the typical Hollywood leading man. Perhaps the greatest revelation, however, was the introduction of Daniel Day-Lewis who, following highly contrasting appearances in *My Beautiful Laundrette* and *A Room with a View* (1985, right), went on to create a legendary performance in *My Left Foot* (1989), taking method acting to new heights and showing that Britain could beat Hollywood at its own game. It secured him a Best Actor Academy Award just a year after Dustin Hoffman had trodden similar ground in *Rain Man* (1988).

During the 1980s, Britain experimented as never before. The financial investment in homegrown productions was symptomatic of Margaret Thatcher's "new enterprise culture" and filmmakers rose to the challenge, producing vital and daring work. When else but in the eighties could a film such as *The Cook, the Thief, His Wife and Her Lover* have been made? A sumptuous, experimental and technical marvel, it revels in the greed and dark underbelly of the era, while condemning rampant indulgence and excess. Equally unexpectedly, ex-Python John Cleese appeared as a romantic hero and Kevin Kline won an Oscar for his crazed performance in *A Fish Called Wanda* (1988, below right)—a last, triumphant hurrah for veteran Ealing director Charles Crichton (1910–99).

During this strange decade of hyperbole, Britain was able to produce cinema that was many things to many audiences yet remained peculiarly British. In 1984, Neil Jordan (b. 1950) made *The Company of Wolves*—a landmark special effects film and a curious participant in the specialist genre of eighties fantasy flicks. A bold look at youth and sex inspired by English writer Angela Carter's eponymous feminist tract, it incorporates the European tradition of Grimm's fairy tales.

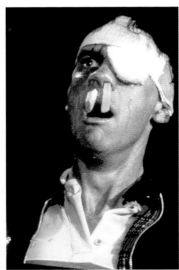

Even unashamedly British productions were praised and welcomed with open arms. In their last feature film outing, the Monty Python team released *The Meaning of Life* (1983), which won the Grand Jury Prize at Cannes. And, crowning twenty years of quality literary adaptations, while bucking filmmaking fashions of the time, Merchant Ivory released *A Room with a View*. The film featured a veritable who's who of British acting talent, with Helena Bonham Carter, Daniel Day-Lewis, Maggie Smith, Simon Callow, Denholm Elliott, and Judi Dench, among others, all turning in restrained performances and all set to become fixtures in British cinema. The film was a hit, beginning a new wave of literary adaptations and establishing a template for costume dramas.

From low budget to lavish, and from genre fare to quirky gems, Britain made films for everyone. In *Rita, Sue and Bob Too* (1986), Alan Clarke (1935–90) crossed ribald comedy with stark realism; Terence Davies (b. 1945) cast an affectionate but cold-eyed memoir of postwar Liverpool in *Distant Voices, Still Lives* (1988, see p. 414); and a year later Michael Caton-Jones (b. 1957) turned back the clocks with *Scandal*, based on the Profumo affair. There is no better document of Britain in the 1980s than the fascinatingly diverse films produced during that decade. **SW**

1984	1984	1985	1986	1987	1987
The Video Recordings Act restricts what can be viewed in the home. The British Board of Film Classification creates the PG, 15, and 18 ratings.	Director Roland Joffé (b. 1945) releases the acclaimed *The Killing Fields*. This powerful drama documents life in Cambodia during "year zero."	Stanley Kubrick (1928–99) begins work on *Full Metal Jacket* by re-creating the United States and Vietnam in London and Cambridgeshire.	Three years before the fall of the Berlin Wall, Ken Loach (b. 1936) delivers his take on socialism and capitalism in *Fatherland*.	Handmade Films, founded by ex-Beatle George Harrison, releases *Withnail and I* (see p. 412), directed by Bruce Robinson (b. 1946) .	Almost twenty years before Daniel Craig reinvents James Bond, Timothy Dalton also explores a darker side of 007 in *The Living Daylights*.

Withnail and I 1987

BRUCE ROBINSON b. 1946

▲ Freshly financed by Uncle Monty, Withnail and "I" head for the nearest pub.

▼ Ralph Steadman provided the poster's appropriately insalubrious artwork.

A gruesome autobiographical exercise from writer-director Bruce Robinson, set in the last days of the 1960s, *Withnail and I* follows a pair of unemployed but ambitious actors who try to live a life of utter indulgence despite dwindling reserves of money. Withnail (Richard E. Grant), an effete hard drinker, pauses in his consumption of ever-more-repulsive booze only to deliver scabrous monologues about his own misunderstood genius. Paul McGann, as Robinson's flashback stand-in (unnamed in the film, but called Marwood in the published script), blinks with babyish puzzlement through John Lennon specs and suffers panic attacks as Withnail gets him into more and more dangerous situations. These range from a possible bar fight to near rape under the considerable bulk of Withnail's Uncle Monty (Richard Griffiths).

What story there is concerns the pair's escape from a sordid, vermin-infested London flat to the savage Cumbrian backwater of Penrith. A sustained gross-out that dwells on messy bodily functions as much as anything by the Farrelly Brothers has, it also sounds a melancholy strain as "I" (who plainly has career prospects) finally rebels and escapes from the self-destructive Withnail.

This thinly plotted movie has survived as a cult film largely because of the quality of the dialogue. Fans cherish Grant's big speeches, relishing every viperish turn of phrase ("We want the finest wines available to humanity. We want them here and we want them now!") and perfectly pronounced curse ("Monty, you terrible cunt!"). And only the Pythons can compete with it for adding bizarre expressions to the language ("I've got a bastard behind the eyes"). **KN**

👁 KEY SCENES

1 A CHILD'S URINE
Withnail explains the workings of his homemade device—fashioned from an old dish-washing liquid bottle—for beating a drunk-driving arrest. Fill it with a child's urine, refuse a breathalyzer test, and use it instead to provide an alcohol-free urine sample.

3 UNCLE MONTY
The frantic young actor has to fend off the libidinous Uncle Monty. The latter has been told by the devious Withnail that his flatmate is a "toilet trader." His initial advances are repelled; Monty persists, declaring, "I mean to have you, even if it must be burglary!"

2 DINNER
The starved Withnail and "I" timidly consider slaughtering a chicken, although "I" is intimidated by its "beady eyes." Withnail proves more resolute ("It's a bloody chicken—just think of it with bacon across its back") and finally dispatches the bird.

4 THE CAMBERWELL CARROT
Withnail and "I" return to the flat in Camden Town. Danny the drug dealer (Ralph Brown) rolls an incredibly potent twelve-skin "Camberwell carrot," so-called because he "invented it in Camberwell and it looks like a carrot."

LOSER BUDDY COMEDY

Comedy double acts such as Withnail and "I" go back to vaudeville and music hall, even to classic archetypes such as Don Quixote and Sancho Panza. Every era of cinema throws up an iconic pairing. The slang, styles, and attitudes may change, but the underlying bond—often as antagonistic as it is mutually dependent—remains the same, whether the duo is Laurel and Hardy, Abbott and Costello, Cheech and Chong (right), Bill and Ted, Wayne and Garth, or Harold and Kumar. There have been one-off attempts at female pairs—Rita Tushingham and Lynn Redgrave in *Smashing Time* (1967), Shelley Long and Bette Midler in *Outrageous Fortune* (1987)—but somehow the world of the loser buddies, as trapped as they are liberated by their own little world, is more aptly male.

Distant Voices, Still Lives 1988

TERENCE DAVIES b. 1945

▲ Maisie (Lorraine Ashbourne) cradles her baby in the street.

▼ The siblings singing at the first of three family weddings depicted in the film.

Terence Davies's *Distant Voices, Still Lives* is a personal account of a postwar working-class childhood in a Liverpool row house. At the center of the film is the dreaded father (Pete Postlethwaite), a morose and violent man who beats up his wife and terrorizes his children. In one of the first sequences, as the family assembles for his funeral, the camera zooms in on a photograph on the wall. This is the only image Davies has of his father. "It's hard to believe that one man could've caused so much suffering and that all these years later I would make a film about it," the director reflected later.

On a formal level, the film is adventurous and accomplished. Davies used a bleach-bypass printing process to give the images a desaturated look. The narrative is elliptical—a series of tableaux based on incidents in the director's childhood and shot to look like posed family photographs. Davies uses popular music from the era, subtle tracking shots that seem to drag viewers back into the past, and a detailed mise-en-scène to bring the material alive.

Reviewers were startled that such an evocative, heartfelt film had been made by a working-class British director. The film was described as "*Coronation Street* directed by Robert Bresson." Such verdicts betray a certain snobbery but this is a film of deep yearning and regret, and Davies controlled every aspect of every shot. Yet this is more than a filmmaker's solipsistic voyage around his childhood. Postlethwaite makes a terrifying patriarch and Freda Dowie brings dignity to the role of the long-suffering mother, while the music, humor, and Davies's idolization of his glamorous sisters keep despair at bay. **GM**

👁 KEY SCENES

1 THE HOUSE
The camera tracks slowly into the family house and then around to show the front room. It is a self-conscious and highly evocative sequence to open a film predicated on memory. The brownish, bleached-out color palette is typical of the film's visual style.

2 THE PATRIARCH
The father beats his daughter with a broom when she has the temerity to ask if she can go to a dance in one of several sequences in which he acts with seemingly random cruelty. Frequently, Davies juxtaposes scenes of violence and happiness.

3 THE MOTHER
Just as Davies detested his father, he adored his mother. Such affection is caught in this sequence, where the camera tracks in toward the gentle, long-suffering woman as she falls asleep by the fire. The vignette captures the essence of a past way of life.

4 SINGSONG IN THE PUB
Much of *Distant Voices, Still Lives* is about loneliness and alienation, so the communal scenes in which music brings everyone together are all the more affecting. Songs are used to evoke memories and many of the sequences were shot in pubs.

🕐 DIRECTOR PROFILE

1945–70
Terence Davies was born in Liverpool into a large working-class family. His work has often drawn on his childhood experiences, both happy and sad, and his films regularly focus on individuals whose emotional and physical endurance are tested to the limit. He has been heavily influenced by his sisters and still speaks with huge affection of trips with them to the local cinemas to see Hollywood musicals.

1971–75
He worked as a clerk in a shipping office and then as a bookkeeper before entering Coventry School of Drama in 1971.

1976–87
Davies made the short film *Children* (1976), writing the screenplay himself and financing the film with money from the British Film Institute. It was the first part of *The Terence Davies Trilogy*, which includes *Madonna and Child* (1980) and *Death and Transfiguration* (1983). Shot in black and white, the trilogy is an anguished account of a gay working-class Catholic boy growing up in Liverpool.

1988–94
Davies won the FIPRESCI Prize for *Distant Voices, Still Lives* at Cannes. He went on to make another autobiographical Liverpool-set story, *The Long Day Closes* (1992).

1995–99
He shot *The Neon Bible* (1995), an adaptation of John Kennedy Toole's novel of 1989 about a boy growing up in Georgia in the 1940s. It explores similar themes to those of his previous work.

2000–present
Davies made an adaptation of Edith Wharton's novel of 1905 *The House of Mirth* (2000). After a long hiatus in his career, during which he failed to find financing for several projects, he made a triumphant comeback with *Of Time and the City* (2008), an evocative low-budget documentary that uses archive footage and period music to bring postwar Liverpool lyrically to life. It premiered at that year's Cannes Film Festival.

PSYCHOLOGICAL DRAMA

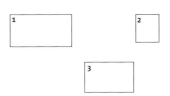

1 Marlon Brando and Maria Schneider clinch in *Last Tango in Paris*, Bernardo Bertolucci's erotic drama.

2 The striking poster for Liliana Cavani's *The Night Porter*, starring Charlotte Rampling and with Dirk Bogarde in the title role.

3 John Baxter (Donald Sutherland) is too late to save his daughter. That is just the start of his problems in the Nicolas Roeg thriller *Don't Look Now*.

arl Jung was fascinated with filmmaking. "The cinema, like the detective story," he observed, "makes it possible to experience without danger all the excitement, passion, and desirousness which must be repressed in a humanitarian ordering of life." This is precisely the role of psychological drama: to explore the internal worlds of the characters (and, by association, the viewers). Sometimes they gain new understanding (*House of Games*, 1987); in *Sous le soleil de Satan* (*Under the Sun of Satan*, 1987) for example, they are destroyed.

In *Sleuth* (1972) the hero's curiosity, greed, and jealousy are his undoing. Jeffrey's odyssey into a nightmarish world in *Blue Velvet* (1986, see p. 418) serves his own fascination: he is at once compelled and repelled. This makes him both protagonist and antagonist—and in doing so confirms humankind as its own worst enemy. As Freud suggests, to understand ourselves we must confront our secret (repressed) desires. Bernardo Bertolucci (b. 1940) was inspired to make *Last Tango in Paris* (1972, above) after fantasizing about anonymous sex with a beautiful woman; the result is a meditation on grief, sexual violence, and fantasy. The director externalized his secret, unexpressed thoughts, and the fact that the film proved so controversial perhaps shows that he struck a nerve in the collective conscious (or unconscious).

In *The Night Porter* (1974, opposite above), director Liliana Cavani (b. 1933) raises questions of power, choice, guilt, and sexual desire. An ex-SS officer is confronted with a figure from his past—a woman with whom he conducted a sadomasochistic affair while she was imprisoned in a concentration camp. For Freud, this is the very essence of repression—a secret history of sexual encounters

KEY EVENTS

1971	1972	1972	1973	1974	1975
Directed by Stanley Kubrick (1928–99), *A Clockwork Orange* raises questions about individual thought, personal choice, and violence.	Psychological thriller *Images*, by Robert Altman (1925–2006), centers on a wealthy housewife who begins to doubt reality and her own sanity.	Andrei Tarkovsky (1932–86) releases *Solaris*. This space-set drama is a meditative reflection on grief, consciousness, and existentialism.	*Don't Look Now* by Nicolas Roeg (b. 1928) explores strong emotions, such as grief. It is an adaptation of a short story by Daphne du Maurier.	In *A Woman under the Influence*, John Cassavetes (1929–89) shows a family coming to terms with the mental decline of the mother and wife.	Laura Mulvey's essay "Visual Pleasure and Narrative Cinema" discusses psychoanalysis and voyeurism, and inspires feminist filmmakers.

and an ongoing struggle to deny or refute them. *The Night Porter* exposes the characters' deep-rooted desires and asks the audience to confront their own.

In his theory of the "mirror stage" in human development, psychoanalyst Jacques Lacan examined the role of a mirror in enabling a young child to think of itself as a discrete being ("I"), separate from its mother and the rest of the world. In film, this concept of a "mirror image" can be expressed metaphorically by exploring the way antagonist and protagonist define each other. In *Manhunter* (1986), the hero gains crucial insights into the minds of killers because he is able to think like them. Hero and villain are like two halves—opposites, but linked—as with Blaney and Rusk in *Frenzy* (1972) by Alfred Hitchcock (1899–1980). In *Blade Runner* (1982), the protagonist, Deckard, understands the struggle of the antagonist, Batty; if we assume that Deckard, like Batty, is a replicant, they are in effect brothers. David Cronenberg (b. 1943) took this to more literal extremes in *Dead Ringers* (1988), in which twin brothers share each other's lives—one whole split in two—and one cannot exist without the other.

Psychological dramas delve into the darkest recesses of the mind. *Spoorloos* (*The Vanishing*, 1988) is a terrifying study of the psyche of a murderer, a family man who has lived a "good life" but whose outer and inner selves are very different. In *Don't Look Now* (1973, below), a grieving couple travel to Venice shortly after the death of their daughter; the husband—who may be psychically gifted—is tantalized by a glimpse of a red-coated figure resembling his daughter. The audience's grasp of events remains as restricted and tentative as that of the bereaved husband and wife. In the words of David Mamet, "The audience members understand themselves to be the protagonist—as, indeed, for the length of the evening they are, for the drama is their dream." **SW**

Blue Velvet 1986

DAVID LYNCH b. 1946

▲ Dorothy (Isabella Rossellini) and the gas-guzzling Frank (Dennis Hopper).

▼ The sensual, dreamlike film poster.

David Lynch conceived *Blue Velvet* in 1973, but did not get the chance to direct it until he had completed the nightmarish *Eraserhead* (1976), the more commercial *The Elephant Man* (1980), and the sci-fi epic *Dune* (1984). The latter was financed by Dino Di Laurentiis, who, undeterred by its failure, gave Lynch final cut on *Blue Velvet* on the condition he halved his salary and made it for $6 million. His faith was justified. The movie was soon recognized as the most daringly subversive of a cluster of films made in 1986 and 1987 that delved beneath the placid surface of life in the US hinterland.

Blue Velvet has the hyperreal dream logic and disorienting sensibility of a perverse 1950s Film Noir (see p. 168), crossed with a beatific early 1960s high-school romance. College student Jeffrey (Kyle MacLachlan) finds a severed human ear and brings it to a detective, whose daughter Sandy (Laura Dern) becomes Jeffrey's fellow sleuth and girlfriend. He decides to investigate and is led to the apartment of a mysterious nightclub chanteuse, Dorothy Vallens (Isabella Rossellini). There he watches her abuse at the hands of the psychopathic Frank Booth (Dennis Hopper) — Lynch's ultimate bogeyman. The kidnapping of Dorothy's son and a drugs deal involving a crooked cop are mere background for one of Hollywood's kinkiest Oedipal triangles. Lynch suggests that every white-picketed garden is a nest of corruption. The film sets out its good-versus-evil morality explicitly while implicating the viewer in Jeffrey's voyeurism, Frank's fetishism, and Dorothy's sadomasochism. *Blue Velvet* is the definitive expression of what lies beneath the surface. **GF**

1 THE BLUE LADY
Investigating the crime of the severed ear, Jeffrey and Sandy go to the Slow Club, where they watch the torch singer Dorothy Vallens perform "Blue Velvet." Sandy is embarrassed by Dorothy's sexual allure and Jeffrey's attraction to her.

3 "CANDY-COLORED CLOWN"
Frank and his crew seize Jeffrey and Dorothy and take them for a "joyride." They stop at the apartment of Frank's effeminate gangster friend, Ben (Dean Stockwell). His lip-synching to a cassette tape of Roy Orbison singing "In Dreams" deeply affects Frank.

2 IN HER INNER SANCTUM
Dorothy catches Jeffrey hiding in her closet, orders him out at knifepoint, and makes him strip. They start to have sex but are interrupted by Frank Booth. Jeffrey hides again and witnesses Frank's abuse of Dorothy.

4 FINAL RECKONING
At Dorothy's apartment, Jeffrey finds Dorothy's husband and the crooked partner of Sandy's dad—both are dead, the latter minus an ear. Frank arrives in disguise. He realizes Jeffrey is in the closet and prepares to shoot him, but Jeffrey has the murdered cop's gun.

HAUNTING SOUNDTRACK

Music sustains *Blue Velvet*'s lush atmosphere. The title song is a Tony Bennett hit from 1951, but it was Bobby Vinton's lachrymose US No. 1 from 1963 that gave Lynch images of "a girl with red lips" in blue velvet in a car "at twilight." As sung by Dorothy, it brings bittersweet memories to Frank Booth, as does Ben's lip-synched rendition of Roy Orbison's "In Dreams" (1963, right). Originally, Dennis Hopper was to have sung "In Dreams," but Dean Stockwell inherited it during rehearsal. Lynch meanwhile used Ketty Lester's "Love Letters" (1962) as a foil to the climactic action. The score, by Lynch's regular composer Angelo Badalamenti, quotes Shostakovich's Fifteenth (and last) Symphony, which Lynch had listened to while writing the screenplay. Badalamenti also gives a brief cameo performance, as the pianist at the Slow Club where Dorothy performs.

EUROPEAN CINEMA

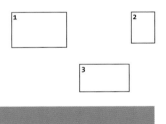

M any established European directors produced excellent films during the 1980s. It was an outstanding decade for two Hungarian directors: István Szabó (b. 1938) made three films starring Klaus Maria Brandauer, including *Mephisto* (1981, see p. 422), while Márta Mészáros (b. 1931) reflected on recent political history with her trilogy *Napló gyermekeimnek* (*Diary for My Children*, 1984), *Napló szerelmeimnek* (*Diary for My Lovers*, 1987) and *Napló apámnak, anyámnak* (*Diary for My Parents*, 1990). Werner Herzog (b. 1942) had his greatest hit with *Fitzcarraldo* (1982), in which deranged visionary Klaus Kinski hauls a ship over a South American mountain, and Bernardo Bertolucci (b. 1940) escaped from the art-house circuit with his Chinese historical saga *The Last Emperor* (1987). Louis Malle (1932–95) began the decade with the finest of his US films, *Atlantic City* (1980), and returned home for the best of his French films, *Au revoir les enfants* (1987, opposite above). Malle drew upon his own childhood experiences during World War II for his moving story about a French Catholic boarding school that gives refuge to Jewish children.

Leading figures of the Nouvelle Vague (see p. 248) were still productive, but with less distinction than in their glory years of the 1960s. The exception was Eric Rohmer (1920–2010), whose witty conversation pieces continued with his "Comédies et Proverbes" series (1980–87). In Germany Margarethe von Trotta (b. 1942) presented a feminist view of her country's history with *Rosa Luxemburg* (1986), and Wim Wenders (b. 1945) scored a hit with his angel-haunted fantasy

1 The voluptuous Béatrice Dalle dazzles in the bittersweet love story *37.2 le matin*.

2 The film poster for *Au revoir les enfants*. Louis Malle wrote, produced, and directed his deeply personal film about a schoolboy friendship in Nazi-occupied France.

3 The poster images of Bogart and Bergman watch over the young Salvatore as he assists the village projectionist Alfredo in *Nuovo Cinema Paradiso*.

KEY EVENTS

1981	1982	1982	1983	1983	1984
Andrzej Wajda (b. 1926) directs *Czlowiek z zelaza* (*Man of Iron*), a film about Poland's Solidarity movement.	Daniel Vigne (b. 1942) directs a medieval identity drama *La retour de Martin Guerre* (*The Return of Martin Guerre*).	A drug overdose kills Rainer Werner Fassbinder, the prolific powerhouse talent who had defined German cinema since 1969.	Maurice Pialat (1925–2003) directs his drama about a sexually promiscuous teenager, *A nos amours* (*To Our Loves*).	Ingmar Bergman (1918–2007) abandons cinema for television after *Fanny och Alexander* (*Fanny and Alexander*). He returns with *Saraband* (2003).	Danish provocateur Lars von Trier (b. 1956) directs his first feature, *Forbrydelsens element* (*The Element of Crime*).

Der Himmel über Berlin (*Wings of Desire*, 1987). Meanwhile, in Spain, Víctor Erice (b. 1940) presented a child's-eye film with *El sur* (*The South*, 1983) and Carlos Saura (b. 1932) adapted Lorca in *Bodas de sangre* (*Blood Wedding*, 1981).

Some of the most popular films were genre pieces: for example, the submarine war film *Das Boot* (*The Boat*, 1981) from Wolfgang Petersen (b. 1941), the evocative Danish period drama *Babettes gæstebud* (*Babette's Feast*, 1987) by Gabriel Axel (b. 1918), and French period pieces *Jean de Florette* and *Manon des sources* (both 1986), directed by Claude Berri (1934–2009). Setting their own trend among younger audiences were the glossy offerings of that quintessential figure of the 1980s Jean-Jacques Beineix (b. 1946), among them *37.2 le matin* (*Betty Blue*, 1986, opposite). Gabriel Yared's haunting piano score and Béatrice Dalle's performance as the free-spirited, unstable Betty electrified audiences.

More lasting reputations were also being established. In Spain Pedro Almodóvar (b. 1949) gave an early indication of his creativity in *Mujeres al borde de un ataque de nervios* (*Women on the Verge of a Nervous Breakdown*, 1988) while Serbian director Emir Kusturica (b. 1954) was attracting notice with *Otac na sluzbenom putu* (*When Father Was Away on Business*, 1985). In nostalgic comedy *Nuovo Cinema Paradiso* (1988, below) by Giuseppe Tornatore (b. 1956), a jaded film director recalls how he first fell in love with films through his friendship with the village cinema projectionist. The finale features a lovely montage of all the kissing scenes the local priest cut from the films the pair screened over the years.

In Poland Krzysztof Kieślowski (1941–96) expanded two films from his television series *Dekalog* for cinema: *Krótki film o zabijaniu* (*A Short Film About Killing*, see p. 424) and *Krótki film o milosci* (*A Short Film About Love*, both 1988). Perhaps the most moving achievement of the decade was the harrowing Holocaust documentary *Shoah* (1985) by Claude Lanzmann (b. 1925). **MS**

1985	1986	1986	1988	1988	1989
Lasse Halström (b. 1946) directs *Mitt liv som hund* (*My Life as a Dog*). *Sans toit ni loi* (*Vagabond*) by Agnès Varda (b. 1928) is her best film of the decade.	An era ends when the Academy Cinema in London's Oxford Street—loving home to many a European film—closes.	Theo Angelopoulos (b. 1935) adds to his gallery of haunting, deliberately paced character studies with *O melissokomos* (*The Beekeeper*).	George Sluizer (b. 1932) directs creepy Franco-Dutch thriller *Spoorloos* (*The Vanishing*).	*Ariel* confirms the skill of Aki Kaurismäki (b. 1957) at capturing a very Finnish blend of deadpan humor and melancholy.	Patrice Leconte (b. 1947) directs unconventional detective story *Monsieur Hire* to wide acclaim.

Mephisto 1981
ISTVÁN SZABÓ b. 1938

▲ The ambitious actor's whole life becomes a performance to please his Nazi patrons.

▼ Höfgen (Brandauer) pictured in his star-making signature role in the film poster.

This big, impressive movie (which earned the Best Foreign Language Film Oscar in 1982) is based on a controversial novel by Klaus Mann. The book was inspired by the life of Gustaf Gründgens, a German theatrical star of the 1930s—best remembered as the criminal mastermind in *M* (1931, see p. 82)—who prospered under the Nazis.

Hendrik Höfgen (Klaus Maria Brandauer), an ambitious and talented young actor, rises to stardom in Berlin with a performance as Mephisto—all the while dabbling in left-wing cabaret and keeping a half-black mistress (Karin Boyd). While not exactly supporting the Nazis when they come to power, he becomes a cultural figurehead for the new Germany. A traditional showbiz movie montage conveying Höfgen's rise features Brandauer in a dizzying variety of stage roles; a later, horribly farcical, parallel shows that under Hitler, Höfgen now has to play all his roles off-stage as he desperately tries to run a theater without losing his life or the last shreds of his integrity. He is not even driven by political conviction: one of the favors done for Höfgen is the murder—in a scene that influenced *Miller's Crossing* (1990)—of a rival actor who has always annoyed the star.

Hungarian director István Szabó, who brings experiences with totalitarian regimes to the table, never lets Brandauer run off with the film. Indeed, the powerful final reels cut the great actor down to size as he is dwarfed by huge swastikas and, finally, by the towering set thrown up for Germany's greatest stage production of the 1930s—the Nuremberg Rally. **KN**

1 HITLERIAN MANNERISMS
While enthusiastically lecturing his leftist theater comrades about his ideas for a new, socially committed production, Höfgen's vocal mannerisms and style of speech prefigure the Führer into whose orbit he will be sucked.

3 THE SWASTIKAS GET BIGGER
A party is thrown to celebrate the opening of Höfgen's "man of action" *Hamlet*. Höfgen has become a big star but he has also become a part of the vast Nazi propaganda machine. The actor becomes diminutive in the frame with the huge swastika banners.

2 MEPHISTO
Ironically Höfgen rises to stardom with his debut role as Mephisto in Goethe's *Faust*. As the audience applauds, he winks at his fellow actor who says: "You were born to play Mephisto." He replies: "You say that with a touch of malice, Dora."

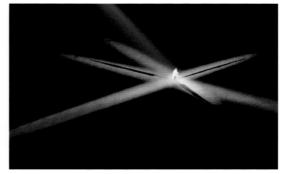

4 "THIS IS THEATER!"
Höfgen's high-ranking Nazi patron takes his pet to the Nuremberg site where Hitler will stage his rally. Höfgen is caught, flinching and tiny, in the intersection of the searchlights. "What do they want of me?" he asks. "After all, I'm only an actor."

NAZI CINEMA

Gustaf Gründgens was not the only actor to prosper under the Nazis. Compare the careers of the stars of *Das Cabinet des Dr. Caligari* (1920, see p. 44): Conrad Veidt left Germany and ironically donned Nazi uniform for roles such as Major Strasser in *Casablanca* (1942, near right); Werner Krauss remained at home and played the despicable rabbi in *Jud Süss* (1940). Nazi-era films (see p. 138) lacked the verve of German experimental cinema. Hitler's rise broke relationships: the half-Jewish Fritz Lang (1890–1976) left for Hollywood while his Nazi party-member wife, writer Thea von Harbou, remained. Hitler and Goebbels felt cinema was important enough to divert funds and manpower to exercises such as *Titanic* (1943), which blamed the disaster on flaws in the British character.

CANADIAN CINEMA

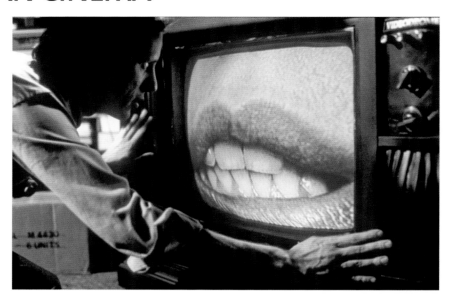

C anadians have to spend a lot of time patiently explaining that they are not Americans. Likewise films made in Canada—with Toronto frequently standing in for New York—are often hard to distinguish from US movies. This may be why certain Canadian directors make a point of creating work that differentiates them from the Hollywood mainstream. Even those whose careers have intermittently taken them to the Los Angeles studios, such as David Cronenberg (b. 1943), have resisted assimilation and continue to make unmistakably individual films, while the output of such Canadian auteurs as Denys Arcand (b. 1941), Guy Maddin (b. 1956), and Atom Egoyan (b. 1960) remains proudly, determinedly idiosyncratic.

David Cronenberg began making zero-budget underground movies but carried his pervasive theme of "body horror" over into the exploitation mainstream with his breakthrough film *Shivers* (1975). In this, as in the surreal *Videodrome* (1983, above), his theme of parasites and other elements that can invade the human body and turn it against itself becomes a metaphor for psychological and social breakdown. Throughout the 1980s, his budgets increased and with them the technical and narrative sophistication of his films, leading to his masterly reimagining of the "teleportation gone wrong" story, *The Fly* (1986, see p. 430)—a rare example of a remake that utterly outstripped the original—and *Dead Ringers* (1988), featuring a career-best double performance from Jeremy Irons as twin gynecologists with increasingly bizarre obsessions.

KEY EVENTS

1968	1971	1972	1974	1975	1976
The Canadian Film Development Corporation is set up by the Canadian government.	*Mon oncle Antoine* wins multiple awards. It observes life in a French-Canadian mining town in the 1940s through the eyes of a preadolescent boy.	Denys Arcand directs his debut feature, the distinctly Québécois thriller *La maudite galette* (*Dirty Money*).	Canadian-born Ted Kotcheff (b. 1931) returns home to direct *The Apprenticeship of Duddy Kravitz*. It wins the Golden Bear at the Berlin Film Festival.	David Cronenberg directs his breakthrough horror film *Shivers*.	The Toronto International Film Festival is founded.

Atom Egoyan similarly started with small-scale experimental films and moved steadily toward the mainstream. Drawing on his own Armenian-Canadian background and turbulent family history, he made a series of films in the 1980s—including *Peep Show* (1981) and *Family Viewing* (1987, opposite below)—that deal insistently with problems of ethnic identity, broken families, alienation, loss, and death. Coupled with these themes is an uneasy fascination with the role of visual media in the modern world. His characters use film and video obsessively to reconstruct reality to fit their own yearnings—identity takes the form of a charade. Egoyan himself has commented: "My films are designed to make the viewer self-conscious. I revel in that."

Unlike Cronenberg and Egoyan, Guy Maddin shows scant interest in making mainstream films. His feature debut, *Tales from the Gimli Hospital* (1988), was weird to the point of defiance, a retro pastiche of silent movie stylization and minimal dialogue, full of narrative nonsequiturs that teased the viewer with shaggy dog logic. Since then he has pursued a consistent course, with films that unabashedly aim at little beyond a cult audience.

Québécois filmmakers, of course, are separated from their US counterparts by language, while remaining too remote and different from their European cousins to risk absorption into the French-language mainstream. Denys Arcand, internationally the best known of French-Canadian directors, started out making documentary shorts for the National Film Board of Canada, but his radical politics and independent nature led to tensions with his paymasters. His first three features, among them *Gina* (1975), used the thriller genre to explore political themes, but his views aroused official mistrust and for some years he had little funding. He bounced back in style with *Le déclin de l'empire américain* (*The Decline of the American Empire*, 1986, see p. 428), which was Oscar-nominated—as was its successor, *Jésus de Montréal* (1989, right), a fable of passionate irony about an actor playing Christ in the city's annual Passion play who finds the role taking over his life.

Arcand has always been too skeptical to identify with the cause of Quebec separatism. His contemporary Jean-Pierre Lefebvre (b. 1941), although never toeing any party line, stands a little closer to the separatist cause. His films use experimental, often avant-garde formal techniques to explore questions of Quebec's history and culture. One of the most highly rated among his prolific output is *Le vieux pays où Rimbaud est mort* (*The Old Country Where Rimbaud Died*, 1977), a meditation on France as viewed from French Canada.

The saddest decline in Canadian cinema is surely that of Claude Jutra (1930–86). In 1971 he directed *Mon oncle Antoine*; showered with awards, in 1984 it was voted the finest Canadian film ever made, but his subsequent work was found disappointing. In the mid-1980s, he was diagnosed with Alzheimer's and in November 1986 he vanished from his home. When the St. Lawrence River thawed in April 1987, his drowned body was discovered. **PK**

1 Sleazy cable TV programer Max Renn (James Woods) is drawn to the charms of Debbie Harry's sadomasochistic psychiatrist in *Videodrome*.

2 In Denys Arcand's witty allegory *Jésus de Montréal*, Daniel (Lothaire Bluteau) answers the question: what would Jesus look like if he walked among us today?

3 Video technology looms ominously over modern family life in Atom Egoyan's *Family Viewing*, a theme reflected in the film's poster.

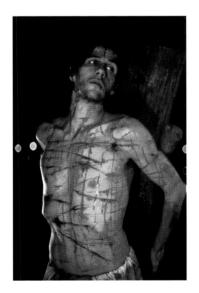

1977	1984	1986	1987	1988	1989
Jean-Pierre Lefebvre directs *Le vieux pays où Rimbaud est mort*.	Atom Egoyan directs Armenian family drama *Next of Kin*.	*Le déclin de l'empire américain* (see p. 428) wins the Jury Prize at Cannes Film Festival and is nominated for an Oscar for Best Foreign Film.	Patricia Rozema (b. 1958) directs her debut feature *I've Heard the Mermaids Singing*. It wins the Youth Award at Cannes.	Kyle McCulloch stars in Guy Maddin's fantasy horror *Tales from the Gimli Hospital*.	*Speaking Parts* features Atom Egoyan's trademark tangle of relationships.

Le déclin de l'empire américain 1986
The Decline of the American Empire   DENYS ARCAND b. 1941

▲ Mario (Gabriel Arcand) makes clear his feelings about the group of intellectuals.

▼ The characters in the poster for *Le déclin de l'empire américain* reveal what is really on their minds.

The first international success of Québécois filmmaker Denys Arcand, *Le déclin de l'empire américain* is a sardonic study in sexual mores where the sex is much more in talk than in action. In a lakeside country house, four male French-Canadian intellectuals prepare a gourmet meal and talk about sex. Meanwhile, the four women who will be their guests meet at a health club in the city—and talk about sex. They all assemble for dinner where the conversations, and the revelations, continue.

Arcand enjoys teasing viewers with the permutations between the characters. Rémy is married to Louise but has slept with countless women, including most of those present. Pierre is in a relationship with the much younger Danielle, whom he met when she serviced him in a massage parlor. Claude is gay; he sleeps around but is terrified of AIDS. Dominique, the oldest woman, ends up bedding the youngest man, Alain. Diane is having an affair with the punkish Mario, who shows up only to express his contempt for these middle-class chatterers.

Early on, Dominique asks whether the "frantic drive for personal happiness" is "linked to the decline of the American empire." Arcand's film ironically explores this question. All the characters, it seems, are hell-bent on finding happiness, yet each one is frustrated and their relationships are disaster areas. This, Arcand hints, is the fallout of a society where sexual gratification is elevated over all other values. The film is at once bleak and funny; the audience may not like these people, but they are fascinating to watch. And every so often the audience are brought up short, recognizing aspects of themselves. **PK**

1 RÉMY'S PHILOSOPHY

As he prepares food, Rémy (Rémy Girard) explains his thinking on sex to the other men: "Lying is the basis of all love affairs—as of our very social existence." The film relishes articulate conversation that reveals the emotional abysses behind the words.

2 SWINGERS

Meanwhile, at the gym, the women recount their own sexual exploits. Louise (Dorothée Berryman) tells the other women about her experiences at a spouse-swap party. Dialogue—witty, erudite, and oblique—drives Arcand's film rather than plot.

3 MARIO'S CONTEMPT

Mario, Diane's lover (Gabriel Arcand), does not fit in at the dinner table: "I've had enough of this. This is a pain. All you do is talk. When I'm horny, I fuck." Interaction between the characters at the table is filmed like a battle with shot and countershot.

4 LOUISE HEARS THE TRUTH

Louise overhears Dominique (Dominique Michel) talking about Louise's husband Rémy: "He's screwed all of Montreal. All the fuckable women in the department, down to the last secretary. He told me he's screwed Louise's sister."

⏱ DIRECTOR PROFILE

1941–71

Denys Arcand was born in Quebec. He attended a Jesuit school in Montreal and later studied history at the Université de Montréal. He worked on the Quebec separatist literary magazine *Parti pris* and in 1963 he joined the National Film Board (NFB) of Canada to make documentary shorts. One of them, *On est au coton* (*We're Fed Up*, 1976), about textile workers in Montreal so offended the NFB with its critical political stance that it was withheld for six years.

1972–85

In 1972 he directed his first feature, *La maudite galette* (*Dirty Money*, 1972), followed by *Réjeanne Padovani* (1973) and *Gina* (1975), thrillers with political overtones put him into official disfavor. He also made programs and commercials for television. In 1981 he made the documentary *Le confort et l'indifférence*.

1986–93

His international breakthrough came with *Le déclin de l'empire américain*—still one of the most profitable Canadian movies ever made—followed by *Jésus de Montréal* (1989), both of which were Oscar-nominated. His first English-language feature, *Love and Human Remains* (1993), the themes of which echoed *Le déclin de l'empire américain*, was a critical and commercial flop.

1994–present

In 1999 Arcand made *15 moments*, a reflection on the media and the cult of celebrity that charted the rise and fall of a supermodel. It was released in a longer version, *Stardom*, in 2000. *Les invasions barbares* (*The Barbarian Invasions*, 2003), a sequel to *Le déclin de l'empire américain*, reunited the same characters (and actors) and earned numerous prizes at Cannes and elsewhere, and won an Academy Award for Best Foreign Film. Arcand's next film, *L'âge des ténèbres* (*The Age of Ignorance*, 2007), was less well received. Arcand's films continue to consistently examine French-Canadian social and political life with wit and insight.

The Fly 1986

DAVID CRONENBERG b. 1943

▲ Seth Brundle (Jeff Goldblum) before his insect metamorphosis.

▼ "Be afraid. Be very afraid," warns the poster.

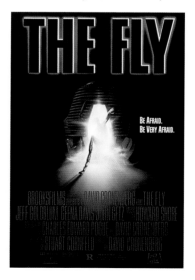

The version of *The Fly* directed by Kurt Neumann (1908–58) in 1958 is a rare property among science fiction films available for remake: it is memorable, full of potential, and deserving of classic status because of a handful of great moments, but not actually terribly good. David Cronenberg's radical rethink is an extension of the mind- and flesh-stretching concerns of his earlier, less mainstream films. Seth Brundle (Jeff Goldblum), the gawky scientist who invents teleportation in order to beat chronic motion sickness, emerges from his experimental telepod fused with the molecules of an interfering fly— not as an insect-headed monstrosity, like the hero of the earlier film, but as a superimproved version of himself. However, after demonstrating prowess as a gymnast, sexual athlete, and barroom arm wrestler, he gradually transforms, decomposes, and loses humanity as he explores his new identity as Brundlefly.

Like many of Cronenberg's rigorously intelligent horrors, it can be read as a metaphor for the processes of disease and aging, and finally comes to an acceptance of the perishability of human tissue as the transformed-beyond-possibility Brundle accepts death at the hands of the one he loves, the neurotic heroine Veronica Quaife (Geena Davis).

The film is surprisingly intimate—it has only three main characters and one primary set. One unnecessary dream sequence involving a maggot baby apart—a similar flaw recurs in Cronenberg's otherwise excellent follow-up *Dead Ringers* (1988)—this is a perfectly structured, tightly inner-directed film, at once funny, poignant, and horrific. **KN**

◉ KEY SCENES

1 FLY IN THE OINTMENT
Seth teleports himself, not noticing the fly in the pod. "A fly got into the transmitter pod with me that first time . . . . It mated us, me and the fly. We hadn't even been properly introduced." Typically for Cronenberg, *The Fly* combines good humor with graphic horror.

2 NEVER WRESTLE A FLY
Suddenly stronger and more dangerous, Seth bests an arm-wrestling champion by snapping his wrist. Cronenberg's film—his biggest production—is a showcase for the makeup and special effects of Chris Walas. He went on to direct sequel *The Fly II* (1989).

3 HYBRID CREATURE
Seth, now a hybrid of human and insect, begins to exhibit flylike characteristics. On video, he demonstrates how "Brundlefly"—the name he has started to call himself—eats, by vomiting digestive fluid on a doughnut.

4 AN ARM AND A LEG
Veronica's ex-lover, Borans (John Getz), tries to rescue her from the lab where Brundlefly is attempting to persuade her not to abort their baby. Brundlefly spits digestive fluid on Borans's foot and hand; they dissolve. His final transformation to monster is nearly complete.

◷ DIRECTOR PROFILE

1943–74
David Cronenberg was born in Toronto, where he still lives. He studied at the University of Toronto, first science, then literature. He directed the experimental art-house shorts *Transfer* (1966) and *From the Drain* (1967) and sci-fi-tinged Canadian underground art movies *Stereo* (1969) and *Crimes of the Future* (1970). For Canadian TV, he made art-themed documentaries and a few episodes of anthology shows.

1975–81
In 1975 he started to make visceral, intelligent horror action films in Toronto, gaining a reputation as the "king of body horror"—starting with *Shivers* (1975), followed by *Rabid* (1977), *The Brood* (1979), and *Scanners* (1981).

1982–90
During this period he worked on a series of varied projects—the personal, bizarre *Videodrome* (1983), the commercial Stephen King adaptation *The Dead Zone* (1983), the sci-fi remake of *The Fly*, and the true crime psychodrama *Dead Ringers*, starring Jeremy Irons in dual roles as twin brothers who work as gynecologists.

1991–present
Cronenberg specializes in filming "the books they said could not be filmed"—these include William S. Burroughs's *Naked Lunch* (1991) and J. G. Ballard's *Crash* (1996). The latter, about a group of individuals who derive sexual pleasure from car crashes, caused controversy on its release, but was awarded the Special Jury Prize at the Cannes Film Festival. Aside from *eXistenZ* (1999), an original Cronenberg script, the director tends to work with the material of others—Patrick McGrath's *Spider* (2002), the crime comic book *A History of Violence* (2005, see p. 552) and Christopher Hampton's play *A Dangerous Method* (2011), for example. Increasingly, he has made films in the United Kingdom, including *Eastern Promises* (2007), in which frequent collaborator Viggo Mortensen also appeared. However, Cronenberg remains a staunchly Canadian filmmaker and prefers to make his films in his home country.

CHINESE CINEMA

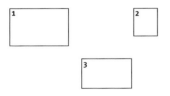

In 1976 the Cultural Revolution ended with the death of Chairman Mao. Few could have predicted that by the end of the 1980s Chinese cinema would be producing some of the world's most original and acclaimed films. The reopening of the Beijing Film Academy paved the way and by the time the first class graduated in 1982, the so-called Fifth Generation filmmakers were preparing to spearhead a revolution in Chinese cinema.

Meanwhile, the older Fourth Generation directors were already reevaluating China's troubled past. Xie Jin (1923–2008) used melodrama to look at the political persecutions of the Cultural Revolution in *Tian yun shan chuan qi* (*The Legend of Tianyun Mountain*, 1980). They also embraced a more innovative form of filmmaking that resulted in a new realism. Zhang Nuanxing (1941–95), for example, opted for a semidocumentary style with *Sha Ou* (*The Drive to Win*, 1981). The Fourth Generation also tackled issues of contemporary relevance. In *Xiangnu xiaoxiao* (*Girl from Hunan*, 1986) Xie Fei (b. 1942) traced the persistence of traditional marriage patterns in rural regions.

Moreover, as teachers at the Beijing Film Academy, the Fourth Generation directors were to influence the next generation of filmmakers. In Zhang Yinjiang's words, "Like their predecessors, the Fifth Generation favored a nondramatic structure and depoliticized narration, but they went further with scant dialogue and music as well as abundant ambiguities in characterization and narration. They insisted on 'showing' their films rather than 'telling' what had happened."

1 Suave counterfeiter Mark Gor (Chow Yun-Fat) lights up in *Ying hung boon sik*.

2 The poster for Edward Yang's urban thriller *Kong bu fen zi*. The film won a Silver Leopard at the Locarno Film Festival.

3 Lush, intense color permeates *Hong gao liang*, Zhang Yimou's exotic parable set in a rural sorghum wine distillery.

KEY EVENTS

1976	1978	1980	1981	1982	1983
Chairman Mao dies and the Chinese Cultural Revolution comes to an end.	The Beijing Film Academy, closed during the Cultural Revolution, accepts its first class of new students.	Xie Jin, who was denounced during the Cultural Revolution, explores the oppression of that period in *Tian yun shan chuan qi*.	Zhang Nuanxing's *Sha Ou* exemplifies the semidocumentary style of the Fourth Generation.	The first post–Cultural Revolution class graduates from the Beijing Film Academy.	Taiwanese filmmaker Hou Hsiao-hsien establishes his mature style with *Feng gui lai de ren* (*The Boys from Fengkuei*).

This new approach came mainly from provincial studios. In 1985 Chen Kaige (b. 1952) made his visually astonishing debut with *Huang tu di* (*Yellow Earth*, see p. 434), at the remote Guangxi Film Studio near the Vietnamese border. Zhang Yimou (b. 1951), who had served as cinematographer on Chen's films, made his own directorial debut with *Hong gao liang* (*Red Sorghum*, 1987, below), a grueling account of China's pre–civil war history. Here, as in his later films, Zhang benefited from the intense performance of his star actress, Gong Li, and made much of the complex visual symbolism of red—a color linked to fire and blood, yet with traditional associations of happiness in China.

Communism, however, did not hold sway over the whole of the Chinese-speaking world. Across the Taiwan straits, the capitalist island of Taiwan was also experiencing a cinematic renaissance with the emergence of a creative and specifically Taiwanese art-house cinema. The leading figure in this renaissance was Hou Hsiao-hsien (b. 1947), whose films are characterized by long takes and long shots reminiscent of classical Japanese cinema. His most significant work is arguably the *Taiwan* trilogy that begins with *Bei qing cheng shi* (*A City of Sadness*, 1989, see p. 436). The other outstanding director of the Taiwanese New Wave was Edward Yang (1947–2007), whose *Kong bu fen zi* (*Terrorizers*, 1986, right) hauntingly explores the theme of urban angst.

Elsewhere, in the Chinese-speaking world, John Woo (b. 1946) changed the face of Hong Kong cinema and deeply influenced international cinema with the small-budget action thriller *Ying hung boon sik* (*A Better Tomorrow*, 1986, opposite). This cool, stylized tale of warring brothers—one a gangster, one a policeman—reignited the stagnating career of Chow Yun-Fat and broke Hong Kong box-office records. **AJ**

1983	1985	1985	1986	1989	1990
Early Fifth Generation films, such as *Yi ge he ba ge* (*One and Eight*) directed by Zheng Junzhao (b. 1952), emerge from provincial studios.	*Dong dong de jia qi* (*A Summer at Grandpa's*, 1984), directed by Hou Hsiao-hsien, wins acclaim at world film festivals.	Edward Yang directs *Qing mei zhu ma* (*Taipei Story*).	*Fu rong zhen* (*Hibiscus Town*), directed by Xie Jin, is released.	Hou Hsiao-hsien directs the first in his *Taiwan* trilogy, *Bei qing cheng shi* (see p. 436). The Tiananmen Square protests and massacre take place in Beijing.	Zhang Yimou's visually extraordinary *Ju Dou* can be seen as a coded response to the atrocities of the previous year.

Huang tu di 1985
Yellow Earth   CHEN KAIGE b. 1952

▲ *Huang tu di* finds the individual story in the grand political and social scene.

▼ The film's key characters are featured in the poster.

In the 1930s, facing defeat at the hands of Chiang Kai-Shek's Nationalists, Mao's Communist Red Army embarked on the epic Long March across China to the inaccessible safe haven of Yan'an in northern Shaanxi Province, which became the base from which, eventually, they would conquer the country. These events form the historical backdrop of *Huang tu di*, the story of a Communist soldier, Gu Qing (Xuegi Wang), sent in 1939 from Yan'an to a nearby farming region to collect folk songs that will be rewritten to inspire the troops.

Director Chen Kaige and cinematographer Zhang Yimou capture both the beauty and the harshness of the landscape, and observe the traditional lifestyles of this remote region with neither condescension nor sentimentality. The plaintive folk songs that punctuate the narrative speak for the plight of the rural poor, but the sensual beauty with which the film records their customs turns it into a celebration of sorts. It is significant that the Communist soldier hopes to enlist China's traditional culture in his cause. Chen and Zhang had both lived through the Cultural Revolution, which mounted a destructive assault on that culture. Here, they proffer the hope that tradition and political progressiveness can be reconciled.

The patient and kind Communist soldier is undoubtedly the hero, but the audience's sympathies rest above all with Cuiqiao (Bai Xue), the farmer's daughter whose unspoken love for the soldier is bound up with her hopes for a freedom unobtainable in the rural community she inhabits. The fatalistic tone of the ending hints at the ultimate inadequacy of political solutions. **AJ**

KEY SCENES

1 THE WEDDING
A wedding procession moves through the hills, red and black specks against the green and brown land. The austere scenery of the loess plateau gives the film its visual grandeur. Such long shots against the immense landscape evoke Chinese landscape painting.

2 THE CONVERSATION
As Cuiqiao works she sees Gu Qing sewing and asks if men can sew too. He tells her that women in the Communist army till the fields and fight the Japanese. Cuiqiao, who is about to be sold into an arranged marriage, yearns for the freedom Gu Qing describes.

3 THE PARTING
On his way to Yan'an, Gu Qing meets Cuiqiao, who begs him to take her with him. He tells her that she must be approved first and promises to return for her. The film subtly criticizes the inflexible party policy that prevents Cuiqiao from joining him in his struggle.

4 THE RAIN DANCE
Local farmers pray to the pagan Dragon King for rain. Meanwhile, Gu Qing returns to the village as promised to collect Ciuqiao. He has come too late, however, because she drowned attempting to cross the Yellow River and reach the Communist camp.

DIRECTOR PROFILE

1952–85
Chen Kaige was born in Beijing. His father was the film director, Chen Huaiai (b. 1912). As a teenager during the Cultural Revolution, Chen joined the Red Guards and denounced his father. After graduating from the Beijing Film Academy in 1982—as part of the so-called Fifth Generation of Chinese directors—he made a stunning debut with the award-winning *Huang tu di*.

1986–91
He greatly expanded his repertoire with the next films he directed. *Da yue bing* (*The Big Parade*, 1986) focused on cadets training for the National Day parade; *Hai zi wang* (*King of the Children*, 1987) centered on a youth teaching in a remote school after being exiled to Yu'nan during the Cultural Revolution; and *Bian zou bian chang* (*Life on a String*, 1991) traced the relationship between an old, blind musician and his pupil.

1992–99
Chen's best-known film in the West, *Ba wang bie ji* (*Farewell My Concubine*, 1993), about the fraught relationship between two stars of the Peking Opera, represented a move from low-key art cinema to epic mode. It was nominated for two Academy Awards and shared the Palme d'Or at the Cannes Film Festival in 1993. Its stars, Leslie Cheung and Gong Li, reunited for the less acclaimed period drama *Feng yue* (*Temptress Moon*, 1996). *Jing Ke ci Qin Wang* (*The Emperor and the Assassin*, 1998) sustained Chen's epic style in the story of Qin Shi Huang, the man who first unified China.

2000–present
In 2002 Chen made his first English-language film with the UK-set, erotic thriller *Killing Me Softly* (2002), starring Heather Graham and Joseph Fiennes, which had a disappointing reception. In 2002 he directed *He ni zai yi qi* (*Together with You*), a drama about a violin prodigy. Back in China he made a move into more commercial cinema with the martial arts movie *Wu ji* (*The Promise*, 2005). In 2008 he made *Mei Lanfang* (*Forever Enthralled*), a biopic of China's greatest opera singer.

Bei qing cheng shi 1989
A City of Sadness   HOU HSIAO-HSIEN b. 1947

▲ Unsure of their future, Wen-ching and his family face the world before them.

▼ The poster for the film references the difficult times the characters live through.

Hou Hsiao-hsien is a leading figure of the Taiwanese New Wave cinema movement—the groundswell of politically engaged and formally daring filmmaking that materialized in 1987 at the end of China's thirty-eight-year imposition of martial law and political suppression in Taiwan.

Bei qing cheng shi offers a mellifluous, impressionistic window view of the events that occurred in Taiwan between 1945 and 1949, when Taiwanese national identity was in a state of violent flux. Fifty years of Japanese occupation ended in 1945 with Japan's surrender at the end of World War II, and Taiwan was ceded to the Chinese Nationalist Party. Taiwan's hopes of reestablishing its cultural autonomy were scuppered under the mainland regime.

Refracting the tragic sweep of history through fragile human experience, Hou's camera flutters between different characters, time frames, and perspectives to trace the fortunes of the individual members of a single extended family. Four brothers act as the film's primary narrative pivots: the swarthy "big brother" Wen-heung (Chen Sown-yung), who opens a gambling parlor named "Little Shanghai" to welcome the island's new rulers; Wen-leung (Jack Kao), a shell-shocked soldier who joins the escalating gangster fraternity; Wen-sun (who never appears on screen), a noted physician who went missing while on maneuvers in the Philippines; and the film's central character, Wen-ching (Tony Leung), a deaf-mute photographer whose tender love affair via handwritten messages with Hinomi (Hsin Shu-fen) establishes the film's dominant theme—the struggle for communication. **DJ**

👁 KEY SCENES

1 BIRTH OF A NATION
Wen-heung prays for his soon-to-be-born son. On the radio, Emperor Hirohito intones his surrender speech in formal Japanese, which no one in the room appears to understand. Hou introduces the notion of family and how the Taiwanese were displaced from political events.

4 FAMILY PORTRAIT
The feelings of the characters are key to the shifting moods within Taiwan itself. The uncertain and anxious expressions on the faces of Wen-ching and his wife Hinomi in this reserved family portrait suggest a tumultuous past and an uncertain future.

2 "DIE LORELEI"
Wen-ching establishes a bond between himself and Hinomi when he puts on a record of the German folk song "Die Lorelei." He recounts memories of being able to hear. He tells a story from childhood about a time when he and his school friends mimicked an opera singer.

3 CULTURAL BARRIERS
Wen-heung meets with a gangster leader in an attempt to have his brother Wen-leung released from custody. His plea is communicated through two translators, adding a tinge of absurd comedy to the scene. A deal is made when Wen-heung places a bribe on the table.

🕒 DIRECTOR PROFILE

1947–79
Born in the province of Guangong in China, Hou Hsiao-hsien moved as an infant with his family to Taiwan to escape the Chinese Civil War. He joined the film program at the National Taiwan Academy of the Arts and graduated in 1972. He worked briefly in sales before starting his film career as a scriptwriter and assistant director.

1980–87
Hou made his directorial debut in 1980 with the romantic musical comedy *Jiu shi liu liu de ta* (*Cute Girl*), although it was his segment in the portmanteau film *Er zi de da wan ou* (*The Sandwich Man*, 1983) that earned him a degree of fame. He formulated his distinctive minimalist style over the remainder of the decade with films such as *Feng gui lai de ren* (*The Boys of Fengkuei*, 1983), *Dong dong de jia qi* (*A Summer at Grandpa's*, 1984), and the masterful childhood scrapbook *Tong nien wang shi* (*A Time to Live and a Time to Die*, 1986). Of the ten films Hou directed between 1980 and 1989, seven received best film or best director awards at international film festivals.

1988–95
Hou directed a trilogy of films about Taiwanese history, beginning with *Bei qing cheng shi*, which won the Golden Lion at the Venice Film Festival in 1989. Meanwhile, he worked in China as executive producer on Zhang Yimou's Chinese drama, *Da hong deng long gao gao gua* (*Raise the Red Lantern*, 1991). The other films in the trilogy were *Xi meng ren sheng* (*The Puppetmaster*, 1993), based on the life of puppeteer Li Tian-Lu, who plays himself in the film, and *Hao nan hao nu* (*Good Men, Good Women*, 1995).

1996–present
In the late 1990s Hou began to make more films outside Taiwan. He directed *Kohi jiko* (*Café Lumière*, 2003) in Japan. He made *Le voyage du ballon rouge* (*Flight of the Red Balloon*, 2007) in Paris, a film commissioned by the Musée d'Orsay and starring Juliette Binoche. Since then he has been working on his first martial arts movie set in eighth-century China.

6 | 1990 TO PRESENT

EUROPEAN PERIOD DRAMA

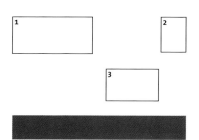

1 Beatrice (Emma Thompson) and Hero (Kate Beckinsale) run through the Tuscan countryside to greet the returning men in Shakespeare's matchmaking comedy, *Much Ado About Nothing*.

2 Ian Hart's unemployed Communist worker is drawn to fight for the Spanish Republicans in *Land and Freedom*.

3 An Italian postman learns to love poetry thanks to an acquaintanceship with a famous Chilean poet in *Il postino*.

Following the collapse of the Soviet Union, Europe entered the 1990s charged, among other things, with the spirit of artistic freedom. However, the economic toll of change was reflected in budgetary restraints placed on film production in certain countries, with costly period dramas mostly restricted to countries with a track record in this genre of cinema. The decade began with a stunning adaptation of *Cyrano de Bergerac* (1990, see p. 442) by Jean-Paul Rappeneau (b. 1932). In a role both he and his proboscis were born to play, Gérard Depardieu gave one of his most likeable performances, conveying wit, intelligence, and emotion through Jean-Claude Carrière's richly textured screenplay. Rappeneau and Carrière teamed up again for *Le hussard sur le toit* (*The Horseman on the Roof*, 1995), which was billed as the most expensive French film ever made, but lacked the depth of their previous collaboration. *La reine Margot* (*Queen Margot*, 1994) fared better. Decadent and bloody, it was more reminiscent of a gangster film than a costume drama.

Ismail Merchant (1936–2005) and James Ivory (b. 1928) continued their dominance of British heritage cinema with two of their best productions— *Howards End* (1992) and *The Remains of the Day* (1993). Nicholas Hytner (b. 1956) oversaw the successful transfer of Alan Bennett's play from stage to screen with *The Madness of King George* (1994). Kenneth Branagh (b. 1960) followed up his mud 'n' blood version of *Henry V* (1989) with *Much Ado About Nothing* (1993, above), the best Shakespeare adaptation of the decade, excepting a brilliant take on *Romeo + Juliet* (1996) from Baz Luhrmann (b. 1962). However,

(1990, see p. 442)

KEY EVENTS

1989	1990	1991	1991	1992	1993
The Berlin Wall falls, prompting the democratization of most countries aligned behind Communism's Iron Curtain.	*Porte aperte*—directed by Gianni Amelio (b. 1945)—recounts a tale of murder set in Sicily during the 1930s.	World War II melodrama *Mediterraneo* wins the Best Foreign Film Oscar.	Cinematographer Sven Nykvist (1922–2006) writes and directs the Swedish nineteenth-century rural drama *Oxen* (*The Ox*).	*Indochine*, directed by Régis Wargnier (b. 1948), is one of the most successful period films of the year. Sally Potter (b. 1949) directs *Orlando*.	*Hedd Wyn* is one of two Welsh period films to receive international distribution during the 1990s.

Branagh's *Hamlet* (1996), the first to use Shakespeare's unabridged text, was only intermittently successful. *Shakespeare in Love* (1998, see p. 444), coscripted by playwright Tom Stoppard, proved more popular, winning over audiences and receiving an Oscar for Best Film and Original Screenplay. Derek Jarman (1942–94) produced one of his best works in 1991, an adaptation of another Elizabethan drama, Christopher Marlowe's *Edward II*.

Many European countries reviewed more recent events in hindsight. *Michael Collins* and *Some Mother's Son* (both 1996) looked back at aspects of the Irish troubles. Germany's small period output during the 1990s, which included *Aimée & Jaguar* (1999) and the tender *Europa Europa* (1990), directed by Agnieska Holland (b. 1948), drew on events from World War II.

Spain's most significant period film of the decade was the Oscar-winning *Belle Epoque* (1992). *La lengua de las mariposas* (*Butterfly's Tongue*, 1999) and *Land and Freedom* (1995, right) by Ken Loach (b. 1936) focused on the Spanish Civil War, while *Vacas* (1992) presented an eccentric history of one Basque family over seven decades. A similar narrative structure, used to explore political realities across various generations, was also adopted by Hungarian director István Szabó (b. 1938) in *Sunshine* (1999) and to better effect by Greece's Theo Angelopoulos (b. 1935) in *To vlemma tou Odyssea* (*Ulysses' Gaze*, 1995).

Il postino (*The Postman*, 1994, below), a fictional account of the encounter between Pablo Neruda and a lovestruck postman, was one of Italy's most successful international productions, although it was soon eclipsed by *La vita è bella* (*Life Is Beautiful*, 1997), directed by and starring Robert Benigni (b. 1952). A comedy drama set mainly in a concentration camp, it was one of the major period successes of the decade; opinions on its merit remain divided. **IHS**

1994	1995	1996	1997	1998	1999
La reine Margot redefines the period costume drama.	*Carrington* depicts the Bloomsbury set. A fictional history of Serbia, *Underground* by Emir Kusturica (b. 1954), wins the Palme d'Or.	*Ridicule* features a sublime performance by Fanny Ardant and one of the most acerbic scripts of the year.	Courtroom drama *Karakter* (*Character*), directed by Mike van Diem (b.1959), is one of the best Dutch films of the decade. *The Wings of the Dove* is released.	Radu Mihaileanu (b. 1958) offers another tragic-comic take on the Holocaust with *Train de vie* (*Train of Life*).	Martha Fiennes (b. 1965) directs Russian Empire drama *Onegin*.

Cyrano de Bergerac 1990
JEAN-PAUL RAPPENEAU b. 1932

▲ Cyrano (Gérard Depardieu) in the throes of a characteristically passionate speech.

▼ In a neat visual conceit, the identity of the ardent lover is hidden on the poster, just as it remains a secret in the movie.

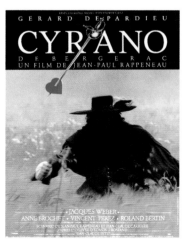

Jean-Paul Rappeneau's *Cyrano de Bergerac* came as something of a pleasant surprise. Here was another version of a well-worn French play, from a far from prolific director best known for romantic comedies. Yet *Cyrano de Bergerac* was a triumph: the film crossed international waters with ease, helped in no small part by Anthony Burgess's English subtitles, which preserve the source play's alexandrines (twelve-syllable rhyming lines). It brought new life to a classic tale, lacing Edmond Rostand's play of 1897 with careful character detail and witty performances. The screenplay by Jean-Claude Carrière and Rappeneau makes subtle changes to the characters of both Roxane and Christian, arguably rendering her more intelligent and him more heroic. Thus there are three central characters to invest in emotionally, creating a love triangle that is imbued with secrets, misunderstandings, and longing.

Key to the film's emotional power is the secret the audience shares with big-nosed hero Cyrano (Gérard Depardieu). He loves Roxane (Anne Brochet), and means every word he pens in the letters purporting to be from Christian (Vincent Perez). The audience are willing him to declare his own love, especially when Roxane unwittingly falls for the letter writer rather than the handsome hero. Fate conspires to keep true soulmates apart—after all, Cyrano is a tragic hero and *Cyrano de Bergerac* is a story of doomed love. But it is also a comedy, a war epic, a morality tale that cautions against judging by appearances. It is this kind of genre-spanning that helped make *Cyrano de Bergerac* accessible and led to its acclaim, also putting Depardieu firmly on the international map. **AS**

👁 KEY SCENES

1 CYRANO VERSUS CHRISTIAN
Cyrano is about to declare his love when Roxane reveals that she has fallen in love with Christian. She asks Cyrano to protect Christian, who is in his regiment. Blinded by her infatuation, she fails to notice Cyrano's anger and disappointment.

2 THE PLAN IS FORMED
Cyrano tells Christian that Roxane loves him and that she requests a letter. Christian claims he cannot write love letters. Cyrano offers to tutor him in eloquence and write his letters. Cyrano now has a safe way to voice his love, and Christian a way to woo his lady.

3 THE FINAL BLOW
Roxane risks her life to visit Christian during a battle. She claims it was his letters that brought her there, and that she was wooed by his soul. Devastated, Christian knows it is Cyrano's soul she loves. He throws himself into the front line of battle and dies.

4 THE REALIZATION
A badly wounded Cyrano visits Roxane at the nunnery where she lives in mourning, and reads her the last letter from "Christian." She realizes he knows the letter by heart. He confesses, she declares her love, but it is too late. Staggering into the moonlight, he dies.

🕐 DIRECTOR PROFILE

1932–65
Jean-Paul Rappeneau was born in Auxerre, Yonne, France. At twenty-eight, he began working as a screenwriter, collaborating with director Louis Malle (1932–95) on the fantasy comedy *Zazie dans le métro* (1960) and *Vie privée* (*A Very Private Affair*, 1962), which starred Brigitte Bardot and Marcello Mastroianni. He also contributed to the screenplay of *L'homme de Rio* (*That Man From Rio*, 1964), for which he received an Oscar nomination.

1966–71
Rappeneau made his directorial debut with *La vie de château* (*A Matter of Resistance*, 1966), a well-received romantic comedy that he had also written, starring Catherine Deneuve. His next directing project came five years later: *Les mariés de l'an II* (*The Scoundrel*, 1971) an action-adventure movie starring Jean-Paul Belmondo.

1972–82
He worked relatively rarely during this period, but continued to maintain a focus on the themes of marriage and relationships. In 1975 Rappeneau was reunited with Catherine Deneuve in making *Le sauvage* (*Call Me Savage*) a screwball romance. *Tout feu, tout flamme* (*All Fired Up*, 1982) followed, starring Yves Montand as a gambling father.

1983–90
After another extensive break from filming, Rappeneau returned with *Cyrano de Bergerac*, which picked up four BAFTAs, one Oscar, one César, a Golden Globe, and a host of other awards.

1991–present
Rappeneau directed Juliette Binoche in war drama *Le hussard sur le toit* (*The Horseman on the Roof*, 1995), which he also wrote, and worked again with Gérard Depardieu on another wartime feature, the well-received *Bon voyage* (2003). This film picked up three César awards in 2004: Most Promising Young Actor, Best Photography, and Best Set Design.

Shakespeare in Love 1998

JOHN MADDEN b. 1949

▲ A young Will Shakespeare (Joseph Fiennes) needs a muse to inspire his work.

▼ An intimate moment—and a stellar cast of actors—adorns the film's poster.

S tar-crossed lovers, misunderstandings, disguises, bawdy brawls—this film could have been written by Shakespeare himself. The script by Marc Norman and Tom Stoppard interweaves the Bard's trademark themes with a fictional story in which the struggling playwright (Joseph Fiennes) takes center stage. He is the romantic whose words woo the woman of his dreams, Viola (Gwyneth Paltrow), but who must face a series of complications that could have been of his own creation. Viola is disguised as a boy when they meet and she is engaged to another man, while Shakespeare has commitments of his own. What is more, Will's reputation and finances rest on the staging of a play, *Romeo and Juliet* (or "Romeo and Ethel, the Pirate's Daughter" as he initially calls it).

Such touches consistently amuse, painting the Bard as a man with human flaws, while setting up an in-joke for modern-day viewers. Although there is much in *Shakespeare in Love* for those familiar with his works, the film is as accessible as it is artful. This Hollywood-friendly movie draws engagingly from Britain's rich cultural history. Small wonder it won seven Academy Awards, including Best Picture. The casting is, of course, key to the film's success: Gwyneth Paltrow was the perfect replacement for Julia Roberts, who dropped out six weeks before filming. Joseph Fiennes brought fresh new talent to the table, while established greats including Judi Dench, Geoffrey Rush, Tom Wilkinson, Imelda Staunton, and Simon Callow brought gravitas. Thanks to John Madden's skillful direction, *Shakespeare in Love* never feels restrictively theatrical. It uses the power of cinema to convey the power of the theater. Shakespeare would surely have approved. **AS**

👁 KEY SCENES

1 THE STAGE IS SET
Viola watches a Shakespeare play with evident delight, her breath quickening as she mouths the words. Back home she shares her excitement with her nurse. She expresses her longing to be involved, setting the stage for her adventure in disguise.

2 WILL MEETS VIOLA
Will follows Viola back home, believing her to be Thomas Kent, her male alter ego. He sneaks into a ball at her home and recognizes her finery as her womanly self. He is instantly smitten—just as Viola's father is making a deal for her hand with Lord Wessex.

3 SHAKESPEARE MAKES LOVE
As they are traveling to Viola's house by boat, Will tells "Thomas Kent" how he feels about Viola. She kisses him while still in disguise. She rushes into the house and the boatman identifies her as Viola. Will rushes after her; they kiss and consummate their love.

4 THE SHOW MUST GO ON
Shakespeare puts on *Romeo and Juliet*, glum at the idea of doing so without Viola, but she replaces the male Juliet at the last minute. The play is a success and gives Will and Viola the chance to express their love before she must depart with her new husband, Wessex.

🕐 DIRECTOR PROFILE

1949–95
Madden attended Clifton College, Bristol, where he befriended future *Notting Hill* director Roger Michell (b. 1956); afterward, Madden went on to study English Literature at Cambridge University. He then moved to the United States, where he worked on radio drama, including adaptations of the original *Star Wars* trilogy for National Public Radio project Earplay. His work on Arthur Kopit's play *Wings* won Madden the Prix Italia in 1978, the most significant radio broadcasting award in the world. He also enjoyed success directing stage plays and taught drama at Yale University, before returning to England and beginning his directing career in television. His work on episodes of *The Adventures of Sherlock Holmes*, *Inspector Morse*, and *Prime Suspect 4: The Lost Child* brought Madden both critical and commercial success. He made the move into directing films with costume drama *Ethan Frome* (1993)—not a commercial success, but proof that he could adapt books to the screen effectively—and crime drama *Golden Gate* (1994).

1996–98
Madden continued to work in television, but finally made his breakthrough in film with *Mrs. Brown* (1997), a biographical drama starring Judi Dench as Queen Victoria that was nominated for two Academy Awards and for which Dench won a Golden Globe. Madden followed it with the enormously popular, award-winning *Shakespeare in Love*, which also featured Dench in the role of a British queen.

1999–present
Madden continued to direct, focusing on the big screen. His films included adaptations of popular works: a version of Louis de Bernières's novel *Captain Corelli's Mandolin* (2001)—which he took over from Roger Michell, after Michell suffered a heart attack prior to the start of production—and an adaptation of David Auburn's play *Proof* (2005), featuring *Shakespeare in Love* star Gwyneth Paltrow. In 2008 he directed *Killshot*, based on an Elmore Leonard novel. He directed the post-World War II thriller *The Debt* in 2010.

HOLLYWOOD DRAMA

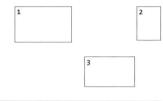

1 Despite having previously costarred in *The Godfather Part II* (1974), Al Pacino and Robert De Niro did not share a scene until *Heat*, a stylish thriller from director Michael Mann (b. 1943).

2 A man for our times: Jim Carrey stars as Truman Burbank in *The Truman Show*, a satire on celebrity and the media and a prophetic look at reality television.

3 Kevin Spacey's Lester Burnham beholds Angela Hayes (Mena Suvari)—a Lolita for the turn of the century—in the Academy Award–winning *American Beauty*.

The 1990s saw strong comebacks for directors and actors who had previously made era-defining films. Long after his 1970s heyday, Robert Altman (1925–2006) returned with the excellent *The Player* (1992) and *Short Cuts* (1993, see p. 448). The latter's patchwork narrative and large ensemble cast drew favorable comparisons with the director's earlier *Nashville* (1975). Terrence Malick (b. 1943), who returned to filmmaking with *The Thin Red Line* (1998) after a twenty-year hiatus, chose to focus on World War II, turning a philosophical lens on the conflict in the Pacific. On the acting side, two giants of cinema shared a scene for the first time when Al Pacino and Robert De Niro starred in the crime epic *Heat* (1995, above). De Niro continued to work with old ally Martin Scorsese (b. 1942) in *Goodfellas* (1990), which saw Scorsese return to the streets of his youth for the first of three films set in New York. *The Age of Innocence* (1993) and *Bringing out the Dead* (1999) followed, but the city's angst was better served by Abel Ferrara (b. 1951). His *King of New York* (1990) and *Bad Lieutenant* (1992) are two of the greatest and bleakest cinematic evocations of the city.

One of New York's most famous sons, Spike Lee (b. 1957), exposed the demand for films portraying the lives of African Americans with *Jungle Fever* (1991), *Malcolm X* (1992), and *Clockers* (1995). *New Jack City* (1991) by Mario van Peebles (b. 1957) and *Menace II Society* (1993) by the Hughes brothers (Albert and Allen, b. 1972) reinforced this interest, although lesser directors seemed intent on glamorizing violence rather than focusing on human drama.

KEY EVENTS

1990	1991	1991	1992	1992	1994
Martin Scorsese's *Goodfellas* is seen as a return to form.	*My Own Private Idaho* by Gus Van Sant (b. 1952) brings gay cinema into the mainstream, with the help of River Phoenix and Keanu Reeves.	*Boyz n the Hood* by John Singleton (b. 1968) is one of the decade's best African American films. Spike Lee directs *Jungle Fever*.	*Bad Lieutenant* and *Glengarry Glen Ross* by David Mamet (b. 1947) witness the breakdowns of two very different men.	Spike Lee's powerful *Malcolm X* biopic courts controversy by using footage of the Rodney King beating in its opening credits.	*Schindler's List* dominates the Oscars and Steven Spielberg is finally given credit as a serious filmmaker.

Combining human drama with blackly comic violence, Quentin Tarantino (b. 1963) easily earned himself the label of US cinema's geeky enfant terrible. The cleverly constructed genre pieces *Reservoir Dogs* (1992), *Pulp Fiction* (1994, see p. 450), and *Jackie Brown* (1997) showed him to be a gifted, if wayward, filmmaker. He also wrote the original script of *Natural Born Killers* (1994), which joined *Reservoir Dogs*, *Bad Lieutenant*, and *Crash* (1996) as the most controversial films of the decade.

Of the mainstream Hollywood dramas, *The Truman Show* (1998, right) offered the perfect platform for Jim Carrey's acting skills and was the best film by Peter Weir since *Witness* (1985). *Titanic* (1997) by James Cameron (b. 1954) topped box-office figures, as well as the Oscars in 1998. However, Cameron's screenplay, the film's weakest element, lost to that of *Good Will Hunting* (1997). Steven Spielberg (b. 1946) balanced the popcorn thrills of *Jurassic Park* (1993) with more serious drama, such as *Schindler's List* (1993), a powerful account of the Holocaust that excelled in its re-creation of the Warsaw ghetto and life in a death camp. The film's documentary style was extended in *Saving Private Ryan* (1998, see p. 452).

Away from these veteran filmmakers, three young directors showed glimpses of future brilliance. *The Usual Suspects* (1995) by Bryan Singer (b. 1965) led the audience through a teasing labyrinth, thanks to a tortuous script from Christopher McQuarrie. Sam Mendes (b. 1965) burst onto the scene in 1999 with *American Beauty* (below), which gave Kevin Spacey the role of his career and took a jaded look at middle age and US domesticity. The remarkably assured *Boogie Nights* (1997) by Paul Thomas Anderson (b. 1970), which re-created the 1970s and 1980s Los Angeles porn scene, hinted at the work that would make him one of the most original filmmakers of the next decade. **IHS**

1995	1995	1996	1997	1998	1999
Forrest Gump wins at the Oscars. *Pulp Fiction* (see p. 450), having won the Palme d'Or at Cannes in 1994, wins the Best Original Screenplay Oscar.	*Heat* and *Se7en* dominate the year's thrillers. Wayne Wang (b. 1949) and Paul Auster (b. 1947) collaborate on *Smoke* and *Blue in the Face*.	Abel Ferrara directs one of the decade's best gangster films, *The Funeral*. *Sydney* is directed by Paul Thomas Anderson.	*The Ice Storm* and *Jackie Brown* are released. *L.A. Confidential* succeeds in bringing James Ellroy to the screen.	*The Thin Red Line* and *Saving Private Ryan* (see p. 452) present two directors' visions of World War II.	*American Beauty* wins at the box office and the Oscars. M. Night Shyamalan (b. 1970) directs the year's big sleeper success, *The Sixth Sense*.

Short Cuts 1993
ROBERT ALTMAN 1925 – 2006

▲ The Piggots (Lily Tomlin and Tom Waits) forget their problems and kick up their heels.

▼ The cast won an award for ensemble acting.

After a busy decade working in television, Robert Altman reestablished himself as a commercial and critical prospect in cinema with *The Player* (1992), which cannily courted Hollywood by reflecting its grandeur—even as it depicted a studio head as a sociopath. The reward was funding for another Los Angeles ensemble piece, which braids a batch of Raymond Carver's spare, disturbing, short stories into a cinematic panorama of disparate, desperate characters caught between two disasters in L.A.—a medfly infestation that necessitates the spraying of neighborhoods with poison and an earthquake.

Drawing on Carver's Midwest setting makes for an odd Los Angeles, with few to no black or Hispanic faces, but this film also avoids *The Player*'s vision of a company town by turning away from the movies. Characters include a singer (Annie Ross) and her classical musician daughter (Lori Singer), and a man (Robert Downey Jr.) who does makeup tests on his wife (Lili Taylor) while his friend's wife (Jennifer Jason Leigh) dispenses phone sex. The film also takes in waitresses, drunks, absent fathers, erring wives, strutting cops, grieving parents, remote doctors, stunned (or dying) children, and a near psychopathically angry baker.

A huge cast (of twenty-two at times tenuously linked principal characters) gives itself over to Altman, whose twinkling, Machiavellian nondirection could always cadge or encourage performances other directors struggled to find in ensemble casts. Here, Lori Singer, who barely registers in most of her credits, is heartbreaking. The film ties up its loose ends, but it is the patterns discerned in chaos that make the film worth revisiting. **KN**

👁 KEY SCENES

1 PHONE SEX
Amid domestic chaos, busy housewife Lois Kaiser (Leigh) looks after her baby while toiling at her part-time job as a telephone sex worker. Meanwhile, Lois's interest in her personal sex life with husband Jerry (Chris Penn) verges on indifference.

2 NOTHING TO HIDE
Marian Wyman (Julianne Moore) and her husband, Ralph (Matthew Modine), prepare for a dinner party. In one of the film's most sparse and theatrical scenes, secrets are revealed and jealousies voiced, with Moore baring herself literally and figuratively.

3 PHOTO MIX-UP
Gordon, who has taken pictures of a corpse found on a camping trip, and Bill, a makeup man who has taken pictures of his wife, Honey, wearing artificial facial bruises, get their photos mixed up. Gordon and Honey draw terrifying conclusions about each other.

4 THE BATCAVE
Jerry Kaiser lures a girl off into the undergrowth with a promise of showing her where the Batcave was in the 1960s *Batman* television series and bludgeons her to death. The earthquake that shakes the city unlocks a terrible yearning in an ordinary man.

🕐 DIRECTOR PROFILE

1925–69
Robert Altman was born in Kansas City, Missouri. After military service in World War II he tried to get started in Hollywood but failed. He returned to his hometown and made sixty-odd industrial films. He directed a couple of exploitation pictures (*The Delinquents*, 1957; *The James Dean Story*, 1957), a lot of episodic television in Hollywood (*Alfred Hitchcock Presents*, *Bonzana*, *Combat*) and some interesting, if commercially unsuccessful, features (*Countdown*, 1968; *That Cold Day in the Park*, 1969).

1970–79
After the huge sleeper success of *MASH* (1970), Altman was able to make a string of distinctive, quirky, ambitious, semi-improvisational features that often used film genres to deconstruct US heroic archetypes (*McCabe & Mrs. Miller*, 1971; *The Long Goodbye*, 1973; *Thieves Like Us*, 1974; *Buffalo Bill and the Indians*, 1976) or the US scene (*Nashville*, 1975; *A Wedding*, 1978). He also made surreal, psychological films (*Brewster McCloud*, 1970; *Images*, 1972; *3 Women*, 1977) and small relationship stories (*California Split*, 1974; *A Perfect Couple*, 1979). Actress Shelley Duvall appeared repeatedly in his films.

1980–91
Popeye (1980), his biggest film, failed and he switched to filmed plays (*Come Back to the Five and Dime, Jimmy Dean, Jimmy Dean*, 1982; *Streamers*, 1983; *Secret Honor*, 1984; *Fool for Love*, 1985; *The Caine Mutiny Court-Martial*, 1988, made for television). His most personal work in this period was the improvised political television series *Tanner '88* (1988).

1992–2006
The Player, a smart "inside Hollywood" picture studded with famous faces, reestablished the Altman style, and he followed up with more ensemble dramas: *Short Cuts*, *Prêt-à-Porter* (1994), *Kansas City* (1996), *Gosford Park* (2001), *The Company* (2003), and *A Prairie Home Companion* (2006). Suffering from leukemia, he died in 2006.

Pulp Fiction 1994
QUENTIN TARANTINO b. 1963

▲ Vincent and Jules are ambushed by a gunman. Incredibly, he misses. They do not.

▼ Uma Thurman dominates the poster for the film that launched her to fame.

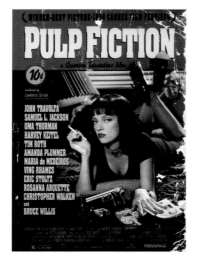

Like one of the pulp magazines referenced in its title, *Pulp Fiction* tells several interlinked stories but tells them out of order. The frame is a holdup in a diner, as petty thieves Pumpkin (Tim Roth) and Honeybunny (Amanda Plummer) pull their guns, only to be faced by professional hitmen Vincent (John Travolta) and Jules (Samuel L. Jackson). In the intervening three stories, we see Vincent spiral (and die) thanks to bad luck and poor judgment, while Jules takes a different lesson from a near-death experience and resolves to quit the business and do good — if he survives the Mexican standoff in the diner.

Having secured a cult following with his debut feature *Reservoir Dogs* (1992), writer-director Quentin Tarantino pulled together a series of stories he had been tinkering with (some in collaboration with writer Roger Avary) for this much more ambitious film. As with *Reservoir Dogs*, the quality of the script — specifically, Tarantino's distinctive, discursive, pop culture–studded, sometimes oddly philosophical line of talk — attracted a diverse cast.

It is a film of archetypal noir situations (the boxer paid to throw a fight, the date that turns disastrous, the body that must be disposed of) but also a set of shaggy dog tales that take off in unexpected ways — as Vincent's "date" with his boss's dangerous wife (Uma Thurman) goes from screwball comedy to junkie nightmare and Butch (Bruce Willis) flees supercrook Marsellus (Ving Rhames) only to drag his enemy into a very bad situation with some unrelated psychopaths. It has black comic violence but also a thread of sweetness and honesty, always privileging characters like Jules who aspire to better things. **KN**

👁 KEY SCENES

1 "ROYALE WITH CHEESE"
Vincent delivers a lengthy riff on Amsterdam hash bars, beer in cinemas, and what a quarter pounder is called in a French McDonald's. Tarantino devotes considerable screen time to the rambling dialogue that reveals the outlook of his characters.

4 "GONNA GET MEDIEVAL ON YOUR ASS!"
Butch and Marsellus chase one another into a pawn shop run by a sadistic psychopath. After Butch decides to save Marsellus, evening the score between them, the latter explains what he is going to do to Zed, the redneck who has just raped him.

2 THE JACKRABBIT SLIM TWIST CONTEST
Vincent escorts his boss's wife, Mia, to a 1950s-themed restaurant where she persuades him to take part in a dance contest. Their distinctive dance moves win them the contest. The film revived Travolta's flagging career and earned him an Oscar nomination.

5 MR. WOLF
Harvey Keitel plays "the cleaner" Winston Wolf who turns up to dispose of the body of an informant, accidentally shot by Vincent in the car. The plum cameo role was specially written for the star, one of Tarantino's favorites, who also appeared in *Reservoir Dogs*.

3 INJECTION OF ADRENALIN
While Vincent debates with himself the wisdom of getting involved with Mia, she overdoses on his heroin. Vincent rushes her to his drug dealer's house. The audience does not actually see the needle go in, but they hear the thump and witness her wild, animal-like reaction.

6 BE COOL
Jules, having had a revelatory near-death experience and intent on changing his ways, talks Pumpkin and Honeybunny, the armed robbers in the diner, out of turning a Mexican standoff into a massacre. Tarantino wrote the part of Jules with Jackson in mind.

Saving Private Ryan 1998

STEVEN SPIELBERG b. 1946

▲ The band of brothers arrive in Ramelle shortly before the film's climactic battle.

▼ Finding individual humanity in war, the value of one life is put into context.

Famed for its visceral D-Day landing opening sequence, Steven Spielberg's World War II opus is one of his most accomplished films. In contrast to *Schindler's List* (1993), which employed its audience as observers of the horror of the Holocaust, *Saving Private Ryan* places them at the heart of a maelstrom, with an intensity few films have achieved.

Cementing his image as the all-American Everyman, Tom Hanks plays Captain Miller, whose orders are to return safely home a young private whose three brothers have been killed in battle. Robert Rodat's screenplay was inspired by the story of the Niland brothers, four siblings who fought in the war, and the sons of Agnes Allison, who died in the American Civil War and who are referenced in one of the film's early scenes.

Critics of the film accused it of jingoism and sentimentality. Certainly, the unit encounters no Allied forces other than Americans on its journey through France, and the framing device, which intimates that the modern-day war veteran in the film's prologue is Miller, only for him to be revealed as Ryan, is just as manipulative as the deployment of the girl with the red dress or the shower sequence in *Schindler's List*. However, these moments are offset by the sheer brutality of the battle scenes, as well as the discussions of the value of a human life and the possible reasons for fighting a war. The film's climax—the defense of a strategically crucial bridge—is more conventional than the earlier battle scenes, but still remains gripping, balancing suspense and narrative drive with emotional engagement. **IHS**

👁 KEY SCENES

1 THE ASSAULT ON OMAHA BEACH
The raw power of this scene, showing the Allied troops' landing on Omaha Beach, is both a gut-wrenching experience and a masterclass in technique. A variety of styles is employed, from hand-held camerawork to slow motion.

2 THE MORALITY OF KILLING
After a "don't shoot, let them burn" comment by one of the US soldiers as Germans engulfed in flames topple out of one of the pillboxes, the debate over what constitutes excessive violence continues when Miller's squad corners a German soldier.

3 THE RETURN OF THE PRISONER
In the film's climactic battle scene, the German prisoner released by Miller is responsible for killing one of his men and finally fatally shooting the captain. Jeremy Davies's translator guns down the soldier, reinforcing the theme of the brutalizing effect of war.

4 THE EPILOGUE
In a devastating and clever narrative maneuver, the old veteran turns out to be Ryan, even though the opening suggested it was Miller. Miller is the film's emotional and moral compass. His death reinforces the film's emphasis on the callousness of war.

🕐 CINEMATOGRAPHER PROFILE: JANUSZ KAMIŃSKI

1959–92
Born in Ziębice, Poland, Janusz Kamiński emigrated to the United States at twenty-one. He completed his BA in cinematography at Chicago's Columbia College, and then studied for his MFA at the American Film Institute. His film career began with low-budget horror films and second unit work on *One False Move* (1992) by Carl Franklin (b. 1949).

1993–2000
His work on *Schindler's List* earned Kamiński his first Academy Award. He went on to collaborate with Steven Spielberg on *The Lost World: Jurassic Park* and *Amistad* (both 1997) and *Saving Private Ryan*, for which he picked up his second Academy Award. For his subsequent work with Spielberg he adopted a darker palette, often with a metallic hue. In 2000 he directed his first feature, *Lost Souls*.

2001–6
Both *Artificial Intelligence: AI* (2001) and *Minority Report* (2002) saw Spielberg and Kamiński's visual style develop in order to capture the morality of futuristic worlds. The palette lightened for *Catch Me If You Can* (2002) and *The Terminal* (2004) before returning to a far darker look for *War of the Worlds* and *Munich* (both 2005).

2007–8
Kamiński's work on *The Diving Bell and the Butterfly* (2007) by Julian Schnabel (b. 1951) saw him feted at Cannes and winning the Independent Spirit Award for Best Cinematography. In the same year he returned to Poland to direct his second film, *Hania*, before reconvening with Spielberg for their least impressive collaboration to date, the long-awaited *Indiana Jones and the Kingdom of the Crystal Skull* (2008).

2009–present
In 2010 he began production on his twelfth Spielberg project, *War Horse*, as well as preparing to shoot his third film, *The Night Witch*.

US INDEPENDENT CINEMA

Although US independent cinema enjoyed a heyday in the 1980s and 1990s, this was by no means strictly a phenomenon of the period. Independent cinema proper—produced outside the studio system—is not new to the United States. Small studios and loners have plied their trade since cinema's early days. Rather than being definable purely by criteria of production and distribution, "indie" cinema is, theoretically at least, independent-minded, resistant to mainstream norms, and vaguely countercultural. US independent film is regarded as being created by filmmakers with distinctive viewpoints, who often produce and retain the rights to their work. This tradition embraces names as varied as Robert Altman (1925–2006), Andy Warhol (1928–87), John Cassavetes (1929–89), and George A. Romero (b. 1940).

US independent film blossomed into a visible culture in the 1980s. Key figures were the versatile John Sayles (b. 1950), making antiauthoritarian dramas such as *Matewan* (1987), and Jim Jarmusch (b. 1953), whose laconic hipster style had its roots in the New York, no-budget scene of the late 1970s. Joel (b. 1954) and Ethan (b. 1957) Coen first made their mark in 1984 with the black comedy *Blood Simple*. A major breakthrough came in 1986 when Spike Lee (b. 1957) emerged with the erotic comedy *She's Gotta Have It*, and his stylistic invention, political provocation, and hard-edged entrepreneurialism spearheaded a new wave of African American directors, including John Singleton (b. 1968), Matty Rich (b. 1971), and twins Albert and Allen Hughes (b. 1972), as well as more experimental voices, such as Julie Dash (b. 1952).

(see p. 460)

KEY EVENTS

1990	1991	1992	1995	1996	1998
Teen musical *Cry-Baby*, directed by John Waters (b. 1946), is released. It features an ensemble cast headed by Johnny Depp.	The Utah/US Film Festival is renamed the Sundance Film Festival: a brand is born.	Quentin Tarantino makes *Reservoir Dogs*, and goes on to become one of the most influential filmmakers of the decade.	Jim Jarmusch's *Dead Man* kicks off the Acid Western genre.	Joel and Ethan Coen achieve a significant crossover hit with *Fargo* (see p. 460), a key film in the career of US indie regular, actor Steve Buscemi.	Gus Van Sant's *Good Will Hunting* (1997) wins an Academy Award for Best Screenplay for writing team Matt Damon and Ben Affleck.

Many of these pioneers have sustained long careers of remarkable variety. Sayles is still making critically acclaimed films, including his unconventional Western, *Lone Star* (1996, see p. 458), and examination of adoption, *Casa de los babys* (2003). Jarmusch continues to break barriers with films such as the gothic Western *Dead Man* (1995, opposite above) and his series of celebrity vignettes *Coffee and Cigarettes* (2003). Lee continued to examine relationships with *Jungle Fever* (1991) and explored documentary with *When the Levees Broke: A Requiem in Four Acts* (2006). The Coen brothers found fame outside the cult circuit with *Barton Fink* (1991) and *Fargo* (1996, see p. 460). The brothers have since worked in a variety of commercial contexts, but the consistent, sometimes perverse, singularity of their vision qualifies them as indie role models. David Lynch (b. 1946) has developed his career in a similar way to the Coen brothers, by beginning as an outsider par excellence with his nightmarish anomaly *Eraserhead* (1976).

Inaugurated in 1982, the Sundance Film Festival—as it has been called since 1991—put the seal on a culture of independent cinema that boomed partly as a reaction to the conservatism prevalent under President Ronald Reagan. Sundance launched the careers of various filmmakers, including Steven Soderbergh (b. 1963), who won the Sundance Audience Award for *sex, lies, and videotape* (1989). The movie drew attention to new low-budget cinema by winning an Oscar nomination and the Palme d'Or at the Cannes Film Festival. Since then, as director and producer, Soderbergh has delved into every kind of genre, at every conceivable budget level, inside and outside the mainstream. Robert Rodríguez (b. 1968) burst on to the scene at Sundance with the action movie *El mariachi* (1992), which was originally intended for the Spanish-language, low-budget, home-video market. After its phenomenal success Rodríguez went on to set up his own mini-studio, becoming a new Roger Corman (b. 1926) with Latino inflections. Kevin Smith (b. 1970) surfaced at Sundance with the boisterous *Clerks* (1994, opposite below), which was shot in the convenience store where he worked. An enthusiastic amateur made good, Smith remains the archetypal fanboy of the indie scene.

Another important development was "New Queer Cinema." An international phenomenon, in the United States trailblazers include Todd Haynes (b. 1961) with *Poison* (1991) and Gus Van Sant (b. 1952) with *Mala Noche* (1986). Both directors went on to transcend this bracket with formally innovative movies. Similarly, women found more space to create distinctive work in the independent sector, among them Allison Anders (b. 1954) with her study of the Los Angeles Hispanic gang scene *Mi vida loca* (1993), and Maggie Greenwald (b. 1955) with her revisionist Western *The Ballad of Little Jo* (1993).

Independent cinema has provided a haven for experimental filmmakers, for example Todd Solondz (b. 1959) with provocative social satires such as *Happiness* (1998, above right), Larry Clark (b. 1943) with his portrayals of urban

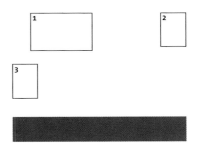

1 William Blake (Johnny Depp) adrift in Jim Jarmusch's take on life in a nineteenth-century frontier town, *Dead Man*.

2 The poster for Todd Solondz's *Happiness* suggests the unhappiness of the movie's grotesque characters.

3 *Clerks* was filmed in black and white and shot at night in the shop Kevin Smith worked in by day.

1998	1999	1999	2003	2003	2007
Happiness, Todd Solondz's hugely controversial film about solitude, depression, and pedophilia in suburbia, is released.	Video-shot horror movie *The Blair Witch Project* becomes the first significant film to achieve major success via Internet promotion.	*Being John Malkovich* by Spike Jonze (b. 1969) launches the eccentric vision of screenwriter Charlie Kaufman.	Edited on iMovie software, *Tarnation*, directed by Jonathan Caouette (b. 1973), shows how new technology can enable filmmaking.	Michael Moore's *Bowling for Columbine* wins an Oscar for Best Documentary.	*Little Miss Sunshine* (2006) by Valerie Faris (b. 1958) and Jonathan Dayton (b. 1957) wins two Oscars, including one for Best Screenplay.

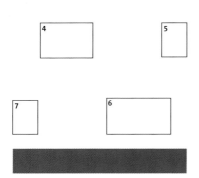

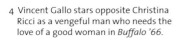

4 Vincent Gallo stars opposite Christina Ricci as a vengeful man who needs the love of a good woman in *Buffalo '66*.

5 The poster for Michael Moore's documentary about the Columbine High School massacre subtly conveys the film's anti-gun message.

6 Unlikely couple Charlotte (Scarlett Johansson) and Bob (Bill Murray) prove to be kindred spirits in *Lost in Translation*.

7 The garish poster for Wes Anderson's *The Royal Tenenbaums* points to the eponymous family's eccentricity.

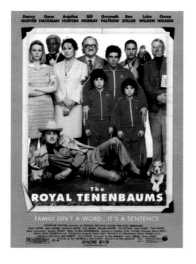

teenagers including the gritty *Kids* (1995), Paul Thomas Anderson (b. 1970) with stylish ensemble pieces such as *Boogie Nights* (1997) and Wes Anderson (b. 1969) with witty fabulist works such as *The Royal Tenenbaums* (2001, left). Vincent Gallo (b. 1961) made his directorial debut with the precocious melodrama about an ex-con's return home, *Buffalo '66* (1998, above), which won him a fan base for its quirky soundtrack and innovative cinematography, and for the director's own hyper-eccentric performance. The comedy *Slacker* (1991) by Richard Linklater (b. 1960) embodied an indie aesthetic and also defined a subculture; his subsequent career includes both commercial films and experimental works, such as the animated *Waking Life* (2001). Sofia Coppola (b. 1971), daughter of Francis Ford Coppola (b. 1939), proved that filmmaking was in her blood with her debut *The Virgin Suicides* (1999), and won an Oscar for Best Original Screenplay with *Lost in Translation* (2003, opposite below). After an experimental costume drama, *Marie Antoinette* (2006), she revisited earlier themes in the sparse *Somewhere* (2010). The king of movie geeks, however, remains Quentin Tarantino (b. 1963), whose obsessional cinephilic energies—first vented in the economically inventive tale of a jewel heist, *Reservoir Dogs* (1992)—led to his being hailed the boy genius of pop-culture cinema. Tarantino's reputation has fluctuated, but he remains a prime reference point for indie fans.

Independent film has also had an impact on documentary, notably the investigative essays from Michael Moore (b. 1954), such as *Roger & Me* (1989) and *Bowling for Columbine* (2002, opposite above). The impact of Moore's work has provided a boost for a wave of extremely diverse documentary, from the traditional social realism of *Hoop Dreams* (1994) by Steve James (b. 1954), to the more narratively distinctive *Capturing the Friedmans* (2003) directed by Andrew Jarecki (b. 1963).

The indie world has been a breeding ground for genre enthusiasms. A pioneering success is the video-shot *The Blair Witch Project* (1999), a horror mock-documentary presaging a new wave of low-budget chillers. Clearly, genre fare can suffer under financial restrictions; effective horror and science fiction can be harder to produce against a level of expectation nurtured by years of multimillion dollar entertainment and increasingly elaborate special effects. Nonetheless, away from the sheen of big budgets, new ideas expressed inventively can transform genre formulae. Albeit very different from each other, *Gattaca* (1997), *Donnie Darko* (2001), and the animated *A Scanner Darkly* (2006) are all independent-minded ventures that echo the knowing use of science fiction in earlier films such as *Alphaville* (1965) by Jean-Luc Godard (b. 1930).

A group of independent production companies became dominant names on the circuit—among them October Films, Good Machine, and the once all-powerful Miramax. Yet with many inferior mainstream films also benefiting from the scene's prestige, eventually the "indie spirit" became a cachet rather than a true ethic. Some of the major studios spun off nominally autonomous subsidiaries, such as Fox Searchlight Pictures, that aimed at corralling something of the indie spirit within their purlieu. Many filmmakers adopt the "one for them, one for me" approach, alternating between a picture made at a studio's behest and one flavored with their own idiosyncrasies. With the *Hellboy* (2004–08) films sandwiching the European-made *El laberinto del fauno* (*Pan's Labyrinth*, 2006), Mexican director Guillermo del Toro (b. 1964) was able to explore a Spanish-language story close to his heart while also producing marketable and distinctive comic book adventures. Rodríguez switched between the family fare of *Spy Kids* (2001) and the more experimental *Sin City* (2005). Similarly, Soderbergh has alternated between knowingly glossy fare (the *Ocean's Eleven* trilogy, 2001–07) and ventures bordering on the outright avant-garde (*The Girlfriend Experience*, 2009). Gus Van Sant also flirted with material close to the mainstream (*Good Will Hunting*, 1997) before returning to more abstract material in *Gerry* (2002) and *Elephant* (2003). In addition, it is not unknown for independent filmmakers to accept lucrative script doctor roles on Hollywood projects, enlivening mainstream fare with more personal writing touches: Tarantino worked on *Crimson Tide* (1995) and Sayles on *Apollo 13* (1995).

Throughout his career writer-actor-director Orson Welles (1915–85) locked horns with studios over creative control. The situation is no different in today's Hollywood, and directors such as the Coen brothers may insist on having the final cut on their work, ensuring that their films stand out in distinction to Hollywood conventions. The challenge for US independent filmmakers is to offer their viewers genuine alternatives to the themes and practices of standard Hollywood output. Indeed, independent films can achieve box-office success: *Little Miss Sunshine* (2006) and the micro-budget horror film *Paranormal Activity* (2007) being recent examples. Another is the Internet-themed *Catfish* (2010), which gained prominence on the back of controversy over its purported documentary nature. Since the turn of the twenty-first century, the health of US independent cinema has waned, but as the cost of equipment drops, the Internet market grows, and Hollywood's creativity stagnates, a resurgence in independent filmmaking in the United States should never be ruled out. **JR**

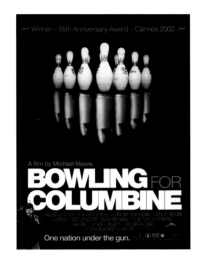

Lone Star 1996
JOHN SAYLES b. 1950

▲ Sheriff Charlie Wade (Kris Kristofferson) personifies institutional racism.

▼ The film's poster pulls no punches.

With *Lone Star* John Sayles returned to the broad canvas, multiple character mode he explored in *City of Hope* (1991). In both films Sayles is intent on tracing lines of tension and interconnection, showing how individuals impinge on each other no matter how they try to hold themselves separate. *Lone Star* is about the artificial divisions, political or social, that must be acknowledged but can still be crossed. In this Texan community close by the American-Mexican border live whites, African Americans, Hispanics, and Native Americans, and, however jealously they guard their identities, proximity and human nature will inevitably erode them.

In its technique, too, the film elides borders. Flashbacks are presented, not by cuts or dissolves but by the camera simply panning or tilting into a different time zone that nonetheless occupies part of the same space. The past is not another country; it is still here and people carry it with them. Similarly, the line between what seemed moral absolutes starts to blur as Sheriff Sam Deeds (Chris Cooper) tries to find out what really happened between his father Buddy (Matthew McConaughey), the previous and near-worshipped sheriff, and Buddy's predecessor, the corrupt and brutal Charlie Wade (Kris Kristofferson).

In turning the conventions of the Western to its own ends, *Lone Star* develops the theme that underpins all of Sayles's work: character as a product of accumulated social and cultural influences, the way people are molded by their pasts and their backgrounds, but are still capable of surmounting that conditioning. As one character observes, "Blood only means what you let it." **PK**

👁 KEY SCENES

1 THE SKULL
The film opens with a grisly discovery. On a disused army rifle range in the desert, a human skull is found—and nearby lies a corroded sheriff's badge. The gruesome find instigates Sheriff Sam Deeds's investigation into the past.

2 THE APOTHEOSIS OF BUDDY DEEDS
A plaque to Sam's father Buddy Deeds, the town's late sheriff, is unveiled. Reluctantly, Sam takes part in the ceremony. The weight of his father's legacy is heavy on Sam's shoulders, and he is all too aware of the upset he may cause by digging up the past.

3 SAM AND PILAR
Sam and schoolteacher Pilar Cruz walk beside the river where they used to meet as teenage sweethearts before Sam's father made them split up. As a teenager, although it was never spoken of, Sam had always presumed that they were separated because of race.

4 THE KILLING OF CHARLIE WADE
In flashback it is revealed that when Charlie Wade was about to gun down Otis (Gabriel Casseus) in cold blood, the corrupt sheriff was shot dead by his deputy Hollis (Jeff Monahan)—and not, as Sam had suspected, by his father Buddy Deeds.

⏱ DIRECTOR PROFILE

1950–80
John Sayles was born in Schenectady, New York, and raised as a Catholic. His first novel, *Pride of the Bimbos*, was published in 1975. In 1977 he began working as a screenwriter for Roger Corman. His screenwriting credits for Corman include the comedy-horror movie *Piranha* (1978) and the gangster film *The Lady in Red* (1979). Sayles made his debut film as a writer-director with the ensemble relationship drama about an activists' reunion *Return of the Secaucus Seven* (1979).

1981–89
The critics praised Sayles's script for the update on a werewolf story *The Howling* (1981) and his writing-direction on *Lianna* (1983). He directed his first Hollywood film for Paramount, a romantic comedy, *Baby, It's You* (1983). Sayles continued to direct his own socially acute, independent films, such as the science fiction movie *The Brother from Another Planet* (1984) and historical drama *Matewan* (1987), which was nominated for an Oscar for Best Cinematography. As well as developing his own projects, Sayles continued to provide scripts for other directors, write plays and novels, and act in small roles.

1990–2001
While continuing to explore his social and political concerns, Sayles's films—financed by his work as a screenwriter for hire—became more technically ambitious with the powerful story of political corruption *City of Hope* featuring regular lead actor Chris Cooper. His drama about a former soap opera star *Passion Fish* (1992) won him a first Oscar nomination for Best Screenplay. Sayles followed up with the strikingly visual *The Secret of Roan Inish* (1994), *Lone Star*, the Latin American–focused *Men with Guns* (1997), and the unconventional thriller *Limbo* (1999).

2002–present
Sayles's fascination with US history and mythology continued to fuel his staunchly independent films *Sunshine State* (2002), *Casa de los Babys* (2003), *Silver City* (2004), *Honeydripper* (2007), and *Amigo* (2010).

Fargo 1996
JOEL COEN b. 1954 ETHAN COEN b. 1957

▲ Frances McDormand's performance as Marge won her a Best Actress Oscar.

▼ The poster emphasizes that even in a small town life can get unpleasant.

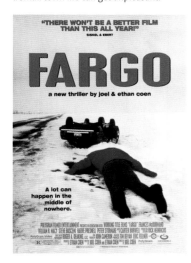

Purporting (mendaciously) to be based on a true story, *Fargo* is similar in its plot essentials to the Coen brothers' first film *Blood Simple* (1984) but has a different tone. Where *Blood Simple* is Texas—heat, passion, cruelty, cowboy hats, bar fights, and plowed fields—*Fargo* is Minnesota—snow, dry wit, stoicism, desperation, earflaps, financial crises, and icy wastes.

Car salesman Jerry Lundegaard (William H. Macy) is frustrated because his rich father-in-law (Harve Presnell) refuses to help him out of debt or invest in his money-making schemes. He goes to the town of Fargo to arrange with petty crooks Carl Showalter (Steve Buscemi) and Gaear Grimsrud (Peter Stormare) the kidnapping of his own wife so he can extort funds from her father. Naturally, with such loose cannons as Carl and Gaear on the case, everything goes wrong. Into this bloody mess comes Marge Gunderson (Frances McDormand), a heavily pregnant small-town sheriff. She pieces together Jerry's story and solves the crime, but misreads people in her personal life. Although Marge lavishes affection on her grumpy husband (John Carroll Lynch), she contemplates a fling with an old college friend (Steve Park), who reveals a depth of despair that rivals Jerry's and turns out to be more disturbed than he seems. The Coen brothers have been accused of being more clever than compassionate, but for all its gruesome humor *Fargo* has a heart as big as Marge's tummy. It does not need speeches from the heroine about how people would be happier if they tried to get along with one another to project a sense of decency struggling with desperation. **KN**

⊙ KEY SCENES

1 MARGE ON THE CASE
The heavily pregnant Marge examines the crime scene and makes sensible deductions: "OK, so we got a trooper pulls someone over, we got a shooting, these folks drive by, there's a high-speed pursuit, ends here, and then this execution-type deal."

2 FRIENDS REUNITED
Marge has a date with an old friend, the fidgety Japanese-American, Mike Yamagita. He has invested a lot more in this meeting than she has and sobs: "You were such a super lady, and I'm . . . I'm so lonely." The trusting Marge believes he is a widower.

3 BURYING TREASURE
Bleeding profusely from a face wound incurred in a shootout with Jerry's father-in-law, Carl buries the bag containing the ransom money in the snow by the highway. Using an ice scraper, Carl leaves a marker in the snow, which is extremely likely to be obscured.

4 RED MIST
In the one element of the film that is based on a true story, Marge discovers Gaear forcing Carl's corpse into a wood chipper. Gaear attempts to escape but a bewildered Marge shoots him in the leg and arrests him, saying, "There's more to life than a little money."

⊙ DIRECTOR PROFILE

1954–89
The brothers were born in Minneapolis to academic parents. In 1984 they collaborated on the hilarious homage to Film Noir (see p. 168) *Blood Simple*. The same year Joel married leading lady Frances McDormand and he has frequently cast her in their movies since. Initially, Joel was listed as director and Ethan as producer and they shared a script credit, but eventually they admitted that they both contributed to all three functions. They followed up with the pyrotechnic comedy *Raising Arizona* (1987), starring Nicolas Cage and Frances McDormand. Both films were so unusual that the duo attracted a cult following.

1990–91
The duo began making their series of distinctive, skewed, intelligent pictures in various genres, often touching on hard-boiled crime—especially kidnapping—and deals with the Devil; starting with the gangster thriller *Miller's Crossing* (1990). They had a breakthrough into the mainstream with their Palme d'Or winner *Barton Fink* (1991).

1992–2002
They continued to mix genres with the screwball comedy *The Hudsucker Proxy* (1994), cult thriller *Fargo*, slapstick comedy with noirish elements *The Big Lebowski* (1998) starring Jeff Bridges, prison break comedy *O Brother, Where Art Thou?* (2000) starring George Clooney, and neo-noir *The Man Who Wasn't There* (2001).

2003–present
After the more commercial—if less memorable—story of gender politics *Intolerable Cruelty* (2003), starring Clooney, and a remake of the classic crime caper, *The Ladykillers* (2004) by Alexander Mackendrick (1912–93), they made *No Country for Old Men* (2007), which is based on a Cormac McCarthy novel and won four Oscars, including Best Picture. The brothers followed up with more original scripts, *Burn After Reading* (2008) and *A Serious Man* (2009), and a remake of a Henry Hathaway (1898–1985) Western, *True Grit* (2010).

AUSTRALASIAN CINEMA

1 P. J. Hogan's charming comedy *Muriel's Wedding*, about an unattractive outcast in Australian suburbia, saw lead Toni Collette win over audiences with her portrayal of a gauche Abba fan.

2 Paul Mercurio and Tara Morice take to the dance floor in Baz Luhrmann's musical *Strictly Ballroom*.

3 Jane Campion's moving story about a mute and her daughter unfolds against a beautiful and dreamy landscape in *The Piano*. The film helped gain a wider audience for cinema from New Zealand.

The defining characteristic of Australasian film of the 1990s is its diversity. The region was becoming increasingly outward looking, open to international collaborations and prepared to redefine its cultural image to illustrate that antipodean life was a far cry from that shown in *Crocodile Dundee* (1986). Prior to this decade, the native film industry had focused on making social realist dramas that were strong on cultural content and less so on nuance. A new generation of Australian actors, including Geoffrey Rush, Nicole Kidman, Cate Blanchett, Toni Collette, and Heath Ledger, also came to the fore in the 1990s in both native and foreign products.

Established Australian director Peter Weir (b. 1944) built on his success with international offerings including the romantic comedy *Green Card* (1990) and the surreal drama *The Truman Show* (1998). Phillip Noyce (b. 1950) parlayed the acclaim he received for his thriller *Dead Calm* (1989) into a role as director of choice for Hollywood vehicles for Harrison Ford: *Patriot Games* (1992) and *Clear and Present Danger* (1994). New Zealander Peter Jackson (b. 1961) changed gear from horror to drama with *Heavenly Creatures* (1994, see p. 466) to find international recognition. Australia also showed its talent for family comedy with the popular tale of an endearing pig that wants to be a sheepdog, *Babe* (1995), directed by Chris Noonan (b. 1952), which grossed AUS $36.77 million.

First-time writer-directors Baz Luhrmann (b. 1962; *Strictly Ballroom*, 1992, opposite above) and Stephan Elliott (b. 1964; *The Adventures of Priscilla, Queen of the Desert*, 1994, see p. 464) helped reinvent the dance and musical genres, reinvigorating Australian cinema along the way. Both films use humor, feel-good music, rich color, and flamboyant characters to portray an Australia that is optimistic and all-embracing. *Strictly Ballroom* follows the fortunes of an obsessive ballroom dancer, Scott Hastings (Paul Mercurio), who breaks with tradition by developing his own spontaneous dance routines, aided by the shy Fran (Tara Morice), a young girl of Spanish descent. Luhrmann's trademark moving camerawork and eye for spectacular costumes make the film a visual gem. His exploration of ethnicity and what defines a contemporary Australian reveals a nation prepared to throw off its British colonial past. *Strictly Ballroom* was a box-office hit in Australia and its international release earned critical plaudits and helped launch its director on the road to Hollywood.

Directed by New Zealander Jane Campion (b. 1954) and shot in New Zealand with Australian, French, and New Zealander backing, art-house movie *The Piano* (1993, below right) was a massive international success both financially and critically. It won the Palme d'Or at Cannes and was nominated for eight Oscars, winning three. A haunting, gothic romance set in the nineteenth century with a score by English composer Michael Nyman and tour de force performances by US actress Holly Hunter as mute Scotswoman Ada McGrath, Canadian-born Anna Paquin as her daughter Flora, New Zealander Sam Neill as her husband Alistair Stewart, and American Harvey Keitel as her lover George Baines, *The Piano* is a truly international film that nevertheless succeeded in putting New Zealand on the cinematic map. Campion's subtle direction also subverts the notion of the female immigrant and mute as downtrodden victim. Like Luhrmann and Elliott, Campion takes the notion of the outsider and makes it mainstream. Campion was reunited with the English-born New Zealander cinematographer with whom she worked on *An Angel at My Table* (1990), Stuart Dryburgh, and his camerawork gives a dreamlike quality to the desolate exteriors of the New Zealand coastline, which emphasize the isolating world where McGrath finds herself.

Filmed on a modest budget, with an Australian cast, setting, crew, and writer-director (P. J. Hogan, b. 1962), *Muriel's Wedding* (1994, opposite) also focuses on an outcast, Muriel Heslop (Toni Collette). A misfit growing up in a provincial backwater, she longs to fit in with her peers. Obsessed with Abba and the idea of getting married, she runs away to Sydney, where her old school chum, Rhonda Epinstalk (Rachel Griffiths), introduces her to big-city life. The film was a surprise hit, particularly given that its two leads were then almost unknown, but audiences warmed to its story of the rebellious ugly duckling who comes good. Hogan's use of popular tunes in the style of Luhrmann and Elliott adds to the movie's appeal, but his script and the performances of the lead actors are what make the movie. *Muriel's Wedding* starts out as a chick-flick comedy but soon takes a more serious turn and becomes a coming-of-age drama, as Muriel deals with the responsibilities and tragedies that real life can bring. **CK**

1996	1996	1997	1997	1999	2000
Babe is nominated for seven Academy Awards, including Best Picture and Best Director.	Peter Jackson directs his first big-budget Hollywood movie, a comedy horror film, *The Frighteners*, which he shoots in New Zealand.	Geoffrey Rush becomes the first Australian-born actor to win an Oscar for Best Actor for his role as a pianist in the drama *Shine*.	Cate Blanchett takes her first leading role, opposite Ralph Fiennes, in literary adaptation *Oscar and Lucinda*, by Gillian Armstrong (b. 1950).	Heath Ledger garners international attention in the teen comedy *10 Things I Hate About You*.	Toni Collette is nominated for an Oscar for Best Actress in a Supporting Role for her part as the mother in the thriller *The Sixth Sense*.

The Adventures of Priscilla, Queen of the Desert 1994
STEPHAN ELLIOTT b. 1964

▲ Adam/Felicia performs on top of the troupe's eponymous bus, Priscilla.

▼ The film poster celebrates the camp exuberance of this Australian road movie.

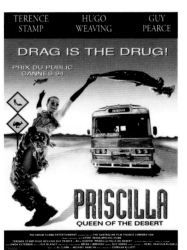

This Australian road-movie musical conceived, written and directed by Stephan Elliott helped revive the musical genre. Featuring songs from 1930s classics to disco hits, *The Adventures of Priscilla, Queen of the Desert* fast became a popular feel-good movie. This was an unexpected outcome for a film that tells the story of three drag queens who journey in a bus from Sydney to Alice Springs, where they perform in a hotel—a theme that might not, at first glance, seem to have such wide appeal. Yet the film is far more than a drag classic. Elliott's witty, fast-paced dialogue, packed with bitchy wisecracks, provides entertaining comedy. Brian J. Breheny's superb cinematography, particularly of the desert landscape, ensures the film is visually lush. Best of all are the scene-stealing costumes, created by Tim Chappel and Lizzy Gardiner, that brought life and color to Australian cinema production, at that time steeped in the dull, brown world of the *Mad Max* (1979–85) action-movie franchise. Chappel and Gardiner's inventiveness is boundless—they even create a dress made from rubber flip-flops.

The movie is also an appeal for tolerance of the oppressed and explores notions of masculinity and normality in a country known for its macho culture. Elliott has said he wanted to depict another side of Australian culture—that of Sydney drag queens. He cast Terence Stamp as Bernadette, Hugo Weaving as Tick/Mitzi, and Guy Pearce as Adam/Felicia; all three put in convincing performances as stiletto-wearing drag queens coming to terms with their identity in what proves to be a life-changing journey. **CK**

⊙ KEY SCENES

1 THE BUS
The "Priscilla" of the film's title is the name of the bus the drag queens use. It is a character in the film, by virtue not only of its name, but also of the changes it undergoes, first when it is ruined with graffiti and later when Adam/Felicia paints it pink.

2 THE DESERT
Elliott, Breheny, and producer Al Clark were keen to use the desert as a location to emphasize the drag queens' isolation and to take advantage of the cinematographic opportunities its topography provides, with its open spaces and striking color palette.

3 SINGING AND DANCING WITH ABORIGINES
The drag queens meet an Aborigine who asks them to join him at a campfire gathering, where they stage an impromptu show to a warm reception. This contrasts with the previous scene, where a white couple are alarmed by the drag queens' appearance and drive off.

4 DRAG SHOW AT ALICE SPRINGS
In this sequence the wild colors of the performers' attire reflect those of the desert, and incorporate motifs such as an emu's head, reflecting the effect that the men's journey has had on them. The film won an Oscar for Best Costume Design.

⏱ DIRECTOR PROFILE

1964–79
Stephan Elliott was born in Sydney, Australia, on August 27, 1964. Fascinated with filmmaking, he was given a camera when he was seven years old and decided that he wanted to direct movies as a career a year later. He began videoing weddings at the age of just thirteen. After high school he studied film editing at North Sydney Technical College.

1980–93
He worked on more than thirty films, often as an assistant director, before making his directorial debut with the black comedy *Frauds* (1993), starring Hugo Weaving and pop musician Phil Collins, which was entered for the Cannes Film Festival.

1994–2003
Elliott came to international attention with his award-winning musical comedy *The Adventures of Priscilla, Queen of the Desert*. He followed this with the musical comedy *Welcome to Woop Woop* (1997), starring Rod Taylor, and an espionage thriller adaptation *Eye of the Beholder* (1999), starring Ewan McGregor. Both were commercial flops, however, bombing at the international box office. Disillusioned, Elliott decided to quit show business.

2004–8
A near-fatal skiing accident, resulting in a lengthy period of hospitalization, helped to reignite Elliott's creative spark and he returned to his biggest success by writing the stage version of *Priscilla*. Following this, he found the will to direct again with *Easy Virtue* (2008), a period comedy based on Noël Coward's play of the same name, starring Colin Firth and Kristin Scott Thomas. It was met with mixed reviews and modest box-office receipts.

2009–present
Elliott returned to familiar territory with *A Few Best Men* (2011), an original comedy concerning a bridegroom who travels to the Australian outback for a wedding, accompanied by his three best men.

Heavenly Creatures 1994

PETER JACKSON b. 1961

▲ Juliet and Pauline create a dangerously seductive, private world for themselves.

▼ *Heavenly Creatures* received an Academy Award for Best Original Screenplay.

It may be the story of a real-life murder but *Heavenly Creatures* is far from a lurid crime thriller. Peter Jackson's sensitive, whimsical drama is a warm and witty depiction of teenage longing and obsessive friendship—albeit a friendship that leads two girls to commit a horrifying act in an effort to avoid being separated.

Given that many viewers will be aware of the fact that Pauline Parker (Melanie Lynskey) and her friend Juliet Hulme (Kate Winslet) murdered Parker's mother, the knowledge of their crime hangs over the film like an ominous specter. Rather than taking away from the girls' innocent, playful friendship, however, this awareness adds another dimension to the film. The viewer watches the girls form a complex shared fantasy and understands their excitement at the discovery of common ground. At no point do Jackson and his fellow screenwriter, wife Fran Walsh, attempt to justify the girls' actions, but the film takes great pains to explore their intense emotions and explain how two young minds could have been quite so deluded.

The filmmakers had several great gifts at their disposal. One was the exceptional cast, including a then-unknown Kate Winslet. Another key find was the journal of Pauline Parker, which is used to narrate the film and lends a compelling degree of authenticity. Walsh and Jackson received deserved acclaim for this award-winning film, which both captures the spirit of imaginative adolescence and sheds light on a mystery that had shocked and fascinated the world some forty years earlier. **AS**

👁 KEY SCENES

1 THE FANTASY BEGINS
Pauline arrives at Juliet's house. Birdsong and a stirring score introduce the viewer to Juliet, who, clad in medieval dress, looks as if she has stepped out of a Romantic painting. This is a strong indication of Pauline's fantasy world and the start of her intense feelings for Juliet.

2 A PASSIONATE NIGHT
After watching *The Third Man*, Pauline and Juliet imagine how their own fictional characters might make love, and enact the scenes themselves. This is a sexual interpretation of Pauline's diary entry for that night, which forms the narration to the scene.

3 THE DEED IS DONE
On a sunny day, Pauline's mother Honora (Sarah Peirse) cheerfully takes her daughter and Juliet for a walk, unaware of the horror that awaits her. Honora stoops to pick up a gem the girls have dropped, and Pauline hits her repeatedly over the head with a brick, killing her.

🕐 DIRECTOR PROFILE

1961–82
Peter Jackson was born to English immigrants in New Zealand. As a young child, he tried to re-create popular films at home using a Super 8 camera and stop-motion models.

1983–87
In 1987 Jackson developed his short film *Bad Taste* into a feature-length horror comedy, made in his time off while working as an apprentice photo engraver at a newspaper.

1988–93
Jackson became known for his horror comedies, dubbed "splatstick." More splatstick films followed, including *Braindead* (1992), as Jackson focused on his film work.

1994–96
Heavenly Creatures saw Jackson working in a very different genre, to great acclaim. Its success helped him make Hollywood film *The Frighteners* (1996), which was less well received.

1997–2004
Jackson won the rights to his childhood favorite story, J. R. R. Tolkien's *The Lord of the Rings* trilogy, and began filming in New Zealand in 1999. The successful trilogy (see p. 530) made Jackson one of the most influential directors of his time.

2005–present
In 2005 Jackson filmed another childhood favorite, *King Kong*, and returned to more contemplative territory with *The Lovely Bones* (2009). His next project is directing a two-film version of Tolkien's *The Hobbit*, due for release in 2012 and 2013.

WHERE ARE THEY NOW?

Pauline Parker and Juliet Hulme (below) were convicted and imprisoned for five years. A condition of their release was that they would never meet again. Their subsequent paths make an interesting postscript to the film. Pauline changed her name to Hilary Nathan and moved to Kent, England, where she taught horse riding. She is said to have converted to Catholicism. A New Zealand journalist has since claimed to have found her living as a recluse on the Orkney Islands. Juliet Hulme

went to the United States and became a Mormon before settling in Scotland. She took the name Anne Perry and, in the late 1970s, began writing detective novels. Anne Perry is now a prolific novelist. Also unmarried, she lives with her brother, who works as her editor. Like Pauline, she is said never to have watched *Heavenly Creatures*.

BRITISH AND IRISH CINEMA

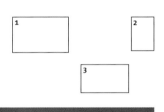

n 1989 British film production was in a trough. Cinema attendance started to climb, but few British films enjoyed commercial success. Yet British acting talent was still to the fore and Daniel Day-Lewis rang in the new decade by winning an Oscar for Best Actor for his role as Christy Brown in *My Left Foot* (1989). Fifteen British and Irish actors won Oscar nominations for Best Actor or Actress in the 1990s, and their success kept Anglo-Irish cinema in the limelight.

The decade saw the demise of one of Britain's most innovative directors, Derek Jarman (1942–94), but fresh talent burst on to the scene in the form of Danny Boyle (b. 1956) with his edgy offerings *Shallow Grave* (1994) and *Trainspotting* (1996, opposite below). Guy Ritchie (b. 1968) reinvigorated the gangster movie with his black comedy about cockney criminals, *Lock, Stock and Two Smoking Barrels* (1998). Meanwhile, Mike Leigh (b. 1943) cemented his position as a major director with three internationally acclaimed films—*Life Is Sweet* (1990), *Naked* (1993), and *Secrets & Lies* (1996, see p. 472). *Secrets & Lies* charted new territory by examining racial barriers and stereotypes, reflecting a contemporary Britain that was trying to integrate a growing multiethnic identity.

Britain said good-bye to Prime Minister Margaret Thatcher in 1990 but Anglo-Irish films continued to reflect on her policies. Neil Jordan (b. 1950), with *The Crying Game* (1992, see p. 470), and Jim Sheridan (b. 1949), with *In the Name of the Father* (1993, above), both explore the effects of the Irish Troubles and put a human face on the conflict. Sheridan's film is based on the real-life

1 Gerry Conlon (Daniel Day-Lewis) is coerced into a confession in *In the Name of the Father*. The screenplay was adapted from Conlon's autobiography.

2 Hugh Grant hides in a hotel bedroom wardrobe in one of the many farcical scenes in *Four Weddings and a Funeral*.

3 The iconic poster for the UK release of *Trainspotting*. The film, based on Irvine Welsh's novel of the same name, has gained a cult following.

KEY EVENTS

1992	1992	1993	1994	1994	1995
The Crying Game (see p. 470) is nominated for six Academy Awards. Neil Jordan wins an Oscar for Best Original Screenplay.	Emma Thompson wins a Best Actress Oscar for *Howards End*; the next year she is nominated for *The Remains of the Day* and *In the Name of the Father*.	Derek Jarman's *Blue* is released four months before his death. He and actors narrate stories of his life against a screen filled with the color blue.	*Four Weddings and a Funeral* becomes the highest-grossing British film to date, with world box-office receipts of more than $245.7 million.	*The Madness of King George* is released. It tells the true story of King George III's battle with mental illness and wins an Oscar for Best Art Direction.	The UK's Conservative government announces that a share of National Lottery revenues will be given to various British film funds.

468 1990–PRESENT

story of the Guildford Four, who were wrongly accused of an IRA pub bombing. It stars Daniel Day-Lewis as one of the accused, Gerry Conlon, and the story focuses on his relationship with his father, Giuseppe (Pete Postlethwaite), who was also imprisoned, and their solicitor Gareth Peirce (Emma Thompson). All the lead actors won Oscar nominations; their heartfelt performances as rebellious son, humble father, and crusading lawyer give the film its poignancy. Directed by Ken Loach (b. 1936), *Land and Freedom* (1995) explores similar themes of identity and idealism set against the backdrop of the Spanish Civil War.

Although costume dramas, such as *Howards End* (1992) and *Shakespeare in Love* (1998, see p. 444), proved still to be a British forte, the most gratifying development in the decade was a resurgence in the popularity of homemade comedy. Romantic comedy *Four Weddings and a Funeral* (1994, right), directed by Mike Newell (b. 1942), was a massive hit and started a collaboration between screenwriter Richard Curtis and actor Hugh Grant that resulted in another hit five years later, *Notting Hill*. Grant's capacity to portray the bumbling but charming middle-class bachelor struck a chord with audiences worldwide, even if such a reserved English stereotype did not always seem recognizable to audiences at home. The success of *Four Weddings and a Funeral* paved the way for more authentic British fare, such as *Brassed Off* (1996) and *The Full Monty* (1997), which showed a working-class Britain that might be down but was not defeated. The resilience of *Brassed Off*'s colliery brass band members in the face of pit closures and *The Full Monty*'s unemployed steelworkers turned strippers appealed to international audiences, proving that Anglo-Irish filmmakers did not have to dilute their own culture to appeal to a US palate. **CK**

1995	1996	1996	1997	1997	1998
Emma Thompson wins an Oscar for her screenplay adaptation of *Sense and Sensibility*; she is also nominated for Best Actress.	*Secrets & Lies* (see p. 472) wins the Palme d'Or at Cannes and is nominated for five Academy Awards including Best Picture and Best Director.	*Trainspotting* is nominated for an Academy Award for Best Adapted Screenplay.	Judi Dench and Billy Connolly star in *Mrs. Brown*. The film focuses on the moving relationship between Queen Victoria and her Scottish servant.	*The Full Monty* is nominated for four Oscars, including Best Director and Best Picture; it wins for Best Original Music Score (Musical or Comedy).	The New Labour government publishes its review of film policy, *A Bigger Picture*. It proposes combining existing institutions as a UK Film Council.

The Crying Game 1992

NEIL JORDAN b. 1950

▲ Cabaret singer Dil caught in mid performance. But as the poster tagline hints, "Nothing is what it seems to be . . . ."

▼ The poster somewhat misleadingly suggests a sultry neo-noir film.

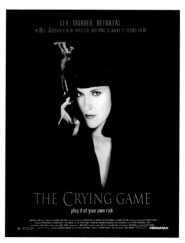

Featuring one of cinema's most notorious surprise twists, *The Crying Game* is a perfect distillation of the elements that make Neil Jordan such a mercurial presence in British and Irish cinema. Following his less successful outing in Hollywood with *High Spirits* (1988) and *We're No Angels* (1989), as well as the commercial failure of *The Miracle* (1991), Jordan returned to the tougher narrative style upon which he had built his reputation.

The Crying Game's brilliance lies in its resistance to being pigeonholed. It is this that is the key to its international success and the reason it rewards repeated viewing. Jordan's story opens conventionally, with the IRA kidnapping a British soldier (inspired by Frank O'Connor's classic short story of 1931, "A Guest of the Nation," about two republican fighters who become friendly with the British soldiers they will have to kill). His death ends what might have been a taut, but conventional, political thriller. Instead, a touching and emotionally engaging love affair develops between Stephen Rea's Irish volunteer, who befriended the hostage, and the dead man's English lover, Dil, played by Jaye Davidson. The two stories intersect for the final, violent act.

The film is ultimately a paean to the irrationality of human love. The whimsical rapport between Fergus and Dil, via a barman-cum-interlocutor at the pub where Dil sings, soon develops into a complex relationship based on the misperception the characters have of each other. Yet, when their truths are revealed, the result is not revulsion but the acknowledgement that the revelations have only deepened the connection between them. **IHS**

KEY SCENES

1 A FRIENDSHIP FORMED
Fergus befriends a British soldier—incongruously played by Forest Whitaker—which leads to a conflict of emotions when the IRA volunteer is ordered to kill him. Fergus finds himself unable to carry out the execution.

2 DIL PERFORMS
Jaye Davidson mimes to the film's eponymous track, further clouding the audience's suspicions prior to Dil's revelation. The lyrics themselves symbolize the depth of emotion evident within all the characters as well as the turbulence of contemporary society.

3 THE TRUTH REVEALED
Fergus discovers Dil's "secret." The scene is even more effective because Dil assumed Fergus had known, their shared surprise allowing the scene to slip between humor and sadness. The twist has often been parodied and referenced, but still retains its power.

4 IN THE NAME OF LOVE
The film's epilogue, in the prison, is both a play on similar scenes in other films and a cementing of the relationship between Fergus and Dil as something more than a dalliance that grew out of grief and guilt. It is an optimistic exchange, hinting at a peaceful future.

DIRECTOR PROFILE

1950–93
Neil Jordan was born in County Sligo, Ireland. His directorial debut, *Angel* (1982), displayed a lyrical visual style evident in his best work. It also marked his first collaboration with actor Stephen Rea, who has appeared in most of his films. An ambitious adaptation of Angela Carter's genre-bending short stories, *The Company of Wolves* (1984), was followed by the hard-hitting gangster drama *Mona Lisa* (1986). Both films exhibit a fascination with sexuality, undermining mainstream conventions within recognizable genres. A brief dalliance with Hollywood proved fruitless by comparison.

1994–95
Following the success of *The Crying Game*, Jordan came unstuck with a big-budget adaptation of Anne Rice's much-loved vampire chronicle *Interview with the Vampire* (1994), starring Tom Cruise, Antonio Banderas, Kirsten Dunst, and Brad Pitt. An extravagant folly, it was undermined by Rice's own slavishly faithful script.

1996–99
The solid, if anonymously directed, *Michael Collins* (1996) featured excellent turns from Liam Neeson and Alan Rickman, but Jordan returned to more familiar ground with the scabrous adaptation of Patrick McCabe's *The Butcher Boy* (1997). Equally impressive was the director's moving adaptation of Graham Greene's *The End of the Affair* (1999). *In Dreams* (1999), starring Robert Downey Jr., was an intriguing misstep.

2000–present
After *The Good Thief* (2002), a stylish remake of *Bob le flambeur* (1956) by Jean-Pierre Melville (1917–73), Jordan reunited with Patrick McCabe for *Breakfast on Pluto* (2005), which starred Cillian Murphy in a transgender role. Less impressive was the Jodie Foster thriller vehicle *The Brave One* (2007). Back in Ireland, Jordan wrote the screenplay for and directed the visually sumptuous, if somewhat slight, *Ondine* (2009), a contemporary fairy tale drawing on Irish mythology.

Secrets & Lies 1996

MIKE LEIGH b. 1943

▲ A tense mother and daughter reunion.

▼ The film's poster depicts a much rosier get-together.

Although *Secrets & Lies* failed to win any of the five Oscars for which it was nominated, Brenda Blethyn did score a BAFTA for her emotionally shattering lead performance, as did Mike Leigh for Best Original Screenplay and Best British Film. As always, Leigh collaborated with his actors in devising the script, instructing them to improvise at length in preparing their characters. This approach led to one of his most memorable scenes to date, when Cynthia (Blethyn) sits in a cafe with Hortense (Marianne Jean-Baptiste), the daughter she gave away for adoption without realizing she was of mixed race. Filmed in one continuous take, it features a painfully intense performance from Blethyn, whose initial polite denial gives way to hysteria and shame as she recalls the incident that led to Hortense's conception. Mixing dark humor with sudden pathos, this typifies the style of Leigh and Blethyn, both keen observers of human behavior and supporters of social realism.

A sympathetic but largely unflattering microcosm of (sub)urban 1990s culture, *Secrets & Lies* focuses on one family while offering brief but no less revealing portraits of other couples and family groups. Leigh's device is to make Cynthia's brother Maurice (Timothy Spall) a studio photographer, putting the viewer behind his lens for portrait sessions. The result is a series of amusing, well-cast vignettes in which the subjects unwittingly reveal their familial strains and affections. Many of the actors involved were already established in their own right and others went on to become familiar faces in British film and on television. *Secrets & Lies* marks a high point in the careers of all those involved. **AS**

⊙ KEY SCENES

1 RACE RELATIONS
Hortense visits the adoption agency and is left alone with her case file. She reads the entry under the name of her mother— "Cynthia Rose Purley"—and begins to cry, having seen that her mother is listed as "white." She is dumbfounded.

2 THE PHONE CALL
Cynthia has just rowed with her daughter Roxanne (Claire Rushbrook) when Hortense telephones. A tearful Cynthia is shocked to hear from the daughter she gave up as a baby and pleads with Hortense not to come to the house.

3 THE PENNY DROPS
Hortense and Cynthia have an awkward conversation in a cafe, with Cynthia under the impression that a mistake has been made on the adoption papers. Then, Cynthia suddenly recalls an unspecified encounter and dissolves into hysterical tears.

4 SECRETS AND LIES
The discovery of Hortense's identity has thrown Roxanne's birthday barbecue into chaos. In the confusion, her uncle Maurice makes a speech denouncing "secrets and lies" and also reveals his wife's fertility problems. Cynthia discloses the identity of Roxanne's father.

⊙ DIRECTOR PROFILE

1943–70
Born in Salford, Lancashire, Mike Leigh won a scholarship to RADA in 1960 and later attended Camberwell School of Arts and Crafts, then Central Saint Martin's College of Art and Design and finally the London Film School. He began to write and direct his own plays in the mid-1960s.

1971–87
The theatrical success of *Bleak Moments* (1971), the story of a London woman looking after her disabled sister, led to its big-screen adaptation by Leigh. Many of Leigh's plays have been filmed for television, including the celebrated *Abigail's Party* (1977). As his distinctive style and thematic concerns developed, he became known for portraying vacuous middle-class characters as well as gritty working-class families.

1988–96
Leigh returned to film with *High Hopes* (1988), a working-class family drama that won him the FIPRESCI Prize at the Venice Film Festival. Backers Channel 4 continued to support him with *Life Is Sweet* (1990) and *Naked* (1993)—a notably darker, more edgy piece, which won a number of awards, including the Best Director prize for Leigh at the Cannes Film Festival. *Secrets & Lies* gained Leigh his first Oscar nomination; Marianne Jean-Baptiste also received a nomination—the first ever for a black British actress. Leigh encouraged his actors to workshop their characters and improvise in all of these films.

1997–2004
After *Career Girls* (1997), the Oscar-nominated period drama *Topsy-Turvy* (1999)—concerning the development of Gilbert and Sullivan's opera *Mikado*—saw Leigh depart from relatively contemporary drama. *All or Nothing* (2002) was followed by abortion drama *Vera Drake* (2004), set in the 1950s.

2005–present
Leigh continued to win acclaim with arguably his most upbeat film to date, *Happy-Go-Lucky* (2008). *Another Year* (2010) was hailed as a success at the Cannes Film Festival.

EUROPEAN CINEMA

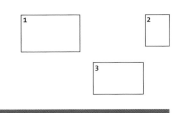

In the 1990s European cinema attempted to establish a continental identity in the face of Hollywood's perceived cultural imperialism. In the new "accession" countries of Central and Eastern Europe, filmmakers struggled to balance a desire for a distinctive national cinema with recognition as part of a European tradition. In part as a result of the Cold War, Central and Eastern Europe countries had longstanding domestic markets for popular product, and it fell to a few directors to produce films with wider appeal.

In Hungary, the epic *Sátántangó* (1994) by Béla Tarr (b. 1955) confirmed the director as the natural successor to Miklós Jancsó (b. 1921) and István Szabó (b. 1938). In the former Yugoslavia Emir Kusturica (b. 1954) deposed Dušan Makavejev (b. 1932) with films such as *Underground* (1995, opposite below)—a surreal comedy about Yugoslavia since World War II. Both Tarr and Kusturica went on to find international acclaim, but with little benefit to their compatriot filmmakers. In Poland Andrzej Wajda (b. 1926) had ceded the national banner to Krzysztof Kieślowski (1941–96) during the 1980s, but their status as national icons was subverted by the fact that each had moved to France for political reasons and financial reward. Their actions were by no means unusual: Kieślowski's trilogy *Trois couleurs: Bleu, Blanc, Rouge* (*Three Colors: Blue, White, Red*, 1993–94, opposite above), named after the colors of the French flag, was produced by Romanian-born Marin Karmitz (b. 1938), the same director who later lured German-Austrian director Michael Haneke (b. 1942) to France. Such

1 The opening scene from *Delicatessen* shows Pascal Benezech in the role of Tried to Escape, who is hiding in a trash can from a cannibal butcher.

2 The poster for *Trois couleurs: Bleu* features French star Juliette Binoche as the grieving widow, Julie de Courcy.

3 The bride Jelena (Milena Pavlovic) flies across the screen like an angel in the wedding scene from Kusturica's witty black comedy *Underground*.

KEY EVENTS

1991	1993	1993	1993	1994	1994
Krzysztof Kieślowski makes his first French-language film, *La double vie de Véronique* (*The Double Life of Veronique*).	The first part of Kieślowski's *Trois couleurs* trilogy, *Bleu*, produced by Marin Karmitz, is released.	The French film industry goes to the European Parliament to demand that cinema not "be treated like a product" in world trade talks.	The General Agreement on Tariffs and Trade talks between the European Union and the United States hit deadlock regarding the export of US films.	US films take 60 percent of the French box office, an all-time high; French films take just 28 percent, an all-time low.	A new generation of Eastern European directors achieves international visibility, led by Hungarian Béla Tarr with *Sátántangó*.

collaborations not only raise questions about a film's nationality—the *Trois couleurs* films are Franco-Polish coproductions, and two are made in French and one primarily in Polish—but also suggest that Europe functions as a microcosm of the international industry: just as Western Europe loses its burgeoning talents to Hollywood, so Eastern Europe loses them to France.

French filmmaking during this period was spearheaded by a series of expensive, large-scale productions that drew on a distinctively French literary and historical tradition and were often star led. The enormous success of *Cyrano de Bergerac* (1990, see p. 442) by Jean-Paul Rappeneau (b. 1932) together with *Jean de Florette* (1986) by Claude Berri (1934–2009) made an international star of Gérard Depardieu. At the same time, a number of low-budget films by younger directors deployed Hollywood techniques to express a unique aesthetic vision. The decade saw the rise of major talents including Jean-Pierre Jeunet (b. 1953) and Marc Caro (b. 1956), who burst onto the international scene with the surreal dark comedy set in a post-apocalyptic France, *Delicatessen* (1991, opposite). The highly stylized depiction of suburban youth by Mathieu Kassovitz (b. 1967) in *La haine* (1995, see p. 478) focuses on issues of social integration that were topical in contemporary France and resonated on an international level. Along with Luc Besson (b. 1959), both Jeunet and Kassovitz went on to make films in the United States.

The siren call of Hollywood had a detrimental impact on Germany because the major talents of the previous decade—Wolfgang Petersen (b. 1941) and Roland Emmerich (b. 1955)—similarly jumped ship. Moreover, the promise and prestige attached to the New German Cinema (see p. 326) of the 1970s was

1995	1997	1997	1998	1999	1999
Danish directors Lars von Trier and Thomas Vinterberg propose the revolutionary *Dogme 95 Manifesto* in Paris.	Jean-Pierre Jeunet directs *Alien: Resurrection* in Hollywood for Twentieth Century Fox.	Michael Haneke says he gave *Funny Games* (see p. 480) an English title to indicate that it says something about mainstream cinema.	The first Dogme films, Thomas Vinterberg's *Festen* and Lars von Trier's *Idioterne*, premiere at the Cannes Film Festival; *Festen* wins the Jury Prize.	*La vita è bella* wins three Academy Awards, including Best Foreign Language Film, and Best Actor for its director and male lead, Roberto Benigni.	The Dogme movement spreads to France and the United States.

La haine 1995

MATHIEU KASSOVITZ b. 1967

▲ The trio of alienated young men pose on the mean streets of Paris in Kassovitz's searing study of race and police violence.

▼ Hatred and disaffection burn from the eyes of Vinz (Vincent Cassel) in the poster.

Mathieu Kassovitz's *La haine* caused uproar when it was released in France in 1995. One of the first films to venture into the *banlieues*—the lawless suburban housing estates on the outskirts of Paris—it opens with newsreel footage of Parisian riots and portrays scenes of horrendous police brutality. The title (meaning "hatred") refers provocatively to the hatred between the racially mixed youths on the estates and the police.

Yet the film is not simply a scathing sociological drama about urban deprivation. Kassovitz's cinematic influences are self-evident. In his depiction of three friends, Vinz (Vincent Cassel), Hubert (Hubert Koundé), and Saïd (Saïd Taghmaoui), Kassovitz is self-consciously invoking the films of Martin Scorsese (b. 1942) and Spike Lee (b. 1957). Cassel plays Vinz as if he were a mix of De Niro's Johnny Boy in *Mean Streets* (1973) and Travis Bickle in *Taxi Driver* (1976, see p. 358). Cassel even reprises the famous "you talking to me?" monologue from *Taxi Driver*.

La haine is set over the course of a day. Kassovitz described it as "the story of a guy who gets up in the morning and by the evening has got himself killed." There's a sense of impending catastrophe as the day progresses. Vinz intends to kill a cop if a young Arab friend in police custody dies. It is almost inevitable that his desire for revenge will rebound on him. The film was shot in color but released in black and white, which Kassovitz felt lent realism and a timeless quality. The freewheeling energy of the filmmaking and blistering performances attracted audiences worldwide. As Kassovitz wryly noted, it helped that the police brutality he depicted was not in any way unique to France. **GM**

1 THE MEDIA COME TO THE ESTATE

"Excuse me, gentlemen. I'm from TV. Did you take part in the riots?" The resentful kids frighten the middle-class journalists away, throwing stones at them and cursing them for treating the kids on the estate as if they are animals in a "drive-in safari park."

4 THE SHAGGY DOG STORY

"Do you believe in God? That's the wrong question. Does God believe in us?" utters an old man the youths meet in a public lavatory. He tells a morbidly odd story about a friend who froze to death. This bleakly comic vignette adds to the film's general fatalism.

2 MUSIC FOR THE MASSES

An early scene features hip-hop DJ Cut Killer's sampling of Edith Piaf's "Non, je ne regrette rien" as the camera sweeps over the high-rises of the estate from above. The film reveals Kassovitz's love of American street style, music, and cinema.

5 THE FATAL BULLET

Vinz is caught by an off-duty cop who threatens him and the cop's gun accidentally goes off. As Vinz drops dead, Hubert points his own gun at the cop. The cop responds in kind. The camera pans away. The audience hears a shot but who fired it?

🕐 DIRECTOR PROFILE

1967–96

Mathieu Kassovitz was born in Paris, the son of a Hungarian-Jewish filmmaker. Mathieu took up acting at the age of eleven. He directed and starred in his first feature in 1993. His second directorial feature, *La haine*, was a huge international success.

1997–2000

His next film *Assassin(s)* (1997) received a muted response. In 2000 he directed *Les rivières pourpres* (*The Crimson Rivers*), which was a big hit in France. He established his own film production company, MNP Entreprise, in 2000.

2001–present

Kassovitz continues to combine his acting and directorial careers. In 2003 he started to direct in the United States and enjoyed mixed fortunes with *Gothika* (2003) and *Babylon AD* (2008). He has yet to make another film that matches *La haine* as a *succès de scandale* or as a critical favorite.

3 THE COW IN THE SUBURBS

The mood in *La haine* is tense and aggressive, and it mounts unbearably as the day unfolds. However, there are rare moments of comic levity, such as this, when a stray cow is suddenly spotted ambling incongruously through the suburban housing estate.

Funny Games 1997
MICHAEL HANEKE b. 1942

▲ Paul (Arno Frisch) with the hooded son Georgie. The next sadistic game involves a counting-out game for who is to die next.

▼ The poster highlights the fact that the film itself is an act of observation.

In a composed and remote introduction, featuring long overhead shots accompanied by classical music, the audience sees a family driving along a woodland road. Then the title appears in large red letters, with jarring rock music, as if pastiching the vicious horror films of the early 1970s.

Middle-class Anna (Susanne Lothar) and Georg (Ulrich Mühe) and their young son are spending a weekend at their isolated lake-front home. Two seemingly well-educated young men, Peter (Frank Giering) and Paul (Arno Frisch), invade their home and subject them to an excruciating if tactfully filmed ordeal. Lothar, whose character suffers most extensively, gives a genuine affecting performance as the innocent who tries to toughen up in extremis, but Haneke shows her as little mercy as the enigmatic home invaders do.

Director Michael Haneke is out to deconstruct and critique almost all previous cinema—confronting the audience with its hypocrisy. The viewer's ability to empathize with suffering characters on the screen does not mitigate a desire to see them put through a wringer (it makes for a better story) as long as he is absolved from guilt by a cathartic final victory. Haneke attacks the suspense thriller but he is paradoxically a talented maker of manipulative, Hitchcockian cinema. Even Brechtian asides to camera ("You want them to win, don't you?") and a major fracturing of mimesis do not undercut the potency of *Funny Games* as a grueling horror film. *Funny Games* is a film that deliberately sets out to confront and provoke the viewer. It is not a pleasant experience but it is a brilliant, necessary movie. **KN**

◉ KEY SCENES

1 EGGS

Two polite young men, dressed in tennis whites (and white gloves), turn up at the family home. Claiming to be friends of the neighbors, they ask to borrow some eggs. They impose themselves on the family and, hinting at what lies ahead, break all the eggs.

3 CAN THEY ESCAPE?

Georgie is shot and the boys leave. In a ten-minute take, Anna struggles to free herself. When the boys return, Paul addresses the audience, pointing out that a final escape attempt was necessary to maintain the sense of drama expected by them as the viewers.

2 GOLF CLUB

Georg is incapacitated after his knee is struck with a golf club. The golf clubs, prominent in the opening credits, are symbolic of the family's plans for a relaxing weekend but in a cruel twist they are used as a weapon against them in Peter and Paul's sadistic games.

4 REWIND

Anna gets hold of a gun and shoots Peter dead, whereupon Paul finds the video remote and rewinds the film to take back her victory and set the audience up for an unhappier ending. Haneke constantly breaks film conventions, finally by having none of the family survive.

US SECOND DRAFTS

In 2007 Michael Haneke made *Funny Games US* (right)—a remake of *Funny Games*, but in English, with a cast including Naomi Watts and Tim Roth. It is a rare instance of a filmmaker not delivering a variation on an earlier work—as Alfred Hitchcock (1899–1980) did with the two versions of *The Man Who Knew Too Much* (1934, 1956)—but trying to reproduce it exactly. Since Haneke claims to be indifferent to commercial success, his purpose appears to be to wag a longer finger at a wider audience. Other directors who have remade their native hits in the United States have tended to be ground up by the system—*The Vanishing* (1993) by George Sluizer (b. 1932) features a travesty of an ending that undermines the power of his original *Spoorloos* (1988).

Todo sobre mi madre 1999

All About My Mother   PEDRO ALMODÓVAR b. 1949

▲ Huma Rojo (Marisa Paredes) attends to her make-up while Manuela (Cecilia Roth) looks on. The color red dominates the film.

▼ The film's poster blends striking art and graphics with strong primary colors.

Already the toast of Spanish cinema, writer-director Pedro Almodóvar gained further acclaim with this rich, moving drama that drew on familiar themes from his own work and that of others. While an early tragedy recalls *Opening Night* (1977), directed by John Cassavetes (1929–89), the ensuing organ donor storyline echoes Almodóvar's *La flor de mi secreto* (*The Flower of My Secret*, 1995). *A Streetcar Named Desire* (1951) and *All About Eve* (1950)—the title of which is echoed here—are referenced liberally, highlighting the script's fascination with theater and sexuality.

Ever the champion of counterculture and contradictory characters, Almodóvar populates his Barcelona with transsexual prostitutes, nuns who prefer Prada, mothers who forge paintings, and dogs who know more than their masters. Bursting with color, Barcelona is a fitting escape for the grieving Manuela (Cecilia Roth), who leaves the more restrained palette of Madrid behind in an attempt to locate her son's father, whom she has not seen for many years.

On its release, many critics praised the film's poignancy and sensitivity compared with Almodóvar's more heightened comic melodramas. Manuela's anguish on losing her son is communicated particularly effectively thanks to a dignified performance from Roth that won her one of the film's many Goyas. Almodóvar's affection for his leading ladies is patent in the film's closing dedication, also a nod to his transgender and maternal themes: "To all actresses who have played actresses. To all women who act. To men who act and become women. To all the people who want to be mothers. To my mother." **AS**

👁 KEY SCENES

1 THE TRAGIC BEGINNING
After a trip to the theater with her son Esteban, Manuela watches as he is tragically run over. In trying to get an autograph, Esteban presses his face against the window of a taxi but it speeds off. Esteban races after it and is struck to the ground by another car.

2 WELCOME TO BARCELONA
Manuela arrives in Barcelona and in a remote car park encounters a group of transsexuals and transvestite prostitutes. Manuela sees a transsexual being assaulted. Hitting the assailant with a rock, Manuela discovers the victim to be her old friend Agrada.

3 THE TRUTH IS OUT
Manuela tells Sister Rosa the story of a "friend" who met her husband after a separation only to discover he had acquired breasts bigger than she had. She left when she was pregnant with his child. Manuela is talking about herself and Lola, the father of Rosa's unborn baby.

4 LOLA IS REVEALED
The hitherto unseen catalyst of the film's dramas finally appears at Rosa's funeral, after her death from AIDS transmitted to her by Lola. Lola expresses regret and the desire to meet his young child. Manuela tells Lola that he fathered another son—hers—who is now dead.

🕑 DIRECTOR PROFILE

1949–77
Pedro Almodóvar was born to an impoverished family in the windswept region of Spain's La Mancha. He moved to Madrid in 1968 and made a living by selling items at a flea market. Unable to afford to study filmmaking, he worked for a telephone company and saved up to buy a Super 8 camera. He began to make short films and became well known in the Madrid "Movida" pop culture movement of the 1970s.

1978–87
Almodóvar wrote and directed his first feature—*Folle...folle... fólleme Tim!* (1978). Seven more followed, establishing recurrent themes in his work including sexuality, family, pop culture, and strong women. In 1987 he formed a production company with his brother Agustín.

1988–98
The success of *Mujeres al borde de un ataque de nervios* (*Women on the Verge of a Nervous Breakdown*, 1988) brought international acclaim, and he explored similar ideas in films including *Tacones lejanos* (*High Heels*, 1991) and *Carne trémula* (*Live Flesh*, 1997).

1999–present
Todo sobre mi madre gained an Oscar for Best Foreign Language Film and a Golden Globe, becoming one of the most honored films in Spain's cinematic history. It starred longtime collaborator Penélope Cruz, who went on to star successfully in many Hollywood films, as well as remaining faithful to Almodóvar. *Todo sobre mi madre* paved the way for an arguably more serious direction with films such as *Hable con ella* (*Talk to Her*, 2002), *La mala educación* (*Bad Education*, 2004), and *Los abrazos rotos* (*Broken Embraces*, 2009). Almodóvar set his sixteenth film, *Volver* (2006)—also featuring Penélope Cruz—in his native La Mancha. The film reunited the director with actress Carmen Maura, who had appeared in several of his early films. Almodóvar's work as an exciting and prolific writer-director continues.

CGI AND SPECIAL EFFECTS

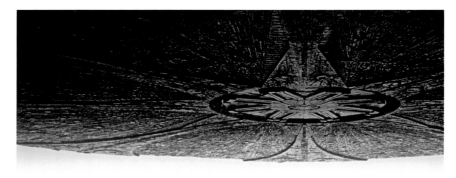

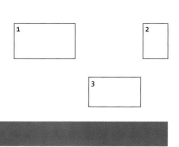

1 An enormous mothership casts its ominous shadow over New York in Roland Emmerich's apocalyptic alien invasion epic *Independence Day*.

2 Dan Shor plays Rinzler in *TRON: Legacy*, the long-awaited sequel to the original *TRON* (1982).

3 Na'vi warrior-princess Neytiri, from James Cameron's record-breaking *Avatar*. The film's making was delayed because then-existing technology was not capable of realizing the director's vision.

Once upon a time, typical movie effects men were Willis O'Brien and Ray Harryhausen, creators of the big ape of *King Kong* (1933) or the skeleton armies of *Jason and the Argonauts* (1963). The last of these geniuses might be Nick Park (b. 1958), the man behind Wallace and Gromit. In the world "ASW" (After *Star Wars*, 1977, see p. 366), special effects men became more like Houston's Mission Control—batteries of desk sitters, working on computers, manipulating pixels, not plasticine, at the service of a visionary director-producer. Like several others, Stan Winston, who handled the Terminator after the Schwarzenegger flesh was stripped from the endoskeleton, began his career working in makeup and puppets and moved into computers. Ironically, when George Lucas (b. 1944) reissued *Star Wars* in 1997, he fiddled with the one aspect of the film everyone had applauded twenty years earlier—the special effects.

CGI (computer-generated imagery) crept into sci-fi films in the 1970s; it was first used by visioneer Michael Crichton (1942–2008) in *Westworld* (1973). The relative commercial failure of *TRON* (1982) and *The Last Starfighter* (1984), the first films to make extensive (and publicized) use of CGI, sidelined the process, though. When James Cameron (b. 1954) used CGI to create a tentacle with Mary Elizabeth Mastrantonio's face in *The Abyss* (1989), the effect was so smooth and striking that audiences at first did not realize that the techniques used were related to the comparatively creaky computer graphics of earlier films. Cameron's *Terminator 2: Judgment Day* (1991) and *Jurassic Park* (1993), by Steven Spielberg (b. 1946), were built around CGI effects, presenting a morphing liquid monster and living prehistoric creatures, respectively, with eye-deceiving verisimilitude.

KEY EVENTS

1989	1991	1992	1995	1996	1997
The "water tentacle" scene in *The Abyss* is the first digital effect in a live-action movie to generate a "How did they do that?" buzz.	The morphing liquid-metal assassin of *Terminator 2: Judgment Day* proves that CGI can create great monsters.	*Let's Kill All the Lawyers* is the first movie edited on the computerized AVID nonlinear editing system—soon to become industry standard.	Pixar's *Toy Story* becomes the first of many effective CGI animated features; the process will all but displace conventional 2-D animation.	*Independence Day* and scenes of *Mars Attacks!* feature mass devastation and alien invasions created with seamless CGI.	The rendering of the numerous scenes of rushing water in *Titanic* demonstrates great advances in CGI.

Filmmakers increasingly looked to CGI. The optical splicing Woody Allen (b. 1935) used in *Zelig* (1983) to appear in Nuremberg Rally footage gave way to the computer-matching that allowed Tom Hanks to meet President Kennedy in *Forrest Gump* (1994). *Gump* director Robert Zemeckis (b. 1951) would later abandon live-action film in favor of CGI (with added 3-D) for subjects that might once have been Harryhausen-style effects films such as *The Polar Express* (2004) and *A Christmas Carol* (2009). The extensive modelwork and physical effects of earlier science fiction, historical spectacle, or disaster movies were replaced by CGI in films such as *Independence Day* (1996, opposite) by Roland Emmerich (b. 1955), *The Perfect Storm* (2000), *Gladiator* (2000), *King Kong* (2005), and *Avatar* (2009, below). As if to underline the point, the 3-D *TRON: Legacy* (right) appeared at the end of 2010. Meanwhile, with its idiosyncratic "bullet-time" and gravity-defying combat, *The Matrix* (1999, see p. 486) was highly influential.

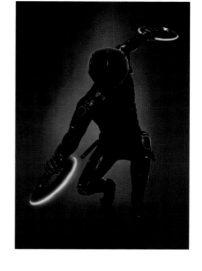

In the *Lord of the Rings* films (2001–03, see p. 530), Peter Jackson (b. 1961) was the first to create a fully integrated CGI character, in Gollum. *S1mone* (2002), a sci-fi film about a computer-generated movie star, perhaps foretells a future of "synthespians." However, it is more usual for real people to act with computer-generated backdrops (*Sky Captain and the World of Tomorrow*, 2004; *Sin City*, 2005; *300*, 2006). The one area in which CGI has attained practical dominance is the feature cartoon. Pixar's *Luxo Jr.* (1986), a computer-generated short that demonstrated that a desk lamp can have a personality, showed off the form, while Disney's traditionally made *Beauty and the Beast* (1991) included a computer-generated set piece. After the success of *Toy Story* (1995, see p. 490), Pixar has become the market leader in the computer-generated toon, despite competition from DreamWorks (*Shrek*, 2001) and others. The CGI cartoon feature is now so common that many filmmakers have to add 3-D to the mix to compete. **KN**

1997	1999	2002	2003	2009	2010
The re-release of the first three *Star Wars* films controversially "updates" the effects by adding CGI creatures, spaceships, and explosions.	*The Matrix* (see p. 486) slows time and explores a computer-generated virtual reality.	Gollum (Andy Serkis) in *The Lord of the Rings: The Two Towers* (see p. 530) is the first CGI-created "character" in mainstream cinema.	The first Best Digital Acting Performance Award from the Broadcast Film Critics Association is won by Andy Serkis in *The Lord of the Rings* trilogy.	*Avatar* popularizes intensely rendered CGI environments in a sophisticated 3-D process. Pixar, DreamWorks, and others follow suit.	*TRON: Legacy* is an effects-driven sequel to a film that used CGI ahead of its time. It costars Jeff Bridges and his computer-generated younger self.

The Matrix 1999

ANDY WACHOWSKI b. 1967, LARRY WACHOWSKI b. 1965

▲ A corridor and three agents, seen as "code"—the underlying workings of reality.

▼ Storms and shades for the movie's poster.

During a pre-millennial summer when Hollywood's expectations were pinned on *Star Wars, Episode I: The Phantom Menace*, the science fiction blockbuster that actually nailed the 1999 zeitgeist was *The Matrix*. In an anonymous, slightly futuristic city (shot in Australian locations), salaryman Thomas Anderson (Keanu Reeves) moonlights as computer hacker Neo. He is approached by leather kung fu babe Trinity (Carrie-Ann Moss) on behalf of mystery rebel Morpheus (Laurence Fishburne). The duo want him to join a revolt against "the Matrix," an organization that fields sinister, indestructible agents in suits and dark glasses led by the snarling Smith (Hugo Weaving).

In the style of Philip K. Dick, the film regularly pulls out the rug of reality. Smith literally wipes Neo's mouth away and bugs him with an (actual) insect implant. Neo wakes up to another, nightmarish, level of reality, where the human race lives in tanks of goo as a power source for a giant computer. From then on, the Wachowski brothers (whose sole previous effort was the low-budget lesbian noir *Bound*, 1996) alternate mind-stretching philosophical science fiction ("there is no spoon") with eye-popping CGI and special effects. Reeves, seriously in shape and doing most of his own ass-kicking in wirework (supervised by fight arranger Yuen Woo-Ping), uses his air of puzzlement well.

Sequels—*The Matrix Reloaded* (2003) and *The Matrix Revolutions* (2003)—upped the astonishment factor while sprawling into head-scratching pretensions that sabotaged the reputation of the original. Like so many zeitgeist works, it still has cult power. **KN**

⬤ KEY SCENES

1 COPS AND KUNG FU
A cadre of fascist policemen close in on Trinity but she sees them off with a display of zero-gravity kung fu—showcasing the Wachowski brothers' newly developed (and newly named) fast photographic process—then escapes via a telephone.

3 BULLET TIME
A form of ultra slo-mo, created using multiple cameras, locks the viewer in the millisecond as Neo dodges a slow bullet. By this means, the audience not only sees split-second action dramatically slowed down, but is also treated to multiple perspectives of the scene.

2 THE REAL WORLD OF 2199
Anderson takes a red pill and wakes up to discover that he is a living power source enslaved by computers. Or, as Morpheus puts it: "The Matrix is a computer-generated dream world built to keep us under control in order to change a human being into [a battery]."

4 SYSTEM FAILURE
The power of the Matrix seems broken. Neo makes one final telephone call and pledges to make everyone caught up in the Matrix understand that there can be "a world where anything is possible." His promise made, Neo zooms up into the sky.

VIRTUAL REALITY

Computer-generated realities were common in written science fiction before *The Matrix*, and had appeared on film (*Welcome to Blood City*, 1977; *TRON*, 1982) and TV (*The Prisoner*; *Star Trek: The Next Generation*). Later variants include the memory-sculpting of *Eternal Sunshine of the Spotless Mind* (2004) and the dream-shaping and tripping of *Inception* (2010, right). Nods to the novel *Alice in Wonderland*, the opera *Orpheus in the Underworld*, and *The Wizard of Oz* (1939) in these films acknowledge some of the precedents for virtual-reality stories. Despite advanced CGI and the interactivity expected by gamers, cinema has not yet found a way to embrace emergent technologies in telling stories. The "feelies" (from Aldous Huxley's *Brave New World*) are still a way off.

Toy Story 1995
JOHN LASSETER b. 1957

▲ Buzz and Woody take a daredevil ride to reach the garbage truck and the other toys.

▼ The poster: a pair of pint-sized heroes.

The first all-CGI animated feature, and foundation stone of the miraculous Pixar empire, *Toy Story* is a paradox. It deploys cutting-edge technology to affirm the worth of hand-stitched stuffed toys beside "Made in Taiwan" plastic high-tech toys, and embeds deep thoughts about the purpose of playthings and changes in the toy industry into an action comedy with heart and charm.

The story is built around the rivalry between Sheriff Woody (Tom Hanks), an old-fashioned stuffed cowboy doll who has hitherto been the favorite of child owner Andy, and state-of-the-art cartoon space ranger Buzz Lightyear (Tim Allen). How it is that an eight-year-old in 1995 has a toy from the 1950s is a question no one asks. Oddly, there is real bite to the conflict: Woody, the ostensible hero, is a paranoid middle-management drone ("Staff meeting, everybody!") so jealous of his pole position in Andy's life that he is willing to murder the naively heroic Buzz (who initially refuses to believe he is not a real space ranger). Despite the horror of Sid, the toy torturer next door, it is Andy who is the monster, turning his toys into emotional wrecks by capriciously bestowing or withholding affection, never aware of the agonies he causes.

Toy Story realizes that kids can love poor-quality toys—the dinosaur whose parts do not quite match ("I'm not actually from Mattel . . . . I'm from a smaller company that got purchased in a leveraged buyout"), the soldiers with bent guns and plastic mold ridges (led by R. Lee Ermey, the drill sergeant from *Full Metal Jacket*, 1987)—because imagination makes them live. Miraculously, Pixar found new things to say in sequels *Toy Story 2* (1999) and *Toy Story 3* (2010). **KN**

👁 KEY SCENES

1 STAFF MEETING
Toy Story is based on the old idea that toys come to life when the children are not looking. Here, Sheriff Woody—very much the "alpha toy" until the unexpected arrival of Buzz Lightyear—gathers the toys together to review the day's play.

3 "THE CLAW CHOOSES WHO WILL GO AND WHO WILL STAY"
A pile of three-eyed aliens worship the grabber that sometimes transports them from their amusement arcade game to the wonders of the outside world. Thinking it is his ticket back home, Buzz climbs in; Woody tries to rescue him. The brattish Sid grabs them both.

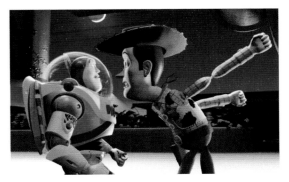

2 CONFRONTATION
Woody and Buzz (whom Woody has knocked out of a window) argue with each other. Woody: "You're a child's plaything." Buzz: "You are a sad, strange little man." Andy heads off to Pizza Planet; after an altercation, Buzz and Woody follow under their own steam.

4 THE NIGHTMARE TOYS
Sid takes Woody and Buzz back to his house, where they encounter both his mutated, hybridized freak toys (who are not nearly as frightening as their appearance might suggest) and his aggressive dog, Scud. Will they ever manage to get back to Andy?

PIXAR

Founded in 1979 as the Graphics Group—a division of effects company Lucasfilm devoted to computer imagery—Pixar has become the leading creative force in computer-generated cartoons. Ironically, its success grew out of a failed attempt to sell computers: the brand did not take off, but John Lasseter's short *Luxo Jr.* (1986)—which introduced the animated lamp that remains the company's logo—showed the potential of computer-generated animation. Following the success of *Toy Story*, Pixar has had an unrivaled series of popular, critically acclaimed hits: *A Bug's Life* (1998), *Toy Story 2* (1999), *Monsters, Inc.* (2001), *Finding Nemo* (2003), *The Incredibles* (2004, right), *Cars* (2006), *Ratatouille* (2007), *WALL-E* (2008), *Up* (2009), and *Toy Story 3* (2010).

Sen to Chihiro no kamikakushi 2001
Spirited Away   MIYAZAKI HAYAO b. 1941

▲ The film's animation brilliantly combines hand drawing and computer graphics.

▼ Miyazaki Hayao's compelling film won the Oscar for Best Animated Film.

I f operatic eco-parable *Mononoke-hime* (*Princess Mononoke*, 1997) marked a breakthrough into the Western market for Japanese animation house Studio Ghibli, its follow-up, *Sen to Chihiro no kamikakushi*, was the work that got Miyazaki Hayao recognized as one of Japan's greatest living writer-directors. With its luxuriant animation style and its violent and scatological undertones, the film challenged the soft-edged hegemony of Disney and its then up-and-coming offshoot, Pixar. Studio Ghibli films featured recurring motifs, such as a young, inquisitive, female protagonist, a vibrant fantasy world rendered with delicate artisanal splendor and—most importantly—the suggestion that what is being seen is possibly a surreal projection of psychological insecurities triggered by life in the real world.

After losing her parents in an alternative spirit world, the heroine Chihiro has to pass various tests to secure her return to normality. Influenced by European literary fabulists such as Lewis Carroll and A. A. Milne as much as by Japanese architecture, design, film, and national character, Miyazaki's film has a cultural otherness to it that allies it to the work of great Japanese directors of the 1950s, such as Ozu (1903–63), Naruse (1905–69), and Mizoguchi (1898–1956). As with Miyazaki's work, a small amount of patience pays dividends, as its meticulous, episodic storyline and cavalcade of exotic characters eventually coalesce into a single, thematically watertight vision. It is about adapting to foreign climes, the consolations of helping others, the effects of ecological devastation and, above all, the importance of remembering who you are and where you came from. **DJ**

👁 KEY SCENES

1 THE ABANDONED THEME PARK
Miyazaki's films often contrast the differing behavior of adults and children. In this opening scene, where Chihiro and her parents explore an abandoned theme park, the reticence and respect of the girl is played off against the greedy self-assurance of her parents.

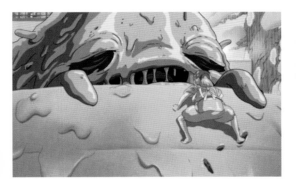

2 WASHING THE STINK SPIRIT
Chihiro (now called Sen) is at the bathhouse where she has to bathe an oversized ball of brown gunk—a stink spirit. She removes a mound of debris attached to the spirit—one of Miyazaki's visual metaphors about collective responsibility for the environment.

3 BLOOD
Miyazaki's use of blood in this scene—where Haku, in the form of a flying dragon, crashes into the side of the bathhouse—is unexpected and audacious. Rarely are the grim realities of violence shown in family movies.

4 SLOW TRAIN COMING
One of the film's most moving scenes is when Sen takes a ghostly train journey to visit Yubaba's sister. It adds nothing crucial to the narrative, but whips up all the exhilaration of solo train journeys. It is the moment when Sen's courage blossoms fully.

5 IDENTITY LOST AND FOUND
Chihiro's paramour is the brooding dragon-boy hybrid Haku, himself under a curse, having forgotten his true identity. When it is revealed that he is a spirit of the Kohaku river, into which Chihiro fell as an infant, the themes of remembrance and identity come to the fore.

🕐 DIRECTOR PROFILE

1941–69
Miyazaki Hayao was born in Tokyo. As a child he devoured anime comic strips and animated films, such as Disney's *Bambi* (1942).

1970–83
In 1971 Miyazaki moved to the A Pro studio with Takahata Isao. His first directorial credit came in 1978, on animated television film *Mirai shonen Konan*.

1984–92
The feisty girl character so beloved of Miyazaki first appeared in his antiwar fantasy *Kaze no tani no Naushika* (*Nausicaä of the Valley of the Wind*, 1984). With Takahata he founded Studio Ghibli in 1985, starting his run of idiosyncratic animated marvels.

1993–present
Sen to Chihiro no kamikakushi is followed by *Hauru no ugoku shiro* (*Howl's Moving Castle*, 2004) and *Gake no ue no Ponyo* (*Ponyo*, 2008), a distinctive take on *The Little Mermaid* story.

HORROR: A NEW BEGINNING

1 Drew Barrymore proves that top billing does not guarantee you a happy ending in the knowing, genre-redefining slasher movie *Scream*.

2 Horror for the Internet age: the poster for low-budget movie *The Blair Witch Project* inspired a cult following online even before the film's release.

3 As with many successful horror films of recent years, *Låt den rätte komma in* uses the genre to address the darker side of contemporary life. The film stars Lina Liandersson as Eli, a young vampire.

Since 1990, the horror movie genre has found itself caught between the old and the new. On the one hand, familiar conventions, such as ghost stories and slasher films, are as prevalent as ever, but on the other hand, new ideas and new technologies have influenced the genre. Legendary directors such as George A. Romero (b. 1940) and John Carpenter (b. 1948) struggled to produce effective cinema in a more horror-savvy era, with Romero revisiting the zombie genre in *Diary of the Dead* (2007) and *Survival of the Dead* (2009), and Carpenter reverting to B movies and overseeing remakes of his more memorable films. However, after a run of forgettable films, such as *Vampire in Brooklyn* (1995), Wes Craven (b. 1939) returned with one of the genre's most influential films, *Scream* (1996, above). This postmodern take on horror successfully managed to ridicule genre conventions as well as being, most importantly, scary. As a subversion of slasher films, it is masterful. Its legacy, however, is less impressive, spawning a host of imitators, such as the *I Know What You Did Last Summer* series (1997–2006), as well as sequels of decreasing quality.

Following such elegant visions of horror as *The Silence of the Lambs* (1991, see p. 496), and the M. Night Shyamalan (b. 1970) blockbuster *The Sixth Sense* (1999), the genre received a fresh helping of plasma from international sources. Japanese horror, or J-horror, made a significant impact at the end of the 1990s, with *Ringu* (*Ring*, 1998), followed by *Honogurai mizu no soko kara* (*Dark Water*, 2003) and *Ju-on* (2003), all of which were adapted by Hollywood. Korean cinema also showed an interest in horror, specifically the dark *Janghwa, Hongryeon*

(*A Tale of Two Sisters*, 2004) and the sardonic *Gwoemul* (*The Host*, 2006). Spanish-language entries included *Tesis* (1996) by Alejandro Amenábar (b.1972) and the films of Guillermo del Toro (b. 1964), such as *Cronos* (1993), *El espinazo del diablo* (*The Devil's Backbone*, 2001), *El laberinto del fauno* (*Pan's Labyrinth*, 2006), and the del Toro-produced *El orfanato* (*The Orphanage*, 2007).

A fascination with the possibilities of the internet for promotion, and low-budget, hand-held filming, gave birth to *[Rec]* (2007), *Paranormal Activity* (2009), *The Last Exorcism* (2010), and the phenomenon that was *The Blair Witch Project* (1999, right). However, classic horror mythology, and vampires in particular, has continued to provide the most popular subject matter. The 1990s gave the world the uneven *Interview with the Vampire* (1994) and *Dracula* (1992), followed in the twenty-first century by the *Twilight* series of films (2008–12) and more original fare, such as *30 Days of Night* (2007) and *Låt den rätte komma in* (*Let the Right One In*, 2008, below).

Scrambling to find the Next Big Thing, attempts at new horror became more extreme, giving rise to the torture porn proliferation and successes such as *Hostel* (2005) and the *Saw* series (2004–10). In reaction to the violent films dominating the market, filmmakers attempted to re-elevate horror to the level of critical acclaim once enjoyed by *The Exorcist* (1973, see p. 336). Frank Darabont (b. 1959) wrote and directed the bleak Stephen King adaptation *The Mist* (2007), Joss Whedon (b. 1964) mentored the subversive *The Cabin in the Woods* (2011), and Kevin Smith (b. 1970) offered the satirical *Red State* (2011). Internationally, *The Descent* (2005), *Los ojos de Julia* (*Julia's Eyes*, 2010), and *Somos lo que hay* (*We Are What We Are*, 2010) all presented variety and originality of vision, showing how, more than any other genre, horror is able to reinvent itself constantly, creating trends, clichés, and classics for every generation. **IHS**

2002	2003	2004	2005	2008	2009
Honogurai mizu no soko kara is another international J-horror success. *Dog Soldiers* launches the career of British director Neil Marshall (b. 1970).	*The Texas Chainsaw Massacre* marks the first of the sanitized remakes of classic 1970s and 1980s horror films.	The *Saw* franchise begins with an inventively gruesome feature debut, directed by James Wan (b. 1977).	Neil Marshall makes one of the 1990s' best British horror films, *The Descent*. *Wolf Creek* is delayed in Australia, so as not to affect the real-life court case.	*Twilight* is released. The first series of *True Blood* is aired.	*Paranormal Activity* becomes one of the decade's low-budget hits.

The Silence of the Lambs 1991
JONATHAN DEMME b. 1944

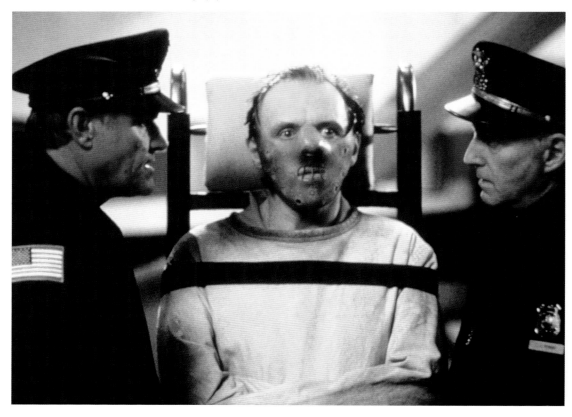

▲ The definitive image of Lecter; the hockey mask is to prevent him biting.

▼ Clarice is "silenced" by a death's-head moth, a motif linked to the killer she seeks.

Joining *It Happened One Night* (1934) and *One Flew Over the Cuckoo's Nest* (1975, see p. 356) as the only films to win the "top five" Oscars (Best Film, Director, Screenplay, Actor, and Actress), *The Silence of the Lambs* was also the first horror film to win the Academy's highest honor. Jonathan Demme's film is a prestigious Hollywood production in every respect except its genre.

Ted Tally's adaptation is an intelligently crafted script, gradually building suspense. Tak Fujimoto's cinematography and Tim Galvin's art direction draw upon a dark, gothic style for many sequences, as evinced by Clarice Starling's first encounter with Hannibal Lecter and Buffalo Bill's labyrinthine dungeon. The film also features Howard Shore's most unsettling score outside his work with David Cronenberg (b. 1943).

Much of the film's pleasure is derived from the contrasting acting styles of the leads. Whereas Jodie Foster's Starling is an impressive exercise in naturalism, Anthony Hopkins delivers something out of Le théâtre du Grand Guignol. His every movement is mannered and lines are uttered as though the fate of those listening to them hangs in the balance. Hopkins's performance might have unbalanced the film had he been present for longer than the sixteen minutes of screen time that he actually occupies. His absence is more than made up for by Ted Levine's chilling portrayal of Jame "Buffalo Bill" Gumb. Demme's interest in strong female characters, apparent throughout his career, pays off here, not only in the development of Starling, but also in highlighting women's difficulties in what is still perceived to be a man's world. **IHS**

KEY SCENES

1 CLARICE MEETS DR. LECTER
Clarice's first encounter with Dr. Lecter offers the suggestion of a bond that may extend beyond the boundaries of the investigation into Buffalo Bill. Lecter's fascination with Clarice forces her to confront the ghosts of her past.

2 A WOMAN IN A MAN'S WORLD
Clarice faces ingrained sexism when Jack Crawford advises police officers to mind what they say in the company of a woman. Her ensuing corralling of the officers and the mild rebuke she gives her superior mark a break in her transformation from rookie to agent.

3 LECTER ESCAPES
Tricking the prison guards, Lecter escapes by removing the face of one of his captors and using it as a disguise over his own. The backup squad assumes Lecter is their fallen colleague and sends him to hospital. En route, he kills the paramedics and disappears.

4 THE DENOUEMENT
In a scene shot in almost complete darkness, with effective use of night-vision technology, Clarice not only kills Buffalo Bill and saves his quarry, but also proves herself as a member of the FBI. She has used her strength and resolve to come through the darkness.

DIRECTOR PROFILE

1944–83
Jonathan Demme was born in 1944. Having graduated from the University of Florida, he began working for Roger Corman (b. 1926), initially producing, then directing, exploitation films such as *Caged Heat* (1974) and *Crazy Mama* (1975). The films displayed Demme's interest in credible female characters, a trait also evident in the widely applauded *Melvin and Howard* (1980), which features an Oscar-winning performance by Mary Steenbergen.

1984
After the lackluster *Swing Shift* (1984), Demme branched into music with *Stop Making Sense* (1984), an acclaimed in-concert film featuring US band Talking Heads.

1985–92
Something Wild (1986) and *Married to the Mob* (1988) saw the director veer closer to the mainstream, a move completed with *The Silence of the Lambs*, which was both a critical and commercial success.

1993–2001
Further Academy Award success followed with *Philadelphia* (1993), starring Tom Hanks and Denzel Washington. Demme also became known for his documentaries, covering everything from life in Haiti to an acclaimed portrait of his pastor relative, *Cousin Bobby* (1992); Demme's cousin has since appeared in a number of his films. In 1998 the director attempted an ambitious and mostly successful adaptation of Toni Morrison's novel *Beloved* (1998).

2002–present
Two remakes—*The Truth About Charlie* (2002) and the more impressive *The Manchurian Candidate* (2004)—were followed by an excellent documentary on the former Democratic president, *Jimmy Carter: Man From Plains* (2007) and one of Demme's best films to date, *Rachel Getting Married* (2008), for which Anne Hathaway received an Oscar nomination. In 2009 he began work on an adaptation of Dave Eggers's *Zeitoun*.

EAST ASIAN CINEMA

1 Gong Li in *Da hong deng long gao gao gua*. She has starred in eight films for director Zhang Yimou.

2 Tony Leung and Maggie Cheung in *Fa yeuhng nihn wah*. The film forms a loose trilogy with *A Fei zheng chuan* (*Days of Being Wild*, 1990) and *2046* (2004).

3 *Oldeuboi* forms part of the *Vengeance* trilogy for director Park Chan-Wook along with *Boksuneun naui geot* (*Sympathy for Mr. Vengeance*, 2002) and *Chinjeolhan geumjassi* (*Lady Vengeance*, 2005).

During the 1990s the major Fifth Generation Chinese filmmakers increasingly sought foreign audiences and courted foreign film festivals even as they faced censorship at home. Zhang Yimou (b. 1951) directed the grim yet opulent account of concubinage in early twentieth-century China *Da hong deng long gao gao gua* (*Raise the Red Lantern*, 1991, above), which won the Silver Lion at Venice. With the Palme d'Or winner *Ba wang bie ji* (*Farewell My Concubine*, 1993), Chen Kaige (b. 1952) traced the relationship of two Beijing opera stars during the Cultural Revolution. Feted abroad, these films were temporarily banned in China. The Fifth Generation provoked hostility and criticism not only from the state, but also from younger filmmakers who desired a more direct engagement with modern Chinese realities. A notable transitional figure was Zhou Xiaowen (b. 1954), who belongs technically to the Fifth Generation, but whose chilling satire *Ermo* (1994) showed the direct engagement with present-day society that would characterize the Sixth.

The Chinese director with the biggest international impact was the Taiwanese Ang Lee (b. 1954), whose early films, *Tui shou* (*Pushing Hands*, 1992) and *Xi yan* (*The Wedding Banquet*, 1993), were both set in the United States and depicted the culture clash between Asia and the West. While other Taiwanese directors were making subtle art films, such as Edward Yang (1947–2007) with *Yi yi* (*A One and a Two*, 2000, see p. 502), Lee directed the stylish martial arts movie *Wo hu cang long* (*Crouching Tiger, Hidden Dragon*, 2000, see p. 500),

KEY EVENTS

1991	1993	1993	1994	1996	1997
Chinese director Zhang Yimou directs *Da hong deng long gao gao gua*.	In Taiwan Tsai Ming-Liang (b. 1957) makes his feature debut with *Qing shao nian nuo zha* (*Rebels of the Neon God*).	*Ba wang bie ji* takes the Palme d'Or at Cannes. It is one of the first films by the Chinese Sixth Generation.	Although his first two films were set in the United States, Ang Lee makes *Yin shi nan nu* (*Eat Drink Man Woman*) in Taiwan.	In South Korea Hong Sang-Soo makes his debut with *Daijiga umule pajinnal*, as does Kim Ki-Duk with *Ag-o* (*Crocodile*).	*Chun guang zha xie* (*Happy Together*), set in Argentina, typifies Wong Kar-Wai's international style.

which inspired *Ying xiong* (*Hero*, 2002) and *Shi mian mai fu* (*House of Flying Daggers*, 2004). These visually splendid epics found eager audiences abroad and testified to the internationalization of East Asian cinema, a development also visible in the work of Hong Kong–based director Wong Kar-Wai (b. 1956), who, in films such as *Fa yeuhng nihn wah* (*In the Mood for Love*, 2000, right), opted for a so-called "MTV aesthetic," eschewing the austerities of Asian art cinema for the style of international commercials and music videos.

While Chinese directors contended with censorship, South Korea's cinema benefited from the liberalization of state controls in the era of democracy. The result was a new maturity in Korean film, which also began to gain international attention. Hong Sang-Soo (b. 1960) won acclaim at home and abroad for his debut, *Daijiga umule pajinnal* (*The Day a Pig Fell into the Well*, 1996), which narrated four loosely connected stories of life in modern Seoul. Park Chan-Wook (b. 1963) took the Grand Prix at Cannes for *Oldeuboi* (*Oldboy*, 2003, below), a brutal story of vengeance. Kim Ki-Duk (b. 1960) won both fame and notoriety for the ultra-violent *Seom* (*The Isle*, 2000), but later opted for a gentler style with the Buddhist parable *Bom yeoreum gaeul gyeoul geurigo bom* (*Spring, Summer, Autumn, Winter...and Spring*, 2003, see p. 504).

The success of these films demonstrated a genuine enthusiasm on the part of Korean audiences for local films. *Seopyeonje* (1993), an understated melodrama about a family of folk singers by Im Kwon-taek (b. 1936), became the most commercially successful Korean film yet, but was overtaken in 1999 by *Shiri*, which in turn conceded the title of highest-grossing Korean film to *Gwoemul* (*The Host*, 2006), a monster movie with political implications. Globalization notwithstanding, Asian cinema can, it seems, sustain Asian audiences. **AJ**

2000	2001	2002	2003	2006	2007
Ang Lee's martial arts extravaganza *Wo hu cang long* (see p. 500) becomes a huge international hit. Edward Yang offers *Yi yi* (see p. 502).	*Shi qi sui de dan che* (*Beijing Bicycle*) by Wang Xiaoshuai (b. 1966) wins acclaim abroad but is banned for a time in China.	Zhang Yimou directs his colorful martial arts epic *Ying xiong*.	Li Yang (b. 1959) makes *Mang jing* (*Blind Shaft*). In Japan Hou Hsiao-hsien (b. 1947) directs *Kohi jiko* (*Café Lumière*).	Sixth Generation director Lou Ye (b. 1965) attracts controversy with *Yihe yuan* (*Summer Palace*), set during the Tiananmen Square massacres.	Ang Lee's sexually explicit *Se, jie* (*Lust, Caution*) wins the Golden Lion at Venice Film Festival.

Wo hu cang long 2000
Crouching Tiger, Hidden Dragon   ANG LEE b. 1954

▲ The breathtaking landscape as captured by cinematographer Peter Pau.

▼ *Wo hu cang long* is the highest-grossing foreign language film in US history.

With *Wo hu cang long* Ang Lee, unpredictable chameleon of filmmaking, pays affectionate homage to the martial arts movies he watched as a boy in Taiwan. The storyline is taken from an epic early twentieth-century novel by Wang Du Lu, set one hundred years previously in a mythical version of late Qing dynasty China. It revolves around two couples—one pair mature and worldly, the other young and impetuous. Li Mu Bai (Chow Yun-Fat) and Shu Lien (Michelle Yeoh) are two of the greatest warriors of their age, seasoned comrades who have never acknowledged their mutual attraction. Li, weary of fighting, entrusts Shu with his mythic sword, Green Destiny, but it is stolen by the young, beautiful Jen (Zhang Ziyi), the governor's daughter. Engaged to a rich dullard, she longs to become a warrior and return to her true love, the dashing bandit Lo (Chang Chen) who once held her captive in the desert.

Granted permission to film all over mainland China, Lee filled the screen with rapturously beautiful shots of jagged mountains and limpid lakes, fronded forests and ochre deserts. The film's fight scenes take on a soaring, balletic grace with combatants skimming the surfaces of lakes as they duel.

With *Wo hu cang long* Lee brings to what was previously seen as a knockabout, down-market genre ("chopsocky" being the dismissive term) his own aesthetic sensibility, care for detail and scrupulously crafted texture, along with a yearning romanticism that transmutes its stock melodrama plot into a blissful meditation on love, loss, honor, and destiny. **PK**

👁 KEY SCENES

1 FIGHT FOR THE SWORD
Shu pursues the masked thief (Jen in disguise), who has stolen the treasured Green Destiny sword. The two women battle in moonlit courtyards, scaling up walls and gliding over rooftops. Jen escapes with the sword.

2 DESERT IDYLL
In a flashback episode, Jen recalls how, when captured by the bandit Lo while traveling through the western desert, she gradually fell in love with her captor. Her sense of freedom with Lo contrasts with her rigid family life and prospects of an arranged marriage.

3 EATING HOUSE RUMBLE
While fleeing from her arranged marriage, Jen is threatened by a gang of heavies in a village eating house. Wielding the Green Destiny sword, she demolishes them and half the building along with them.

4 TREETOP DUEL
Li and Jen finally confront each other in a breathtakingly elegant airborne duel fought out on the green tops of a bamboo forest. The martial arts choreographer Yuen Woo-ping also brought his gravity-defying skills to *The Matrix* (1999, see p. 486).

🕐 DIRECTOR PROFILE

1954–92
Ang Lee was born in Pingtung, Taiwan. After graduating from Taiwan College of Arts, he traveled to the United States in 1978 to study theater production and film direction. He served as assistant director to Spike Lee (b. 1957) on *Joe's Bed-Stuy Barbershop: We Cut Heads* (1983). In 1992 he directed his debut feature, *Tui shou* (*Pushing Hands*).

1993–95
Lee completed his "Father Knows Best" trilogy about generational conflict in Chinese families with *Xi yan* (*The Wedding Banquet*, 1993) and *Yin shi nan nu* (*Eat Drink Man Woman*, 1994). In England he directed an adaptation of Jane Austen's *Sense and Sensibility* (1995), which won a Best Screenplay Oscar for star and screenwriter Emma Thompson.

1996–99
In the United States he directed *The Ice Storm* (1997), adapted from Rick Moody's novel about troubled families in 1970s New England. He followed this with *Ride with the Devil* (1999), an American Civil War story, starring Tobey Maguire.

2000–04
Lee's return to Chinese-language filmmaking, *Wo hu cang long*, won four Oscars, several more nominations and inspired a raft of imitators. Lee shifted genres once more when he directed the comic book adaptation *Hulk* (2003). This attempt at a Hollywood action movie was not well received.

2005–present
Combining the visual scope of a John Ford (1894–1973) Western with the emotional engagement of his earlier work, Lee directed *Brokeback Mountain* (2005). Starring Heath Ledger and Jake Gyllenhaal, this sweeping romance triumphed at the Oscars, winning Lee Best Director. He followed this with the wartime espionage thriller *Se, jie* (*Lust, Caution*, 2007), which aroused controversy for its graphic portrayal of sex. In 2009 he directed the period comedy *Taking Woodstock* (2009), and then began work on a screen adaptation of Yann Martel's Booker Prize-winning novel *Life of Pi*.

Yi yi 2000
A One and a Two   EDWARD YANG 1947 – 2007

▲ Many of the film's events are seen through the eyes of eight-year-old Yang-Yang.

▼ The camera is pointed at the viewer, asking them to empathize with the film.

As writer and critic Saul Austerlitz comments, Edward Yang's work seeks "to filter the experience of the Taiwanese journey to modernity through the twin sieves of the romantic couple and the family." This aim was fully realized in *Yi yi*, one of the outstanding achievements of modern Taiwanese cinema, a film that is intimate in focus but epic in length and scope. Beginning with a wedding, incorporating a birth, and ending with a funeral, the film comprehends the experiences of three generations and spans the familial, romantic, and professional travails of a middle-aged man, N.J. (Nien-Jen Wu), and of those around him.

Despite its melancholy tone, Yang's bleak vision of life in modern Taipei is never depressing, and although the director often keeps his camera at a distance, the viewer never feels removed from the emotions of his characters. Nor is the film without touches of humor, many of them revolving around N.J.'s inquiring eight-year-old son, Yang-Yang (Jonathan Chang), who takes photographs of the backs of people's heads to show them something "they can't see themselves." In using the experiences of one family to explore the wider experience of life as a whole, this subtle and profound study of the modern Asian urban experience is also a universal film—an account of the physical and emotional trials that are an inevitable part of the human condition. This universality surely accounts for the movie's international success. All the more ironic that in Taiwan it was denied a proper release and all the more tragic that it was to prove the director's last film before his death. **AJ**

KEY SCENES

1 THE MEETING
Waiting for a lift with his son, Yang-Yang, N.J. encounters his first love, Sherry (Su-Yun Ko), who emerges from the lift. Yang-Yang watches as they exchange pleasantries. She leaves, then abruptly returns to ask, "Why didn't you come that day? I never got over it."

2 "IF YOU HAVE QUESTIONS, YOU CAN'T ASK"
As their grandmother lies unconscious in bed, members of her family visit her room to talk to her. Her son visits, as does her granddaughter, but her grandson, Yang-Yang, refuses to speak with her because "she can't see what I tell her."

3 IN JAPAN
After N.J. and Sherry have checked into separate rooms in a Japanese hotel, Sherry knocks at N.J.'s door, offering to divorce her husband and start again with him. She breaks down, and he embraces her. "Why do I always make the same mistake?" she asks.

DIRECTOR PROFILE

1947–81
Born in Shanghai, Edward Yang grew up in Taiwan. He studied electrical engineering at the University of Florida, and, despite briefly enrolling at USC Film School, aspired to a career in the technology industry.

1982–84
His passion for film was rekindled and he returned to Taiwan to contribute a sequence to a portmanteau movie, *Guang yin de gu shi* (*In Our Time*, 1982). His first big screen solo feature was *Hai tan de yi tian* (*That Day, on the Beach*, 1983), which concerned families and relationships, and was told through a fractured narrative.

1985–91
Qing mei zhu ma (*Taipei Story*, 1985), starring fellow director Hou Hsiao-hsien, and *Kon bu fen zi* (1986) explored the theme of urban alienation in contemporary Taiwan. By contrast, *Gu ling jie shao nian sha ren shi jian* (*Brighter Summer Day*, 1991) focuses on an alienated teenager in the early 1960s.

1992–2007
Yang returned to the present with *Du li shi dai* (*A Confucian Confusion*, 1994) and *Mahjong* (1996). In 2000 he made *Yi yi*, which became his most widely acclaimed film, winning the Best Director award at the Cannes Film Festival. He then established Miluku Technology and Entertainment, with the aim of developing digital technology and producing animated films. Its first film, *The Wind*, was postponed due to Yang's illness. In 2007 he succumbed to cancer, at fifty-nine.

ART CINEMA IN TAIWAN

Taiwan found its commercial film industry in decline after restrictions on imported cinema were lifted in 1994. However, the island continued to produce distinguished art-house films that focused both on specifically Taiwanese concerns and on broader themes of urban life in the modern world. The two leading figures of the 1980s New Wave movement continued to produce outstanding work: Hou Hsiao-hsien completed his *Taiwan* trilogy with *Xi meng ren sheng* (*The Puppetmaster*, 1993) and *Hao nan hao nu* (*Good Men, Good Women*, 1995), while Edward Yang made the

epic *Gu ling jie shao nian sha ren shi jian* (*A Brighter Summer Day*, 1991, left). In such films as *Ai qing wan sui* (*Vive l'amour*, 1994) and *He liu* (*The River*, 1997), Tsai Ming-Liang focused on urban alienation and homosexuality, employing an austere style typified by long takes and minimal camera movement.

Bom yeoreum gaeul gyeoul geurigo bom 2003
Spring, Summer, Autumn, Winter...and Spring   KIM KI-DUK b. 1960

▲ Seo Kyung-Jae and Ha Jin-Yeo in the tranquil setting of the lake and temple.

▼ The poster for this extraordinary and lovely study of life and religious devotion.

Among the most beautiful and haunting of modern Korean films, Kim Ki-Duk's remarkable movie has a deliberate simplicity and concision. It unfolds entirely at and around a temple in the middle of a lake, where a Buddhist priest lives with his acolyte, a small boy. In spring, the mischievous boy ties stones to three creatures—a fish, a frog, and a snake. These acts of cruelty set in motion a bleak chain of events that unfolds through the seasons and down the years.

Although the title implies that the events of the film will take place in a single year, the movie in fact follows the life story of its protagonist from childhood to middle age, and the coda, set in another spring, sees the wayward acolyte inheriting the place of his late master. Kim, who himself plays the protagonist in adulthood, draws meanings and implications from the seasonal changes in the appearance of the lake. Other motifs, too, recur and accrue new meanings as the film progresses. For instance, although in spring a snake was one of the boy's victims, in summer the sight of snakes mating heralds the now adolescent acolyte's first sexual experience.

The film's theme is a Buddhist one—the working out of karma—and much of its symbolism is steeped in Buddhist teaching and theology. Even for spectators with little knowledge of the cultural and religious context, its visual beauty and formal precision are spellbinding. Viewers nervous of approaching a religious tradition from the outside may take comfort in the fact that this haunting exposition of Buddhist doctrine was directed by a Christian. **AJ**

👁 KEY SCENES

1 SPRING
At the lakeside, the boy chases butterflies and throws stones at fish in the water. Paddling in the water, he catches a small fish with his hands. The priest observes from a distance as the boy ties a stone to the fish and puts it back into the water.

2 SUMMER
Watched by the girl who has been sent to the temple to recover from an illness, the now adolescent acolyte pilots the craft round in circles before jumping into the lake. He pulls her in, before clambering back into the boat and hoisting her in after him.

3 AUTUMN
The acolyte, at his master's instructions, is carving a Buddhist sutra into the floorboards of the temple when the police arrive to arrest him. At first, he threatens them with the knife, while they level their guns at him, but at his master's command he returns to his carving.

4 WINTER
After his master's suicide and having completed his own jail sentence, the acolyte returns to the temple. He ties a stone to his body and carries a Buddhist statue across the frozen lake and up the snow-covered mountain at the lakeside.

🕐 DIRECTOR PROFILE

1960–97
Kim Ki-Duk was born in Bonghwa, South Korea. After becoming interested in cinema during a period spent in Paris, he began to write screenplays, several of which won prizes. In 1996 he made his low-budget debut *Ag-o* (*Crocodile*). Concerning the relationship that develops between a homeless man and a suicidal woman, the film received positive reviews. He followed this in 1997 with the crime drama *Yasaeng dongmul bohoguyeog* (*Wild Animals*), for which he drew inspiration from his time in Paris.

1998–2002
Although it was not a hit in South Korea, *Paran daemun* (*Birdcage Inn*, 1998) brought Kim his first international notice when it played at the Karlovy Vary Film Festival and the Berlin International Film Festival. The ultra-violent *Seom* (*The Isle*, 2000) sparked controversy when it played in competition at the Venice Film Festival. It contains graphic violence and scenes featuring cruelty to animals—scenes that Kim claims were real. He followed this with *Shilje sanghwang* (*Real Fiction*, 2000), an intense crime drama. In 2001 he released *Suchwiin bulmyeong* (*Address Unknown*), which looked at the effects of both the Korean and the Cold Wars. The violent and psychological *Nabbeun namja* (*Bad Guy*, 2001) became Kim's first domestic hit, and *Hae anseon* (*The Coast Guard*, 2002) garnered numerous awards and nominations.

2003–present
With *Bom yeoreum gaeul gyeoul geurigo bom*, Kim opted for a gentler, more restrained mode of filmmaking. In 2004 he released the relationship drama and road movie *Samaria* (*Samaritan Girl*), which won the Silver Bear at Berlin. In the same year *Bin-jip* (*3-Iron*) scooped him the Special Director's Award at Venice. *Hwal* (*The Bow*, 2005) examines the relationship between a sixty-year-old man and the child he has been raising to one day become his wife. Subsequent films include *Shi gan* (*Time*, 2006), the Palme d'Or–nominated *Soom* (*Breath*, 2007), and *Bi-mong* (*Dream*, 2008).

IRANIAN NEW WAVE

The Iranian Revolution that overthrew Mohammad Rezā Shāh Pahlavi, shah of Iran, and installed the Ayatollah Khomeini as the supreme leader in 1979 followed a year of violent demonstrations. Because of its association with the old order, activity in cinema pretty much came to a standstill. With the new order installed, anger erupted over what was seen as the medium's role as a tool of the old regime. By the time the revolution ended, 180 cinemas had been destroyed. Over the next few years, only a very small number of films were produced. In 1983 the government set up the Farabi Cinema Foundation, which oversaw film production and played a major role in ensuring that films were made in accordance with the values enshrined in Islamic culture. By the end of the year, twenty-two features had been produced.

The most significant new filmmaker to appear after the revolution was Mohsen Makhmalbaf (b. 1957). A militant Islamist in the 1970s, he had been imprisoned for four years by the shah. After the Iranian Revolution, he turned his hand to filmmaking, having already made his name as a writer. *Dastforoush* (*The Peddler*, 1989), a series of vignettes exploring the plight of Iran's urban poor, brought him to international attention. Mohsen's work became increasingly liberal and even critical of the state. *Nobat e asheghi* (*Time of Love*, 1990) was banned domestically, but like the films of a number of his colleagues, Mohsen's work became recognized worldwide as that of a major filmmaker. *Gabbeh* (1996), *Nun va Goldoon* (*A Moment of Innocence*, 1996), and *Sokout* (*The Silence*, 1998, opposite above) all evince a lyrical visual style that appealed to audiences around the world. His often breathtaking approach

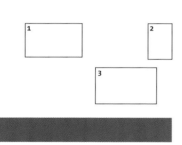

1 Abbas Kiarostami used long shots in *Ta'm e guilass* to establish a visual distance so that the audience is brought to reflect on the actions of the film's characters.

2 In Mohsen Makhmalbaf's lyrical *Sokout*, a blind boy, Khorshid (Tahmineh Normatova), works tuning instruments.

3 A woman decides to enter a bicycle race against her husband's wishes in Marzieh Makhmalbaf's *Roozi ke zan shodam*.

KEY EVENTS

1990	1990	1990	1995	1997	2000
Hamoun, directed by Dariush Mehrjui, is released.	*Nobat e asheghi*, directed by Mohsen Makhmalbaf, is banned by the Iranian government because of its treatment of female adultery.	Mohsen Makhmalbaf plays himself in Abbas Kiarostami's film about human identity, *Nema-ye nazdik*.	Rakhshan Bani Etemad attracts international attention for her story of a widower who falls in love with a poor young girl, *Rusari abi*.	Abbas Kiarostami wins the Palme d'Or at the Cannes Film Festival for *Ta'm e guilass*.	Marzieh Makhmalbaf makes an impressive debut with *Roozi ke zan shodam*, which wins the award for Best First Film at the Venice Film Festival.

merged with a more urgent polemic in the powerful *Safar e Ghandehar* (*Kandahar*, 2001) about Afghan society, the relevance of which increased after the attack on New York's World Trade Center on September 11, 2001.

No filmmaker has become more identified with Iranian film internationally than Abbas Kiarostami (b. 1940). His most acclaimed work in the post-revolution years was the "Koker" trilogy: *Khane-ye doust kodjast?* (*Where Is the Friend's Home?*, 1987), *Zendegi va digar hich* (*Life and Nothing More*, 1992), and *Zire darakhatan zeyton* (*Through the Olive Trees*, 1994, see p. 510), in which a blend of fiction and documentary blurs the lines between the story presented and the process of making it. The sparse style of these films was taken further in the Palme d'Or–winning *Ta'm e guilass* (*Taste of Cherry*, 1997, opposite) about a middle-aged man (Homayoun Ershadi) hellbent on taking his own life and *Bad ma ra khahad bord* (*The Wind Will Carry Us*, 1999), which tells the story of a clash of worlds when a city engineer (Behzad Dorani) goes to a remote Kurdish village to attend the vigil of a dying woman.

The role of women became more significant after the revolution. Prominent female filmmakers to emerge include Mohsen Makhmalbaf's wife Marzieh (b. 1969) and two daughters, Samira (b. 1980) and Hana (b. 1988). Marzieh wrote and directed her first film in 2000, *Roozi ke zan shodam* (*The Day I Became a Woman*, below), which was produced by her husband. It depicts three Iranian women at varying stages of life: the first is a young girl, Hava (Fatemeh Cherag Akhar), who is declared "a woman" on her ninth birthday and

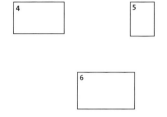

4 Set in Afghanistan after the Taliban
regime fell, Samira Makhmalbaf's *Panj
é asr* follows the idealistic and ambitious
Nogreh (Agheleh Rezaie) as she trades
her burkah for an umbrella.

5 Jafar Panahi's *Offside* tells the story of
girls who disguise themselves as boys
in order to watch a soccer match.

6 In Hana Makhmalbaf's *Buda as sharm
foru rikht*, a young girl Bakhtay (Nikbakht
Noruz), is desperate to learn to read
and write.

consequently is required to wear a chador and is no longer allowed to speak to boys, including her best friend; the second is a rebellious young woman, Ahoo (Shabnam Toloui), who is threatened with divorce by her husband because she wants to participate in a bicycle race; and the last is a wealthy widow, Hoora (Azizeh Sedighi), who is finally free from the constraints of society. Marzieh went on to make *Sag-haye velgard* (*Stray Dogs*, 2004), a reflection on European and Hollywood cinema and life for children orphaned in post-Taliban Afghanistan, and with her husband she codirected *The Man Who Came with the Snow* (2009), a drama set in the former Soviet Union.

Samira won international acclaim with her debut, *Sib* (*The Apple*, 1998), about the real-life story of two sisters, Massoumeh and Zahra Naderi, who were locked up for years by their parents and then released into the world. Some critics saw the film as harking back to Iran's first indigenous release, *Khaneh siah ast* (*The House Is Black*, 1963), a short documentary directed by controversial female poet Forugh Farrokhzad (1935–67) about a colony of lepers and featuring lyrical narration by the poet. The narrative structure of *Sib* is more complex than that of *Khaneh siyah ast*; in *Sib* the characters from the story play themselves in the film, mirroring the style of Kiarostami's earlier *Nema-ye nazdik* (*Close-Up*, 1990), in which Mohsen Makhmalbaf played himself in a film concerning a real-life case where someone tried to impersonate him. Samira then directed the gritty and moving *Takhté siah* (*Blackboards*, 2000), which follows the journey of itinerant Kurdish teachers during the Iran-Iraq War. Her *Panj é asr* (*At Five in the Afternoon*, 2003, above) won the Jury Prize at the Cannes Film Festival and follows the struggle of Nogreh (Agheleh Rezaie), a young woman in contemporary Afghanistan, as she tries to get an education. In yet another cinematic and self-referential twist, the making of *Panj é asr* in Kabul after the fall of the Taliban regime became the subject of Samira's sister Hana's documentary, *Lezate divanegi* (*Joy of Madness*, 2003), shot when Hana was only fourteen years old.

One of the youngest directors in world cinema, Hana has since adopted a similar minimalist style to her older sister, directing *Buda as sharm foru rikht* (*Buddha Collapsed Out of Shame*, 2007, opposite below), which examines the life of a five-year-old Afghani girl, Bakhtay (Nikbakht Noruz), who lives in the caves under the remains of the Buddhas of Bamyan that were destroyed by the Taliban in 2001. Hana's *Green Days* (2009) began life as a drama featuring the contemporary Iranian election but grew into part documentary when violence broke out after the disputed result, incorporating anonymous amateur videos.

Iran's most prominent female director is Rakhshan Bani Etemad (b. 1954). A graduate of Tehran University's Faculty of Dramatic Arts, she initially worked in television before directing a series of short documentaries. Bani Etemad's first three features, *Kharej az mahdudeh* (*Off-Limits*, 1986), *Zard-e ghanari* (1988), and *Pul-e khareji* (*Foreign Currency*, 1989), resemble her documentary work in their concern with lives at the lower end of the social spectrum. However, in their focus on the protagonists as victims of social or criminal circumstances, they differ from the more personal, emotional drama of her later work, which she also wrote, such as *Nargess* (1992), *Rusari abi* (*The Blue-Veiled*, 1995), *Banoo-ye ordibehesht* (*The May Lady*, 1998), *Zir-e poost-e shahr* (*Under the City's Skin*, 2001), and *Khoon bazi* (*Mainline*, 2006). Her films have garnered international recognition for their depiction of women attempting to forge their identity in an Islamic state. But her complex, sometimes satirical, works also critique how women are treated in general and strike a universal chord.

The most acclaimed director of the latest generation of Iranian filmmakers is Jafar Panahi (b. 1960). He served as first assistant director on Kiarostami's *Zire darakhatan zeyton*, and the veteran director has written a number of screenplays for Panahi's own movies since. A strong narrative pervades Panahi's best work, such as his debut feature *Badkonake sefid* (*The White Balloon*, 1995) and *Ayneh* (*The Mirror*, 1997), which are hushed, deeply symbolic ruminations on, respectively, childhood innocence and the artifice of cinema. *Dayereh* (*The Circle*, 2000, see p. 512) marked a very different tenor of filmmaking for Panahi, and both it and *Offside* (2006, right) are critical of Iran's patriarchal society. As a result, Panahi has been regularly censured by the authorities. An attempt to make a film about the events surrounding the presidential election in 2009 resulted in Panahi's imprisonment. He was freed but had his passport revoked by the Iranian government. In early 2010 he was arrested after applying to travel to the Berlin Film Festival to participate in a panel discussion on Iranian cinema; this galvanized the film world to demand his freedom and he was released.

Like the founders of Iran's intellectual New Cinema, Farokh Ghafari (1921–2006), Bahram Beizai (b. 1938), and Parviz Kimiavi (b. 1939), and pioneering Iranian New Wave directors such as Dariush Mehrjui (b. 1939) and Amir Naderi (b. 1946), Panahi sees cinema as a powerful tool by which he can expose injustice and, ideally, prompt change. **IHS**

Zire darakhatan zeyton 1994
Through the Olive Trees   ABBAS KIAROSTAMI b. 1940

▲ Like many of Abbas Kiarostami's films, *Zire darakhatan zeyton* is filmed in a minimalist, naturalistic way.

▼ The poster style reflects the poetic imagery within film's landscape.

It pays to have seen the first two installments of Abbas Kiarostami's "Koker" trilogy—*Khane-ye doust kodjast?* (*Where Is the Friend's Home?*, 1987) and *Zendegi va digar hich* (*Life and Nothing More*, 1992)—before settling down to his bucolic rumination on love, landscape, and the moral responsibilities of filmmaking—*Zire darakhatan zeyton*. It is not that the three films offer separate fragments of a linear storyline, but rather each subsequent film borrows from and adds to the cinematic DNA of the previous one. All are set in and around the precipitous northern Iranian village of Koker, and *Khane-ye doust kodjast* concerns a boy's (Babek Ahmed Poor) quest to return a schoolbook to a classmate. *Zendegi va digar hich* follows a filmmaker (Farhad Kheradmand) and his son (Buba Bayour) as they try to locate the lead actor from *Khane-ye doust kodjast* after the area has been devastated by an earthquake. *Zire darakhatan zeyton* sees a film crew return to the area and make a movie based on the aforementioned filmmaker's experiences.

The quest element in *Zire darakhatan zeyton* is born out of the strained on-set relationship between two of the film's lead actors, illiterate stonemason Hossein (Hossein Rezai) and his introverted student Tahereh (Tahereh Ladanian), for whom he yearns. Consisting of a sequence of long, often static and ironically composed takes with much of the crucial sound and dialogue emanating from off-screen, the film examines the toil of filmmaking, cinema's role as a chronicler of real life, and the possibilities of love in a world where poetry and death hang symbiotically in the atmosphere. **DJ**

👁 KEY SCENES

1 DRIVING

The audience sees the countryside and an occasional wanderer, who has most likely been displaced by the earthquake. There are slightly muffled radio broadcasts and two voices from behind the camera discussing the making of *Khane-ye doust kodjast*.

2 IS THIS LOVE?

The seed of the film's love story is planted when, in trying to discover why Hossein keeps fumbling his lines, the director of the film learns that his sweetly earnest actor views his costar as "the kind of girl I could conceive of marrying."

3 THE FEELING IS MUTUAL

Tahereh resists Hossain's advances, even when he asks her to turn the page of her book to show that she shares his affection. She starts to fumble her lines, confirming to the viewer that while not responding to Hossein's calls for marriage, she does hear them.

4 FIELD OF DREAMS

The ambiguous final scene captures the "lovers" in long shot (possibly from the perspective of the director, who has turned voyeur to their courtship) as Hossein runs up to Tahereh, and then they part, leaving the audience to ponder their future together.

🕐 DIRECTOR PROFILE

1940–69

Abbas Kiarostami was born in Tehran into a large family. He did not excel at school and worked for a time as a traffic policeman before eventually studying fine art at the University of Tehran. Kiarostami worked as a graphic designer and then joined the Center for Intellectual Development of Children and Young Adults, where he started a film section.

1970–86

He made his celebrated first short, *Nan va koutcheh* (*The Bread and Alley*) about a boy trying to take some bread past an aggressive dog in an alley. Its concise structure, focus on children, depiction of an everyday event, and simple moral lesson forged the template for much of the director's work (mainly shorts) up to and including *Khane-ye doust kodjast*.

1987–96

Kiarostami made the first of his "Koker" trilogy, which introduced audiences to his concerns about the nature of cinematic artifice and the interplay between fiction and reality. In this period he made two other key works, the documentary *Mashgh-e shab* (*Homework*, 1989), featuring young boys talking about their homework, and *Nema-ye nazdik* (*Close-up*, 1990), which tells the real-life story of a man who impersonated a filmmaker.

1997–2000

He gained international recognition in 1997 by winning the Palme d'Or for his drama *Ta'm e guilass* (*Taste of Cherry*) about a man planning to commit suicide. His drama following the story of a city engineer's visit to a village to attend a vigil for a dying woman, *Bad ma ra khahad bord* (*The Wind Will Carry Us*, 1999), confirmed Kiarostami's status as a cinematic master.

2001–present

The documentary *ABC Africa* (2001) marked Kiarostami's first use of a digital camera. He used the medium to revolutionary effect in *Ten* (2002) and in the next year in *Five Dedicated to Ozu*. This period of experimentation ended in 2010 with his Tuscany-set thinkpiece *Copie conforme* (*Certified Copy*).

Dayereh 2000
The Circle   JAFAR PANAHI b. 1960

▲ Amateur actress Mamizadeh plays the troubled Nargess, alone and on the run.

▼ The poster includes the poignant tagline "Her only crime was being a woman."

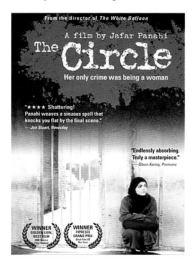

This hard-hitting anthology of contemporary tales from the streets of Tehran is the third feature from Iranian New Wave alumnus Jafar Panahi. Instilled with a rough-hewn urgency and a sober political message that could have been torn from the pages of Franz Kafka or George Orwell, *Dayereh* bravely blows the whistle on a society that imposes draconian and often discriminatory laws upon its populace.

The film is specifically about the curse of being born a woman in Iran and the cruelty and humiliation that results from a system where female expression, independence, and sexuality are violently quashed by male oppressors. It marked a very different tenor of filmmaking for Panahi, and *Dayereh* is raw, outspoken and palpably enraged by its surroundings.

Weaving together five curt, loosely linked vignettes, Panahi employs this free-flowing structure to comment on a variety of difficulties that Iranian women invariably have to face, such as how to obtain an abortion, how to leave town without spousal supervision, and even how to converse discreetly with like-minded souls. Panahi's close-quarters, *vérité* technique imbues the film with a sense of immediacy and terror, augmented very considerably by the naturalistic playing of his mostly amateur cast and his willingness to keep the camera rolling at particularly agonizing moments. The film won the Golden Lion at the Venice Film Festival but was banned in Iran. The courage needed to make such a film stands as rousing testament to both the gravity of its subject matter and the zeal of its director. **DJ**

⊙ KEY SCENES

1 THE HATCH
The film's themes are introduced in its opening scene where a woman is informed through a hatch in a hospital door that her daughter has given birth to a baby girl. Her response is one of grief: "The in-laws will be furious!" she yowls. "They'll want a divorce!"

2 THE WAIT
Arezou (Maryiam Palvin Almani) and Nargess (Nargess Mamizadeh) are two escaped female convicts looking to make money. Arezou resorts to selling her body. Panahi shows Nargess as she waits, her isolation and distress making her a likely target for the police.

3 THE SHOP
Nargess must get on the bus to escape, but she does not have the correct papers, so she heads into a clothing shop to gather her thoughts. A man behind the counter attempts to sell her a shirt; his slimy sales tactics are patronizing and insidiously chauvinistic.

4 THE CHILD
Pari (Fereshteh Sadre Orafaiy) is unable to get an abortion. She bumps into a small girl abandoned by her mother, who is watching from behind a taxi across the road. She has been in Pari's situation and hopes her daughter will be picked up by the police as an orphan.

5 THE BRIDE
A prostitute, waiting to be taken to prison, leans against a car and lights a cigarette. Another car covered in streamers passes, carrying a bride on her wedding day. The prostitute considers an alternative future of docile drudgery that would keep her out of jail.

⊕ DIRECTOR PROFILE

1960–93
Jafar Panahi was born in Mianeh, Iran. He learned the technical aspects of filmmaking at Tehran's College of Cinema and Television, before fighting in the Iran-Iraq War, about which he made a documentary.

1994–95
He served as first assistant director on *Zire darakhatan zeyton* (*Through the Olive Trees*, 1994, see p. 510). In 1995 he directed his breakthrough hit, *Badkonake sefid* (*The White Balloon*).

1996–present
Panahi moved away from making films about abstract concerns with his droll study of directorial etiquette, *Ayneh* (*The Mirror*, 1997) and more overtly political works such as *Dayereh* and *Offside* (2006), about female soccer fans. He was arrested in early 2010 by the Iranian government but released in May. He continues to make shorts and features in Iran.

LATIN AMERICAN CINEMA

1 Street punk Jarocho (Gustavo Sánchez Parra) lines up another of his dogs for canine combat in *Amores perros*.

2 Ivan (Marco Ricca) finds his life getting out of control when a hitman he hires starts making demands of his own in Beto Brant's *O invasor*.

3 Anapola Mushkadiz is the poster star for Carlos Reygadas's *Batalla en el cielo*, a controversial exploration of moral responsibility and faith.

In the new millennium, Latin American cinema emerged as among the best in the world. A generation of filmmakers from Mexico, Brazil, Argentina, Chile, and Peru have made films that resonate for both local and global audiences; they have won major prizes, and some are using their international status to act as ambassadors for their national industries. In the early 1990s this positive state of affairs was unimaginable.

In Mexico, years of ill-conceived state involvement, along with distribution problems, had denuded local cinema of its quality and identity. In the mid-1990s film production fell to 1930s figures. Alfonso Cuarón (b. 1961) and Guillermo del Toro (b. 1964) were just two of the directors who broke through—with *Sólo con tu pareja* (*Only With Your Partner*, 1991) and *Cronos* (1993) respectively—but felt the only way to move on was to decamp to Hollywood.

The problems experienced by the film industries of South America were inextricably linked to the tumultuous recent history of those societies. Dictatorship, institutional corruption, and misadventures in neo-liberalism all had an effect on cinema, ranging from censorship and lack of funding to exile and even murder. It summed up the continent's cultural turmoil that thousands of cinemas were converted into evangelical churches.

A bitter irony for Brazil, Argentina, and Mexico, the traditional powerhouses of Latin cinema, was that their dictatorships were followed by democratically elected but philistine presidents who proved equally damaging to the national film industries. During the reign of Brazil's president Fernando Collor de Mello,

KEY EVENTS

1990	1991	1993	1994	1998	1999
The Brazilian president withdraws all state funding of cinema and film production grinds to a standstill. Chile returns to democracy.	The Fundacion Universidad del Cine, Argentina's signature film school, opens in Buenos Aires. Alfonso Cuarón's *Sólo con tu pareja* is released.	The newly elected Brazilian government's Cinema Rescue Act creates grants for ninety projects. Guillermo del Toro's *Cronos* is released.	The Brazilian Audiovisual Law and Argentine New Cinema Law are introduced.	*Central do Brasil* (see p. 518) wins Berlin's Golden Bear. *Pizza, birra, faso* (*Pizza, Beer, Cigarettes*) announces New Argentine Cinema.	Pablo Trapero's *Mundo grúa* wins Best Director and Best Actor prizes at the inaugural Buenos Aires Independent Film Festival.

the country's film production fell to one feature in three years and in 1991 director Héctor Babenco (b.1946) declared: "Brazilian cinema is dead." This makes the subsequent turnaround in the region remarkable.

In South America the revival has coincided with the onset of improving political democracy and economies across the continent. Brazil and Argentina were the first to introduce new film laws: Brazil offered tax breaks in return for private investment in local films, while Argentina rebuilt the eroded system of state subsidy. Other countries have followed suit slowly.

The first sign of rejuvenation came in 1998, when *Central do Brasil* (*Central Station*, see p. 518) by Walter Salles (b. 1956) won the Golden Bear at the Berlin Film Festival. Salles's film was quickly followed by two from Mexico, *Amores perros* (*Love Dogs* or *Love's a Bitch*, 2000, opposite) by Alejandro González Iñárritu (b. 1963) and Cuarón's *Y tu mamá también* (2001, see p. 520), then *Cidade de Deus* (*City of God*, 2002, see p. 522) by Brazilian Fernando Meirelles (b. 1955). This quartet of films announced the *buena onda* (good wave) to the world.

Behind the *buena onda* were a number of specific 'waves' or movements: Brazil's *retomada da produção* (resumption of production), the *nuevo cine mexicano*, *nuevo cine argentino*, and *nuevo cine chileno*. In Brazil there is a palpable sense of a film community, in part derived from the influence of director-producers Salles and Meirelles, who nurture young directors through their companies—respectively, Rio-based VideoFilmes and O2 Filmes in São Paulo. A key theme of the work is the desire for purpose and fulfillment as seen in *O céu de Suely* (*Suely in the Sky*, 2006), a poetic film by Karim Aïnouz (b. 1966), centering on a single mother's attempt at self-determination; the disquieting *Deserto feliz* (*Happy Desert*, 2007) by Paulo Caldas (b. 1964), about a girl's slide into, and attempted escape from, prostitution; and *Antônia* (2006) by Tata Amaral (b. 1961), a tale of a São Paulo girl band's efforts to sing their way out of the slums.

The subjects of São Paulo's brilliant, provocative maverick Beto Brant (b. 1964) range from the criminal underworld of *O invasor* (*The Trespasser*, 2002, above right) and the rich brew of art, disability, and sexual obsession in *Crime delicado* (*Delicate Crime*, 2005) to tragic love story *Cão sem dono* (2007).

The Mexicans, whose success sprang from the enterprise of producers and financiers rather than a sound industrial infrastructure, were the ebullient face of the *buena onda*. *Amores perros* was an electric shock of a film: structurally ambitious, visceral, unsettling, it launched the international careers of González Iñárritu, writer Guillermo Arriaga, and their star Gael García Bernal. Bernal also featured, with Diego Luna, in *Y tu mamá también*, whose director had returned to Mexico after two Hollywood pictures and produced a film that was road movie, rites of passage, and state of the nation, all rolled into one sexy package.

The rigorous art-house blend of sex, faith, and meticulous aesthetic in *Japón* (*Japan*, 2002), *Batalla en el cielo* (*Battle in Heaven*, 2005, right), and *Stellet licht* (*Silent Light*, 2007) by Carlos Reygadas (b. 1971), elicited praise and sparked

2001	2002	2004	2006	2009	2010
Alejandro González Iñárritu's *Amores perros* and Alfonso Cuarón's *Y tu mamá también* (see p. 520) are the twin faces of New Mexican Cinema.	Fernando Meirelles's *Cidade de Deus* (see p. 522) is released.	Walter Salles's *Diarios de motocicleta* (*The Motorcycle Diaries*) is released. Cuarón directs *Harry Potter and the Prisoner of Azkaban*.	Venezuelan president Hugo Chavez opens the state film studio.	Claudia Llosa's *La teta asustada* wins the Golden Bear at Berlin Film Festival.	*El secreto de sus ojos* (*The Secret in their Eyes*), by the Argentine Juan José Campanella (b. 1959), wins the Oscar for Best Foreign Language Film.

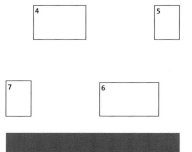

4 A startling and memorable image: the child-devouring Pale Man, from Guillermo del Toro's *El laberinto del fauno*, wakes up.

5 Julia (Martina Gusman) struggles to bring up her son in prison in *Leonera*, directed by Pablo Trapero.

6 Sayra (Paulina Gaitán) and her family are part of a stream of illegal immigrants riding the trains to the United States in Cary Fukunaga's *Sin nombre*.

7 A serial killer's infatuation with John Travolta's role in *Saturday Night Fever* (1977) provides the offbeat premise for Pablo Larraín's *Tony Manero*.

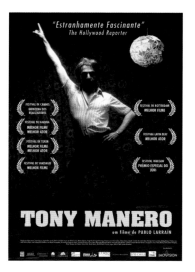

controversy. *Temporada de patos* (*Duck Season*, 2004) by Fernando Eimbcke (b. 1970) was a glorious, hugely popular comedy about adolescence. Del Toro has divided his time between US and Spanish-Mexican projects, his command of fantasy allowing for the escapism of *Hellboy* (2004) as well as the frightening, profound *El laberinto del fauno* (*Pan's Labyrinth*, 2006, above). *Sin nombre* (2009, opposite below), by Cary Fukunaga (b. 1977), a moving tale of gang culture and illegal immigrants, attracted two awards at the Sundance Film Festival.

Many of the political and social experiences are common, but the continent's cinema is understandably diverse. In Argentina, which is richest in world-class directors, that variety is extraordinary. Pablo Trapero (b. 1971) epitomizes the resourceful generation emerging from the country's newly established state-run and private film schools. His *vérité* approach, using nonactors and drawing subjects from real life, has proved extremely versatile: from his debut *Mundo grúa* (*Crane World*, 1999), a bittersweet tale of a man trying to rebuild his life in middle age, to the road movie *Familia rodante* (*Rolling Family*, 2004) and the women's prison drama *Leonera* (*Lion's Den*, 2008, opposite above).

Carlos Sorín (b. 1944) and Lisandro Alonso (b. 1975) also cast nonactors, the former in warm-hearted comedies about poor, provincial Argentines propped up by dreams (*Bombón: El perro*, 2004), the latter using a minimalist style to explore the isolation and alienation of people on the fringes of society in films such as *La libertad* (*Freedom*, 2001) and *Los muertos* (*The Dead*, 2004). In contrast, Daniel Burman (b. 1973) has created wry investigations of Jewish identity and father-son relationships—*Esperando al mesías* (*Waiting for the Messiah*, 2000), *El abrazo partido* (*Lost Embrace*, 2004), and *Derecho de familia* (*Family Law*, 2006)—that have earned him the sobriquet "the Woody Allen of Buenos Aires." And the polished, sensorial style of Lucrecia Martel (b. 1966) in *La ciénaga* (*The Swamp*, 2001), *La niña santa* (*The Holy Girl*, 2004), and *La mujer sin cabeza* (*The Headless Woman*, 2008) frames piquant views on family, sexuality, religion, and her country's stagnating bourgeoisie.

Machuca (2004), by Chile's Andrés Wood (b. 1965), focused on the events leading to Pinochet's coup. Bucking the local trend for imports, it inspired a younger generation of directors to greater originality—with one eye on overseas festivals and markets. Many of these investigate the contemporary Chilean experience, notably Alicia Scherson (b. 1974) with the enigmatic *Play* (2005) and Sebastián Silva (b. 1979) in complex black comedy *La nana* (*The Maid*, 2009). In the deliciously twisted *Tony Manero* (2008, left) and *Post Mortem* (2010), Pablo Larraín (b. 1976) offered chilling glimpses of life during the dictatorship.

One of the most popular films of the era was melancholy Uruguayan comedy *Whisky* (2004), by Juan Pablo Rebella (1974–2006) and Pablo Stoll (b. 1974). Peru's Claudia Llosa (b. 1976) deservedly won the Golden Bear with *La teta asustada* (*The Milk of Sorrow*, 2009), about the clash between city life and rural superstition.

The common denominator between all these directors is not style but attitude. Uninterested in genre or in aping Hollywood, they make personal films faithful to their own experience, preoccupations, and cinematic language. The strongest influence on the continent is probably that of Italian Neo-Realism (see p. 178). Although not polemic, these Latin films shine a light on the political, social, even psychological problems in their countries, considering what it means to be Latin American after years of strife. While their stories are ostensibly local, they are told with a skill that makes them universal. This Latin renaissance is marked by an unusually large number of women directors, a thriving documentary scene, and a spirit of collaboration within and across borders.

Despite the Mexican government being slow to catch up (it increased the state film budget only in 2004), there is a feisty entrepreneurial spirit among the country's filmmakers—González Iñárritu, Cuarón, and Del Toro joining forces with the production company Cha Cha Cha; the actors García Bernal and Luna and producer Pablo Cruz with Canana. Similarly, Salles and Meirelles successfully juggle international careers with local production.

In 2003 the Colombian government introduced laws to support local cinema and a film fund to boost Colombian production. The result is a rising output and increased international presence. Two notable films, both released in 2009, are *El vuelco del cangrejo* (*Crab Trap*) by Oscar Ruiz Navia (b. 1982), an atmospheric, beautifully photographed clash of old traditions and new in a Colombian coastal village, and *Los viajes del viento* (*The Wind Journeys*) by Ciro Guerra (b. 1981), a characterful fable about a legendary accordion player, with performance sequences that are both cinematic and a musical tour de force.

In Venezuela, President Hugo Chavez is seeking to counter "the dictatorship of Hollywood" with a new, state-owned film studio, Villa del Cine, to produce local features and documentaries. There are funds for independent filmmakers and exhibition regulations compelling the screening of every Venezuelan film.

A quiet revolution is already sweeping through Latin America—not political, but cultural—which promises to overcome Hollywood's stranglehold on cinemas and popularize Latin films among their own audiences. As this struggle continues, the best of these filmmakers are telling their own stories, in their own ways, and finding that the rest of the world is watching. **DM**

Central do Brasil 1998
Central Station WALTER SALLES b. 1956

▲ After the trail of Josué's father goes cold, Dora invites the boy to live with her.

▼ The sunbleached film poster captures a moment at the end of a long day for the weary duo.

When Walter Salles's third feature, *Central do Brasil*, won the Golden Bear in Berlin, its success heralded the return of Brazilian cinema to the world stage after years in the doldrums. Fernanda Montenegro was Oscar-nominated for her performance as the cynical Dora, a retired schoolteacher who reluctantly helps a homeless boy, Josué, search for the father he has never known—and rediscovers her humanity in the process. At the same time, Salles uses his preferred mode—the road movie—to explore a country still finding its feet after years of dictatorship and hardship.

The film opens in the eponymous Rio train station, where Dora plies a dishonest trade writing letters for the city's illiterates, whose heartfelt messages she never posts. It eventually follows the irascible woman and her sulking charge as they travel—by bus and hitchhiking, soon without a coin in their pockets—into the country's arid northeastern hinterland, the *sertão*. Displaying his experience as a documentary maker, Salles constantly allows true life to enter the frame, notably when Dora and Josué encounter a pilgrimage: the whirl of preachers, fortune-tellers, musicians, and hawkers is patently real.

Anthony Minghella (1954–2008) said of *Central do Brasil*: "That small Brazilian movie touched more hearts than almost any other movie I know of. It announced a real voice in international cinema." Among its many awards was the British Academy Award for Best Foreign Film. But perhaps its greatest success was that it saw Salles enter the ranks of viable international directors, able to influence and support his fellow filmmakers in Brazil. **DM**

👁 KEY SCENES

1 LETTERS
The Central do Brasil train station in Rio de Janeiro. A series of people dictate letters to Dora, who offers to send them on to friends and loved ones. The last of these is a woman, with her son Josué beside her. She declares, "Jesus, you're the worst thing to happen to me."

2 ESCAPE
Dora has left Josué with child traffickers, using the money she receives to buy a television. Overnight, she is overcome by guilt, and the next morning returns to the traffickers' apartment. Dora enters the apartment, finds Josué, and flees with him.

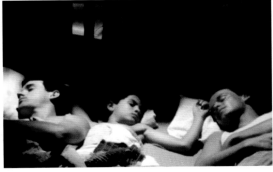

3 BROTHERS
It turns out that Jesus had left his home some months earlier. But Dora and Josué have found his two older sons, who take an instant liking to the boy. Dora is content that Josué has found the family he needs. At dawn, as the three brothers sleep side by side, she leaves.

🕐 DIRECTOR PROFILE

1956–2000
Walter Salles was born in Rio de Janeiro. He began to direct documentaries for Brazilian television in his twenties. With his brother, filmmaker João Moreira Salles (b. 1962), he founded the production and distribution company VideoFilmes. In 1991 he directed his first feature, the thriller *A grande arte* (*Exposure*, 1991). His second feature, *Terra estrangeira* (*Foreign Land*, 1996), codirected with Daniela Thomas (b. 1959), dealt with the exodus after Brazil's economic crisis of the early nineties. *Central do Brasil* won the Golden Bear in Berlin.

2001–5
Salles directed *Abril despedaçado* (*Behind the Sun*, 2001) and then championed its two screenwriters as directors, producing *Madame Satã* (2002) by Karim Aïnouz and *Cidade baixa* (*Lower City*, 2005) by Sérgio Machado (b. 1968). He was executive producer on *Cidade de Deus* (*City of God*, 2002, see p. 522), by Fernando Meirelles. *Diarios de motocicleta* (*The Motorcycle Diaries*, 2004), based on the memoir by Che Guevara, was Salles's biggest international success. He then made his first feature in the United States, horror film *Dark Water* (2005).

2006–present
After coproducing two films by the Argentine director Pablo Trapero—*Nacido y criado* (*Born and Bred*, 2006) and *Leonera* (*Lion's Den*, 2008)—Salles directed his second film with Daniela Thomas, *Linha de Passe* (2008). In 2010 he began shooting his long-planned adaptation of Jack Kerouac's novel *On the Road*, executive produced by Francis Ford Coppola (b. 1939).

FACT TO FICTION

Walter Salles's documentary roots provided the initial idea for *Central do Brasil*—and a hidden poignancy in its opening sequence. His documentary *Socorro Nobre* (*Life Somewhere Else*, 1995) concerned the unusual relationship between a female prison inmate, Socorro Nobre, and an elderly sculptor, Franz Krajcberg (below). The woman had read an article about Krajcberg's work, was moved by it, and wrote a letter to him. The artist replied, prompting a regular correspondence. Commented Salles: "I was shocked that on the verge

of the twenty-first century, in the age of the Internet, lives could still be changed by a letter. I started to wonder what could happen if letters were written, but did not reach their destination. And what if this was on purpose? This is how the story of *Central Station* was born."

Y tu mamá también 2001

ALFONSO CUARÓN b. 1961

▲ A masterclass in unobtrusive camerawork and measured storytelling.

▼ Important connections involving water are referenced on the film's poster.

Tenoch (Diego Luna) and Julio (Gael García Bernal) have just graduated from school. They spend their days discussing sex, smoking weed, and being bored. Upon meeting the older Luisa (Maribel Verdú) they invite her to join them on a trip to Heaven's Mouth—a beach paradise dreamed up only moments before. After receiving results from medical tests and learning that her husband has been cheating on her, Luisa takes the boys up on the offer and the three of them set off to find this imaginary, perfect place.

At first the film seems to be simply an exploration of sex, with graphic scenes depicting sex as both powerful and trivial. There is, however, more to this film than that. Director Alfonso Cuarón paints a rich, naturalistic picture of Mexico, showing different social classes and the changing political landscape, while the lead characters reveal secrets, expose bitter jealousies, discover the world around them, and let go of their old way of life.

For Tenoch and Julio this is the last summer before adulthood. They are full of giggly excitement, bursting with sexual tension and blind to the larger events happening around them: beggars go largely unnoticed, and although Tenoch's father wants to involve him in society and Julio's sister is a political activist, none of this concerns the boys. As they begin to understand the world in all its beauty and harshness, Luisa is embracing what experiences and happiness she can before leaving it all behind. The film is a playful and thoughtful study of life, death, and relationships and was a groundbreaking hit internationally for Latin American cinema. **SW**

◉ KEY SCENES

1 THE ROAD TRIP STARTS
Assured of their sexual prowess and bond of friendship, Tenoch and Julio set out with the object of their infatuation—Luisa, who becomes both a lover and maternal figure to the boys. The actors complement each other, their arcs portrayed naturalistically.

4 LUISA WALKS AWAY FROM LIFE
While the boys' euphemistic destination is far from what they expected, Luisa finds peace, walking into the sea, giving herself over to a literal and spiritual Heaven's Mouth. The last thing she tells them is: "Life is like the surf, so give yourselves away like the sea."

2 A TRYST
Luisa and Tenoch make love, while, unbeknown to them, Julio watches. It is messy, brief, and far from glamorous, ending with Luisa stifling a laugh. She sees herself as passing on wisdom, being adventurous, while the boys' loyalties are about to be tested.

◷ DIRECTOR PROFILE

1961—94
Alfonso Cuarón was born in Mexico City. After studying philosophy and film studies, he won jobs as a technician and director for Mexican television and as assistant director for films such as *Gaby: A True Story* (1987) before working on his debut feature, *Sólo con tu pareja* (*Only With Your Partner*, 1991). This sex comedy was a success in Mexico and attracted the attention of Sydney Pollack (1934–2008), who invited Cuarón to direct an episode of the US cable show *Fallen Angels*.

1995—2001
Cuarón's first two US feature films were the literary adaptations *A Little Princess* (1995) and a modernized take on *Great Expectations* (1998), starring Ethan Hawke, Gwyneth Paltrow, Chris Cooper, and Robert De Niro. Cuarón returned to Mexico for the acclaimed part erotic drama, part road movie *Y tu mamá también*, which earned an Academy Award nomination for Best Original Screenplay and Golden Globe and BAFTA nominations for Best Film Not in the English Language.

2002—3
The genre-shifting director took on his biggest film to date, *Harry Potter and the Prisoner of Azkaban* (2004)—the third film in the series. A darker and tighter adaptation than the previous Potter films, it earned positive reviews both from critics and from the books' author, J. K. Rowling.

2004—present
In 2006 Cuarón released the acclaimed, Academy Award-nominated, science fiction thriller *Children of Men*. Starring Clive Owen and Julianne Moore, the film drew praise for its dystopian setting and long, single-shot sequences. In 2008, along with friends and fellow directors Guillermo del Toro and Alejandro González Iñárritu, Cuarón established the production company Cha Cha Cha Films. The first film released by Cha Cha Cha was *Rudo y Cursi* (2008). Cuarón began work in 2010 on his seventh feature, *Gravity*—an ambitious science fiction drama.

3 LUISA DANCES
Free from emotional burdens, Luisa's dance serves as a prelude to the climactic sex scene. This is the end of the trip, the end of Luisa's travels, and the end of the boys' friendship. Is the use of a threesome and same-sex experience a fitting ending or too predictable?

Cidade de Deus 2002
City of God   FERNANDO MEIRELLES b. 1955

▲ The tense, quickfire opening cuts to a flashback of a young Rocket playing soccer.

▼ The dynamic but ominous poster references a pivotal scene early in the film.

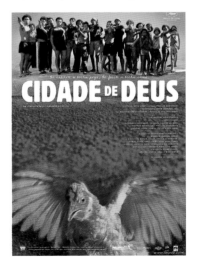

Cidade de Deus is arguably the most important Latin American film of the past twenty years, a dazzling, vibrant piece of cinema that was also socially significant and a box-office hit. That it was only Meirelles's second feature, and that its cast was dominated by nonprofessional child actors, makes it all the more remarkable. Adapted from the novel by Paulo Lins, who grew up in the real favela suburb of Cidade de Deus, it concerns three phases in the life of the slum (one in the 1960s, two in the 1970s). The community is transformed by poverty, by ever more congested living space and by crime, as drug dealing leads to armed gang warfare.

From the novel's vast cast of characters, Meirelles and scriptwriter Bráulio Mantovani chose as their narrator Rocket (Alexandre Rodrigues), who dreams of being a photographer and escaping the favela. The other characters knee deep in the mess include: psychopathic drug dealer Li'l Zé (Leandro Firmino da Hora), his right-hand man and jovial party animal Bené (Phellipe Haagensen), and Knockout Ned (Seu Jorge), a peaceful ex-soldier drawn into a war with Li'l Zé.

Key collaborators included executive producer Walter Salles, codirector Kátia Lund (b. 1966), who was central in training the young actors, cinematographer César Charlone, editor Daniel Rezende, and scriptwriter Mantovani. Their bravura narrative style featured voice-over, captions, split-screen, slow motion, and freeze frame, flashing backward, forward, sideways. But at the heart of the film are the mesmerizing performances from the boys, speaking in the expressive patois of the favela, a veritable choir of angels with dirty faces. **DM**

1 CHASING THE CHICKEN

Li'l Zé and his gang jokingly chase a chicken through the favela. The chicken and the gang stop in front of Rocket, as police arrive behind him. Guns are raised. He is about to be caught in the crossfire. The film jumps back in time, but returns to this showdown for its climax.

2 THE DEATH OF BENÉ

Bené plans to leave the favela. During his farewell party, a former gang member with a grudge tries to shoot Li'l Zé, but hits and kills Bené instead. At the same party, Knockout Ned suffers the first of the humiliations that will turn him into Li'l Zé's nemesis.

3 THE CYCLE CONTINUES

During a final shootout, Knockout Ned is killed, while Li'l Zé and his rival Carrot are arrested by police; Li'l Zé pays a bribe for his freedom. After the police have left, he is riddled with bullets by "the runts," the youngest tearaways in the favela, who declare: "The business is ours."

⏱ DIRECTOR PROFILE

1955–90

Fernando Meirelles was born in São Paulo. While still an architecture student, he began making animated films. On graduation, he and some friends formed Olhar Eletronico, first making experimental videos, then working in independent television for several years, creating a show for teenagers, *Crag-Ra*, and the children's program *Rá-Tim-Bum*, of which Meirelles directed 180 episodes. In 1990 he cofounded O2 Filmes, which became Brazil's biggest advertising company.

1991–2005

In 1998 Meirelles directed the short *E no meio pass um trem*, followed by his first feature, *Menino maluquinho 2: A aventura* (*The Nutty Boy 2*, 1998). He and Kátia Lund made the short film *Palace II* (2000), as a rehearsal for *Cidade de Deus*. His second feature as sole director was *Domésticas* (*Maids*, 2001), based on a stage play. Afterward, Meirelles produced the television series *Cidade dos Homens* (*City of Men*, 2002–05).

2006–8

Meirelles coproduced *O ano em que meus pais saíram de férias* (*The Year My Parents Went on Vacation*), directed by Cao Hamburger (b. 1962), and *Antônia* (both 2006) by Tata Amaral (b. 1961). He directed *The Constant Gardener* (2005), based on a John Le Carré novel. *Blindness* (2008) was based on the novel by Portuguese Nobel laureate José Saramago.

2009–present

Meirelles directed and produced two television series in Brazil and began preparing a biopic of the singer Janis Joplin.

LIVES ON SCREEN

Integral to the veracity of *Cidade de Deus* was the decision of director Fernando Meirelles (below) to find his cast in the favelas, training boys who would bring their life experience to the screen. Many came from the We of the Hillside theater workshop, joined by others who responded to an offer, made on the favelas' loudspeaker systems, to attend an acting class. Some four hundred boys were chosen, of which two hundred attended workshops for three months. "Five were drug dealers themselves," the director recalls. "We had this rule: you participate here, or you deal drugs, but you can't do both. So three boys stayed, and two left."

POSTMILLENNIAL BRITISH CINEMA

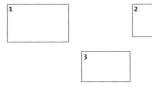

1 Jamie Bell takes off in the lead role of *Billy Elliot*. Billy is torn between his passion for dance and his militant mining family.

2 *Wallace & Gromit: The Curse of the Were-Rabbit* provided Nick Park with his fourth Oscar. He was awarded his first for *Creature Comforts* (1989).

3 The Queen reads of the death of Diana, Princess of Wales. Dame Helen Mirren's commanding performance secured many awards, including a BAFTA and an Oscar.

The first decade of the twenty-first century saw British films scoop a host of awards and director Danny Boyle (b. 1956) venture into Bollywood territory: *Slumdog Millionaire* (2008) made headlines when it won eight Oscars, including one for Best Picture. Established film director Mike Leigh (b. 1943) found success with his tale of a 1950s abortionist, *Vera Drake* (2004), while new talent Stephen Daldry (b. 1961) broke onto the scene with *Billy Elliot* (2000, above), a feel-good drama about a boy from a mining community who learns to dance. The film gained worldwide critical plaudits and Hollywood's attention. British society and social mores came under the lens of Paweł Pawlikowski (b. 1957) in the bittersweet story of teenage romance, *My Summer of Love* (2004, see p. 526), as they did from a very different angle in the French-backed drama about the death of Princess Diana directed by Stephen Frears (b. 1941), *The Queen* (2006, opposite below).

Independent production companies such as Working Title Films built on the comedy and costume drama hits of the 1990s to gain distribution deals with US studios and make more, including *Bridget Jones's Diary* (2001), *Love Actually* (2003), *Pride & Prejudice* (2005), and *Atonement* (2007). Although US-backed, the *Harry Potter* (2001–11) franchise was made in the United Kingdom at Hertfordshire's Leavesden Film Studios and starred homegrown talent, with Englishmen Mike Newell (b. 1942) and David Yates (b. 1963) among the directors. The epic story of a young wizard is the world's highest-grossing film series to date.

KEY EVENTS

2000	2000	2003	2004	2005	2006
The UK Film Council is created to develop the film industry in the UK. It supports film societies, independent film venues, and UK film festivals.	Stephen Daldry wins the first of three Oscar nominations, for *Billy Elliot*. He is later nominated for *The Hours* (2002) and *The Reader* (2008).	Richard Curtis (b. 1958) makes his directorial debut with a romantic comedy, *Love Actually*, which grosses $239 million.	*Vera Drake* wins the Golden Lion for Best Film at the Venice Film Festival and secures three BAFTAs and three Academy Award nominations.	*Pride & Prejudice*, the feature debut by Joe Wright (b. 1972), is nominated for four Oscars. His follow-up, *Atonement* (2007), is nominated for six.	*Wallace & Gromit: The Curse of the Were-Rabbit* wins an Oscar for Best Animated Feature Film for its makers, Park and Box.

Of the award-winning films of the new millennium, the most idiosyncratic was the Claymation *Wallace & Gromit: The Curse of the Were-Rabbit* (2005, right), by Nick Park (b. 1958) and Steve Box (b. 1967). Produced by Bristol-based Aardman Features and DreamWorks Animation, this imaginative and hilarious movie, full of absent-minded inventor Wallace's strange contraptions, slapstick humor, and cinematic in-jokes, appeals to adults and children alike.

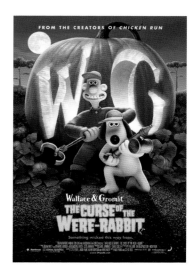

A British film that charted more familiar territory, *The Constant Gardener* (2005), won multiple awards on account of its strong performances. It features Ralph Fiennes as disillusioned British diplomat Justin Quayle, who wants to find out the truth about the murder of his idealistic wife (Rachel Weisz), a human-rights activist, after she stumbles upon the devious working practices of a large pharmaceutical company in Kenya. Despite a complicated plot, Brazilian director Fernando Meirelles (b. 1955) does an excellent job of exposition without slowing down the pace of the narrative.

While the 1990s saw a renaissance in British film revolving around costume dramas and romantic comedies, the 2000s saw more hard-hitting films, and a Britain prepared to reflect on its not-so-distant colonial past in *The Last King of Scotland* (2006), directed by Scot Kevin Macdonald (b. 1967). This low-budget movie became a box-office triumph thanks to a screenplay cowritten by *The Queen*'s scriptwriter Peter Morgan, and an Oscar-winning powerhouse performance by Forest Whitaker as Ugandan dictator General Idi Amin. The mesmerizing Whitaker manages to project the deranged leader's capricious bullying and murderous nature in such a manner that he emerges as a deeply flawed human being rather than a stereotypical figure of evil. **CK**

2006	2008	2009	2009	2009	2010
Dame Helen Mirren wins a Best Actress Oscar for her convincing portrayal of Queen Elizabeth II in *The Queen*.	The British film industry earns an all-time-high export income of more than £1.3 billion from film rights and production services.	*Slumdog Millionaire* is nominated for ten Academy Awards and wins eight, including Best Director for Danny Boyle.	*Harry Potter and the Half-Blood Prince* is the year's second highest-grossing film at the worldwide box office, earning more than $900 million.	More than 173.5 million people go to the cinema in the UK. British films take 17 percent of the UK box office and 7 percent worldwide.	To cut costs, the British government abolishes the UK Film Council. It had funded 900 films, including *The Last King of Scotland* and *The Constant Gardener*.

My Summer of Love 2004

PAWEŁ PAWLIKOWSKI b. 1957

▲ Tamsin and Mona set off to a river, where they take their first steps toward intimacy.

▼ Natalie Press and Emily Blunt on a poster redolent with implied longing.

Polish-born writer-director Paweł Pawlikowski's second (and first independently produced) feature, *My Summer of Love*, announced the arrival of a challenging and original voice. His thematically rich, highly cinematic version of Helen Cross's Yorkshire-set novel, about two fifteen-year-old girls of different classes who engage in a brief and dangerously passionate summer affair, brought his "internationalist" sensibility and iconoclastic, boundary-crossing mentality to bear on some of the conventions—literary, romantic, social realist—within early twenty-first-century British cinema.

Pawlikowski employs the expressive cinematography and saturated color palette of fellow Pole Ryszard Lenczewski to highlight the contrasts between the natural and man-made environments of West Yorkshire's semirural Hebden Bridge area, where fantasist private schoolgirl Tamsin (Emily Blunt) and "near orphan" Mona (Natalie Press) meet and form a relationship built on shared rebellious curiosity, personal estrangement, and undeclared need. The director's preference for relatively unknown actors led to a nine-month search until he came up trumps with Natalie Press as the ingenuous Mona and Emily Blunt as the more imperious, sexually provocative Tamsin. He shot in sequence, on a modest budget, but employed a sometimes elliptical editing style.

Pawlikowski almost seamlessly combines sensuality, realist detail, and lyrical flights of fancy—not to mention religious and psychological symbolism, moments of tongue-in-cheek horror, and a genuine sense of threat—while staying faithful to the emotional rhythms pulsing in the hearts of his two young leads. **WH**

KEY SCENES

1 FATEFUL MEETING

Tamsin invites her less socially favored neighbor Mona to visit the big house. Tamsin's mother is a bohemian actress and her father a wealthy businessman, whereas Mona lives, parentless, in a rundown pub with her ex-inmate, born-again Christian brother.

2 HEARTBREAK HOUSE

Seduced by Tamsin's serenade featuring a Saint-Saëns cello piece, intrigued by her romantic readings of Nietzsche, and intoxicated by copious drafts of brandy, Mona is led into a dance to Edith Piaf's tragic Argentine waltz, "La Foule."

3 KISS ME DEADLY

Having taken seriously their mutual promise to kill each other should either lover leave, Mona discovers that Tamsin is returning to school. Mona kisses Tamsin farewell, pretends to strangle her, and then submerges her in the river where they first declared their eternal love.

DIRECTOR PROFILE

1957–88

Paweł Pawlikowski was born in Poland, but later settled in England. In 1987 he joined the BBC and made *Lucifer over Lancashire* (1987) and *Palace Life* (1988) for the broadcasting corporation's Community Programme and Bookmark documentary strands.

1989–97

Pawlikowski embarked on a series of sometimes controversial, Emmy-winning documentaries in Central and Eastern Europe, examining themes of exile and Russian culture, including *From Moscow to Pietushki* (1991), *Dostoevsky's Travels* (1992), *Serbian Epics* (1992), and *Tripping with Zhirinovsky* (1995).

1998–2000

From 1998 Pawlikowski moved into more drama-based BBC projects, such as *Twockers* (1998) and *The Stringer* (1998). *Last Resort* (2000), his touching drama about a young Russian immigrant mother's experiences in Margate, won Best New British Feature at the Edinburgh Film Festival.

2001–present

My Summer of Love won BAFTA's award for Best British Film. A period of abandoned or aborted film projects followed during the illness and eventual death of Pawlikowski's wife—including his adaptation of Magnus Mills's debut novel *The Restraint of Beasts*. In 2010 Pawlikowski completed the shooting in Paris of *The Woman in the Fifth*, an adaptation of Douglas Kennedy's novel, starring Ethan Hawke and Kristin Scott Thomas.

PAGE TO SCREEN

Pawlikowski made extensive changes to Helen Cross's Betty Trask Award–winning novel, which was published in 2001. He considered it "busy" and "too specific and at the same time too generic." With cowriter Michael Wynne, he stripped from the novel most of its peripheral characters and its specific references—the 1980s miners' strike, the Yorkshire Ripper—at the same time adding the character of Phil, Mona's evangelical convert brother played by Paddy Considine. In so doing he introduced to the film the notion of an ideal or "absolute" love to set alongside the young women's more chaotic, ambivalent love. The resulting script allowed Pawlikowski greater scope to explore more fully the emotional development of the characters; it also allowed the central actors themselves to develop their relationship in the spirit, rather than the letter, of the book through workshops and improvisation. This bold but sympathetic essentialist attitude to literary adaptation is one of the defining qualities of Pawlikowski's contribution to narrative cinema.

FAMILY BLOCKBUSTERS

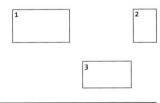

1 Captain Jack Sparrow (Johnny Depp) and Will Turner (Orlando Bloom) flourish their cutlasses in *Pirates of the Caribbean: The Curse of the Black Pearl*.

2 Harry Potter (Daniel Radcliffe) and Ron Weasley (Rupert Grint) in *Harry Potter and the Half-Blood Prince*, the sixth entry in the magical hit series and the second to be directed by David Yates.

3 Iron Man (Robert Downey Jr.) launches a trademark repulsor ray at his enemy Ivan Vanko (Mickey Rourke) at the Monaco Grand Prix in *Iron Man 2*.

Since the release of *Jaws* (1975, see p. 364), the summer blockbuster has been aimed at a younger audience. Gone are the epics and dramas aimed at adults: the last thirty years have been dominated by family entertainment. For the industry, this shift has seen the growth of revenue streams beyond box-office receipts, from toys and other merchandising to video and DVD sales that often account for more income than the theatrical release does. Disney understood the value of family entertainment from the start. *Snow White and the Seven Dwarfs* (1937, see p. 146) was the year's most successful movie, its hand-drawn animation setting a trend that lasted almost fifty years. The last conventional Disney cartoon to dominate the box office was *The Lion King* in 1994, the year before a young upstart entered the fray.

No studio has held sway over family entertainment in the last decade as strongly as Pixar. Although the studio came under the auspices of The Walt Disney Company in 2006, its brand is so strong that it is still regarded as a separate creative entity. In the eleven films it has produced between 1995 and 2010, its signature blend of stunning animation with savvy, emotionally engaging scripts that appeal to all ages has proven almost unbeatable with audiences and critics. In Blue Sky Studio's *Ice Age* and DreamWorks's *Shrek* series the originality of each of the first movies, particularly *Shrek* (2001) with its deconstruction of fairy tales, paled in the inevitable sequels. The classical hand-drawn animation of *The Princess and the Frog* (2009) marked a stunning return to a style that Disney had all but given up on. It was left to directors such as Sylvain Chomet (b. 1963) and Miyazaki Hayao (b. 1941) to fill this gap.

KEY EVENTS

1995	2000	2001	2001	2002	2003
Disney Pixar's *Toy Story* begins the studio's domination of family-oriented entertainment.	The success of *X-Men*, directed by Bryan Singer (b. 1965), ushers in a new age in comic book adaptations.	*Harry Potter and the Philosopher's Stone* and *The Lord of the Rings: The Fellowship of the Ring* are released.	Disney Pixar's *Monsters, Inc.* wins the Oscar for Best Animated Feature but is less successful than *Shrek* at the box office.	The global box office is dominated by *The Lord of the Rings: The Two Towers* (see p. 530), *Harry Potter and the Chamber of Secrets*, and *Spider-Man*.	*Pirates of the Caribbean: The Curse of the Black Pearl* is released.

Disney's most successful blockbusters of the first decade of the twenty-first century began, incongruously, with a theme-park ride. Inspired by the last ride designed with Disney's input, producer Jerry Bruckheimer transformed it into the *Pirates of the Caribbean* franchise. The first film, *The Curse of the Black Pearl* (2003, opposite), proved a surprisingly entertaining summer hit, harking back to the swashbuckling adventures of Hollywood's golden age, with an eccentric turn from Johnny Depp as the permanently inebriated Captain Jack Sparrow. Sadly the sequels became longer, louder, and seemingly never-ending.

Two literary sources were behind the decade's most successful franchises. J. K. Rowling's *Harry Potter* series (right) got off to a shaky start thanks to the unimaginative direction of Chris Columbus (b. 1958), but became stronger in the dark *Harry Potter and the Prisoner of Azkaban* (2004), directed by Alfonso Cuarón (b. 1961). Meanwhile, Peter Jackson (b. 1961) directed the impressive *Lord of the Rings* trilogy (2001–03, see p. 530), brilliantly adapted by Jackson himself, Fran Walsh, and Philippa Boyens. Skillful writing was sadly absent from the ludicrous, but highly successful, space-bound follies *The Phantom Menace* (1999), *Attack of the Clones* (2002), and *Revenge of the Sith* (2005), which continued the *Star Wars* saga from George Lucas (b. 1944).

The other dominant forces at the box office during this period were the revitalized houses of DC and Marvel. With the success of *X-Men* (2000), *Spider-Man* (2002), and the *Iron Man* movies (below), Marvel was now able to afford to fund its own films. DC was a little slower off the mark, but *Batman Begins* (2005, see p. 532) and *The Dark Knight* (2008), both directed by Christopher Nolan (b. 1970), set the standard for future comic adaptations. In *Avatar* (2009), the most commercially successful film to date, James Cameron (b. 1954) presented an impressive spectacle in 3-D. The movie also carried a message about protecting the environment, in contrast to most previous blockbusters of its type. **IHS**

2003	2004	2006	2008	2009	2010
The Lord of the Rings: Return of the King becomes the most successful film of the *Lord of the Rings* series and picks up a total of eleven Oscars.	Sequels *Shrek 2* and *Spider-Man 2*, directed like *Spider-Man* by Sam Raimi (b. 1959), dominate the global box office.	Pixar is taken over by Disney. George Lucas announces *Revenge of the Sith* will be the last in the *Star Wars* saga.	*The Dark Knight* is the year's biggest box-office hit. *Iron Man* and the disappointing *Indiana Jones and the Kingdom of the Crystal Skull* are released.	*Avatar* becomes the greatest box-office success to date. This suggests 3-D cinema is here to stay. Pixar's *Up* is nominated for the Best Film Oscar.	*Toy Story 3* maintains the high standard set by the first two films in the series. *Shrek Forever After* is the fourth entry in a now-tired franchise.

The Lord of the Rings: The Two Towers 2002

PETER JACKSON b. 1961

▲ The hardship Frodo suffers in his quest to destroy the ring gives him heroic stature.

▼ A poster montage of the ensemble cast.

It remains to be seen whether it proves to be the defining cinematic moment of the twenty-first century's first decade, but *The Lord of the Rings* was certainly one of the boldest and most ambitious undertakings since the silent era. In adapting, with relative faithfulness, J. R. R. Tolkien's sprawling and complex fantasy trilogy, director Peter Jackson and independent studio New Line staked not just their reputations but their creative futures on a single, shaky enterprise. There was a strong chance the public would not want anything to do with this violent, backstory-heavy, sword-and-sorcery adventure, however popular the source material.

The Lord of the Rings: The Two Towers marks the peak of Jackson's powers as a filmmaker to date. It is a masterly blend of epic scale and emotional intimacy. As the central core of an ongoing story—which itself contains three separate narrative threads, one featuring Frodo's (Elijah Wood) quest to destroy the One Ring—the film might lack either a strong opening or a satisfying climax, and could easily have proved confusing for viewers. Yet Jackson and his cowriters Fran Walsh and Philippa Boyens were astute in their adaptation, and the resulting film is a triumph of the storyteller's art, with a complex series of cross-cuts, flashbacks, and montage sequences giving it its own rounded structure.

The Two Towers was a huge success and although it was left unrewarded on Oscar night that oversight was atoned for the following year when the last film in the trilogy, *The Return of the King*, swept the board. *The Lord of the Rings* remains a pinnacle of mainstream cinema in the twenty-first century. **TH**

👁 KEY SCENES

1 THE BALROG
The opening scene throws audiences straight into the action. To allow the Fellowship of the Ring to escape, Gandalf (Ian McKellen) battles the monstrous Balrog. The two plummet through mile after mile of computer-generated underground chasm.

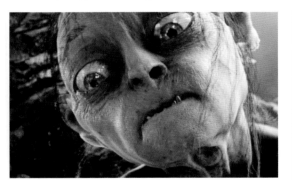

2 THE TAMING OF SMÉAGOL/GOLLUM
The film was groundbreaking for its use of computer graphics (using voice and motion capture) to realize fully formed characters such as Sméagol/Gollum (Andy Serkis), whose helpless, addictive lust for the ring makes him the tragic antihero of the trilogy.

3 GANDALF THE WHITE
Aragorn, Gimli, and Legolas face down the mysterious White Rider only to find themselves reunited with Gandalf. Gandalf the Grey, the leader of the Fellowship, has been reborn as Gandalf the White. He returns more powerful than ever to fight the evil Sauron.

4 THE GOLDEN HALL OF EDORAS
Jackson's commitment to mixing modern CGI techniques with old-fashioned sets and miniatures lends the film its realistic quality. This full-scale Saxon hall was built on the peak of Mount Sunday in New Zealand's South Island. It was dismantled when filming finished.

5 THE BATTLE OF HELM'S DEEP
Jackson took inspiration from the movie *Zulu* (1964) for the film's epic centerpiece, in which hundreds of extras—and thousands of CGI characters—fight for control of the stone fortress at Helm's Deep. The grueling filming took place at night over four months.

6 "THE STORIES THAT MEANT SOMETHING"
Jackson's greatest achievement is in fusing the epic with the intimate. In the closing scenes the hobbit Sam's words demonstrate Jackson's fidelity to emotional storytelling, and his debt to the great myths and tales that inspired Tolkien and the screenwriters.

Batman Begins 2005

CHRISTOPHER NOLAN b. 1970

▲ To summon Batman, Lieutenant Gordon devises—naturally enough—a Bat-signal.

▼ The apocalyptic poster presents Nolan's Batman as a menacing gothic avenger.

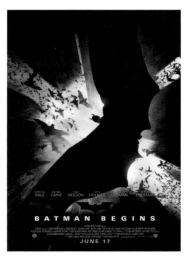

Oddly, none of the previous television or film versions of DC Comics's caped crusader explored Batman's origin. Half of this film elapses before Bruce Wayne (Christian Bale) puts on the cloak and mask and sets out to terrorize the criminals of blighted Gotham City, revealing the journey the bereaved billionaire takes from orphaned child to vigilante hero.

Previous Batman films—and even Christopher Nolan's follow-up *The Dark Knight* (2008)—undervalue the lead character and play him as a straight man to star-turn villains such as the Joker (Jack Nicholson or Heath Ledger). Here, Bruce/Batman unquestionably takes center stage, supported by martial arts teacher Henri Ducard (Liam Neeson), his enabling butler (Michael Caine), underrated no-questions-asked inventor Lucius Fox (Morgan Freeman), and the lone honest cop in town Jim Gordon (Gary Oldman). Bale, showing the sleek physicality of *American Psycho* (2000), takes the role uncommonly seriously, but brings humor to his characterization in a way that has seldom been seen since the 1940s: Bruce Wayne, drunken playboy idiot. Other Batman films make Bruce so heroic he barely seems to be a secret identity.

Pitted against him is a series of interlocked criminals, from a scared gunman in an alley to an old-fashioned organized crime boss (Tom Wilkinson), a flamboyant and demented supervillain (Cillian Murphy), and a Fu Manchu–like mastermind (Ken Watanabe), who turns out to be behind every other evil in a long-standing attempt to destroy Gotham. One of the best structured comic book action films, *Batman Begins* also has depth and resonance. **KN**

1 THE BIRTH OF THE BATMAN
In an alleyway outside the opera, mugger Joe Chill (Richard Brake) tries to hold up Thomas and Martha Wayne and, in panic, shoots the couple dead in front of their young son, Bruce (Gus Lewis). It is left to the family butler, Alfred, to bring up the orphaned boy.

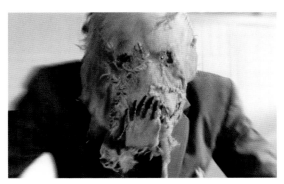

3 "WOULD YOU LIKE TO SEE MY MASK?"
Criminal psychiatrist Dr. Jonathan Crane (Murphy) produces a scarecrow mask, supposedly for use in radical therapy—but actually counters the first strike of the Batman by becoming the first of Gotham's equally freakish villains.

2 THE DEBUT OF THE DARK KNIGHT
A frightening figure appears out of the darkness and assaults a gang of criminals, announcing that there is a new force out to clean up Gotham City. A childhood phobia prompts the costume design: Bruce swears to make evildoers fear him as he once feared bats.

4 A CALLING CARD
Newly promoted Captain Gordon muses on the response of the city's criminals to the masked hero and hands over a piece of evidence: a playing card, the joker, left at the scene of a violent armed robbery. "Got a taste for the theatrical, like you."

BATMAN ON FILM

Created by writer Bill Finger and artist Bob Kane, Batman debuted in *Detective Comics* in 1939. The character appeared in the serials *Batman* (1943) and *Batman and Robin* (1949), but crossed into pop culture immortality when played by Adam West in the television show and movie *Batman* (1966). Tim Burton (b. 1958) directed the gothic, expressionistic *Batman* (1989) and *Batman Returns* (1992), but Joel Schumacher (b. 1939) struck a lighter approach (*Batman Forever*, 1995; *Batman & Robin*, 1997) that disappointed. Even before Christopher Nolan reimagined the character in *Batman Begins* and *The Dark Knight* (right) there were animated television takes on Gotham, including *Batman: Mask of the Phantasm* (1993).

POSTMILLENNIAL EUROPEAN CINEMA

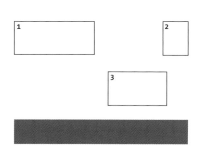

1 Björk picked up the Best Actress award at Cannes for her performance in *Dancer in the Dark*, although critical opinion on the film was strongly divided.

2 In *Good Bye Lenin!*, East German siblings try to turn back time by hiding the fall of the Berlin Wall from their fragile mother who has been in a coma.

3 Noomi Rapace in the adaptation of *The Girl With the Dragon Tattoo*. Despite a limited US release, in just 202 cinemas, it has taken more than $10 million.

When future generations look back on the first decade of the twenty-first century, they might well see it as something of a golden age for European cinema. For this was a time when the EU incentives introduced since 1990 finally came to fruition, as the evidence of the material advantages accruing to directors and producers when working on a Europe-wide basis led to coproductions becoming the norm, rather than the exception. Yet the coproductions of the new century are a far cry from the badly dubbed Euro-puddings of the 1990s. With the odd exception, such as the clunky melting-pot films *L'auberge espagnole* (*Pot Luck*, 2002) and *Les poupées russes* (*Russian Dolls*, 2005) by Cédric Klapisch (b. 1961), the resulting films betray little external sign of their mixed heritage, which was restricted in the main to an exchange of funds and occasionally production personnel.

The director is no longer necessarily a national figure. Filmmakers such as Michael Haneke (b. 1942) and Paul Verhoeven (b. 1938) can glide back and forth between different countries—including the United States—without losing their authorial identities. *Antichrist* (2009), by Lars von Trier (b. 1956), was European-financed but shot in English; its leads were French and American. Yet between that and *Dogville* (2003), Von Trier had made *De fem benspænd* (*The Five Obstructions*, 2003) and *Direktøren for det hele* (*The Boss of it All*, 2006), the two films in his oeuvre most concerned with Denmark. Von Trier may be the epitome of this fluid approach to nationality and auteurism. Although he had produced an English-language film in 1996—*Breaking the Waves*—2000 saw the release of his first truly international venture, *Dancer in the Dark* (above). It starred Björk and won two awards at Cannes that year—including the

KEY EVENTS

2000	2004	2004	2005	2005	2006
Dancer in the Dark wins the Palme d'Or. Its funders include Denmark, Italy, Germany, the United States, the United Kingdom, and France.	Fatih Akin's German-Turkish *Gegen die Wand* raises questions regarding nation, immigration, and integration.	Signs of a sea change in Italian film come with Marco Bellocchio's *Buongiorno, notte* and Paolo Sorrentini's *Le consequenze dell'amore* (see p. 538).	*L'enfant*, by the Dardenne brothers, beats Michael Haneke's *Caché* (see p. 560) to the Palme d'Or, but the latter film does better commercially.	As a coproduction, *Caché* is ineligible for Oscar contention.	*Das Leben der Anderen* (see p. 540) causes controversy with its sensitive characterization of a Stasi officer.

Palme d'Or. More recently, Danish film *The Girl With the Dragon Tattoo* (2009, below), adapted by director Niels Arden Oplev (b. 1961) from the novel by fellow Scandinavian Stieg Larsson, proved a hit with critics and cinemagoers alike; a US adaptation was swiftly planned for 2011.

The two countries that had struggled to find a coherent cinematic identity in the 1980s and 1990s—Germany and Italy—gave birth to two very distinctive, if very divergent, film movements in the 2000s. From Germany came a series of high-budget films that were historical but by no means nostalgic, dominated by a concern with the country's conflicted past. Having directed the latter-day *Das Experiment* (2001), a contemporaneous look at Nazi-esque psychology, in 2004 Oliver Hirschbiegel (b. 1957) made *Der Untergang* (*Downfall*), which documented Hitler's last days. This was followed in 2005 by World War II drama *Sophie Scholl*, directed by Marc Rothemund (b. 1968). In 2003 Wolfgang Becker (b. 1954) took a witty look at the consequences of reunification in the fondly comic *Good Bye Lenin!* (right) and Uli Edel (b. 1947) turned to the 1970s and the terrorist actions of the Red Army Faction for *Der Baader Meinhof Komplex* in 2008. But it was Cold War surveillance drama *Das Leben der Anderen* (*The Lives of Others*, 2006, see p. 540), directed by Florian Henckel von Donnersmarck (b. 1973), that arguably defined German cinema in the 2000s. The film gained huge popularity worldwide and garnered an Oscar, but equally caused controversy with its extremely moving, sympathetic portrayal of a Stasi officer.

For proponents of these films, they marked a long overdue coming to terms by Germany's film industry with the Fascist past; opponents, on the other hand, declaimed them as cynical and insensitive attempts to cash in on it. The Austro-

DANIEL BRÜHL
KATRIN SASS

GOOD BYE
LENIN!

EIN FILM VON
WOLFGANG BECKER

www.79qmDDR.de

2006	2007	2007	2009	2009	2009
Rachid Bouchareb opens up questions of French nationalism and identity with *Indigènes*, an Algerian-French-Moroccan-Belgian production.	Romanian cinema emerges with the world release of *4 luni, 3 saptamâni si 2 zile* (*4 Months, 3 Weeks and 2 days*) by Cristian Mungiu (b. 1968).	*Das Leben der Anderen* wins a Best Foreign Language Film Oscar.	Michael Haneke finally wins the Palme d'Or for *Das weisse Band*, his first German-language film in more than a decade.	Michele Placido's *Il grande sogno* and Marco Bellocchio's *Vincere* are released.	Niels Arden Oplev's *The Girl With the Dragon Tattoo* is an international hit. Its accolades include two Guldbagge awards from Sweden.

Le conseguenze dell'amore 2004
The Consequences of Love   PAOLO SORRENTINO b. 1970

▲ A study of Di Girolamo (Toni Servillo) and the hotel barmaid Sofia (Olivia Magnani).

▼ Titta Di Girolamo, a man alone, on the poster for Sorrentino's psychological thriller.

The new millennium saw promise of a renaissance in Italian film, with one of the most gifted contemporary directors in the vanguard. Paolo Sorrentino is a visual stylist and unique storyteller and *Le conseguenze dell'amore* is his most beguiling film. An existential character study dressed as a Mafia drama (or vice versa), the film stars Toni Servillo as Titta Di Girolamo, a permanent resident of a Lugano hotel in Switzerland. Sorrentino allows viewers no knowledge of the man's life, other than the odd scraps of information passed to them through Di Girolamo's sparse voice-over. The film asks the audience to look beyond the surface banality of people's lives, to discover simmering emotions, past betrayals, failed dreams, and fading hopes. The air of detachment that Sorrentino creates underpins the journey that Di Girolamo takes, from a lack of concern for himself and the world around him to finally reaching out, at first to Sofia (Olivia Magnani), the beautiful hotel barmaid, then to other residents whose lives are shattered, but not beyond repair.

Le conseguenze dell'amore being called a Mafia film, albeit one of the most esoteric Mafia-related films ever made, is only justified in the film's last act. Sorrentino moves from a narrative with little action or drama to one that features a shootout, a car crash, and a prolonged, suspenseful confrontation with the head of the crime syndicate, without ever betraying the film's lugubrious mood. Then, as Di Girolamo faces his fate, Sorrentino extends his narrative, confronting the loneliness we all feel and the comfort and security that comes from knowing we may be cared for and thought about by others. **IHS**

KEY SCENES

1 AN INTRODUCTION
Di Girolamo introduces himself and proffers his opinion on another one of the hotel's permanent residents. In doing so, he succeeds in drawing attention away from his past and focusing instead on the banality of his present situation.

2 A SECRET REVEALED
Di Girolamo admits that for more than two decades he has injected himself with heroin at the same time every Wednesday. The scene is played out with the appearance—via a dream—of three clerical figures on the adjacent bed.

3 THE FIRST BANK VISIT
When a case appears in Di Girolamo's hotel room, the mystery surrounding his life in Lugano increases. He subsequently takes the case, which contains millions of US dollars, to be deposited in a bank.

4 THE HIT
The arrival of two "stock" gangster characters is the first concrete reference to the world that Di Girolamo may have come from (or may still be involved in)—although in what capacity remains unclear. The killings suggest that Di Girolamo may not be in Lugano by choice.

5 A DISHONORABLE DEATH
Unwilling to play by the Mafia's rules anymore, Di Girolamo pays the ultimate price for his actions. But his sacrifice sees him become human once more, his act (theft) benefiting those in need and his last thoughts about others in the world rather than himself.

DIRECTOR PROFILE

1970–2003
Paolo Sorrentino was born in Naples in 1970. His first feature script, *Polvere di Napoli* (1998), was directed by Antonio Capuano (b. 1940). Sorrentino followed it with the short films *L'amore non ha confini* (1998) and *La notte lunga* (2001). His feature debut was *L'uomo in più* (*One Man Up*, 2001).

2004–present
Sorrentino achieved international recognition with *Le conseguenze dell'amore*, which was nominated for the Palme d'Or at the Cannes Film Festival. *L'amico di famiglia* (*The Family Friend*, 2006) was a character study of a misanthropic moneylender. After the portmanteau documentary *Napoli 24* (2010), Sorrentino embarked on his first English-language film—*This Must Be the Place* (2011, working title), starring Sean Penn as a fading rock star who sets out to find the Nazi officer responsible for his father's death in Auschwitz.

Das Leben der Anderen 2006
The Lives of Others   FLORIAN HENCKEL VON DONNERSMARCK b. 1973

▲ The East German actor Ulrich Mühe
plays Stasi surveillance officer Wiesler.

▼ On the poster Wiesler appears as a
disembodied voyeur in the shadows.

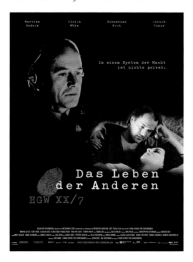

Florian Henckel von Donnersmarck's *Das Leben der Anderen* is one of
the few post-reunification films to acknowledge the nightmarishness
of life in Communist East Germany. The Stasi, the army of a hundred
thousand state-trained spies, investigated every aspect of the lives of their
fellow citizens, and this film attempts to illustrate frankly the devastating
effects of a surveillance society run mad.

Despite the dour settings, the director was determined to make a film
with sweep and emotional impact. He researched the film extensively,
speaking both to Stasi victims and to members of the secret police. The
re-creation of 1980s East Berlin in all its gray oppression was meticulous.
"This small state had its own world of colors and forms," the director later
said. "Almost every piece of furniture was angular, sharp-cornered, and thin.
The colors, whether of cars or textiles, were curiously pale and desaturated."

Stasi spy Wiesler (Ulrich Mühe) becomes obsessed by the richness of the
life of the writer he is shadowing. Dreyman (Sebastian Koch), a seemingly
model playwright about whom the state is suspicious, is a passionate man,
enthused by literature, music, and ideas. Slowly, Wiesler begins to realize how
squalid his own existence as state-licensed eavesdropper and voyeur is by
comparison. Wiesler is the loyal party man who "turns"—the cunning, low-
minded apparatchik who discovers he has a soul after all. Mühe, who had
himself been under Stasi surveillance, plays Wiesler brilliantly, conveying
both self-loathing and nobility. **GM**

👁 KEY SCENES

1 BREAKING A SUSPECT
Wiesler gives a masterclass. Sit the suspect down, question him relentlessly, deny him sleep. An innocent prisoner will shout and rage, but a guilty prisoner will calmly repeat his prepared lies. Threaten to arrest his wife and put his kids into state care. Then he will talk.

2 LENIN'S WEAKNESS
Von Donnersmarck's original inspiration for the film came from a remark Lenin made about Beethoven's *Apassionata Sonata*: "If I keep listening to it, I won't finish the revolution." When Wiesler hears Dreyman playing classical music, he too begins to waver.

3 SEEING OURSELVES AS OTHERS SEE US
Wiesler is startled when an angelic child tells him his father says the Stasi are "bad men who put people in prison." He begins to ask for the boy's father's name, but does not finish the question. Wiesler is starting to doubt what the Stasi are doing.

4 THE STASI ERA IS OVER
The Berlin Wall has come down and playwright Dreyman is able to consult his Stasi files and find out who protected him all those years ago—none other than the Stasi spy Wiesler. The film's final scene packs a powerful emotional punch.

🕑 DIRECTOR PROFILE

1973–90
Florian Henckel von Donnersmarck was born in Cologne, West Germany. His mother was East German, his father, from an aristocratic background, worked as a senior manager at the airline Lufthansa. He had an international upbringing, spending various parts of his childhood in New York, Berlin, and Brussels.

1991–96
He studied Russian literature in Leningrad for two years and then moved to England. While studying politics, philosophy and economics at Oxford University, he won a competition set up by visiting teacher Richard Attenborough (b. 1923) to become an intern on Attenborough's new film *In Love and War* (1996).

1997–2005
While at the Munich Film School he began to direct short films. His short film *Dobermann* (1999)—on which he served as writer, director, producer, and editor—broke records for awards garnered by a student production and was feted on the international festival circuit.

2006–7
Das Leben der Anderen—Von Donnersmarck's debut feature—was made on a small budget, with no distributor attached and the cast having to defer their fees. Eventually, Buena Vista took the German rights. The film became a runaway success in Germany, secured a number of international film awards, and went on to win an Oscar for Best Foreign Language Film. Amid the near universal praise, ex-Stasi members offered perhaps the only dissenting voices, insisting that they had "only been following orders." The film's lead actor Ulrich Mühe died of stomach cancer in 2007.

2008–present
Production began on Von Donnersmarck's second feature, *The Tourist*, for which he also cowrote the screenplay. It is a remake of the French romance thriller *Anthony Zimmer* (2005) and stars Johnny Depp and Angelina Jolie.

BOLLYWOOD

The origin of the term "Bollywood"—combining the Hindi-language film industry based in what was then Bombay with "Hollywood"—dates back to the 1970s. Many of the industry's stars—including the biggest of them all, Amitabh Bachchan—abhor the usage, preferring instead to replace it with "Indian film industry." However, Bachchan is wrong. Although in the West "Bollywood" remains synonymous with Indian cinema, in truth Bollywood is merely a fraction of the vast ocean that is the Indian film industry. Bollywood produces a mere quarter of the thousand-odd films that India produces annually. The South Indian film industry (comprising the Tamil, Telugu, Malayalam, and Kannada language industries) accounts for more than 75 percent of all Indian film production and revenues, according to an Ernst & Young report in 2009, with Tamil and Telugu film production rivaling if not surpassing Bollywood. Nonetheless, even though Bombay is now Mumbai and Hindi cinema, while made in India's national language, is not representative of the country as a whole, Bollywood remains India's most visible and celebrated film export. Today Bollywood movies are more accessible to international audiences than they were a decade ago thanks to their cross-cultural appeal outside the Indian diaspora.

The first Indian film to enter the UK Top 10 box-office charts, *Dil se* (1998, left) directed by Mani Ratnam (b. 1956), starred then superstar in the making Shah Rukh Khan. It also featured chartbusting music by A. R. Rahman, who would go on to win a BAFTA and a brace of Oscars and Grammys a decade

1995	1998	2000	2001	2001	2002
Dilwale dulhania le jayenge scores with the South Asian diaspora, paving the way for many more such NRI films.	*Dil se* becomes the first Bollywood film to enter the UK Top 10.	*Kaho naa...pyaar hai* launches director Roshan's son Hrithik as a superstar alternative to the Shah Rukh, Aamir, and Salman Khan triumvirate.	*Lagaan: Once Upon a Time in India* is released. *Dil chahta hai* generates a wave of films aimed solely at urban audiences.	*Asoka* wins international acclaim. *Kabhi khushi kabhie gham* debuts at No. 3 in the United Kingdom, the highest placing for an Indian film.	*Devdas* is a hit across Europe and is nominated for a BAFTA in 2003.

later for *Slumdog Millionaire* (2008) by Danny Boyle (b. 1956). During the 2000s the Hindi film industry moved away from the staple song-and-dance romantic melodramas and gore-soaked revenge dramas of the preceding two decades. Some of the biggest hits of the decade were Non-Resident Indian (NRI) romances—films featuring protagonists who lived in foreign cities, such as London or New York, yet espoused Indian moral values. These films, dear to first-generation Indian immigrants living in the United Kingdom and United States, owe their box-office successes as much to the Indian domestic market as to the NRI viewers buying tickets in pounds and dollars. *Kabhi khushi kabhie gham* (2001, opposite) directed by Karan Johar (b. 1972), and *Kal ho naa ho* (2003, below) directed by Nikhil Advani (b. 1971) were two of the most successful NRI films.

Although films were increasingly set in India, the thirst of audiences for watching foreign locales, pioneered by Raj Kapoor (1924–88) in *Sangam* (1964), meant that many of the successes of the decade include at least a few song-and-dance sequences shot elsewhere in the world. The two major hits of 2000, *Kaho naa...pyaar hai* and *Mohabbatein* (*Love Stories*), both featured extensive shooting outside India. The former, although a standard issue, all-singing all-dancing potboiler shot largely in New Zealand by actor turned director Rakesh Roshan (b. 1949), introduced his son Hrithik Roshan as a viable heroic alternative in an industry otherwise dominated by the Khans—Shah Rukh, Aamir, and Salman. The film *Kaho naa...pyaar hai* was also responsible for New Zealand becoming a tourist destination for well-heeled Indians, something that veteran producer-director Yash Chopra (b. 1932) acheived for Switzerland

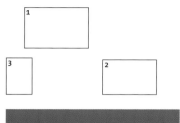

1 Kareena Kapoor (center) in the midst of a spectacular dance sequence in the generational romance drama *Kabhi khushi kabhie gham*.

2 Saif Ali Khan (front and center) in *Kal ho naa ho*. The film was a critical and financial success, gaining many awards and nominations at the International Indian Film Academy Awards.

3 A suitably sweeping and romantic poster for *Dil se*, starring Shah Rukh Khan and Manisha Koirala.

2004	2006	2007	2008	2009	2010
Main hoon naa marks the debut of choreographer Farah Khan (b. 1965) as a rarity—a female director in Bollywood.	*Krrish*, directed by Rakesh Roshan, becomes modern Bollywood's first superhero film.	Retro comedy drama *Om shanti om* is another huge hit for Shah Rukh Khan. Rakesh Mehra's *Rang de basanti* wins a BAFTA nomination.	*Singh is kinng* sees the rise of Akshay Kumar as a rival to the Khans and Roshan. *Dostana* becomes Bollywood's first mainstream, gay-themed film.	*Ajab prem ki ghazab kahani* launches Ranbir Kapoor as the star for the next decade.	*Udaan* is a surprise box-office hit and is also India's first Cannes Film Festival selection in sixteen years.

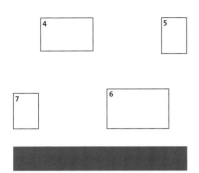

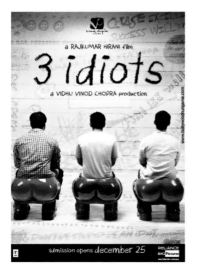

4 Aamir Khan in *Rang de basanti*. The film was controversial and provoked scrutiny from the Indian censor board.

5 The poster for *Love, sex aur dhokha*. This critically well-received film is a satire about media consumption.

6 *Peepli Live* is a comic satire, a comment on contemporary society, and was the first Indian film to compete at the Sundance Film Festival.

7 *3 Idiots* was a box-office hit, although it created controversy for its relation to the source novel *Five Point Someone*.

by using it as a location in several of his films from the 1970s to the present day. Unusually for Bollywood, *Mohabbatein*, directed by Chopra's son Aditya (b. 1971), is set entirely in a school (in India but filmed in the United Kingdom), and for the first time pitted current superstar Shah Rukh Khan as a crusader for young love against a stern headmaster, played by the superstar of an earlier generation, Amitabh Bachchan. The pair appeared together throughout the decade in a string of hits, notably in *Kabhi khushi kabhie gham*, where Khan played an estranged son facing up to his stern father played by Bachchan.

The following year saw the release of several films that greatly influenced the Bollywood industry throughout the next decade. A four-hour epic about cricket set during the British Raj in the 1890s, *Lagaan: Once Upon a Time in India* (2001, see p. 548) initially attracted no backers. Cricket-themed films had not fared well at the box office, despite the game's huge popularity on the subcontinent. Eventually, the film's star Aamir Khan decided to take the gamble and produce it himself. The film, which was directed by Ashutosh Gowariker (b. 1964), became a massive hit and gained an Academy Award nomination for Best Foreign Language Film.

The lesson Aamir Khan—renowned as a romantic hero throughout the 1990s—took from *Lagaan: Once Upon a Time in India* was to take on fewer films as an actor, choosing only those subjects that eschewed the usual Bollywood formula, and produce films that were offbeat. His new mantra resulted in films such as *3 Idiots* (2009, left), directed by Rajkumar Hirani (b. 1962), which challenged the Indian educational system and became Bollywood's highest-grossing film of all time; his own *Taare zameen par* (*Like Stars on Earth*, 2007), which looked at dyslexia; *Rang de basanti* (2006, above) by Rakeysh Mehra (b. 1963), which focuses on dissatisfaction among India's youth; and the debut by Anusha Rizvi (b. 1978), *Peepli Live* (2010, opposite), which skewered India's byte-hungry electronic media while at the same time highlighting the country's endemic issue of suicide among farmers. The film became a box-office success without Khan's or any other recognized star's presence in front of the camera.

Dil chahta hai (*D.C.H./Do Your Thing*), directed by Farhan Akhtar (b. 1974) and starring Aamir Khan and Saif Ali Khan, was also released in 2001. The film centers on the lives of three male friends and was remarkable as one of the first to cater unabashedly to an urban audience. Previously Bollywood had produced "pan-India" films, movies with something for everyone, from a corporate high-flyer to a housewife to a taxi driver. Akhtar recognized that the highest income would be generated in the burgeoning urban multiplex culture where people would pay far higher ticket prices to sit in air-conditioned luxury and watch movies about people like themselves. This paved the way for a boom in city-themed films and, inevitably, to the rise of young directors who had different, nonformulaic stories to tell.

In the vanguard of this movement were directors Anurag Kashyap (b. 1972) and Dibakar Banerjee (b. 1969) who, despite working within the Bollywood system, told stunningly different stories produced on a micro-budget. Banerjee's debut *Khosla ka ghosla!* (*Khosla's Nest*, 2006) concerned an ordinary family dealing with Delhi land-grabbers, while *Love, sex aur dhokha* (*Love, Sex and Deceit*, 2010, right) explores the emotions of love, sex, and betrayal as seen through handycams, spycams, mobile cameras, and security cameras. Kashyap's *Dev.D* (2009) takes the classic, oft-filmed love triangle novel *Devdas* and turns it into a sex- and drugs-drenched descent into hell.

The usual staple melodramas and action films continued to be produced by Bollywood. Shah Rukh Khan appeared in a number of these, such as *Main hoon naa*, *Veer-zaara* (both 2004), and *Kabhi alvida naa kehna* (2006), consolidating his superstar position. However, audiences rejected him when he tried to play offbeat characters in films such as *Asoka* (2001, see p. 546) and *Paheli* (2005). The former was a largely fictional, historical drama about the life of the ancient Indian emperor Asoka the Great (Khan), who converted to Buddhism, and was directed by Santosh Sivan (b. 1961). Jingoism was also seen to be alive and well, with slogan-spewing action hero Sunny Deol walking into Pakistan and taking on the entire army while saving his kidnapped wife and son in *Gadar: ek prem katha* (*Mutiny: A Love Story*, 2001).

The 2000s witnessed a sharp upswing in Bollywood comedies catering to India's large youthful population. However, it was the transformation of erstwhile action hero Akshay Kumar into a full-blown comic star that took the industry by surprise. He appeared in a string of broad, loud comedies that harked back to the "everything but the kitchen sink" films of earlier decades: *Namastey London*, *Heyy babyy*, *Bhool bhulaiyaa* (*Maze*), *Welcome* (all 2007), *Singh is kinng* (2008), *Kambakkht ishq* (*Incredible Love*, 2009), and *Housefull* (2010) were all massive successes, proving that there continues to be a significant market for old-fashioned Bollywood. **NR**

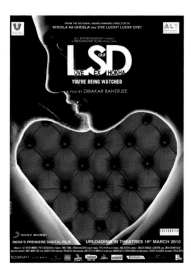

Asoka 2001

SANTOSH SIVAN b. 1961

▲ Superstar Shah Rukh Khan in the brooding and troubled role of Asoka.

▼ The poster for the historical epic.

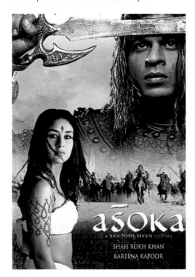

Ace cinematographer Santosh Sivan won international acclaim with his third directorial venture *Theeviravaathi: The Terrorist* (1998) about a female suicide bomber. His follow-up, *Asoka*, could not be more different in theme and style as Sivan shifts gear to create a grand historical spectacle that recounts the story of the young and bloodthirsty eponymous third-century BCE monarch.

Sivan's fictitious account of Asoka's early years has leading man and producer Shah Rukh Khan playing the Mauryan dynasty prince, the heir to the throne of Magadha. When the battle for the throne turns bloody, Asoka's mother persuades him to go into exile as a commoner for his own safety. He meets the fugitive princess from Kalinga, Kaurwaki, and they fall in love. Ensuing events lead Asoka to believe that Kaurwaki is dead and he returns to Magadha and marries the Buddhist girl Devi. Asoka begins to ruthlessly eliminate his enemies, including his brother, and assumes power. His final bloody act is to unify the disputed lands surrounding the kingdom.

Sivan creates a film that is bursting with stunning imagery and is at the same time a powerful fable about the folly of violence. The battle scenes in particular are equal to any that Western cinema has produced, all achieved without the aid of special effects. Curiously, the film was labeled a flop, although with a budget of just more than $3 million (a high figure in India in 2001) it went on to gross more than $12 million worldwide, the bulk of its revenues coming from its home country. **NR**

◉ KEY SCENES

1 THE SEED IS SOWN
The young boy Asoka practices with the sword that his pacifist father had thrown away and he has retrieved. Legend states that the sword craves blood. Asoka throws the sword in the air, killing a nestful of birds.

2 A GLIMPSE OF HIS PROWESS
Asoka demonstrates his skill in the ancient Indian martial art of *kalaripayattu*, wielding the sinuous Urumi sword to bring down his attackers. The prince thrives on victory and shows himself to be a formidable opponent.

3 ENTER THE WOMAN
Asoka spots and is entranced by Kaurwaki bathing. Little does he know she is the runaway princess of Kalinga. Despite coming from rival families, the two fall in love and when she is attacked by soldiers he defends her.

4 NUMBING LOSS
After being tricked back to his kingdom by his manipulative mother, Asoka returns to search for Kaurwaki. He is mistakenly told she has been killed in a fire and he smears ash on his face. In his grief, he begins a campaign of mindless violence.

5 REMORSE
Asoka sees the violence he has wreaked and is struck by remorse. He walks through the sea of bodies and finds a dying Kaurwaki. Devastated by this discovery and all the bloodshed, he renounces violence and decides to preach pacifism and the Buddhist faith.

◷ STAR PROFILE: SHAH RUKH KHAN

1965–91
Shah Rukh Khan was born in New Delhi, India, into a middle-class Muslim family. After working in Delhi theater, he made his television debut in 1988 with *Fauji*. In 1991 he moved to Mumbai and married the Hindu Gauri Chibber.

1992–97
His first two features were *Deewana* (*Crazy*) and *Raju ban gaya gentleman* (both 1992). *Dilwale Dulhania Le Jayenge* (1995) established him as Bollywood's most popular hero.

1998–present
Kuch kuch hota hai (*Something Is Happening*, 1998) marked the beginning of his association with director Karan Johar (b. 1972). *Kabhi khushi kabhie gham* (2001) debuted in the United Kingdom at No. 3. In 2007 he replaced Amitabh Bachchan as host of the Indian version of *Who Wants to Be A Millionaire?*.

Lagaan: Once Upon a Time in India 2001
ASHUTOSH GOWARIKER b. 1964

▲ Actors Aamir Khan and Gracy Singh in the lead roles of Bhuvan and Gauri.

▼ *Lagaan* was nominated for the Best Foreign Language Film Academy Award.

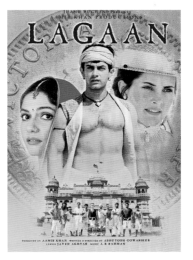

Actor turned director Ashutosh Gowariker's *Lagaan: Once Upon a Time in India*, produced by its star Aamir Khan, is an Asterix-like fable about the people of a small village in India during the British Raj uniting to beat their colonial masters at their own game: cricket. Although cricket is immensely popular on the subcontinent, cricket-themed films such as *Kabhi ajnabi the* (1985), featuring members of India's World Cup-winning team of 1983, and *Awwal number* (1990) had failed at the box office. Gowariker's film was therefore a risky and expensive proposition—especially given that it was a period piece. However, Gowariker and Khan assembled an experienced team including cinematographer Anil Mehta and composer A. R. Rahman, shooting the film on location in the sandy reaches of the western state of Gujarat.

The film centers on the villagers of Champaner, who cannot pay the steep British land tax because they are suffering from a drought. The upright villager Bhuvan (Khan) witnesses a cricket match being played by the British, led by Captain Russell (Paul Blackthorne), and mocks it. An enraged Russell challenges Bhuvan to a game of cricket on condition that if the Indians win their taxes will be waived for three years, but if they lose they must pay three times the normal amount. Helped by Russell's sister Elizabeth (Rachel Shelley), who has a crush on Bhuvan, the villagers prepare for the big game—leading to a fairy-tale finish.

Khan's gamble paid off handsomely at the box office. *Lagaan: Once Upon a Time in India* was made for $5.5 million (expensive for a Bollywood film at the time) and collected $45 million worldwide. **NR**

⊙ KEY SCENES

1 FALSE HOPE
In the drought-hit village, the villagers spot distant rain clouds and sing and dance in anticipatory celebration, only for their hopes to be dashed when the clouds move away. Their crops will dry up and they will have no means of paying the *lagaan* (land tax).

2 THROWING DOWN THE GAUNTLET
Captain Russell challenges Bhuvan to a high-stakes game of cricket. Bhuvan accepts. The malnourished, ill-equipped, barefoot villagers must compete against their sleek, well-shod masters. The future of the village hangs in the balance.

3 DIVINE INTERVENTION
With the British ahead and India's numbers dwindling, the villagers are on the verge of losing the cricket match. In a moving scene, Bhuvan's mother leads the village in a prayer song that builds up to a rousing finale. It now all depends on the gods.

4 THE WINNING MOMENT
The last hour of the film follows the agony and the ecstasy of the match. It is closely fought until Bhuvan hits the final ball of the match into the air. Captain Russell catches it, only to realize that he has crossed the boundary. It is a six, giving the villagers their victory.

⟳ DIRECTOR PROFILE

1964–92
Ashutosh Gowariker was born in Mumbai, India, into a middle-class family. He began his career in entertainment modeling in television commercials. He first worked as an actor in *Holi* (1984), which was directed by Ketan Mehta (b. 1952). Over the next decade he starred in numerous television shows, as well as films including *Naam* (1986) and *Chamatkar* (1992).

1993–95
Gowariker acted in *Kabhi haan kabhi naa* and directed his first feature film *Pehla nasha* (both 1993) about a struggling actor who gets drawn into a murder investigation. Inspired by *Body Double* (1984) directed by Brian De Palma (b. 1940), it is notable for being the last occasion when Shah Rukh Khan, Aamir Khan, and Saif Ali Khan appeared together in the same film. The film was not a success at the box office. Gowariker's second feature, *Baazi* (1995), was a drama, again starring Aamir Khan. It also failed at the box office.

1996–2000
His various acting roles during this time included *Sarkarnama* (1998) and two television series—the acclaimed *Woh* (1998) and *C.I.D.* (1998–99).

2001–7
Gowariker returned to directing and Aamir Khan agreed to produce and act in the director's most successful film to date *Lagaan: Once Upon a Time in India*. Gowariker followed this in 2004 with *Swades: We, the People*, starring Shah Rukh Khan, which was admired by the critics.

2008–present
After a four-year hiatus he returned to directing with the historical epic *Jodhaa akbar* (2008), starring box-office draws Hrithik Roshan and Aishwarya Rai. The film was well received. In 2009 he released the romantic comedy *What's Your Raashee?* It stalled at the box office. He returned to period films in 2010 with *Khelein hum jee jaan sey* and began pre-production on a mega-budget biopic of the Buddha.

POST 9/11 US DRAMA

1 Edward Norton and Barry Pepper in *25th Hour*. The film was based on the novel by David Benioff and its message was updated in the wake of 9/11.

2 The moody poster for Steven Spielberg's dark and allegorical *Munich*. The Israeli operations portrayed in the film are known as Operation Wrath of God.

3 Daniel Day-Lewis won an Academy Award for his searing performance in *There Will Be Blood*.

In the aftermath of the terrorist attacks in 2001, there were visible signs of soul-searching in US cinema. Spike Lee (b. 1957) responded with the heartfelt *25th Hour* (2002, above). Focusing on the final day of freedom for a man about to be sent to prison, the film is a love letter to Lee's beloved New York, as well as a study of consequences and responsibility. The dramatic reenactments of what took place on September 11 were dominated by the harrowing *United 93* (2006) by Paul Greengrass (b. 1955); *World Trade Center* (2006) by Oliver Stone (b. 1946) incurred criticism from all sides. Stone was also criticized for his George W. Bush biopic, *W.* (2008). Although far from the damning indictment some had hoped for, Stone's aim could be seen as more ambitious, questioning how the system could allow such a man to reach the Oval Office.

The ensuing conflicts in Afghanistan and Iraq were dealt with in a variety of films, but even with the presence of major stars, *Syriana* (2005), *Good Night, and Good Luck* (2005)—a clever allusion to the McCarthy witch hunts that was reflected in the Bush administration's "either you're with us or against us" rhetoric—*Home of the Brave* (2006), *In the Valley of Elah*, *Grace Is Gone* (both 2007), and *Stop-Loss* (2008) all failed to attract large audiences. The Oscar-winning *The Hurt Locker* (2008, see p. 554) could be read as an endorsement of either right- or left-wing attitudes to the conflict in Iraq. Ridley Scott (b. 1937) weighed in with *Body of Lies* (2008), an old-fashioned thriller updated to

KEY EVENTS

2001	2001	2002	2003	2003	2004
Terrorists attack the World Trade Center and Pentagon on September 11. The Twin Towers are removed from posters for *Spider-Man* (2002).	Woody Allen (b. 1935) makes his first appearance at an Academy Awards ceremony as a show of unity following 9/11.	Action thriller *The Sum of All Fears* depicts a nuclear bomb attack on Baltimore.	Operation Iraqi Freedom begins when US and allied forces invade Iraq.	*House of Sand and Fog* becomes one of the first films to deal with cultural differences in the light of 9/11.	M. Night Shyamalan (b. 1970) calls the United States a sheltered community in historical drama *The Village*.

explore the CIA's current overseas dealings, while David Cronenberg (b. 1943) reminded audiences in 2005 of homegrown evil and the darkness lurking in everyday lives with the classy *A History of Violence* (see p. 552).

Blockbusters by Steven Spielberg (b. 1946), such as *Minority Report* (2002) and *War of the Worlds* (2005)—the apocalyptic early scenes of which recalled Manhattan immediately after the airplane attacks—were no longer so different from his more "serious" work. If *AI: Artificial Intelligence* (2001) divided audiences and critics concerning its quality, the debate over *Munich* (2005, right) played out in the political arena. Whatever dissatisfaction there was about the film's message, which inflamed both pro- and anti-Israel factions, Spielberg and writer Tony Kushner's account of the Mossad agents hunting down those responsible for the massacre at the Olympics in 1972 is powerful cinema. The film raises questions about retaliation and draws parallels to the attack on the World Trade Center and the US government's response to it.

In the wake of 9/11 filmmakers found themselves looking back at US history and the roots of the national psyche. Paul Thomas Anderson (b. 1970) directed *There Will Be Blood* (2007, below) and drove home the message that many contemporary films had explored during the Bush administration—that power corrupts and engenders paranoia and fear in those who exploit it. With *Gangs of New York* (2002) and *The Aviator* (2004), Martin Scorsese (b. 1942) examined the birth of the modern United States—capitalism, the racial divide, and, in the characters of the brutal Bill the Butcher and the unstable millionaire Howard Hughes, the dangers of greed and isolationism. **IHS**

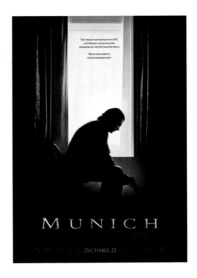

2004	2006	2007	2007	2008	2008
Michael Moore (b. 1954) releases his biting study of the War on Terror and George W. Bush's presidency, *Fahrenheit 9/11*.	*Brokeback Mountain* (2005) is widely acclaimed and controversy erupts when it loses the Best Film Oscar to the racial drama *Crash* (2004).	Martin Scorsese finally wins an Oscar, for *The Departed*. *There Will Be Blood* confirms Paul Thomas Anderson as an important director.	*No Country for Old Men*, by Joel (b. 1954) and Ethan (b. 1957) Coen, reflects on changing times and the cycle of violence.	Gus Van Sant (b. 1952) examines inequality and social politics in the biopic *Milk*.	Matt Reeves (b. 1966) depicts an attack on New York in monster movie *Cloverfield*.

A History of Violence 2005

DAVID CRONENBERG b. 1943

▲ Tom's violent past catches up with him.

▼ The film was based on John Wagner and Vince Locke's graphic novel.

Canadian director David Cronenberg is generally associated with a subgenre of cinema that he virtually created—the viscerally graphic "body horror." However, *A History of Violence* offers a subtler, more philosophical inquiry into humanity's atavistic inner nature. This elegant, controlled drama is set in an archetypal US small town, where Tom Stall (Viggo Mortensen) runs a diner. When a couple of hoodlums start trouble, Tom defends his territory with startling decisiveness.

This quiet-spoken family man is hailed as an "American hero," but the exposure attracts a mobster (Ed Harris), who wants revenge on the man he recognizes as Joey Cusack. Tom, it turns out, has a previous life as a violent Philadelphia criminal: "Tom Stall" is an identity that he has invented, and, once unearthed, Tom/Joey's violent past affects his wife Edie (Maria Bello) and family.

The film is not without Cronenberg's trademark extremity—grisly makeup effects are used sparingly to show the reality of violence. Yet the film is unusually subtle and contemplative for a thriller—concise, slow paced, and built as much on domestic drama as on action. The drama's emotional core lies in Tom's changing relationship with Edie, and is mapped around two very differently inflected sex scenes, before and after she discovers his secret.

Intensely intelligent, the film constantly tests the viewer's attitude to violence. It stands very much as a critique of US society, questioning the accepted understanding that it is every individual's right to keep the peace in their own home, through gun-related violence if necessary. **JR**

👁 KEY SCENES

1 THE SETUP
The nature of violence is established in a slow-burning scene that begins under the opening credits. Two hoodlums check out of a motel, and the audience sees the damage they do. Two extended shots lead to a shocking—but calmly presented—payoff.

3 THE MOMENT OF TRUTH
Edie confronts Tom having discovered that he is not the man she married. This scene offers borderline-humorous mundanity ("You didn't grow up in Portland," Edie realizes), and captures the film's melding of reassuring everyday reality with hard-boiled thriller.

2 THE SHOWDOWN
The hoodlums (Stephen McHattie and Greg Bryk) arrive at Tom's diner at closing time and start throwing their weight around. When the interlopers physically menace the diner waitress, Tom responds with lightning speed and deadly accuracy, killing both men.

4 THE BROTHERS MEET
Joey confronts his past when he visits the Philadelphia mansion of his gangster brother Richie (a scene-stealing William Hurt). At first affable and affectionate, Richie soon reveals that he wants payback for the damage that Joey has done to his criminal career.

WESTERN-THRILLER HYBRIDS

Ostensibly a modern-day thriller, *A History of Violence* is also a cross-genre hybrid, with its roots in the Western. Mortensen's taciturn man of mystery is modeled on the noble tight-lipped Western hero exemplified by Gary Cooper. The film can be seen as a contemporary variant on *Unforgiven* (1992) by Clint Eastwood (b. 1930), another story of a reformed man forced to embrace violence one last time. The long tradition of Western-thriller crossovers includes the modern-day crime story in a Western setting *Bad Day at Black Rock* (1955), the hugely influential *Bring Me the Head of Alfredo Garcia* (1974), and *No Country for Old Men* (2007, right), a bleak parable of the uncontainable nature of violence and something of a companion piece to Cronenberg's film.

The Hurt Locker 2008

KATHRYN BIGELOW b. 1951

▲ The film's biggest "name" actor, Guy Pearce, appears only in a cameo role.

▼ The film's poster is gritty and textured.

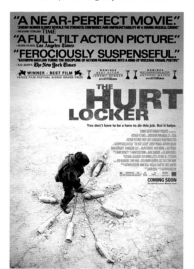

Set in Iraq in 2004, Kathryn Bigelow's *The Hurt Locker* focuses on the work of a three-man US Army bomb squad. When the sergeant in charge (a brief cameo from Guy Pearce) is killed by a roadside bomb, a new disposal expert, Sgt. William James (Jeremy Renner), comes in to replace him. His two colleagues soon realize that James, although instinctively brilliant at his job, is a reckless wild card, high on adrenaline and endangering them all. Their company is nearing the end of its tour of duty and an on-screen countdown of days heightens the suspense.

The Hurt Locker opens with a quote from *The New York Times* war correspondent Chris Hedges: "The rush of battle is often a potent and lethal addiction, for war is a drug." Unlike other Iraq movies, *The Hurt Locker* passes no comment on the rightness or otherwise of the US-led invasion. Bigelow, who insisted on shooting in Jordan near the Iraqi border, rather than in Morocco, South Africa, or other less logistically problematic locations, simply aims, with visceral immediacy, to get viewers inside the heads of soldiers operating with that degree of danger in grueling, always potentially hostile terrain.

From the outset of her career Bigelow has shown a fascination with the testosterone-fueled world of masculinity and violence, always tempered by a certain ironic critical distance. As ever, her action sequences are textbook examples of clarity, pace, timing, and gut-churning tension. The nearest hint of a political comment comes when James arrives at what he thinks is Camp Liberty, to be told it has been renamed Camp Victory because "it sounds better." **PK**

KEY SCENES

1 DEATH OF SGT. THOMPSON
The film is set in Baghdad in 2004, after the invasion of Iraq by US-led forces. The catalyst for the action is the demise of Sgt. Thompson (Guy Pearce), who, when trying to defuse a bomb, is blown up by a booby trap improvised explosive device (IED).

2 SIX TIMES THE DANGER
Thompson's successor, the obsessive, driven Sgt. James, finds that what he thought was one IED is in fact six. Bigelow has commented about the film: "War's dirty little secret is that some men love it. I'm trying to unpack why, to look at what it means to be a hero."

3 UNDER FIRE IN THE DESERT
Sgt. James's team comes across a group of British contractors in the desert. Both groups come under attack from hostile Iraqis. The scene is a frantic, chaotic firefight with the handheld camerawork perfectly capturing the unpredictable nature of warfare.

4 FORCED SUICIDE BOMBER
An Iraqi who has a bomb padlocked to him begs the bomb squad to save him. The squad debates over whether it is worth trying to help ("Can't we just shoot him?") before Sgt. James attempts to remove the device. He fails and the man dies.

DIRECTOR PROFILE

1951–81
Kathryn Bigelow was born in San Carlos, California, to a prosperous, middle-class family. She studied painting at the San Francisco Art Institute, and, at age nineteen, won a scholarship to the Whitney Museum in New York. During her time there she became active in the city's avant-garde art scene. Increasingly drawn to cinema, Bigelow enrolled at Columbia University's Graduate School of Film. In 1978 she made her graduate film, the seventeen-minute study of violence, *The Set-Up*.

1982–94
Bigelow co directed her debut feature with Monty Montgomery (b. 1963), and the result, *The Loveless* (1982), is a biker movie that subverts genre expectations. She followed it with a series of genre-bending films: *Near Dark* (1987), a vampire Western; *Blue Steel* (1989), a police drama with horror movie elements; and *Point Break* (1991), a heist thriller crossed with a surfing movie. The latter film particularly had a lasting legacy, influencing such action films as *The Fast and the Furious* (2001) and homages such as *Hot Fuzz* (2007). From 1989 to 1991 she was married to James Cameron (b. 1954). By the early 1990s Bigelow had established herself as one of Hollywood's few female top action directors.

1995–2002
The failure of her ambitious, complex, futuristic drama *Strange Days* (1995) badly dented her career. Her long-planned Joan of Arc movie, *The Company of Angels*, was taken away from her by its producer, Luc Besson (b. 1959), who directed it as *Joan of Arc* (1999). Her next two films, the period drama *The Weight of Water* (2000) and the mega-budget submarine drama *K19: The Widowmaker* (2002), both flopped.

2003–present
After six years in the wilderness, she directed *The Hurt Locker*, which took the top prize at the Venice Film Festival and won six Oscars, including Best Picture and Best Director—making Bigelow the first woman to win a Best Director Oscar.

POSTMILLENNIAL FRENCH CINEMA

1 Ludivine Sagnier, Virginie Ledoyen, Catherine Deneuve, Danielle Darrieux, Isabelle Huppert, Firmine Richard, and Emmanuelle Béart are seven of the titular *8 femmes* (*8 Women*).

2 *La môme* features an Oscar-winning performance by Marion Cotillard as singer Edith Piaf.

3 Mathieu Amalric and Marie-Josee Croze star in the award-winning *The Diving Bell and the Butterfly*, an adaptation of Jean-Dominique Bauby's powerful and moving memoir.

uring the first decade of the twenty-first century the French film industry appeared to be in crisis, with radical funding cuts in both the private and public sectors. Despite this, the period produced some of the most successful movies—at home and abroad—since the heritage film boom of the late 1980s. The films released have been eclectic in nature. François Ozon (b. 1967) combined generic pastiches such as the musical *8 femmes* (*8 Women*, 2002, above) with intimate character studies, including *Sous le sable* (*Under the Sand*, 2000) and *5x2* (2005). Christophe Honoré (b. 1970) moved from the incestuous Bataille adaptation *Ma mère* (*My Mother*, 2004) to a chirpy piece of modern-day nouvelle vaguerie, *Dans Paris* (*Inside Paris*, 2006), whereas Laurent Cantet (b. 1961) veered from an examination of female sex tourists in Haiti starring Charlotte Rampling, *Vers le sud* (*Heading South*, 2005), to the thought-provoking schoolroom drama *Entre les murs* (*The Class*, 2008).

Most of the decade's export successes embraced ciné-tourism, rehearsing clichés about Frenchness. The apotheoses of this tradition were *Le fabuleux destin d'Amélie Poulain* (*Amélie*, 2001, see p. 558) and *Un long dimanche de fiançailles* (*A Very Long Engagement*, 2004), films directed by Jean-Pierre Jeunet (b. 1953) that traded, respectively, on postcard images of a sanitized Montmartre and a Gallic rural idyll. In the latter half of the decade a biopic of Edith Piaf, *La môme* (*La vie en rose*, 2007, opposite above), likewise traded on familiar French exoticism for its success.

KEY EVENTS

2000	2000	2001	2002	2002	2004
Coralie Trinh-Thi and Virginie Despentes's *Baise-Moi!* opens in Paris with a "16+" rating. Following right-wing pressure, it is reclassified "X."	Marin Karmitz defies censors to show *Baise-Moi!* at his MK2 cinemas.	*A ma soeur!* (*Fat Girl*) by Catherine Breillat (b. 1948) and *Le pornographe* (*The Pornographer*) by Bertrand Bonello (b. 1968) are released.	Jean-Pierre Jeunet's *Amélie* becomes the highest-grossing French film of all time at the international box office.	The chameleonic Olivier Assayas (b. 1955) produces *Demonlover*, an examination of Japanese S&M anime and torture websites.	*Dans ma peau* (*In My Skin*) by Marina de Van (b. 1971), *Process* by C. S. Leigh (b. 1964), and Breillat's *Anatomie de l'enfer* (*Anatomy of Hell*) are all released.

An alternative perspective was offered by outsiders coming to work in France. Algerian Rachid Bouchareb (b. 1959) and Austrian Michael Haneke (b. 1942) cast two very different gazes on France's colonial history with *Indigènes* (*Days of Glory*, 2006) and *Caché* (*Hidden*, 2005, see p. 560), two films that, along with *De battre mon coeur s'est arrêté* (*The Beat That My Heart Skipped*, 2005) and *Un prophète* (*A Prophet*, 2009, see p. 562) directed by Jacques Audiard (b. 1952), combined an auteurist aesthetic with a keen awareness of genre convention. Meanwhile US painter-filmmaker Julian Schnabel (b. 1951) brought Jean-Dominique Bauby's moving memoir, *Le scaphandre et le papillon* (*The Diving Bell and the Butterfly*, 2007, below), to startling, vivid-hued life.

Much of the decade was overshadowed by filmic portrayals of graphic sexuality, violence, and social apocalypse, dubbed "the new French extremity" by James Quandt. This theme emerged in earnest in 2000 when Coralie Trinh-Thi (b. 1976) and Virginie Despentes (b. 1969) codirected the rape-revenge movie *Baise-moi!* (*Fuck Me!*). In 2002 Philippe Grandrieux (b. 1954) explored sex trafficking in *La vie nouvelle* (*A New Life*), which culminates in a man being torn apart by dogs. The most notorious example was directed by Gaspar Noé (b. 1963); his brutal *Irréversible* (2002) became infamous for its nine-minute rape scene. The New French Extremism created heated debate among critics but it did not pack in audiences. Two of the era's biggest successes were a documentary about penguins—*La marche de l'empereur* (*March of the Penguins*, 2005)—and an animation directed by Luc Besson (b. 1959), *Arthur et les Minimoys* (*Arthur and the Invisibles*, 2006). If this was indeed the time of crisis that some commentators have suggested, it proves the maxim that adversity breeds creation. **CW**

2004	2004	2006	2007	2008	2009
Writing in *Artforum* magazine, James Quandt coins the term the "New French Extremity," referring to works by Noé and Breillat, among others.	Jean-Pierre Jeunet's *Un long dimanche de fiançailles* is coproduced by Warner Bros.	Popular comedies *Brice de Nice* (*The Brice Man*) and *Les bronzés 3* (*French Fried Vacation*) dominate the domestic box office.	Directed by Guillaume Canet (b. 1973), *Ne le dis à personne* (*Tell No One*) combines a "Frenchness" with genre convention to great effect.	Marion Cotillard wins a Best Actress Oscar for her performance as Edith Piaf in *La môme*.	Breillat produces *Barbe Bleue* (*Bluebeard*) and Claire Denis (b. 1948) *35 rhums* (*35 Shots of Rum*); both films are a far cry from the New French Extremism.

Le fabuleux destin d'Amélie Poulain 2001

Amélie   JEAN-PIERRE JEUNET b. 1953

▲ Jeunet cast the elfish Tautou for her ability to combine comedy and drama.

▼ The film is shot mostly in Montmartre, the Parisian district where Amélie works.

French director Jean-Pierre Jeunet once revealed that he and writing partner Guillaume Laurant would scribble down idle thoughts and curious facts on slips of paper and toss them into a big bowl. When it was full, they would ransack the bowl for ideas and begin making the movie. Sepia-hued charmer *Le fabuleux destin d'Amélie Poulain* feels every bit the product of this method: a serendipitous romantic comedy showcasing a delight in trivia, wordplay, and quixotic ruminations on the arcane mysteries of the world. The audience learns, through a series of choreographed flashbacks and André Dussollier's drily intoned narration, that Amélie, played by then-unknown actress Audrey Tautou, was not a happy child. Her parents' neglect left her unschooled in the art of forming meaningful human relationships. She now works as a waitress in Montmartre and dedicates her spare time to general philanthropy. Yet she becomes determined to contrive a meeting with similarly rootless dreamer Nino (Mathieu Kassovitz), who spends his time collecting and reassembling torn-up photographs.

Le fabuleux destin d'Amélie Poulain represents the apotheosis of Jeunet's fastidious, yet unabashedly romanticized, visual mode. His snowglobe rendering of Paris is stuffed fit to burst with tourist locations, immaculate exteriors, and a coterie of oddball characters. Yann Tiersen binds the film together with his ultra-melodic accordion-driven score, while every shard of light captured by Bruno Delbonnel's camera is tweaked to perfection, so that *American Cinematographer* magazine crowned this the best-shot film of the decade. **DJ**

KEY SCENES

1 UP IN THE CLOUDS
With a camera given to her by her mother, Amélie proceeds to photograph the figure of a rabbit she sees in the clouds. Jeunet uses such small "secret" moments to draw viewers into her world and convinces the viewer that Amélie is not a normal girl.

2 THE LONELY PAINTER
Amélie visits artist Raymond Dufayel, who continually repaints a Renoir work, anxious that he can never do it justice. His character voices many of the film's themes, notably that it can be acceptable to overlook the finer details in order to savor the bigger picture.

3 DREAM SEQUENCE
While waiting for Nino, Amélie fears that he may not have found her clues to a surreal flight of fancy involving bank robbers, a bungled heist, and a prison escape, all rendered in a dream sequence that is assembled brilliantly from archive footage.

4 THE KISS
Amélie manages her self-doubt by forcing boyfriend-to-be Nino to jump through various hoops before they meet. When they finally get together, Jeunet slows the tempo right down as the pair unleash their feelings for each other in a series of slow, sensual kisses.

DIRECTOR PROFILE

1953–80
Born in France's Loire region, Jean-Pierre Jeunet never attended film school. His cinematic influences were directors Marcel Carné (1906–96) and René Clair (1898–1981), as well as screenwriter and wit Jacques Prevért. Jeunet produced his first two, puppet-based, animated shorts with collaborator Marc Caro—*L'évasion* (1978) and the César-winning *Le manège* (1980).

1981–89
Working with Caro, he moved into live action with his sci-fi short *Le bunker de la dernière rafale* (*The Bunker of the Last Gunshots*, 1981). The versatile pair made every detail of the film themselves, including its costumes and sets. Jeunet continued to make television advertisements and music promos.

1990–99
Jeunet and Caro worked together on two feature films: the surreal horror-comedy *Delicatessen* (1991) and the similarly styled, dark fairy tale *La cité des enfants perdus* (*The City of Lost Children*, 1995). Jeunet left France for the United States to direct *Alien: Resurrection* (1997), his first (and to date, only) English-language feature. Collaborator Marc Caro followed.

2000–3
Jeunet returned to France to make the whimsical romantic comedy *Le fabuleux destin d'Amélie Poulain*. Although it was rejected by Cannes selector Gilles Jacob, the film became a global sensation.

2004–7
The director reunited his regular favorite actors Dominique Pinon and Audrey Tautou to make the World War II saga *Un long dimanche de fiançailles* (*A Very Long Engagement*, 2004). He then spent two years preparing an adaptation of Yann Martel's conceptual novel *The Life of Pi* but was unable to secure funding.

2008–present
Jeunet made the Ealingesque heist movie *Micmacs à tire-larigot* (*Micmacs*), which premiered at the Toronto Film Festival in 2009.

Caché 2005
Hidden MICHAEL HANEKE b. 1942

▲ Daniel Auteuil and Juliette Binoche in a scene where Georges's tension and anger reaches breaking point.

▼ The horror movie–style poster alludes to a key moment in the film.

In *Caché* Michael Haneke delivers one of his best films, although the hook (if not the development) is lifted from another movie, *Lost Highway* (1997), directed by David Lynch (b. 1946). Did Haneke coincidentally come up with his MacGuffin without having seen Lynch's film? Or was he inspired—fascinated by a plot direction Lynch did not take and driven to spin his own story from the same starting point?

Georges Laurent (Daniel Auteuil), a pundit who hosts a bookish intellectual chat show, is happily married to publisher Anne (Juliette Binoche) and has a comfortable, bourgeois lifestyle, which is disturbed when a series of surveillance tapes is delivered. Videotapes are left repeatedly on Laurent's doorstep, sometimes wrapped in bloody child's drawings. At first the tapes simply show two hours of a fixed shot of the exterior of the building. Later tapes make odder links, to the farm estate in the country where Georges grew up and to a less salubrious apartment in another part of town. There, Georges finds Majid (Maurice Bénichou), an Algerian whom Georges's parents briefly considered adopting after his own parents (who worked for them) were killed by police during a (real-life) demonstration in 1961. A primal betrayal is remembered.

Caché pretends to be a suspense thriller even if some aspects of the film suggest otherwise. Two instances of appalling violence remind us how far Haneke is willing to go to shock the audience, despite most of the movie consisting of flat medium shots that, unnervingly, seem to be taken from the point of view of a hidden camera. **KN**

👁 KEY SCENES

1 VIDEO SURVEILLANCE
The Laurents watch a videotape left outside their home and are disturbed by the intrusion: without knowing it, they have been filmed, all their comings and goings captured by the unwavering gaze of a camera.

2 PRIMAL GUILT
In menacing flashback sequences Georges revisits a defining moment of his childhood. Duped by the young Georges, Majid kills a chicken. Georges tells his parents that this was done to scare him, and Majid loses his chance of adoption by the Laurent family.

3 SELF-MURDER
Majid commits suicide suddenly, cutting his throat as he had once killed the chicken. It is a vivid, brutal moment, with the blood shooting out geyserlike. Georges and the audience are left shocked and speechless.

4 CONTINUING MYSTERY
A long-held final shot of random Parisians might contain a vital clue to the unresolved enigma. Two characters meet and hold a conversation, but the sound is indiscernible. Haneke has discussed the scene in depth, but its ambiguity remains.

🕒 DIRECTOR PROFILE

1942–88
Michael Haneke was born in Munich, the son of actors. He studied philosophy, drama, and psychology at the University of Vienna before graduating and finding work as a film critic, playwright, and theater director. In 1974 he made his debut as a television director.

1989
His feature film debut was *Der siebente Kontinent* (*The Seventh Continent*). Inspired by a true story, it serves as an examination of Austrian middle-class life.

1990–96
Haneke completed his trilogy of Austrian films about violence in contemporary society that started with *Der siebente Kontinent*. The second and third films are *Benny's Video* (1992) and *71 Fragmente einer Chronologie des Zufalls* (*71 Fragments of a Chronology of Chance*, 1994). These controversial films brought his work to a wider audience.

1997–98
Haneke released *Funny Games* (1997, see p. 480), a brutal look at violence in the media and an effective horror-thriller that condemns audiences for enjoying horror-thrillers.

1999–2005
Haneke worked in France, bringing his mix of icy art-house style and confrontational material to *Code inconnu* (*Code Unknown*, 2000), *La pianiste* (*The Piano Teacher*, 2001), *Le temps du loup* (*Time of the Wolf*, 2003), and *Caché*.

2006–present
In the United States Haneke remade *Funny Games* in English, virtually shot for shot, as *Funny Games US* (2008), starring Tim Roth and Naomi Watts. In Germany he made the epic-length black-and-white period drama *Das weisse Band* (*The White Ribbon*, 2009). Concerning a pre-World War I German village, it is a study of the roots of Fascism. It went on to win the Palme d'Or at Cannes in 2009, and was nominated for Best Foreign Language Film at the Academy Awards in 2010.

Un prophète 2009

A Prophet   JACQUES AUDIARD b. 1952

▲ Tahar Rahim gives a riveting central performance as the troubled, conflicted Malik El Djebena.

▼ Physical and mental imprisonment is conveyed by the French poster.

A long with Michael Mann (b. 1943), Jacques Audiard has done more than any other contemporary director to transform the crime film into an art form. Like his predecessor Jean-Pierre Melville (1917–73), he has written and directed an impressive body of work, in which the action and tough talk illustrate the complex and troubled lives of his characters.

Already celebrated as one of the best prison dramas ever made, *Un prophète* traces the story of a young Muslim man's descent into a moral abyss and his subsequent rise through the jail's pecking order. As with the central characters in all Audiard's films, the metaphysical well-being of Malik is as important as his mental and physical health. He is tormented by having killed a man on the orders of the prison's dominant Corsican gang. A fellow Muslim, the man's ghost haunts Malik's waking hours, like a consigliere from beyond the grave, chiding him for his inaction and questioning his allegiance to the Corsicans.

Audiard employed a long shooting schedule to allow time for the actors to grasp the psychological impact of long-term imprisonment. Although the film is the most physically contained that Audiard has shot to date, it is arguably the director's most expansive work. While remaining primarily a character piece, the film also works as a microcosm of society, although Audiard has gone to great lengths to distance his film from any claims to realism. Like Melville's best films, it is patently the work of a stylist unafraid to explore the margins of society, but who ultimately produces a fiction. **IHS**

👁 KEY SCENES

1 AN OFFER YOU CANNOT REFUSE
The Corsicans order Malik to execute Reyeb (Hichem Yacoubi), a Muslim snitch. He will not be allowed to live if he refuses. The scene prompts Malik's descent into hell, simultaneously forging the character that will undo the stranglehold of life in the prison.

2 A GUILTY CONSCIENCE
After the murder of Reyeb, Malik dreams he is in bed with him. The sequence highlights Audiard's fascination with violence and sensuality, often blurring the lines between the two. In the dream, a sexual act could easily be mistaken for a fight.

3 A PRISON COUP
Having double-crossed Luciani (Niels Arestrup) Malik arrives back at the prison after his deadline and sits out the battle between gangs in solitary confinement. He hears the result of his subterfuge and knows he will be the kingpin on his release.

4 UNLUCKY LUCIANI
Luciani approaches Malik, now surrounded by his Muslim brothers. Refused an audience, the Corsican is then punched by one of Malik's soldiers. Alone and unprotected, Luciani has reached the bottom of the prison's pecking order.

🕐 DIRECTOR PROFILE

1952–93
Jacques Audiard was born in Paris. As a writer, he contributed to thirteen films and one television series, including *Mortelle randonnée* (*Deadly Circuit*, 1983), *Réveillon chez Bob* (1984), *Saxo* (1987), and *Fréquence meurtre* (*Frequent Death*, 1988), starring Catherine Deneuve. His first script, *Bons baisers...à lundi* (*Kisses till Monday*, 1974), was a collaboration with his father, screenwriter and director Michel Audiard (1920–85).

1994–96
In his directorial debut, *Regarde les hommes tomber* (*See How They Fall*, 1994), Audiard continued his exploration of the underworld. The film won the César award for best first film. He was joined by the stars of that film—Mathieu Kassovitz and Jean-Louis Trintignant—for his second feature, *Un héros très discret* (*A Self-Made Hero*, 1996), based on the novel by Jean-François Deniau. Like *Lacombe Lucien* (1974) directed by Louis Malle (1932–95), Audiard's film dared to suggest that not everyone in France had been a member of the Resistance during World War II.

1997–2001
After writing the script for *Vénus beauté (institut)* (*Venus Beauty Salon*, 1999), directed by Tonie Marshall (b. 1951) and starring Audrey Tautou, Audiard returned to directing with *Sur mes lèvres* (*Read My Lips*, 2001). The relationship between an ex-con and his deaf office manager in the film allowed the director to explore further a sensuous style of filmmaking. The film won three Césars, including one for best screenplay.

2002–present
An imaginative reworking of the ambitious *Fingers* (1978) directed by James Toback (b. 1944), *De battre mon coeur s'est arrêté* (*The Beat That My Heart Skipped*, 2005) attracted international acclaim, winning the director awards for his portrayal of a thug whose despondency about his life is mitigated by his desire to follow in his mother's footsteps and become a pianist. *Un prophète* further established Audiard's status as one of his generation's most accomplished filmmakers.

GLOSSARY

Anime
A popular style of Japanese animation, originating from comic book cartoons.

Art house
Typically refers to noncommercial, independently made films aimed at a niche rather than a mass audience.

Cahiers du cinéma
Influential French film journal founded in 1951 and for which many of the early directors of the Nouvelle Vague film movement wrote.

Cinéma-vérité
French term meaning "cinema of truth"; refers to a style of documentary filmmaking that appears to be realistic, showing ordinary people in ordinary situations with minimal filmmaking techniques, such as voice-over.

Close-up
A camera shot used to emphasize the importance of its subject or to show detail. The close-up tightly frames the subject, typically an actor's face.

CGI
Computer-generated imagery, such as 3D computer graphics, used for special effects in movies.

Cross-cutting
An editing technique used to interweave between shots that occur simultaneously. The pace of cutting between the shots is varied to create dramatic tension or to emphasize a theme.

Dolly shot
Also known as a tracking shot, the camera is mounted on a truck that is moved along rails while the shot is being filmed. The technique is used to focus in on, or pull away from, the action. It is subtly different from a zoom shot.

Double take
A delayed reaction indicating surprise or disbelief, usually for comic effect.

Expressionism
An artistic movement in the early 20th century in which expression of the artist's subjective inner experiences was emphasized. From the 1920s German Expressionist filmmakers developed a style of cinema focusing on the darker fringes of human experience by using symbolism, shadowy lighting and *mise en scène*.

Film Noir
Genre of film, made originally between 1940 and 1969 in the United States, characterized by low-key lighting and depicting dark, bleak themes. Noir films are marked by their cynical characters and mood of pessimism.

Giallo
Italy's particular twist on the mystery genre is dominated by elaborate, show-stopping murder sequences and an overwhelming air of perversity.

Grand Guignol
A style of macabre, horrific melodrama developed in France, notably at the Théâtre du Grand-Guignol.

Hays Code
Also known as the Motion Picture Production Code, the Hays Code was a set of regulatory guidelines drawn up in the 1930s to censor the US film industry. The regulations were strict and made clear that the depiction of sex, crime, violence, and other such activities was not morally acceptable on-screen. The code was abandoned in the late 1960s.

Intercutting
A process of editing that alternates between scenes from one sequence and scenes from another film sequence, so that shots from separate narrative storylines are used.

Intertitles
A title card with text that appears in between scenes or shots of a film. Commonly used in silent films for dialogue or to clarify action.

Jump cut
A cut in film editing in which two sequential shots of the same subject are taken from camera positions that vary only slightly. For example, a shot of a character opening a car door followed by a shot of him or her driving the car; the audience does not see the character actually getting into the car. The jump cut compresses time and the result on-screen is abrupt and jerky.

J-horror
A Japanese horror genre that focuses on psychological drama and high levels of tension. The films are often remakes of classic horror movies and tell tales of ghosts and spirits rather than blood and gore.

Macguffin
A term used by Alfred Hitchcock to refer to an element of a film that catches the attention of the viewer or drives the plot. Examples include the statue with the microfilms in *North by Northwest* (1959).

Mise en scène
The artistic elements that contribute to the visual appearance or mood of a shot or scene, including the set, props, costumes, and types of camera shots used.

Montage
A cinematic device for creating the artistic look or feel of a scene through the use of visual editing.

Neo-Realism
Italian film movement after World War II characterized by starkly realistic, humanistic stories, documentary-like camera style and the use of non-professional actors.

New French Extremity
Term coined by critic James Quandt for a collection of transgressive films by French directors at the turn of the 21st century.

Nouvelle Vague
Term (meaning "new wave") for an informal group of French filmmakers of the late 1950s and 1960s influenced by Italian Neo-Realism and classic Hollywood cinema. Nouvelle Vague cinema placed the director at the center of the filmmaking process and was shot in real locations with innovative use of lightweight cameras and featured existential themes.

Palme d'Or
Or Golden Palm is the most prestigious prize awarded at the Cannes Film Festival.

Polyvision
A specialized film format devised for the filming and projection of Abel Gance's *Napoléon* (1927, see p.32).

Pre-Code
Movies made in the 1920s and 1930s before the Hays Code was enforced in 1934. Typically the films enjoyed risqué subject matter and a liberal attitude to moral correctness.

Schlock
A term used to describe something cheap, exploitative, and lacking in substance, for example, a schlock horror film.

Sensurround
A process developed in the 1970s by Universal Studios to enhance the audio experience in movies.

Set piece
An eye-catching scene or sequence with heightened stakes and production values. For example, in an action film a set piece may be a helicopter chase amid skyscrapers.

Stop-motion animation
An animation technique using 3D figures made from clay or plasticine that are photographed frame by frame as they are physically manipulated.

Surrealism
A 20th-century artistic movement that attempted to express the workings of the subconscious. Surrealist works are characterized by fantastic images and incongruous juxtapositions.

Talkie
Early term for a film with sound and especially one with recorded spoken dialogue. It is typically used to make a distinction between silent and sound films made in the late 1920s and early 1930s when sound films were establishing their marketplace dominance.

Technicolor
A trademarked method of making movies in which films sensitive to different primary colors are exposed simultaneously and later superimposed to produce a full-color print.

Wuxia
A martial arts genre that uses figures from Chinese mythology. Skillful swordsmanship and impressive flying sequences also feature.

CONTRIBUTORS

JB
James Bell is the features editor at *Sight & Sound* magazine.

GB
Guy Barefoot is a lecturer in film studies at the University of Leicester, UK. He is the author of *Gaslight Melodrama: From Victorian London to 1940s Hollywood* (Continuum, 2001).

JC
James Chapman is Professor of Film Studies at the University of Leicester. He is an authority on British cinema whose books include *Licence To Thrill: A Cultural History of the James Bond Films* (1999; 2007), *Past and Present: National Identity and the British Historical Film* (2005), and (with Nicholas J. Cull) *Projecting Empire: Imperialism and Popular Cinema* (2009).

RC
Richard Chatten has written about film for different publications, including *The Times*, the *Independent*, *Film Dope*, the *International Dictionary of Films & Filmmakers*, and the *Journal of Popular British Cinema*. He was a contributor to *The Encyclopedia of British Film*.

GF
Graham Fuller has written about cinema for a number of publications, including *Sight & Sound*, *Film Comment*, *Cineaste*, *The New York Times*, the *Guardian*, and *Vanity Fair*. He was the film columnist for *Interview* from 1991 to 2008 and is the editor of *Potter on Potter* and *Loach on Loach* (both Faber & Faber). His website is www.inalonelyplace.com.

JG
Jamie Graham is Deputy Editor of *Total Film* and has contributed to the *Sunday Times*, the *Daily Telegraph*, and *Sight & Sound*.

WH
Wally Hammond has been a film writer for many years during which he has contributed to a number of periodicals including *Time Out*, where he spent twenty-five years as a staff writer and film critic. He is a regular contributor to *Sight & Sound*.

TH
Tom Huddleston is a writer and critic for *Time Out London*.

RH
Russ Hunter is a lecturer in film and television at Northumbria University, UK. His research interests include film reception, popular Italian cinema, and the horror film.

AJ
Alexander Jacoby is a writer who lectures on Japanese film and manga at Oxford Brookes University, UK. He is the author of *A Critical Handbook of Japanese Film Directors* (Stone Bridge Press, 2008). His articles have appeared in print and online in *CineAction*, *Sight & Sound*, *Film Criticism*, *The Times*, *The Times Literary Supplement*, and *The Japan Times*. He was a contributor to *Japanese Cinema: Texts and Contexts* (Routledge, 2007).

NJ
Nick James is editor of *Sight & Sound*. He has written on film, literature, and art for the *Guardian*, the *Observer*, *Time Out*, *The London Review of Books*, and *The Literary Review*. He is the author of a book on Michael Mann's *Heat* and presented the BBC TV documentary *British Cinema: The End of the Affair* (both 2002). He is currently editing a British Film Criticism Reader.

DJ
David Jenkins started his career as deputy editor of *Little White Lies* and is now a writer and critic for the film section of *Time Out London*.

PK
Philip Kemp is a freelance film reviewer and historian, and a regular contributor to *Sight & Sound*, *Total Film*, and *DVD Review*. He teaches film journalism at the University of Leicester, UK.

CK
Carol King is a freelance writer and editor who fell in love with cinema on her first trip to the movies to see *Snow White and the Seven Dwarfs*. She is the author of *As Much As I Can*, a biography of actor and director Peter Glenville.

GM
Geoffrey Macnab is a London-based freelance author and journalist. He is a UK correspondent for *Screen International* and also writes for the *Independent*, the *Guardian*, and *Sight & Sound*. His books include *J. Arthur Rank and the British Film Industry* (1993), *The Making of Taxi Driver* (2006), *Ingmar Bergman: The Life and Films of the Last Great European Director* (2009), and *Screen Epiphanies: Filmmakers on the Films that Inspired Them* (2009).

DM
Demetrios Matheou is a film journalist, writer and programmer. He is the film critic for the *Sunday Herald* and also contributes to the *Independent on Sunday*, *The Times*, *Sight & Sound*, and the BBC. He is the author of *The Faber Book of New South American Cinema* and penned the title entry of *Ten Bad Dates with De Niro*.

KN
Kim Newman is a novelist, critic, and broadcaster. He is a contributing editor to *Empire* and *Sight & Sound*. His latest books are *Nightmare Movies* and *The Hound of the d'Urbervilles*.

DP
Dominic Power is Head of Screen Arts at the National Film and Television School. He is a radio dramatist whose work is regularly broadcast on BBC radio and he is co-editor of the journal *The New Soundtrack*.

NR
Naman Ramachandran writes on South Asian cinema for *Sight & Sound*, *Total Film*, and *Variety*. He covers South Asia for *Variety* and the UK and Ireland for Cineuropa. He is the author of *Lights, Camera, Masala! Making Movies in Mumbai*.

JR
Jonathan Romney is film critic of the *Independent on Sunday*, a contributing editor to *Sight & Sound* and program adviser on French cinema for the London Film Festival. He is the author of *Short Orders* and a monograph on Atom Egoyan (BFI World Directors series).

AS
Anna Smith is a film critic and broadcaster. She is a regular contributor to *Empire*, *Time Out*, *ELLE*, *Sight & Sound*, Sky News, and BBC TV and radio. She is currently vice chair of the Critics' Circle Film Section.

IHS
Ian Haydn Smith is the editor of the *International Film Guide*. He is also the series editor of *24 Frames*, published by Wallflower Press, and runs the Screen Salon series of events at London cinemas.

MS
Mansel Stimpson is the co-editor and chief reviewer for Film Review Annual, chair of the Eastbourne Film Society, and regularly interviews artists at ROH Covent Garden for the Web Site Classical Source.

SW
Simon Ward is a writer and editor working in London. He has won awards for his short story work and has written extensively on cinema and comic books.

CW
Catherine Wheatley is a lecturer in film and media studies at the University of East London. Her film criticism has appeared in numerous publications, including *Sight & Sound*. She has also written books on the films of Michael Haneke and on Anglo-French film relations.

SOURCES OF QUOTATIONS

p.10 "Sinful and abominable rubbish" *British Cinema and Middlebrow Culture in the Interwar Years*, Lawrence Napper, University of Exeter Press, 2009

p.13 "the truth . . . a second" Jean-Luc Godard's screenplay *Le petit soldat* (1963)

p.13 "a battleground . . . emotion" Sam Fuller in *Pierrot le fou* (1965) by Jean-Luc Godard

p.27 "$18,000 Used for . . . Great Air Battle." *La Crosse Tribune*, 2 October 1916

p.30 "saved the South . . . black rule". Intertitle to *Birth of a Nation*

p.41 "For four years . . . desperation and death." *The Films of Fritz Lang*, Frederick W. Ott, Citadel Press, 1979

p.46 "there blows a chill draught from the world beyond." *The Haunted Screen: Expressionism in the German Cinema and the Influence of Max Reinhardt*, Lotte H. Eisner, Thames & Hudson, 2008

p.46 "Murnau's greatness lies . . . subjective qualities." David Thomson, *A Biographical Dictionary of Film*, Andre Deutsch, 1994

p.55 "father of Russian cinema" http://www.filmreference.com/Directors-Jo-Ku/Kuleshov-Lev.html

p.64 "the picture . . . remembered by". *Chaplin and American Culture: The Evolution of a Star Image*, Charles J. Maland, Princeton University Press, 1989

p.68 "the director's pencil" *The Haunted Screen: Expressionism in the German Cinema and the Influence of Max Reinhardt*, Lotte H. Eisner, Thames & Hudson, 2008

p.69 "It is possible . . . medium seemed a mess." *The American Cinema: Directors and Directions, 1929–1968*, Andrew Sarris, Da Capo Press, 1996

p.78 "a date enshrined . . . and Pearl Harbor" *You Ain't Heard Nothing Yet: The American Talking Film, History & Memory, 1927–1949*, Andrew Sarris, Oxford University Press, 1998

p.79 "*The Jazz Singer* . . . whole goddam tide." *The Speed of Sound: Hollywood and the Talkie Revolution, 1926–1930*, Scott Eyman, Simon & Schuster, 1997

p.94 "Give me something . . . out-horror Frankenstein" *The MGM Story: The Complete History of Fifty Roaring Years*, John Douglas Eames, Crown Publishers, 1976

p.96 "An idea came . . . villains and bawds." *Film: An Anthology*, ed. Daniel Talbot, University of California Press, 1959

p.96 "As a newspaperman . . . as their sadism." *Framework: A History of Screenwriting*

in the American Film, Tom Stempel, Syracuse University Press, 2000

p.97 "torn from the headlines" *You Must Remember This: The Warner Bros. Story*, Richard Schickel, PBS, 2008

p.97 "I would like to . . . down in Chicago." *Howard Hawks: Interviews*, ed. Scott Breivold, University Press of Mississippi, 2006

p.97 "The American public . . . in the cinema" *The New Censors: Movies and the Culture Wars*, Charles Lyons, Temple University Press, 1997

p.98 "an expression. . . rejects Americanism", "a cheerful view of life", "The gangster is the man. . . a placard, a club." "The Gangster as Tragic Hero" in *The Immediate Experience: Movies, Comics, Theater, and Other Aspects of Popular Culture*, Robert Warshow, Doubleday, 1962

p.99 "great gangster film . . . Film Noir" *A Personal Journey with Martin Scorsese Through American Movies* (1995)

p.100 "Every other underworld . . . go over big" *The Motion Picture Guide*, Jay Robert Nash, Stanley Ralph Ross, Cinebooks, 1988

p.104 "when the whole . . . out of windows" *The Genius of the System: Hollywood Filmmaking in the Studio Era*, Thomas Schatz, Pantheon, 1988

p.105 "his ability . . . dramatized on the screen" *Master Space: Film Images of Capra, Lubitsch, Sternberg and Wyler*, Barbara Bowman, Greenwood Press, 1992

p.105 "Go to see . . . your own song" *Woody Sez*, Woody Guthrie, Grosset & Dunlap, 1975

p.113 "We told stars . . . we knew best" *The Fame Formula: How Hollywood's Fixers, Fakers and Star Makers Created the Celebrity Industry*, Mark Borkowski, Pan Macmillan, 2009

p.114 "an emotionalized background . . . into my foreground" http://archive.sensesofcinema.com/contents/01/19/sternberg.html

p.115 "Count to six . . . live without it" http://archive.sensesofcinema.com/contents/01/19/sternberg.html

p.124 "a society dancing on a volcano" *Expressionism Reassessed*, Shulamith Behr, David Fanning, Douglas Jarman, Manchester University Press, 1993

p.132 "Either the camera . . . or I do." *Fred Astaire*, Benny Green, Exeter Books, 1979

p.136 "He gives her class . . . gives him sex" http://www.time.com/time/arts/article/0,8599,265339,00.html

p.138 "the one notable exception . . . is Leni Riefenstahl" *Visions of Yesterday*, Jeffrey Richards, Routledge & Kegan Paul, 1973

p.139 "post-war years . . . Soviet cinema" *The Film Encyclopedia*, Ephraim Katz, HarperPerennial, 1979

p.139 "The style in which . . . or humanity" *Film*, Roger Manvell, Pelican Books, 1950

p.139 "Among the ten . . . Soviet cinema" *Dictionary of Film Makers*, Georges Sadoul, Peter Morris, University of California Press, 1972

p.139 "It is to be all . . . for a long while" *The Graham Greene Film Reader*, Graham Greene, David Parkinson, Applause Theatre Book Publishers, 1994

p.140 "a peculiar mystique" *The Story of Cinema*, David Shipman, St Martin's Press, 1982

p.140 "was probably . . . to most audiences" *Film in the Third Reich*, David Stewart Hull, University of California Press, 1969

p.140 "All this rubbish . . . how could you fail?" Brian Winston's letter to the *Guardian*, 21 December 1988

p.141 "one of the . . . film history" *Leni: The Life and Work of Leni Riefenstahl*, Steven Bach, Alfred A. Knopf, 2007

p.142 "found the third . . . dreaming of"; "a man of fine musical understanding"; "never becomes...dynamic structure" *Sergei Prokofiev: A Biography*, Harlow Robinson, Northeastern University Press, 2002

p.145 "Sometimes it is, frankly . . . its generation" *Chestnuts in Her Lap, 1936–1946*, Caroline Alice Lejeune, Phoenix House, 1947

p.148 "a whole genre . . . by aggravation" *Screwball: Hollywood's Madcap Romantic Comedies*, Ed Sikov, Crown Publishers, 1989

p.158 "Hitler's mistake . . . gorgeous opportunity" *The Long View*, Basil Wright, Secker & Warburg, 1974

p.158 "Had I known . . . of the Nazis" *My Autobiography*, Charles Chaplin, Penguin Books, 1992

p.159 "It really is . . . for a long time" *The Unsung Artistry of George Orwell*, Lorraine Saunders, Ashgate Publishing, 2008

p.162 "It's for the mothers . . . to hit back" *Searching for John Ford*, Joseph McBride, Faber & Faber, 2004

p.171 "The meanings spoken . . . the human condition" *An Introduction to Studying Popular Culture*, Dominic Strinati, Routledge, 2000 p.175 "more aggravation . . . worked with"; "an agonizing . . . my life"; "as much about screenwriting as I am capable of learning" *City of Nets: A Portrait of Hollywood in the 1940s*, Otto Friedrich, Harper & Row, 1986

p.178 "Set up a camera . . . elementary actions" *A History of the Cinema: From its Origins to 1970*, Eric Rhode, Allen Lane, 1976

p.180 "Usually the film . . . scene was over"; "I try . . . nothing else" http://www.imdb.com/name/nm0744023/bio

p.182 "a simple workman . . . face to me"; "He is the most . . . in the world" "A Note by De Sica", *Sight & Sound*, Vol. 19, No. 1, March 1950

p.185 "can make any subject . . . spent on it" *Halliwell's Film Guide*, Leslie Halliwell, HarperPerennial, 1995

p.188 "paid no regard . . . a mass murderer" http://www.criterion.com/current/posts/414-kind-hearts-and-coronets-ealings-shadow-side

p.190 "A great many . . . French filmmaking" www.independent.co.uk 27 January 2011

p.192 "a bomb on non-conformity" *The Independent*, 6 March 2009 http://www.independen.co.uk/arts-entertainment/films/features/from-new-wave-to-tedious-old-hat-1638216.html

p.192 "Truffaut misfired . . . most open" http://www.guardian.co.uk/film/2002/oct/23/artsfeatures.france

p.193 "One of those films . . . collection of images" *The Films in My Life*, Francois Truffaut, Da Capo Press, 1994

p.194 "I wanted my actors . . . wearing costumes" www.criterion.com/current/posts/679-casque-dor-tenderness-and-violence

p.196 "has some claim . . . Damocles's sword" http://thefedorachronicles.com/hollywood/Movies/WagesofFear.html

p.196 "Dialogue . . . in the background" *Dictionary of Film Makers*, Georges Sadoul, Peter Morris, University of California Press, 1972

p.196 "holds the balance . . . of the journey" *Punch* Vol. 226, 1954

p.197 "the gingerly . . . to explode" *New York Times*, 17 February 1955

p.214 "had but one subject . . . its dissolution" *The Donald Richie Reader: 50 years of writing on Japan*, Donald Richie, ed. Arturo Silva, Stone Bridge Press, 2001

p.214 "the most Japanese of Japanese directors" *Ozu: His Life and Films*, Donald

Richie, University of Carolina Press, 1977

p.221 "I could answer . . . in the morning" Brian W. Fairbanks, Writings, Lulu.com, 2005

p.221 "Naturally, men scared . . . slaughter for you" *The Cold War Romance of Lillian Hellman and John Melby*, Robert P. Newman, University of North Carolina Press, 1989

p.228 "And she was . . . the laugh was" *Conversations with Wilder*, Cameron Crowe, Knopf, 1999

p.258 "every beard . . . seemed to converge" http://filmstore.bfi.org.uk/acatalog/info_150.html

p.259 "a minimum of . . . unmade-up look" *The Cinema of Tony Richardson: Essays and Interviews*, James Michael Welsh, John C. Tibbetts, State University of New York Press, 1999

p.260 "A lot of people . . . not my wife"; "You had . . . in snooker" www.screenonline.org.uk/audio/id/956482/

p.262 "It has a blow . . . English character" *Searching for Stars: Rethinking British Cinema*, Geoffrey Macnab, Cassell, 2000

p.262 "had a great . . . hardly aware" http://eltj.oxfordjournals.org/content/XX/3/273.extract

p.262 "the physicality . . . locker room" *Brief Encounters: Lesbians and Gays in British Cinema, 1930–1971*, Stephen Bourne, Cassell, 1996

p.264 "an idea . . . the hand" *Film Theory: An Introduction*, Robert Stam, Blackwell Publishing, 2000

p.268 "The feast of metaphors...colonial anthropology" http://www.culturebase.net/artist.php?656

p.269 "all great deeds . . . ridiculous beginning" *Le Mythe de Sisyphe*, Albert Camus, 1942

p.296 "to put the audience through it" http://hitchcock.tv/quotes/quotes.html

p.296 "to be able to use the cinematic . . . by pure film" *The Art Question*, Nigel Warburton, Routledge, 2003

p.308 "The true poetry . . . and tragedy" http://www.guardian.co.uk/film/1999/oct/07/derekmalcolmscenturyoffilm

p.309 "a merciless portrait . . . produced before" *The Most Important Art: Eastern European Film after 1945*, Mira Liehm, Antonin J. Liehm, University of California Press, 1977

p.323 "everything else . . . creation" *Making Pictures: A Century of European Cinematography*, Aurum Press, 2003

p.334 "You watch these movies . . . of a maniac"; "It's all about bad...go somewhere" *The American Nightmare*, a documentary by Adam Simon, 2000

p.371 "All that we seem . . . within a dream" Edgar Allan Poe, "Dream Within a Dream", first published 1849

p.376 "the least appreciated . . . film history" *Cinema Taiwan: Politics, popularity and state of the art*, Darrell William Davis, Ruxiu Chen, Routledge, 2007

p.383 "I am a camera . . . not thinking" *Goodbye to Berlin*, Christopher Isherwood, Hogarth Press, 1939

p.384 "tears up the screen . . . seen in film" *African Cinema: Politics and Culture*, Manthia Diawara, Indiana University Press, 1992

p.384 "Africa's equivalent . . . *A bout de souffle*" Mark Cousins, *Sight & Sound*, February 2007

p.394 "My film is not about Vietnam . . . we went insane" *Tangled Memories: the Vietnam War, the AIDS epidemic and the politics of remembering*, Marita Sturken, University of California Press, 1997

p.414 "It's hard to believe . . . a film about it" Terence Davies in the DVD commentary to *Distant Voices, Still Lives* (1988)

p.416 "The cinema . . . ordering of life" *Modern Man in Search of a Soul*, Carl Jung, Routledge, 2001

p.417 "The audience members . . . is their dream" *Theatre*, David Mamet, Faber, 2010

p.424 "Everybody's life . . . scrutiny" http://frank.mtsu.edu/~cfrost/god/decalogue.htm

p.427 "My films . . . revel in that" www.filmreference.com/Directors-Du-Fr/Egoyan-Atom.html

p.502 "to filter the experience . . . and the family" www.sensesofcinema.com/2002/great-directors/yang/

p.527 "busy . . . too specific . . . too generic" "A Quick Chat with Pawel Pawlikowski" by Jason Wood, http://www.kamera.co.uk/interviews/a_quick_chat_with_pawel_pawlikowski.php

p.554 "The rush of battle . . . a drug" *War is a Force That Gives Us Meaning*, Chris Hedges, Random House, 2002

p.555 "War's dirty . . . a hero" *Kathryn Bigelow: Love and War* by Geoffrey Macnab, *The Independent*, 23 January 2010

p.557 "the new French extremity" "Flesh & Blood: Sex and violence in recent French cinema", James Quandt, *Artforum*, February 2004

INDEX

PICTURE CREDITS

Many of the images in this book are from the archives of The Kobal Collection, which owes its existence to the vision, courage, talent, and energy of the men and women who created the movie industry and whose legacies live on through the films they made, the studios they built, and the publicity photographs they took. Kobal collects, preserves, organizes, and makes these photographs available. Quintessence wishes to thank all the film distribution and production companies and apologizes in advance for any omissions or neglect, and will be pleased to make any necessary changes in future editions. (Key: top = t; center = c; bottom = b; left = l; right = r)

8 b Keystone **10 b** Warner Bros. **11 t** Paramount **11 b** Selznick/MGM **12 t** Chaumiane/Film Studio **13 b** Taplin-Perry-Scorsese **13** Lorimar **14** and **15** Chapter Opener Nero **16** Pathé Brothers **17 b** Star Film **17 t** Pathé Brothers **18** Gaumont **19 b** MGM (Turner Ent./Warner Bros.) **19 t** Gaumont **20 b** Star Film/Méliès **20 t** Star Film/Méliès **21 stills** Star Film/Méliès **22 t** Edison **22 b** Edison **23 stills** Edison **24 t** Société Des Etablissements/Gaumont **24 b** Société Des Etablissements/Gaumont **25 stills** Société Des Etablissements/Gaumont **26** Cines Co, Roma **27 t** Thomas Ince **27 b** MGM/Samuel Bronston Productions **28 t** Itala Film Torino **28 b** Itala Film Torino **29** still **2** Itala Film Torino **29 stills 1** and **3** Itala Film Torino **30 t** Epoch/DWG **30 b** Epoch/DWG **31 stills** Epoch/DWG **32 t** Films Abel Gance/Société Générale Des Films **32 b** Films Abel Gance/Société Générale Des Films **33 stills** Films Abel Gance/Société Générale Des Films **34** Fox Films Witzel **35 t** MGM **35 b** Nero **36 t** Fox Films **36 b** Fox Films **37 panel** MGM **37 stills** Fox Films **38 t** Paramount **38 b** Paramount **39 stills** Paramount **40** Svensk Filmindustri **41 t** UFA **41 b** Kinugasa Productions **42 t** Universal **42 b** H.R. Sokal-Film Gmbh **43 t** Neumann-Film-Produktion **43 b** Universal **44 t** Decla-Bioscop **44 b** Decla-Bioscop **45 stills** Decla-Bioscop **46 t** Prana-Film **46 b** Prana-Film **47 stills** Prana-Film **48** United Artists **49 b** MGM **49 t** Paramount **50 t** Famous Players/Paramount **51** Famous Players/Paramount **51 stills** Famous Players/Paramount **52 t** United Artists **52 b** United Artists **53 stills** Douglas Fairbanks Pictures/United Artists **54** Mehzrabpom, Moscow **55 t** Goskino **56** Goskino **57 t** Vufku **57 b** Sovkino **58 t** Goskino **58 b** Goskino **59 stills** Goskino **59 panel** Paramount **60 t** Vufku **60 b** Vufku **61 stills** Vufku **62** Hal Roach/Pathe Exchange Kornman, Gene **63 t** Charles Chaplin/First National **63 b** D.W.Griffith **64 t** Charles Chaplin/U.A. **64 b** Charles Chaplin/U.A. **65** still **3** Charles Chaplin/U.A. **65 panel** Charles Chaplin Productions/U.A. (Roy Export) **65 stills 1** and **2** Charles Chaplin Productions/U.A. (Roy Export) **66 t** Buster Keaton/Joseph M. Schenck/U.A. **66 b** Buster Keaton/Joseph M. Schenck/U.A. **67 stills** Buster Keaton/Joseph M. Schenck/U.A. **68** UFA **69 t** Decla-Bioscop **69 b** UFA **70 t** Fox Films **70 b** Fox Films **71 panel** Warner Bros. **71 stills** Fox Films **72 t** Société Générale Des Films (Gaumont) **72 b** Société Générale Des Films (Gaumont) **73 stills** Société Générale Des Films (Gaumont) **75 t** Vicomte Charles De Noailles **76 t** Bunuel-Dali **76 b** Bunuel-Dali **77 stills** Bunuel-Dali **79 b** MGM **79 t** Warner Bros. **80 t** BIP (ITV Global) **80 b** Ufa Ewald, Kar **81 t** Vicomte Charles De Noailles **81 b** Films Sonores Tobis **82 t** Nero-Film Ag **82 b** Nero-Film Ag **83 stills** Nero-Film Ag **84 t** Paramount Pictures (Emka Ltd) **84 b** Paramount Pictures (Emka Ltd) **85 stills** Paramount Pictures (Emka Ltd) **87** and **88** Chapter Opener RKO **88** Paramount **89 t** Universal **89 b** Universal **90** RKO **91 b** Universal **91 t** Universal **92 t** Universal **92 b** Universal **93 panel** Universal **93 stills** Universal **94 t** MGM (Turner Ent./Warner Bros.) **95 stills** MGM (Turner Ent./Warner Bros.) **96** United Artists **97 t** Paramount **97 b** Warner Bros./First National **98** Warner Bros. **99 b** Warner Bros. **100 t** Warner Bros./First National **100 b** Warner Bros./First National **101 stills** Warner Bros./First National **102 t** Warner Bros. **102 b** Warner Bros. **103 stills** Warner Bros. **104** Warner Bros. **105 b** MGM **105 t** Columbia **106 t** MGM (Turner Ent./Warner Bros.) **106 b** MGM (Turner Ent./Warner Bros.) **107 stills** MGM (Turner Ent./Warner Bros.) **108 t** Paramount **108 b** Paramount **109 panel** Kobal Collection **109 stills** Paramount Pictures **110 t** RKO Kahle, Alex **110 b** RKO **111 stills** RKO **112** Warner Bros./First National **113 b** United Artists (ITV Global) **113 t** MGM Hurrell, George **114 t** Paramount Pictures (Universal) English, Don **114 b** Paramount Pictures (Universal) **115 panel** Paramount **115 stills** Paramount Pictures (Universal) **116 t** MGM (Turner Ent./Warner Bros.) Bull, Clarence Sinclair **116 b** MGM (Turner Ent./Warner Bros.) **117 stills** MGM (Turner Ent./Warner Bros.) **118** Films Sonores Tobis **119 t** Films Marcel Pagnol **119 b** Cinéas **120** Films Hakim/Paris Film **121 b** Corniglion-Molinier **121 t** Realisations D'Art Cinematographique **122 t** GFFA **123 stills** GFFA **124 t** Nouvelles Éditions Francais **124 b** Nouvelles Éditions Francais **125 panel** USA Films/Capitol Films/Film Council Tillie, Mark **125 stills** Nouvelles Éditions Francais **126** Paramount **127 b** Columbia **127 t** Paramount **128 t** Hal Roach/MGM **129 panel** Hal Roach/MGM **129 stills** Hal Roach/MGM **130 t** Paramount Pictures (Emka Ltd) **130 b** Paramount Pictures (Emka Ltd) **131 panel** MGM (Turner Ent./Warner Bros.) **131 stills** Paramount Pictures (Emka Ltd) **132** Warner Bros. **133 t** Warner Bros. **133 b** RKO **134 t** Warner Bros. **134 b** Warner Bros. **135 stills** Warner Bros. **136 t** RKO **136 b** RKO **137 stills** RKO **138 l** Vufku-Kino-Ukrain/Amkino **138 c** DFG **138 r** Mezhrabpom **139 b** Lenfilm **139 t** Olympia-Film **140 t** Leni Riefenstahl-NSDAP **140 b** Leni Riefenstahl-NSDAP **141 stills** Leni Riefenstahl-NSDAP **42 t** Mosfilm **142 b** Mosfilm **3 stills** Mosfilm **144** Comenius-Film **145 t** © Disney **145 b** Paramount **146 b** © Disney **148** Columbia **149 t** Universal **149 b** MGM (Turner Ent./Warner Bros.) **150 t** RKO **150 b** RKO **151 stills** RKO **152 t** Paramount Pictures (Universal) **152 b** Paramount Pictures (Universal) **153 stills** Paramount Pictures (Universal) **154** Universal **155 b** Warner Bros. Hurrell, George **155 t** Universal **156 t** Walter Wagner Productions/U.A. **156 b** Walter Wagner Productions/U.A. **157 stills** Walter Wagner Productions/U.A. **158 t** Charles Chaplin Productions/U.A. (Roy Export) **158 b** Charles Chaplin Productions/U.A. (Roy Export) **159 panel** Paramount **159 stills** Charles Chaplin Productions/U.A. (Roy Export) **160** and **161** Chapter Opener MGM **162 t** Itv Global (Two Cities) **163 t** MGM (Turner Ent./Warner Bros.) **163 b** U.S. War Department **164 t** Ealing Studios (Canal+ Image UK Ltd) **165 stills** Ealing Studios (Canal+ Image UK Ltd) **166 t** Arnold Pressburger Productions Inc **166 b** Arnold Pressburger Productions Inc**167 stills** Arnold Pressburger Productions Inc **168 t** RKO **169 b** 20th Century Fox **169 t** Universal **170 t** Paramount Schafer, A.L. 'Whitey' **170 b** Warner Bros. **171 t** RKO **171 b** RKO **172 t** Warner Bros./First National **173 b** Warner Bros./First National **173 t** Warner Bros./First National Elliott, Mack **173 c** Warner Bros./First National **174 t** Paramount **174 b** Paramount **175 c** Paramount **176 t** London Film Productions/British Lion (Canal+ Image UK Ltd) **176 b** London Film Productions/British Lion (Canal+ Image UK Ltd) **177 b** London Film Productions/British Lion (Canal+ Image UK Ltd) **177 stills** London Film Productions/British Lion (Canal+ Image UK Ltd) **178 t** Industria Cinematografica Italiana **179 t** Tevere/UGC **179 b** Berit Films **180 t** Excelsa Film **180 b** Excelsa Film **181 stills** Excelsa Film **182 t** Produzioni De Sica **182 b** Produzioni De Sica **183 stills** Produzioni De Sica **185 b** Hammer **185 t** Associated British (Canal+ Image UK Ltd) **186 b** Cineguild (ITV Global) **187 stills** Cineguild (ITV Global) **188 t** Ealing Studios (Canal+ Image UK Ltd) **188 b** Ealing Studios (Canal+ Image UK Ltd) **189 stills** Ealing Studios (Canal+ Image UK Ltd) **190 t** Sacha Gordine Productions **191 b** Filmsonor **192 b** OGC/Studios Jenner/Play Art/La Cyme **192 t** Indus/Pathé/Prima **193 t** Gaumont **193 b** Cady/Discina/Specta **194 t** Robert Et Raymond Hakim (StudioCanal Image) **194 b** Robert Et Raymond Hakim (StudioCanal Image) **195 stills** Robert Et Raymond Hakim (StudioCanal Image) **196 t** CICC/Filmsonor/Vera Films/Fono Roma **196 b** CICC/Filmsonor/Vera Films/Fono Roma **197 panel** Universal**197 stills** CICC/Filmsonor/Vera Films/Fono Roma **198 t** Warner Bros. **199 t** MGM (Turner Ent./Warner Bros.) **199 b** MGM (Turner Ent./Warner Bros.) **200 t** MGM (Turner Ent./Warner Bros.) Carpenter, Eric **200 b** Paramount **201 t** MGM (Turner Ent./Warner Bros.) **201 b** 20th Century Fox **202 t** MGM (Turner Ent./Warner Bros.) Hubbell, Eddie **202 b** MGM (Turner Ent./Warner Bros.) **203 panel** Touchstone **203 stills** MGM (Turner Ent./Warner Bros.) **205 b** Terrafilm **206 t** Palladium Film **206 b** Palladium Film **207 stills** Palladium Film **209 stills** Svensk Filmindustri **210 t** Daiei **11 b** Shochiku **211 t** Daiei **212 t** Junli Zheng **212 b** Han Hyeong-Mo Productions **213 b** RK Films **213 t** Ajanta Pictures **214 t** Shochiku Eiga **214 b** Shochiku Eiga **215 panel** Shochiku Eiga **215 stills** Shochiku Eiga **216 b** Toho Company **216 t** Toho Company **217 stills** Toho Company **218 b** Satyajit Ray Productions/Govt. Of West Bengal **218 t** Satyajit Ray Productions/Govt. Of West Bengal **219 stills** Satyajit Ray Productions/Govt. Of West Bengal **221 t** Columbia **221 b** 20th Century Fox SHAW, SAM **222 t** Universal **222 b** Warner Bros. **223 b** MGM (Turner Ent./Warner Bros.) **223 t** United Artists **224 t** Liberty Films **224 b** Liberty Films **225 t l** Liberty Films **225 stills** Liberty Films **226 t** MGM (Turner Ent./Warner Bros.) **226 b** MGM (Turner Ent./Warner Bros.) **227 stills** MGM (Turner Ent./Warner Bros.) **228 t** Ashton Productions/Mirisch Corporation (MGM) **228 b** Ashton Productions/Mirisch Corporation (MGM) **229 stills** Ashton Productions/Mirisch Corporation (MGM) **230 t** Warner Bros. **231 b** MGM (Turner Ent./Warner Bros.) **231 t** MGM (Turner Ent./Warner Bros.) **232 t** Stanley Kramer Productions/Columbia Pictures **232 b** Stanley Kramer Productions/Columbia Pictures **233 panel** Columbia **233 c** Stanley Kramer Productions/Columbia Pictures **233 stills** Stanley Kramer Productions/Columbia Pictures **234 b** Warner Bros. **235 stills** Warner Bros. **236 t** Universal **237 b** Universal **237 t** Warner Bros. **238 t** 20th Century Fox **238 b** 20th Century Fox **239 stills** 20th Century Fox **240 t** Walter Wagner Productions/Allied Artists **240 b** Walter Wagner Productions/Allied Artists **241 stills** Walter Wagner Productions/Allied Artists **242 t** Stanley Kramer/U.A. **243 t** Universal **243 b** United Artists **244 b** Republic **244 t** Warner Bros. **245 t** Warner Bros. **246 t** CV Whitney Pictures/Warner Bros. Pictures **246 b** CV Whitney Pictures/Warner Bros. Pictures**247 panel** CV Whitney Pictures/Warner Bros. Pictures **247 stills** CV Whitney Pictures/Warner Bros. Pictures **248 t** Les Films De La Pleiade/Pathe **249 t** Ayjm/CGCF **249 b** Ajym/Les Films Du Carosse Pierre, Georges **250 t** Cocinor/Terra/Cormoran Film Pierre, Georges **251 t** Anouchka/Orsay **252 b** Les Films Du Carrosse/Sédif Productions **253 stills** Les Films Du Carrosse/Sédif Productions **254 b** Georges De Beauregard/SNC (StudioCanal Image) **255 stills** Georges De Beauregard/SNC (StudioCanal Image) **256** and **257** Chapter Opener Paris Film/Five Film **258 t** Woodfall **259 b** Jospeh Janni (Canal+ Image UK Ltd) **259 t** Vic Films/Waterhall (Canal+ Image UK Ltd) **260 t** Woodfall Film Productions **260 b** Woodfall Film Productions **261 stills** Woodfall Film Productions **262 b** ITV Global (Rank) **263 stills** ITV Global (Rank) **264 t** Glauber Rocha/Mapa **265 b** Sino Filmes/Luiz Carlos Barreto Prod.**266 t** Mosfilm/Icaic (Cuba) **267 b** Grupo Cine Liberacion **267 t** G. Alatriste **268 t** Copacabana Filmes/Luiz Augusto Mendes **268 b** Copacabana Filmes/Luiz Augusto Mendes**269 stills** Copacabana Filmes/Luiz Augusto Mendes **270 t** ICAIC/Cuban State Film **270 b** ICAIC/Cuban State Film **271 stills** ICAIC/Cuban State Film **272 t** United Artists **273 t** Paramount **273 b** Warner Bros. **274 b** Mirisch/United Artists **274 t** MGM (Turner Ent./Warner Bros.) **275 t** Warner Bros. **275 b** Jerome Hellman/U.A. **276 t** Columbia Pictures/Hawk Films **276 b** Columbia Pictures/Hawk Films **277 stills** Columbia Pictures/Hawk Films **278 t** Tatira-Hiller Productions/Warner Bros./Seven Arts **279 stills** Tatira-Hiller Productions/Warner Bros./Seven Arts **280 t** Sandrews **281 b** Paramount **281 t** MGM (Turner Ent./Warner Bros.) **282 t** Robert Et Raymond Hakim/Paris Film/Five Film (StudioCanal Image) **282 b** Robert Et Raymond Hakim/Paris Film/Five Film (StudioCanal Image) **283 stills** Robert Et Raymond Hakim/Paris Film/Five Film (StudioCanal Image) **284 t** Embassy/Laurence Turman (Canal+ Image UK Ltd) **284 b** Embassy/Laurence Turman (Canal+ Image UK Ltd) **285 b** Embassy/Laurence Turman (Canal+ Image UK Ltd) **285 stills** Embassy/Laurence Turman (Canal+ Image UK Ltd) **287 b** Paramount **287 t** Paramount**288 b** Danjaq LLC/Eon Productions **289 stills** Danjaq LLC/Eon Productions **290 t** MGM (Turner Ent./Warner Bros.) **291 t** Chaumiane/Film Studio **291 b** 20th Century Fox **292 t** MGM (Turner Ent./Warner Bros.) **293 stills** MGM (Turner Ent./Warner Bros.) **294 b** Universal **294 t** MGM (Turner Ent./Warner Bros.) **295 t** Image Ten **296 t** Shamley Productions (Universal) **296 b** Shamley Productions (Universal) **297 stills** Shamley Productions (Universal) **298 t** William Castle Productions/Paramount **298 b** William Castle Productions/Paramount **299 panel** Union-Carolco/Tri Star **299 stills** William Castle Productions/Paramount **300 t** Interopa-Cineriz-Paris/Times **301 b** Parc/Madeleine/Beta Film **301 t** Specta **302 t** Cineriz **302 b** Film Polski **303 t** Casbah/Igor **303 b** Paris Europa/Ficit/Hisa **304 t** Riama/Grey/Pathé Pierluigi **304 b** Riama/Grey/Pathé **305 stills** Riama/Grey/Pathé **306 t** Mosfilm**307 stills** Mosfilm **308 t** Filmové Studio Barrandov **308 b** Filmové Studio Barrandov **309 panel** United Artists **309 stills** Filmové Studio Barrandov **310 t** Paramount/Rafran **311 t** BRC/Tesica **312 t** Alberto Grimaldi/Arturo González/Constantin/PEA **312 b** Alberto Grimaldi/Arturo González/Constantin/PEA **313 stills** Alberto Grimaldi/Arturo González/Constantin/PEA **314** and **315** Chapter Opener Universal **317 b** Alfa Cinematografica **317 t** Greenwich Film Productions **318 t** F.C. Rome/P.E.C.F.Paris **319 b** Artistes Associès/PEA **319 t** Elias Querejeta Prods **320 t** Les Films Du Losange **320 b** Les Films Du Losange **321 stills** Les Films Du Losange **322 t** Mars Film/Marianne Productions/Maran Film **322 b** Mars Film/Marianne Productions/Maran Film **323 panel** 20th Century Fox **323 stills** Mars Film/Marianne Productions/Maran Film **324 b** Cinematograph AB/SFI **325 stills** Cinematograph AB/SFI **326 t** Werner Herzog Filmproduktion **327 b** Filmverlag Der Autoren **327 t** Bioskop/Paramount-Orion/WDR **328 t** Filmverlag Der Autoren **328 b** Trio/Albatros/WDR **329 b** Bavaria/Radiant **329 t** Seitz/Bioskop/Hallelujah **330 t** Filmverlag Der Autoren/Tango Film/Fassbinder Foundation **330 b** Filmverlag Der Autoren/Tango Film/Fassbinder Foundation **331 stills** Filmverlag Der Autoren/Tango Film/Fassbinder Foundation **333 stills** Filmverlag Der Autoren/Werner Herzog/ZDF **334 t** Falcon International **335 t** United Artists **335 b** Warner Bros. **336 b** Warner Bros./Hoya Productions **336 t** Warner Bros./Hoya Productions **337 stills** Warner Bros./Hoya Productions **338 t** British Lion (Canal+ Images UK Ltd) **339 stills** British Lion (Canal+ Images UK Ltd) **340 t** Warner Bros. **341 b** 20th Century Fox **341 t** MGM (Turner Ent./Warner Bros.) **342 t** Paramount **342 b** Paramount **343 stills** Paramount **344 t** Paramount Pictures/Penthouse/Long Road Prods. **344 b** Paramount Pictures/Penthouse/Long Road Prods. **345 stills** Paramount Pictures/Penthouse/Long Road Prods.**346 t** MGM (Turner Ent./Warner Bros.) **347 b** Paramount **347 t** Paramount **348 b** Paramount **349 panel** MGM (Turner Ent./

Warner Bros.) **349 stills** Paramount/Zoetrope/The Coppola Company **350 t** Warner Bros./Wildwood **350 b** Warner Bros./Wildwood **351 stills** Warner Bros./Wildwood **352 t** 20th Century Fox **353 b** Paramount **353 t** Universal **354 b** Paramount **354 t** United Artists **355 t** Columbia **355 b** United Artists Hamill, Brian **356 t** Fantasy Films/Saul Zaentz Co **356 b** Fantasy Films/Saul Zaentz Co **357 stills** Fantasy Films/Saul Zaentz Co **358 t** Columbia Pictures Industries Inc **358 b** Columbia Pictures Industries Inc **359 stills** Columbia Pictures Industries Inc **360 t** Columbia **361 t** 20th Century Fox **361 b** Warner Bros./Dc Comics **362 t** 20th Century Fox/Warner Bros. **362 b** 20th Century Fox/Warner Bros. **363 stills** 20th Century Fox/Warner Bros. **364 t** Zanuck/Brown/Universal Pictures **364 b** Zanuck/Brown/Universal Pictures **365 c** Zanuck/Brown/Universal Pictures **365 stills** Zanuck/Brown/Universal Pictures **366 t** Lucasfilm Ltd/20th Century Fox **366 b** Lucasfilm Ltd/20th Century Fox **367 stills** Lucasfilm Ltd/20th Century Fox **368 t** Film House-Australia **369 b** Paramount **369 t** Aip-Filmways **370 t** Australian Film Comm./South Australian Film Corp./B.E.F. KYNOCH, DAVID **370 b** Australian Film Comm./South Australian Film Corp./B.E.F. **371 stills** Australian Film Comm./South Australian Film Corp./B.E.F. **372 t** Margaret Fink Prods./GUO/NSW Film Corp. **372 b** Margaret Fink Prods./GUO/NSW Film Corp. **373 stills** Margaret Fink Prods./GUO/NSW Film Corp. **374 t** Sozosha **375 b** Devki Chitra **375 t** Golden Harvest **376 b** Lian Bang/Union Film/IFC **376 t** Lian Bang/Union Film/IFC **377 stills** Lian Bang/Union Film/IFC **378 t** Oshima/Argos Films/Shibata Organisation **378 b** Oshima/Argos Films/Shibata Organisation **379 stills** Oshima/Argos Films/Shibata Organisation **380 t** Paramount **380 b** United Artists **381 t** Vestron **381 b** Paramount **382 t** ABC Pictures/Allied Artists **382 b** ABC Pictures/Allied Artists **383 stills** ABC Pictures/Allied Artists **385 t** Cinegrit/Studio Kankourama **386 t** Films Soleil O/Cinematographie Nationale **387 t** Souleymane Cissé Films **387 b** Films De L'Avenir/Thelma/Arcadia **389 stills** Films Domireew **390 t** Les Films Cissé/Atriascop Paris/Cnc/Les Films Du Carrosse **391 stills** Les Films Cissé/Atriascop Paris/Cnc/Les Films Du Carrosse **393 b** Warner Bros. **393 t** Enigma/Goldcrest **394 t** Omni Zoetrope Studios **394 b** Omni Zoetrope Studios **395 stills** Omni Zoetrope Studios **396 t** Hemdale Film Corporation **396 b** Hemdale Film Corporation **397 stills** Hemdale Film Corporation **399 t** 20th Century Fox **399 b** 20th Century Fox **400 t** Lucasfilm Ltd./Paramount Pictures **400 b** Lucasfilm Ltd./Paramount Pictures **401 stills** Lucasfilm Ltd./Paramount Pictures **402 t** Hemdale Film/Cinema 84/Greenberg Brothers **402 b** Hemdale Film/Cinema 84/Greenberg Brothers **403 stills** Hemdale Film/Cinema 84/Greenberg Brothers **404 t** Paramount **404 b** Paramount **405 b** Castle Rock/Nelson/Columbia **406 t** Spinal Tap Prod./Embassy Pictures (StudioCanal) **406 b** Spinal Tap Prod./Embassy Pictures (StudioCanal) **407 panel** Castle Rock/Warner Bros. Gregory, Doane **407 stills** Spinal Tap Prod./Embassy Pictures (StudioCanal) **408 t** Amblin Ent./Silver Screen Partners Iii/Touchstone Pictures **408 b** Amblin Ent./Silver Screen Partners Iii/Touchstone Pictures **409 stills** Amblin Ent./Silver Screen Partners Iii/Touchstone Pictures **410 t** 20th Century Fox/Allied Stars/Enigma **411 b** MGM/UA **411 t** Merchant Ivory/Goldcrest **412 t** Handmade Films **412 b** Handmade Films **413 panel** Paramount **413 stills** Handmade Films **414 b** BFI/Channel Four Films **415 stills** BFI/Channel Four Films **416 t** U.A./P.A.A./P.E.A. (Rome) **417 b** Casey Prod.-Eldorado Films (Canal+ Image UK Ltd) **417 t** Italonegglio/Lotar Film **418 t** De Laurentiis Entertainment Group **418 b** De Laurentiis Entertainment Group **419 c l** De Laurentiis Entertainment Group **419 stills** De Laurentiis Entertainment Group **420 t** Gaumont/Cargo Films **421 t** Nouvelles Editions/Mk2/Stella/Nef **421 b** Cristaldifilm/Films Ariane **422 t** HR/Mafilm/Durniok/Objektiv Film **422 b** HR/Mafilm/Durniok/Objektiv Film **423 panel** Warner Bros. **423 stills** HR/Mafilm/Durniok/Objektiv Film **424 b** Zespol Filmowy-Tor **425 stills** Zespol Filmowy-Tor **426 b** Ego-Canada Council-Ontario Arts Council **426 t** Universal **427 b** Max Films/Gerard Mital **428 b** Corporation Image M&M/Office National Du Film Du Canada **429 stills** Corporation Image M&M/Office National Du Film Du Canada **430 t** Brooksfilms/20th Century Fox **430 b** Brooksfilms/20th Century Fox **431 stills** Brooksfilms/20th Century Fox **433 b** Xi'An Film Studio **433 t** Golden Harvest Group **434 b** Guangxi Film Studio **435 stills** Guangxi Film Studio **436 b** 3-H Films/Era International **437 stills** 3-H Films/Era International **438** and **439** Chapter Opener Warner Bros./Village Roadshow Films **440 t** Sam Goldwyn/Renaissance Films/BBC Coote, Clive **441 t** Parallax **441 b** Cecchi Gori/Tiger/Canal + **442 t** Caméra One/CNC/Dd Prods/Films A2/UGC/ Hachette Premiere **442 b** Caméra One/CNC/Dd Prods/Films A2/UGC/ Hachette Premiere **443 stills** Caméra One/CNC/Dd Prods/Films A2/UGC/ Hachette Premiere **444 t** Universal Pictures/Miramax Films/Bedford Falls Prods. Sparham, Laurie **444 b** Universal Pictures/Miramax Films/Bedford Falls Prods. **445 stills** Universal Pictures/Miramax Films/Bedford Falls Prods. **447 b** Dreamworks/Jinks/Cohen Sebastian, Lorey **447 t** Paramount **448 b** Avenue Pictures/Fine Line Features/Spelling Entertainment **449 stills** Avenue Pictures/Fine Line Features/Spelling Entertainment **450 t** A Band Apart/Jersey Films/Miramax Films **450 b** A Band Apart/Jersey Films/Miramax Films **451 stills** A Band Apart/Jersey Films/Miramax Films **452 t** Amblin Entertainment/Dreamworks/Paramount Pictures James, David **452 b** Amblin Entertainment/Dreamworks/Paramount Pictures **453 stills** Amblin Entertainment/Dreamworks/Paramount Pictures **454 b** View Askew **454 t** 12-Gauge Productions/Pandora**455 t** October Films **456 t** Cinepix Film **456 b** Touchstone Pictures **457 t** Alliance Atlantis/Dog Eat Dog/United Broadcasting **457 b** Focus Features Sato, Yoshio **458 t** Castle Rock Entertainment/Rio Dulce/Columbia Pictures **458 b** Castle Rock Entertainment/Rio Dulce/Columbia Pictures **459 stills** Castle Rock Entertainment/Rio Dulce/Columbia Pictures **460 t** Working Title/Polygram **460 b** Working Title/Polygram **461 stills** Working Title/Polygram **462 t** Ciby 2000 **463 b** Jan Chapman Prods/Ciby 2000 **463 t** M & A Film Corp **464 t** Polygram/Affc/Latent Image/Specific Films Lockwood, Elise **464 b** Polygram/Affc/Latent Image/Specific Films **465 stills** Polygram/Affc/Latent Image/Specific Films **466 t** Wingnut/Fontana **466 t** Wingnut/Fontana **467** still Fontana Prod/WingNut Films/New Zealand Film Commission **468 t** Universal HESSION, JONATHAN **469 t** Polygram/Channel 4/Working Title **469 b** Figment/Noel Gay/Channel 4 **470 t** Palace Pictures/Channel Four Films Hilton, Tom **470 b** Palace Pictures/Channel Four Films **471 stills** Palace Pictures/Channel Four Films **472 t** Channel Four Films/Ciby 2000/Thin Man Films **472 b** Channel Four Films/Ciby 2000/Thin Man Films **473 stills** Channel Four Films/Ciby 2000/Thin Man Films **474 t** Constellation/UGC/Hachette Premiere **475 t** Mk2/Ced/Cab **475 b** Barrandov/Ciby 2000 **476 t** Sogetel/Le Films Alain Sarde/Canal+ Espana **477 t** Theo Angelopoulos **478 t** Prods. Lazennec/StudioCanal/ Sept Cinema/Kasso Inc. **478 b** Prods. Lazennec/StudioCanal/ Sept Cinema/Kasso Inc. **479 stills** Prods. Lazennec/StudioCanal/ Sept Cinema/Kasso Inc. **480 t** Wega Film **480 b** Wega Film **481 panel** Dreamachine **481 stills** Wega Film **482 t** El Deseo/Renn Productions/France 2 Cinéma **482 b** El Deseo/Renn Productions/France 2 Cinéma **483 stills** El Deseo/Renn Productions/France 2 Cinéma **484 t** 20th Century Fox **485 t** © Disney **485 b** Twentieth Century-Fox Film Corporation **486 t** Warner Bros./Village Roadshow Films **487 panel** Warner Bros./Village Roadshow Films **487 stills** Warner Bros./Village Roadshow Films **489 b** Focus Features **489 t** Pathé/Django Films **491 stills** Pixar Animation Studios/Walt Disney Pictures **492 t** Studio Ghibli (Nibariki) **492 b** Studio Ghibli (Nibariki) **493 t l** Studio Ghibli (Nibariki) **493 stills** Studio Ghibli (Nibariki) **494 t** Miramax **495 t** Artisan Pics **495 b** Fido Film AB **496 t** Orion Pictures/Strong Heart/Demme Production Regan, Ken **496 b** Orion Pictures/Strong Heart/Demme Production **497 stills** Orion Pictures/Strong Heart/Demme Production **498 t** Era International **499 t** Block 2 Pics/Jet Tone **499 b** Egg Films/Show East **500 t** UCV/China Film /Columbia/Edko/Good Machine/Sony Pictures Chuen, Chan Kam **500 b** UCV/China Film /Columbia/Edko/Good Machine/Sony Pictures **501 stills** UCV/China Film /Columbia/Edko/Good Machine/Sony Pictures **502 t** Atomfilms/Omega/Pony Canyon Inc **502 b** Atomfilms/Omega/Pony Canyon Inc **503 panel** Yang & His Gang **503 stills** Atom/Nemuru Otoko Seisaku Linkai/Omega/Pony Canyon **504 t** Korea Pictures/Lj Film/Pandora/Cineclick Asia **504 b** Korea Pictures/Lj Film/Pandora/Cineclick Asia **505 stills** Korea Pictures/Lj Film/Pandora/Cineclick Asia **506 t** Abbas Kiarostami **509 b** Makhmalbaf Film House **509 t** Jafar Panahi Film Productions **510 t** Abbas Kiarostami/Ciby 2000/Farabi Cinema Foundation **510 b** Abbas Kiarostami/Ciby 2000/Farabi Cinema Foundation **511 stills** Abbas Kiarostami/Ciby 2000/Farabi Cinema Foundation **512 t** Jafar Panahi Prods./Lumière & Co./Mikado Film **512 b** Jafar Panahi Prods./Lumière & Co./Mikado Film **513 stills** Jafar Panahi Prods./Lumière & Co./Mikado Film **514 t** Alta Vista **515 b** Mantarraya Productions **515 t** Drama Filmes **516 t** Tequila Gang/WB **516 b** Prodigital **517 t** Matanza Cine **517 b** Canana Films **518 t** Mact Prods./Riofilme/Videofilmes/Canal+ Carvalho, Walter **518 b** Mact Prods./Riofilme/Videofilmes/Canal+ **519 stills** Mact Prods./Riofilme/Videofilmes/Canal+ **520 t** Besame Mucho Pictures/Producciones Anhelo **520 b** Besame Mucho Pictures/Producciones Anhelo **521 stills** Besame Mucho Pictures/Producciones Anhelo **522 t** O2 Filmes/Videofilmes/Hank Levine **522 b** O2 Filmes/Videofilmes/Hank Levine **523 panel** O2 Filmes/Videofilmes/Hank Levine**523 stills** O2 Filmes/Videofilmes/Hank Levine **524 t** Tiger Aspect Pictures Keyte, Giles **525 b** Pathé Sparham, Laurie **525 t** Dreamworks/Aardman Animations **526 t** Apocalypso/BBC Films/Baker Street/Take Partnership **526 b** Apocalypso/BBC Films/Baker Street/Take Partnership **527 stills** Apocalypso/BBC Films/Baker Street/Take Partnership **528 t** © Disney **529 b** Marvel Productions **530 t** New Line Cinema/Wingnut Films/The Saul Zaentz Company Vinet, Pierre **530 b** New Line Cinema/Wingnut Films/The Saul Zaentz Company **531 stills** New Line Cinema/Wingnut Films/The Saul Zaentz Company **532 t** Warner Bros./Syncopy/Dc Comics/Patalex Prods. James, David **532 b** Warner Bros./Syncopy/Dc Comics/Patalex Prods. **533 stills** Warner Bros./Syncopy/Dc Comics/Patalex Prods. **533 panel** Warner Bros./Dc Comics **534 t** Arte France/Blind Spot/Dinovi **535 t** WDR/X-Filme **535 b** Nordisk Film **536 t** Babelsberg Film **536 b** Lucky Red **537 t** Fandango **538 t** Fandango/Indigo Film/Medusa Film **538 b** Fandango/Indigo Film/Medusa Film **539 stills** Fandango/Indigo Film/Medusa Film **540 t** Arte/Br/Creado Film/Wiedemann & Berg Filmproduktion Keller, Hagen **540 b** Arte/Br/Creado Film/Wiedemann & Berg Filmproduktion **541 stills** Arte/Br/Creado Film/Wiedemann & Berg Filmproduktion **542 t** Dharma Productions **543 b** Dharma Productions **544 t** Flicks/UTV **544 b** Eros/Reliance Big Pictures **545 t** Balaji Telefilms **545 b** Aamir Khan Productions **546 t** Arclightz And Films/Dreamz Unlimited **546 b** Arclightz And Films/Dreamz Unlimited **547 stills** Arclightz And Films/Dreamz Unlimited **548 t** Aamir Khan/Ashutosh Gowariker Prods Singh Sachdev, Hardeep **548 b** Aamir Khan/Ashutosh Gowariker Prods **549 stills** Aamir Khan/Ashutosh Gowariker Prods **551 t** Dreamworks/Universal **551 b** Paramount/Vantage **552 t** New Line Productions/Media 1 Seida, Takashi **552 b** New Line Productions/Media 1 **553 panel** Paramount/Miramax **553 stills** New Line Productions/Media 1 **554 t** The Hurt Locker LLC **554 b** The Hurt Locker LLC **555 stills** The Hurt Locker LLC **556 t** Bim/Canal+/CNC Moireau, Jean-Claude **557 b** Pathé Renn/France 3 Prods. **557 t** Legende/Tfi International **558 t** Victoires/Tapioca/UGC/France 3/Mmc Independent **558 b** Victoires/Tapioca/UGC/France 3/Mmc Independent **559 stills** Victoires/Tapioca/UGC/France 3/Mmc Independent **560 t** Les Films Du Losange/Wega/Bavaria Film/Sony Pictures **560 b** Les Films Du Losange/Wega/Bavaria Film/Sony Pictures **561 stills** Les Films Du Losange/Wega/Bavaria Film/Sony Pictures **562 t** Why Not/Chic/Page 114/France 2/Bim/UGC/Celluloid Dreams **562 b** Why Not/Chic/Page 114/France 2/Bim/UGC/Celluloid Dreams **563 stills** Why Not/Chic/Page 114/France 2/Bim/UGC/Celluloid Dreams

Other images in this book have been provided by the picture libraries listed below.

2 Private Collection/Archives Charmet/The Bridgeman Art Library **9** Bettmann/Corbis **23 panel** Private collection **29 panel** akg-images **45 panel** Offentliche Kunstsammlung, Basel, Switzerland/The Bridgeman Art Library **47 panel** Private collection **51 panel** Allstar/Cinetext **55 b** RIA Novosti **61 panel** Photo Scala, Florence 2005 **74** BFI Stills **75 b** BFI Stills **78** Pictorial Press Ltd/Alamy **94 b** Everett Collection/Rex Features **99 t** Bettmann/Corbis **122 b** Everett Collection/Rex Features **128 b** Private collection **141 panel** Corbis **143 panel** Private collection **146 t** © Disney. Supplied by Pictorial Press Ltd/Alamy **153 panel** RA/Lebrecht Music & Arts **164 b** Private collection **167 panel** Photos 12/Alamy **172 b** Snap/Rex Features **173 panel** Private collection **175 stills** Royal Books **184 t** BFI Stills **186 t** Moviestore Collection Ltd/Alamy **189 panel** Private collection **191 t** Everett Collection/Rex Features **204 t** AF archive/Alamy **205 t** Photos 12/Alamy **207 panel** Private collection **208 t** Moviestore Collection Ltd/Alam **208 b** Pictorial Press Ltd/Alamy **209 t r** AF archive/Alamy **209 c** Photos **12**/Alamy **219 panel** Private collection **220 t** BFI Stills **234 t** Sunset Boulevard/Corbis **250 b** RA/Lebrecht Music & Arts**251 b** Moviestore Collection Ltd/Alamy **252 t** Allstar/Cinetext/The Criterion Collection **254 t** © Raymon Cauchetier. Supplied by RA/Lebrecht Music & Arts **261 panel** Private collection **262 t** Moviestore Collection Ltd/Alamy **265 t** Private collection **278 b** Snap/Rex Features **285 panel** Private collection **286 t** Moviestore Collection Ltd**/**Alamy **288 t** AF archive/Alamy **289 panel** Private collection **92 b** Allstar/MGM **293 panel** Lebrecht Music & Arts **311 b** Photos 12/Alamy **316 t** RA/Lebrecht Music & Arts **324 t** AF archive/Alamy **325 panel** Photos 12/Alamy **332 t** RA/Lebrecht Music & Arts **332 b** Private collection **348 t** AF archive/Alamy **383 panel** Private collection **384 t** RA/Lebrecht Music & Arts **385 b** BFI Stills **388 t** BFI Stills **388 b** Private collection **389 panel** Private collection**390 b** Photos **12**/Alamy **392 t** Moviestore collection Ltd/Alamy **398 t** BFI Stills **414 t** Photos 12/Alamy **419 panel** Private collection **424 t** Photos **12**/Alamy **428 t** RA/Lebrecht Music & Arts **432 t** AF archive/Alamy **434 t** Photos 12/Alamy **436 t** Private collection **446 t** Warner Brothers/Everett/Rex Features **467 panel** Bettmann/Corbis **477 b** AF archive/Alamy **486 b** Warner Brothers/Everett/Rex Features **488 t** © 2009 Disney/Pixar. Supplied by Moviestore Collection Ltd/Alamy **490 b** © 2005 Disney. Slinky ® Dog © James Industries. Mr. Potato Head ® and Mrs Potato Head ® are resgistered trademarks of Hasbro, Inc. Used with permission. © Hasbro, Inc. All rights reserved. Troll Doll © Russ Berrie and Company, Inc. Supplied by Moviestore Collection Ltd/Alamy **490 t** © 2005 Disney. Supplied by AF Archive/Alamy **491 panel** © 2004 Disney/Pixar. Supplied by AF archive/Alamy **507 t** Photos 12/Alamy **507 b** BFI Stills **508 t** AF archive/Alamy **519 panel** Pierre Boulat/Time Life Pictures/Getty Images **527 panel** Private collection **529 t** BFI Stills **533 panel** Private collection **542 b** BFI Stills **550 t** BFI Stills